BIG IDEAS MATH®

COURSE 1

Virginia Edition

Ron Larson
Laurie Boswell

BIG IDEAS LEARNING®
Erie, Pennsylvania
BigIdeasLearning.com

Big Ideas Learning, LLC
1762 Norcross Road
Erie, PA 16510-3838
USA

For product information and customer support, contact Big Ideas Learning
at **1-877-552-7766** or visit us at ***BigIdeasLearning.com***.

Cover Image
Richard Cummins/Lonely Planet Images/Getty Images

Printed in the U.S.A.

ISBN 13: 978-1-63598-096-7
ISBN 10: 1-63598-096-8

3 4 5 6 7 8 9 10 WEB 21 20 19 18

AUTHORS

Ron Larson is well known as the lead author of a comprehensive program for mathematics that spans middle school, high school, and college courses. His middle school and high school programs are published by Big Ideas Learning, and his college and Advanced Placement books are published by Cengage Learning. He holds the distinction of Professor Emeritus from Penn State Erie, The Behrend College, where he taught for nearly 40 years. He received his Ph.D. in mathematics from the University of Colorado. Dr. Larson's numerous professional activities keep him actively involved in the mathematics education community and allow him to fully understand the needs of students, teachers, supervisors, and administrators.

Laurie Boswell is the former Head of School at Riverside School in Lyndonville, Vermont. In addition to textbook authoring, she provides mathematics consulting and embedded coaching sessions. Dr. Boswell received her Ed.D. from the University of Vermont in 2010. She is a recipient of the Presidential Award for Excellence in Mathematics Teaching and is a Tandy Technology Scholar. Laurie has taught math to students at all levels, elementary through college. In addition, Laurie has served on the NCTM Board of Directors and as a Regional Director for NCSM. Along with Ron, Laurie has co-authored numerous math programs and has become a popular national speaker.

ABOUT THE BOOK

Big Ideas Math: Virginia Edition was developed using the same research-based strategy of a balanced approach that has become synonymous with the *Big Ideas Math* series. This approach opens doors to abstract thought, reasoning, and inquiry as students persevere to answer the Essential Questions that introduce each section.

From start to finish, this program was designed with the student in mind. Students are subtly introduced to "Habits of Mind" that help them internalize concepts for a greater depth of understanding. These habits serve students well not only in mathematics, but across all curricula throughout their academic careers. *Big Ideas Math: Virginia Edition* exposes students to highly motivating and relevant problems. Woven throughout the program are the depth and rigor students need to prepare for career-readiness and other college-level courses.

We consider the *Big Ideas Math* series to be the crowning jewel of 30 years of achievement in writing educational materials.

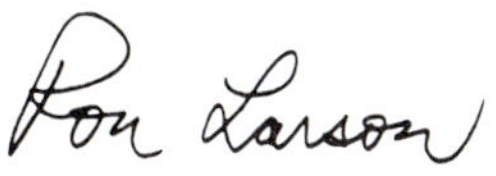

TEACHER REVIEWERS

- Lisa Amspacher
  Milton Hershey School
  Hershey, PA
- Mary Ballerina
  Orange County Public Schools
  Orlando, FL
- Lisa Bubello
  School District of Palm Beach County
  Lake Worth, FL
- Sam Coffman
  North East School District
  North East, PA
- Sally Griffith
  Staunton City Public Schools
  Staunton, VA
- Kristen Karbon
  Troy School District
  Rochester Hills, MI
- Laurie Mallis
  Westglades Middle School
  Coral Springs, FL
- Dave Morris
  Union City Area School District
  Union City, PA
- Michael Ormsmith, Ph.D.
  Staunton City Public Schools
  Staunton, VA
- Bonnie Pendergast
  Tolleson Union High School District
  Tolleson, AZ
- Ian Shenk
  Hanover County Public Schools
  Ashland, VA
- Molly L. Sullivan
  Chesapeake Public Schools
  Chesapeake, VA
- Valerie Sullivan
  Lamoille South Supervisory Union
  Morrisville, VT
- Becky Walker
  Appleton Area School District
  Appleton, WI
- Zena Wiltshire
  Dade County Public Schools
  Miami, FL

STUDENT REVIEWERS

- Mike Carter
- Matthew Cauley
- Amelia Davis
- Wisdom Dowds
- John Flatley
- Nick Ganger
- Hannah Iadeluca
- Paige Lavine
- Emma Louie
- David Nichols
- Mikala Parnell
- Jordan Pashupathi
- Stephen Piglowski
- Robby Quinn
- Michael Rawlings
- Garrett Sample
- Andrew Samuels
- Addie Sedelmyer
- Tyler Steffy
- Erin Taylor
- Reid Wilson

CONSULTANTS

- Patsy Davis
  Educational Consultant
  Knoxville, Tennessee
- Bob Fulenwider
  Mathematics Consultant
  Bakersfield, California
- Linda Hall
  Mathematics Assessment Consultant
  Norman, Oklahoma
- Ryan Keating
  Special Education Advisor
  Gilbert, Arizona
- Michael McDowell
  Project-Based Instruction Specialist
  Fairfax, California
- Sean McKeighan
  Interdisciplinary Advisor
  Norman, Oklahoma
- Bonnie Spence
  Differentiated Instruction Consultant
  Missoula, Montana

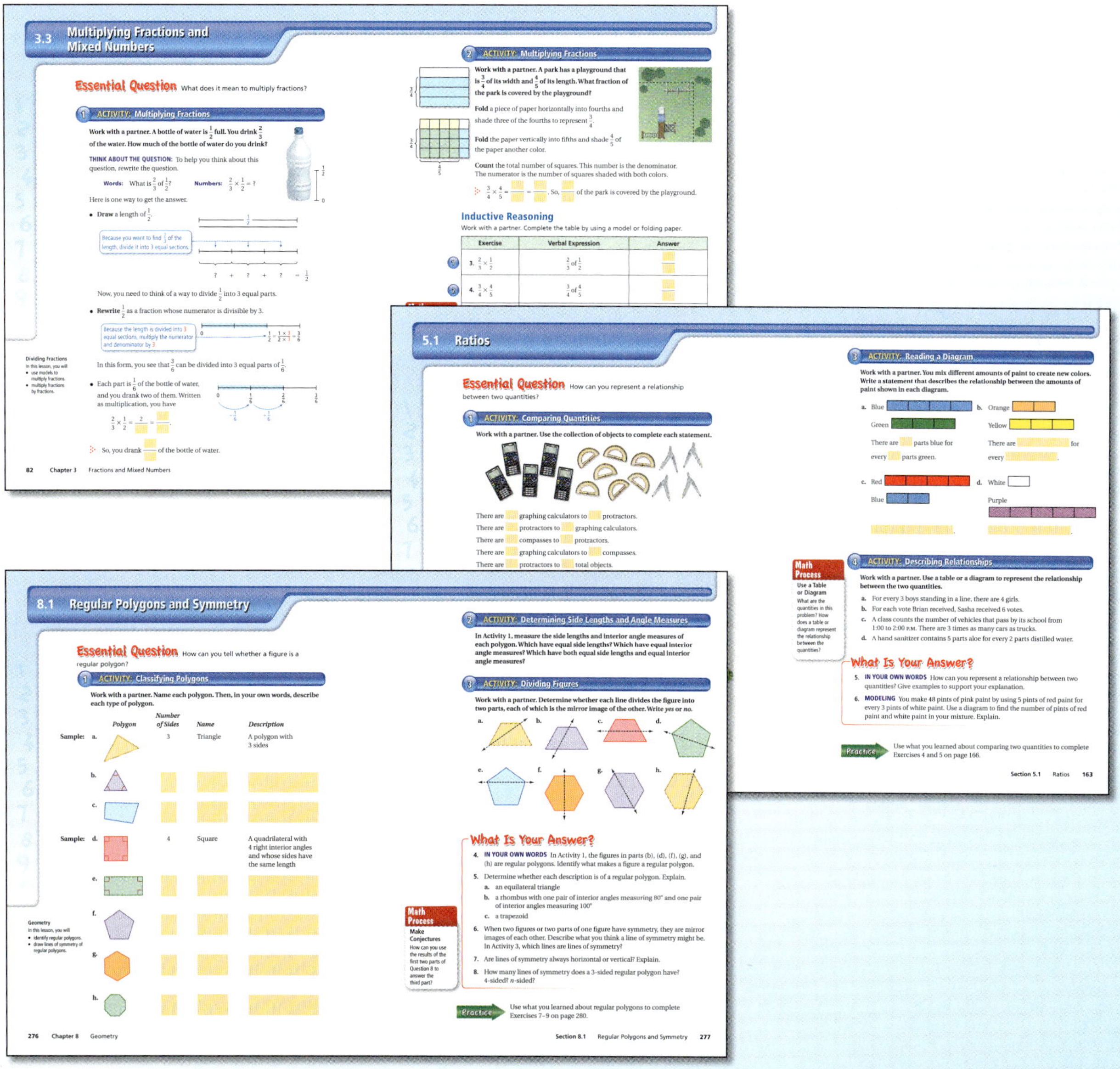

Mathematical Process Goals for Students

Mathematical Problem Solving

- Real-life problems are provided to help students learn to apply the mathematics that they are learning to everyday life.
- Real-life problems help students use the structure of mathematics to break down and solve more difficult problems.
- *In Your Own Words* provide opportunities for students to look for meaning and entry points to a problem.
- Students are continually encouraged to check for reasonableness in their solutions.

Mathematical Communication

- Cooperative learning opportunities support precise communication.
- *Essential Questions* help students focus and analyze.
- *On Your Own* questions encourage students to formulate consistent and appropriate reasoning.

Mathematical Reasoning

- *Inductive Reasoning* activities help students make conjectures and build a logical progression of statements to explore their conjecture.
- *Error Analysis*; *Different Words, Same Question*; and *Which One Doesn't Belong* features provide students the opportunity to construct arguments and critique the reasoning of others.
- Opportunities are provided to help students make generalizations.

Mathematical Connections

- Prior knowledge is continually brought back and tied in with current learning.
- Real-life problems incorporate other disciplines to help students see that math is used across content areas.
- *Inductive Reasoning* activities provide students the opportunity to see patterns and structure in mathematics.

Mathematical Representations

- Real-life problems are translated into diagrams, tables, equations, and graphs to help students analyze relations and to draw conclusions.
- Visual problem-solving models help students create a coherent representation of the problem.
- Multiple representations are presented to help students move from concrete to representative and into abstract thinking.

Mathematical Content

Chapter Coverage

1 – **2** – 3 – **4** – **5** – 6 – 7 – 8 – 9

Number and Number Sense

- Represent relationships between quantities using ratios.
- Extend understanding of numbers to integers and positive rational numbers expressed as fractions, mixed numbers, decimals, and percents.
- Investigate patterns with whole number exponents and perfect squares.

1 – **2** – **3** – **4** – 5 – **6** – 7 – 8 – 9

Computation and Estimation

- Solve problems involving operations with (a) integers and (b) positive rational numbers expressed as fractions, mixed numbers, and decimals.

1 – 2 – 3 – 4 – 5 – 6 – 7 – **8** – 9

Measurement and Geometry

- Solve problems involving circumference and area of circles, and perimeter and area of triangles and rectangles.
- Develop an understanding of the coordinate plane.
- Determine congruence of segments, angles, and polygons.

1 – 2 – 3 – 4 – 5 – 6 – 7 – 8 – **9**

Probability and Statistics

- Create and analyze circle graphs.
- Develop concepts regarding measures of center.

1 – 2 – 3 – 4 – **5** – **6** – **7** – 8 – 9

Patterns, Functions, and Algebra

- Investigate and represent proportional relationships.
- Identify examples of and use algebraic terminology.
- Write linear equations and inequalities. Solve one-step linear equations, and one-step inequalities involving addition and subtraction.

1

Integers

“I like talking about math, and working with a partner allows me to do that.”

Operations with Integers

Fractions and Mixed Numbers

“I like that the Essential Question helps me begin thinking about the lesson.”

Decimals, Fractions, and Percents

4

"I like how I can click on the words in the eBook and hear how to pronounce the words correctly."

5

Ratios, Rates and Proportions

"I like Newton and Descartes! The cartoons are funny and I like that they model the math that we are learning."

Geometry

8

"I like playing the games in the Game Closet! They are a fun way to practice concepts we are learning in class."

9 Statistical Measures and Data Analysis

"With the BigIdeasMath.com website I don't have to worry if I forget my book or my workbook at school."

How to Use Your Math Book

- Read the **Essential Question** in the activity.

  Discuss the **Math Process** question with your partner.

  Work with a partner to decide **What Is Your Answer?**

  Now you are ready to do the **Practice** problems.

- Find the **Key Vocabulary** words, **highlighted in yellow**.

  Read their definitions. Study the concepts in each **Key Idea**.

  If you forget a definition, you can look it up online in the

  Multi-Language Glossary at BigIdeasMath.com.

- After you study each **EXAMPLE**, do the exercises in the **On Your Own**.

  Now You're Ready to do the exercises that correspond to the example.

  As you study, look for a **Study Tip** or a **Common Error**.

- The exercises are divided into 3 parts.

  Vocabulary and Concept Check

  Practice and Problem Solving

  Fair Game Review

  If an exercise has a 1 next to it, look back at Example 1 for help with that exercise.

  More help is available at **Check It Out Lesson Tutorials BigIdeasMath.com**.

- Find a STEM VIDEO. Scan the Real-Life STEM Video QR Code® to view a video and the corresponding Performance Task.

- To help study for your test, use the **Study Help** and **Chapter Review**.

SCAVENGER HUNT

Use this *Scavenger Hunt* to find where things are in **Chapter 1**.

Newton

- Find an **Essential Question**.
- Find a **Math Process**.
- Find a **Practice**.
- Find the definition of **absolute value**.
- Find the **Key Idea** The Coordinate Plane. Use the index in the back of the book.
- Find an **EXAMPLE** of graphing integers.
- Find an **On Your Own** about ordering $-2, -3, 3, 1, -1$.
- Find **Now You're Ready** Exercises 16–23.
- Find a **Remember** about number lines.
- Find a **Vocabulary** question about the number of quadrants in a coordinate plane.
- Find a **Problem Solving** question about **ELEVATION**. Find the answer in the back of the book.
- Which examples **?** help with Exercise 4 on page 12?
- How many questions are on the **Chapter Review**?

Descartes

1 Integers

"Don't worry. At negative 20 miles per hour, we're still under the speed limit."

"Dear Sir: You asked me to 'find' the opposite of −1."

"I didn't know it was missing."

What You Learned Before

"The Dog License Department wrote and said that it has run out of positive license numbers. So, they assigned me negative 3."

Ordering Decimals

Example 1 Use a number line to order 0.25, 1.15, 0.2, and 0.34 from least to greatest.

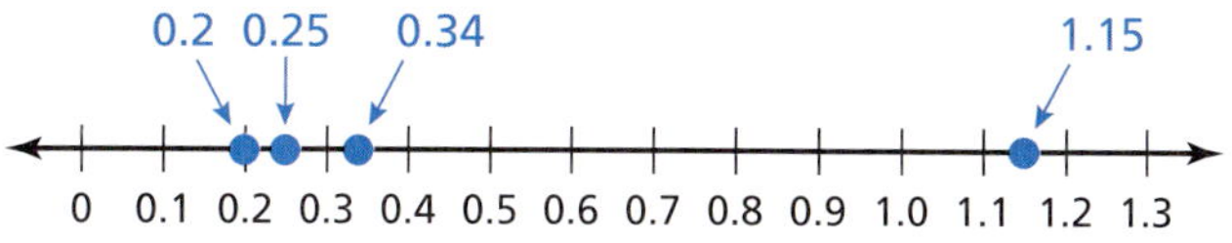

Try It Yourself

Use a number line to order the numbers from least to greatest.

1. 0.01, 0.42, 0.2, 0.5

2. 1.05, 0.95, 0.75, 1.01

Comparing Numbers

Complete the number sentence with <, >, or =.

Example 2 10 ____ 15

On a number line, 10 is closer to zero than 15.

So, $10 < 15$.

Example 3 0.875 ____ $\frac{7}{8}$

$$0.875 = \frac{875}{1000} = \frac{875 \div 125}{1000 \div 125} = \frac{7}{8}$$

So, $0.875 = \frac{7}{8}$.

Example 4 Find three numbers that make the number sentence $1\frac{2}{5} \leq$ ____ true.

Sample answer: $1\frac{3}{5}, \frac{5}{2}, 2$

Try It Yourself

Complete the number sentence with <, >, or =.

3. 2.01 ____ 2.001

4. 4.5 ____ $\frac{9}{2}$

5. 3.18 ____ 3.2

Find three numbers that make the number sentence true.

6. $\frac{17}{2} \leq$ ____

7. $1\frac{1}{2} >$ ____

8. $0.75 \geq$ ____

1.1 Integers

Essential Question How can you represent numbers that are less than 0?

1 ACTIVITY: Reading Thermometers

Work with a partner. The thermometers show the temperatures in four cities.

Honolulu, Hawaii — *Anchorage, Alaska*

Death Valley, California — *Seattle, Washington*

Write each temperature. Then match each temperature with its most appropriate location.

a.

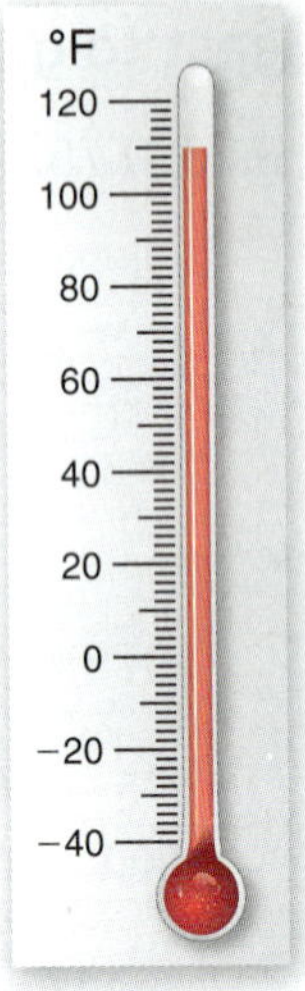

b.

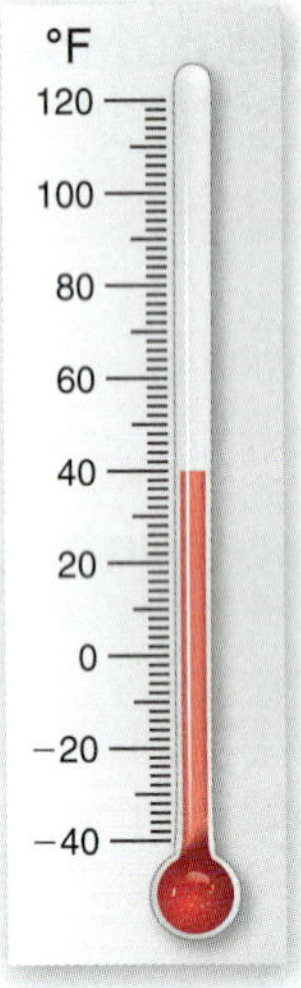

c.

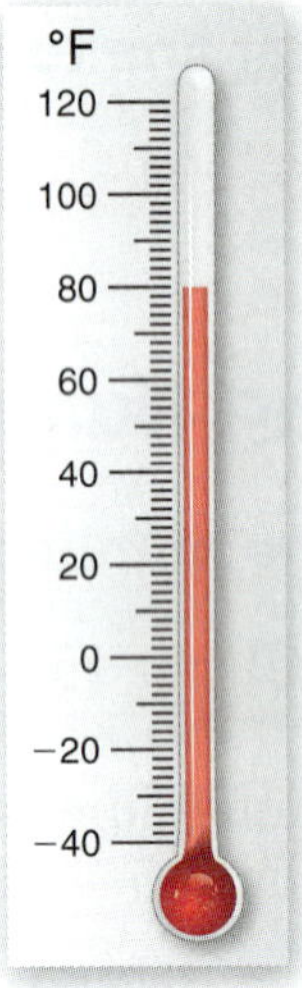

d.

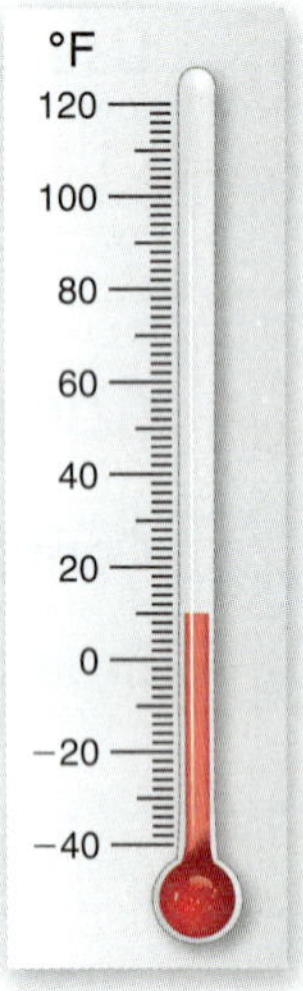

e. How would you describe all the temperatures in relation to 0°F?

2 ACTIVITY: Describing a Temperature

Integers

In this lesson, you will

- understand positive and negative integers and use them to describe real-life situations.
- graph integers on a number line.

Work with a partner. The thermometer shows the coldest temperature ever recorded in Seattle, Washington.

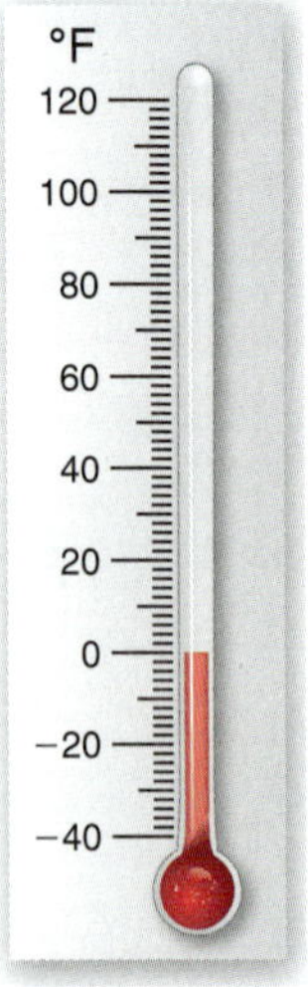

a. What is the temperature?

b. How do you write temperatures that are colder than this?

c. Suppose the record for the coldest temperature in Seattle is broken by 10 degrees. What is the new coldest temperature? Draw a thermometer that shows the new coldest temperature.

d. How is the new coldest temperature different from the temperatures in Activity 1?

3 ACTIVITY: Extending the System of Whole Numbers

Math Process

Maintain Oversight

How does this activity help you represent numbers less than 0?

Work with a partner.

a. Copy and complete the number line using whole numbers only.

b. Fold the paper with your number line around 0 so that the lines overlap. Make tick marks on the other side of the number line to match the tick marks for the whole numbers.

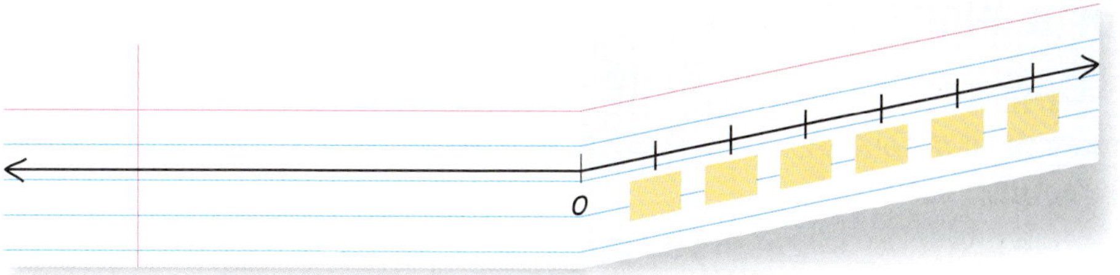

c. **STRUCTURE** Compare this number line to the thermometers from Activities 1 and 2. What do you think the new tick marks represent? How would you label them?

What Is Your Answer?

4. **IN YOUR OWN WORDS** How can you represent numbers that are less than 0?
5. Describe another real-life example that uses numbers that are less than 0.
6. **REASONING** How are the temperatures shown by the thermometers at the right similar? How are they different?
7. **WRITING** The temperature in a town on Thursday evening is 25°F. On Sunday morning, the temperature drops below 0°F. Write a story to describe what may have happened in the town. Be sure to include the temperatures for each day.

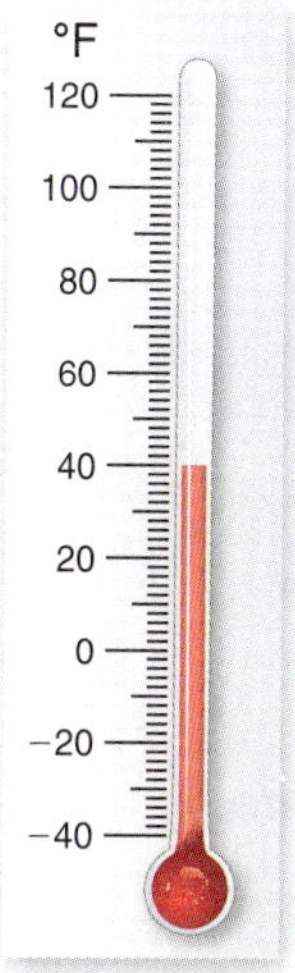

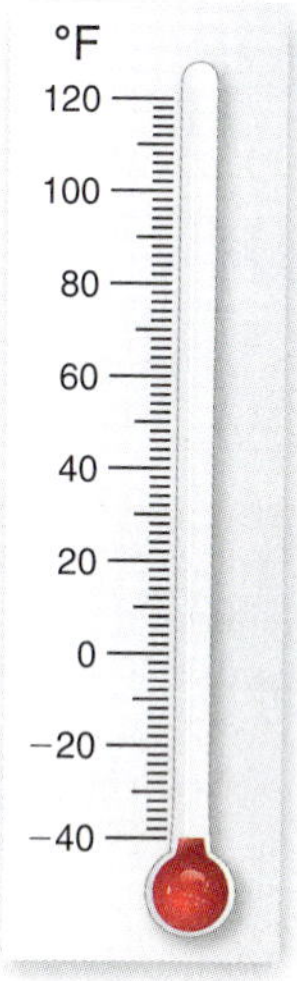

Practice Use what you learned about positive and negative numbers to complete Exercises 4–7 on page 6.

1.1 Lesson

Check It Out
Lesson Tutorials
BigIdeasMath.com

Key Vocabulary
positive numbers, *p. 4*
negative numbers, *p. 4*
opposites, *p. 4*
integers, *p. 4*

Positive numbers are greater than 0. They can be written with or without a positive sign (+).

$+1 \qquad 5 \qquad +20 \qquad 10{,}000$

Negative numbers are less than 0. They are written with a negative sign (−).

$-1 \qquad -5 \qquad -20 \qquad -10{,}000$

Two numbers that are the same distance from 0 on a number line, but on opposite sides of 0, are called **opposites**. The opposite of 0 is 0.

The Meaning of a Word

Opposite

When you sit across from your friend at the lunch table, you sit **opposite** your friend.

Key Idea

Integers

Words **Integers** are the set of whole numbers and their opposites.

Graph

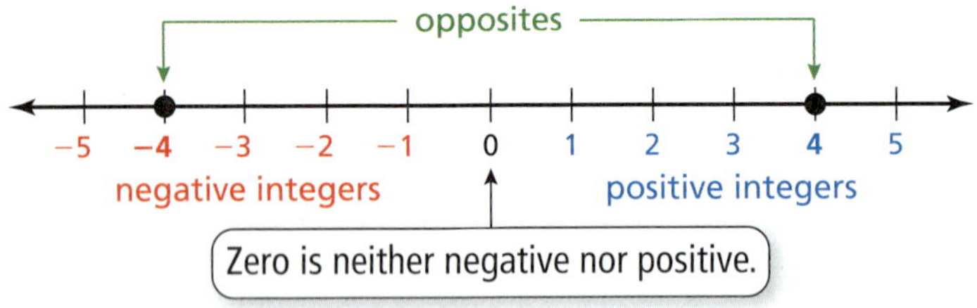

EXAMPLE 1 Writing Positive and Negative Integers

Write a positive or negative integer that represents the situation.

a. A contestant gains 250 points on a game show.

Gains indicates a number greater than 0. So, use a positive integer.

+250, or 250

b. Gasoline freezes at 40 degrees below zero.

Below zero indicates a number less than 0. So, use a negative integer.

−40

On Your Own

Now You're Ready
Exercises 8–13

Write a positive or negative integer that represents the situation.

1. A hiker climbs 900 feet up a mountain.
2. You have a debt of $24.
3. A student loses 5 points for being late to class.
4. A savings account earns $10.

Multi-Language Glossary at BigIdeasMath.com

EXAMPLE 2 Graphing Integers

Graph each integer and its opposite.

a. 3

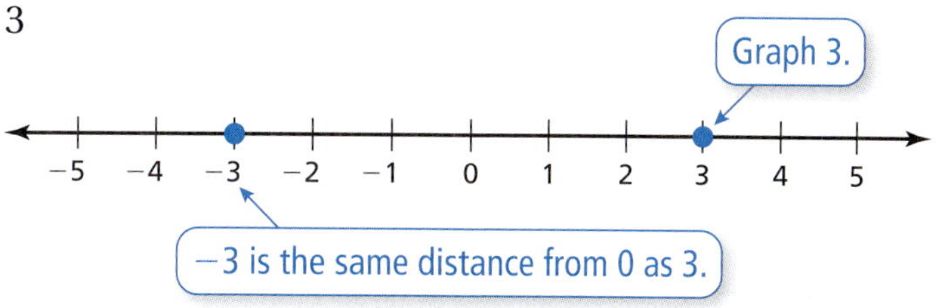

b. −2

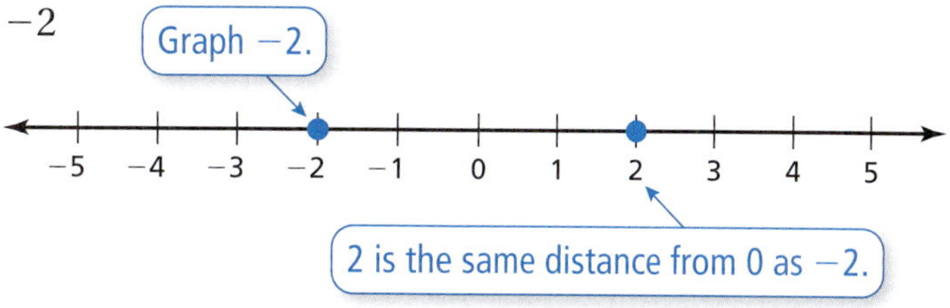

Reading

You can think of the negative sign (−) as referring to the opposite of a number. In Example 2(b), you can read −2 as "the opposite of 2."

EXAMPLE 3 Real-Life Application

You deliver flowers to an office building. You enter at ground level and go down 2 floors to make the first delivery. Then you go up 7 floors to make the second delivery.

a. Write an integer that represents each position.

Position	*Integer*
You enter at ground level.	0
You go down 2 floors.	−2
You go up 7 floors.	+7

b. Write an integer that represents how you return to ground level.

Use a number line to model your movement, as shown.

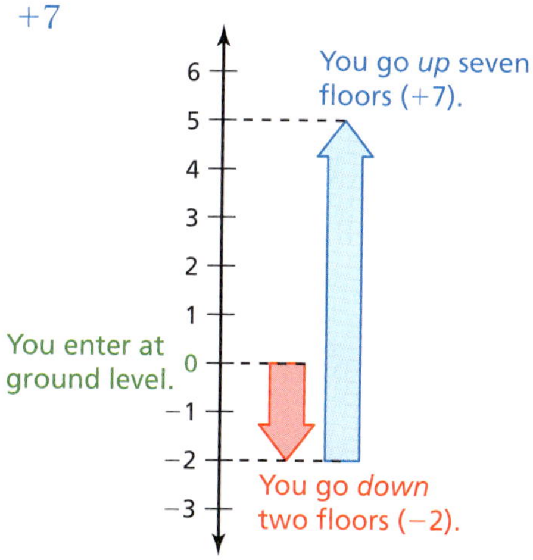

The second delivery is on the fifth floor. You must go down 5 floors to return to ground level.

∴ The integer representing "down 5 floors" is −5.

On Your Own

Now You're Ready
Exercises 16–23

Graph the integer and its opposite.

5. 6 **6.** −4 **7.** −12 **8.** 1

9. **WHAT IF?** In Example 3, you go up 9 floors to make the second delivery. Write an integer that represents how you return to ground level.

1.1 Exercises

Check It Out
Help with Homework
BigIdeasMath.com

Vocabulary and Concept Check

1. **VOCABULARY** Which of the following numbers are integers?

$$8, -4.1, -9, \frac{1}{6}, 1.75, 22$$

2. **OPEN-ENDED** Describe a real-life example that you can represent by -1200.
3. **VOCABULARY** List three words or phrases used in real life that indicate negative numbers.

Practice and Problem Solving

Graph the number that represents the situation on a number line.

4. A football team loses 3 yards.
5. The temperature is 6 degrees below zero.
6. A person climbs 600 feet up a mountain.
7. You earn $15 raking leaves.

Write a positive or negative integer that represents the situation.

(1) 8. You withdraw $42 from an account.
9. An airplane climbs to 37,500 feet.
10. The temperature rises 17 degrees.
11. You lose 56 points in a video game.
12. A ball falls 350 centimeters.
13. You receive 5 bonus points in class.

14. **STOCK MARKET** A stock market gains 83 points. The next day, the stock market loses 47 points. Write each amount as an integer.
15. **SCUBA DIVING** The world record for scuba diving is 318 meters below sea level. Write this as an integer.

Graph the integer and its opposite.

(2) 16. -5
17. -8
18. 14
19. 9
20. 30
21. -150
22. -32
23. 400

24. **ERROR ANALYSIS** Describe and correct the error in describing positive integers.

✗ The positive integers are 0, 1, 2, 3, ...

25. **TEMPERATURE** The highest temperature in February is 25°F. The lowest temperature in February is the opposite of the highest temperature. Graph both temperatures.

Identify the integer represented by the point on the number line.

26. A **27.** B **28.** C **29.** D

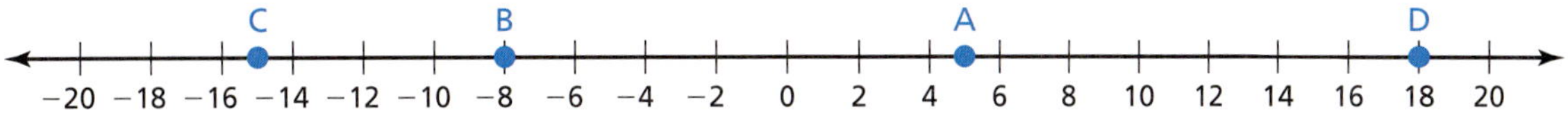

30. **TIDES** Use the information below.

- Low tide is 1 foot below the average water level.
- High tide is 5 feet higher than low tide.

Write an integer that represents the average water level relative to high tide.

31. **REPEATED REASONING** Choose any positive integer.

a. Find the opposite of the integer. **b.** Find the opposite of the integer in part (a).

c. What can you conclude about the opposite of the opposite of the integer? Is this true for all integers? Use a number line to justify your answer.

d. Describe the meaning of $-(-(-6))$. Find its value.

32. Number Sense In a game of tug-of-war, a team wins by pulling the flag over its goal line. The flag begins at 0. During a game, the flag moves 8 feet to the right, 12 feet to the left, and 13 feet back to the right. Did a team win? Explain.

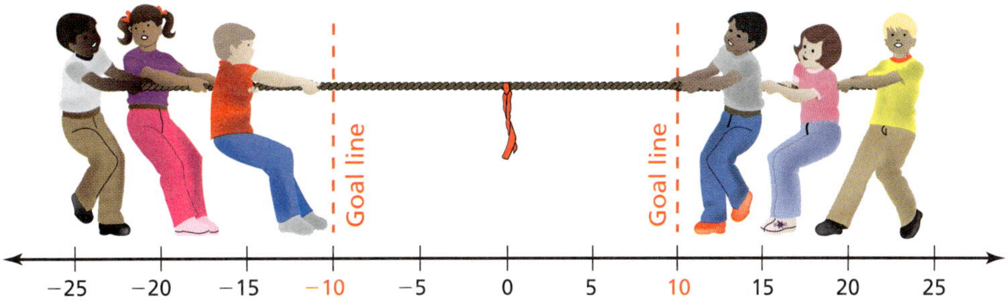

Fair Game Review What you learned in previous grades & lessons

Order the numbers from least to greatest.

33. $\frac{7}{8}, \frac{1}{2}, \frac{3}{8}, \frac{3}{4}$ **34.** 4.5, 4.316, 4.32, 4.312

35. **MULTIPLE CHOICE** The height of a statue is 710 centimeters. What is the height of the statue in meters? (One meter is equal to 100 centimeters.)

Ⓐ 0.71 m Ⓑ 7.1 m Ⓒ 7100 m Ⓓ 71,000 m

1.2 Comparing and Ordering Integers

Essential Question How can you use a number line to order real-life events?

1 ACTIVITY: Seconds to Takeoff

Work with a partner. You are listening to a command center before the liftoff of a rocket.

You hear the following:

> **"T minus 10 seconds . . . go for main engine start . . . T minus 9 . . . 8 . . . 7 . . . 6 . . . 5 . . . 4 . . . 3 . . . 2 . . . 1 . . . we have liftoff."**

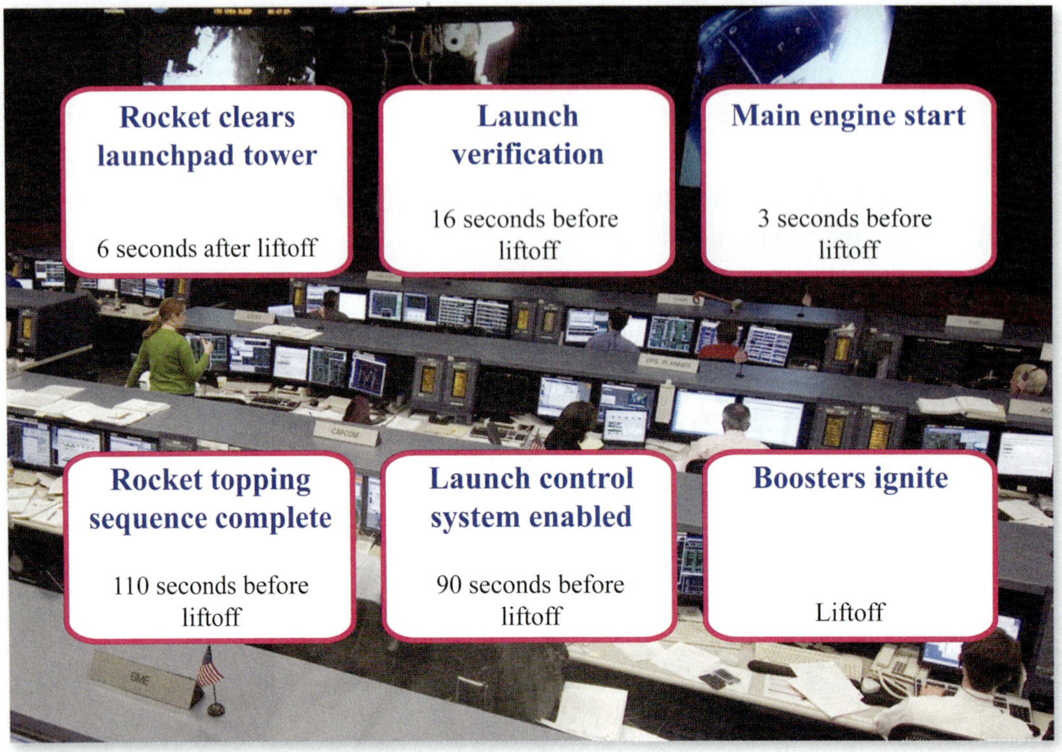

Integers

In this lesson, you will
- use a number line to compare positive and negative integers.
- use a number line to order positive and negative integers for real-life situations.

a. Draw a number line. Then locate the events shown above at appropriate points on the number line.

b. Which event occurs at zero on your number line? Explain.

c. Which of the events occurs first? Which of the events occurs last? How do you know?

d. List the events in the order they occurred.

2 ACTIVITY: Being Careful with Terminology

Work with a partner.

a. Use a number line to show that the phrase "3 seconds away from liftoff" can have two meanings.

b. Reword the phrase "3 seconds away from liftoff" in two ways so that each meaning is absolutely clear.

c. Explain why you must be very careful with terminology if you are working in the command center for a rocket launch.

3 ACTIVITY: A Day in the Life of an Astronaut

Math Process

Recognize the Usefulness of Tools

Which sources would give you the most accurate information? How do you know you can trust the information you find?

Make a time line that shows a day in the life of an astronaut. Use the Internet or another reference source to gather information.

- Use a number line with units representing hours. Start at 12 hours before liftoff and end at 12 hours after liftoff. Locate the liftoff at 0. Assume liftoff occurs at noon.
- Include at least five events before liftoff, such as when the astronauts suit up.
- Include at least five events after liftoff, such as when the rocket enters Earth's orbit.
- How do you determine where each event occurs on the number line?

What Is Your Answer?

4. **IN YOUR OWN WORDS** How can you use a number line to order real-life events?

5. Describe how you can use a number line to create a time line.

Practice Use what you learned about number lines to complete Exercises 4–7 on page 12.

1.2 Lesson

Check It Out
Lesson Tutorials
BigIdeasMath.com

On a horizontal number line, numbers to the left are less than numbers to the right. Numbers to the right are greater than numbers to the left.

EXAMPLE 1 Comparing Integers on a Horizontal Number Line

Compare 2 and -6.

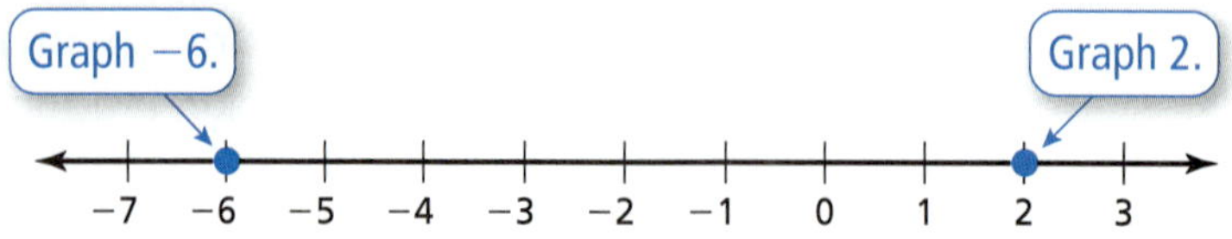

∴ 2 is to the right of -6. So, $2 > -6$.

On a vertical number line, numbers below are less than numbers above. Numbers above are greater than numbers below.

EXAMPLE 2 Comparing Integers on a Vertical Number Line

Compare -5 and -3.

∴ -5 is below -3. So, $-5 < -3$.

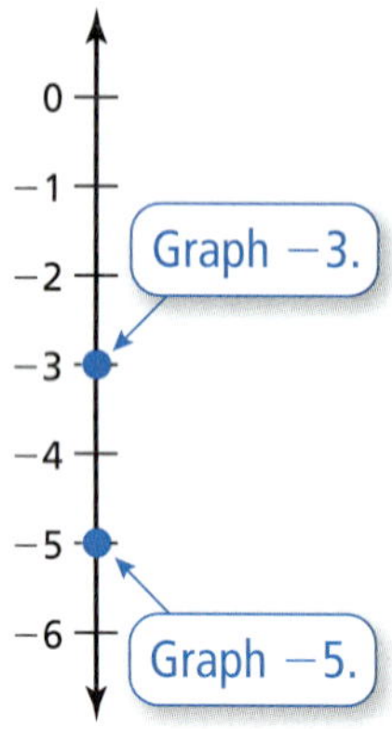

On Your Own

Now You're Ready
Exercises 4–11

Copy and complete the statement using < or >.

1. 0 ___ -4 **2.** -5 ___ 5 **3.** -8 ___ -7

EXAMPLE 3 Ordering Integers

Order $-4, 3, 0, -1, -2$ from least to greatest.

Graph each integer on a number line.

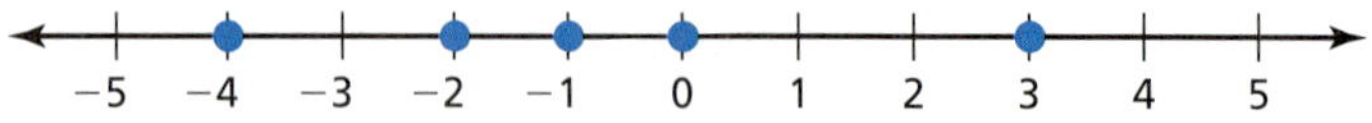

Write the integers as they appear on the number line from left to right.

∴ So, the order from least to greatest is $-4, -2, -1, 0, 3$.

EXAMPLE 4 Reasoning with Integers

A number is greater than −8 and less than 0. What is the greatest possible integer value of this number?

Ⓐ −10 Ⓑ −7 Ⓒ −1 Ⓓ 2

> **Study Tip**
> In Example 4, you can eliminate Choices A and D because −10 is to the left of −8 and 2 is to the right of 0.

The number is greater than −8 and less than 0. So, the number must be to the right of −8 and to the left of 0 on a horizontal number line.

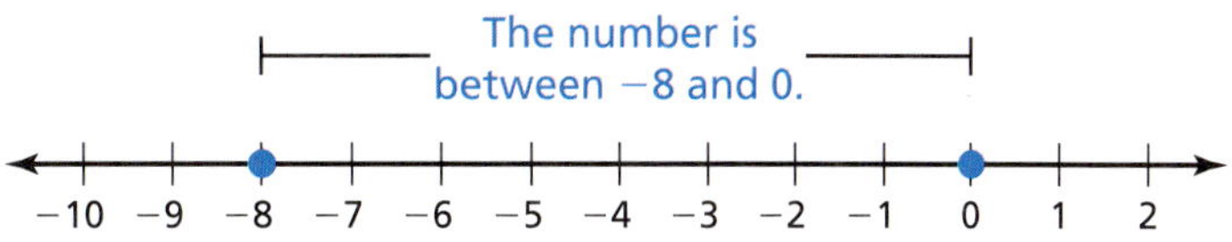

The greatest possible integer value between −8 and 0 is the integer farthest to the right on the number line between these values, which is −1.

So, the correct answer is Ⓒ.

EXAMPLE 5 Real-Life Application

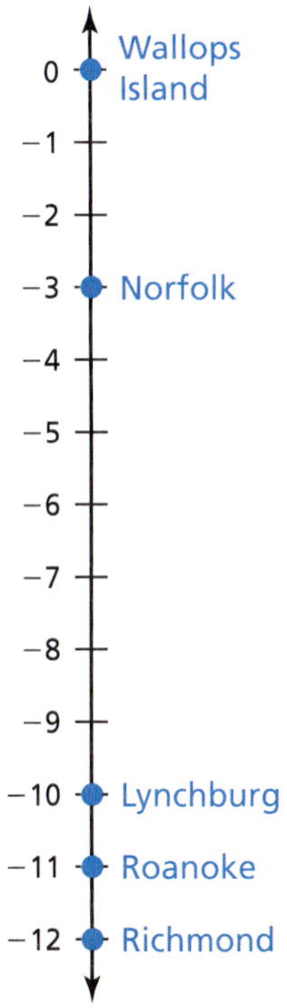

The diagram shows the coldest recorded temperatures for several cities in Virginia.

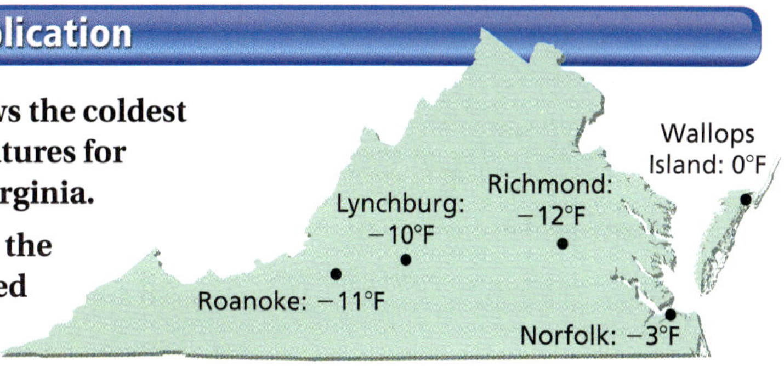

a. Which city has the coldest recorded temperature?

Graph each integer on a vertical number line.

−12 is the lowest on the number line. So, Richmond has the coldest recorded temperature.

b. Has a negative Fahrenheit temperature ever been recorded on Wallops Island? Explain.

The coldest recorded temperature on Wallops Island is 0°F, which is greater than every negative temperature. So, a negative temperature has never been recorded on Wallops Island.

On Your Own

Now You're Ready Exercises 14–19 and 22

Order the integers from least to greatest.

4. −2, −3, 3, 1, −1
5. 4, −7, −8, 6, 1
6. In Example 4, what is the least possible integer value of the number?
7. In Example 5, Norfolk recorded a new record low last night. The new record low is greater than the record low in Lynchburg. What integers can represent the new record low in Norfolk?

1.2 Exercises

Check It Out
Help with Homework
BigIdeasMath.com

Vocabulary and Concept Check

1. **WRITING** Explain how to use a number line to compare two integers.

2. **REASONING** The positions of four fish are shown.

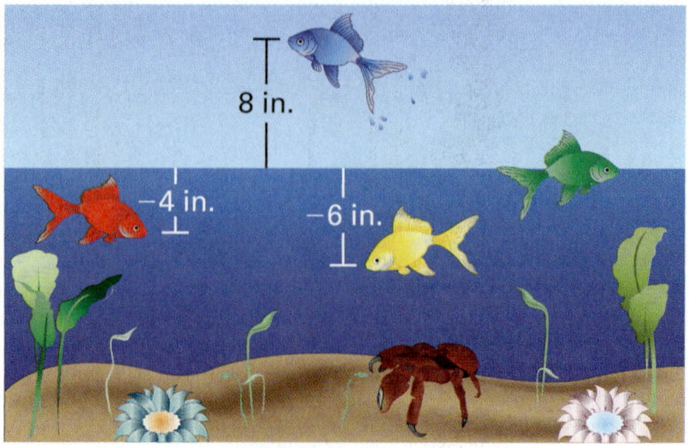

   a. Use red, blue, yellow, and green dots to graph the positions of the fish on a horizontal number line and a vertical number line.

   b. Explain how to use the number lines from part (a) to order the positions from least to greatest.

3. **NUMBER SENSE** a and b are negative integers. Compare a and b. Explain your reasoning.

Practice and Problem Solving

Copy and complete the statement using < or >.

(1) (2) **4.** $3 \ \square\ 0$ **5.** $-2 \ \square\ 0$ **6.** $6 \ \square\ -6$ **7.** $3 \ \square\ -4$

8. $-1 \ \square\ 4$ **9.** $-7 \ \square\ -8$ **10.** $-3 \ \square\ -2$ **11.** $-5 \ \square\ -10$

ERROR ANALYSIS **Describe and correct the error in comparing the negative numbers.**

12. ✗ Compare −3 and −1.
3 > 1. So, −3 > −1.

13. ✗ Compare −7 and −3.
Because −7 < −3, −7 is to the right of −3 on a number line.

Order the integers from least to greatest.

(3) **14.** 0, −1, 2, 3, −3 **15.** −4, −2, −3, 2, 1 **16.** −2, 3, −3, −4, 4

17. −7, 2, 6, −4, 3 **18.** 10, −10, 30, −30, −50 **19.** −5, 15, −10, −20, 25

20. **ARCHAEOLOGY** An archaeologist discovers the two artifacts shown.

   a. What integer represents ground level?

   b. A dinosaur bone is found 42 centimeters below ground level. Is it deeper than both of the artifacts?

21. **TEMPERATURE** The freezing temperature of nitrogen is −210°C, and the freezing temperature of oxygen is −223°C. Which temperature is colder?

④ **22.** **REASONING** A number is between −2 and −10. What is the least possible integer value of this number? What is the greatest possible integer value of this number?

Tell whether the statement is *always*, *sometimes*, or *never* true. Explain.

23. A positive integer is greater than its opposite.

24. An integer is less than its opposite and greater than 0.

25. **ELEVATION** The table shows the highest and lowest elevations for five states.

a. Order the states by their highest elevations, from least to greatest.

b. Order the states by their lowest elevations, from least to greatest.

c. What does the lowest elevation for Florida represent?

State	Highest Elevation (feet)	Lowest Elevation (feet)
Arkansas	2,753	55
California	14,494	−282
Florida	345	0
Louisiana	535	−8
Tennessee	6,643	178

26. **NUMBER LINE** Point *A* is on a number line halfway between −17 and 5. Point *B* is halfway between point *A* and 0. What integer does point *B* represent?

27. **TEMPERATURE** Eleven Fahrenheit temperatures are shown on a map during a weather report. When the temperatures are ordered from least to greatest, the middle temperature is below 0°F. Do you know exactly how many of the temperatures are represented by negative numbers? Explain.

28. Puzzle Nine students choose integers. Here are seven of them:

5, −8, 10, −1, −12, −20, and 1.

a. When all nine integers are ordered from least to greatest, the middle integer is 1. Describe the integers chosen by the other two students.

b. When all nine integers are ordered from least to greatest, the middle integer is –3. Describe the integers chosen by the other two students.

Fair Game Review What you learned in previous grades & lessons

Graph the decimal on a number line.

29. 2.4 **30.** 1.3 **31.** 0.65 **32.** 2.45

33. **MULTIPLE CHOICE** What is the perimeter of the trapezoid?

Ⓐ 16 ft Ⓑ 30 ft
Ⓒ 34 ft Ⓓ 48 ft

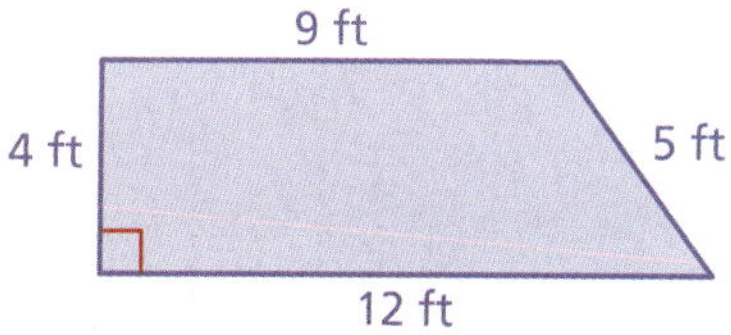

1.3 Integers and Absolute Value

Essential Question How can you use integers to represent the velocity and the speed of an object?

On these two pages, you will investigate vertical motion (up or down).

- Speed tells how fast an object is moving, but it does not tell the direction.
- Velocity tells how fast an object is moving, and it also tells the direction.

  When velocity is positive, the object is moving up.

  When velocity is negative, the object is moving down.

1 ACTIVITY: Falling Parachute

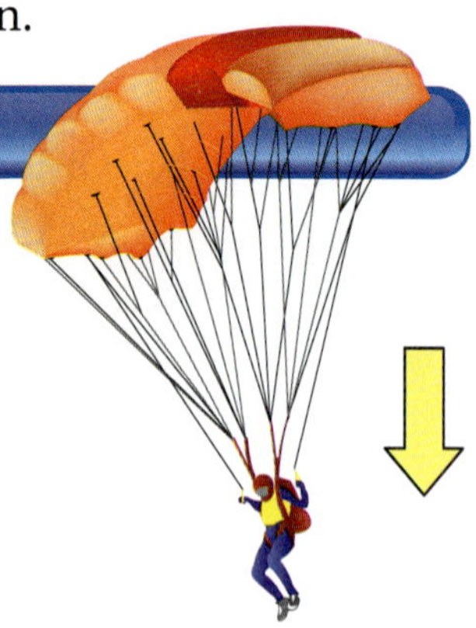

Work with a partner. You are gliding to the ground wearing a parachute. The table shows your height above the ground at different times.

Time (seconds)	0	1	2	3
Height (feet)	90	75	60	45

a. Describe the pattern in the table. How many feet do you move each second? After how many seconds will you land on the ground?

b. What integer represents your speed? Give the units.

c. Do you think your velocity should be represented by a positive or negative integer? Explain your reasoning.

d. What integer represents your velocity? Give the units.

2 ACTIVITY: Rising Balloons

Work with a partner. You release a group of balloons. The table shows the height of the balloons above the ground at different times.

Time (seconds)	0	1	2	3
Height (feet)	8	12	16	20

a. Describe the pattern in the table. How many feet do the balloons move each second? After how many seconds will the balloons be at a height of 40 feet?

b. What integer represents the speed of the balloons? Give the units.

c. Do you think the velocity of the balloons should be represented by a positive or negative integer? Explain your reasoning.

d. What integer represents the velocity of the balloons? Give the units.

Integers

In this lesson, you will

- define the absolute value of a number.
- find absolute values of numbers.
- solve real-life problems.

3 ACTIVITY: Firework Parachute

Work with a partner. The table shows the height of a firework's parachute above the ground at different times.

Time (seconds)	Height (feet)
0	480
1	360
2	240
3	120
4	0

Math Process

Use Clear Definitions

What information can you use to support your answer?

a. Describe the pattern in the table. How many feet does the parachute move each second?

b. What integer represents the speed of the parachute? What integer represents the velocity? How are these integers similar in their relation to 0 on a number line?

Inductive Reasoning

4. Copy and complete the table.

Velocity (feet per second)	-14	20	-2	0	25	-15
Speed (feet per second)						

5. Find two different velocities for which the speed is 16 feet per second.

6. Which number is greater: -4 or 3? Use a number line to explain your reasoning.

7. One object has a velocity of -4 feet per second. Another object has a velocity of 3 feet per second. Which object has the greater speed? Explain your answer.

What Is Your Answer?

8. **IN YOUR OWN WORDS** How can you use integers to represent the velocity and the speed of an object?

9. **LOGIC** In this lesson, you will study *absolute value*. Here are some examples:

$|-16| = 16$ $\quad |16| = 16$ $\quad |0| = 0$ $\quad |-2| = 2$

Which of the following is a true statement? Explain your reasoning.

$|\text{velocity}| = \text{speed}$ $\quad |\text{speed}| = \text{velocity}$

Practice Use what you learned about absolute value to complete Exercises 4–11 on page 18.

1.3 Lesson

Check It Out
Lesson Tutorials
BigIdeasMath.com

Key Vocabulary
absolute value, *p. 16*

The following numbers are integers:

$\ldots, -3, -2, -1, 0, 1, 2, 3, \ldots$

Key Idea

Absolute Value

Words The **absolute value** of an integer is the distance between the number and 0 on a number line. The absolute value of a number a is written as $|a|$.

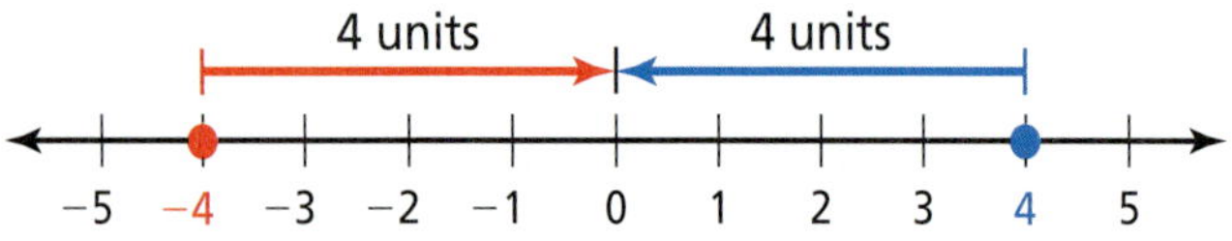

Numbers $|-4| = 4$ $|4| = 4$

EXAMPLE 1 Finding Absolute Value

Find the absolute value of 2.

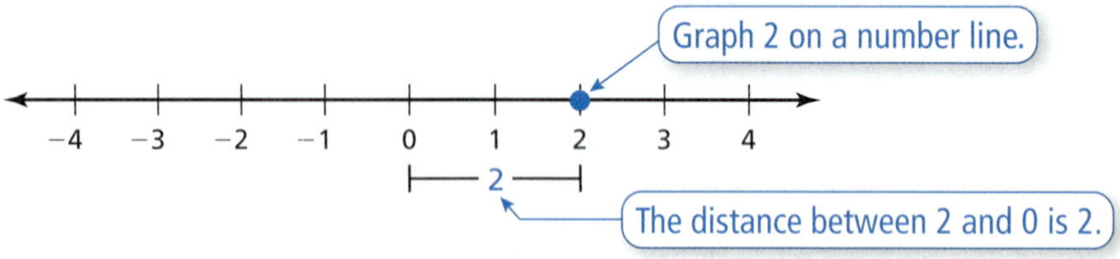

So, $|2| = 2$.

EXAMPLE 2 Finding Absolute Value

Find the absolute value of −3.

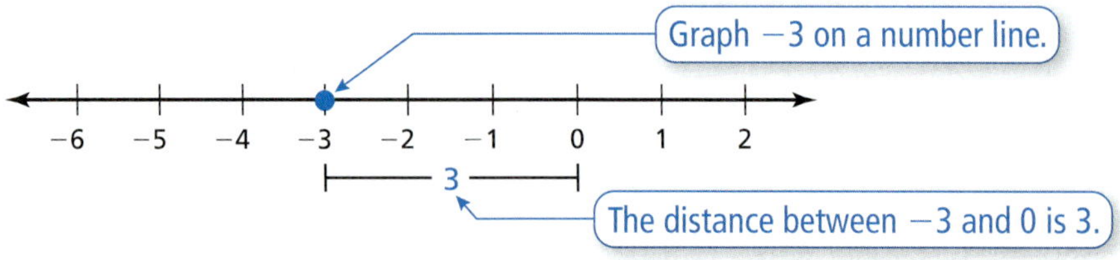

So, $|-3| = 3$.

On Your Own

Now You're Ready
Exercises 4–19

Find the absolute value.

1. $|7|$ **2.** $|-1|$ **3.** $|-5|$ **4.** $|14|$

EXAMPLE 3 Comparing Values

Remember

A number line can be used to compare and order integers. Numbers to the left are less than numbers to the right. Numbers to the right are greater than numbers to the left.

Compare 1 and $|-4|$.

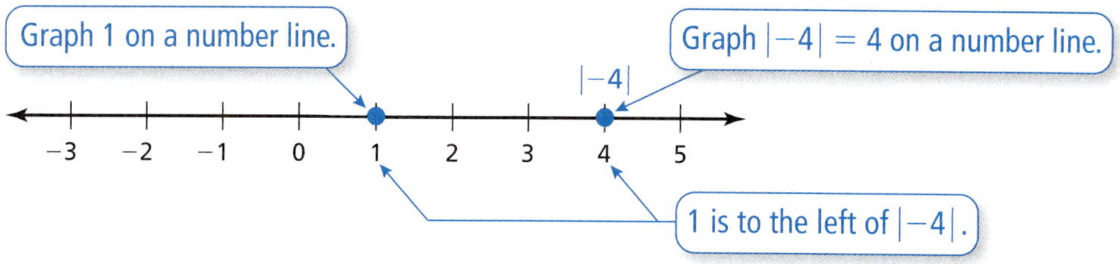

So, $1 < |-4|$.

On Your Own

Now You're Ready
Exercises 20–25

Copy and complete the statement using <, >, or =.

5. $|-2|$ ☐ -1

6. -7 ☐ $|6|$

7. $|10|$ ☐ 11

8. 9 ☐ $|-9|$

EXAMPLE 4 Real-Life Application

Substance	Freezing Point (°C)
Butter	35
Airplane fuel	−53
Honey	−3
Mercury	−39
Candle wax	55

STEM VIDEO

The *freezing point* is the temperature at which a liquid becomes a solid.

a. **Which substance in the table has the lowest freezing point?**

b. **Is the freezing point of mercury or butter closer to the freezing point of water, 0°C?**

a. Graph each freezing point.

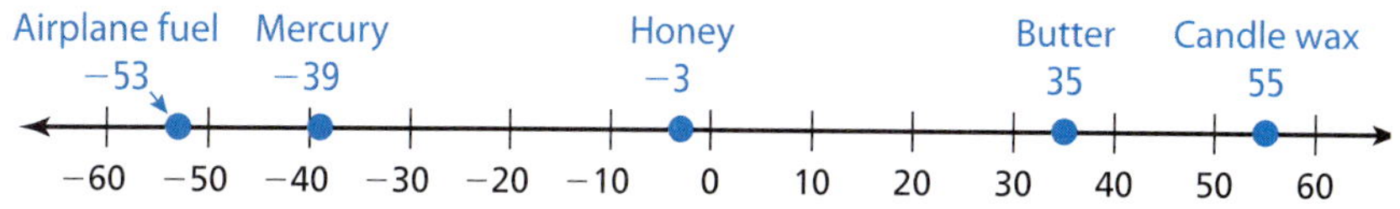

Airplane fuel has the lowest freezing point, −53°C.

b. The freezing point of water is 0°C, so you can use absolute values.

Mercury: $|-39| = 39$ **Butter:** $|35| = 35$

Because 35 is less than 39, the freezing point of butter is closer to the freezing point of water.

On Your Own

9. Is the freezing point of airplane fuel or candle wax closer to the freezing point of water? Explain your reasoning.

1.3 Exercises

Check It Out
Help with Homework
BigIdeasMath.com

Vocabulary and Concept Check

1. **VOCABULARY** Which of the following numbers are integers?

$$9,\ 3.2,\ -1,\ \frac{1}{2},\ -0.25,\ 15$$

2. **VOCABULARY** What is the absolute value of an integer?

3. **WHICH ONE DOESN'T BELONG?** Which expression does *not* belong with the other three? Explain your reasoning.

$|6|$ 6 -6 $|-6|$

Practice and Problem Solving

Find the absolute value.

1 2 4. $|9|$ 5. $|-6|$ 6. $|-10|$ 7. $|10|$

8. $|-15|$ 9. $|13|$ 10. $|-7|$ 11. $|-12|$

12. $|5|$ 13. $|-8|$ 14. $|0|$ 15. $|18|$

16. $|-24|$ 17. $|-45|$ 18. $|60|$ 19. $|-125|$

Copy and complete the statement using <, >, or =.

3 20. 2 ▢ $|-5|$ 21. $|-4|$ ▢ 7 22. -5 ▢ $|-9|$

23. $|-4|$ ▢ -6 24. $|-1|$ ▢ $|-8|$ 25. $|5|$ ▢ $|-5|$

ERROR ANALYSIS **Describe and correct the error.**

26. ✗ $|10| = -10$

27. ✗ $|-5| < 4$

28. **SAVINGS** You deposit \$50 in your savings account. One week later, you withdraw \$20. Write each amount as an integer.

29. **ELEVATOR** You go down 8 floors in an elevator. Your friend goes up 5 floors in an elevator. Write each amount as an integer.

Order the values from least to greatest.

30. $8, |3|, -5, |-2|, -2$ 31. $|-6|, -7, 8, |5|, -6$

32. $-12, |-26|, -15, |-12|, |10|$ 33. $|-34|, 21, -17, |20|, |-11|$

Simplify the expression.

34. $|-30|$ 35. $-|4|$ 36. $-|-15|$

37. **PUZZLE** Use a number line.

a. Graph and label the following points on a number line: $A = -3$, $E = 2$, $M = -6$, $T = 0$. What word do the letters spell?

b. Graph and label the absolute value of each point in part (a). What word do the letters spell now?

38. **OPEN-ENDED** Write a negative integer whose absolute value is greater than 3.

REASONING Determine whether $n \geq 0$ or $n \leq 0$.

39. $n + |-n| = 2n$

40. $n + |-n| = 0$

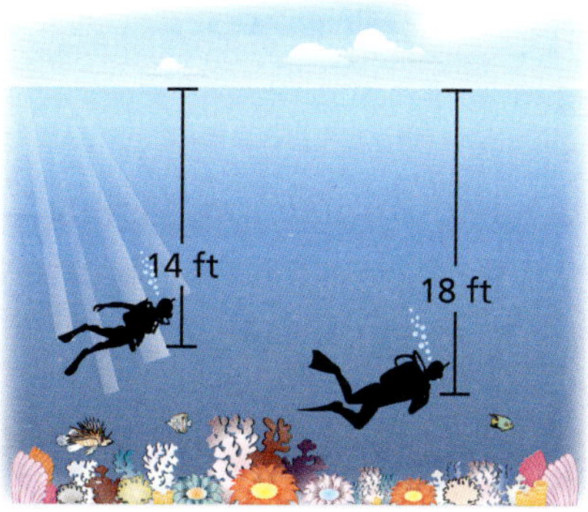

41. **CORAL REEF** The depths of two scuba divers exploring a living coral reef are shown.

a. Write an integer for the position of each diver relative to sea level.

b. Which integer in part (a) is greater?

c. Which integer in part (a) has the greater absolute value? Compare this absolute value with the depth of that diver.

42. **VOLCANOES** The *summit elevation* of a volcano is the elevation of the top of the volcano relative to sea level. The summit elevation of the volcano Kilauea in Hawaii is 1277 meters. The summit elevation of the underwater volcano Loihi in the Pacific Ocean is -969 meters. Which summit is closer to sea level?

43. **MINIATURE GOLF** The table shows golf scores, relative to *par*.

a. The player with the lowest score wins. Which player wins?

b. Which player is at par?

c. Which player is farthest from par?

Player	Score
1	+5
2	0
3	−4
4	−1
5	+2

True or False? **Determine whether the statement is *true* or *false*. Explain your reasoning.**

44. If $x < 0$, then $|x| = -x$.

45. The absolute value of every integer is positive.

Fair Game Review What you learned in previous grades & lessons

Add.

46. $19 + 32$

47. $50 + 94$

48. $181 + 217$

49. $1149 + 2021$

50. **MULTIPLE CHOICE** Which value is *not* a whole number?

Ⓐ -5 Ⓑ 0 Ⓒ 4 Ⓓ 113

1.4 The Coordinate Plane

Essential Question How can you graph and locate points in a coordinate plane?

In Activity 1, you will form the coordinate plane.

1 ACTIVITY: Forming the Entire Coordinate Plane

Work with a partner.

a. In the middle of a sheet of grid paper, construct a horizontal number line as shown. Label the tick marks. On a different sheet of grid paper, construct and label a similar vertical number line.

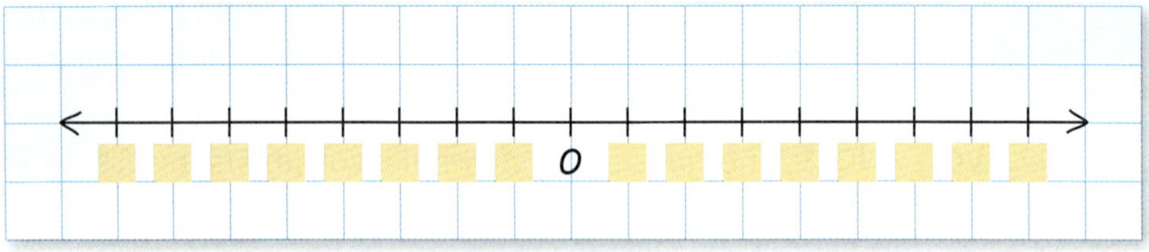

b. Cut out the vertical number line and tape it on top of the horizontal number line so that the zeros overlap. Make sure the number lines are perpendicular to one another. How many regions did you form by doing this?

c. **REASONING** What ordered pair represents the point where the number lines intersect? Why do you think this point is called the *origin*? Explain.

2 ACTIVITY: Describing Points in the Coordinate Plane

Work with a partner. Use your perpendicular number lines from Activity 1.

a. Plot and label (3, 2) on your coordinate plane. Shade this region in your coordinate plane. What do you notice about the integers along the number lines that surround (3, 2)?

b. Can you plot a point in your coordinate plane so that it is surrounded by negative numbers on the axes? If so, where is this point? Use a different color to shade this region in your coordinate plane.

c. What do you notice about the integers along the number lines for points in the regions that are not shaded?

d. **STRUCTURE** Describe how you would plot $(-3, -2)$. How is plotting this point similar to plotting (3, 2)? Plot $(-3, -2)$ in your coordinate plane.

e. **REASONING** Where in your coordinate plane do you plot $(2, -4)$? Where do you plot $(-2, 4)$? Explain your reasoning.

Coordinate Plane

In this lesson, you will

- describe the locations of points in the coordinate plane.
- plot points in the coordinate plane given ordered pairs.
- find distances between points in the coordinate plane.

3 ACTIVITY: Plotting Points in a Coordinate Plane

Math Process

Check Progress

How can you check your progress to make sure you are accurately drawing the picture?

Work with a partner. Plot and connect the points to make a picture. Describe and color the picture when you are done.

1(6, 9)	2(4, 11)	3(2, 12)	4(0, 11)	5(−2, 9)
6(−6, 2)	7(−9, 1)	8(−11, −3)	9(−7, 0)	10(−5, −1)
11(−5, −5)	12(−4, −8)	13(−6, −10)	14(−3, −9)	15(−3, −10)
16(−4, −11)	17(−4, −12)	18(−3, −11)	19(−2, −12)	20(−2, −11)
21(−1, −12)	22(−1, −11)	23(−2, −10)	24(−2, −9)	25(1, −9)
26(2, −8)	27(2, −10)	28(1, −11)	29(1, −12)	30(2, −11)
31(3, −12)	32(3, −11)	33(4, −12)	34(4, −11)	35(3, −10)
36(3, −8)	37(4, −6)	38(6, 0)	39(9, −3)	40(9, −1)
41(8, 1)	42(5, 3)	43(3, 6)	44(3, 7)	45(4, 8)

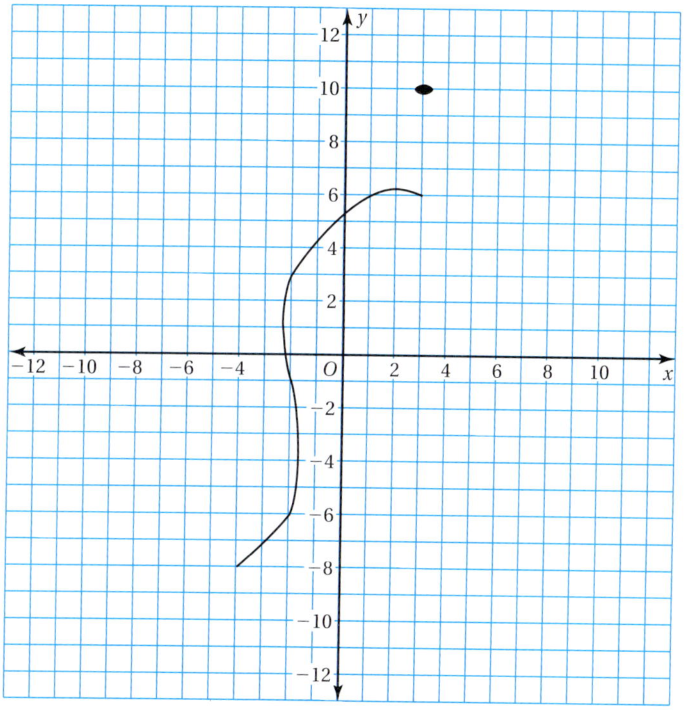

What Is Your Answer?

4. **IN YOUR OWN WORDS** How can you graph and locate points in a coordinate plane?

5. Make up your own "dot-to-dot" picture. Use at least 20 points. Your picture should have at least two points in each region of the coordinate plane.

Practice Use what you learned about the coordinate plane to complete Exercise 4 on page 25.

1.4 Lesson

Check It Out
Lesson Tutorials
BigIdeasMath.com

Key Vocabulary
coordinate plane, *p. 22*
origin, *p. 22*
quadrants, *p. 22*

In this lesson, you will plot points with positive and negative coordinates.

Key Idea

The Coordinate Plane

A **coordinate plane** is formed by the intersection of a horizontal number line and a vertical number line. The number lines intersect at the **origin** and separate the coordinate plane into four regions called **quadrants**.

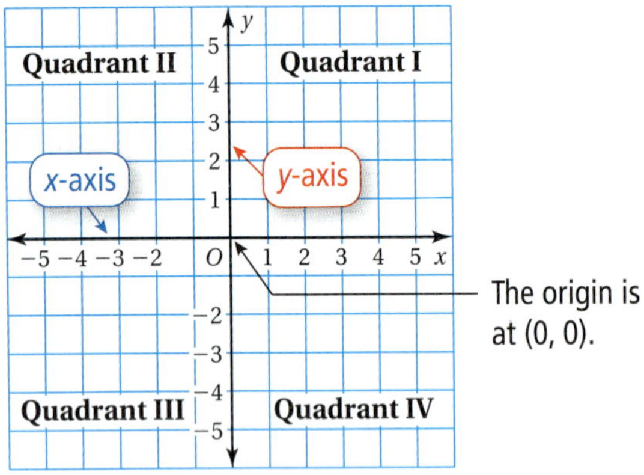

An *ordered pair* is used to locate a point in a coordinate plane.

ordered pair: (4, −2)

x-coordinate → 4; *y*-coordinate → −2

EXAMPLE 1 Identifying an Ordered Pair

Which ordered pair corresponds to point *T*?

Ⓐ (−3, −3) Ⓑ (−3, 3)

Ⓒ (3, −3) Ⓓ (3, 3)

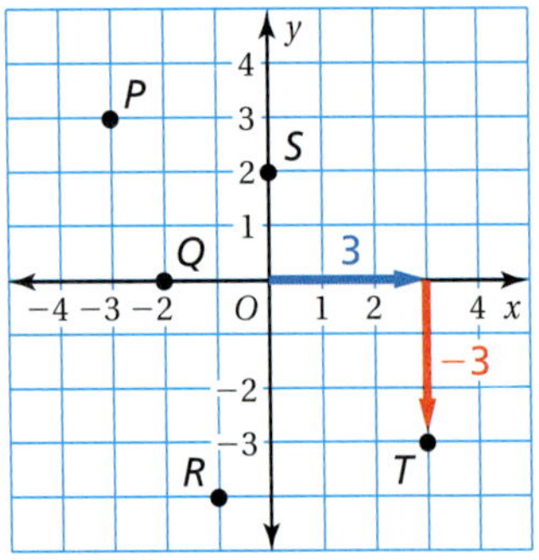

Point *T* is 3 units to the right of the origin and 3 units down. So, the *x*-coordinate is 3 and the *y*-coordinate is −3.

∴ The ordered pair (3, −3) corresponds to point *T*. The correct answer is Ⓒ.

On Your Own

Now You're Ready
Exercises 5–14

Use the graph in Example 1 to write an ordered pair corresponding to the point.

1. Point *P*
2. Point *Q*
3. Point *R*
4. Point *S*

Multi-Language Glossary at BigIdeasMath.com

EXAMPLE 2 Plotting Ordered Pairs

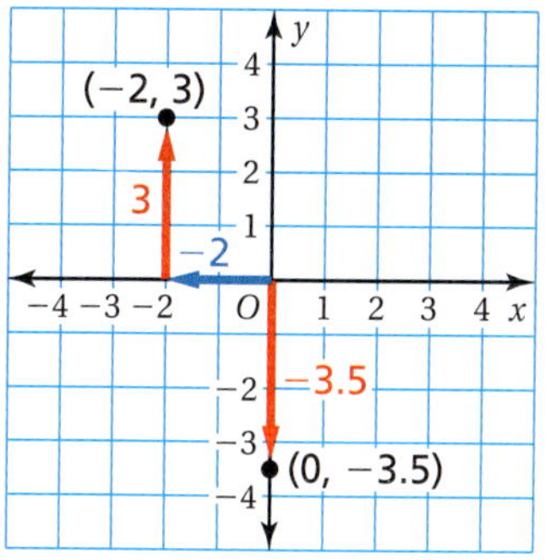

Plot (a) $(-2, 3)$ and (b) $(0, -3.5)$ in a coordinate plane. Describe the location of each point.

a. Start at the origin. Move 2 units left and 3 units up. Then plot the point.

The point is in Quadrant II.

b. Start at the origin. Move 3.5 units down. Then plot the point.

The point is on the y-axis.

On Your Own

Now You're Ready
Exercises 15–22

Plot the ordered pair in a coordinate plane. Describe the location of the point.

5. $(3, -1)$ **6.** $(-5, 0)$ **7.** $(-2.5, -1)$ **8.** $\left(-1\frac{1}{2}, \frac{1}{2}\right)$

EXAMPLE 3 Finding Distances in the Coordinate Plane

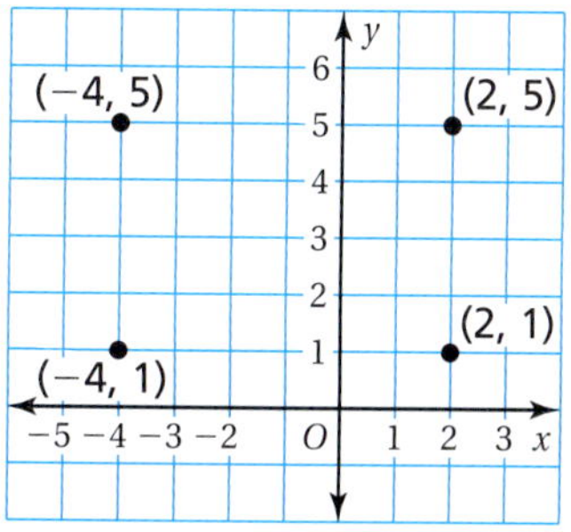

An *archaeologist* divides an area using a coordinate plane in which each unit represents 1 meter. The corners of a secret chamber are shown in the graph. What are the dimensions of the secret chamber?

The length of the chamber is the distance between $(-4, 5)$ and $(2, 5)$. The width of the chamber is the distance between $(2, 5)$ and $(2, 1)$.

You can use absolute values to find the distances between the points.

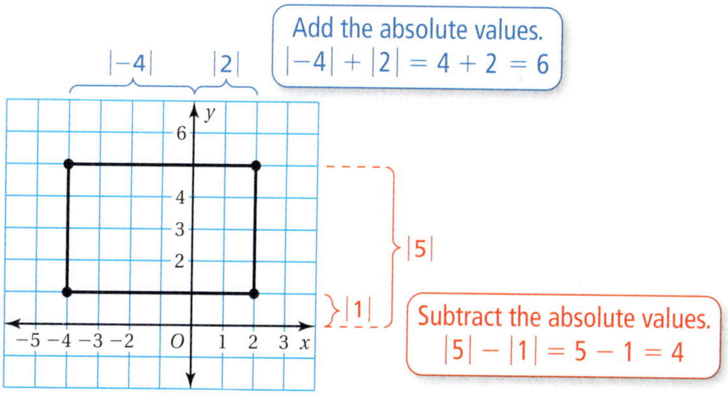

Reading

An **archaeologist** studies ancient ruins and objects to learn about people and cultures.

The secret chamber is 6 meters long and 4 meters wide.

On Your Own

Now You're Ready
Exercises 25–30

9. In Example 3, the archaeologist finds a gold coin at $(-1, 4)$, a silver coin at $(-4, 2)$, and pottery at $(-4, 4)$. How much closer is the pottery to the silver coin than to the gold coin?

You can use line graphs to display data that is collected over a period of time. Graphing and connecting the ordered pairs can show patterns or trends in the data. This type of line graph is also called a *time series graph*.

EXAMPLE 4 Real-Life Application

A blizzard hits a town at midnight. The table shows the hourly temperatures from midnight to 8:00 A.M.

Hours after Midnight, x	0	1	2	3	4	5	6	7	8
Temperature, y	7°F	5°F	3°F	0°F	−1°F	−4°F	−5°F	−2°F	2°F

a. Display the data in a line graph.

Write the ordered pairs.

(0, 7) (1, 5) (2, 3)

(3, 0) (4, −1) (5, −4)

(6, −5) (7, −2) (8, 2)

Plot and label the ordered pairs. Then connect the ordered pairs with line segments.

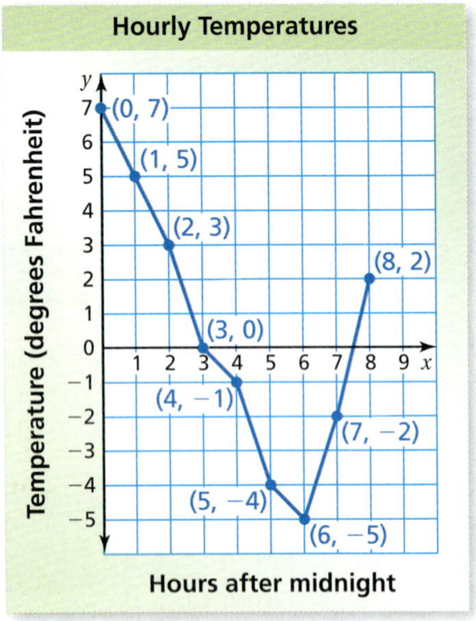

b. Make three observations from the graph.

Three possible observations follow:

- The hourly temperatures decrease from midnight to 6:00 A.M.
- The hourly temperatures increase from 6:00 A.M. to 8:00 A.M.
- The greatest decrease in hourly temperatures from one hour to the next is 3°F. This happens twice: from 2:00 A.M. to 3:00 A.M. and from 4:00 A.M. to 5:00 A.M.

Study Tip

The observations given in Example 4(b) are sample answers. You can make many other correct observations.

On Your Own

10. In Example 4, the blizzard hits another town at noon. The table shows the hourly temperatures from noon to 6:00 P.M.

Hours after Noon	0	1	2	3	4	5	6
Temperature	6°F	7°F	5°F	1°F	1°F	0°F	−3°F

a. Display the data in a line graph.

b. Make three observations from the graph.

1.4 Exercises

Check It Out
Help with Homework
BigIdeasMath.com

Vocabulary and Concept Check

1. **VOCABULARY** How many quadrants are in a coordinate plane?
2. **VOCABULARY** Is the point $(0, -7)$ on the x-axis or the y-axis?
3. **WHICH ONE DOESN'T BELONG?** Which point does *not* belong with the other three? Explain your reasoning.

$(-2, 1)$ $\quad$ $(-4, 5)$ $\quad$ $(2, -3)$ $\quad$ $(-1, 3)$

Practice and Problem Solving

4. Plot and connect the points to make a picture.

1 $(5, 0)$	**2** $(2, -3)$	**3** $(2, -2)$	**4** $(0, -2)$	**5** $(-3, -2)$
6 $(-3, 0)$	**7** $(-3, 2)$	**8** $(0, 2)$	**9** $(2, 2)$	**10** $(2, 3)$

Write an ordered pair corresponding to the point.

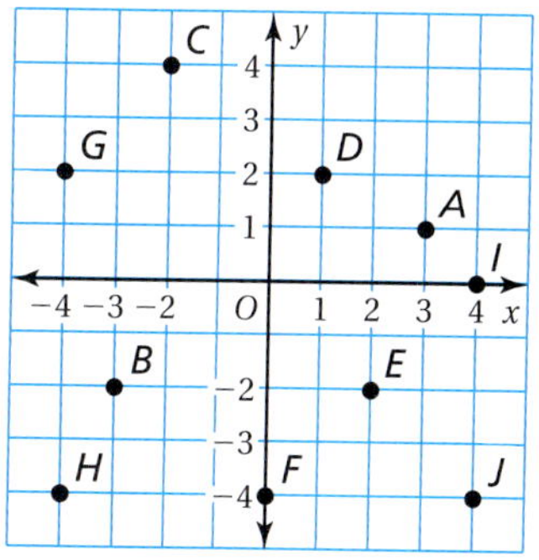

1 5. Point A
6. Point B
7. Point C
8. Point D
9. Point E
10. Point F
11. Point G
12. Point H
13. Point I
14. Point J

Plot the ordered pair in a coordinate plane. Describe the location of the point.

2 15. $K(4, 3)$
16. $L(-1, 2)$
17. $M(0, -6)$
18. $N(3.5, -1.5)$
19. $P(2, -4)$
20. $R(-4, 1)$
21. $S\left(2\frac{1}{2}, 0\right)$
22. $T(-4, -5)$

ERROR ANALYSIS **Describe and correct the error in the solution.**

23. ✗ To plot (4, 5), start at (0, 0) and move 5 units right and 4 units up.

24. ✗ To plot (−6, 3), start at (0, 0) and move 6 units right and 3 units down.

Plot the points and find the distance between the points.

3 25. $(2, -3), (6, -3)$
26. $(4, 2), (4, -1)$
27. $(-1, 1), (-1, 7)$
28. $(-5, -2), (4, -2)$
29. $(-3, 4), (5, 4)$
30. $(-2, -4), (-2, 1)$

31. **REASONING** The coordinates of three vertices of a square are shown in the figure. What are the coordinates of the fourth vertex?

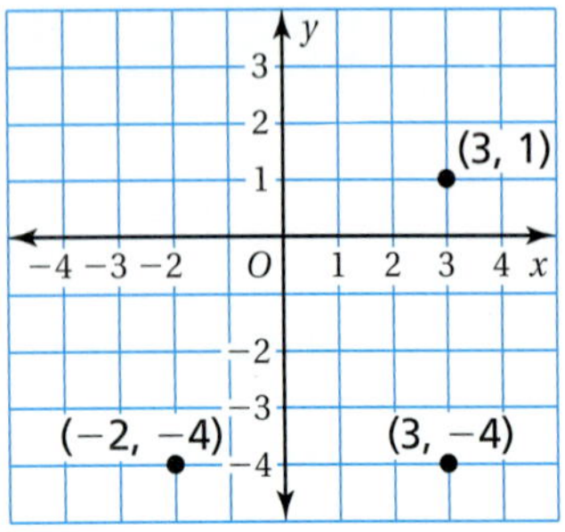

Draw the figure with the given vertices in a coordinate plane. Find the perimeter and the area of the figure.

32. $D(1, 1)$, $E(1, -2)$, $F(-2, -2)$, $G(-2, 1)$

33. $P(-2, 3)$, $Q(5, 3)$, $R(5, -1)$, $S(-2, -1)$

34. $W(-3, 2)$, $X(2, 2)$, $Y(2, -7)$, $Z(-3, -7)$

35. **POPULATION** The line graph shows the population of a city from 2005 to 2013.

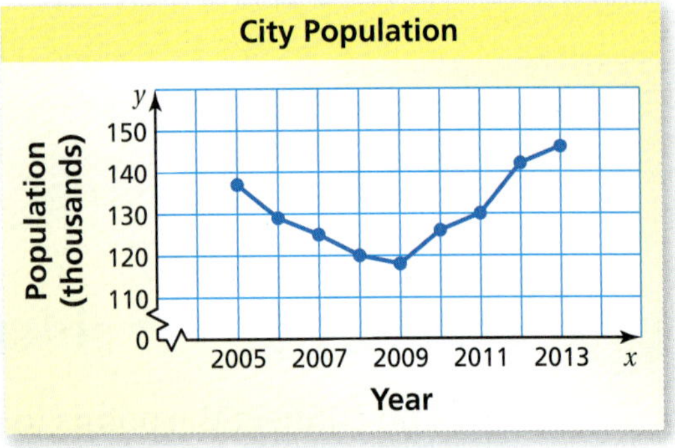

a. Estimate the population of the city in 2012.

b. Between which two years did the population increase the most?

c. Estimate the total change in population from 2005 to 2013.

36. **MODELING** The table shows the total miles run through 18 weeks for a marathon training program.

Week	1	2	3	4	5	6	7	8	9
Total Miles	22	46	72	96	124	151	181	211	244

Week	10	11	12	13	14	15	16	17	18
Total Miles	279	317	357	397	437	473	506	530	544

a. Create a table for the distance run during each week of training.

b. Display the data from part (a) in a line graph.

c. Make three observations from the graph.

d. Explain the pattern shown in the graph.

37. **PROFITS** The table shows the profits of a company from 2007 to 2013.

Years since 2000, x	7	8	9	10	11	12	13
Profit (millions of dollars), y	0.6	−0.2	−1.2	1.2	0.8	1	−0.6

a. Display the data in a line graph.

b. Make three observations from the graph.

c. How could you include profits from the years 1990 to 2006 on your graph? Explain.

Describe the possible location(s) of the point (x, y).

38. $x > 0, y > 0$

39. $x < 0, y < 0$

40. $x > 0, y < 0$

41. $x > 0$

42. $y < 0$

43. $x = 0, y = 0$

Tell whether the statement is *sometimes*, *always*, or *never* true. Explain your reasoning.

44. The x-coordinate of a point on the x-axis is zero.

45. The y-coordinates of points in Quadrant III are positive.

46. The x-coordinate of a point in Quadrant II has the same sign as the y-coordinate of a point in Quadrant IV.

ZOO **In Exercises 47–51, use the map of the zoo.**

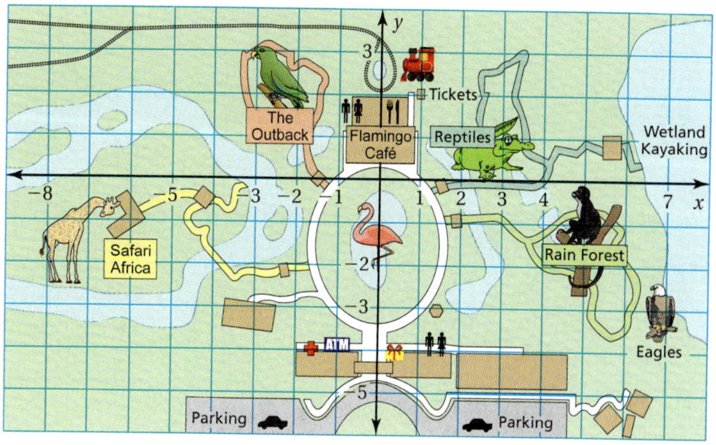

47. Which exhibit is located at (2, 1)?

48. Name an attraction on the positive y-axis.

49. Is parking available in Quadrant II? If not, name a quadrant in which you can park.

50. Write two different ordered pairs that represent the location of the Rain Forest.

51. Which exhibit is closest to (−8, −3)?

52. **NUMBER SENSE** Name the ordered pair that is 5 units right and 2 units down from (−3, 4).

53. **OPEN-ENDED** The vertices of triangle ABC are $A(-6, -3)$ and $B(2, -3)$. List four possible coordinates of the third vertex so that the triangle has an area of 24 square units.

54. **Reasoning** Your school is located at (2, −1), which is 2 blocks east and 1 block south of the center of town. To get from your house to the school, you walk 5 blocks west and 2 blocks north.

a. What ordered pair corresponds to the location of your house?

b. Is your house or your school closer to the center of town? Explain.

c. You can only walk along streets that are north and south or streets that are east and west. You are at the center of town and decide to take the shortest path home that passes by the school. When you are at the school, what percent of the walk home remains?

Fair Game Review What you learned in previous grades & lessons

Evaluate the expression.

55. $7 + 3 \times 9$

56. $24 - 14 \div 2$

57. $30 \div (4 + 2)$

58. $4 \times (10 - 3)$

59. **MULTIPLE CHOICE** What is the perimeter of the rectangle?

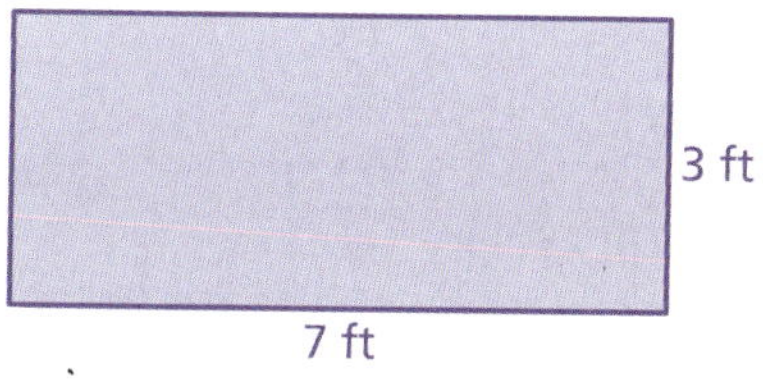

Ⓐ 10 ft

Ⓑ 11.5 ft

Ⓒ 20 ft

Ⓓ 21 ft

1 Study Help

Check It Out
Graphic Organizer
BigIdeasMath.com

You can use a **summary triangle** to explain a concept. Here is an example of a summary triangle for integers.

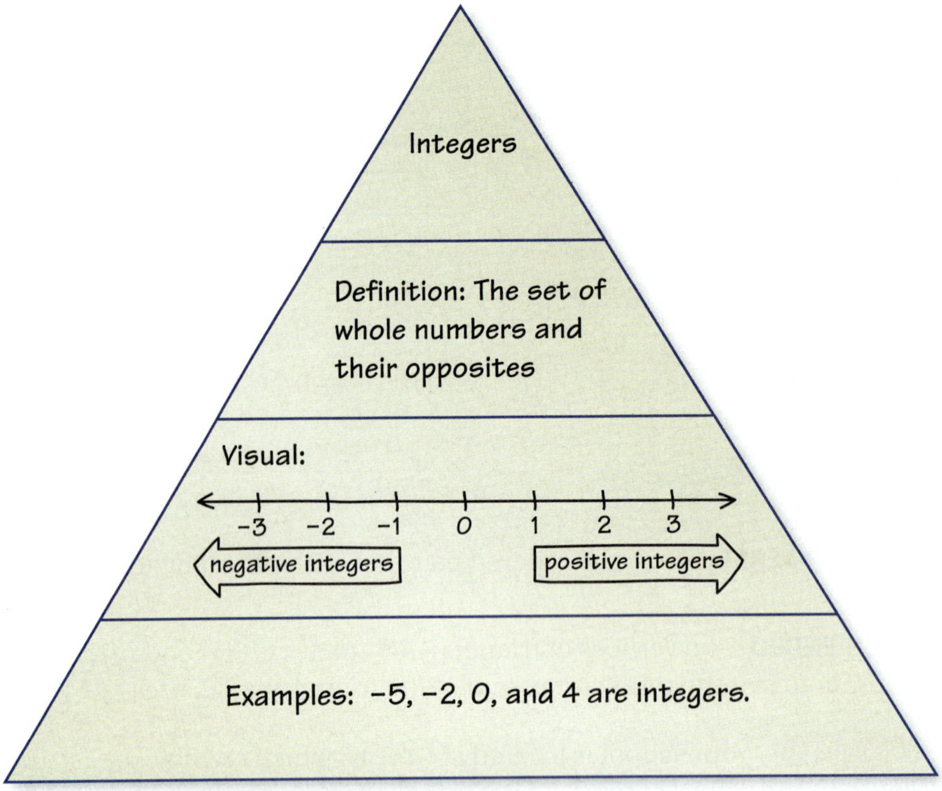

On Your Own

Make summary triangles to help you study these topics.

1. positive integers
2. negative integers
3. opposites
4. absolute value
5. coordinate plane
6. origin
7. quadrants

"I'm posting my new summary triangle on my daily blog. Do you think it will get me more hits?"

1 Chapter Review

Check It Out
Vocabulary Help
BigIdeasMath.com

Review Key Vocabulary

positive numbers, *p. 4*
negative numbers, *p. 4*
opposites, *p. 4*
integers, *p. 4*
absolute value, *p. 16*
coordinate plane, *p. 22*
origin, *p. 22*
quadrants, *p. 22*

Review Examples and Exercises

1.1 Integers *(pp. 2–7)*

Write a positive or negative integer to represent losing 150 points in a pinball game.

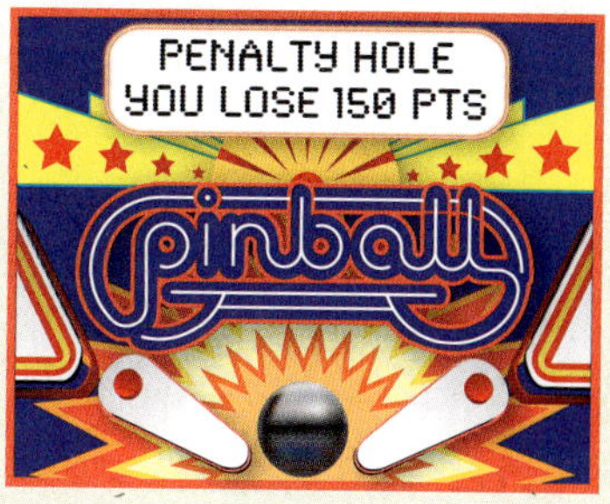

"Lose" indicates a number less than 0. So, use a negative integer.

∴ −150

Exercises

Write a positive or negative integer that represents the situation.

1. An elevator goes down 8 floors.

2. You earn $12.

Graph the integer and its opposite.

3. −7

4. 13

5. 4

6. −100

1.2 Comparing and Ordering Integers *(pp. 8–13)*

Order −3, −4, 2, 0, −1 from least to greatest.

Graph each integer on a number line.

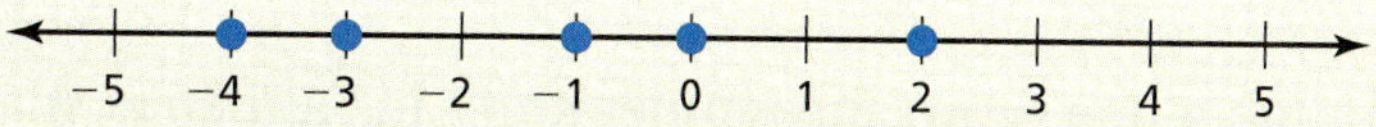

Write the integers as they appear on the number line from left to right.

∴ So, the order from least to greatest is −4, −3, −1, 0, 2.

Exercises

Order the integers from least to greatest.

7. −5, 4, 2, −3, −1

8. 5, −20, −10, 10, 15

9. Order the temperatures −3°C, 8°C, −12°C, −7°C, and 0°C from coldest to warmest.

1.3 Integers and Absolute Value (pp. 14–19)

Find the absolute value of −2.

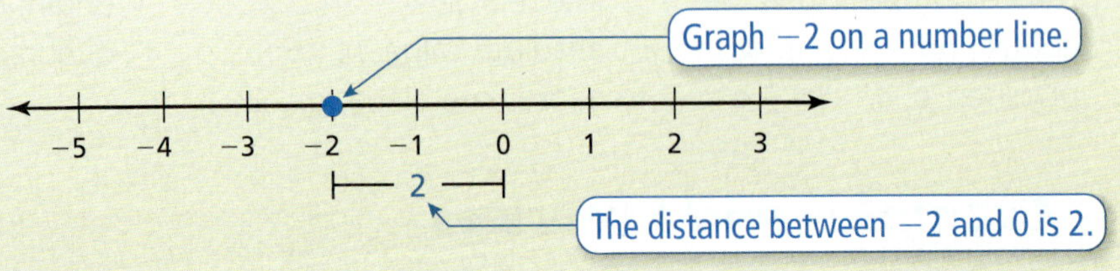

So, $|-2| = 2$.

Exercises

Find the absolute value.

10. $|3|$

11. $|-9|$

12. $|-17|$

13. $|8|$

14. $|0|$

15. $|-36|$

16. $|114|$

17. $|-87|$

Copy and complete the statement using <, >, or =.

18. $|4| \; \square \; |3|$

19. $|6| \; \square \; |-6|$

20. $|-8| \; \square \; |5|$

21. $|-2| \; \square \; |7|$

22. $|-6| \; \square \; |-10|$

23. $|-1| \; \square \; |0|$

24. **ELEVATION** The elevation of Death Valley, California, is −282 feet. The Mississippi River in Illinois has an elevation of 279 feet. Which is closer to sea level?

25. The number line shows the temperatures in Fairbanks, Alaska and Richmond, Virginia. Which temperature is closer to the freezing point of water, 0°C?

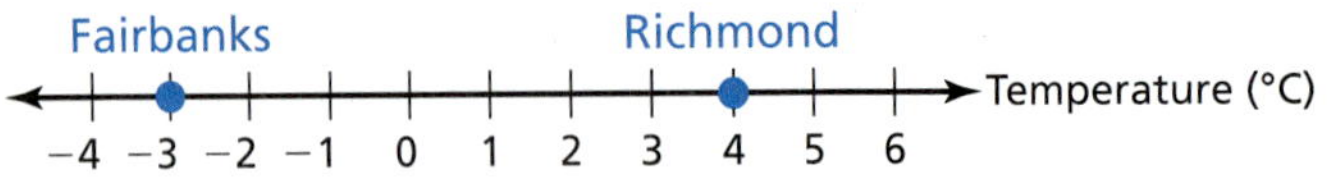

1.4 The Coordinate Plane (pp. 20–27)

a. Plot (−3, 0) and (4, −4) in a coordinate plane. Describe the location of each point.

To plot (−3, 0), start at the origin. Move 3 units left. Then plot the point.

To plot (4, −4), start at the origin. Move 4 units right and 4 units down. Then plot the point.

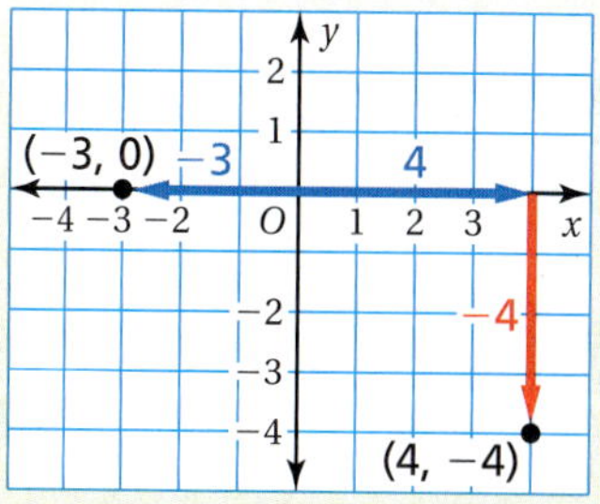

∴ The point (−3, 0) is on the x-axis.
The point (4, −4) is in Quadrant IV.

b. Plot (2, 3) and (2, −3) in a coordinate plane. Then find the distance between the points.

Plot (2, 3) and (2, −3).

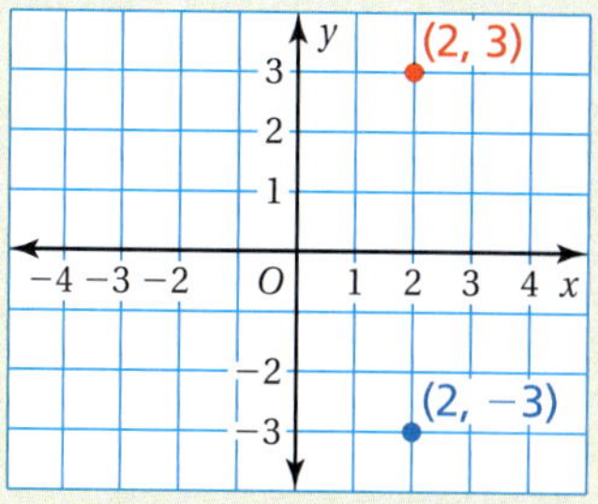

You can use absolute values to find the distances between the points.

$$|3| + |-3| = 3 + 3 = 6$$

∴ So, the distance between the points is 6 units.

c. Plot (2, −3) and (−2, −3) in a coordinate plane. Then find the distance between the points.

Plot (2, −3) and (−2, −3).

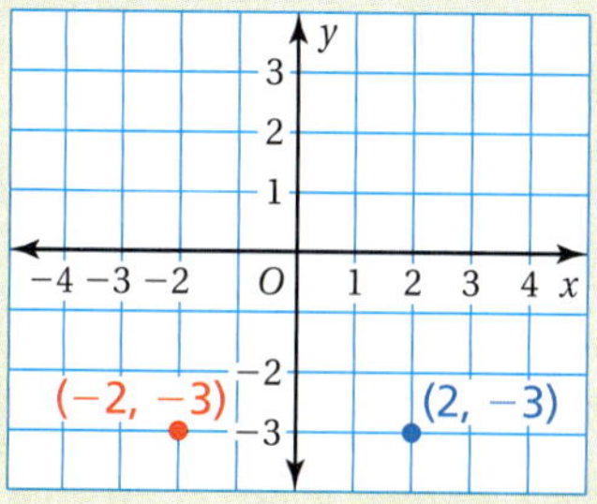

You can use absolute values to find the distances between the points.

$$|-2| + |2| = 2 + 2 = 4$$

∴ So, the distance between the points is 4 units.

Exercises

Plot the ordered pair in a coordinate plane. Describe the location of the point.

26. $A(1, 3)$

27. $B(0, -3)$

28. $C(-4, -2)$

29. $D(-1, 2)$

Plot the points and find the distance between the points.

30. (4, 1), (4, 6)

31. (−2, 3), (−6, 3)

32. (2, −5), (−7, −5)

33. (−3.5, −2.5), (−3.5, 4)

34. (1, 2), (1, −9)

35. $(-4, 6), \left(-\frac{1}{2}, 6\right)$

36. $(3, -4), \left(3, -1\frac{1}{2}\right)$

37. $(-3, -3), \left(-3, 2\frac{1}{2}\right)$

2 Operations with Integers

"Look, subtraction is not that difficult. Imagine that you have five squeaky mouse toys."

"After your friend Fluffy comes over for a visit, you notice that one of the squeaky toys is missing."

"Now, you go over to Fluffy's and retrieve the missing squeaky mouse toy. It's easy."

"Dear Sir: You asked me to 'find' the opposite of −1."

"I didn't know it was missing."

What You Learned Before

"I liked it because it is the opposite of the freezing point on the Fahrenheit temperature scale."

Commutative and Associative Properties

Example 1 **a. Simplify the expression 6 + (14 + 9).**

$6 + (14 + 9) = (6 + 14) + 9$ — Associative Property of Addition

$= 20 + 9$ — Add 6 and 14.

$= 29$ — Add 20 and 9.

b. Simplify the expression (2 + 57) + 8.

$(2 + 57) + 8 = (57 + 2) + 8$ — Commutative Property of Addition

$= 57 + (2 + 8)$ — Associative Property of Addition

$= 57 + 10$ — Add 2 and 8.

$= 67$ — Add 57 and 10.

c. Simplify the expression 20 × (5 × 17).

$20 \times (5 \times 17) = (20 \times 5) \times 17$ — Associative Property of Multiplication

$= 100 \times 17$ — Multiply 20 and 5.

$= 1700$ — Multiply 100 and 17.

Try It Yourself

Simplify the expression. Explain each step.

1. $3 + (17 + 8)$ **2.** $(4 + 27) + 6$ **3.** $50 \times (2 \times 9)$

Properties of Zero and One

Example 2 **a. Simplify the expression 6 • 0 • 38.**

$6 \cdot 0 \cdot 38 = (6 \cdot 0) \cdot 38$ — Associative Property of Multiplication

$= 0 \cdot 38 = 0$ — Multiplication Property of Zero

b. Simplify the expression 8 • 5 • 1.

$8 \cdot 5 \cdot 1 = 8 \cdot (5 \cdot 1)$ — Associative Property of Multiplication

$= 8 \cdot 5$ — Multiplication Property of One

$= 40$ — Multiply 8 and 5.

Try It Yourself

Simplify the expression. Explain each step.

4. $13 \cdot 4 \cdot 0$ **5.** $1 \cdot 6 \cdot 5$ **6.** $(36 + 14) + 0$

2.1 Adding Integers

Essential Question Is the sum of two integers *positive*, *negative*, or *zero*? How can you tell?

1 ACTIVITY: Adding Integers with the Same Sign

Work with a partner. Use integer counters to find $-4 + (-3)$.

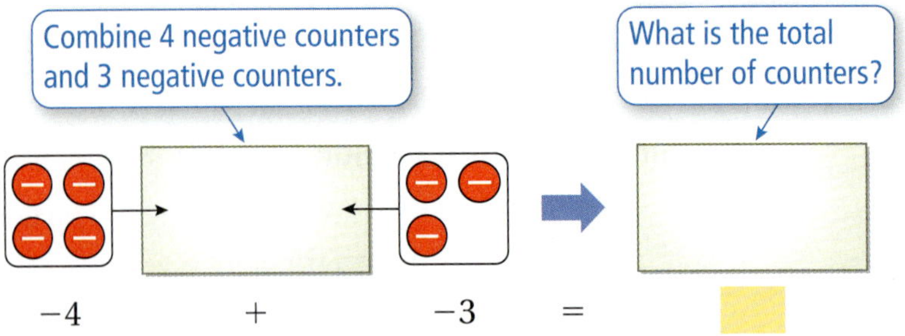

So, $-4 + (-3) =$ ______.

2 ACTIVITY: Adding Integers with Different Signs

Work with a partner. Use integer counters to find $-3 + 2$.

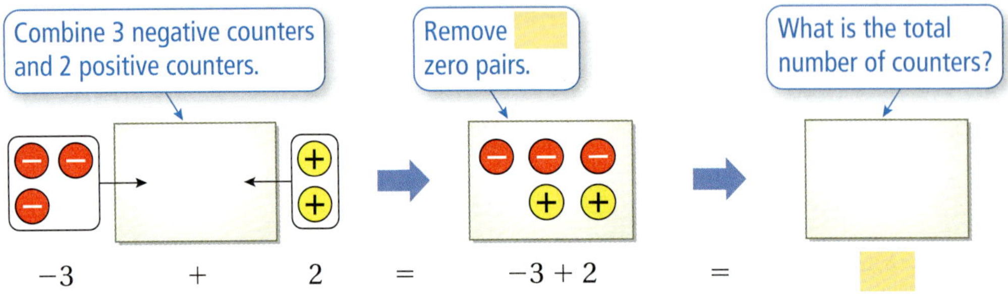

So, $-3 + 2 =$ ______.

Integers

In this lesson, you will

- add integers.
- show that the sum of a number and its opposite is 0.
- solve real-life problems.

3 ACTIVITY: Adding Integers with Different Signs

Work with a partner. Use a number line to find $5 + (-3)$.

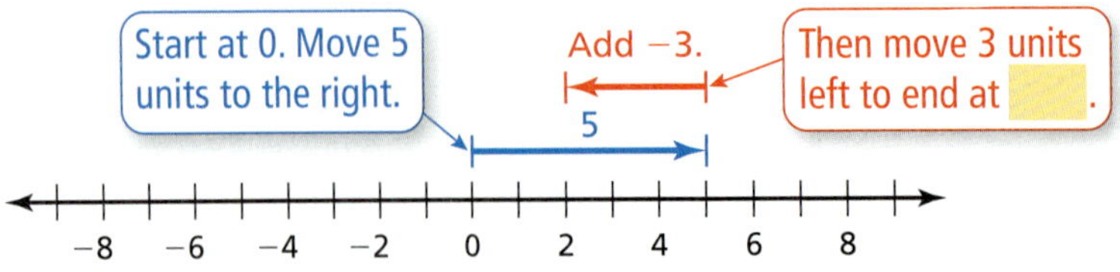

So, $5 + (-3) =$ ______.

4 ACTIVITY: Adding Integers with Different Signs

Math Process

Make Conjectures

How can the relationship between the integers help you write a rule?

Work with a partner. Write the addition expression shown. Then find the sum. How are the integers in the expression related to 0 on a number line?

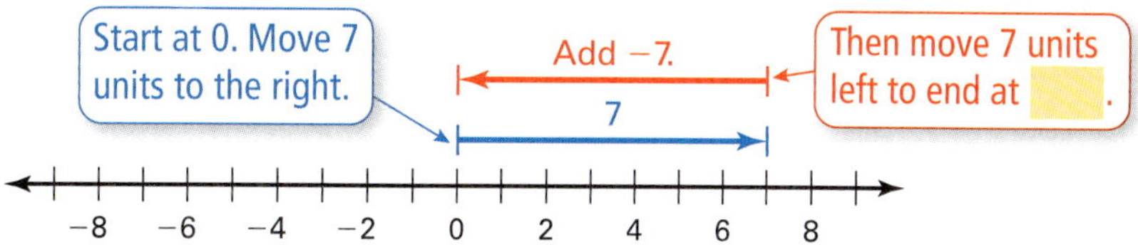

Inductive Reasoning

Work with a partner. Use integer counters or a number line to complete the table.

	Exercise	Type of Sum	Sum	Sum: Positive, Negative, or Zero
1	**5.** $-4 + (-3)$	Integers with the same sign		
2	**6.** $-3 + 2$			
3	**7.** $5 + (-3)$			
4	**8.** $7 + (-7)$			
	9. $2 + 4$			
	10. $-6 + (-2)$			
	11. $-5 + 9$			
	12. $15 + (-9)$			
	13. $-10 + 10$			
	14. $-6 + (-6)$			
	15. $13 + (-13)$			

What Is Your Answer?

16. **IN YOUR OWN WORDS** Is the sum of two integers *positive*, *negative*, or *zero*? How can you tell?

17. **STRUCTURE** Write general rules for adding (a) two integers with the same sign, (b) two integers with different signs, and (c) two integers that vary only in sign.

Practice Use what you learned about adding integers to complete Exercises 8–15 on page 38.

2.1 Lesson

Key Vocabulary
additive inverse, *p. 36*

Key Idea

Adding Integers with the Same Sign

Words Add the absolute values of the integers. Then use the common sign.

Numbers $2 + 5 = 7$ $\quad -2 + (-5) = -7$

EXAMPLE 1 Adding Integers with the Same Sign

Find $-2 + (-4)$. Use a number line to check your answer.

$-2 + (-4) = -6$ Add $|-2|$ and $|-4|$.

Use the common sign.

∴ The sum is -6.

Check

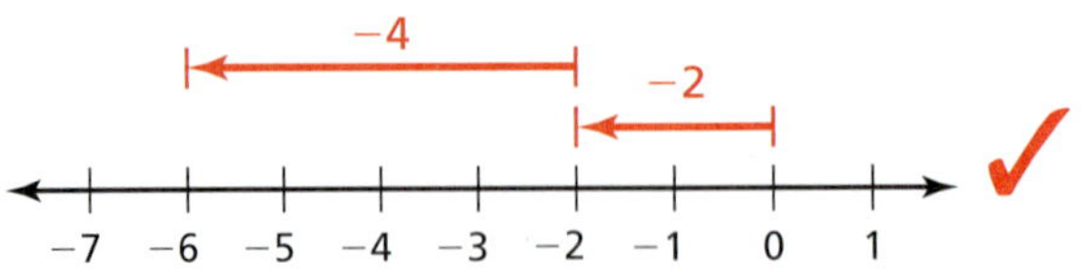

On Your Own

Add.

1. $7 + 13$ **2.** $-8 + (-5)$ **3.** $-20 + (-15)$

Two numbers that are the same distance from 0, but on opposite sides of 0, are called *opposites*. For example, -3 and 3 are opposites.

Key Ideas

Adding Integers with Different Signs

Words Subtract the lesser absolute value from the greater absolute value. Then use the sign of the integer with the greater absolute value.

Numbers $8 + (-10) = -2$ $\quad -13 + 17 = 4$

Additive Inverse Property

Words The sum of an integer and its **additive inverse**, or opposite, is 0.

Numbers $6 + (-6) = 0$ $\quad -25 + 25 = 0$ **Algebra** $a + (-a) = 0$

EXAMPLE 2 Adding Integers with Different Signs

a. Find 5 + (−10).

$5 + (-10) = -5$ — $|-10| > |5|$. So, subtract $|5|$ from $|-10|$.

Use the sign of −10.

The sum is −5.

b. Find −3 + 7.

$-3 + 7 = 4$ — $|7| > |-3|$. So, subtract $|-3|$ from $|7|$.

Use the sign of 7.

The sum is 4.

c. Find −12 + 12.

$-12 + 12 = 0$ — The sum is 0 by the Additive Inverse Property.

−12 and 12 are opposites.

The sum is 0.

EXAMPLE 3 Adding More Than Two Integers

The list shows four bank account transactions in July. Find the change C in the account balance.

JULY TRANSACTIONS	
Withdrawal	-$40
Deposit	$50
Deposit	$75
Withdrawal	-$50

Study Tip

A deposit of $50 and a withdrawal of $50 represent opposite quantities, +50 and −50, which have a sum of 0.

Find the sum of the four transactions.

$C = -40 + 50 + 75 + (-50)$ — Write the sum.

$= -40 + 75 + 50 + (-50)$ — Commutative Property of Addition

$= -40 + 75 + [50 + (-50)]$ — Associative Property of Addition

$= -40 + 75 + 0$ — Additive Inverse Property

$= 35 + 0$ — Add −40 and 75.

$= 35$ — Addition Property of Zero

Because $C = 35$, the account balance increased $35 in July.

On Your Own

Now You're Ready
Exercises 8–23 and 28–39

Add.

4. $-2 + 11$ **5.** $9 + (-10)$ **6.** $-31 + 31$

7. WHAT IF? In Example 3, the deposit amounts are $30 and $40. Find the change C in the account balance.

2.1 Exercises

Check It Out
Help with Homework
BigIdeasMath.com

Vocabulary and Concept Check

1. **WRITING** How do you find the additive inverse of an integer?

2. **NUMBER SENSE** Is $3 + (-4)$ the same as $-4 + 3$? Explain.

Tell whether the sum is *positive*, *negative*, or *zero* without adding. Explain your reasoning.

3. $-8 + 20$
4. $30 + (-30)$
5. $-10 + (-18)$

Tell whether the statement is *true* or *false*. Explain your reasoning.

6. The sum of two negative integers is always negative.

7. An integer and its absolute value are always opposites.

Practice and Problem Solving

Add.

1 2

8. $6 + 4$
9. $-4 + (-6)$
10. $-2 + (-3)$
11. $-5 + 12$
12. $5 + (-7)$
13. $8 + (-8)$
14. $9 + (-11)$
15. $-3 + 13$
16. $-4 + (-16)$
17. $-3 + (-1)$
18. $14 + (-5)$
19. $0 + (-11)$
20. $-10 + (-15)$
21. $-13 + 9$
22. $18 + (-18)$
23. $-25 + (-9)$

ERROR ANALYSIS **Describe and correct the error in finding the sum.**

24. ✗ $9 + (-6) = -3$

25. ✗ $-10 + (-10) = 0$

26. **TEMPERATURE** The temperature is −3°F at 7:00 A.M. During the next 4 hours, the temperature increases 21°F. What is the temperature at 11:00 A.M.?

27. **BANKING** Your bank account has a balance of −\$12. You deposit \$60. What is your new balance?

Tell how the Commutative and Associative Properties of Addition can help you find the sum mentally. Then find the sum.

3

28. $9 + 6 + (-6)$
29. $-8 + 13 + (-13)$
30. $9 + (-17) + (-9)$
31. $7 + (-12) + (-7)$
32. $-12 + 25 + (-15)$
33. $6 + (-9) + 14$

Add.

34. $13 + (-21) + 16$
35. $22 + (-14) + (-35)$
36. $-13 + 27 + (-18)$
37. $-19 + 26 + 14$
38. $-32 + (-17) + 42$
39. $-41 + (-15) + (-29)$

40. **SCIENCE** A lithium atom has positively charged protons and negatively charged electrons. The sum of the charges represents the charge of the lithium atom. Find the charge of the atom.

Lithium Atom

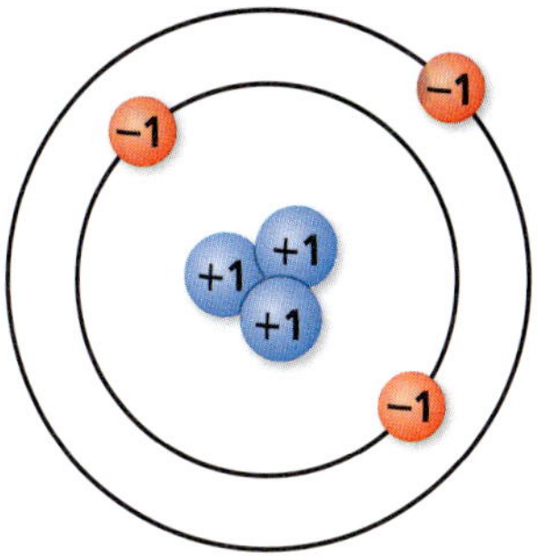

41. **OPEN-ENDED** Write two integers with different signs that have a sum of -25. Write two integers with the same sign that have a sum of -25.

ALGEBRA Evaluate the expression when $a = 4$, $b = -5$, and $c = -8$.

42. $a + b$

43. $-b + c$

44. $|a + b + c|$

MENTAL MATH Use mental math to solve the equation.

45. $d + 12 = 2$

46. $b + (-2) = 0$

47. $-8 + m = -15$

48. **PROBLEM SOLVING** Starting at point A, the path of a dolphin jumping out of the water is shown.

a. Is the dolphin deeper at point C or point E? Explain your reasoning.

b. Is the dolphin higher at point B or point D? Explain your reasoning.

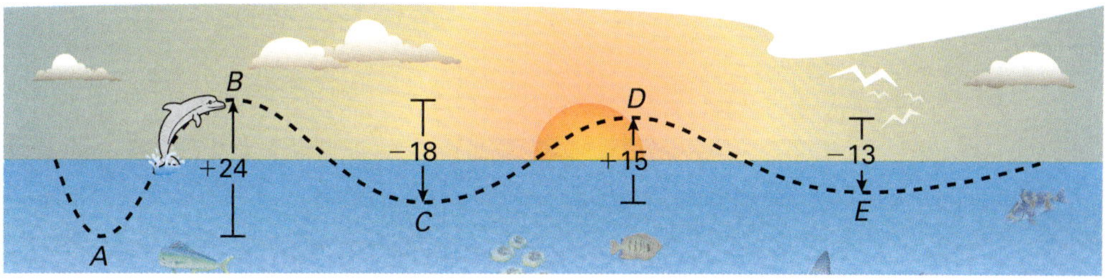

49. **Puzzle** According to a legend, the Chinese Emperor Yu-Huang saw a magic square on the back of a turtle. In a *magic square*, the numbers in each row and in each column have the same sum. This sum is called the *magic sum*.

STEM VIDEO

Copy and complete the magic square so that each row and each column has a magic sum of 0. Use each integer from -4 to 4 exactly once.

Fair Game Review What you learned in previous grades & lessons

Subtract.

50. 69 – 38

51. 82 – 74

52. 177 – 63

53. 451 – 268

54. **MULTIPLE CHOICE** What is the range of the numbers below?

12, 8, 17, 12, 15, 18, 30

Ⓐ 12 Ⓑ 15 Ⓒ 18 Ⓓ 22

2.2 Subtracting Integers

Essential Question How are adding integers and subtracting integers related?

1 ACTIVITY: Subtracting Integers

Work with a partner. Use integer counters to find $4 - 2$.

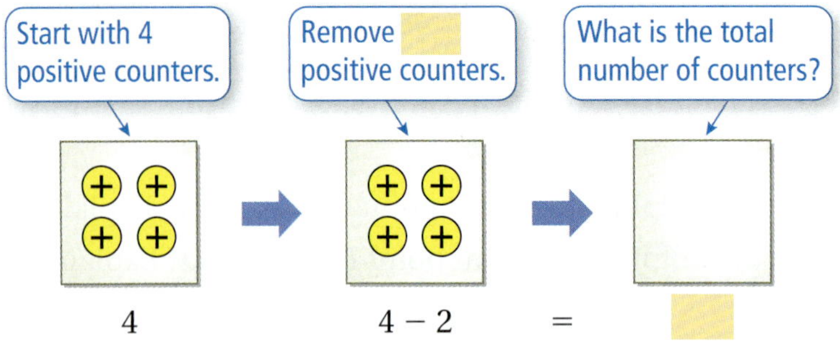

So, $4 - 2 =$ ____.

2 ACTIVITY: Adding Integers

Work with a partner. Use integer counters to find $4 + (-2)$.

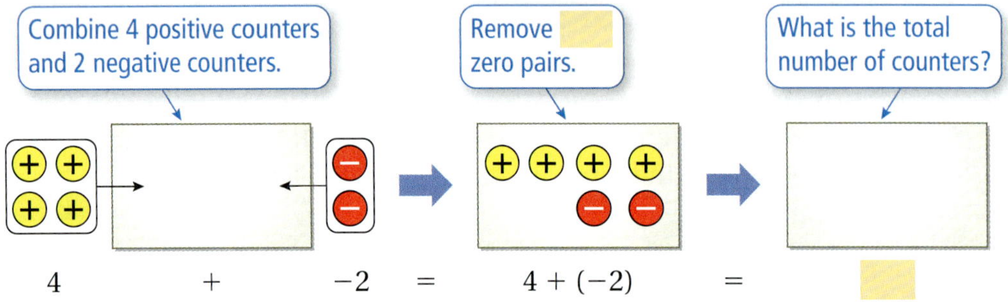

So, $4 + (-2) =$ ____.

Integers

In this lesson, you will

- subtract integers.
- solve real-life problems.

3 ACTIVITY: Subtracting Integers

Work with a partner. Use a number line to find $-3 - 1$.

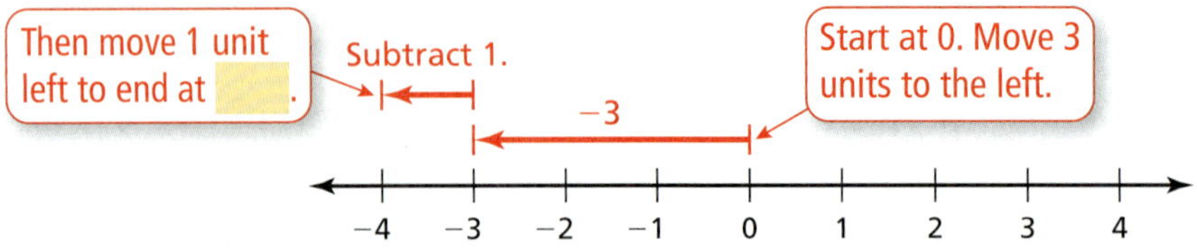

So, $-3 - 1 =$ ____.

4 ACTIVITY: Adding Integers

Math Process

Make Sense of Quantities

What integers will you use in your addition expression?

Work with a partner. Write the addition expression shown. Then find the sum.

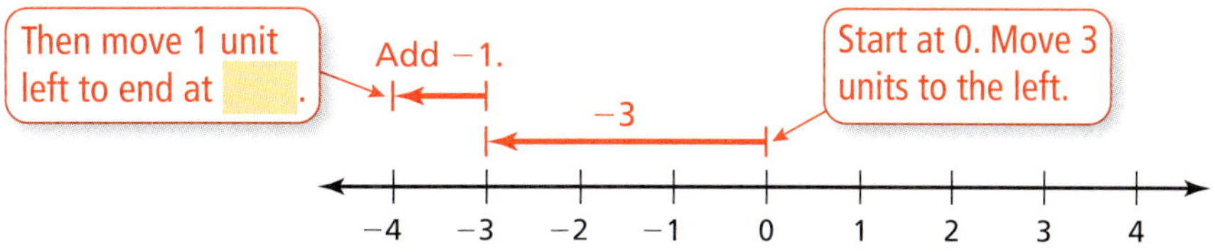

Inductive Reasoning

Work with a partner. Use integer counters or a number line to complete the table.

Exercise	Operation: Add or Subtract	Answer
1 **5.** $4 - 2$	Subtract 2	
2 **6.** $4 + (-2)$		
3 **7.** $-3 - 1$		
4 **8.** $-3 + (-1)$		
9. $3 - 8$		
10. $3 + (-8)$		
11. $9 - 13$		
12. $9 + (-13)$		
13. $-6 - (-3)$		
14. $-6 + 3$		
15. $-5 - (-12)$		
16. $-5 + 12$		

What Is Your Answer?

17. **IN YOUR OWN WORDS** How are adding integers and subtracting integers related?

18. **STRUCTURE** Write a general rule for subtracting integers.

19. Use a number line to find the value of the expression $-4 + 4 - 9$. What property can you use to make your calculation easier? Explain.

Practice Use what you learned about subtracting integers to complete Exercises 8–15 on page 44.

2.2 Lesson

Check It Out
Lesson Tutorials
BigIdeasMath.com

Key Idea

Subtracting Integers

Words To subtract an integer, add its opposite.

Numbers $3 - 4 = 3 + (-4) = -1$

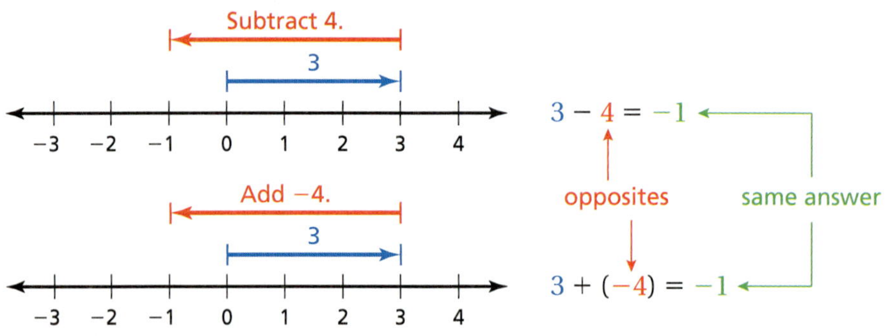

EXAMPLE 1 Subtracting Integers

a. Find 3 − 12.

$3 - 12 = 3 + (-12)$ Add the opposite of 12.

$= -9$ Add.

The difference is −9.

b. Find −8 − (−13).

$-8 - (-13) = -8 + 13$ Add the opposite of −13.

$= 5$ Add.

The difference is 5.

c. Find 5 − (−4).

$5 - (-4) = 5 + 4$ Add the opposite of −4.

$= 9$ Add.

The difference is 9.

On Your Own

Now You're Ready
Exercises 8–23

Subtract.

1. $8 - 3$ **2.** $9 - 17$ **3.** $-3 - 3$

4. $-14 - 9$ **5.** $9 - (-8)$ **6.** $-12 - (-12)$

EXAMPLE 2 Subtracting Integers

Evaluate $-7 - (-12) - 14$.

$-7 - (-12) - 14 = -7 + 12 - 14$	Add the opposite of −12.
$= 5 - 14$	Add −7 and 12.
$= 5 + (-14)$	Add the opposite of 14.
$= -9$	Add.

So, $-7 - (-12) - 14 = -9$.

On Your Own

Now You're Ready
Exercises 27–32

Evaluate the expression.

7. $-9 - 16 - 8$

8. $-4 - 20 - 9$

9. $0 - 9 - (-5)$

10. $-8 - (-6) - 0$

11. $15 - (-20) - 20$

12. $-14 - 9 - 36$

EXAMPLE 3 Real-Life Application

Which continent has the greater range of elevations?

	North America	Africa
Highest Elevation	6198 m	5895 m
Lowest Elevation	−86 m	−155 m

To find the range of elevations for each continent, subtract the lowest elevation from the highest elevation.

North America

$$\text{range} = 6198 - (-86)$$
$$= 6198 + 86$$
$$= 6284 \text{ m}$$

Africa

$$\text{range} = 5895 - (-155)$$
$$= 5895 + 155$$
$$= 6050 \text{ m}$$

Because 6284 is greater than 6050, North America has the greater range of elevations.

On Your Own

13. The highest elevation in Mexico is 5700 meters, on Pico de Orizaba. The lowest elevation in Mexico is −10 meters, in Laguna Salada. Find the range of elevations in Mexico.

2.2 Exercises

Check It Out
Help with Homework
BigIdeasMath.com

Vocabulary and Concept Check

1. **WRITING** How do you subtract one integer from another?
2. **OPEN-ENDED** Write two integers that are opposites.
3. **DIFFERENT WORDS, SAME QUESTION** Which is different? Find "both" answers.

Find the difference of 3 and -2.	What is 3 less than -2?
How much less is -2 than 3?	Subtract -2 from 3.

MATCHING **Match the subtraction expression with the corresponding addition expression.**

4. $9 - (-5)$
5. $-9 - 5$
6. $-9 - (-5)$
7. $9 - 5$

A. $-9 + 5$
B. $9 + (-5)$
C. $-9 + (-5)$
D. $9 + 5$

Practice and Problem Solving

Subtract.

(1) 8. $4 - 7$
9. $8 - (-5)$
10. $-6 - (-7)$
11. $-2 - 3$
12. $5 - 8$
13. $-4 - 6$
14. $-8 - (-3)$
15. $10 - 7$
16. $-8 - 13$
17. $15 - (-2)$
18. $-9 - (-13)$
19. $-7 - (-8)$
20. $-6 - (-6)$
21. $-10 - 12$
22. $32 - (-6)$
23. $0 - 20$

24. **ERROR ANALYSIS** Describe and correct the error in finding the difference $7 - (-12)$.

✗ $7 - (-12) = 7 + (-12) = -5$

25. **SWIMMING POOL** The floor of the shallow end of a swimming pool is at -3 feet. The floor of the deep end is 9 feet deeper. Which expression can be used to find the depth of the deep end?

$-3 + 9$ $\quad$ $-3 - 9$ $\quad$ $9 - 3$

26. **SHARKS** A shark is at -80 feet. It swims up and jumps out of the water to a height of 15 feet. Write a subtraction expression for the vertical distance the shark travels.

Evaluate the expression.

(2) 27. $-2 - 7 + 15$
28. $-9 + 6 - (-2)$
29. $12 - (-5) - 8$
30. $-87 - 5 - 13$
31. $-6 - (-8) + 6$
32. $-15 - 7 - (-11)$

MENTAL MATH **Use mental math to solve the equation.**

33. $m - 5 = 9$ **34.** $w - (-3) = 7$ **35.** $6 - c = -9$

ALGEBRA **Evaluate the expression when $k = -3$, $m = -6$, and $n = 9$.**

36. $4 - n$ **37.** $m - (-8)$

38. $-5 + k - n$ **39.** $|m - k|$

40. **PLATFORM DIVING** The figure shows a diver diving from a platform. The diver reaches a depth of 4 meters. What is the change in elevation of the diver?

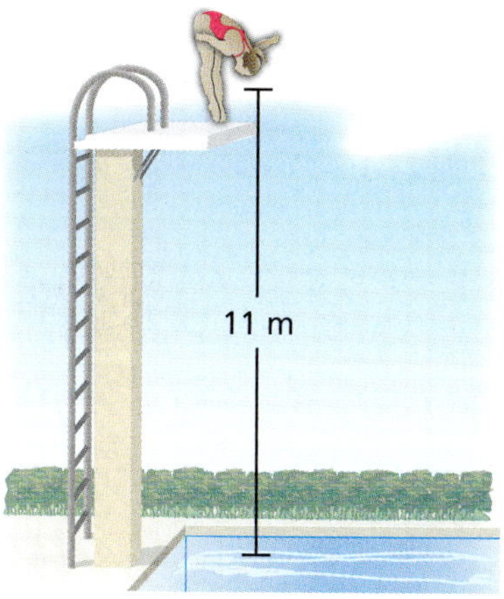

41. **OPEN-ENDED** Write two different pairs of negative integers, x and y, that make the statement $x - y = -1$ true.

42. **TEMPERATURE** The table shows the record monthly high and low temperatures for a city in Alaska.

	Jan	Feb	Mar	Apr	May	Jun	Jul	Aug	Sep	Oct	Nov	Dec
High (°F)	56	57	56	72	82	92	84	85	73	64	62	53
Low (°F)	−35	−38	−24	−15	1	29	34	31	19	−6	−21	−36

a. Find the range of temperatures for each month.

b. What are the all-time high and all-time low temperatures?

c. What is the range of the temperatures in part (b)?

REASONING **Tell whether the difference between the two integers is *always*, *sometimes*, or *never* positive. Explain your reasoning.**

43. two positive integers **44.** two negative integers

45. a positive integer and a negative integer **46.** a negative integer and a positive integer

Number Sense **For what values of a and b is the statement true?**

47. $|a - b| = |b - a|$ **48.** $|a + b| = |a| + |b|$ **49.** $|a - b| = |a| - |b|$

Fair Game Review What you learned in previous grades & lessons

Add.

50. $-5 + (-5) + (-5) + (-5)$ **51.** $-9 + (-9) + (-9) + (-9) + (-9)$

Multiply.

52. 8×5 **53.** 6×78 **54.** 36×41 **55.** 82×29

56. **MULTIPLE CHOICE** Which of the following is a composite number?

Ⓐ 3 Ⓑ 7 Ⓒ 9 Ⓓ 13

2.3 Multiplying and Dividing Integers

Essential Question How can you multiply and divide integers?

1 ACTIVITY: Multiplying Integers with Different Signs

Work with a partner. Use repeated addition to find $3 \cdot (-2)$.

$3 \cdot (-2)$ means to add 3 groups of -2.

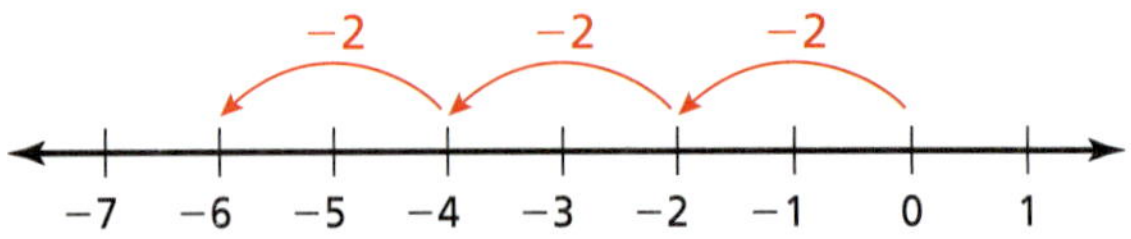

Now you can write

$3 \cdot (-2) =$ ____ + ____ + ____

= ____.

So, $3 \cdot (-2) =$ ____.

2 ACTIVITY: Multiplying Integers with the Same Sign

Work with a partner. Use a table to find $-3 \cdot (-2)$.

Describe the pattern of the products in the table. Then complete the table.

−3	•	3	=	−9
−3	•	2	=	−6
−3	•	1	=	−3
−3	•	0	=	____
−3	•	−1	=	____
−3	•	−2	=	____

Math Process

Look for Patterns

How can you use the pattern to complete the table?

So, $-3 \cdot (-2) =$ ____.

3 ACTIVITY: Dividing Integers Using Manipulatives

Integers

In this lesson, you will

- multiply integers.
- divide integers.
- solve real-life problems.

Work with a partner. Use integer counters to find $-15 \div 3$.

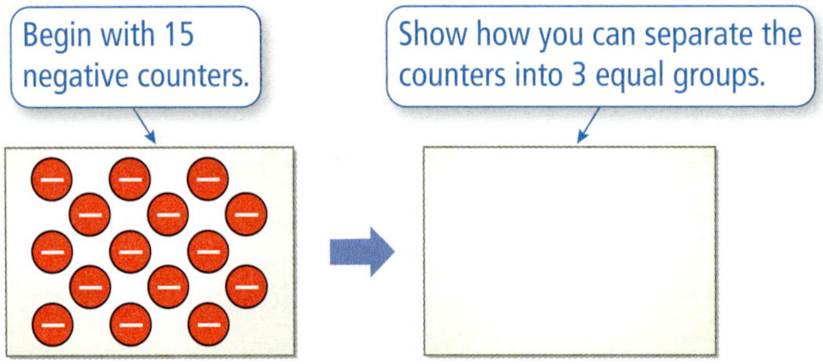

Because there are ____ negative counters in each group, $-15 \div 3 =$ ____.

4 ACTIVITY: Rewriting a Product as a Quotient

Math Process
Maintain Oversight
How do you know what the sign will be when you divide two integers?

Work with a partner. Rewrite the product $3 \cdot (-4) = -12$ as a quotient in two different ways. What can you conclude?

First Way

$-12 \div (\ \_\_\_\ ) = \_\_\_$

Second Way

$-12 \div (\ \_\_\_\ ) = \_\_\_$

When you divide a ______ integer by a ______ integer, you get a ______ integer. When you divide a ______ integer by a ______ integer, you get a ______ integer.

Inductive Reasoning

Work with a partner. Complete the table.

Exercise	Type of Product or Quotient	Product or Quotient	Product or Quotient: Positive, Negative, or Zero
5. $6 \cdot 3$	Integers with the same sign		
6. $2 \cdot (-5)$			
7. $-6 \cdot 5$			
8. $-5 \cdot (-3)$			
9. $0 \cdot (-5)$			
10. $-6 \div 2$			
11. $-21 \div (-7)$			
12. $10 \div (-2)$			
13. $12 \div (-6)$			
14. $0 \div (-15)$			

What Is Your Answer?

15. IN YOUR OWN WORDS Is the product (or quotient) of two integers *positive*, *negative*, or *zero*? How can you tell?

16. STRUCTURE Write general rules for multiplying and dividing (a) two integers with the same sign and (b) two integers with different signs.

Practice Use what you learned about multiplying and dividing integers to complete Exercises 8–23 on page 50.

2.3 Lesson

Check It Out
Lesson Tutorials
BigIdeasMath.com

Key Ideas

Remember

Division by 0 is undefined.

Multiplying and Dividing Integers with the Same Sign

Words The product (or quotient) of two integers with the same sign is positive.

Numbers $8 \cdot 2 = 16$ $\quad -8 \cdot (-2) = 16$

$8 \div 2 = 4$ $\quad -8 \div (-2) = 4$

Multiplying and Dividing Integers with Different Signs

Words The product (or quotient) of two integers with different signs is negative.

Numbers $8 \cdot (-2) = -16$ $\quad -8 \cdot 2 = -16$

$8 \div (-2) = -4$ $\quad -8 \div 2 = -4$

EXAMPLE 1 Multiplying and Dividing Integers with the Same Sign

Multiply or divide.

a. $-5 \cdot (-6)$ **b.** $-18 \div (-6)$

The integers have the same sign.

$-5 \cdot (-6) = 30$ $\quad -18 \div (-6) = 3$

The product and quotient are positive.

The product is 30. The quotient is 3.

EXAMPLE 2 Multiplying and Dividing Integers with Different Signs

Multiply or divide.

a. $3(-4)$ **b.** $\frac{75}{-25}$

The integers have different signs.

$3(-4) = -12$ $\quad \frac{75}{-25} = -3$

The product and quotient are negative.

The product is -12. The quotient is -3.

On Your Own

Now You're Ready
Exercises 8–23

Multiply or divide.

1. $5 \cdot 5$ **2.** $-7(-8)$ **3.** $12 \cdot (-2)$

4. $14 \div 2$ **5.** $\frac{-32}{-4}$ **6.** $-40 \div (8)$

EXAMPLE 3 Multiplying Integers

Multiply.

a. $(-3) \cdot (2) \cdot (-7)$

$$(-3) \cdot (2) \cdot (-7) = -6 \cdot (-7)$$
$$= 42$$

b. $(-4) \cdot (-5) \cdot (-9)$

$$(-4) \cdot (-5) \cdot (-9) = 20 \cdot (-9)$$
$$= -180$$

On Your Own

Now You're Ready
Exercises 24–29

Evaluate the expression.

7. $(6)(2)(-1)$ **8.** $(-7)(3)(-7)$ **9.** $(8)(-3)(-2)$ **10.** $(6)(2)(-9)$

EXAMPLE 4 Real-Life Application

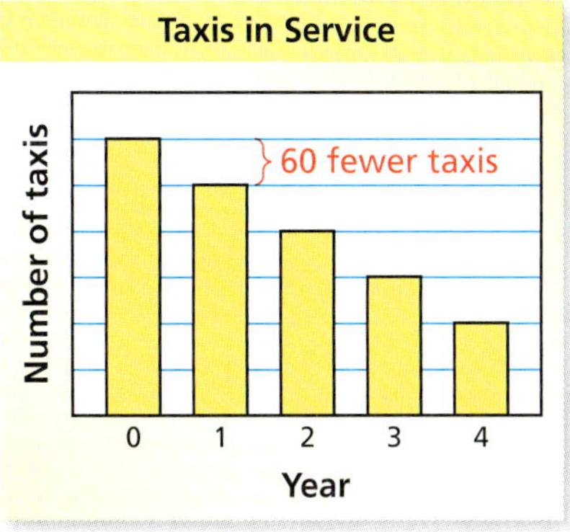

The bar graph shows the number of taxis a company has in service. The number of taxis decreases by the same amount each year for 4 years.

a. Find the total change in the number of taxis.

b. What is the mean monthly change in the number of taxis?

a. The bar graph shows that the number of taxis in service decreases by 60 each year. Use a model to solve the problem.

total change = change per year • number of years

$= -60 \cdot 4$

Use −60 for the change per year because the number *decreases* each year.

$= -240$

The total change in the number of taxis is −240.

b. Use a model to solve the problem.

mean change per month = total change ÷ number of months

$= -240 \div 48$

$= -5$

The mean change in the number of taxis is −5 taxis per month.

On Your Own

11. A cardinal population decreases by 24 cardinals each year for 3 years. Find the total change in the cardinal population. Then find the mean monthly change.

2.3 Exercises

Vocabulary and Concept Check

1. **WRITING** What can you conclude about the signs of two integers whose product (or quotient) is (a) positive and (b) negative?
2. **OPEN-ENDED** Write two integers whose product and quotient are negative.

Tell whether the product or quotient is *positive* or *negative* without multiplying or dividing. Explain your reasoning.

3. $4(-8)$
4. $-5(-7)$
5. $-42 \div (14)$

Tell whether the statement is *true* or *false*. Explain your reasoning.

6. The product of three positive integers is positive.
7. The product of three negative integers is positive.

Practice and Problem Solving

Multiply or divide.

(1) (2)

8. $6(4)$
9. $-6 \cdot 9$
10. $3 \cdot 9$
11. $8(-11)$
12. $-1(-13)$
13. $-9(9)$
14. $-10 \cdot 11$
15. $0 \cdot (-4)$
16. $4 \div (-2)$
17. $\frac{21}{-7}$
18. $-20 \div 4$
19. $-18 \div (-3)$
20. $-33 \div 11$
21. $\frac{-49}{-7}$
22. $\frac{0}{-2}$
23. $\frac{60}{-6}$

Multiply.

(3)

24. $3 \cdot (-8) \cdot (-2)$
25. $6(-9)(-1)$
26. $-3(-5)(-4)$
27. $(-5)(-7)(-20)$
28. $-6 \cdot 3 \cdot (-2)$
29. $3 \cdot (-12) \cdot 0$

30. **JOGGING** You burn 10 calories each minute you jog. What integer represents the change in your calories after you jog for 20 minutes?

31. **WETLANDS** About 60,000 acres of wetlands are lost each year in the United States. What integer represents the change in wetlands after 4 years?

32. **SNOWBOARDING** A snowboarder descends a 1200-foot hill in 3 minutes. What is the mean change in elevation per minute?

33. **ALLIGATORS** An alligator population in a nature preserve in the Everglades decreases by 60 alligators over 5 years. What is the mean yearly change in the alligator population?

ERROR ANALYSIS **Describe and correct the error in evaluating the expression.**

34. ✗ $-2(-7) = -14$

35. ✗ $0 \div (-5) = -5$

NUMBER SENSE **Find the next two numbers in the pattern.**

36. $-12, 60, -300, 1500, \ldots$

37. $-128, 64, -32, 16, \ldots$

38. **GOLF** The table shows a golfer's score for each round of a tournament.

a. What was the golfer's total score?

b. What was the golfer's mean score per round?

Scorecard	
Round 1	-2
Round 2	-6
Round 3	-7
Round 4	-3

39. **INLINE SKATES** In June, the price of a pair of inline skates is $165. The price changes each of the next 3 months.

a. Copy and complete the table.

Month	Price of Skates
June	$165 \qquad\quad = \$165$
July	$165 + (-12) = \$\_\_\_\_$
August	$165 + 2(-12) = \$\_\_\_\_$
September	$165 + 3(-12) = \$\_\_\_\_$

b. Describe the change in the price of the inline skates for each month.

c. The table at the right shows the amount of money you save each month to buy the inline skates. Do you have enough money saved to buy the inline skates in August? September? Explain your reasoning.

Amount Saved	
June	$35
July	$55
August	$45
September	$18

40. Number Sense Write five different integers that have a mean of -10. Explain how you found your answer.

Fair Game Review What you learned in previous grades & lessons

Graph the values on a number line. Then order the values from least to greatest.

41. $-6, 4, |2|, -1, |-10|$

42. $3, |0|, |-4|, -3, -8$

43. $|5|, -2, -5, |-2|, -7$

44. **MULTIPLE CHOICE** What is the prime factorization of 84?

Ⓐ $2^2 \times 3^2$ Ⓑ $2^3 \times 7$ Ⓒ $3^3 \times 7$ Ⓓ $2^2 \times 3 \times 7$

2.4 Powers and Exponents

Essential Question How can you use repeated factors in real-life situations?

As I was going to St. Ives
I met a man with seven wives
Each wife had seven sacks
Each sack had seven cats
Each cat had seven kits
Kits, cats, sacks, wives
How many were going to St. Ives? Nursery Rhyme, 1730

1 ACTIVITY: Analyzing a Math Poem

Work with a partner. Here is a "St. Ives" poem written by two students. Answer the question in the poem.

As I was walking into town
I met a ringmaster with five clowns
Each clown had five magicians
Each magician had five bunnies
Each bunny had five fleas
Fleas, bunnies, magicians, clowns
How many were going into town?

Numerical Expressions
In this lesson, you will
- write expressions as powers.
- find values of powers.

Number of clowns:	5	$=$ ______
Number of magicians:	5×5	$=$ ______
Number of bunnies:	$5 \times 5 \times 5$	$=$ ______
Number of fleas:	$5 \times 5 \times 5 \times 5$	$=$ ______

So, the number of fleas, bunnies, magicians, and clowns is ______. Explain how you found your answer.

2 ACTIVITY: Writing Repeated Factors

Math Process

Repeat Calculations

What patterns do you notice with each problem? How does this help you write exponents?

Work with a partner. Copy and complete the table.

Repeated Factors	Using an Exponent	Value
a. 4×4		
b. 6×6		
c. $10 \times 10 \times 10$		
d. $100 \times 100 \times 100$		
e. $3 \times 3 \times 3 \times 3$		
f. $4 \times 4 \times 4 \times 4 \times 4$		
g. $2 \times 2 \times 2 \times 2 \times 2 \times 2$		

h. In your own words, describe what the two numbers in the expression 3^5 mean.

3 ACTIVITY: Writing and Analyzing a Math Poem

Work with a partner.

a. Write your own "St. Ives" poem.

b. Draw pictures for your poem.

c. Answer the question in your poem.

d. Show how you can use exponents to write your answer.

What Is Your Answer?

4. IN YOUR OWN WORDS How can you use repeated factors in real-life situations? Give an example.

5. STRUCTURE Use exponents to complete the table. Describe the pattern.

10	100	1000	10,000	100,000	1,000,000
10^1	10^2				

Practice

Use what you learned about exponents to complete Exercises 4–6 on page 56.

2.4 Lesson

Check It Out
Lesson Tutorials
BigIdeasMath.com

Key Vocabulary
power, *p. 54*
base, *p. 54*
exponent, *p. 54*
perfect square, *p. 55*

A **power** is a product of repeated factors. The **base** of a power is the repeated factor. The **exponent** of a power indicates the number of times the base is used as a factor.

base → exponent

$3^4 = 3 \cdot 3 \cdot 3 \cdot 3$

power — 3 is used as a factor 4 times.

Power	Words
3^2	Three *squared*, or three to the second
3^3	Three *cubed*, or three to the third
3^4	Three to the fourth

The value of any power, whose base is not 0, with an exponent of 0 is 1. For example, $1^0 = 1$ and $3^0 = 1$. Zero to the zero, 0^0 is undefined.

EXAMPLE 1 Writing Expressions as Powers

Math Process
Choose Tools
Why are calculators more efficient when finding the values of expressions involving exponents?

Write each product as a power.

a. $4 \cdot 4 \cdot 4 \cdot 4 \cdot 4$

Because 4 is used as a factor 5 times, its exponent is 5.

So, $4 \cdot 4 \cdot 4 \cdot 4 \cdot 4 = 4^5$.

b. $12 \times 12 \times 12$

Because 12 is used as a factor 3 times, its exponent is 3.

So, $12 \times 12 \times 12 = 12^3$.

On Your Own

Now You're Ready
Exercises 4–12

Write the product as a power.

1. $6 \cdot 6 \cdot 6 \cdot 6 \cdot 6 \cdot 6$

2. $15 \times 15 \times 15 \times 15$

EXAMPLE 2 Finding Values of Powers

Find the value of each power.

a. 7^2

$7^2 = 7 \cdot 7$ — Write as repeated multiplication.

$= 49$ — Simplify.

b. 5^3

$5^3 = 5 \cdot 5 \cdot 5$

$= 125$

The square of a whole number is a **perfect square**.

EXAMPLE 3 Identifying Perfect Squares

Determine whether each number is a perfect square.

a. 64

Because $8^2 = 64$, 64 is a perfect square.

b. 20

No whole number squared equals 20. So, 20 is not a perfect square.

On Your Own

Now You're Ready
Exercises 14–21 and 25–32

Find the value of the power.

3. 6^3 **4.** 9^2 **5.** 7^0 **6.** 18^2

Determine whether the number is a perfect square.

7. 25 **8.** 2 **9.** 99 **10.** 100

Remember

The *area* of a figure is the amount of surface it covers. Area is measured in square units.

The area of a square is equal to its side length squared.

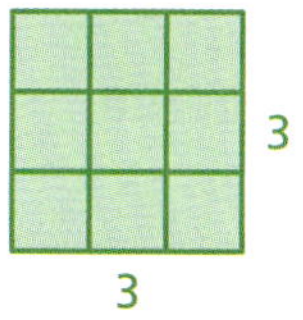

Area $= 3^2 = 9$ square units

EXAMPLE 4 Real-Life Application

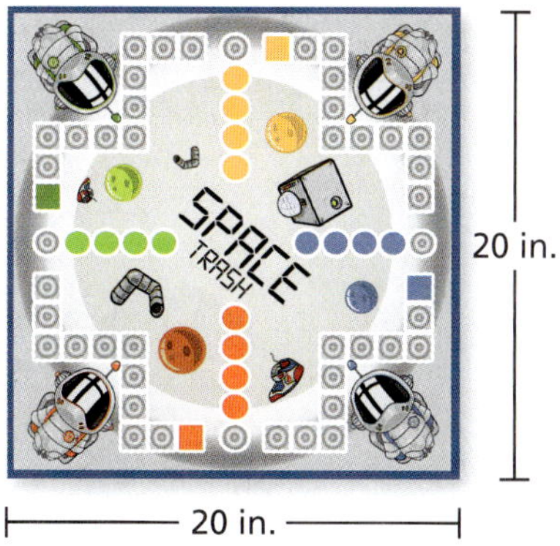

A game board is a square with a side length of 20 inches. What is the area of the game board?

Use a verbal model to solve the problem.

$$\text{area of game board} = (\text{side length})^2$$

$$= 20^2 \quad \text{Substitute 20 for side length.}$$

$$= 400 \quad \text{Multiply.}$$

The area of the game board is 400 square inches.

On Your Own

11. What is the area of the square traffic sign in square inches? in square feet?

2.4 Exercises

Check It Out
Help with Homework
BigIdeasMath.com

Vocabulary and Concept Check

1. **VOCABULARY** How are exponents and powers different?
2. **VOCABULARY** Is 10 a perfect square? Is 100 a perfect square? Explain.
3. **WHICH ONE DOESN'T BELONG?** Which one does *not* belong with the other three? Explain your reasoning.

$2^4 = 2 \times 2 \times 2 \times 2$	$3 + 3 + 3 + 3 = 3(4)$	$3^2 = 3 \times 3$	$5 \cdot 5 \cdot 5 = 5^3$

Practice and Problem Solving

Write the product as a power.

1 4. 9×9 5. 13×13 6. $15 \times 15 \times 15$

7. $2 \cdot 2 \cdot 2 \cdot 2 \cdot 2$ 8. $14 \times 14 \times 14$ 9. $8 \cdot 8 \cdot 8 \cdot 8$

10. $11 \times 11 \times 11 \times 11 \times 11$ 11. $7 \cdot 7 \cdot 7 \cdot 7 \cdot 7 \cdot 7$ 12. $16 \cdot 16 \cdot 16 \cdot 16$

13. **ERROR ANALYSIS** Describe and correct the error in writing the product as a power.

✗ $4 \cdot 4 \cdot 4 = 3^4$

Find the value of the power.

2 14. 5^2 15. 4^3 16. 2^5 17. 4^0

Use a calculator to find the value of the power.

18. 7^6 19. 4^8 20. 12^4 21. 17^5

22. **ERROR ANALYSIS** Describe and correct the error in finding the value of the power.

✗ $8^3 = 8 \cdot 3 = 24$

23. **POPULATION** The population of Virginia is about 8×10^6. About how many people live in Virginia?

24. **FIGURINES** The smallest figurine in a gift shop is 2 inches tall. The height of each figurine is twice the height of the previous figurine. Write a power to represent the height of the tallest figurine. Then find the height.

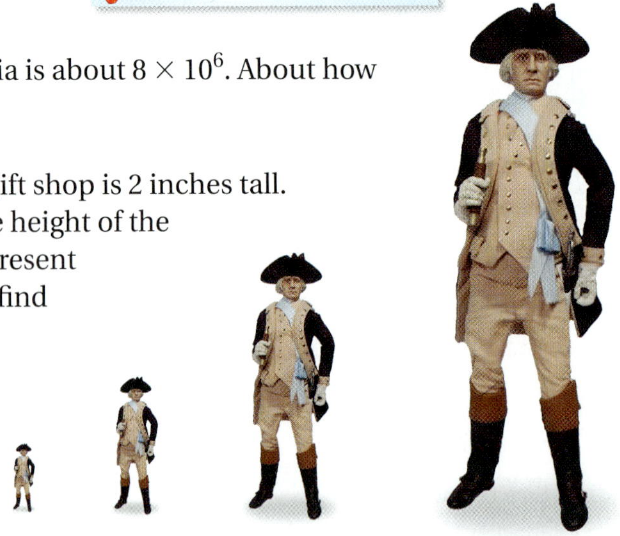

Determine whether the number is a perfect square.

3 **25.** 8　　**26.** 4　　**27.** 81　　**28.** 44

29. 49　　**30.** 125　　**31.** 150　　**32.** 144

33. **PAINTING** A square painting measures 2 meters on each side. What is the area of the painting in square centimeters?

34. **NUMBER SENSE** Write three powers that have values greater than 120 and less than 130.

35. **CHECKERS** A checkers board has 64 squares. How many squares are in each row?

36. **PATIO** A landscaper has 125 tiles to build a square patio. The patio must have an area of at least 80 square feet.

a. What are the possible arrangements for the patio?

b. How many tiles are not used in each arrangement?

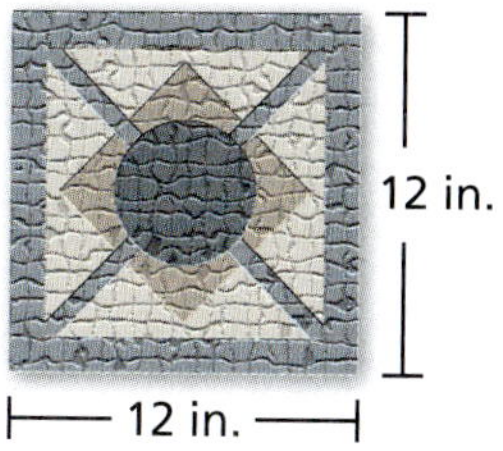

37. **PATTERNS** Copy and complete the table. Describe what happens to the value of the power as the exponent decreases. Use this pattern to find the value of 4^0.

Power	4^6	4^5	4^4	4^3	4^2	4^1
Value	4096	1024				

38. **REASONING** Consider the equation $56 = \square^2$. The missing number is between what two whole numbers?

39. Repeated Reasoning How many blocks do you need to add to Square 6 to get Square 7? to Square 9 to get Square 10? to Square 19 to get Square 20? Explain.

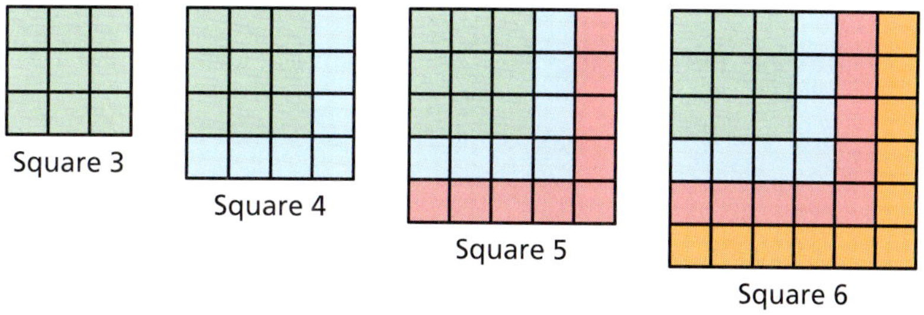

Fair Game Review What you learned in previous grades & lessons

Find the value of the expression.

40. 6×14　　**41.** 11×15　　**42.** $56 \div 7$　　**43.** $112 \div 16$

44. **MULTIPLE CHOICE** You buy a box of gum that has 12 packs. Each pack has 5 pieces. Which expression represents the total number of pieces of gum?

Ⓐ $12 + 5$　　Ⓑ $12 - 5$　　Ⓒ 12×5　　Ⓓ $12 \div 5$

2.5 Order of Operations

Essential Question What is the effect of inserting parentheses into a numerical expression?

1 ACTIVITY: Comparing Different Orders

Work with a partner. Find the value of the expression by using different orders of operations. Are your answers the same? (Circle *yes* or *no.*)

a. Add, then multiply. | Multiply, then add. | Same?

$3 + 4 \times 2 =$ ____ | $3 + 4 \times 2 =$ ____ | Yes No

b. Add, then subtract. | Subtract, then add. | Same?

$5 + 3 - 1 =$ ____ | $5 + 3 - 1 =$ ____ | Yes No

c. Divide, then multiply. | Multiply, then divide. | Same?

$12 \div 3 \cdot 2 =$ ____ | $12 \div 3 \cdot 2 =$ ____ | Yes No

d. Divide, then add. | Add, then divide. | Same?

$16 \div 4 + 4 =$ ____ | $16 \div 4 + 4 =$ ____ | Yes No

e. Multiply, then subtract. | Subtract, then multiply. | Same?

$8 \times 4 - 2 =$ ____ | $8 \times 4 - 2 =$ ____ | Yes No

f. Multiply, then divide. | Divide, then multiply. | Same?

$8 \cdot 4 \div 2 =$ ____ | $8 \cdot 4 \div 2 =$ ____ | Yes No

g. Subtract, then add. | Add, then subtract. | Same?

$13 - 4 + 6 =$ ____ | $13 - 4 + 6 =$ ____ | Yes No

h. Multiply, then add. | Add, then multiply. | Same?

$1 \times 2 + 3 =$ ____ | $1 \times 2 + 3 =$ ____ | Yes No

Numerical Expressions

In this lesson, you will

- evaluate numerical expressions with whole-number exponents.

2 ACTIVITY: Using Parentheses

Work with a partner. Use all the symbols and numbers to write an expression that has the given value.

	Symbols and Numbers	*Value*	*Expression*
a.	( ), +, ÷, 3, 4, 5	3	
b.	( ), −, ×, 2, 5, 8	11	
c.	( ), ×, ÷, 4, 4, 16	16	
d.	( ), −, ÷, 3, 8, 11	1	
e.	( ), +, ×, 2, 5, 10	70	

3 ACTIVITY: Reviewing Fractions and Decimals

Math Process

Use Operations

How do you know which operation to perform first?

Work with a partner. Evaluate the expression.

a. $\frac{3}{4} - \left(\frac{1}{4} + \frac{1}{2}\right) =$

b. $\left(\frac{5}{6} - \frac{1}{6}\right) - \frac{1}{12} =$

c. $7.4 - (3.5 - 3.1) =$

d. $10.4 - (8.6 + 0.9) =$

e. $(\$7.23 + \$2.32) - \$5.40 =$

f. $\$124.60 - (\$72.41 + \$5.67) =$

What Is Your Answer?

4. In an expression with two or more operations, why is it necessary to agree on an order of operations? Give examples to support your explanation.

5. **IN YOUR OWN WORDS** What is the effect of inserting parentheses into a numerical expression?

Practice Use what you learned about the order of operations to complete Exercises 3–5 on page 62.

2.5 Lesson

Check It Out
Lesson Tutorials
BigIdeasMath.com

Key Vocabulary
numerical expression, *p. 60*
evaluate, *p. 60*
order of operations, *p. 60*

A **numerical expression** is an expression that contains only numbers and operations. To **evaluate**, or find the value of, a numerical expression, use a set of rules called the **order of operations**.

Key Idea

Order of Operations

1. Perform operations in **P**arentheses and other grouping symbols.
2. Evaluate numbers with **E**xponents.
3. **M**ultiply or **D**ivide from left to right.
4. **A**dd or **S**ubtract from left to right.

EXAMPLE 1 Using Order of Operations

a. Evaluate $12 - 2 \times 4$.

$12 - 2 \times 4 = 12 - 8$ Multiply 2 and 4.

$= 4$ Subtract 8 from 12.

b. Evaluate $7 + 60 \div (-5 \times 3)$.

$7 + 60 \div (-5 \times 3) = 7 + 60 \div (-15)$ Perform operation in parentheses.

$= 7 + (-4)$ Divide 60 by -15.

$= 3$ Add 7 and -4.

EXAMPLE 2 Using Order of Operations with Exponents

Study Tip
Remember to multiply and divide from left to right. In Example 2, you should divide before multiplying because the division symbol comes first when reading from left to right.

Evaluate $-24 \div 2^3 \times 6$.

Evaluate the power in parentheses first.

$-24 \div 2^3 \times 6 = -24 \div 8 \times 6$ Evaluate 2^3.

$= -3 \times 6$ Divide -24 by 8.

$= -18$ Multiply -3 and 6.

On Your Own

Now You're Ready
Exercises 6–14

Evaluate the expression.

1. $7 \cdot 5 + 3$
2. $(20 - 28) \div 4$
3. $6 \times 15 - 10 \div 2$
4. $6 + 2^3 - 1$
5. $(-4) \cdot 3^2 + 18$
6. $(5^2 - 7) \div (-3)$

The symbols × and • are used to indicate multiplication. You can also use parentheses to indicate multiplication. For example, $3(2 + 7)$ is the same as $3 \times (2 + 7)$.

EXAMPLE 3 Using Order of Operations

a. Evaluate $9 + |7(-3)|$.

$$9 + |7(-3)| = 9 + |-21|$$ Multiply 7 and −3.

$$= 9 + 21$$ Find the absolute value of −21.

$$= 30$$ Add 9 and 21.

b. Evaluate $15 - 4(6 + 1) \div 2^2$.

$$15 - 4(6 + 1) \div 2^2 = 15 - 4(7) \div 2^2$$ Perform operation in parentheses.

$$= 15 - 4(7) \div 4$$ Evaluate 2^2.

$$= 15 - 28 \div 4$$ Multiply 4 and 7.

$$= 15 - 7$$ Divide 28 by 4.

$$= 8$$ Subtract 7 from 15.

EXAMPLE 4 Real-Life Application

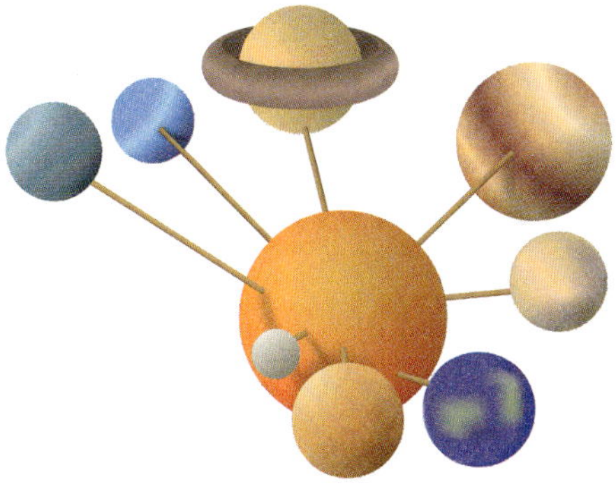

You buy foam spheres, paint bottles, and wooden rods to construct a model of our solar system. What is your total cost?

Item	Quantity	Cost per Item
Spheres	9	\$2
Paint	6	\$3
Rods	8	\$1

Use a verbal model to solve the problem.

cost of 9 spheres + cost of 6 paint bottles + cost of 8 rods

$9 \cdot 2 \quad + \quad 6 \cdot 3 \quad + \quad 8 \cdot 1$

$$9 \cdot 2 + 6 \cdot 3 + 8 \cdot 1 = 18 + 18 + 8$$ Multiply.

$$= 44$$ Add.

Your total cost is \$44.

On Your Own

Now You're Ready
Exercises 18–23

Evaluate the expression.

7. $|8(5)| - 7$

8. $5^2 - 5(10)$

9. $\dfrac{8(3 + 4)}{7}$

10. WHAT IF? In Example 4, you add the dwarf planet Pluto to your model. Use a verbal model to find your total cost assuming you do not need more paint. Explain.

2.5 Exercises

Check It Out
Help with Homework
BigIdeasMath.com

Vocabulary and Concept Check

1. **WRITING** Why does $12 - 8 \div 2 = 8$, but $(12 - 8) \div 2 = 2$?
2. **REASONING** Describe the steps in evaluating the expression $8 \div (-4) + 3^2$.

Practice and Problem Solving

Find the value of the expression.

3. $(4 \times 15) - 3$
4. $10 - (7 + 1)$
5. $18 \div (6 + 3)$

Evaluate the expression.

1 2
6. $5 + 18 \div 6$
7. $(3 - 11) \div 2 + 1$
8. $45 \div 9 \times 12$
9. $6^2 - 3 \cdot 4$
10. $42 \div (15 - 2^3)$
11. $2^2 + 8 \cdot (-7)$
12. $5^2 \div 5 \times (-2)$
13. $(10 + 4) \div (26 - 19)$
14. $(4 - 3^3) \cdot 2$

ERROR ANALYSIS **Describe and correct the error in evaluating the expression.**

15. ✗ $9 + (-2) \times 3 = 7 \times 3$
$= 21$

16. ✗ $19 - 6 + 12 = 19 - 18$
$= 1$

17. **POETRY** You need to read 20 poems in 5 days for an English project. Each poem is 2 pages long. Evaluate the expression $20 \times 2 \div 5$ to find how many pages you need to read each day.

Evaluate the expression.

3
18. $4^2 - 8(1 + 3)$
19. $7(6) - 5^2$
20. $|-5 + 8| \times 5$
21. $3 - |2(-9)|$
22. $8(7.3 + 3.7) - 14 \div 2$
23. $7^2 - 2\left(\frac{11}{8} - \frac{3}{8}\right)$

24. **MONEY** You have four \$10 bills and eighteen \$5 bills in your piggy bank. How much money do you have?

25. **THEATER** Before a show, there are 8 people in a theater. Five groups of 4 people enter, and then three groups of 2 people leave. Evaluate the expression $8 + 5(4) - 3(2)$ to find how many people are in the theater.

4(\$10) + 18(\$5)

Evaluate the expression.

26. $\dfrac{6(3+5)}{4}$ **27.** $\dfrac{2-130}{8^2}$ **28.** $\dfrac{72}{3^2-3}$

29. FIELD TRIP Eighty students are going on a field trip to a history museum. The total cost includes

- 2 bus rentals and
- $10 per student for lunch.

What is the total cost per student?

30. OPEN-ENDED Use all four operations without parentheses to write an expression that has a value of 100.

31. SHOPPING You buy 6 notebooks, 10 folders, 1 pack of pencils, and 1 lunch box for school. After using a $10 gift card, how much do you owe? Explain how you solved the problem.

32. LITTER CLEANUP Two groups collect litter along the side of a road. It takes each group 5 minutes to clean up a 200-yard section. How long does it take to clean up 2 *miles*? Explain how you solved the problem.

33. Number Sense Copy each statement. Insert +, −, ×, or ÷ symbols to make each statement true.

a. $27 \;\square\; 3 \;\square\; 5 \;\square\; 2 = 19$ **b.** $9^2 \;\square\; 11 \;\square\; 8 \;\square\; 4 \;\square\; 1 = 60$

c. $5 \;\square\; 6 \;\square\; 15 \;\square\; 9 = 24$ **d.** $14 \;\square\; 2 \;\square\; 7 \;\square\; 3 \;\square\; 9 = 10$

Fair Game Review What you learned in previous grades & lessons

Add or subtract.

34. $5.2 + 0.5$ **35.** $8 - 1.9$ **36.** $12.6 - 3$ **37.** $0.7 + 0.2$

38. MULTIPLE CHOICE You are making two recipes. One recipe calls for $2\frac{1}{3}$ cups of flour. The other recipe calls for $1\frac{1}{4}$ cups of flour. How much flour do you need to make both recipes?

Ⓐ $1\frac{1}{12}$ cups Ⓑ $3\frac{1}{12}$ cups Ⓒ $3\frac{2}{7}$ cups Ⓓ $3\frac{7}{12}$ cups

2 Study Help

Check It Out
Graphic Organizer
BigIdeasMath.com

You can use an **information frame** to help you organize and remember concepts. Here is an example of an information frame for powers.

Words:
A *power* is a product of repeated factors. The *base* of a power is the common factor. The *exponent* of a power indicates the number of times the base is used as a factor.

Numbers:
$5^2 = 5 \cdot 5$

Powers

Numbers:
$4^3 = 4 \cdot 4 \cdot 4$

Example:

Find the value of the power.

$2^4 = 2 \cdot 2 \cdot 2 \cdot 2 = 16$

On Your Own

Make information frames to help you study these topics.

1. adding integers
2. Additive Inverse Property
3. subtracting integers
4. multiplying integers
5. dividing integers
6. order of operations

"Dear Mom, I am sending you an information frame card for Mother's Day!"

2 Chapter Review

Check It Out
Vocabulary Help
BigIdeasMath.com

Review Key Vocabulary

additive inverse, *p. 36*
power, *p. 54*
base, *p. 54*
exponent, *p. 54*
perfect square, *p. 55*
numerical expression, *p. 60*
evaluate, *p. 60*
order of operations, *p. 60*

Review Examples and Exercises

2.1 Adding Integers *(pp. 34–39)*

Find $6 + (-14)$.

$6 + (-14) = -8$ $\quad |-14| > |6|$. So, subtract $|6|$ from $|-14|$.

Use the sign of -14.

∴ The sum is -8.

Exercises

Add.

1. $-16 + (-11)$
2. $-15 + 5$
3. $100 + (-75)$
4. $-32 + (-2)$

2.2 Subtracting Integers *(pp. 40–45)*

Subtract.

a. $7 - 19 = 7 + (-19)$ Add the opposite of 19.

$= -12$ Add.

∴ The difference is -12.

b. $-6 - (-10) = -6 + 10$ Add the opposite of -10.

$= 4$ Add.

∴ The difference is 4.

Exercises

Subtract.

5. $8 - 18$
6. $-16 - (-5)$
7. $-18 - 7$
8. $-12 - (-27)$
9. **GAME SHOW** Your score on a game show is -300. You answer the final question incorrectly, so you lose 400 points. What is your final score?

2.3 Multiplying and Dividing Integers (pp. 46–51)

a. Find $-7 \cdot (-9)$.

The integers have the same sign.

$$-7 \cdot (-9) = 63$$

The product is positive.

The product is 63.

b. Find $30 \div (-10)$.

The integers have different signs.

$$30 \div (-10) = -3$$

The quotient is negative.

The quotient is -3.

c. Find $\frac{-72}{-9}$.

The integers have the same sign.

$$\frac{-72}{-9} = 8$$

The quotient is positive.

The quotient is 8.

Exercises

Multiply.

10. $-8 \cdot 6$ **11.** $10(-7)$ **12.** $-3 \cdot (-6)$ **13.** $-12(5)$

Divide.

14. $-18 \div 9$ **15.** $\frac{-42}{-6}$ **16.** $\frac{-30}{6}$ **17.** $84 \div (-7)$

Multiply.

18. $-6 \cdot 3 \cdot (-4)$ **19.** $(-7) \cdot 2 \cdot (-1)$ **20.** $(-4) \cdot (-4) \cdot (-5)$

Find the mean of the integers.

21. −3, −8, 12, −15, 9

22. −54, −32, −70, −25, −65, −42

23. PROFITS The table shows the weekly profits of a fruit vendor. What is the mean profit for these weeks?

Week	1	2	3	4
Profit	−$125	−$86	$54	−$35

24. RETURNS You return several shirts to a store. The receipt shows that the amount placed back on your credit card is −$30.60. Each shirt is −$6.12. How many shirts did you return?

2.4 Powers and Exponents *(pp. 52–57)*

Evaluate 6^2.

$6^2 = 6 \cdot 6 = 36$ — Write as repeated multiplication and simplify.

Exercises

Find the value of the power.

25. 7^3

26. 2^6

27. 4^4

2.5 Order of Operations *(pp. 58–63)*

Evaluate $4^3 - 15 \div (-3)$.

$4^3 - 15 \div (-3) = 64 - 15 \div (-3)$ — Evaluate 4^3.

$= 64 - (-5)$ — Divide 15 by −3.

$= 64 + 5$ — Add the opposite of −5.

$= 69$ — Add 64 and 5.

Exercises

Evaluate the expression.

28. $3 \times (-6) - 12 \div 4$

29. $(-20) \times (3^2 - 4)$

30. $6 - (4 - 1) \div |-3|$

3 Fractions and Mixed Numbers

What You Learned Before

"On a scale from 1 to 10, how do you like my painting?"

Estimating Whole Number Products and Quotients

Example 1 Estimate 32 × 88.

32 is close to 30.

$$32 \times 88 \approx 30 \times 90 = 2700$$

88 is close to 90.

Example 2 Estimate 176 ÷ 57.

176 is close to 180.

$$176 \div 57 \approx 180 \div 60 = 3$$

57 is close to 60.

Try It Yourself

Estimate the product or the quotient.

1. 9×23
2. 19×22
3. 49×21
4. 38×61
5. $38 \div 9$
6. $63 \div 22$
7. $118 \div 19$
8. $245 \div 62$

Multiplying and Dividing Whole Numbers

Example 3 Find 356 × 21.

$$\begin{array}{r} {\scriptstyle 1\,1} \\ 356 \\ \times\ \ 21 \\ \hline 356 \\ +\ 7120 \\ \hline 7476 \end{array}$$

Example 4 Find 765 ÷ 3.

$$\begin{array}{r} 255 \\ 3\overline{)765} \\ -\ 6 \\ \hline 16 \\ -\ 15 \\ \hline 15 \\ -\ 15 \\ \hline 0 \end{array}$$

Try It Yourself

Find the product or the quotient.

9. $\begin{array}{r} 425 \\ \times\ \ 9 \\ \hline \end{array}$
10. $\begin{array}{r} 721 \\ \times\ 18 \\ \hline \end{array}$
11. $\begin{array}{r} 599 \\ \times\ 29 \\ \hline \end{array}$
12. $\begin{array}{r} 503 \\ \times\ 12 \\ \hline \end{array}$
13. $7\overline{)280}$
14. $4\overline{)428}$
15. $14\overline{)532}$
16. $23\overline{)8303}$

3.1 Adding Fractions and Mixed Numbers

Essential Question How can you add fractions and mixed numbers?

1 ACTIVITY: Adding Fractions

Work with a partner. Use a number line to find the sum.

a. $\frac{3}{10} + \frac{9}{10}$

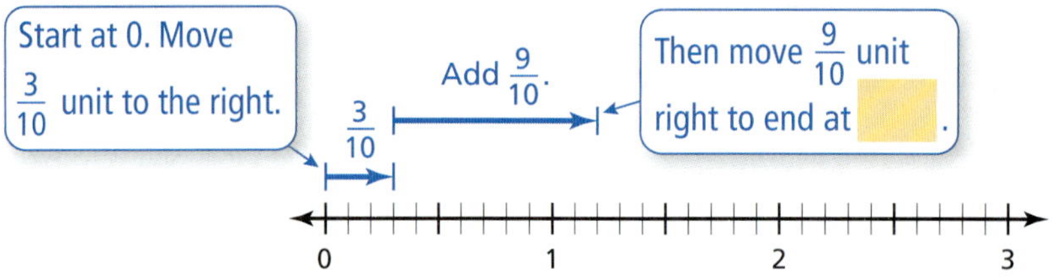

So, $\frac{3}{10} + \frac{9}{10} =$ ___.

b. $\frac{1}{4} + \frac{1}{4}$

c. $\frac{2}{7} + \frac{5}{7}$

d. $\frac{5}{8} + \frac{1}{8}$

e. $\frac{2}{5} + \frac{4}{5}$

2 ACTIVITY: Adding Mixed Numbers

Work with a partner. Use a number line to find the sum.

a. $1\frac{3}{8} + \frac{5}{8}$

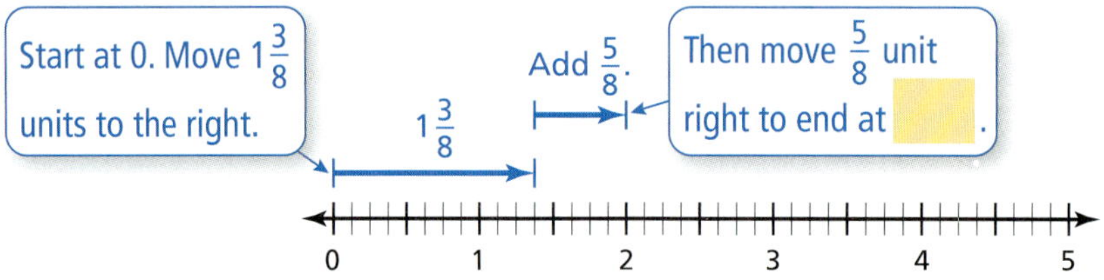

So, $1\frac{3}{8} + \frac{5}{8} =$ ___.

b. $4\frac{2}{5} + 3\frac{1}{5}$

c. $3\frac{7}{10} + 3\frac{1}{10}$

d. $7\frac{3}{4} + \frac{1}{4}$

e. $2\frac{2}{3} + 1\frac{2}{3}$

Fractions and Mixed Numbers

In this lesson, you will

- add fractions and mixed numbers.
- solve real-life problems.

3 ACTIVITY: Writing Expressions

Work with a partner. Write the addition expression shown. Then find the sum.

> **Math Process**
> **Use Operations**
> What operation is represented in each number line? How does this help you write an expression?

a.

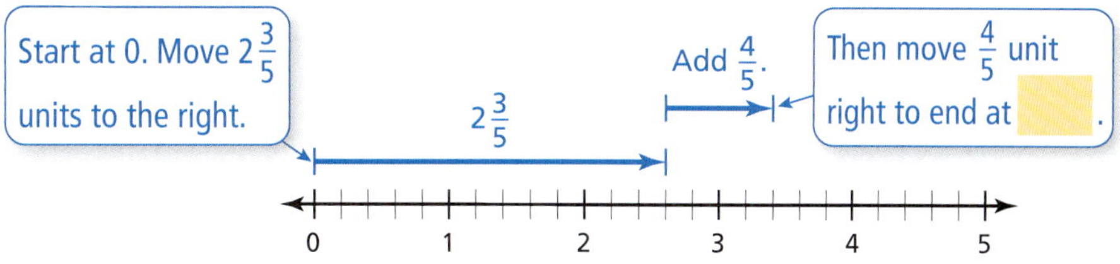

b.

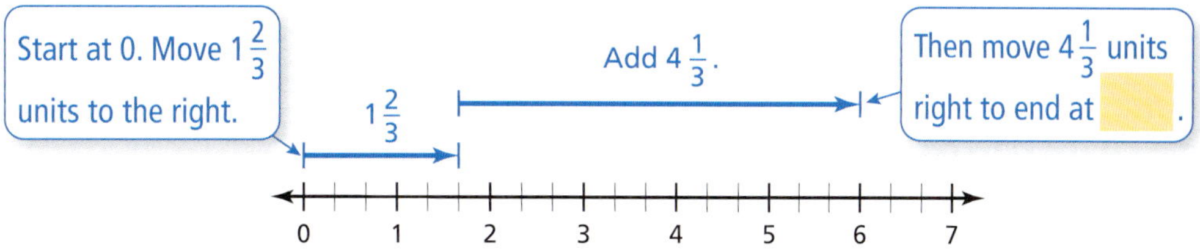

c.

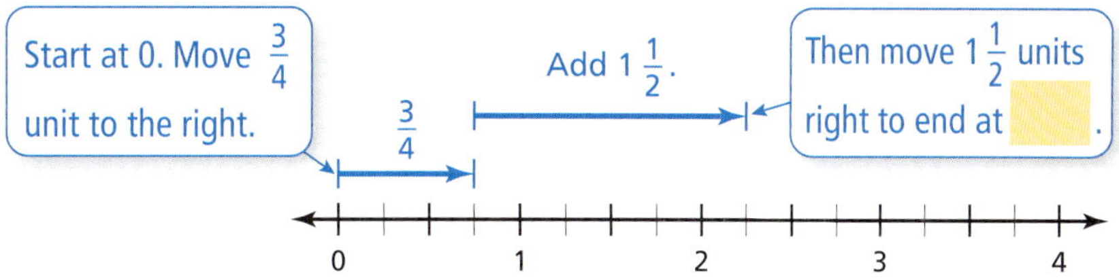

What Is Your Answer?

4. **IN YOUR OWN WORDS** How can you add fractions and mixed numbers?

PUZZLE **Find a path through the table so that the numbers add up to the sum. You can move horizontally and vertically.**

5. Sum: $\frac{9}{10}$

Start →

$\frac{1}{10}$	$\frac{2}{5}$	$\frac{1}{10}$
$\frac{7}{10}$	$\frac{1}{5}$	$\frac{3}{10}$

← End

6. Sum: $5\frac{3}{8}$

Start →

$1\frac{1}{2}$	$1\frac{1}{4}$	$\frac{3}{8}$
$\frac{7}{8}$	$2\frac{1}{2}$	$\frac{1}{8}$

← End

Practice Use what you learned about adding fractions and mixed numbers to complete Exercises 4–6 on page 74.

3.1 Lesson

Check It Out
Lesson Tutorials
BigIdeasMath.com

Key Idea

Adding Fractions and Mixed Numbers

Words To add fractions and mixed numbers, find a common denominator.

Numbers $\frac{2}{3} + 2\frac{3}{4} = \frac{8}{12} + 2\frac{9}{12} = 2\frac{17}{12} = 3\frac{5}{12}$

EXAMPLE 1 Adding Fractions and Mixed Numbers

Remember

The least common denominator (LCD) of two or more fractions is the least common multiple (LCM) of the denominators.

Find $2\frac{1}{3} + \frac{5}{6}$.

Estimate $2 + 1 = 3$

$2\frac{1}{3} + \frac{5}{6} = 2\frac{2}{6} + \frac{5}{6}$ Rewrite using the LCD.

$= 2\frac{7}{6}$ Add the whole numbers and add the fractions.

$= 3\frac{1}{6}$ Simplify.

The sum is $3\frac{1}{6}$.

Reasonable? $3\frac{1}{6} \approx 3$ ✓

EXAMPLE 2 Adding Fractions and Mixed Numbers

Find $2\frac{1}{4} + 5\frac{1}{3} + \frac{3}{8}$.

$2\frac{1}{4} + 5\frac{1}{3} + \frac{3}{8} = 2\frac{6}{24} + 5\frac{8}{24} + \frac{9}{24}$ Rewrite using the LCD.

$= 7\frac{23}{24}$ Add the whole numbers and add the fractions.

The sum is $7\frac{23}{24}$.

On Your Own

Now You're Ready
Exercises 4–12

Add.

1. $6\frac{1}{3} + \frac{2}{9}$
2. $4\frac{3}{5} + \frac{2}{7}$
3. $1\frac{3}{5} + \frac{1}{10} + \frac{3}{4}$

EXAMPLE 3 Real-Life Application

You study for $1\frac{2}{3}$ hours before dinner and $\frac{3}{5}$ hour after dinner. Find the total amount of time you spend studying.

$$\text{Total time} = 1\frac{2}{3} + \frac{3}{5} \quad \text{Write the sum.}$$

$$= 1\frac{10}{15} + \frac{9}{15} \quad \text{Rewrite using the LCD.}$$

$$= 1\frac{19}{15} \quad \text{Add the whole numbers and add the fractions.}$$

$$= 2\frac{4}{15} \quad \text{Simplify.}$$

You study for a total of $2\frac{4}{15}$ hours.

Study Tip

In Example 3, you could also add by first writing the mixed number as an improper fraction.

$$1\frac{2}{3} + \frac{3}{5} = \frac{5}{3} + \frac{3}{5}$$

$$= \frac{25}{15} + \frac{9}{15}$$

$$= \frac{34}{15}, \text{ or } 2\frac{4}{15}$$

EXAMPLE 4 Real-Life Application

The table shows the weights (in pounds) of the items on a shelf in a pottery store. What is the total weight of the items on the shelf?

Item	Weight (pounds)
Mug	$2\frac{3}{4}$
Plate	$2\frac{1}{8}$
Vase	$3\frac{1}{4}$
Bowl	$1\frac{3}{8}$

$$\text{Total weight} = 2\frac{3}{4} + 2\frac{1}{8} + 3\frac{1}{4} + 1\frac{3}{8} \quad \text{Write the sum.}$$

$$= 2\frac{3}{4} + 3\frac{1}{4} + 2\frac{1}{8} + 1\frac{3}{8} \quad \text{Commutative Property of Addition}$$

$$= \left(2\frac{3}{4} + 3\frac{1}{4}\right) + \left(2\frac{1}{8} + 1\frac{3}{8}\right) \quad \text{Associative Property of Addition}$$

$$= 5\frac{4}{4} + 3\frac{4}{8} \quad \text{Add within the parentheses.}$$

$$= 6 + 3\frac{1}{2} \quad \text{Simplify.}$$

$$= 9\frac{1}{2} \quad \text{Add.}$$

The total weight is $9\frac{1}{2}$ pounds.

On Your Own

4. You run $\frac{3}{2}$ miles, stop to drink some water, and then run another $\frac{3}{4}$ mile. Find the total distance you run.

5. **WHAT IF?** In Example 4, a bowl that weighs $2\frac{2}{3}$ pounds is added to the shelf. What is the new total weight of the items on the shelf?

3.1 Exercises

Check It Out
Help with Homework
BigIdeasMath.com

Vocabulary and Concept Check

1. **WRITING** Explain how to find the sum $2\frac{7}{8} + \frac{3}{4}$.

2. **OPEN-ENDED** Write an addition expression using fractions that equals $\frac{1}{2}$.

3. **DIFFERENT WORDS, SAME QUESTION** Which is different? Find "both" answers.

Add $4\frac{6}{7}$ and $\frac{3}{7}$.	What is the distance between $4\frac{6}{7}$ and $\frac{3}{7}$?
What is $4\frac{6}{7}$ increased by $\frac{3}{7}$?	Find the sum of $4\frac{6}{7}$ and $\frac{3}{7}$.

Practice and Problem Solving

Add. Write fractions in simplest form.

1 2

4. $\frac{11}{12} + \frac{7}{12}$
5. $1\frac{1}{5} + \frac{3}{5}$
6. $4\frac{1}{6} + 3\frac{5}{6}$
7. $\frac{9}{14} + \frac{2}{7}$
8. $4 + 1\frac{2}{3}$
9. $\frac{15}{4} + 4\frac{1}{3}$
10. $4\frac{1}{3} + 2\frac{3}{5} + \frac{1}{5}$
11. $\frac{5}{3} + 3\frac{7}{8} + 1\frac{1}{6}$
12. $1\frac{3}{4} + 9\frac{4}{5} + \frac{7}{10}$

ERROR ANALYSIS **Describe and correct the error in finding the sum.**

13. ✗ $2\frac{4}{9} + 2\frac{1}{3} = 2\frac{4}{9} + 2\frac{3}{9}$
$= 2\frac{7}{9}$

14. ✗ $1\frac{3}{4} + \frac{1}{5} = 1\frac{4}{9}$

15. **THEATER** This week, the students in a school play rehearsed $2\frac{1}{2}$ hours on Tuesday and $1\frac{2}{3}$ hours on Thursday. How many hours did the students rehearse this week?

16. **HOT DOGS** You eat $\frac{3}{10}$ of a pack of hot dogs. Your friend eats $\frac{1}{5}$ of the pack of hot dogs. What fraction of the pack of hot dogs do you and your friend eat?

Fill in the blank.

17. $\frac{3}{\square} + 3\frac{1}{7} = 3\frac{4}{7}$

18. $2\frac{3}{4} + \frac{\square}{4} = 3$

19. $9\frac{5}{12} + \frac{\square}{6} = 9\frac{7}{12}$

20. **NUMBER SENSE** When is the sum of two mixed numbers an integer?

21. **WRITING** You are adding two fractions with different denominators. Explain how to find the sum.

June	July	August
$7\frac{9}{16}$	$4\frac{1}{4}$	$3\frac{3}{4}$

22. **RAINFALL** The table at the left shows the amounts of rainfall (in inches) measured at a reservoir for three months. Was the total amount of rainfall during the three-month period more than 16 inches? Explain.

23. **TREES** The table at the right shows the growth (in feet) of a tree each year from 2013 to 2017. How many feet did the tree grow in 2017 if its total growth over the five-year period was 10 feet?

Year	Growth (feet)
2013	$1\frac{3}{4}$
2014	$2\frac{1}{2}$
2015	$2\frac{1}{4}$
2016	$1\frac{1}{2}$
2017	?

24. **REASONING** Without adding, determine whether the sum $\frac{5}{12} + \frac{3}{8}$ is *greater than* or *less than* 1. Explain your reasoning.

25. Repeated Reasoning Evaluate the expression.

$$\frac{1}{10} + \frac{2}{10} + \frac{3}{10} + \cdots + \frac{8}{10} + \frac{9}{10} + \frac{10}{10}$$

Fair Game Review What you learned in previous grades & lessons

Identify the property. Then simplify.

26. $8 + (-3) + 2 = 8 + 2 + (-3)$

27. $-2 \cdot (4 \cdot 9) = (-2 \cdot 4) \cdot 9$

28. $\frac{1}{4} + \left(\frac{3}{4} + \frac{1}{8}\right) = \left(\frac{1}{4} + \frac{3}{4}\right) + \frac{1}{8}$

29. $\frac{3}{7} \cdot \frac{4}{5} = \frac{4}{5} \cdot \frac{3}{7}$

30. **MULTIPLE CHOICE** Your bank account balance is −\$16. You deposit \$21. What is your new balance?

Ⓐ −\$37 Ⓑ −\$5 Ⓒ \$5 Ⓓ \$37

3.2 Subtracting Fractions and Mixed Numbers

Essential Question How can you subtract fractions and mixed numbers?

1 ACTIVITY: Subtracting Fractions

Work with a partner. Use a number line to find the difference.

a. $\frac{7}{8} - \frac{3}{8}$

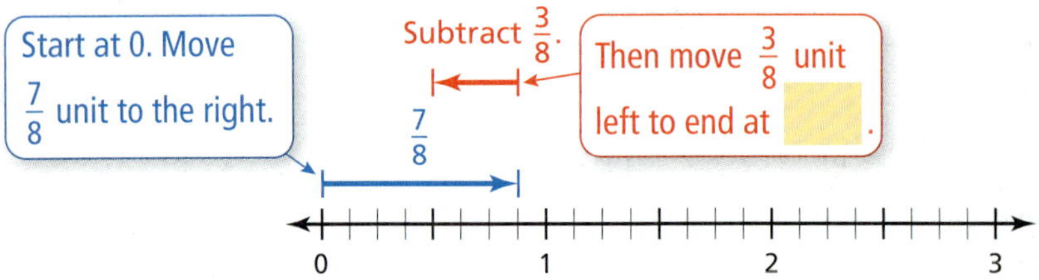

So, $\frac{7}{8} - \frac{3}{8} =$ ___.

b. $\frac{9}{10} - \frac{6}{10}$

c. $\frac{4}{5} - \frac{1}{5}$

d. $\frac{5}{3} - \frac{2}{3}$

e. $\frac{7}{9} - \frac{4}{9}$

2 ACTIVITY: Subtracting Mixed Numbers

Work with a partner. Use a number line to find the difference.

a. $1\frac{1}{4} - \frac{3}{4}$

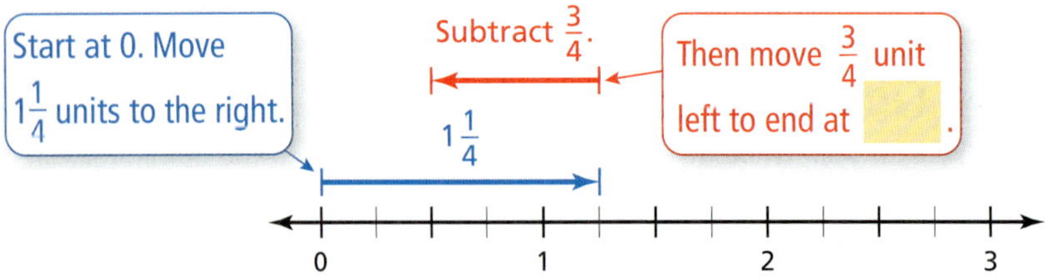

So, $1\frac{1}{4} - \frac{3}{4} =$ ___.

b. $1\frac{4}{5} - \frac{2}{5}$

c. $1\frac{7}{10} - \frac{3}{10}$

d. $2\frac{1}{3} - 1\frac{2}{3}$

e. $3\frac{1}{8} - 1\frac{3}{8}$

Fractions and Mixed Numbers

In this lesson, you will

- subtract fractions and mixed numbers.
- solve real-life problems.

3 ACTIVITY: Restaurant

Work with a partner. The table shows the weights of vegetables a restaurant chef has ordered for Tuesday.

Vegetable	Weight (pounds)
Broccoli	$5\frac{1}{2}$
Zucchini	$8\frac{3}{4}$
Tomatoes	$10\frac{1}{2}$
Cucumber	$4\frac{1}{8}$
Green peppers	$6\frac{3}{8}$
Cauliflower	$5\frac{1}{4}$
Yellow squash	$6\frac{5}{8}$

a. The chef plans to order a total of 50 pounds of vegetables for Tuesday. How many more pounds of vegetables should the chef order?

b. How did you find your answer in part (a)?

c. If the chef adds $5\frac{5}{6}$ pounds of onions to the original order, how much over 50 pounds is the new order?

d. When the original order arrives, the chef discovers that all the cucumbers are rotten and must be thrown out. How many pounds of vegetables are left from the original order?

Math Process

Interpret Results

What does your answer represent? Does your answer make sense?

What Is Your Answer?

4. **IN YOUR OWN WORDS** How can you use what you know about subtracting integers to subtract fractions and mixed numbers?

5. Give two real-life examples of subtracting fractions or mixed numbers.

Practice Use what you learned about subtracting two fractions and mixed numbers to complete Exercises 3–5 on page 80.

3.2 Lesson

Check It Out
Lesson Tutorials
BigIdeasMath.com

Key Idea

Subtracting Fractions and Mixed Numbers

Words To subtract fractions and mixed numbers, find a common denominator.

Numbers $2\frac{3}{10} - \frac{4}{5} = \frac{23}{10} - \frac{4}{5} = \frac{23}{10} - \frac{8}{10} = \frac{15}{10} = 1\frac{5}{10} = 1\frac{1}{2}$

EXAMPLE 1 Subtracting Fractions

Find $\frac{5}{6} - \frac{3}{4}$.

$\frac{5}{6} - \frac{3}{4} = \frac{10}{12} - \frac{9}{12}$ Rewrite using the LCD.

$= \frac{1}{12}$ Subtract.

∴ The difference is $\frac{1}{12}$.

EXAMPLE 2 Subtracting Mixed Numbers

Find $3\frac{1}{9} - 1\frac{5}{6}$. **Estimate** $3 - 2 = 1$

$3\frac{1}{9} - 1\frac{5}{6} = 3\frac{2}{18} - 1\frac{15}{18}$ Rewrite using the LCD.

$= 2\frac{20}{18} - 1\frac{15}{18}$ Rewrite $3\frac{2}{18}$ as $2\frac{20}{18}$.

$= 1\frac{5}{18}$ Write the improper fraction as a mixed number. Subtract the whole numbers and subtract the fractions.

∴ The difference is $1\frac{5}{18}$. **Reasonable?** $1\frac{5}{18} \approx 1$ ✓

Study Tip

Example 2 shows a method for subtracting mixed numbers without first rewriting the mixed numbers as improper fractions. After solving with one method, you can use the other method to check your answer.

On Your Own

Now You're Ready
Exercises 3–11

1. $\frac{3}{5} - \frac{1}{2}$
2. $5\frac{1}{3} - \frac{5}{8}$
3. $2\frac{1}{4} - 1\frac{1}{5}$
4. $4\frac{6}{7} - 1\frac{1}{2}$
5. $8 - \frac{6}{5}$
6. $3\frac{7}{9} - 2\frac{4}{5}$

EXAMPLE 3 Finding Distances Between Numbers on a Number Line

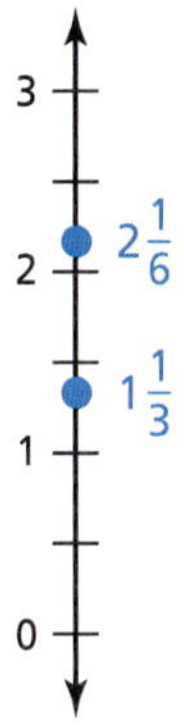

Find the distance between the two numbers on the number line.

To find the distance between the numbers, subtract the smaller number from the larger number.

$2\frac{1}{6} - 1\frac{1}{3} = \frac{13}{6} - \frac{4}{3}$ — Write the mixed numbers as improper fractions.

$= \frac{13}{6} - \frac{8}{6}$ — Rewrite using the LCD.

$= \frac{5}{6}$ — Subtract.

∴ The distance between $2\frac{1}{6}$ and $1\frac{1}{3}$ is $\frac{5}{6}$.

EXAMPLE 4 Real-Life Application

Clearance: $11\frac{2}{3}$ ft

The height of a boat is $9\frac{1}{2}$ feet. Towed on a trailer, the bottom of the boat is $1\frac{1}{2}$ feet above the ground. How much space is between the top of the boat and the bottom of the bridge when the trailer passes under the bridge?

Step 1: Find the height h of the boat and trailer.

$h = 9\frac{1}{2} + 1\frac{1}{2}$ — Add the height of the boat to the height of the trailer.

$= 10\frac{2}{2}$, or 11 — Add and simplify.

Step 2: Find the distance d between the top of the boat and the bottom of the bridge.

$d = 11\frac{2}{3} - 11$ — Subtract the height of the boat and trailer from the height of the bottom of the bridge.

$= \frac{2}{3}$ — Subtract.

∴ When the trailer passes under the bridge, the space between the top of the boat and the bottom of the bridge is $\frac{2}{3}$ foot.

On Your Own

Now You're Ready
Exercises 13–15

7. Find the distance between $5\frac{4}{5}$ and $2\frac{1}{4}$ on a number line.

8. **WHAT IF?** In Example 4, the clearance is $13\frac{1}{4}$ feet. How much space is between the top of the boat and the bottom of the bridge when the trailer passes under the bridge?

3.2 Exercises

Check It Out
Help with Homework
BigIdeasMath.com

Vocabulary and Concept Check

1. **WRITING** Explain how to find the difference $3\frac{1}{5} - \frac{2}{3}$.

2. **WHICH ONE DOESN'T BELONG?** Which expression does *not* belong with the other three? Explain your reasoning.

$\frac{5}{9} - \frac{1}{4}$ $\qquad$ $\frac{20-9}{36}$ $\qquad$ $\frac{5-1}{9-4}$ $\qquad$ $\frac{20}{36} - \frac{9}{36}$

Practice and Problem Solving

Subtract. Write fractions in simplest form.

1 2 3. $\frac{7}{8} - \frac{5}{8}$ 4. $1\frac{2}{3} - 1\frac{1}{3}$ 5. $\frac{21}{5} - 2\frac{3}{5}$

6. $4\frac{3}{10} - 1\frac{4}{5}$ 7. $10\frac{1}{6} - 8\frac{3}{8}$ 8. $\frac{5}{9} - \frac{1}{2}$

9. $5 - \frac{5}{3}$ 10. $3\frac{1}{4} - \frac{3}{5}$ 11. $7\frac{1}{4} - \frac{9}{10}$

12. **ERROR ANALYSIS** Describe and correct the error in finding the difference.

$$\frac{9}{4} - \frac{1}{2} = \frac{9-1}{4-2} = \frac{8}{2} = 4$$

Find the distance between the two numbers on a number line.

3 13. $2\frac{1}{2}, 5\frac{3}{4}$ 14. $7, 3\frac{2}{3}$ 15. $1\frac{1}{8}, 3\frac{2}{5}$

16. **SPORTS DRINK** Your sports drink bottle is $\frac{5}{6}$ full. After practice, the bottle is $\frac{3}{8}$ full. Write the difference of the amounts before practice and after practice.

17. **HOT-AIR BALLOON** The figure shows the heights of a hot-air balloon.

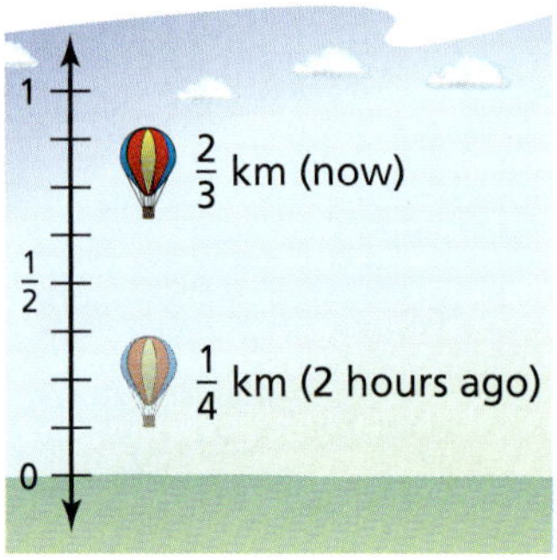

a. Find the vertical distance traveled by hot-air balloon.

b. Find the mean hourly vertical distance traveled by the hot-air balloon.

Evaluate.

18. $2\frac{1}{6} - \frac{5}{3} + 2\frac{4}{9}$ 19. $8 - \left(2\frac{1}{4} - 1\frac{7}{8}\right)$ 20. $\frac{32}{5} - \frac{13}{6} - 3\frac{2}{3}$

21. **REASONING** When is the difference of two mixed numbers an integer? Explain.

22. **RECIPE** A cook has $2\frac{2}{3}$ cups of flour. A recipe calls for $2\frac{3}{4}$ cups of flour. Does the cook have enough flour? If not, how much more flour is needed?

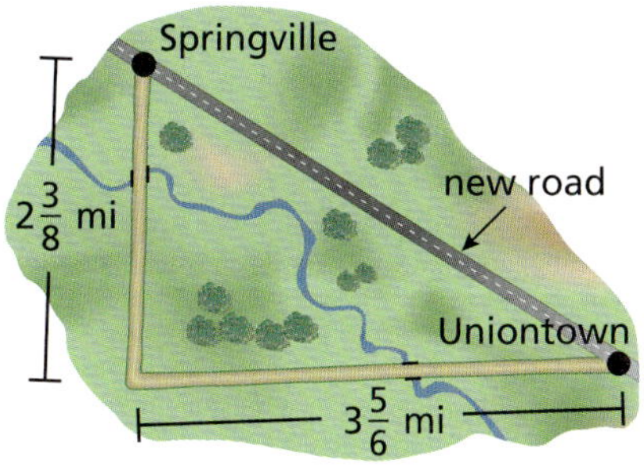

23. **ROADWAY** A new road that connects Uniontown to Springville is $4\frac{1}{3}$ miles long. How much shorter is the distance when using the new road instead of the dirt roads?

RAINFALL In Exercises 24–26, the table shows a city's rainfall in one year.

24. How much more rainfall did the city receive in August than in November?

25. What is the difference in the amounts of rainfall between September and February?

STEM VIDEO

26. How much less was the amount of rainfall in January than in May?

Monthly Rainfall

Month	Rainfall (in.)	Month	Rainfall (in.)
Jan	$\frac{1}{8}$	Jul	$5\frac{7}{8}$
Feb	$\frac{1}{10}$	Aug	6
Mar	$\frac{1}{8}$	Sep	$8\frac{1}{3}$
Apr	$\frac{1}{8}$	Oct	$7\frac{3}{4}$
May	$5\frac{1}{2}$	Nov	$2\frac{1}{5}$
Jun	$7\frac{3}{4}$	Dec	$\frac{3}{4}$

REASONING Without subtracting, tell whether the difference between the two numbers is greater than or less than 1. Explain your reasoning.

27. $2\frac{3}{4} - 1\frac{1}{3}$

28. $2\frac{1}{5} - 1\frac{4}{7}$

29. **Structure** Fill in the blanks to make the solution correct.

$$2\frac{\square}{5} - 1\frac{1}{\square} = 1\frac{1}{2}$$

Fair Game Review What you learned in previous grades & lessons

Evaluate.

30. $15 \cdot (-6)$

31. $-78 \div (-3)$

32. $-20 \cdot (-12)$

33. $64 \div (-4)$

34. **MULTIPLE CHOICE** A sports store has 116 soccer balls. Over 6 months, it sells 8 soccer balls per month. How many soccer balls are in inventory at the end of the 6 months?

Ⓐ −48 Ⓑ 48 Ⓒ 68 Ⓓ 108

3.3 Multiplying Fractions and Mixed Numbers

Essential Question What does it mean to multiply fractions?

1 ACTIVITY: Multiplying Fractions

Work with a partner. A bottle of water is $\frac{1}{2}$ full. You drink $\frac{2}{3}$ of the water. How much of the bottle of water do you drink?

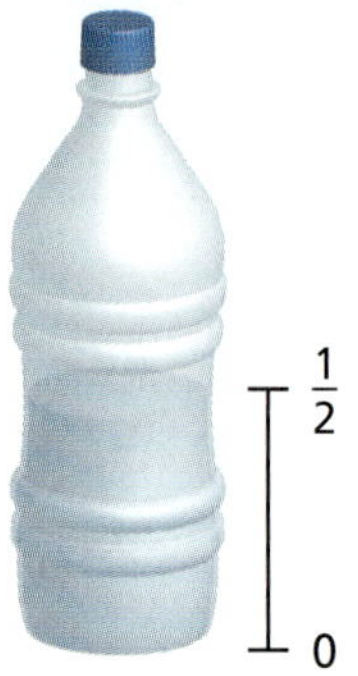

THINK ABOUT THE QUESTION: To help you think about this question, rewrite the question.

Words: What is $\frac{2}{3}$ of $\frac{1}{2}$? **Numbers:** $\frac{2}{3} \times \frac{1}{2} = ?$

Here is one way to get the answer.

- **Draw** a length of $\frac{1}{2}$.

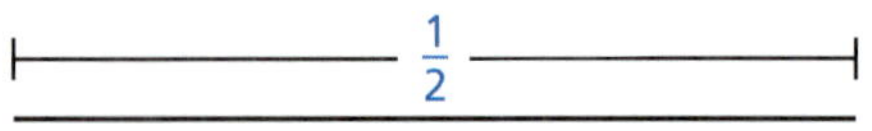

Because you want to find $\frac{2}{3}$ of the length, divide it into 3 equal sections.

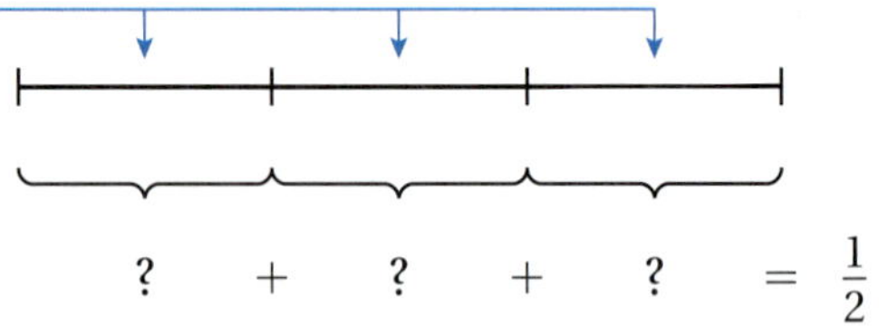

Now, you need to think of a way to divide $\frac{1}{2}$ into 3 equal parts.

- **Rewrite** $\frac{1}{2}$ as a fraction whose numerator is divisible by 3.

Because the length is divided into 3 equal sections, multiply the numerator and denominator by 3.

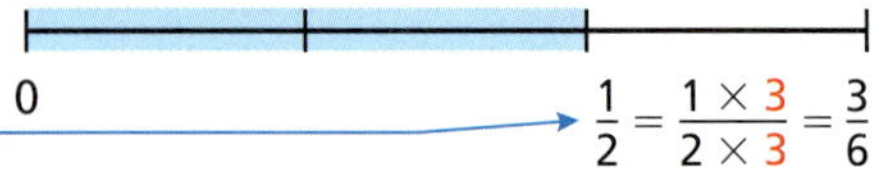

Dividing Fractions
In this lesson, you will
- use models to multiply fractions.
- multiply fractions by fractions.

In this form, you see that $\frac{3}{6}$ can be divided into 3 equal parts of $\frac{1}{6}$.

- Each part is $\frac{1}{6}$ of the bottle of water, and you drank two of them. Written as multiplication, you have

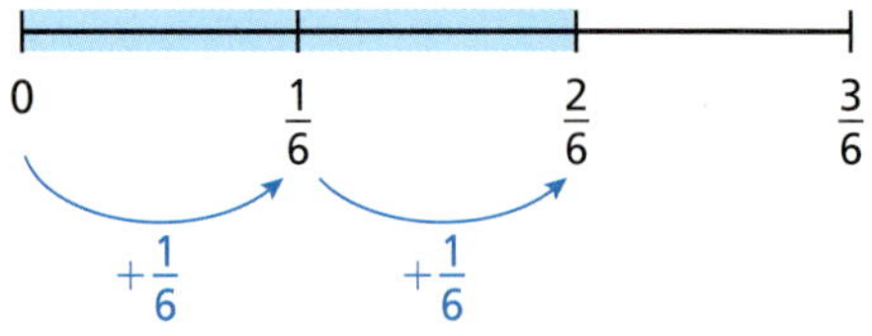

$$\frac{2}{3} \times \frac{1}{2} = \frac{2}{\square} = \frac{\square}{\square}.$$

So, you drank $\frac{\square}{\square}$ of the bottle of water.

2 ACTIVITY: Multiplying Fractions

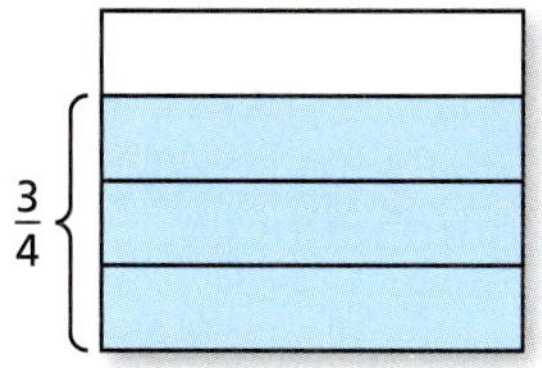

Work with a partner. A park has a playground that is $\frac{3}{4}$ of its width and $\frac{4}{5}$ of its length. What fraction of the park is covered by the playground?

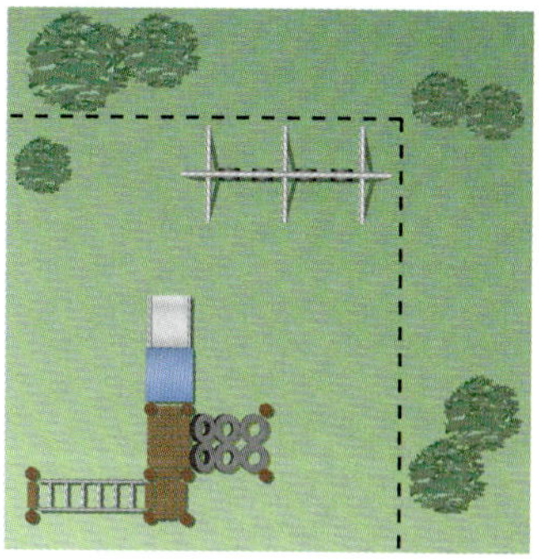

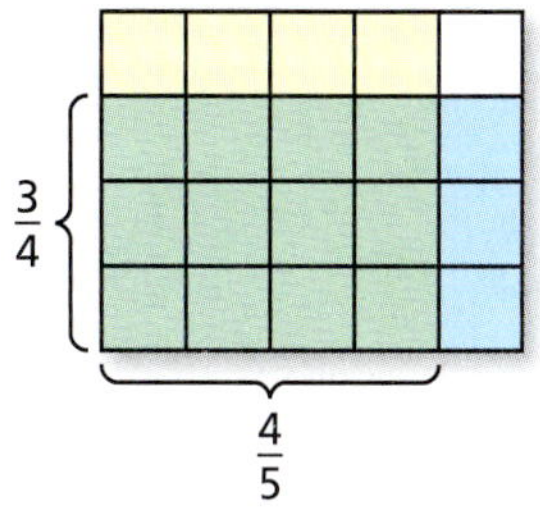

Fold a piece of paper horizontally into fourths and shade three of the fourths to represent $\frac{3}{4}$.

Fold the paper vertically into fifths and shade $\frac{4}{5}$ of the paper another color.

Count the total number of squares. This number is the denominator. The numerator is the number of squares shaded with both colors.

$\frac{3}{4} \times \frac{4}{5} = \frac{\square}{\square} = \frac{\square}{\square}$. So, $\frac{\square}{\square}$ of the park is covered by the playground.

Inductive Reasoning

Work with a partner. Complete the table by using a model or folding paper.

	Exercise	Verbal Expression	Answer
1	3. $\frac{2}{3} \times \frac{1}{2}$	$\frac{2}{3}$ of $\frac{1}{2}$	$\frac{\square}{\square}$
2	4. $\frac{3}{4} \times \frac{4}{5}$	$\frac{3}{4}$ of $\frac{4}{5}$	$\frac{\square}{\square}$
	5. $\frac{2}{3} \times \frac{5}{6}$		
	6. $\frac{1}{6} \times \frac{1}{4}$		
	7. $\frac{2}{5} \times \frac{1}{2}$		
	8. $\frac{5}{8} \times \frac{4}{5}$		

Math Process

Consider Similar Problems

What are the similarities in constructing the models for each problem? What are the differences?

What Is Your Answer?

9. **IN YOUR OWN WORDS** What does it mean to multiply fractions?

10. **STRUCTURE** Write a general rule for multiplying fractions.

Practice Use what you learned about multiplying fractions to complete Exercises 4–11 on page 87.

3.3 Lesson

Check It Out
Lesson Tutorials
BigIdeasMath.com

Key Idea

Multiplying Fractions

Words Multiply the numerators and multiply the denominators.

Numbers $\frac{3}{7} \times \frac{1}{2} = \frac{3 \times 1}{7 \times 2} = \frac{3}{14}$

Algebra $\frac{a}{b} \cdot \frac{c}{d} = \frac{a \cdot c}{b \cdot d}$, where $b, d \neq 0$

EXAMPLE 1 Multiplying Fractions

Find $\frac{1}{5} \times \frac{1}{3}$.

$\frac{1}{5} \times \frac{1}{3} = \frac{1 \times 1}{5 \times 3}$ — Multiply the numerators. Multiply the denominators.

$= \frac{1}{15}$ — Simplify.

EXAMPLE 2 Multiplying Fractions with Common Factors

Find $\frac{8}{9} \times \frac{3}{4}$. **Estimate** $1 \times \frac{3}{4} = \frac{3}{4}$

$\frac{8}{9} \times \frac{3}{4} = \frac{8 \times 3}{9 \times 4}$ — Multiply the numerators. Multiply the denominators.

$= \frac{\overset{2}{\cancel{8}} \times \overset{1}{\cancel{3}}}{\underset{3}{\cancel{9}} \times \underset{1}{\cancel{4}}}$ — Divide out common factors.

$= \frac{2}{3}$ — Simplify.

∴ The product is $\frac{2}{3}$. **Reasonable?** $\frac{2}{3} \approx \frac{3}{4}$ ✓

Study Tip

When the numerator of one fraction is the same as the denominator of another fraction, you can use mental math to multiply. For example, $\frac{4}{5} \times \frac{5}{9} = \frac{4}{9}$ because you can divide out the common factor 5.

On Your Own

Now You're Ready
Exercises 4–19

Multiply. Write the answer in simplest form.

1. $\frac{1}{2} \times \frac{5}{6}$
2. $\frac{7}{8} \times \frac{1}{4}$
3. $\frac{3}{7} \times \frac{2}{3}$
4. $\frac{4}{9} \times \frac{3}{10}$

EXAMPLE 3 Real-Life Application

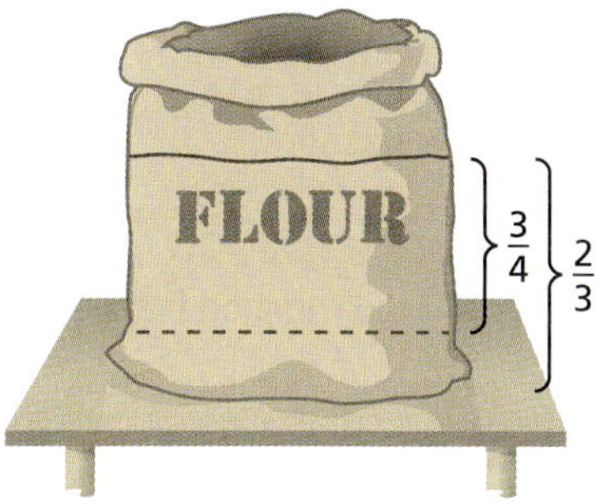

You have $\frac{2}{3}$ of a bag of flour. You use $\frac{3}{4}$ of the flour to make empanada dough. How much of the entire bag do you use to make the dough?

Method 1: Use a model. Six of the 12 squares have both types of shading.

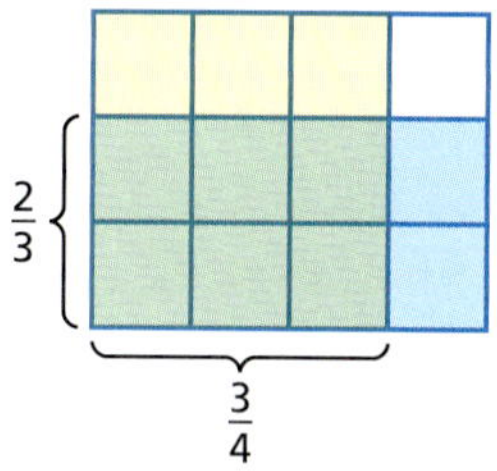

∴ So, you use $\frac{6}{12} = \frac{1}{2}$ of the entire bag.

Method 2: To find $\frac{3}{4}$ of $\frac{2}{3}$, multiply.

$$\frac{3}{4} \times \frac{2}{3} = \frac{\cancel{3}^{1} \times \cancel{2}^{1}}{\cancel{4}_{2} \times \cancel{3}_{1}}$$ Multiply the numerators and the denominators. Divide out common factors.

$$= \frac{1}{2}$$ Simplify.

∴ So, you use $\frac{1}{2}$ of the entire bag.

On Your Own

5. **WHAT IF?** In Example 3, you use $\frac{1}{4}$ of the flour to make the dough. How much of the entire bag do you use to make the dough?

Key Idea

Multiplying Mixed Numbers

Write each mixed number as an improper fraction. Then multiply as you would with fractions.

EXAMPLE 4 Multiplying a Fraction and a Mixed Number

Find $\frac{1}{2} \times 2\frac{3}{4}$.

Estimate $\frac{1}{2} \times 3 = 1\frac{1}{2}$

$$\frac{1}{2} \times 2\frac{3}{4} = \frac{1}{2} \times \frac{11}{4}$$ Write $2\frac{3}{4}$ as the improper fraction $\frac{11}{4}$.

$$= \frac{1 \times 11}{2 \times 4}$$ Multiply the numerators and the denominators.

$$= \frac{11}{8}, \text{ or } 1\frac{3}{8}$$ Simplify.

∴ The product is $1\frac{3}{8}$.

Reasonable? $1\frac{3}{8} \approx 1\frac{1}{2}$ ✓

EXAMPLE 5 Multiplying Mixed Numbers

Find $1\frac{4}{5} \times 3\frac{2}{3}$.

Estimate $2 \times 4 = 8$

$1\frac{4}{5} \times 3\frac{2}{3} = \frac{9}{5} \times \frac{11}{3}$ Write $1\frac{4}{5}$ and $3\frac{2}{3}$ as improper fractions.

$= \frac{\overset{3}{\cancel{9}} \times 11}{5 \times \underset{1}{\cancel{3}}}$ Multiply fractions. Divide out the common factor 3.

$= \frac{33}{5}$, or $6\frac{3}{5}$ Simplify.

The product is $6\frac{3}{5}$.

Reasonable? $6\frac{3}{5} \approx 8$ ✓

On Your Own

Now You're Ready
Exercises 26–41

Multiply. Write the answer in simplest form.

6. $\frac{1}{3} \times 1\frac{1}{6}$ **7.** $3\frac{1}{2} \times \frac{4}{9}$ **8.** $1\frac{7}{8} \times 2\frac{2}{5}$ **9.** $5\frac{5}{7} \times 2\frac{1}{10}$

EXAMPLE 6 Real-Life Application

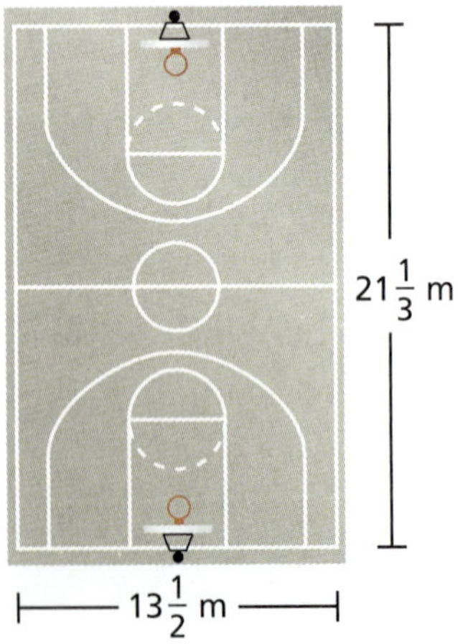

A city is resurfacing a basketball court. Find the area of the court.

Estimate $21 \times 14 = 294$

$A = \ell w$ Write the formula for the area of a rectangle.

$= 21\frac{1}{3} \times 13\frac{1}{2}$ Substitute $21\frac{1}{3}$ for ℓ and $13\frac{1}{2}$ for w.

$= \frac{64}{3} \times \frac{27}{2}$ Write $21\frac{1}{3}$ and $13\frac{1}{2}$ as improper fractions.

$= \frac{\overset{32}{\cancel{64}} \times \overset{9}{\cancel{27}}}{\underset{1}{\cancel{3}} \times \underset{1}{\cancel{2}}}$ Multiply fractions. Divide out common factors.

$= 288$ Simplify.

So, the area of the court is 288 square meters.

Reasonable? $288 \approx 294$ ✓

On Your Own

10. Find the area of a rectangular air hockey table that is $8\frac{1}{4}$ feet by $4\frac{3}{8}$ feet.

3.3 Exercises

Check It Out
Help with Homework
BigIdeasMath.com

Vocabulary and Concept Check

1. **WRITING** Explain how to multiply two fractions.
2. **REASONING** Name the missing denominator.

   $\frac{3}{7} \times \frac{1}{\square} = \frac{3}{28}$

3. **OPEN-ENDED** Write two mixed numbers between 3 and 4 that have a product between 9 and 12.

Practice and Problem Solving

Multiply. Write the answer in simplest form.

1 2 **4.** $\frac{1}{7} \times \frac{2}{3}$ **5.** $\frac{5}{8} \times \frac{1}{2}$ **6.** $\frac{1}{4} \times \frac{2}{5}$ **7.** $\frac{3}{7} \times \frac{1}{4}$

8. $\frac{2}{3} \times \frac{4}{7}$ **9.** $\frac{5}{7} \times \frac{7}{8}$ **10.** $\frac{3}{8} \times \frac{1}{9}$ **11.** $\frac{5}{6} \times \frac{2}{5}$

12. $\frac{5}{12} \times 10$ **13.** $6 \times \frac{7}{8}$ **14.** $\frac{3}{4} \times \frac{8}{15}$ **15.** $\frac{4}{9} \times \frac{4}{5}$

16. $\frac{3}{7} \times \frac{3}{7}$ **17.** $\frac{5}{6} \times \frac{2}{9}$ **18.** $\frac{13}{18} \times \frac{6}{7}$ **19.** $\frac{7}{9} \times \frac{21}{10}$

20. ERROR ANALYSIS Describe and correct the error in finding the product.

$$\frac{2}{5} \times \frac{3}{10} = \frac{4}{10} \times \frac{3}{10} = \frac{4 \times 3}{10} = \frac{12}{10} = 1\frac{1}{5}$$

21. AQUARIUM In an aquarium, $\frac{2}{5}$ of the fish are surgeonfish. Of these, $\frac{3}{4}$ are yellow tangs. What fraction of all fish in the aquarium are yellow tangs?

22. JUMP ROPE You exercise for $\frac{3}{4}$ of an hour. You jump rope for $\frac{1}{3}$ of that time. What fraction of the hour do you spend jumping rope?

Without finding the product, copy and complete the statement using <, >, or =. Explain your reasoning.

23. $\frac{4}{7} \ \square \ \left(\frac{9}{10} \times \frac{4}{7}\right)$ **24.** $\left(\frac{5}{8} \times \frac{22}{15}\right) \ \square \ \frac{5}{8}$ **25.** $\frac{5}{6} \ \square \ \left(\frac{5}{6} \times \frac{7}{7}\right)$

Multiply. Write the answer in simplest form.

4 5 **26.** $1\frac{1}{3} \times \frac{2}{3}$ **27.** $6\frac{2}{3} \times \frac{3}{10}$ **28.** $2\frac{1}{2} \times \frac{4}{5}$ **29.** $\frac{3}{5} \times 3\frac{1}{3}$

30. $7\frac{1}{2} \times \frac{2}{3}$ **31.** $\frac{5}{9} \times 3\frac{3}{5}$ **32.** $\frac{3}{4} \times 1\frac{1}{3}$ **33.** $3\frac{3}{4} \times \frac{2}{5}$

34. $4\frac{3}{8} \times \frac{4}{5}$ **35.** $\frac{3}{7} \times 2\frac{5}{6}$ **36.** $1\frac{3}{10} \times 18$ **37.** $15 \times 2\frac{4}{9}$

38. $1\frac{1}{6} \times 6\frac{3}{4}$ **39.** $2\frac{5}{12} \times 2\frac{2}{3}$ **40.** $5\frac{5}{7} \times 3\frac{1}{8}$ **41.** $2\frac{4}{5} \times 4\frac{1}{16}$

ERROR ANALYSIS **Describe and correct the error in finding the product.**

42. ✗ $4 \times 3\frac{7}{10} = 12\frac{7}{10}$

43. ✗ $2\frac{1}{2} \times 7\frac{4}{5} = (2 \times 7) + \left(\frac{1}{2} \times \frac{4}{5}\right)$

$= 14 + \frac{2}{5} = 14\frac{2}{5}$

44. VITAMIN C A vitamin C tablet contains $\frac{1}{40}$ of a gram of vitamin C. You take $1\frac{1}{2}$ tablets every day. How many grams of vitamin C do you take every day?

45. SCHOOL BANNER You make a banner for a football rally.

a. What is the area of the banner?

b. You add a $\frac{1}{4}$-foot border on each side. What is the new area of the banner?

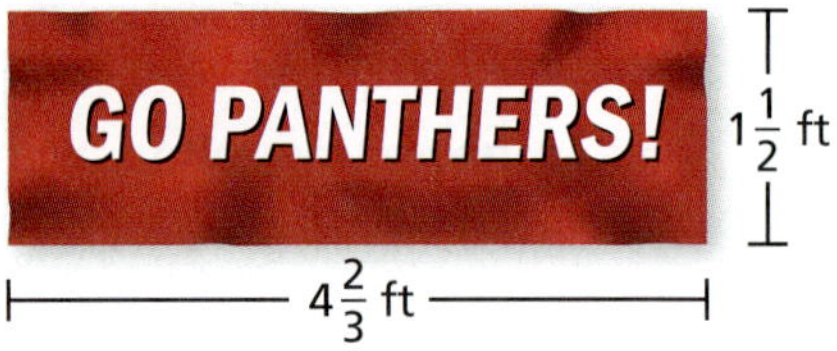

46. NUMBER SENSE Without calculating, is $1\frac{1}{6} \cdot \frac{4}{5}$ less than or greater than $1\frac{1}{6}$? Is the product less than or greater than $\frac{4}{5}$? Explain your reasoning.

Multiply. Write the answer in simplest form.

47. $\frac{1}{2} \times \frac{3}{5} \times \frac{4}{9}$ **48.** $\frac{4}{7} \times 4\frac{3}{8} \times \frac{5}{6}$ **49.** $1\frac{1}{15} \times 5\frac{2}{5} \times 4\frac{7}{12}$

50. $\left(\frac{3}{5}\right)^3$ **51.** $\left(\frac{4}{5}\right)^2 \times \left(\frac{3}{4}\right)^2$ **52.** $\left(\frac{5}{6}\right)^2 \times \left(1\frac{1}{10}\right)^2$

53. PICTURES Three pictures hang side by side on a wall. What is the total area of the wall that the pictures cover?

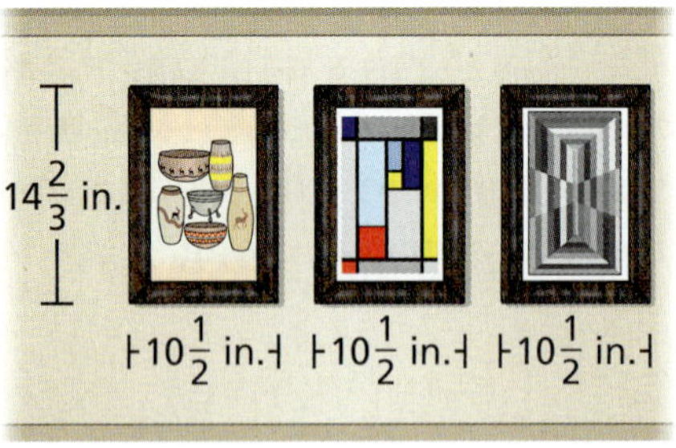

54. OPEN-ENDED Find a fraction that, when multiplied by $\frac{1}{2}$, is less than $\frac{1}{4}$.

55. DISTANCES You are in a bike race. When you get to the first checkpoint, you are $\frac{2}{5}$ of the distance to the second checkpoint. When you get to the second checkpoint, you are $\frac{1}{4}$ of the distance to the finish. What is the distance from the start to the first checkpoint?

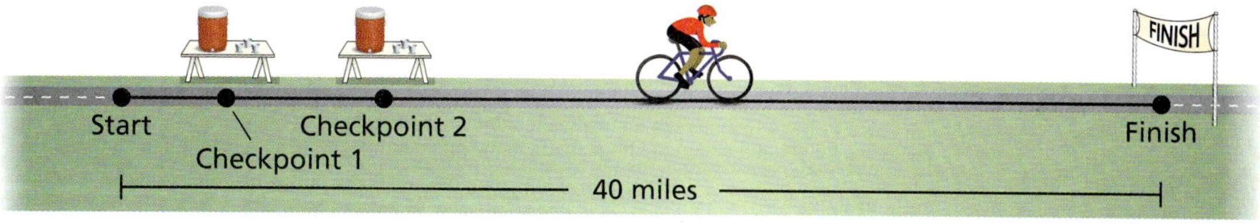

56. NUMBER SENSE Is the product of two positive mixed numbers ever less than 1? Explain.

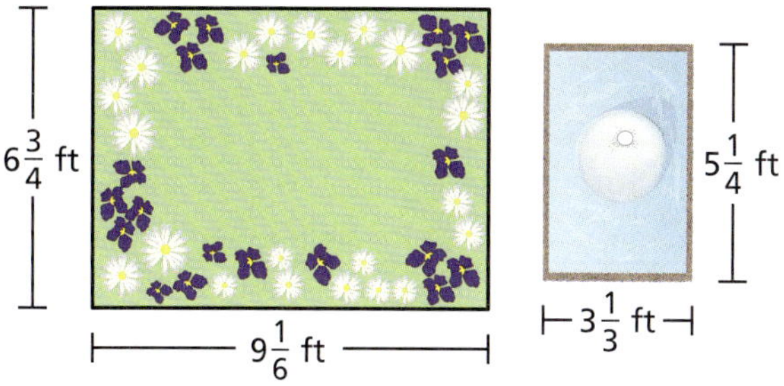

57. MODELING You plan to add a fountain to your garden.

a. Draw a diagram of the fountain in the garden. Label the dimensions.

b. Describe two methods for finding the area of the garden that surrounds the fountain.

c. Find the area. Which method did you use, and why?

58. COOKING The cooking time for a ham is $\frac{2}{5}$ of an hour for each pound.

a. How long should you cook a ham that weighs $12\frac{3}{4}$ pounds?

b. Dinner time is 4:45 P.M. What time should you start cooking the ham?

59. PETS You ask 150 people about their pets. The results show that $\frac{9}{25}$ of the people own a dog. Of the people who own a dog, $\frac{1}{6}$ of them also own a cat.

a. What fraction of the people own a dog and a cat?

b. Reasoning How many people own a dog but not a cat? Explain.

Fair Game Review What you learned in previous grades & lessons

Find the prime factorization of the number.

60. 24 **61.** 45 **62.** 53 **63.** 60

64. MULTIPLE CHOICE A science experiment calls for $\frac{3}{4}$ cup of baking powder. You have $\frac{1}{3}$ cup of baking powder. How much more baking powder do you need?

Ⓐ $\frac{1}{4}$ cup Ⓑ $\frac{5}{12}$ cup Ⓒ $\frac{4}{7}$ cup Ⓓ $1\frac{1}{12}$ cups

3.4 Dividing Fractions

Essential Question How can you divide by a fraction?

1 ACTIVITY: Dividing by a Fraction

Work with a partner. Write the division problem and solve it using a model.

a. How many two-thirds are in three?

The division problem is ___ ÷ $\frac{\_\_}{\_\_}$.

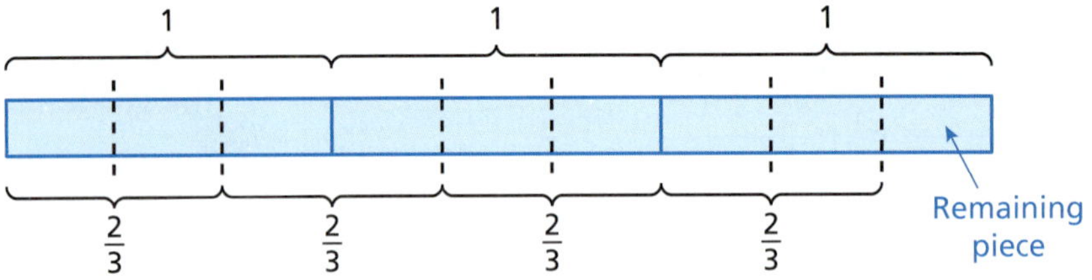

How many groups of $\frac{2}{3}$ are in 3? ___

The remaining piece represents $\frac{\_\_}{\_\_}$ of $\frac{2}{3}$.

So, there are ___ $\frac{\_\_}{\_\_}$ groups of $\frac{2}{3}$ in 3.

So, ___ ÷ $\frac{\_\_}{\_\_}$ = ___ $\frac{\_\_}{\_\_}$.

b. How many halves are in five halves?

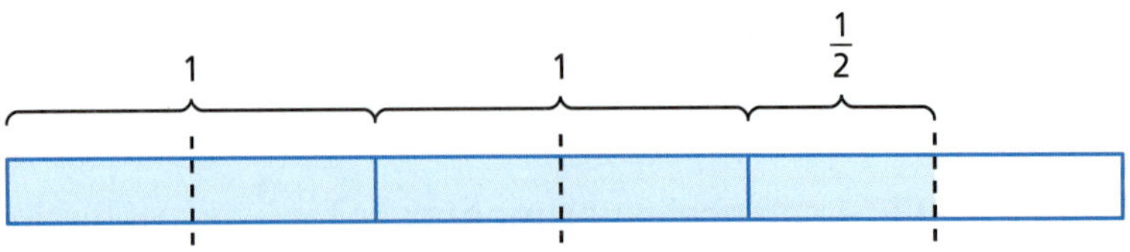

c. How many four-fifths are in eight?

d. How many one-thirds are in seven halves?

e. How many three-fourths are in five halves?

Dividing Fractions

In this lesson, you will
- write reciprocals of numbers.
- use models to divide fractions.
- divide fractions by fractions.
- solve real-life problems.

2 ACTIVITY: Using Tables to Recognize a Pattern

Work with a partner.

a. Complete each table.

Division Table

$8 \div 16$	$\frac{1}{2}$
$8 \div 8$	1
$8 \div 4$	2
$8 \div 2$	4
$8 \div 1$	8
$8 \div \frac{1}{2}$	
$8 \div \frac{1}{4}$	
$8 \div \frac{1}{8}$	

Multiplication Table

$8 \times \frac{1}{16}$	$\frac{1}{2}$
$8 \times \frac{1}{8}$	1
$8 \times \frac{1}{4}$	2
$8 \times \frac{1}{2}$	4
8×1	8
8×2	
8×4	
8×8	

Math Process

Analyze Relationships

How is multiplying numbers similar to dividing numbers?

b. Describe the relationship between the red numbers in the division table and the red numbers in the multiplication table.

c. Describe the relationship between the blue numbers in the division table and the blue numbers in the multiplication table.

d. **STRUCTURE** Make a conjecture about how you can use multiplication to divide by a fraction.

e. Test your conjecture using the problems in Activity 1.

What Is Your Answer?

3. **IN YOUR OWN WORDS** How can you divide by a fraction? Give an example.

4. How many halves are in a fourth? Explain how you found your answer.

Practice Use what you learned about dividing fractions to complete Exercises 11–18 on page 95.

3.4 Lesson

Check It Out
Lesson Tutorials
BigIdeasMath.com

Key Vocabulary
reciprocals, *p. 92*

Two numbers whose product is 1 are **reciprocals**. To write the reciprocal of a number, write the number as a fraction. Then invert the fraction. So, the reciprocal of a fraction $\frac{a}{b}$ is $\frac{b}{a}$, where a and $b \neq 0$.

The Meaning of a Word ● Invert

When you **invert** a glass, you turn it over.

Study Tip

The product of a nonzero number and its reciprocal is 1.

$$\frac{a}{b} \cdot \frac{b}{a} = 1$$

This is called the *Multiplicative Inverse Property*. You will learn more about this property in Chapter 7.

EXAMPLE 1 Writing Reciprocals

	Original Number	*Fraction*	*Reciprocal*	*Check*
a.	$\frac{3}{5}$	$\frac{3}{5}$	$\frac{5}{3}$	$\frac{3}{5} \times \frac{5}{3} = 1$
b.	$\frac{9}{5}$	$\frac{9}{5}$	$\frac{5}{9}$	$\frac{9}{5} \times \frac{5}{9} = 1$
c.	2	$\frac{2}{1}$	$\frac{1}{2}$	$\frac{2}{1} \times \frac{1}{2} = 1$

Study Tip

When any number is multiplied by 0, the product is 0. So, the number 0 does not have a reciprocal.

On Your Own

Now You're Ready
Exercises 7–10

Write the reciprocal of the number.

1. $\frac{3}{4}$ **2.** 5 **3.** $\frac{7}{2}$ **4.** $\frac{4}{9}$

Key Idea

Dividing Fractions

Words To divide a number by a fraction, multiply the number by the reciprocal of the fraction.

Numbers $\frac{1}{5} \div \frac{3}{4} = \frac{1}{5} \times \frac{4}{3} = \frac{1 \times 4}{5 \times 3}$

Algebra $\frac{a}{b} \div \frac{c}{d} = \frac{a}{b} \cdot \frac{d}{c} = \frac{a \cdot d}{b \cdot c}$, where b, c, and $d \neq 0$

EXAMPLE 2 Dividing a Fraction by a Fraction

Find $\frac{1}{6} \div \frac{2}{3}$.

$\frac{1}{6} \div \frac{2}{3} = \frac{1}{6} \times \frac{3}{2}$ — Multiply by the reciprocal of $\frac{2}{3}$, which is $\frac{3}{2}$.

$= \frac{1 \times \cancel{3}^{1}}{\cancel{6}_{2} \times 2}$ — Multiply fractions. Divide out the common factor 3.

$= \frac{1}{4}$ — Simplify.

EXAMPLE 3 Dividing a Whole Number by a Fraction

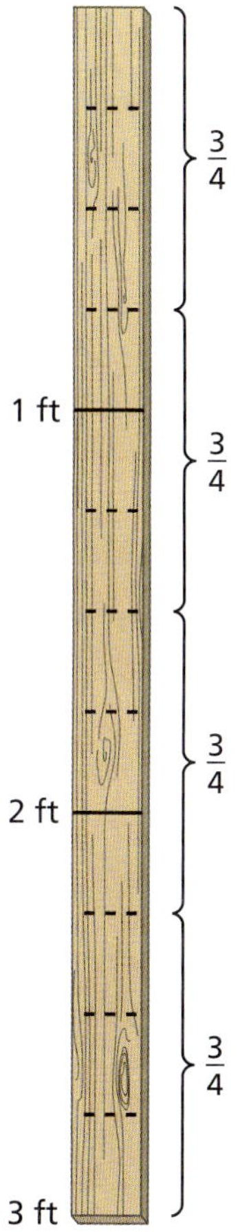

A piece of wood is 3 feet long. How many $\frac{3}{4}$-foot pieces can you cut from the piece of wood?

Method 1: Draw a diagram. Mark each foot on the diagram. Then divide each foot into $\frac{1}{4}$-foot sections.

Count the number of $\frac{3}{4}$-foot pieces of wood. There are four.

∴ So, you can cut four $\frac{3}{4}$-foot pieces from the piece of wood.

Method 2: Divide 3 by $\frac{3}{4}$ to find the number of $\frac{3}{4}$-foot pieces.

$3 \div \frac{3}{4} = 3 \times \frac{4}{3}$ — Multiply by the reciprocal of $\frac{3}{4}$, which is $\frac{4}{3}$.

$= \frac{\cancel{3}^{1} \times 4}{\cancel{3}_{1}}$ — Multiply. Divide out the common factor 3.

$= 4$ — Simplify.

∴ So, you can cut four $\frac{3}{4}$-foot pieces from the piece of wood.

On Your Own

Divide. Write the answer in simplest form.

5. $\frac{2}{7} \div \frac{1}{3}$ **6.** $\frac{1}{2} \div \frac{1}{8}$ **7.** $\frac{3}{8} \div \frac{1}{4}$ **8.** $\frac{2}{5} \div \frac{3}{10}$

9. How many $\frac{1}{2}$-foot pieces can you cut from a 7-foot piece of wood?

EXAMPLE 4 Dividing a Fraction by a Whole Number

Find $\frac{4}{5} \div 2$.

$\frac{4}{5} \div 2 = \frac{4}{5} \div \frac{2}{1}$ Write 2 as an improper fraction.

$= \frac{4}{5} \times \frac{1}{2}$ Multiply by the reciprocal of $\frac{2}{1}$, which is $\frac{1}{2}$.

$= \frac{\overset{2}{\cancel{4}} \times 1}{5 \times \underset{1}{\cancel{2}}}$ Multiply fractions. Divide out the common factor 2.

$= \frac{2}{5}$ Simplify.

On Your Own

Now You're Ready
Exercises 11–26

Divide. Write the answer in simplest form.

10. $\frac{1}{2} \div 3$

11. $\frac{2}{3} \div 10$

12. $\frac{5}{8} \div 4$

13. $\frac{6}{7} \div 4$

EXAMPLE 5 Using Order of Operations

Evaluate $\frac{3}{8} + \frac{5}{6} \div 5$.

$\frac{3}{8} + \frac{5}{6} \div 5 = \frac{3}{8} + \frac{5}{6} \times \frac{1}{5}$ Multiply by the reciprocal of 5, which is $\frac{1}{5}$.

$= \frac{3}{8} + \frac{\overset{1}{\cancel{5}} \times 1}{6 \times \underset{1}{\cancel{5}}}$ Multiply $\frac{5}{6}$ and $\frac{1}{5}$. Divide out the common factor 5.

$= \frac{3}{8} + \frac{1}{6}$ Simplify.

$= \frac{18}{48} + \frac{8}{48}$ Rewrite fractions using a common denominator.

$= \frac{26}{48}$, or $\frac{13}{24}$ Simplify.

Study Tip

You can use the LCD, 24, to add the fractions in Example 5.

$\frac{3}{8} + \frac{1}{6} = \frac{9}{24} + \frac{4}{24} = \frac{13}{24}$

On Your Own

Now You're Ready
Exercises 43–51

Evaluate the expression. Write the answer in simplest form.

14. $\frac{4}{5} + \frac{2}{5} \div 4$

15. $\frac{3}{8} \div \frac{3}{4} - \frac{1}{6}$

16. $\frac{8}{9} \div 2 \div 8$

3.4 Exercises

Check It Out
Help with Homework
BigIdeasMath.com

Vocabulary and Concept Check

1. **OPEN-ENDED** Write a fraction and its reciprocal.

2. **WHICH ONE DOESN'T BELONG?** Which of the following does *not* belong with the other three? Explain your reasoning.

$\frac{1}{3}$ $\quad\frac{1}{6}$ $\quad\frac{2}{9}$ $\quad\frac{1}{8}$

MATCHING **Match the expression with its value.**

3. $\frac{2}{5} \div \frac{8}{15}$
4. $\frac{8}{15} \div \frac{2}{5}$
5. $\frac{2}{15} \div \frac{8}{5}$
6. $\frac{8}{5} \div \frac{2}{15}$

A. $\frac{1}{12}$ B. $\frac{3}{4}$ C. 12 D. $1\frac{1}{3}$

Practice and Problem Solving

Write the reciprocal of the number.

(1) 7. 8 8. $\frac{6}{7}$ 9. $\frac{2}{5}$ 10. $\frac{8}{11}$

Divide. Write the answer in simplest form.

(2) (3) (4) 11. $\frac{1}{8} \div \frac{1}{4}$ 12. $\frac{5}{6} \div \frac{2}{7}$ 13. $12 \div \frac{3}{4}$ 14. $8 \div \frac{2}{5}$

15. $\frac{3}{7} \div 6$ 16. $\frac{12}{25} \div 4$ 17. $\frac{2}{9} \div \frac{2}{3}$ 18. $\frac{8}{15} \div \frac{4}{5}$

19. $\frac{1}{3} \div \frac{1}{9}$ 20. $\frac{7}{10} \div \frac{3}{8}$ 21. $\frac{14}{27} \div 7$ 22. $\frac{5}{8} \div 15$

23. $\frac{27}{32} \div \frac{7}{8}$ 24. $\frac{4}{15} \div \frac{10}{13}$ 25. $9 \div \frac{4}{9}$ 26. $10 \div \frac{5}{12}$

ERROR ANALYSIS **Describe and correct the error in finding the quotient.**

27. ✗
$$\frac{4}{7} \div \frac{13}{28} = \frac{4}{7} \times \frac{13}{28} = \frac{\overset{1}{\cancel{4}} \times 13}{7 \times \underset{7}{\cancel{28}}} = \frac{13}{49}$$

28. ✗
$$\frac{2}{5} \div \frac{8}{9} = \frac{5}{2} \times \frac{8}{9} = \frac{5 \times \overset{4}{\cancel{8}}}{\underset{1}{\cancel{2}} \times 9} = \frac{20}{9}$$

29. **REASONING** How can you use estimation to show that the quotient in Exercise 28 is incorrect?

30. **APPLE PIE** You have $\frac{3}{5}$ of an apple pie. You divide the remaining pie into 5 equal slices. What fraction of the original pie is each slice?

31. **ANIMALS** How many times longer is the baby alligator than the baby gecko?

Determine whether the numbers are reciprocals. If not, write the reciprocal of each number.

32. $9, \frac{1}{9}$

33. $\frac{4}{5}, \frac{10}{8}$

34. $\frac{5}{6}, \frac{15}{18}$

35. $\frac{6}{5}, \frac{5}{6}$

Copy and complete the statement.

36. $\frac{5}{12} \times \square = 1$

37. $3 \times \square = 1$

38. $7 \div \square = 56$

Without finding the quotient, copy and complete the statement using <, >, or =. Explain your reasoning.

39. $5 \div \frac{7}{9} \ \square \ 5$

40. $\frac{3}{7} \div 1 \ \square \ \frac{3}{7}$

41. $8 \div \frac{3}{4} \ \square \ 8$

42. $\frac{5}{6} \div \frac{7}{8} \ \square \ \frac{5}{6}$

Evaluate the expression. Write the answer in simplest form.

5 43. $\frac{1}{6} \div 6 \div 6$

44. $\frac{7}{12} \div 14 \div 6$

45. $\frac{3}{5} \div \frac{4}{7} \div \frac{9}{10}$

46. $4 \div \frac{8}{9} - \frac{1}{2}$

47. $\frac{3}{4} + \frac{5}{6} \div \frac{2}{3}$

48. $\frac{7}{8} - \frac{3}{8} \div 9$

49. $\frac{9}{16} \div \frac{3}{4} \cdot \frac{2}{13}$

50. $\frac{3}{14} \cdot \frac{2}{5} \div \frac{6}{7}$

51. $\frac{10}{27} \cdot \left(\frac{3}{8} \div \frac{5}{24}\right)$

52. **REASONING** Use a model to evaluate the quotient $\frac{1}{2} \div \frac{1}{6}$. Explain.

53. **VIDEO CHATTING** You use $\frac{1}{8}$ of your battery for every $\frac{2}{5}$ of an hour that you video chat. You use $\frac{3}{4}$ of your battery video chatting. How long did you video chat?

54. **NUMBER SENSE** When is the reciprocal of a fraction a whole number? Explain.

55. **BUDGETS** The table shows the portions of a family budget that are spent on several expenses.

Expense	Portion of Budget
Housing	$\frac{1}{4}$
Food	$\frac{1}{12}$
Automobiles	$\frac{1}{15}$
Recreation	$\frac{1}{40}$

   a. How many times more is the expense for housing than for automobiles?

   b. How many times more is the expense for food than for recreation?

   c. The expense for automobile fuel is $\frac{1}{60}$ of the total expenses. What fraction of the automobile expense is spent on fuel?

56. **PROBLEM SOLVING** You have 6 pints of glaze. It takes $\frac{7}{8}$ of a pint to glaze a bowl and $\frac{9}{16}$ of a pint to glaze a plate.

   a. How many bowls could you glaze? How many plates could you glaze?

   b. You want to glaze 5 bowls, and then use the rest for plates. How many plates can you glaze? How much glaze will be left over?

   c. How many of each object could you glaze so that there is no glaze left over? Explain how you found your answer.

57. **Reasoning** A water tank is $\frac{1}{8}$ full. The tank is $\frac{3}{4}$ full when 42 gallons of water are added to the tank.

   a. How much water can the tank hold?

   b. How much water was originally in the tank?

   c. How much water is in the tank when it is $\frac{1}{2}$ full?

Fair Game Review What you learned in previous grades & lessons

Find the GCF of the numbers.

58. 8, 16 59. 24, 66 60. 48, 80 61. 15, 45, 100

62. **MULTIPLE CHOICE** How many inches are in $5\frac{1}{2}$ yards? (One yard is equal to 36 inches.)

Ⓐ $15\frac{1}{2}$ Ⓑ $16\frac{1}{2}$ Ⓒ 66 Ⓓ 198

3.5 Dividing Mixed Numbers

Essential Question How can you model division by a mixed number?

1 ACTIVITY: Writing a Story

Work with a partner. Think of a story that uses division by a mixed number.

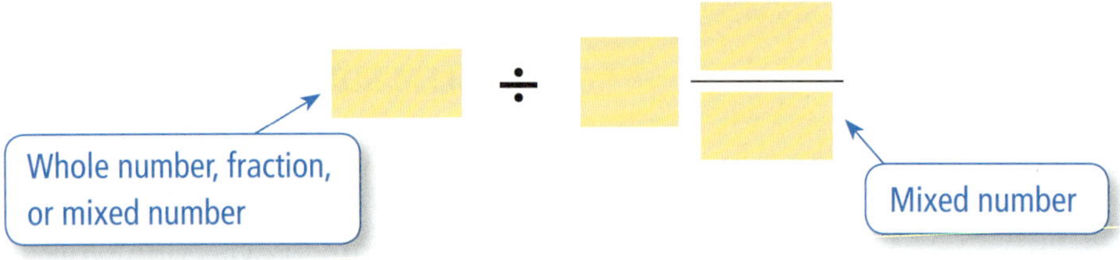

a. Write your story. Then draw pictures for your story.

b. Solve the division problem and use the answer in your story. Include a diagram of the division problem.

There are many possible stories. Here is one that uses $6 \div 1\frac{1}{2}$.

Joe goes on a camping trip with his aunt, his uncle, and three cousins. They leave at 5:00 P.M. and drive 2 hours to the campground.

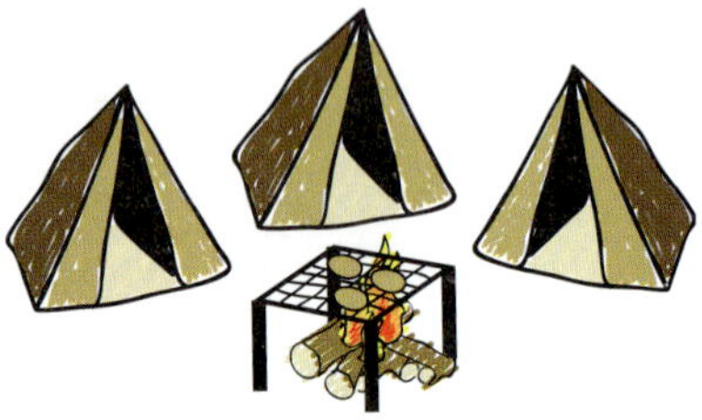

Joe helps his uncle put up three tents. His aunt cooks hamburgers on a grill that is over a fire.

In the morning, Joe tells his aunt that he is making pancakes. He decides to triple the recipe so there will be plenty of pancakes for everyone. A single recipe uses 2 cups of water, so he needs a total of 6 cups.

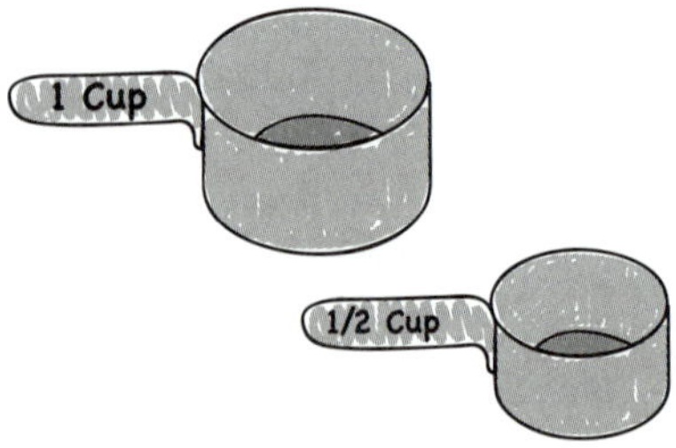

Joe's aunt has a 1-cup measuring cup and a ½-cup measuring cup. The water faucet is about 50 yards from the campsite. Joe tells his cousins that he can get 6 cups of water in only 4 trips.

When his cousins ask him how he knows that, he uses a stick to draw a diagram in the dirt. Joe says, "This diagram shows that there are four 1½s in 6." In other words, $6 \div 1\frac{1}{2} = 4$.

Dividing Fractions

In this lesson, you will
- use models to divide mixed numbers.
- divide mixed numbers.
- solve real-life problems.

2 ACTIVITY: Dividing Mixed Numbers

Work with a partner. Write the division problem and solve it using a model.

Math Process

Make Sense of Quantities

What values do the parts of the model represent?

a. How many three-fourths are in four and one-half?

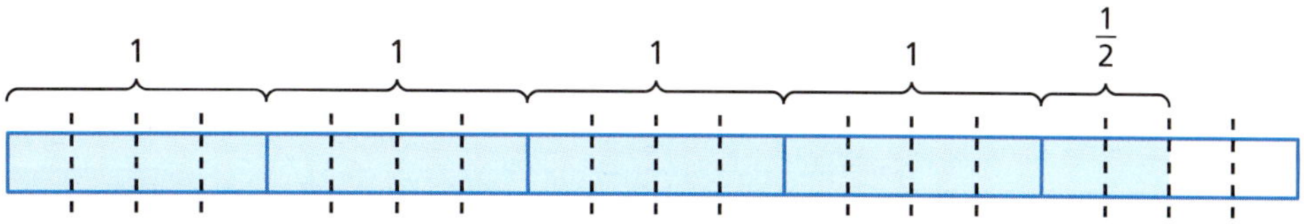

b. How many five-sixths are in three and one-third?

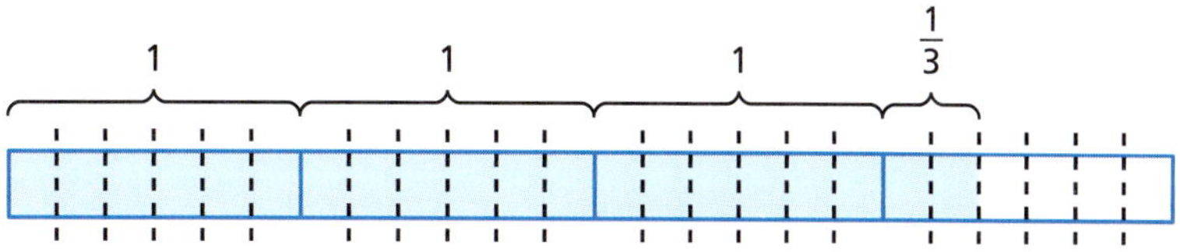

c. How many three-eighths are in three and three-fourths?

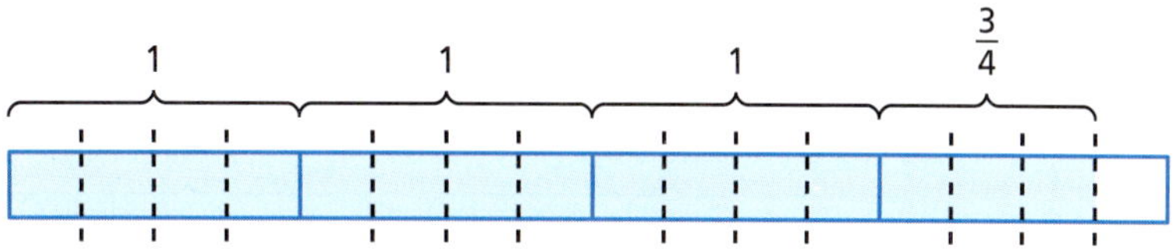

d. How many one and one-halves are in six?

e. How many one and one-fifths are in five?

f. How many one and one-fourths are in four and one-half?

g. How many two and one-thirds are in five and five-sixths?

What Is Your Answer?

3. **IN YOUR OWN WORDS** How can you model division by a mixed number?

4. Can you think of another method you can use to obtain your answers in Activity 2?

Practice Use what you learned about dividing mixed numbers to complete Exercises 5–12 on page 102.

3.5 Lesson

Check It Out
Lesson Tutorials
BigIdeasMath.com

Key Idea

Dividing Mixed Numbers

Write each mixed number as an improper fraction. Then divide as you would with proper fractions.

EXAMPLE 1 Dividing a Mixed Number by a Fraction

Find $2\frac{1}{4} \div \frac{3}{8}$.

$2\frac{1}{4} \div \frac{3}{8} = \frac{9}{4} \div \frac{3}{8}$ — Write $2\frac{1}{4}$ as the improper fraction $\frac{9}{4}$.

$= \frac{9}{4} \times \frac{8}{3}$ — Multiply by the reciprocal of $\frac{3}{8}$, which is $\frac{8}{3}$.

$= \frac{\overset{3}{\cancel{9}} \times \overset{2}{\cancel{8}}}{\underset{1}{\cancel{4}} \times \underset{1}{\cancel{3}}}$ — Multiply fractions. Divide out common factors.

$= 6$ — Simplify.

Check

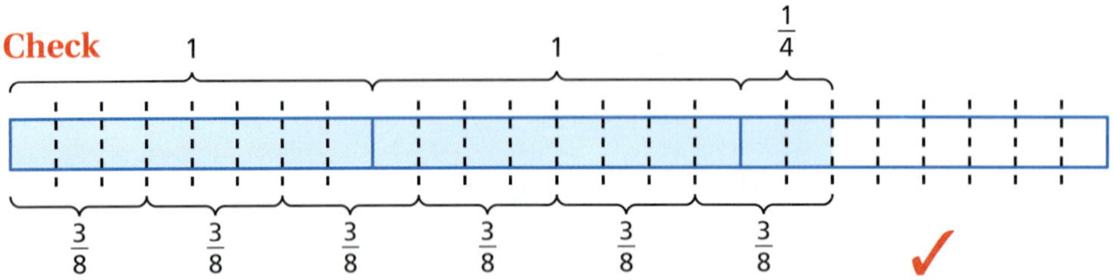

EXAMPLE 2 Dividing Mixed Numbers

Find $3\frac{5}{6} \div 1\frac{2}{3}$.

Estimate $4 \div 2 = 2$

$3\frac{5}{6} \div 1\frac{2}{3} = \frac{23}{6} \div \frac{5}{3}$ — Write each mixed number as an improper fraction.

$= \frac{23}{6} \times \frac{3}{5}$ — Multiply by the reciprocal of $\frac{5}{3}$, which is $\frac{3}{5}$.

$= \frac{23 \times \overset{1}{\cancel{3}}}{\underset{2}{\cancel{6}} \times 5}$ — Multiply fractions. Divide out common factors.

$= \frac{23}{10}$, or $2\frac{3}{10}$ — Simplify.

So, the quotient is $2\frac{3}{10}$.

Reasonable? $2\frac{3}{10} \approx 2$ ✓

On Your Own

Now You're Ready
Exercises 5–20

Divide. Write the answer in simplest form.

1. $1\frac{3}{7} \div \frac{2}{3}$
2. $2\frac{1}{6} \div \frac{3}{4}$
3. $8\frac{1}{4} \div 1\frac{1}{2}$
4. $6\frac{4}{5} \div 2\frac{1}{8}$

EXAMPLE 3 Using Order of Operations

Evaluate $5\frac{1}{4} \div 1\frac{1}{8} - \frac{2}{3}$.

$$5\frac{1}{4} \div 1\frac{1}{8} - \frac{2}{3} = \frac{21}{4} \div \frac{9}{8} - \frac{2}{3}$$ Write each mixed number as an improper fraction.

$$= \frac{21}{4} \times \frac{8}{9} - \frac{2}{3}$$ Multiply by the reciprocal of $\frac{9}{8}$, which is $\frac{8}{9}$.

$$= \frac{\overset{7}{\cancel{21}} \times \overset{2}{\cancel{8}}}{\underset{1}{\cancel{4}} \times \underset{3}{\cancel{9}}} - \frac{2}{3}$$ Multiply $\frac{21}{4}$ and $\frac{8}{9}$. Divide out common factors.

$$= \frac{14}{3} - \frac{2}{3}$$ Simplify.

$$= \frac{12}{3}, \text{ or } 4$$ Subtract.

Remember

Be sure to check your answers whenever possible. In Example 3, you can use estimation to check that your answer is reasonable.

$5\frac{1}{4} \div 1\frac{1}{8} - \frac{2}{3}$

$\approx 5 \div 1 - 1$

$= 5 - 1$

$= 4$ ✓

EXAMPLE 4 Real-Life Application

One serving of tortilla soup is $1\frac{2}{3}$ cups. A restaurant cook makes 50 cups of soup. Is there enough to serve 35 people? Explain.

Divide 50 by $1\frac{2}{3}$ to find the number of available servings.

$$50 \div 1\frac{2}{3} = \frac{50}{1} \div \frac{5}{3}$$ Rewrite each number as an improper fraction.

$$= \frac{50}{1} \cdot \frac{3}{5}$$ Multiply by the reciprocal of $\frac{5}{3}$, which is $\frac{3}{5}$.

$$= \frac{\overset{10}{\cancel{50}} \cdot 3}{1 \cdot \underset{1}{\cancel{5}}}$$ Multiply fractions. Divide out common factors.

$$= 30$$ Simplify.

No. Because 30 is less than 35, there is not enough soup to serve 35 people.

On Your Own

Now You're Ready Exercises 26–37

Evaluate the expression. Write the answer in simplest form.

5. $1\frac{1}{2} \div \frac{1}{6} - \frac{7}{8}$

6. $3\frac{1}{3} \div \frac{5}{6} + \frac{8}{9}$

7. $\frac{2}{5} + 2\frac{4}{5} \div 1\frac{3}{4}$

8. $\frac{2}{3} - 1\frac{4}{7} \div 4\frac{5}{7}$

9. In Example 4, can 30 cups of tortilla soup serve 15 people? Explain.

3.5 Exercises

Check It Out
Help with Homework
BigIdeasMath.com

Vocabulary and Concept Check

1. **VOCABULARY** What is the reciprocal of $7\frac{1}{3}$?

2. **NUMBER SENSE** Is $5\frac{1}{4} \div 3\frac{1}{2}$ the same as $3\frac{1}{2} \div 5\frac{1}{4}$? Explain.

3. **NUMBER SENSE** Is the reciprocal of an improper fraction *sometimes*, *always*, or *never* a proper fraction? Explain.

4. **DIFFERENT WORDS, SAME QUESTION** Which is different? Find "both" answers.

What is $5\frac{1}{2}$ divided by $\frac{1}{8}$?	Find the quotient of $5\frac{1}{2}$ and $\frac{1}{8}$.
What is $5\frac{1}{2}$ times 8?	Find the product of $5\frac{1}{2}$ and $\frac{1}{8}$.

Practice and Problem Solving

Divide. Write the answer in simplest form.

1 2

5. $2\frac{1}{4} \div \frac{3}{4}$

6. $3\frac{4}{5} \div \frac{2}{5}$

7. $8\frac{1}{8} \div \frac{5}{6}$

8. $7\frac{5}{9} \div \frac{4}{7}$

9. $7\frac{1}{2} \div 1\frac{9}{10}$

10. $3\frac{3}{4} \div 2\frac{1}{12}$

11. $7\frac{1}{5} \div 8$

12. $8\frac{4}{7} \div 15$

13. $8\frac{1}{3} \div \frac{2}{3}$

14. $9\frac{1}{6} \div \frac{5}{6}$

15. $13 \div 10\frac{5}{6}$

16. $12 \div 5\frac{9}{11}$

17. $\frac{7}{8} \div 3\frac{1}{16}$

18. $\frac{4}{9} \div 1\frac{7}{15}$

19. $4\frac{5}{16} \div 3\frac{3}{8}$

20. $6\frac{2}{9} \div 5\frac{5}{6}$

21. **ERROR ANALYSIS** Describe and correct the error in finding the quotient.

$$3\frac{1}{2} \div 1\frac{2}{3} = 3\frac{1}{2} \times 1\frac{3}{2} = \frac{7}{2} \times \frac{5}{2} = \frac{35}{4} = 8\frac{3}{4}$$

22. **DOG FOOD** A bag contains 42 cups of dog food. Your dog eats $2\frac{1}{3}$ cups of dog food each day. How many days does the bag of dog food last?

23. **HAMBURGERS** How many $\frac{1}{4}$-pound hamburgers can you make from $3\frac{1}{2}$ pounds of ground beef?

24. **BOOKS** How many $1\frac{3}{5}$-inch-thick books can fit on a $14\frac{1}{2}$-inch-long bookshelf?

25. **LOGIC** Alexei uses the model shown to state that $2\frac{1}{2} \div 1\frac{1}{6} = 2\frac{1}{6}$. Is Alexei correct? Justify your answer using the model.

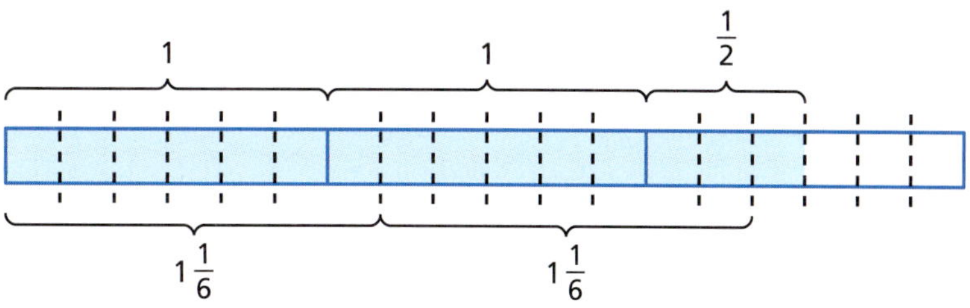

Evaluate the expression. Write the answer in simplest form.

3 26. $3 \div 1\frac{1}{5} + \frac{1}{2}$

27. $4\frac{2}{3} - 1\frac{1}{3} \div 2$

28. $\frac{2}{5} + 2\frac{1}{6} \div \frac{5}{6}$

29. $5\frac{5}{6} \div 3\frac{3}{4} - \frac{2}{9}$

30. $6\frac{1}{2} - \frac{7}{8} \div 5\frac{11}{16}$

31. $9\frac{1}{6} \div 5 + 3\frac{1}{3}$

32. $3\frac{3}{5} + 4\frac{4}{15} \div \frac{4}{9}$

33. $\frac{3}{5} \times \frac{7}{12} \div 2\frac{7}{10}$

34. $4\frac{3}{8} \div \frac{3}{4} \times \frac{4}{7}$

35. $1\frac{9}{11} \times 4\frac{7}{12} \div \frac{2}{3}$

36. $3\frac{4}{15} \div \left(8 \times 6\frac{3}{10}\right)$

37. $2\frac{5}{14} \div \left(2\frac{5}{8} \times 1\frac{3}{7}\right)$

38. **TRAIL MIX** You have 12 cups of granola and $8\frac{1}{2}$ cups of peanuts to make trail mix. What is the greatest number of full batches of trail mix you can make? Explain how you found your answer.

39. **RAMPS** You make skateboard ramps by cutting pieces from a board that is $12\frac{1}{2}$ feet long.

a. Estimate how many ramps you can cut from the board. Is your estimate reasonable? Explain.

b. How many ramps can you cut from the board? How much wood is left over?

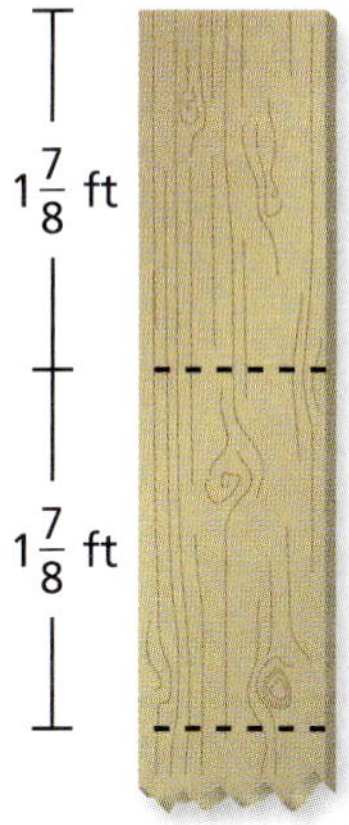

40. **Reasoning** At a track meet, the longest shot-put throw by a boy is 25 feet 8 inches. The longest shot-put throw by a girl is 19 feet 3 inches. How many times greater is the longest shot-put throw by the boy than by the girl?

Fair Game Review What you learned in previous grades & lessons

Write the number as a decimal.

41. forty-three hundredths

42. thirteen thousandths

43. three and eight tenths

44. seven and nine thousandths

45. **MULTIPLE CHOICE** The winner in a vote for class president received $\frac{3}{4}$ of the 240 votes. How many votes did the winner receive?

(A) 60 (B) 150 (C) 180 (D) 320

3 Study Help

Check It Out
Graphic Organizer
BigIdeasMath.com

You can use a **notetaking organizer** to write notes, vocabulary, and questions about a topic. Here is an example of a notetaking organizer for dividing fractions.

Write important vocabulary or formulas in this space. →

$$\frac{a}{b} \div \frac{c}{d} = \frac{a}{b} \cdot \frac{d}{c} = \frac{a \cdot d}{b \cdot c}$$

(where b, c, and $d \neq 0$)

Dividing fractions

To divide a number by a fraction, multiply the number by the reciprocal of the fraction.

Example:

$$\frac{1}{5} \div \frac{3}{4} = \frac{1}{5} \times \frac{4}{3} = \frac{1 \times 4}{5 \times 3} = \frac{4}{15}$$

← Write your notes about the topic in this space.

How do you divide a mixed number by a fraction?

← Write your questions about the topic in this space.

On Your Own

Make notetaking organizers to help you study these topics.

1. adding fractions
2. adding mixed numbers
3. subtracting fractions
4. subtracting mixed numbers
5. multiplying fractions
6. multiplying mixed numbers
7. dividing mixed numbers

"The notetaking organizer in my math class gave me an idea of how to organize my doggy biscuits."

3 Chapter Review

Check It Out
Vocabulary Help
BigIdeasMath.com

Review Key Vocabulary

reciprocals, *p. 92*

Review Examples and Exercises

3.1 Adding Fractions and Mixed Numbers *(pp. 70–75)*

Find $\frac{5}{8} + \frac{5}{6}$.

$\frac{5}{8} + \frac{5}{6} = \frac{15}{24} + \frac{20}{24}$ Rewrite using the LCD (least common denominator).

$= \frac{15 + 20}{24}$ Write the sum of the numerators over the common denominator.

$= \frac{35}{24}$ Add the numerators.

$= 1\frac{11}{24}$ Write the improper fraction as a mixed number.

Exercises

Add. Write fractions in simplest form.

1. $\frac{9}{10} + \frac{4}{5}$ **2.** $4\frac{5}{7} + \frac{1}{7}$ **3.** $2\frac{5}{6} + 5\frac{4}{9}$

4. ALMONDS Two bags of almonds that weigh $3\frac{1}{4}$ pounds and $1\frac{7}{8}$ pounds are combined into a large bag. What is the total weight of the large bag?

3.2 Subtracting Fractions and Mixed Numbers *(pp. 76–81)*

Find $4\frac{2}{5} - \frac{3}{5}$.

$4\frac{2}{5} - \frac{3}{5} = \frac{22}{5} - \frac{3}{5}$ Write the mixed number as an improper fraction.

$= \frac{22 - 3}{5}$ Write the difference of the numerators over the common denominator.

$= \frac{19}{5}$ Subtract.

$= 3\frac{4}{5}$ Write the improper fraction as a mixed number.

Exercises

Subtract. Write fractions in simplest form.

5. $\frac{4}{5} - \frac{3}{10}$

6. $4\frac{5}{9} - \frac{8}{9}$

7. $7\frac{1}{6} - 3\frac{3}{4}$

8. Evaluate $\frac{17}{3} + \frac{5}{6} - 2\frac{5}{12}$.

9. **SLOTH** A sloth is in a tree $20\frac{5}{6}$ inches above the ground. He slowly climbs up to a height of $32\frac{1}{4}$ inches. What is the change in the sloth's height?

3.3 Multiplying Fractions and Mixed Numbers *(pp. 82–89)*

a. Find $\frac{1}{4} \times \frac{3}{5}$.

$\frac{1}{4} \times \frac{3}{5} = \frac{1 \times 3}{4 \times 5} = \frac{3}{20}$ — Multiply the numerators and the denominators.

b. Find $\frac{3}{5} \times 1\frac{1}{8}$.

$\frac{3}{5} \times 1\frac{1}{8} = \frac{3}{5} \times \frac{9}{8}$ — Write $1\frac{1}{8}$ as the improper fraction $\frac{9}{8}$.

$= \frac{3 \times 9}{5 \times 8} = \frac{27}{40}$ — Multiply the numerators and the denominators.

Exercises

Multiply. Write the answer in simplest form.

10. $\frac{1}{8} \times \frac{5}{7}$

11. $\frac{3}{5} \times \frac{1}{2}$

12. $\frac{2}{9} \times \frac{3}{4}$

13. $\frac{3}{10} \times \frac{4}{5}$

14. $2\frac{2}{3} \times \frac{4}{5}$

15. $\frac{2}{7} \times 4\frac{4}{9}$

16. $1\frac{5}{6} \times 2\frac{3}{8}$

17. $2\frac{3}{10} \times 5\frac{1}{3}$

3.4 Dividing Fractions *(pp. 90–97)*

Find $\frac{3}{7} \div \frac{5}{8}$.

$\frac{3}{7} \div \frac{5}{8} = \frac{3}{7} \times \frac{8}{5}$ — Multiply by the reciprocal of $\frac{5}{8}$, which is $\frac{8}{5}$.

$= \frac{3 \times 8}{7 \times 5}$ — Multiply fractions.

$= \frac{24}{35}$ — Simplify.

Exercises

Divide. Write the answer in simplest form.

18. $\frac{1}{9} \div \frac{2}{5}$

19. $\frac{3}{4} \div \frac{5}{6}$

20. $5 \div \frac{1}{3}$

21. $\frac{8}{9} \div \frac{3}{10}$

3.5 Dividing Mixed Numbers (pp. 98–103)

a. Find $2\frac{1}{5} \div \frac{2}{3}$.

$2\frac{1}{5} \div \frac{2}{3} = \frac{11}{5} \div \frac{2}{3}$ Write the mixed number as an improper fraction.

$= \frac{11}{5} \times \frac{3}{2}$ Multiply by the reciprocal of $\frac{2}{3}$, which is $\frac{3}{2}$.

$= \frac{11 \times 3}{5 \times 2}$ Multiply fractions.

$= \frac{33}{10}$, or $3\frac{3}{10}$ Simplify.

b. Find $3\frac{3}{4} \div 1\frac{1}{2}$.

$3\frac{3}{4} \div 1\frac{1}{2} = \frac{15}{4} \div \frac{3}{2}$ Write each mixed number as an improper fraction.

$= \frac{15}{4} \times \frac{2}{3}$ Multiply by the reciprocal of $\frac{3}{2}$, which is $\frac{2}{3}$.

$= \frac{\overset{5}{\cancel{15}} \times \overset{1}{\cancel{2}}}{\underset{2}{\cancel{4}} \times \underset{1}{\cancel{3}}}$ Multiply fractions. Divide out common factors.

$= \frac{5}{2}$, or $2\frac{1}{2}$ Simplify.

Exercises

Divide. Write the answer in simplest form.

22. $1\frac{2}{5} \div \frac{4}{7}$

23. $2\frac{3}{8} \div \frac{3}{5}$

24. $4\frac{1}{8} \div 2\frac{1}{4}$

25. $5\frac{5}{8} \div 1\frac{2}{9}$

26. **PANCAKES** A box contains 10 cups of pancake mix. You use $\frac{2}{3}$ cup each time you make pancakes. How many times can you make pancakes?

4 Decimals, Fractions, and Percents

4.1 Adding and Subtracting Decimals
4.2 Multiplying Decimals
4.3 Dividing Decimals
4.4 Rational Numbers
4.5 Percents
4.6 Percents and Decimals
4.7 Comparing and Ordering Fractions, Decimals, and Percents

What You Learned Before

"Let's play a game. The goal is to say a positive rational number that is less than the other pet's number... You go first."

Writing Fractions as Decimals

Example 1 Write $\frac{3}{20}$ as a decimal.

$$\frac{3}{20} = \frac{3 \cdot 5}{20 \cdot 5} = \frac{15}{100} = 0.15$$

Example 2 Write $\frac{3}{5}$ as a decimal.

$$\frac{3}{5} = \frac{3 \cdot 2}{5 \cdot 2} = \frac{6}{10} = 0.6$$

Try It Yourself

Write the fraction as a decimal.

1. $\frac{7}{10}$ **2.** $\frac{9}{25}$ **3.** $\frac{4}{5}$ **4.** $\frac{27}{50}$

Estimating Sums and Differences of Decimals

Example 3 Estimate 6.23 + 3.79.

6.23 is close to 6.

$$6.23 + 3.79 \approx 6 + 4 = 10$$

3.79 is close to 4.

Example 4 Estimate 8.845 − 5.117.

8.845 is close to 9.

$$8.845 - 5.117 \approx 9 - 5 = 4$$

5.117 is close to 5.

Estimating Products and Quotients of Decimals

Example 5 Estimate 7.6 × 5.9.

7.6 is close to 8.

$$7.6 \times 5.9 \approx 8 \times 6 = 48$$

5.9 is close to 6.

Example 6 Estimate 15.31 ÷ 2.7.

15.31 is close to 15.

$$15.31 \div 2.7 \approx 15 \div 3 = 5$$

2.7 is close to 3.

Try It Yourself

Estimate the value of the expression.

5. $5.912 + 1.787$ **6.** $11.04 - 7.72$ **7.** 8.34×5.2 **8.** $27.9 \div 4.15$

4.1 Adding and Subtracting Decimals

Essential Question How can you add and subtract decimals?

Base ten blocks can be used to model numbers.

1 one 1 tenth 1 hundredth

1 ACTIVITY: Modeling a Sum

Work with a partner. Use base ten blocks to find the sum.

a. 1.23 + 0.87

Which base ten blocks do you need to model the numbers in the sum? How many of each do you need?

+

1.23 + 0.87

How many of each base ten block do you have when you combine the blocks?

____ ones ____ tenths ____ hundredths

How many of each base ten block do you have when you trade the blocks?

____ ones ____ tenths ____ hundredths

So, 1.23 + 0.87 = ____.

b. 1.25 + 1.35 **c.** 2.14 + 0.92 **d.** 0.73 + 0.86

2 ACTIVITY: Modeling a Difference

Work with a partner. Use base ten blocks to find the difference.

a. 2.43 − 0.73

Which number is shown by the model? ____

Circle the portion of the model that represents 0.73.

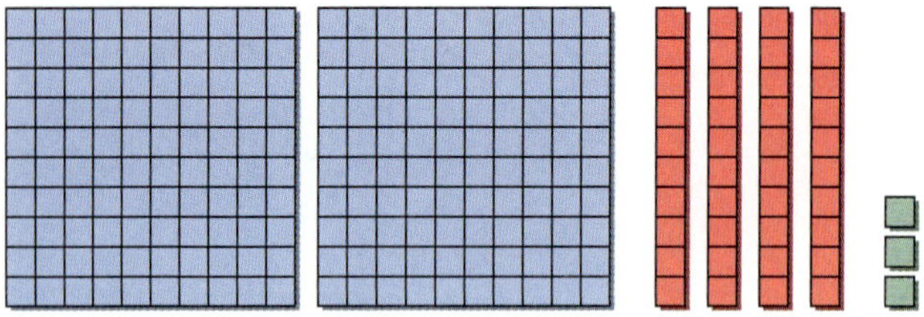

So, 2.43 − 0.73 = ____.

b. 1.86 − 1.26 **c.** 3.72 − 0.5 **d.** 1.58 − 0.09

Adding and Subtracting Decimals

In this lesson, you will

- use models to add and subtract decimals.
- add and subtract decimals.

3 ACTIVITY: Making a Conjecture

Work with a partner.

a. Find each sum or difference.

$123 + 87$	$125 + 135$	$214 + 92$	$73 + 86$
$243 - 73$	$186 - 126$	$372 - 50$	$158 - 9$

b. How are the numerical expressions in part (a) related to the numerical expressions in Activities 1 and 2? How are the sums and differences related?

c. **STRUCTURE** There is a relationship between adding and subtracting decimals and adding and subtracting whole numbers. What conjecture can you make about this relationship?

4 ACTIVITY: Using a Place Value Chart

Work with a partner. Use the place value chart to find the sum or difference.

Math Process

Analyze Conjectures

How can the conjecture you wrote in Activity 3 help you to solve these problems?

Place Value Chart

millions	hundred thousands	ten thousands	thousands	hundreds	tens	ones	and	tenths	hundredths	thousandths	ten-thousandths	hundred-thousandths	millionths
							.						
							.						
							.						

a. $16.05 + 2.94$

b. $7.421 + 92.55$

c. $38.72 - 8.61$

d. $64.968 - 51.167$

What Is Your Answer?

5. **MODELING** Describe two real-life examples of when you would need to add and subtract decimals.

6. **IN YOUR OWN WORDS** How can you add and subtract decimals?

Practice Use what you learned about adding and subtracting decimals to complete Exercises 3–4 on page 114.

4.1 Lesson

Check It Out
Lesson Tutorials
BigIdeasMath.com

Key Idea

Adding and Subtracting Decimals

To add or subtract decimals, write the numbers vertically and line up the decimal points. Then bring down the decimal point and add or subtract as you would with whole numbers.

EXAMPLE 1 Adding Decimals

a. Add 8.13 + 2.76.

Estimate $8.13 + 2.76 \approx 8 + 3 = 11$

Line up the decimal points.

$$\begin{array}{r} 8.13 \\ +\ 2.76 \\ \hline 10.89 \end{array}$$

Add as you would with whole numbers.

Reasonable? $10.89 \approx 11$ ✓

Study Tip

Be sure to add or subtract only digits that have the same place value.

b. Add 1.459 + 23.7.

$$\begin{array}{r} \scriptstyle 1 \\ 1.459 \\ +\ 23.700 \\ \hline 25.159 \end{array}$$

Insert zeros so that both numbers have the same number of decimal places.

EXAMPLE 2 Subtracting Decimals

a. Subtract 5.508 − 3.174.

Estimate $5.508 - 3.174 \approx 6 - 3 = 3$

Line up the decimal points.

$$\begin{array}{r} \scriptstyle 4\ 10 \\ 5.\not{5}\not{0}8 \\ -\ 3.174 \\ \hline 2.334 \end{array}$$

Subtract as you would with whole numbers.

Reasonable? $2.334 \approx 3$ ✓

b. Subtract 21.9 − 1.605.

$$\begin{array}{r} \scriptstyle 9 \\ \scriptstyle 8\ 10\ 10 \\ 21.\not{9}\not{0}\not{0} \\ -\ 1.605 \\ \hline 20.295 \end{array}$$

Insert zeros so that both numbers have the same number of decimal places.

On Your Own

Now You're Ready
Exercises 5–16

Add or subtract.

1. 4.206 + 10.85
2. 15.5 + 8.229
3. 78.41 + 90.99
4. 6.34 − 5.33
5. 27.9 − 0.905
6. 18.626 − 13.88

EXAMPLE 3 Real-Life Application

Your meal at the school cafeteria costs \$3.45. Your friend's meal costs \$3.90. You pay for both meals with a \$10 bill. How much change do you receive?

Use a verbal model to solve the problem.

$$\text{amount of change} = \text{amount given} - \left(\text{cost of your meal} + \text{cost of friend's meal}\right)$$

$$= 10.00 - (3.45 + 3.90) \qquad \text{Substitute values.}$$

$$= 10.00 - 7.35 \qquad \text{Add inside parentheses.}$$

$$= 2.65 \qquad \text{Subtract.}$$

∴ So, you receive \$2.65.

EXAMPLE 4 Real-Life Application

The Lincoln Memorial Reflecting Pool is approximately rectangular. Its width is 50.9 meters, and its length is 618.44 meters. You walk the perimeter of the pool. About how many meters do you walk?

Draw a diagram and label the dimensions.

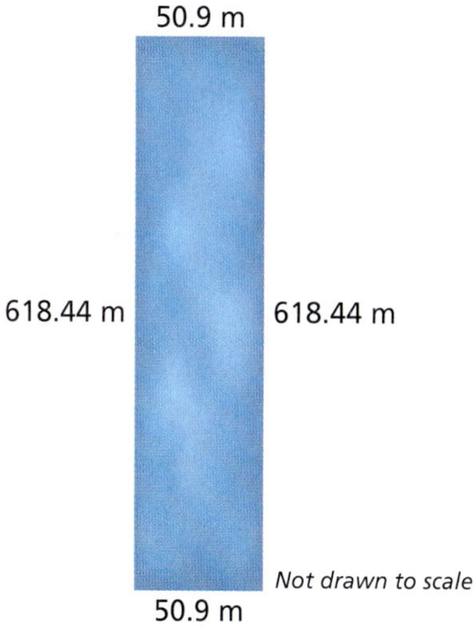

Find the sum of the side lengths.

$$\begin{array}{r} {\scriptstyle 1\,1\,2} \\ 618.44 \\ 50.90 \\ 618.44 \\ +\quad 50.90 \\ \hline 1338.68 \end{array}$$

∴ So, you walk about 1339 meters.

On Your Own

Now You're Ready
Exercises 21–26

7. **WHAT IF?** In Example 3, your meal costs \$4.10 and your friend's meal costs \$3.65. You pay for both meals with a \$20 bill. How much change do you receive?

8. Find the perimeter of the triangle.

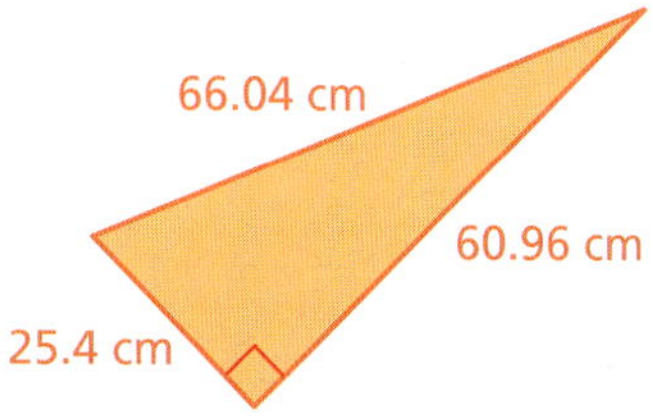

4.1 Exercises

Vocabulary and Concept Check

1. **CHOOSE TOOLS** Why is it helpful to estimate the answer before adding or subtracting decimals?

2. **WRITING** When adding or subtracting decimals, how can you be sure to add or subtract only digits that have the same place value?

Practice and Problem Solving

Write and evaluate the numerical expression modeled by the base ten blocks.

3. 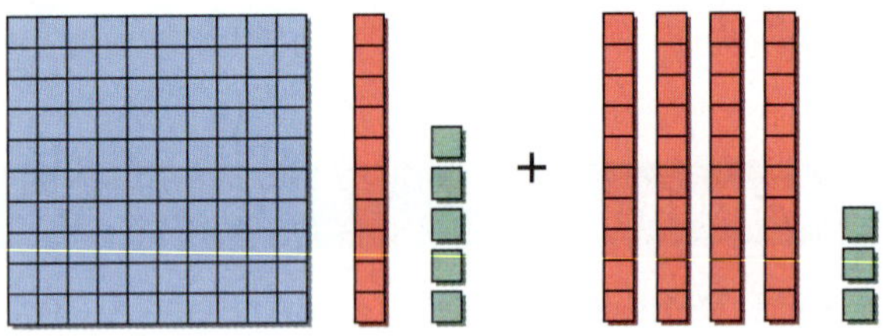

4. 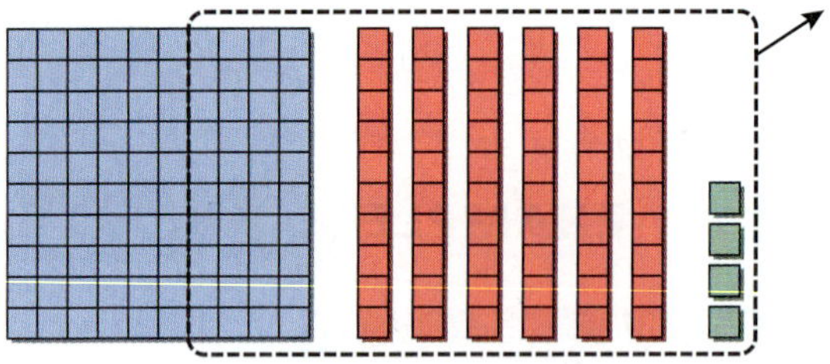

Add.

① 5. 7.82 + 3.209
6. 3.7 + 2.774
7. 12.829 + 10.07
8. 20.35 + 13.748
9. 17.440 + 12.497
10. 15.255 + 19.058

Subtract.

② 11. 4.58 − 3.12
12. 8.629 − 5.309
13. 6.98 − 2.614
14. 15.131 − 11.57
15. 13.5 − 10.856
16. 25.82 − 22.936

ERROR ANALYSIS **Describe and correct the error in the solution.**

17. ✗
$$\begin{array}{r} 6.058 \\ +\ 3.95 \\ \hline 6.453 \end{array}$$

18. ✗
$$\begin{array}{r} 9.5 \\ -\ 7.18 \\ \hline 2.48 \end{array}$$

Breakfast Menu
7:30 A.M. to 11:00 A.M.

2 Eggs (any style)	$^{\$}2^{95}$	Bacon & Eggs	$^{\$}3^{95}$
Steak & Eggs	$^{\$}6^{25}$	Cheese Omelet	$^{\$}3^{55}$
Ham & Eggs	$^{\$}3^{95}$	Ham Omelet	$^{\$}4^{35}$
Sausage & Eggs	$^{\$}3^{95}$	Ham & Cheese Omelet	$^{\$}4^{95}$
Salami & Eggs	$^{\$}3^{95}$		

19. **BREAKFAST** You order the sausage and eggs breakfast, and your friend orders the ham omelet. How much is the bill before taxes and tip?

20. **HAM & CHEESE** How much more does the ham and cheese omelet cost than the cheese omelet?

Evaluate the expression.

③ **21.** $6.105 + 10.4 + 3.075$

22. $22.6 - 12.286 - 3.542$

23. $15.35 + 7.604 - 12.954$

24. $16.5 - 13.45 + 7.293$

25. $25.92 - 18.478 + 8.164$

26. $23.45 + 17.75 - 19.618$

27. **STRUCTURE** When is the sum of two decimals equal to a whole number? When is the difference of two decimals equal to a whole number?

28. **OPEN-ENDED** Write three decimals that have a sum of 27.905.

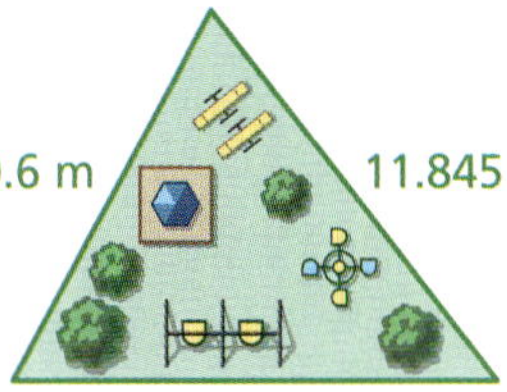

29. **DAY CARE** A day-care center is building a new outdoor play area. The diagram shows the dimensions in meters. How much fencing is needed to enclose the play area?

30. **HOMEWORK** You work 1.15 hours on English homework and 1.75 hours on math homework. Your science homework takes 1.05 hours less than your math homework. How many hours do you work on homework?

STEM VIDEO

ASTRONOMY An astronomical unit (AU) is the average distance of Earth from the Sun. In Exercises 31–34, use the table that shows the average distance of each planet in our solar system from the Sun.

31. How much farther is Jupiter from the Sun than Mercury?

32. How much farther is Neptune from the Sun than Mars?

33. Estimate the greatest distance between Earth and Uranus.

34. Estimate the greatest distance between Venus and Saturn.

Planet	Average Distance from the Sun (AU)
Mercury	0.387
Venus	0.723
Earth	1.000
Mars	1.524
Jupiter	5.203
Saturn	9.537
Uranus	19.189
Neptune	30.07

35. Critical Thinking The length of a rectangle is twice the width. The perimeter of the rectangle can be expressed as $3 \cdot 13.7$. What is the width?

Fair Game Review What you learned in previous grades & lessons

Multiply. Write the answer in simplest form.

36. $\frac{7}{10} \times \frac{5}{7}$

37. $\frac{5}{6} \times \frac{3}{10}$

38. $\frac{3}{4} \times \frac{2}{9}$

39. $\frac{2}{5} \times \frac{1}{8}$

40. **MULTIPLE CHOICE** What is the LCM of 6, 12, and 18?

Ⓐ 6 Ⓑ 18 Ⓒ 36 Ⓓ 72

4.2 Multiplying Decimals

Essential Question How can you multiply decimals?

1 ACTIVITY: Multiplying Decimals Using a Rectangle

Work with a partner. Use a rectangle to find the product.

a. 2.7 • 1.3

Arrange base ten blocks to form a rectangle of length 2.7 units and width 1.3 units.

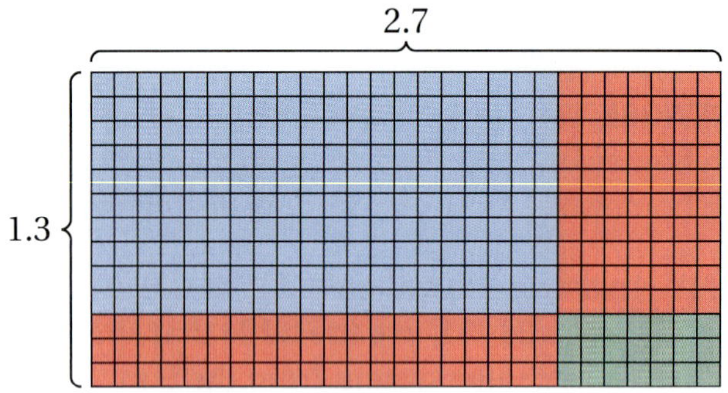

The area of the rectangle represents the product.

Find the total area represented by each grouping of base ten blocks.

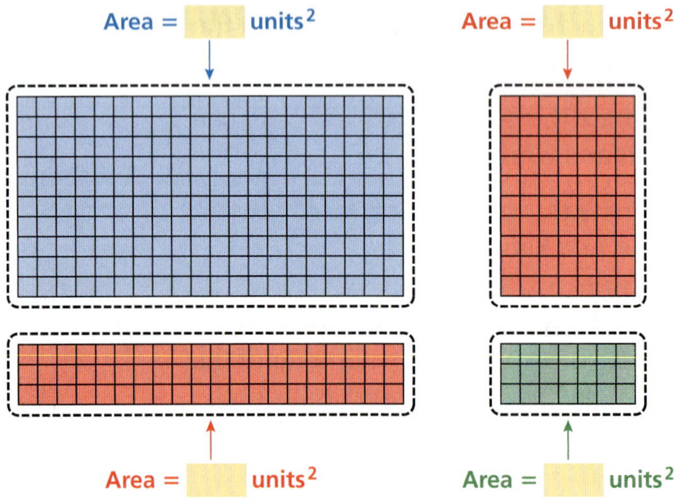

The area of the rectangle is:

+

units^2

So, 2.7 • 1.3 = ____.

b. 1.8 • 1.1 **c.** 4.6 • 1.2 **d.** 3.2 • 2.4

Multiplying Decimals

In this lesson, you will

- use models to multiply decimals.
- multiply decimals.

2 ACTIVITY: Multiplying Decimals Using an Area Model

Work with a partner. Use an area model to find the product. Explain your reasoning.

a. $0.8 \cdot 0.5$

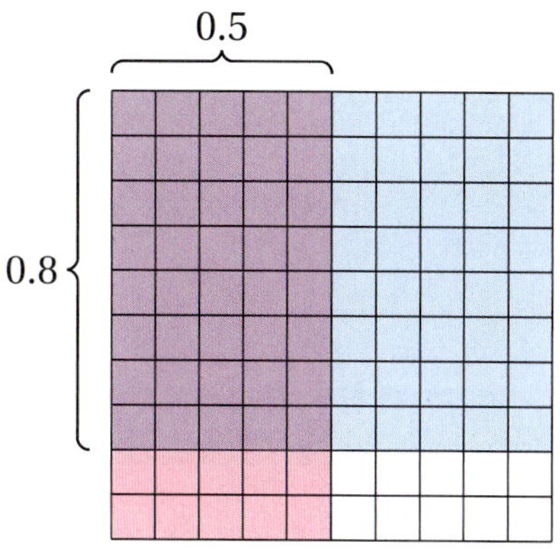

Because ___ hundredths are shaded with both colors, the product is

$\dfrac{\square}{100} = \square$.

So, $0.8 \cdot 0.5 = \square$.

b. $0.3 \cdot 0.5$ **c.** $0.7 \cdot 0.6$ **d.** $0.2 \cdot 0.9$

Math Process

View as Components

How can you use an area model to find the product?

3 ACTIVITY: Making a Conjecture

Work with a partner.

a. Find each product.

$27 \cdot 13$	$18 \cdot 11$	$46 \cdot 12$	$32 \cdot 24$
$8 \cdot 5$	$3 \cdot 5$	$7 \cdot 6$	$2 \cdot 9$

b. How are the numerical expressions in part (a) related to the numerical expressions in Activities 1 and 2? How are the products related?

c. **STRUCTURE** What conjecture can you make about the relationship between multiplying decimals and multiplying whole numbers?

What Is Your Answer?

4. **IN YOUR OWN WORDS** How can you multiply decimals?

Practice Use what you learned about multiplying decimals to complete Exercises 9–12 on page 121.

Check It Out
Lesson Tutorials
BigIdeasMath.com

Key Idea

Multiplying Decimals by Whole Numbers

Words Multiply as you would with whole numbers. Then count the number of decimal places in the decimal factor. The product has the same number of decimal places.

Numbers

$$\begin{array}{r} 13.91 \\ \times\quad 7 \\ \hline 97.37 \end{array}$$ 2 decimal places

$$\begin{array}{r} 6.218 \\ \times\quad 4 \\ \hline 24.872 \end{array}$$ 3 decimal places

EXAMPLE 1 Multiplying Decimals and Whole Numbers

a. Find 6 × 3.91.

Estimate $6 \times 4 = 24$

$$\begin{array}{r} \overset{5}{3}.91 \\ \times\quad 6 \\ \hline 23.46 \end{array}$$

3.91 ← 2 decimal places

23.46 ← Count 2 decimal places from right to left.

So, $6 \times 3.91 = 23.46$.

Reasonable? $23.46 \approx 24$ ✓

b. Find 3 × 0.016.

Estimate $3 \times 0 = 0$

$$\begin{array}{r} 0.0\overset{1}{1}6 \\ \times\quad 3 \\ \hline 0.048 \end{array}$$

0.016 ← 3 decimal places

0.048 ← To have 3 decimal places, insert zeros to the left of 48.

So, $3 \times 0.016 = 0.048$.

Reasonable? $0.048 \approx 0$ ✓

EXAMPLE 2 Use Mental Math

How high is a stack of 100 dimes?

1.35 millimeters

Method 1: Multiply 1.35 by 100.

$$\begin{array}{r} 1.35 \\ \times\ 1\,00 \\ \hline 0\,00 \\ 00\,0 \\ 135 \\ \hline 135.00 \end{array}$$

2 decimal places

Method 2: You are multiplying by a power of 10. Use mental math.

There are two zeros in 100. So, move the decimal point in 1.35 two places to the right.

$1.35 \times 100 = 135. = 135$

So, a stack of 100 dimes is 135 millimeters high.

On Your Own

Now You're Ready
Exercises 13–24

Multiply. Use estimation to check your answer.

1. 12.3×8 **2.** 5×14.51 **3.** 0.88×9 **4.** 0.003×10

5. A quarter is 1.75 millimeters thick. How high is a stack of 1000 quarters? Solve using both methods.

The rule for multiplying two decimals is similar to the rule for multiplying a decimal by a whole number.

Key Idea

Multiplying Decimals by Decimals

Words Multiply as you would with whole numbers. Then add the number of decimal places in the factors. The sum is the number of decimal places in the product.

Numbers

$$\begin{array}{r l} 4.716 & \leftarrow \text{3 decimal places} \\ \times \quad 0.2 & \leftarrow +\text{ 1 decimal place} \\ \hline 0.9432 & \leftarrow \text{4 decimal places} \end{array}$$

EXAMPLE 3 Multiplying Decimals

a. Multiply 4.8 × 7.2. **Estimate** $5 \times 7 = 35$

$$\begin{array}{r l} 4.8 & \leftarrow \text{1 decimal place} \\ \times 7.2 & \leftarrow +\text{ 1 decimal place} \\ \hline 96 & \\ 336 & \\ \hline 34.56 & \leftarrow \text{2 decimal places} \end{array}$$

So, $4.8 \times 7.2 = 34.56$. **Reasonable?** $34.56 \approx 35$ ✓

b. Multiply 3.1 × 0.05. **Estimate** $3 \times 0 = 0$

$$\begin{array}{r l} 3.1 & \leftarrow \text{1 decimal place} \\ \times 0.05 & \leftarrow +\text{ 2 decimal places} \\ \hline 0.155 & \leftarrow \text{3 decimal places} \end{array}$$

So, $3.1 \times 0.05 = 0.155$. **Reasonable?** $0.155 \approx 0$ ✓

On Your Own

Now You're Ready
Exercises 30–45

Multiply. Use estimation to check your answer.

6. 8.1×5.6

7. 2.7×9.04

8. 6.32×0.09

9. 1.785×0.2

EXAMPLE 4 Evaluating an Expression

What is the value of 2.44(4.5 − 3.175)?

(A) 3.233 (B) 3.599 (C) 7.805 (D) 32.33

Step 1: Subtract first because the minus sign is in parentheses.

$$\begin{array}{r} 4.500 \\ -\ 3.175 \\ \hline 1.325 \end{array}$$

(borrowing marks: 4 10 10, 9)

So, $2.44(4.5 - 3.175) = 2.44(1.325)$.

Step 2: Multiply the result from Step 1 by 2.44.

$$\begin{array}{r} 1.325 \\ \times\ 2.44 \\ \hline 5300 \\ 5300 \\ 2650 \\ \hline 3.23300 \end{array}$$

∴ The correct answer is (A).

On Your Own

Now You're Ready
Exercises 52–60

Evaluate the expression.

10. $12.67 + 8.2 \cdot 1.9$

11. $6.4(1.8 \cdot 7.5)$

EXAMPLE 5 Real-Life Application

You buy 2.75 pounds of tomatoes. You hand the cashier a $10 bill. How much change will you receive?

Step 1: Find the cost of the tomatoes. Multiply 1.89 by 2.75.

$$\begin{array}{rl} 1.89 & \leftarrow \text{2 decimal places} \\ \times\ 2.75 & \leftarrow +\ \text{2 decimal places} \\ \hline 945 & \\ 1323 & \\ 378 & \\ \hline 5.1975 & \leftarrow \text{4 decimal places} \end{array}$$

The cost of 2.75 pounds of tomatoes is $5.20.

Step 2: Subtract the cost of the tomatoes from the amount of money you hand the cashier.

10.00 − 5.20 = $4.80

∴ So, you will receive $4.80 in change.

On Your Own

12. **WHAT IF?** You buy 2.25 pounds of grapes. You hand the cashier a $5 bill. How much change will you receive?

4.2 Exercises

Check It Out
Help with Homework
BigIdeasMath.com

Vocabulary and Concept Check

1. **NUMBER SENSE** If you know $12 \times 24 = 288$, how can you find 1.2×2.4?
2. **NUMBER SENSE** Is the product 1.23×8 greater than or less than 8? Explain.

Copy the problem and place the decimal point in the product.

3. $\begin{array}{r} 1.78 \\ \times\ \ 4.9 \\ \hline 8722 \end{array}$

4. $\begin{array}{r} 9.24 \\ \times\ \ 0.68 \\ \hline 62832 \end{array}$

5. $\begin{array}{r} 3.75 \\ \times\ \ 5.22 \\ \hline 195750 \end{array}$

How many decimal places are in the product?

6. 6.17×8.2
7. 1.684×10.2
8. 0.053×2.78

Practice and Problem Solving

Use base ten blocks or an area model to find the product.

9. $\begin{array}{r} 2.1 \\ \times 1.5 \\ \hline \end{array}$

10. $\begin{array}{r} 0.6 \\ \times 0.4 \\ \hline \end{array}$

11. $\begin{array}{r} 0.7 \\ \times 0.3 \\ \hline \end{array}$

12. $\begin{array}{r} 2.7 \\ \times 2.3 \\ \hline \end{array}$

Multiply. Use estimation to check your answer.

13. $\begin{array}{r} 4.8 \\ \times\ \ 7 \\ \hline \end{array}$

14. $\begin{array}{r} 6.3 \\ \times\ \ 5 \\ \hline \end{array}$

15. $\begin{array}{r} 7.19 \\ \times\ \ 16 \\ \hline \end{array}$

16. $\begin{array}{r} 0.87 \\ \times\ \ 21 \\ \hline \end{array}$

17. $\begin{array}{r} 1.95 \\ \times\ \ 11 \\ \hline \end{array}$

18. $\begin{array}{r} 5.89 \\ \times\ \ 5 \\ \hline \end{array}$

19. $\begin{array}{r} 3.472 \\ \times\ \ 4 \\ \hline \end{array}$

20. $\begin{array}{r} 8.188 \\ \times\ \ 12 \\ \hline \end{array}$

21. 100×0.024
22. 19×0.004
23. 0.0038×9
24. 10×0.0093

ERROR ANALYSIS **Describe and correct the error in the solution.**

25. ✗ $\begin{array}{r} 0.0045 \\ \times\ \ 9 \\ \hline 4.05 \end{array}$

26. ✗ $\begin{array}{r} 0.32 \\ \times\ \ 5 \\ \hline 0.160 \end{array}$

27. **MOON** The weight of an object on the Moon is about 0.167 of its weight on Earth. How much does a 180-pound astronaut weigh on the Moon?
28. **BAMBOO** A bamboo plant grows about 1.25 feet each day. Find the growth in one week.
29. **NAILS** A fingernail grows about 0.1 millimeter each day. How much does a fingernail grow in 30 days? 90 days?

Multiply.

③ 30. $\begin{array}{r} 0.7 \\ \times\ 0.2 \\ \hline \end{array}$

31. $\begin{array}{r} 0.08 \\ \times\ 0.3 \\ \hline \end{array}$

32. $\begin{array}{r} 0.007 \\ \times\ 0.03 \\ \hline \end{array}$

33. $\begin{array}{r} 0.0008 \\ \times\ \ 0.09 \\ \hline \end{array}$

34. $\begin{array}{r} 0.004 \\ \times\ \ 0.9 \\ \hline \end{array}$

35. $\begin{array}{r} 0.06 \\ \times\ 0.5 \\ \hline \end{array}$

36. $\begin{array}{r} 0.0008 \\ \times\ 0.004 \\ \hline \end{array}$

37. $\begin{array}{r} 0.0002 \\ \times\ \ 0.06 \\ \hline \end{array}$

38. 12.4×0.2

39. 18.6×5.9

40. 7.91×0.72

41. 1.16×3.35

42. 6.478×18.21

43. 1.9×7.216

44. 0.0021×18.2

45. 6.109×8.4

46. **ERROR ANALYSIS** Describe and correct the error in the solution.

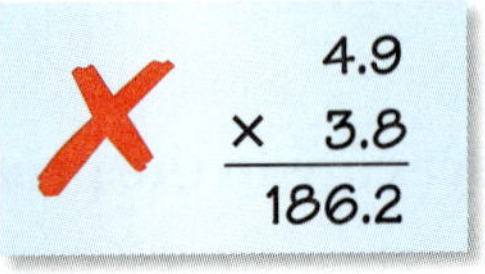

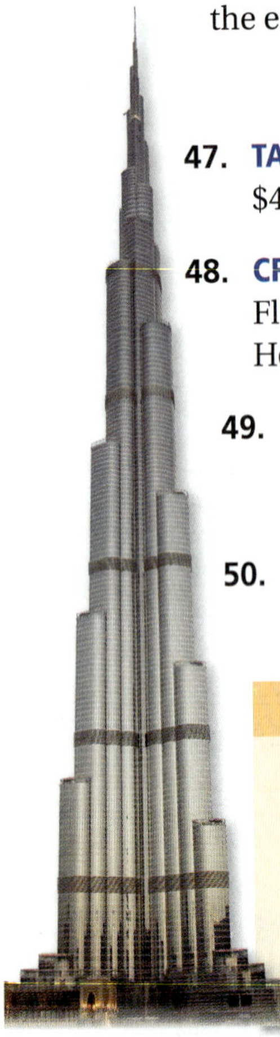

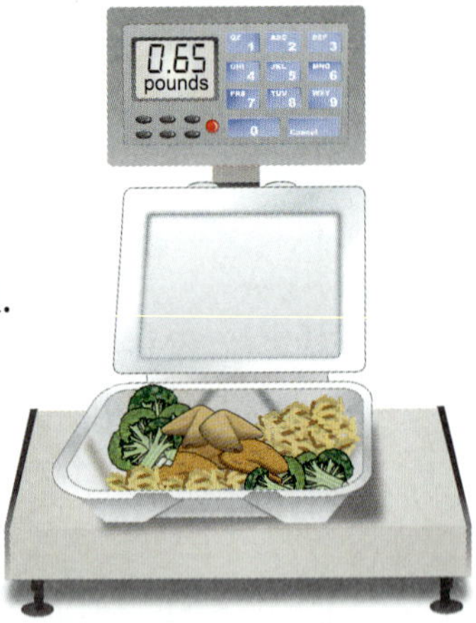

47. **TAKEOUT** A Chinese restaurant offers buffet takeout for $4.99 per pound. How much does your takeout meal cost?

48. **CROPLAND** Alabama has about 2.51 million acres of cropland. Florida has about 1.15 times as much cropland as Alabama. How much cropland does Florida have?

49. **GOLD** On a tour of an old gold mine, you find a nugget containing 0.82 ounce of gold. Gold is worth $1566.80 per ounce. How much is your nugget worth?

50. **BUILDING HEIGHTS** One meter is approximately 3.28 feet. Find the height of each building in feet by multiplying its height in meters by 3.28.

Continent	Tallest Building	Height (meters)
Africa	Carlton Centre Office Tower	223
Asia	Burj Khalifa	828
Australia	Q1 Tower	323
Europe	The Shard	310
North America	Willis Tower	442
South America	Gran Torre	300

51. **REASONING** Show how to evaluate $7.12 \times 8.22 \times 100$ without multiplying the two decimals.

ORDER OF OPERATIONS **Evaluate the expression.**

④ 52. $2.4 \times 16 + 7$

53. $6.85 \times 2 \times 10$

54. $1.047 \times 5 - 0.88$

55. $4.32(3.7 + 1.65)$

56. $23.98 - 1.7^2 \cdot 7.6$

57. $12 \cdot 5.16 + 10.064$

58. $0.9(8.2 \cdot 20.35)$

59. $7.5^2(6.084 - 5.44)$

60. $6.8 \cdot 2.18 \cdot 3.95$

61. **REASONING** Without multiplying, how many decimal places does 3.4^2 have? 3.4^3? 3.4^4? Explain your reasoning.

REPEATED REASONING **Describe the pattern. Find the next three numbers.**

62. 1, 0.6, 0.36, 0.216, . . .

63. 15, 1.5, 0.15, 0.015, . . .

64. 0.04, 0.02, 0.01, 0.005, . . .

65. 5, 7.5, 11.25, 16.875, . . .

66. **FOOD** You buy 2.6 pounds of apples and 1.475 pounds of peaches. You hand the cashier a $20 bill. How much change will you receive?

67. **MILEAGE** A car can travel 22.36 miles on one gallon of gasoline.

   a. How far can the car travel on 8.5 gallons of gasoline?

   b. A hybrid car can travel 33.1 miles on one gallon of gasoline. How much farther can the hybrid car travel on 8.5 gallons of gasoline?

68. **OPEN-ENDED** You and four friends have dinner at a restaurant.

   a. Draw a restaurant menu that has main items, desserts, and beverages, with their prices.

   b. Write a guest check that shows what each of you ate. Find the subtotal.

   c. Multiply by 0.07 to find the tax. Then find the total.

   d. Round the total to the nearest whole number. Multiply by 0.20 to estimate a tip. Including the tip, how much did you spend?

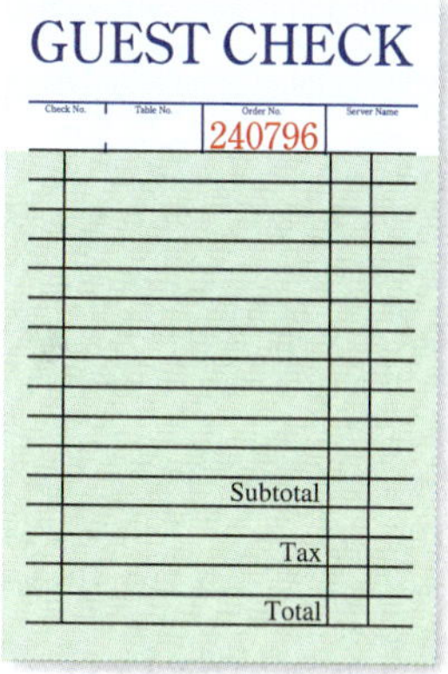

69. Geometry A rectangular painting has an area of 9.52 square feet.

   a. Draw three different ways in which this can happen.

   b. The cost of a frame depends on the perimeter of the painting. Which of your drawings from part (a) is the least expensive to frame? Explain your reasoning.

   c. The thin, black framing costs $1 per foot. The fancy framing costs $5 per foot. Will the fancy framing cost five times as much as the black framing? Explain why or why not.

   d. Suppose the cost of a frame depends on the outside perimeter of the frame. Does this change your answer to part (c)? Explain why or why not.

Fair Game Review What you learned in previous grades & lessons

Divide.

70. 78 ÷ 3

71. 65 ÷ 13

72. 57 ÷ 19

73. 84 ÷ 12

74. **MULTIPLE CHOICE** How many edges does the rectangular prism at the right have?

Ⓐ 4 Ⓑ 6

Ⓒ 8 Ⓓ 12

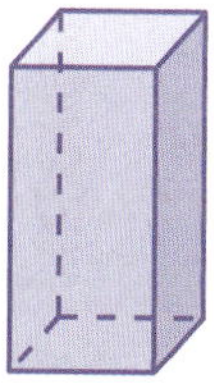

4.3 Dividing Decimals

Essential Question How can you use base ten blocks to model decimal division?

1 ACTIVITY: Dividing Decimals

Work with a partner. Use base ten blocks to model the division. Then find the quotient.

a. 2.4 ÷ 0.6

Begin by modeling 2.4.

2.4

How many of each base ten block did you use?

____ ones

____ tenths

____ hundredths

Next, think of the division problem 2.4 ÷ 0.6 as the question,

"How can you divide 2.4 into groups of 0.6?"

Rearrange the model for 2.4 into groups of 0.6. There are ____ groups of 0.6.

So, 2.4 ÷ 0.6 = ____.

Dividing Decimals

In this lesson, you will

- use models to divide decimals.
- divide decimals.

b. 1.8 ÷ 2 **c.** 3.9 ÷ 3 **d.** 2.8 ÷ 0.7 **e.** 3.2 ÷ 0.4

f. Write and solve the division problem represented by the model.

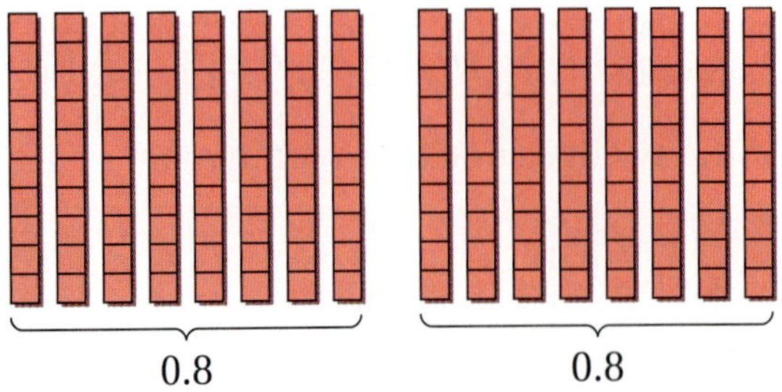

2 ACTIVITY: Dividing Decimals

Work with a partner. Use base ten blocks to model the division. Then find the quotient.

Math Process

Evaluate Results

What can you do to check the reasonableness of your answer?

a. 0.3 ÷ 0.06

Model 0.3. | Replace tenths with hundredths. | How many 0.06s are in 0.3? Divide hundredths into groups of 0.06.

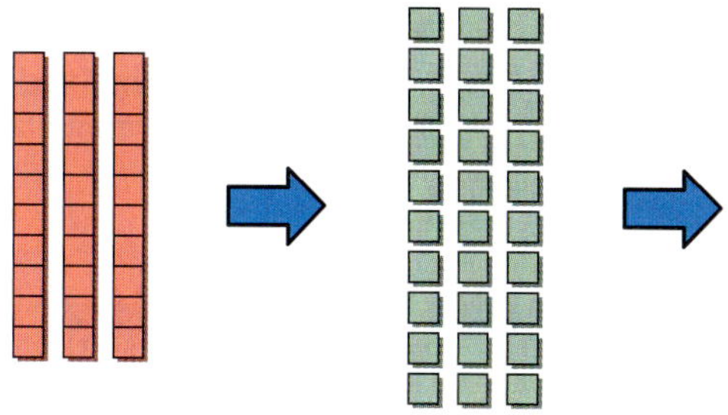

There are ___ groups of 0.06. So, 0.3 ÷ 0.06 = ___.

b. 0.2 ÷ 0.04

c. 0.6 ÷ 0.01

d. 0.16 ÷ 0.08

e. 0.28 ÷ 0.07

What Is Your Answer?

3. **IN YOUR OWN WORDS** How can you use base ten blocks to model decimal division? Use examples from Activity 1 and Activity 2 as part of your answer.

4. **WRITING** Newton's poem is about dividing fractions. Write a poem about dividing decimals.

"When you must divide a fraction, do this very simple action: Flip what you're dividing BY, and then it's easy—multiply!"

5. Think of your own cartoon about dividing decimals. Draw your cartoon.

Practice Use what you learned about dividing decimals to complete Exercises 8–11 on page 129.

Check It Out
Lesson Tutorials
BigIdeasMath.com

Key Idea

Dividing Decimals by Whole Numbers

Words Place the decimal point in the quotient above the decimal point in the dividend. Then divide as you would with whole numbers. Continue until there is no remainder.

Numbers

$$4\overline{)7.32}\quad\text{quotient: } 1.83$$

Place the decimal point in the quotient above the decimal point in the dividend.

EXAMPLE 1 Dividing Decimals by Whole Numbers

a. Find 7.6 ÷ 4. **Estimate** $8 \div 4 = 2$

$$\begin{array}{r} 1.9 \\ 4\overline{)7.6} \\ -\,4 \\ 3\,6 \\ -\,3\,6 \\ \hline 0 \end{array}$$

Place the decimal point in the quotient above the decimal point in the dividend.

So, 7.6 ÷ 4 = 1.9. **Reasonable?** $1.9 \approx 2$ ✓

b. Find 4.38 ÷ 12.

$$\begin{array}{r} 0.365 \\ 12\overline{)4.380} \\ -\,3\,6 \\ 78 \\ -\,72 \\ 60 \\ -\,60 \\ \hline 0 \end{array}$$

Place the decimal point in the quotient above the decimal point in the dividend.

Insert a zero and continue to divide.

So, 4.38 ÷ 12 = 0.365. **Check** $0.365 \times 12 = 4.38$ ✓

On Your Own

Now You're Ready
Exercises 12–23

Divide. Use estimation to check your answer.

1. 36.4 ÷ 2
2. 22.2 ÷ 6
3. 59.64 ÷ 7
4. 43.26 ÷ 14
5. 6.2 ÷ 4
6. 3.12 ÷ 16

Key Idea

Dividing Decimals by Decimals

Words Multiply the divisor *and* the dividend by a power of 10 to make the divisor a whole number. Then place the decimal point in the quotient and divide as you would with whole numbers. Continue until there is no remainder.

Numbers $1.2\overline{)4.56} \rightarrow 12\overline{)45.6}$ with quotient 3.8

Multiply each number by 10.

Place the decimal point above the decimal point in the dividend 45.6.

EXAMPLE 2 Dividing Decimals

a. Find 18.2 ÷ 1.4.

$1.4\overline{)18.2} \rightarrow 14\overline{)182.}$

$$\begin{array}{r} 13.\\ 14\overline{)182.}\\ -14\\ \hline 42\\ -42\\ \hline 0 \end{array}$$

Multiply each number by 10.

Place the decimal point above the decimal point in the dividend 182.

So, 18.2 ÷ 1.4 = 13.

Check $13 \times 1.4 = 18.2$ ✓

Study Tip

Multiplying the divisor and the dividend by a power of 10 does not change the quotient.

For example:

18.2 ÷ 1.4 = 13

182 ÷ 14 = 13

1820 ÷ 140 = 13

b. Find 0.273 ÷ 0.39.

$0.39\overline{)0.273} \rightarrow 39\overline{)27.3}$

$$\begin{array}{r} 0.7\\ 39\overline{)27.3}\\ -27.3\\ \hline 0 \end{array}$$

Multiply each number by 100.

So, 0.273 ÷ 0.39 = 0.7.

Check $0.7 \times 0.39 = 0.273$ ✓

On Your Own

Now You're Ready
Exercises 36–39

Divide. Check your answer.

7. $1.2\overline{)9.6}$

8. $3.4\overline{)57.8}$

9. 21.643 ÷ 2.3

10. 0.459 ÷ 0.51

EXAMPLE 3 Inserting Zeros in the Dividend and the Quotient

Divide 2.45 ÷ 0.007.

Study Tip

Remember to check your answer by multiplying the quotient by the divisor.

$0.007\overline{)2.450}$ ⟶ $7\overline{)2450}$

Multiply each number by 1000. Insert a zero in the dividend.

```
   350
7)2450
 -21
   35
  -35
   00  ← Because 0 ÷ 7 = 0, insert a zero in the quotient.
```

So, 2.45 ÷ 0.007 = 350.

On Your Own

Now You're Ready Exercises 40–43

Divide. Check your answer.

11. 3.8 ÷ 0.16

12. 15.6 ÷ 0.78

13. 7.2 ÷ 0.048

14. 0.18 ÷ 0.003

EXAMPLE 4 Real-Life Application

How many times more cellular phone subscribers were there in 2011 than in 1991? Round to the nearest whole number.

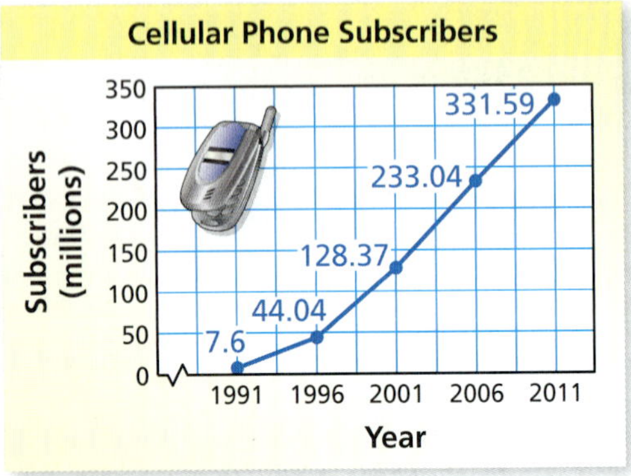

From the graph, there were 331.59 million subscribers in 2011 and 7.6 million in 1991. So, divide 331.59 by 7.6.

Estimate **320 ÷ 8 = 40**

$7.6\overline{)331.59}$ ⟶ $76\overline{)3315.9}$

```
      43.6   ← Rounds to 44.
76)3315.9
  -304
    275
   -228
    47 9
   -45 6
     2 3
```

So, there were about 44 times more subscribers in 2011 than in 1991.

Reasonable? **44 ≈ 40** ✓

On Your Own

15. How many times more subscribers were there in 2006 than in 1996? Round to the nearest whole number.

4.3 Exercises

Check It Out
Help with Homework
BigIdeasMath.com

Vocabulary and Concept Check

1. **NUMBER SENSE** Fix the one that is not correct.

$4\overline{)24.4}$ = 6.1 $4\overline{)244}$ = 61 $4\overline{)2.44}$ = 6.1

Copy the problem and place the decimal point in the correct location.

2. $18.6 \div 4 = 465$
3. $6.38 \div 11 = 58$
4. $88.27 \div 7 = 1261$

Rewrite the problem so that the divisor is a whole number.

5. $4.7\overline{)13.6}$
6. $0.21\overline{)17.66}$
7. $2.16\overline{)18.5}$

Practice and Problem Solving

Use base ten blocks to find the quotient.

8. $3.6 \div 0.3$
9. $2.6 \div 0.2$
10. $0.72 \div 0.06$
11. $0.36 \div 0.04$

Divide. Use estimation to check your answer.

1 12. $6\overline{)25.2}$
13. $5\overline{)33.5}$
14. $7\overline{)3.5}$
15. $8\overline{)10.4}$
16. $38.7 \div 9$
17. $37.6 \div 4$
18. $43.4 \div 7$
19. $25.6 \div 8$
20. $44.64 \div 8$
21. $0.294 \div 3$
22. $3.6 \div 24$
23. $64.26 \div 18$

ERROR ANALYSIS **Describe and correct the error in finding the quotient.**

24.

✗
3.922
9)28.008
27
1 00
81
198
198
0

25.

✗
0.86
6)0.516
48
36
36
0

26. **TEXT MESSAGING** You send 40 text messages in one month. The total cost is $4.80. How much does each text message cost?

27. **SUNBLOCK** Of the two bottles of sunblock shown, which is the better buy? Explain.

4-ounce bottle $8.49   5-ounce bottle $10.29

ORDER OF OPERATIONS Evaluate the expression.

28. $7.68 + 3.18 \div 12$ **29.** $10.56 \div 3 - 1.9$ **30.** $19.6 \div 7 \times 9$

31. $5.5 \times 16.56 \div 9$ **32.** $35.25 \div 5 \div 3$ **33.** $13.41 \times (5.4 \div 9)$

34. FRUIT PUNCH Which pack of fruit punch is the best buy? Explain.

35. SALE You buy 3 pairs of jeans for $35.95 each and get a fourth pair for free. What is your cost per pair of jeans?

Divide. Check your answer.

2 **36.** $2.1\overline{)25.2}$ **37.** $3.8\overline{)34.2}$ **38.** $36.47 \div 0.7$ **39.** $0.984 \div 12.3$

3 **40.** $4.23 \div 0.012$ **41.** $0.52 \div 0.0013$ **42.** $95.04 \div 0.0132$ **43.** $32.2 \div 0.07$

Divide. Round to the nearest hundredth if necessary.

44. $80.88 \div 8.425$ **45.** $0.8 \div 0.6$ **46.** $38.9 \div 6.44$ **47.** $11.6 \div 0.95$

48. ERROR ANALYSIS Describe and correct the error in rewriting the problem.

✗ $0.32\overline{)146.4} \rightarrow 32\overline{)1.464}$

49. TICKETS Tickets to the school musical cost $6.25. The amount received from ticket sales is $706.25. How many tickets were sold?

50. HEIGHT A person's running stride is about 1.14 times the person's height. Your friend's stride is 5.472 feet. How tall is your friend?

51. MP3 PLAYER You have 3.4 gigabytes available on your MP3 player. Each song is about 0.004 gigabyte. How many more songs can you download onto your MP3 player?

52. SWIMMING The table shows the top three times in a swimming event at the Summer Olympics. The event consists of a team of four women swimming 100 meters each.

Women's 4 × 100 Freestyle Relay		
Medal	**Country**	**Time (seconds)**
Gold	Australia	215.94
Silver	United States	216.39
Bronze	Netherlands	217.59

a. Suppose the times of all four swimmers on each team were the same. For each team, how much time does it take a swimmer to swim 100 meters?

b. Suppose each U.S. swimmer completed 100 meters a quarter second faster. Would the U.S. team have won the gold medal? Explain your reasoning.

Without finding the quotient, copy and complete the statement using <, >, or =.

53. $6.66 \div 0.74$ ▭ $66.6 \div 7.4$

54. $32.2 \div 0.7$ ▭ $3.22 \div 7$

55. $160.72 \div 16.4$ ▭ $160.72 \div 1.64$

56. $75.6 \div 63$ ▭ $7.56 \div 0.63$

57. **BEES** To approximate the number of bees in a hive, multiply the number of bees that leave the hive in one minute by 3 and divide by 0.014. You count 25 bees leaving a hive in one minute. How many bees are in the hive?

58. **PROBLEM SOLVING** You are saving money to buy a new bicycle that costs \$155.75. You have \$30 and plan to save \$5 each week. Your aunt decides to give you an additional \$10 each week.

a. How many weeks will you have to save until you have enough money to buy the bicycle?

b. How many more weeks would you have to save to buy a new bicycle that costs \$203.89? Explain how you found your answer.

Applesauce	
3.9-ounce bowl	\$0.52
24-ounce jar	\$2.63

59. **PRECISION** A store sells applesauce in two sizes.

a. How many *bowls* of applesauce fit in a *jar*? Round your answer to the nearest hundredth.

b. Explain two ways to find the better buy.

c. What is the better buy?

60. **Geometry** The large rectangle's dimensions are three times the dimensions of the small rectangle.

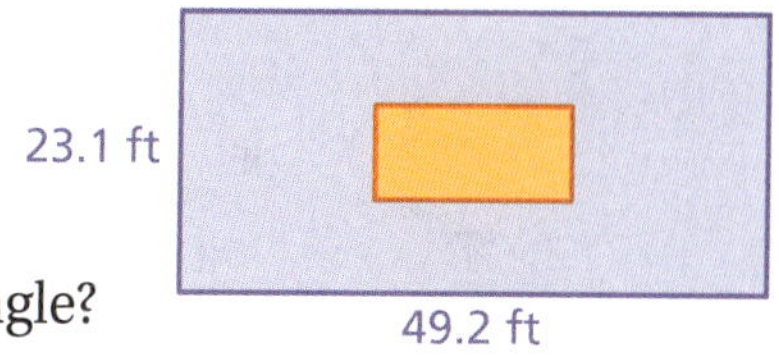

a. How many times greater is the perimeter of the large rectangle compared to the perimeter of the small rectangle?

b. How many times greater is the area of the large rectangle compared to the area of the small rectangle?

c. Are the answers to parts (a) and (b) the same? *Explain* why or why not.

d. What happens in parts (a) and (b) if the dimensions of the large rectangle are two times the dimensions of the small rectangle?

Fair Game Review What you learned in previous grades & lessons

Add or subtract. Write your answer in simplest form.

61. $\frac{1}{2} + \frac{2}{3}$

62. $\frac{2}{5} + \frac{3}{4}$

63. $\frac{3}{10} - \frac{1}{4}$

64. $\frac{11}{12} - \frac{7}{8}$

65. **MULTIPLE CHOICE** Melissa earns \$7.40 an hour working at a grocery store. She works 14.25 hours this week. How much does she earn?

Ⓐ \$83.13 Ⓑ \$105.45 Ⓒ \$156.75 Ⓓ \$1054.50

4.4 Rational Numbers

Essential Question How can you use a number line to order rational numbers?

1 ACTIVITY: Ordering Rational Numbers

Work in groups of four. Order the numbers from least to greatest.

- Use masking tape and a marker to make a number line on the floor similar to the one shown.

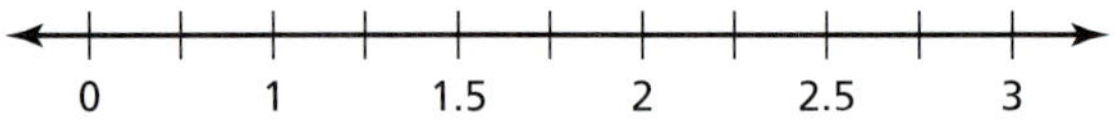

- Write the numbers on pieces of paper. Then each person should choose one.
- Stand on the location of your number on the number line.
- Use your positions to order the numbers from least to greatest.

a. $1.25, \frac{1}{3}, 0.5, \frac{5}{3}$

b. $\frac{7}{4}, 1.1, \frac{1}{2}, 1.3$

c. $1.4, \frac{3}{5}, \frac{1}{4}, 0.9$

d. $\frac{5}{4}, 0.75, 0.8, 1.1$

e. $\frac{5}{2}, 0.5, 1\frac{3}{4}, \frac{2}{3}$

f. $\frac{9}{5}, 1.9, 0.7, \frac{2}{5}$

Rational Numbers

In this lesson, you will

- understand that a rational number is an integer divided by an integer.
- convert rational numbers to decimals.

2 ACTIVITY: The Game of Math Card War

Math Process

Consider Similar Problems

What are some ways to determine which number is greater?

Preparation:

- Cut index cards to make 40 playing cards.
- Write each number in the table on a card.

To Play:

- Play with a partner.
- Deal 20 cards to each player facedown.
- Each player turns one card faceup. The player with the greater number wins. The winner collects both cards and places them at the bottom of his or her cards.
- Suppose there is a tie. Each player lays three cards facedown, then a new card faceup. The player with the greater of these new cards wins. The winner collects all ten cards and places them at the bottom of his or her cards.
- Continue playing until one player has all the cards. This player wins the game.

0.55	$\frac{3}{10}$	$\frac{1}{10}$	0.35	1.25	1.75	$\frac{5}{4}$	$\frac{3}{5}$	$\frac{1}{20}$	$\frac{7}{20}$
$\frac{3}{20}$	$\frac{8}{5}$	$\frac{1}{4}$	$\frac{19}{10}$	0.75	$\frac{4}{5}$	$\frac{1}{2}$	$\frac{7}{4}$	1.2	0.3
1.5	1.9	0.05	0.1	$\frac{3}{4}$	$\frac{1}{5}$	0.5	$\frac{2}{5}$	0.2	$\frac{11}{20}$
$\frac{6}{5}$	$\frac{9}{20}$	1.6	0.25	0.6	0.15	$\frac{3}{2}$	0.8	0.4	0.45

What Is Your Answer?

3. **IN YOUR OWN WORDS** How can you use a number line to order rational numbers? Give an example.

The numbers are in order from least to greatest. Fill in the blank spaces with rational numbers.

4. $\frac{1}{3}$, ____, $\frac{7}{5}$, ____

5. $\frac{2}{3}$, ____, $\frac{5}{2}$, ____

6. ____, 0.1, ____, $\frac{4}{5}$

7. 1.5, ____, 2.2, ____

Practice Use what you learned about ordering rational numbers to complete Exercises 28–30 on page 136.

Check It Out
Lesson Tutorials
BigIdeasMath.com

Key Vocabulary
rational number, p. 134
terminating decimal, p. 134
repeating decimal, p. 134

Key Idea

Rational Numbers

A **rational number** is a number that can be written as $\frac{a}{b}$ where a and b are integers and $b \neq 0$.

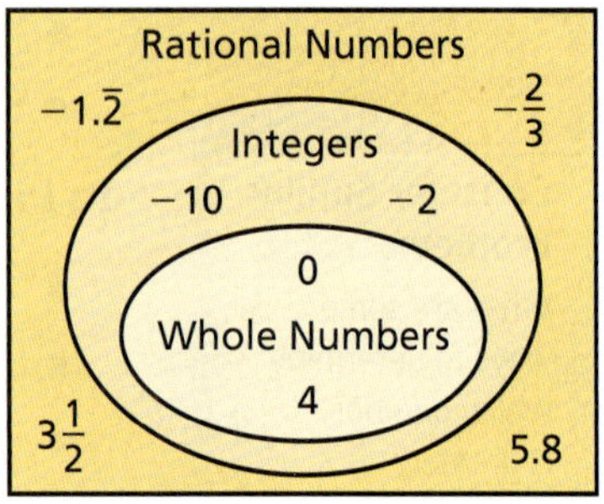

Because you can divide any integer by any nonzero integer, you can use long division to write fractions and mixed numbers as decimals. These decimals are also rational numbers and will either *terminate* or *repeat.*

A **terminating decimal** is a decimal that ends.

1.5, 0.25, 10.625

A **repeating decimal** is a decimal that has a pattern that repeats.

$1.333\ldots = 1.\overline{3}$

$0.151515\ldots = 0.\overline{15}$

Use *bar notation* to show which of the digits repeat.

EXAMPLE 1 Writing Rational Numbers as Decimals

a. Write $2\frac{1}{4}$ as a decimal.

Notice that $2\frac{1}{4} = \frac{9}{4}$.

Divide 9 by 4.

$$\begin{array}{r} 2.25 \\ 4\overline{)9.00} \\ -\underline{8} \\ 1\,0 \\ -\underline{8} \\ 20 \\ -\underline{20} \\ 0 \end{array}$$

The remainder is 0. So, it is a terminating decimal.

So, $2\frac{1}{4} = 2.25$.

b. Write $\frac{5}{11}$ as a decimal.

Divide 5 by 11.

$$\begin{array}{r} 0.4545 \\ 11\overline{)5.0000} \\ -\underline{4\,4} \\ 60 \\ -\underline{55} \\ 50 \\ -\underline{44} \\ 60 \\ -\underline{55} \\ 5 \end{array}$$

The remainder repeats. So, it is a repeating decimal.

So, $\frac{5}{11} = 0.\overline{45}$.

On Your Own

Now You're Ready
Exercises 11–18

Write the rational number as a decimal.

1. $\frac{6}{5}$ **2.** $7\frac{3}{8}$ **3.** $\frac{3}{11}$ **4.** $1\frac{5}{27}$

Multi-Language Glossary at BigIdeasMath.com

EXAMPLE 2 Writing a Decimal as a Fraction

Write 0.26 as a fraction in simplest form.

$$0.26 = \frac{26}{100}$$

Write the digits after the decimal point in the numerator.

The last digit is in the hundredths place. So, use 100 in the denominator.

$$= \frac{13}{50}$$

Simplify.

On Your Own

Now You're Ready
Exercises 20–27

Write the decimal as a fraction or a mixed number in simplest form.

5. 0.7 **6.** 0.125 **7.** 3.1 **8.** 10.25

EXAMPLE 3 Ordering Rational Numbers

Activity	Portion of Students
Band	0.14
Chorus	$\frac{3}{25}$
Debate	$\frac{1}{20}$
Gymnastics	0.11

The table shows the portions of students in your grade that participate in four activities. List the activities in order by number of students from least to greatest.

Write each rational number as a decimal.

$$\frac{3}{25} = \frac{3 \times 4}{25 \times 4} = \frac{12}{100} = 0.12$$

$$\frac{1}{20} = \frac{1 \times 5}{20 \times 5} = \frac{5}{100} = 0.05$$

Then graph each decimal on a number line.

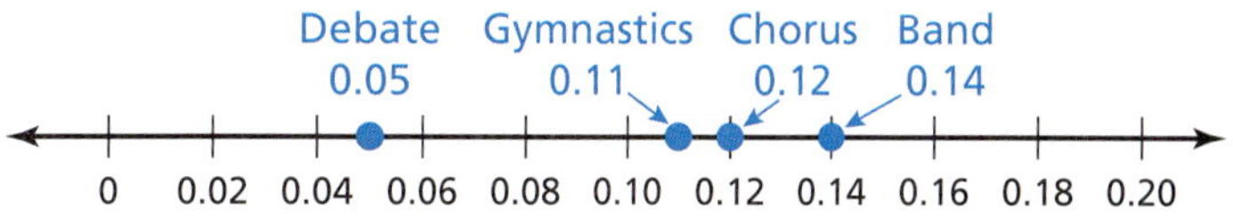

∴ The activities in order by number of students from least to greatest are debate, gymnastics, chorus, and band.

On Your Own

Now You're Ready
Exercises 28–33

9. **WHAT IF?** The portion of students in your grade that participate in theater is $\frac{2}{25}$. Which of the activities in Example 3 have more students than theater?

4.4 Exercises

Check It Out
Help with Homework
BigIdeasMath.com

Vocabulary and Concept Check

1. **VOCABULARY** Is the quotient of two integers always a rational number? Explain.
2. **WRITING** Are all terminating and repeating decimals rational numbers? Explain.

Tell whether the number belongs to each of the following number sets: *rational numbers, integers, whole numbers.*

3. -5
4. $2.1\overline{6}$
5. 12
6. 0

Tell whether the decimal is *terminating* or *repeating*.

7. 0.4848 . . .
8. 0.151
9. 72.72
10. $5.2\overline{36}$

Practice and Problem Solving

Write the rational number as a decimal.

11. $\frac{7}{8}$ (1)
12. $\frac{1}{11}$
13. $\frac{7}{9}$
14. $\frac{17}{40}$
15. $1\frac{5}{6}$
16. $2\frac{17}{18}$
17. $5\frac{7}{12}$
18. $8\frac{15}{22}$
19. **ERROR ANALYSIS** Describe and correct the error in writing the rational number as a decimal.

✗ $\frac{7}{11} = 0.6\overline{3}$

Write the decimal as a fraction or a mixed number in simplest form.

20. 0.9 (2)
21. 0.45
22. 0.258
23. 0.312
24. 2.32
25. 1.64
26. 6.012
27. 12.405

Order the numbers from least to greatest.

28. $\frac{3}{4}$, 0.5, $\frac{2}{3}$, 1.2 (3)
29. $\frac{9}{5}$, 2.5, 1.1, 0.8
30. 1.4, $\frac{8}{5}$, 0.6, $\frac{1}{4}$
31. 2.1, $\frac{6}{10}$, $\frac{9}{4}$, $\frac{5}{3}$
32. $\frac{7}{2}$, $\frac{5}{4}$, $\frac{4}{3}$, 1.3
33. 2.4, 1.6, $\frac{15}{10}$, 2.25
34. **COINS** You have one quarter, two dimes, and two nickels.
    a. Write the amount as a decimal.
    b. Write the amount as a fraction in simplest form.
35. **NESTS** A house finch builds a nest $8\frac{5}{8}$ feet above the ground. A robin builds a nest $8\frac{2}{3}$ feet above the ground. Which nest is higher?

Copy and complete the statement using <, >, or =.

36. $2.2 \;\square\; 2.42$ **37.** $1.82 \;\square\; 1.81$ **38.** $\frac{15}{8} \;\square\; 1\frac{7}{8}$

39. $4\frac{6}{10} \;\square\; 4.65$ **40.** $5\frac{3}{11} \;\square\; 5.\overline{2}$ **41.** $2\frac{13}{16} \;\square\; 2\frac{11}{14}$

42. **OPEN-ENDED** Find one terminating decimal and one repeating decimal between $\frac{1}{3}$ and $\frac{1}{2}$.

Player	Hits	At Bats
Eva	42	90
Michelle	38	80

43. **SOFTBALL** In softball, a batting average is the number of hits divided by the number of times at bat. Does Eva or Michelle have the higher batting average?

44. **PROBLEM SOLVING** You miss 3 out of 10 questions on a science quiz and 4 out of 15 questions on a math quiz. Which quiz has a higher percent of correct answers?

45. **SKATING** Is the half pipe deeper than the skating pool? Explain.

46. **ENVIRONMENT** The table shows the changes from the average water level of a pond over several weeks. Order the numbers from least to greatest.

Week	1	2	3	4
Change (inches)	$\frac{7}{5}$	$1\frac{5}{11}$	1.45	$1\frac{91}{200}$

47. Critical Thinking Given: a and b are integers.

a. When is $-\frac{1}{a}$ positive? **b.** When is $\frac{1}{ab}$ positive?

Fair Game Review What you learned in previous grades & lessons

Add or subtract.

48. $\frac{3}{5} + \frac{2}{7}$ **49.** $\frac{9}{10} - \frac{2}{3}$ **50.** $8.79 - 4.07$ **51.** $11.81 + 9.34$

52. **MULTIPLE CHOICE** In one year, a company has a profit of −$2 million. In the next year, the company has a profit of $7 million. How much more profit did the company make the second year?

Ⓐ $2 million Ⓑ $5 million Ⓒ $7 million Ⓓ $9 million

4.5 Percents

Essential Question What is the connection between fractions and percents?

1 ACTIVITY: Writing Fractions

Work with a partner.

- **Write the number of squares that are shaded.**
- **Write the total number of squares.**
- **Write the fraction of the squares that are shaded.**
- **What type of relationship do the fractions represent?**

a.

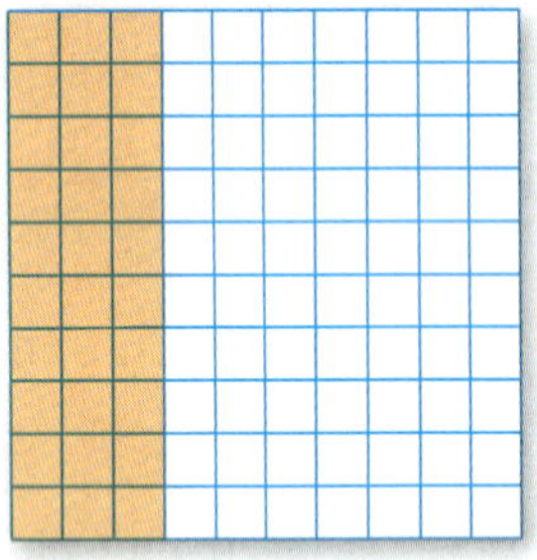

b.

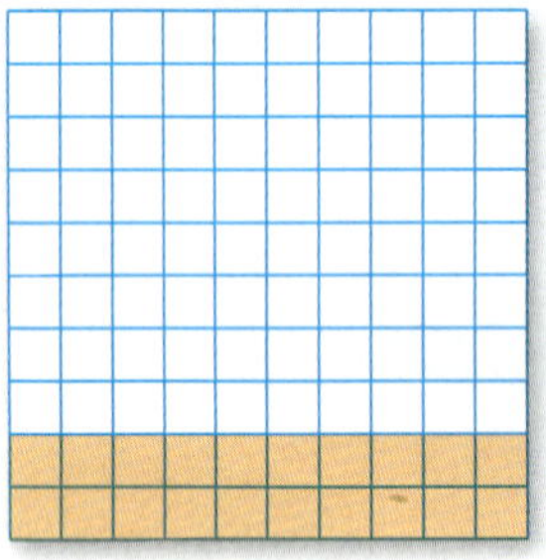

c.

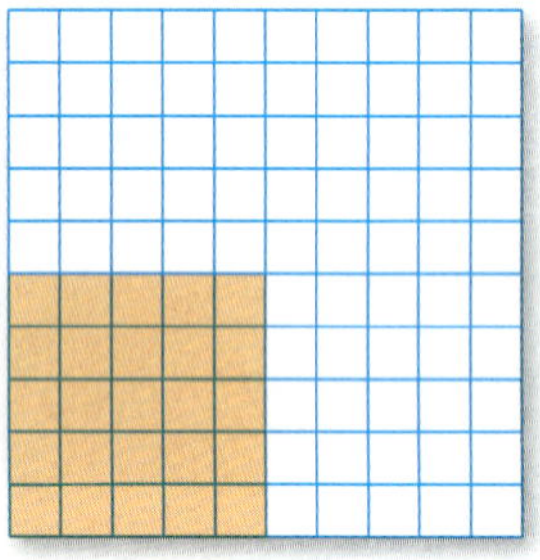

The Meaning of a Word ● Percent

A century is 100 years.

A cent is one hundredth of a dollar.

In Mexico, a centavo is one hundredth of a peso.

Percents

In this lesson, you will
- write percents as fractions with denominators of 100.
- write fractions as percents.

Cent means *one hundred*, so **percent** means *per one hundred*. The symbol for percent is %.

2 ACTIVITY: Writing Percents as Fractions

Work with a partner.

- What percent of each diagram in Activity 1 is shaded?
- What percent of each diagram below is shaded? Write each percent as a fraction in simplest form.

a.

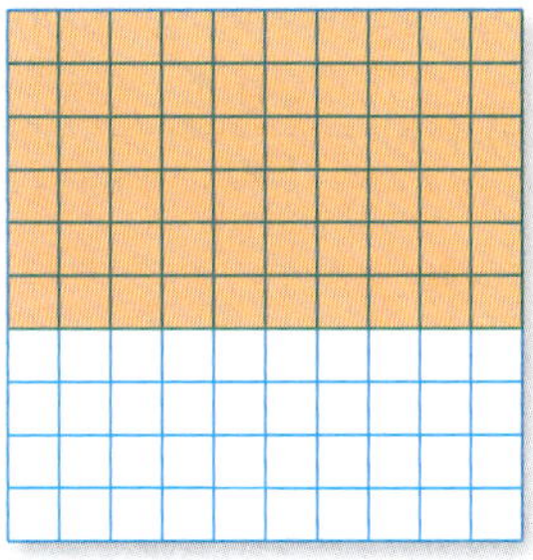

b.

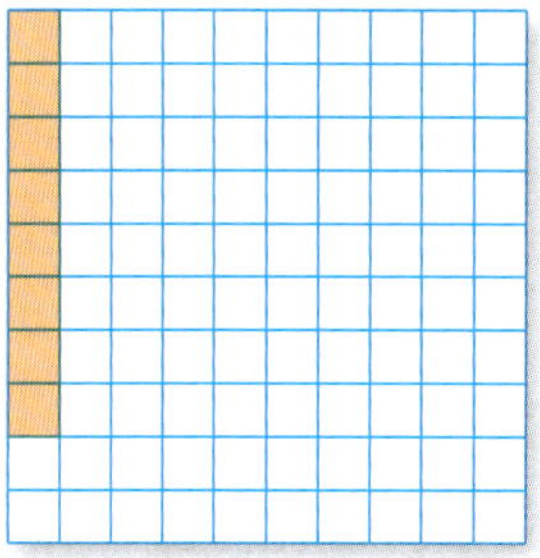

c.

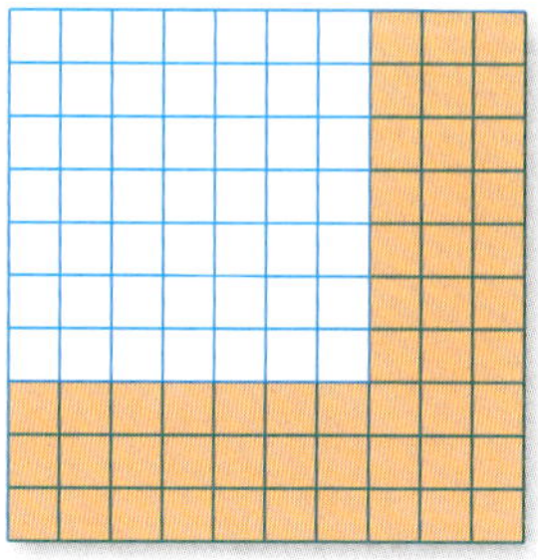

3 ACTIVITY: Writing Fractions as Percents

Work with a partner. Draw a model to represent the fraction. How can you write the fraction as a percent?

a. $\frac{2}{5} = \frac{\square}{100} = \square\%$

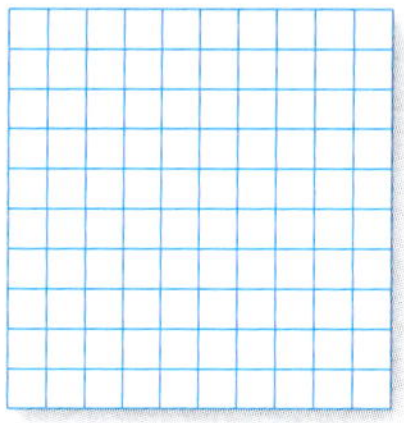

b. $\frac{7}{10}$

c. $\frac{3}{5}$

d. $\frac{3}{4}$

e. $\frac{3}{25}$

Math Process

Consider Similar Problems

How is this problem similar to ones you have seen before? How does this help you find the solution?

What Is Your Answer?

4. **IN YOUR OWN WORDS** What is the connection between fractions and percents? Give an example with your answer.

5. **REASONING** Your score on a test is 110%. What does this mean?

Practice Use what you learned about percents to complete Exercises 5–7 on page 142.

Check It Out
Lesson Tutorials
BigIdeasMath.com

Key Vocabulary
percent, *p. 140*

Key Idea

Writing Percents as Fractions

Words A **percent** is a part-to-whole relationship where the whole is 100. So, you can write a percent as a fraction with a denominator of 100.

Numbers $60\% = 60 \text{ out of } 100 = \frac{60}{100}$ (60: part; fraction bar: per; 100: one hundred (whole))

Algebra $n\% = \frac{n}{100}$

EXAMPLE 1 Writing Percents as Fractions

Study Tip
Equivalent fractions and percents represent the same number using different notations.

a. Write 35% as a fraction in simplest form.

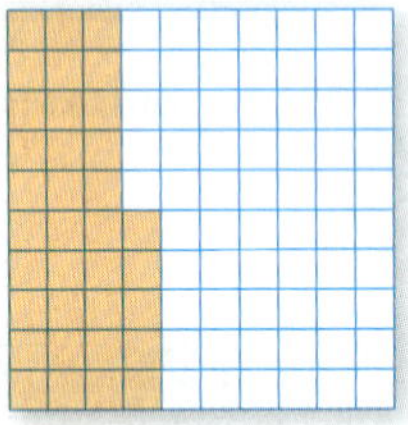

$35\% = \frac{35}{100}$ Write as a fraction with a denominator of 100.

$= \frac{7}{20}$ Simplify.

So, $35\% = \frac{7}{20}$.

b. Write 100% as a fraction in simplest form.

$100\% = \frac{100}{100}$ Write as a fraction with a denominator of 100.

$= 1$ Simplify.

So, $100\% = 1$.

c. Write 174% as a mixed number in simplest form.

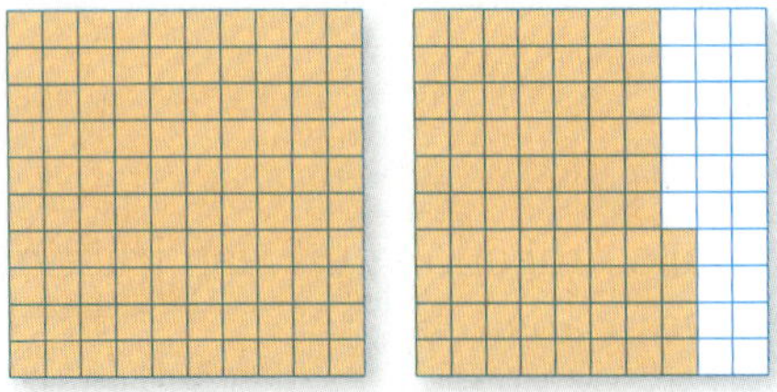

$174\% = \frac{174}{100}$ Write as a fraction with a denominator of 100.

$= \frac{87}{50}$, or $1\frac{37}{50}$ Simplify.

So, $174\% = 1\frac{37}{50}$.

On Your Own

Now You're Ready
Exercises 8–19

Write the percent as a fraction or mixed number in simplest form.

1. 5% **2.** 168% **3.** 36% **4.** 83%

Multi-Language Glossary at BigIdeasMath.com

Key Idea

Writing Fractions as Percents

Words Write an equivalent fraction with a denominator of 100. Then write the numerator with the percent symbol.

Numbers $\frac{1}{4} = \frac{25}{100} = 25\%$ (multiply numerator and denominator by $\times 25$)

EXAMPLE 2 Writing a Fraction as a Percent

Write $\frac{3}{50}$ as a percent.

$\frac{3}{50} = \frac{6}{100} = 6\%$ (numerator and denominator $\times 2$)

Because $50 \times 2 = 100$, multiply the numerator and denominator by 2. Write the numerator with a percent symbol.

EXAMPLE 3 Real-Life Application

A drought affects 9 out of 12 midwestern states. What percent of the midwestern states are affected by the drought?

Midwestern United States

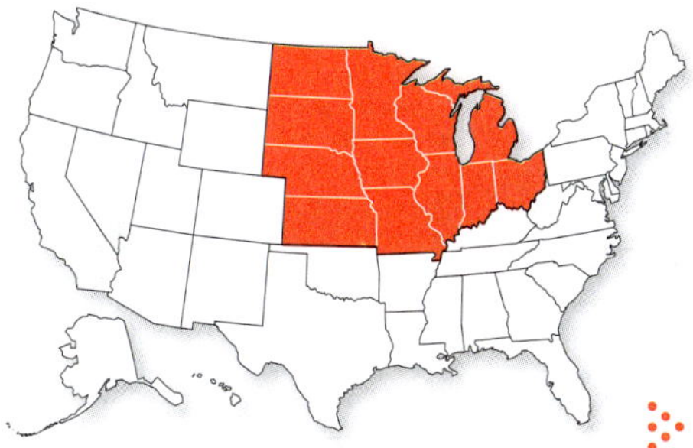

$\frac{9}{12} = \frac{3}{4}$ Simplify.

$= \frac{75}{100}$ ← $\frac{3 \times 25}{4 \times 25} = \frac{75}{100}$

$= 75\%$ Write the numerator with a percent symbol.

∴ So, 75% of the midwestern states are affected by the drought.

On Your Own

Now You're Ready
Exercises 21–28

Write the fraction or mixed number as a percent.

5. $\frac{31}{50}$ **6.** $\frac{7}{25}$ **7.** $\frac{19}{20}$ **8.** $1\frac{1}{2}$

9. WHAT IF? In Example 3, it rains in all the midwestern states. In what percent of the states affected by drought does it rain?

4.5 Exercises

Check It Out
Help with Homework
BigIdeasMath.com

Vocabulary and Concept Check

1. **WRITING** Explain how you can use a 10-by-10 grid to model 42%.
2. **WHICH ONE DOESN'T BELONG?** Which one does *not* have the same value as the other three? Explain your reasoning.

   $\frac{10}{100}$ 10% $\frac{1}{10}$ 0.01

3. **OPEN-ENDED** Write three different fractions that are less than 40%.
4. **NUMBER SENSE** Can $1\frac{1}{4}$ be written as a percent? Explain.

Practice and Problem Solving

Use a 10-by-10 grid to model the percent.

5. 10%
6. 55%
7. 35%

Write the percent as a fraction or mixed number in simplest form.

(1) 8. 45%
9. 90%
10. 15%
11. 7%
12. 34%
13. 79%
14. 77.5%
15. 188%
16. 8%
17. 224%
18. 0.25%
19. 0.4%

20. **ERROR ANALYSIS** Describe and correct the error in writing 225% as a fraction.

   ✗ $225\% = \frac{225}{1000} = \frac{9}{40}$

Write the fraction or mixed number as a percent.

(2) 21. $\frac{1}{10}$
22. $\frac{1}{5}$
23. $\frac{11}{20}$
24. $\frac{2}{25}$
25. $\frac{27}{50}$
26. $\frac{18}{25}$
27. $1\frac{17}{20}$
28. $2\frac{41}{50}$

29. **ERROR ANALYSIS** Describe and correct the error in writing $\frac{14}{25}$ as a percent.

   ✗ $\frac{14}{25} = \frac{14 \times 4}{25 \times 4} = \frac{56}{100} = 0.56\%$

30. **LEFT-HANDED** Of the students in your class, 12% are left-handed. What *fraction* of the students are left-handed? Are there more right-handed or left-handed students? Explain.
31. **ARCADE** You have 125% of the tickets required for a souvenir. What *fraction* of the required tickets do you have? Do you need more tickets for the souvenir? Explain.

Find the percent.

32. 3 is what percent of 8?

33. 13 is what percent of 16?

34. 9 is what percent of 16?

35. 33 is what percent of 40?

36. **SOCIAL NETWORKING** A survey asked students to choose their favorite social networking website. The results are shown in the table.

a. What fraction of the students chose Website A?

b. What percent of the students chose Website C?

Social Networking Website	Number of Students
Website A	35
Website B	13
Website C	22
Website D	10

37. **GEOGRAPHY** The percent of the total area of the United States that is in each of four states is shown.

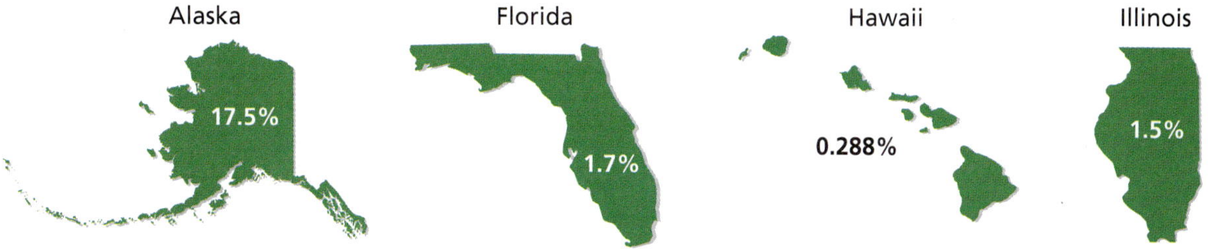

a. Write the percents as fractions in simplest form.

b. How many times larger is Illinois than Hawaii?

c. Compared to the map of Florida, is the map of Alaska the correct size? Explain your reasoning.

d. **RESEARCH** Which of the 50 states are larger than Illinois?

38. **CRITICAL THINKING** A school fundraiser raised 120% of its goal last year and 125% of its goal this year. Did the fundraiser raise more money this year? Explain your reasoning.

39. **CRITICAL THINKING** How can you use a 10-by-10 grid to model $\frac{1}{2}$%?

40. Reasoning Write $\frac{1}{12}$ as a percent. Explain how you found your answer.

Fair Game Review What you learned in previous grades & lessons

Divide. Write the answer in simplest form.

41. $\frac{1}{6} \div \frac{1}{3}$

42. $9 \div \frac{3}{4}$

43. $10 \div \frac{5}{8}$

44. $\frac{1}{6} \div 2$

45. **MULTIPLE CHOICE** Which of the following is *not* equal to 15?

Ⓐ $\frac{3}{4} \cdot 20$ Ⓑ $\frac{5}{9} \cdot 27$ Ⓒ $35 \cdot \frac{3}{7}$ Ⓓ $28 \cdot \frac{5}{7}$

4.6 Percents and Decimals

Essential Question How does the decimal point move when you rewrite a percent as a decimal and when you rewrite a decimal as a percent?

1 ACTIVITY: Writing Percents as Decimals

Work with a partner. Write the percent shown by the model. Write the percent as a decimal.

a.

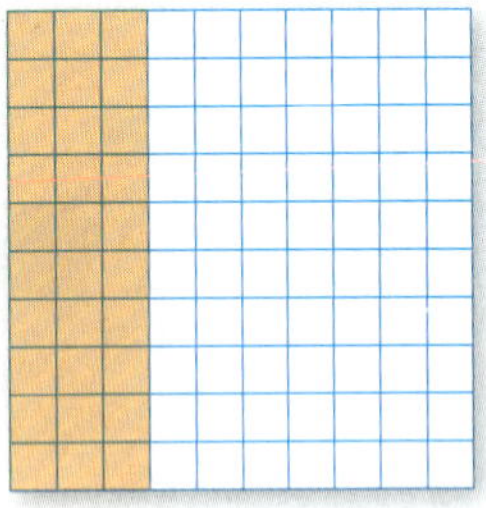

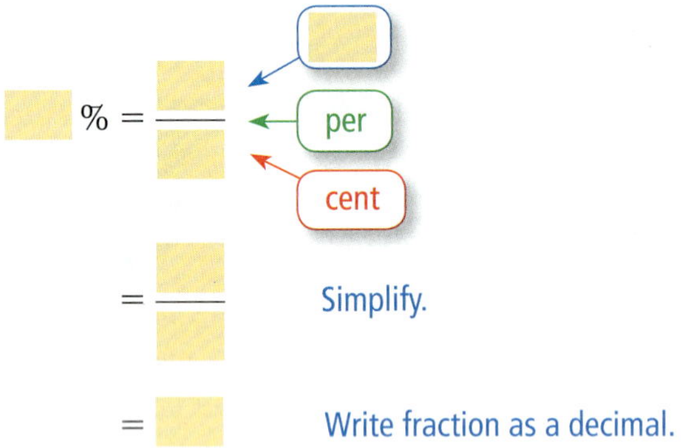

b.

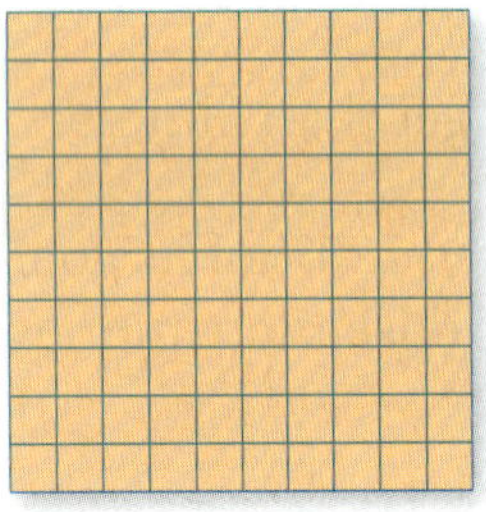

c.

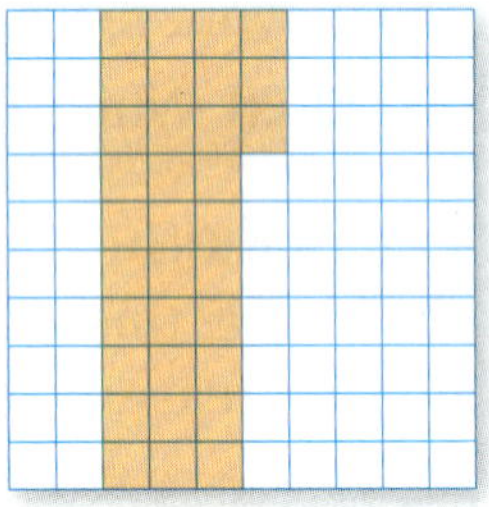

d.

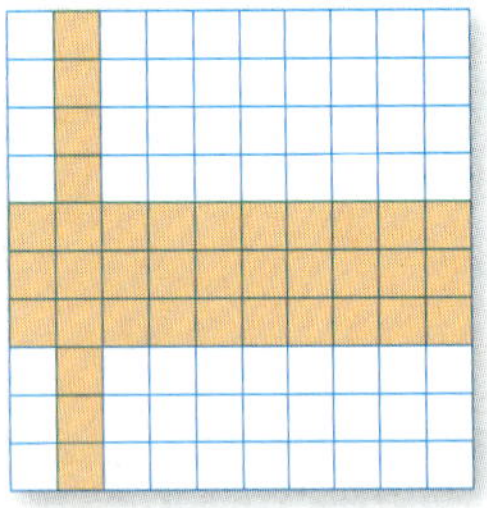

e.

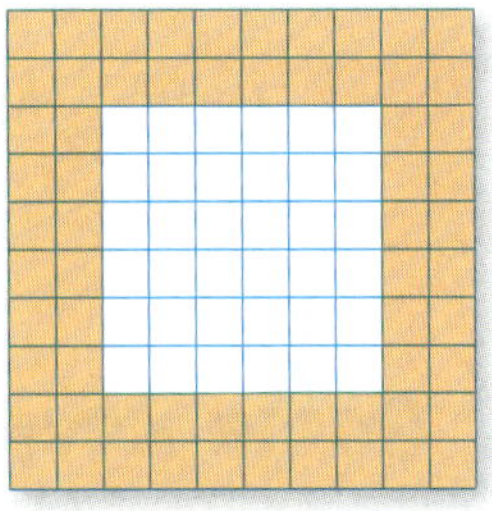

f.

g.

Percents and Decimals

In this lesson, you will

- write percents as decimals.
- write decimals as percents.
- solve real-life problems.

2 ACTIVITY: Writing Percents as Decimals

> **Math Process**
> **Communicate Precisely**
> How can reading the fraction aloud help you write it as a decimal?

Work with a partner. Write the percent as a decimal.

a. 13.5%

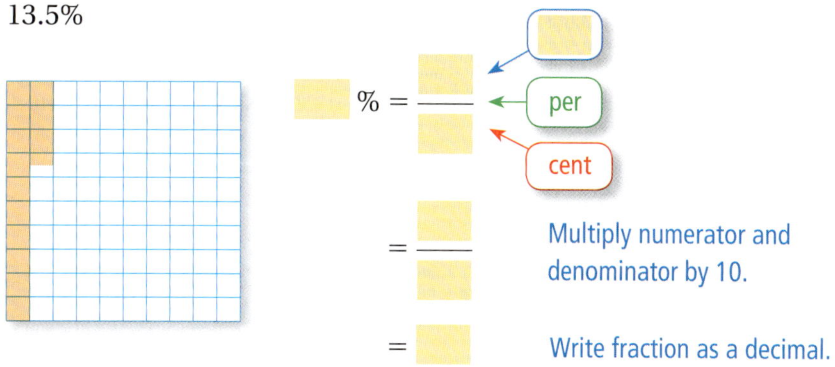

b. 12.5% **c.** 3.8% **d.** 0.5%

3 ACTIVITY: Writing Decimals as Percents

Work with a partner. Draw a model to represent the decimal. Write the decimal as a percent.

a. 0.1

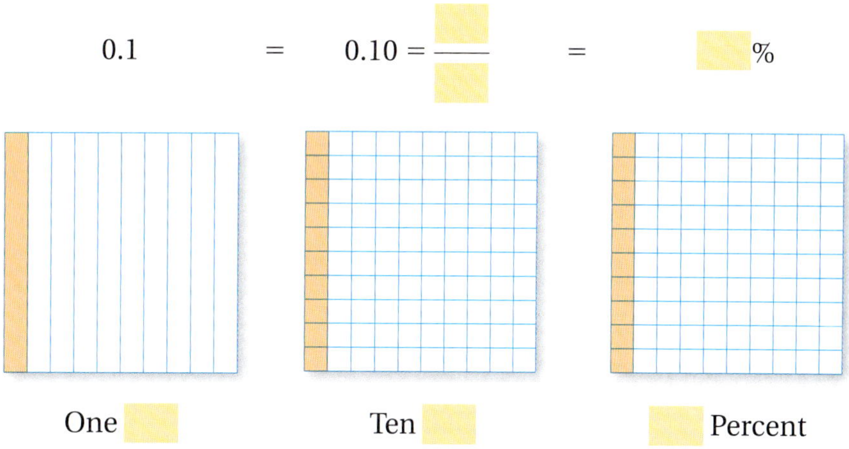

b. 0.24 **c.** 0.58 **d.** 0.05

What Is Your Answer?

4. **IN YOUR OWN WORDS** How does the decimal point move when you rewrite a percent as a decimal and when you rewrite a decimal as a percent?

5. Explain why the decimal point moves when you rewrite a percent as a decimal and when you rewrite a decimal as a percent.

Practice Use what you learned about percents and decimals to complete Exercises 7–12 and 19–24 on page 148.

4.6 Lesson

Check It Out
Lesson Tutorials
BigIdeasMath.com

Key Idea

Writing Percents as Decimals

Words Remove the percent symbol. Then divide by 100, or just move the decimal point two places to the left.

Numbers $23\% = 23.\% = 0.23$

EXAMPLE 1 Writing Percents as Decimals

a. Write 52% as a decimal.

$52\% = 52.\% = 0.52$

Check

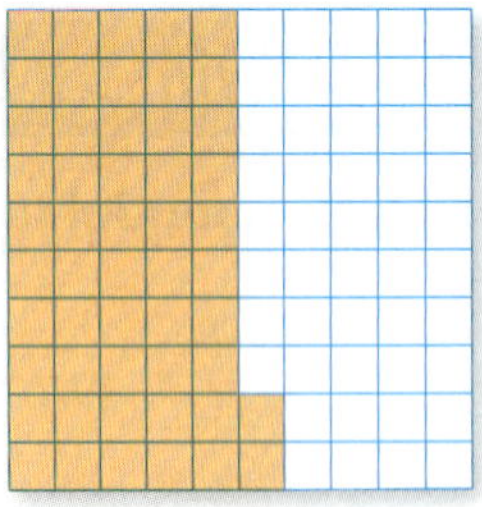

b. Write 7% as a decimal.

$7\% = 07.\% = 0.07$

Check

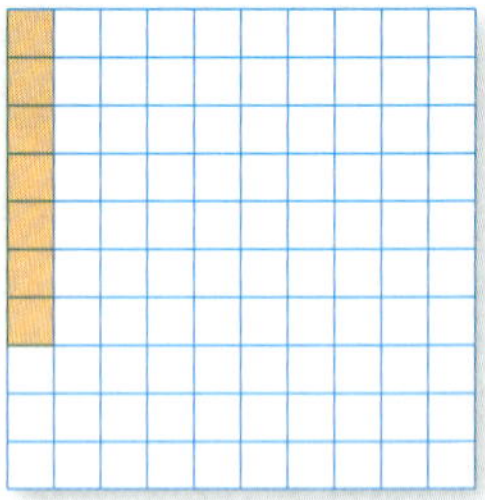

Study Tip

When moving the decimal point, you may need to place one or more zeros in the number.

On Your Own

Now You're Ready
Exercises 7–18

Write the percent as a decimal. Use a model to check your answer.

1. 24%
2. 3%
3. 107%
4. 92.7%

Key Idea

Writing Decimals as Percents

Words Multiply by 100, or just move the decimal point two places to the right. Then add a percent symbol.

Numbers $0.36 = 0.36 = 36\%$

EXAMPLE 2 Writing Decimals as Percents

a. Write 0.47 as a percent.

$0.47 = 0.47 = 47\%$

b. Write 0.663 as a percent.

$0.663 = 0.663 = 66.3\%$

c. Write 1.8 as a percent.

$1.8 = 1.80 = 180\%$

d. Write 0.009 as a percent.

$0.009 = 0.009 = 0.9\%$

On Your Own

Now You're Ready
Exercises 19–30

Write the decimal as a percent. Use a model to check your answer.

5. 0.94 **6.** 1.2 **7.** 0.316 **8.** 0.005

EXAMPLE 3 Writing a Fraction as a Percent and a Decimal

On a math test, you get 92 out of a possible 100 points. Which of the following is *not* another way of expressing 92 out of 100?

Ⓐ $\frac{23}{25}$ Ⓑ 92% Ⓒ $\frac{17}{20}$ Ⓓ 0.92

92 out of 100 $= \frac{92}{100}$

→ $= 92\%$ Eliminate Choice B.

→ $= \frac{23}{25}$ Eliminate Choice A.

→ $= 0.92$ Eliminate Choice D.

So, the correct answer is Ⓒ.

EXAMPLE 4 Real-Life Application

The figure shows the portions of ultraviolet (UV) rays reflected by four different surfaces. How many times more UV rays are reflected by water than by sea foam?

Write 25% and $\frac{21}{25}$ as decimals.

Sea foam: $25\% = 25.\% = 0.25$ **Water:** $\frac{21}{25} = \frac{84}{100} = 0.84$

Divide 0.84 by 0.25: $0.25\overline{)0.84} \rightarrow 25\overline{)84.00}$ = 3.36

So, water reflects about 3.4 times more UV rays than sea foam.

On Your Own

9. Write "18 out of 100" as a percent, a fraction, and a decimal.

10. In Example 4, how many times more UV rays are reflected by water than by sand?

4.6 Exercises

Check It Out
Help with Homework
BigIdeasMath.com

Vocabulary and Concept Check

MATCHING **Match the decimal with its equivalent percent.**

1. 0.42
2. 4.02
3. 0.042
4. 0.0402

A. 4.02%
B. 42%
C. 4.2%
D. 402%

5. **OPEN-ENDED** Write three different decimals that are between 10% and 20%.
6. **WHICH ONE DOESN'T BELONG?** Which one does *not* belong with the other three? Explain your reasoning.

70% | 0.7 | $\frac{7}{10}$ | 0.07

Practice and Problem Solving

Write the percent as a decimal.

(1)
7. 78%
8. 55%
9. 18.5%
10. 57.4%
11. 33%
12. 9%
13. 47.63%
14. 91.25%
15. 166%
16. 217%
17. 0.06%
18. 0.034%

Write the decimal as a percent.

(2)
19. 0.74
20. 0.52
21. 0.89
22. 0.768
23. 0.99
24. 0.49
25. 0.487
26. 0.128
27. 3.68
28. 5.12
29. 0.0371
30. 0.0046

31. **ERROR ANALYSIS** Describe and correct the error in writing 0.86 as a percent.

✗ $0.86 = 00.86 = 0.0086\%$

32. **MUSIC** Thirty-six percent of the songs on your MP3 player are pop songs. Write this percent as a decimal.
33. **CAT** About 0.34 of the length of a cat is its tail. Write this decimal as a percent.
34. **COMPUTER** Write the percent of free space on the computer as a decimal.

Volume	Capacity	Free Space	% Free Space
(C:)	149 GB	133 GB	89%

Write the percent as a fraction in simplest form and as a decimal.

35. 36%
36. 23.5%
37. 16.24%

38. **SCHOOL** The percents of students who travel to school by car, bus, and bicycle are shown for a school of 825 students.

Car: 20%

School bus: 48%

Bicycle: 8%

a. Write the percents as decimals.

b. Write the percents as fractions.

c. What percent of students use another method to travel to school?

d. **RESEARCH** Make a bar graph that represents how the students in your class travel to school.

39. **ELECTIONS** In an election, the winning candidate receives 60% of the votes. What percent of the votes does the other candidate receive?

40. **COLORS** Students in a class were asked to tell their favorite color.

a. What percent said red, blue, or yellow?

b. How many times more students said red than yellow?

c. Use two methods to find the percent of students who said green. Which method do you prefer?

Favorite Color

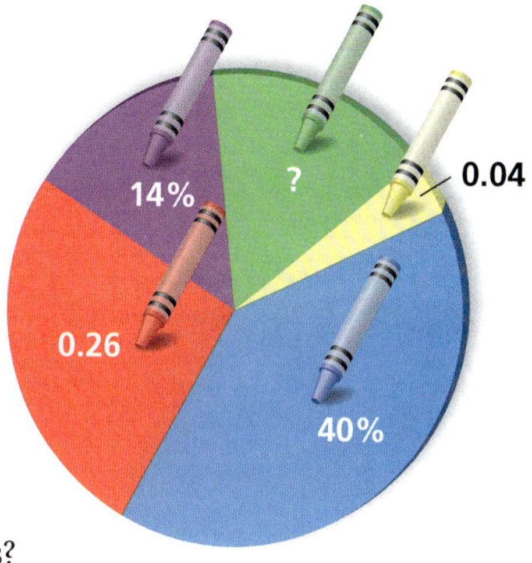

41. Problem Solving In the first 42 Super Bowls, $0.1\overline{6}$ of the MVPs (most valuable players) were running backs.

a. What percent of the MVPs were running backs?

b. What fraction of the MVPs were *not* running backs?

Fair Game Review What you learned in previous grades & lessons

Write the decimal as a fraction or mixed number in simplest form.

42. 0.46 **43.** 0.31 **44.** 2.2 **45.** 4.32

Copy and complete the statement using <, >, or =.

46. $5 \ \square \ |-8|$ **47.** $|-6| \ \square \ 6$

48. $-11 \ \square \ |-12|$ **49.** $|-3| \ \square \ |-1|$

50. **MULTIPLE CHOICE** Ham costs \$4.48 per pound. Cheese costs \$6.36 per pound. You buy 1.5 pounds of ham and 0.75 pound of cheese. How much more do you pay for the ham?

Ⓐ \$1.41 Ⓑ \$1.95 Ⓒ \$4.77 Ⓓ \$6.18

4.7 Comparing and Ordering Fractions, Decimals, and Percents

Essential Question How can you order numbers that are written as fractions, decimals, and percents?

1 ACTIVITY: Using Fractions, Decimals, and Percents

Work with a partner. Decide which number form (fraction, decimal, or percent) is more common. Then find which is greater.

a. 7% sales tax or $\frac{1}{20}$ sales tax

b. 0.37 cup of flour or $\frac{1}{3}$ cup of flour

c. $\frac{5}{8}$-inch wrench or 0.375-inch wrench

d. $12\frac{3}{5}$ dollars or 12.56 dollars

e. 93% test score or $\frac{7}{8}$ test score

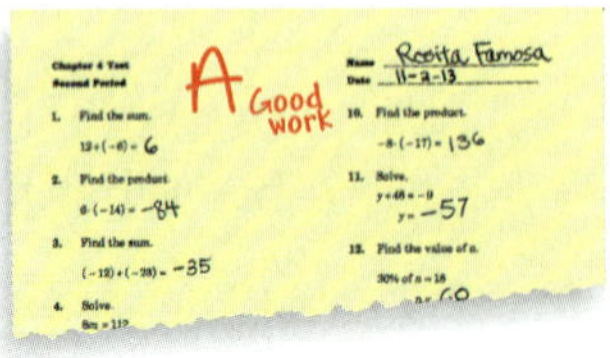

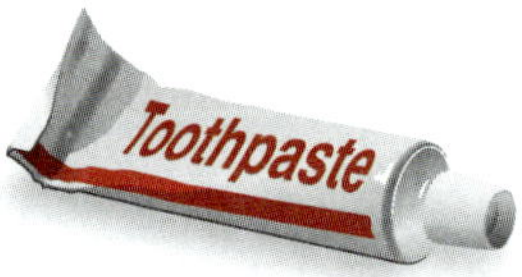

f. $5\frac{5}{6}$ fluid ounces or 5.6 fluid ounces

Fractions, Decimals, and Percents

In this lesson, you will

- compare and order fractions, decimals, and percents.
- solve real-life problems.

2 ACTIVITY: Ordering Numbers

Work with a partner to order the following numbers.

$\frac{1}{8}$ 11% $\frac{3}{20}$ 0.172 0.32 43% 7% 0.7 $\frac{5}{6}$

a. Decide on a strategy for ordering the numbers. Will you write them all as fractions, decimals, or percents?

b. Use your strategy and a number line to order the numbers from least to greatest. (Note: Label the number line appropriately.)

3 ACTIVITY: The Game of Math Card War

Math Process

Make Sense of Quantities

What strategies can you use to determine which number is greater?

Preparation:

- Cut index cards to make 40 playing cards.
- Write each number in the table onto a card.

To Play:

- Play with a partner.
- Deal 20 cards facedown to each player.
- Each player turns one card faceup. The player with the greater number wins. The winner collects both cards and places them at the bottom of his or her cards.
- Suppose there is a tie. Each player lays three cards facedown, then a new card faceup. The player with the greater of these new cards wins. The winner collects all 10 cards and places them at the bottom of his or her cards.
- Continue playing until one player has all the cards. This player wins the game.

75%	$\frac{3}{4}$	$\frac{1}{3}$	$\frac{3}{10}$	0.3	25%	0.4	0.25	100%	0.27
0.75	$66\frac{2}{3}\%$	12.5%	40%	$\frac{1}{4}$	4%	0.5%	0.04	$\frac{1}{100}$	$\frac{2}{3}$
0	30%	5%	$\frac{27}{100}$	0.05	$33\frac{1}{3}\%$	$\frac{2}{5}$	0.333. . .	27%	1%
1	0.01	$\frac{1}{20}$	$\frac{1}{8}$	0.125	$\frac{1}{25}$	$\frac{1}{200}$	0.005	0.666. . .	0%

What Is Your Answer?

4. **IN YOUR OWN WORDS** How can you order numbers that are written as fractions, decimals, and percents? Give an example with your answer.

5. All but one of the U.S. coins shown has a name that is related to its value. Which one is it? How are the names of the others related to their values?

Practice Use what you learned about ordering numbers to complete Exercises 4–7, 16, and 17 on page 154.

4.7 Lesson

Check It Out
Lesson Tutorials
BigIdeasMath.com

When comparing and ordering fractions, decimals, and percents, write the numbers as all fractions, all decimals, or all percents.

EXAMPLE 1 Comparing Fractions, Decimals, and Percents

a. Which is greater, $\frac{3}{20}$ or 16%?

Write $\frac{3}{20}$ as a percent: $\frac{3}{20} = \frac{15}{100} = 15\%$ (numerator and denominator × 5)

15% is less than 16%. So, 16% is the greater number.

Study Tip

It is usually easier to order decimals or percents than to order fractions.

b. Which is greater, 79% or 0.08?

Write 79% as a decimal: 79% = 79.% = 0.79

0.79 is greater than 0.08. So, 79% is the greater number.

On Your Own

Now You're Ready
Exercises 4–15

1. Which is greater, 25% or $\frac{7}{25}$?
2. Which is greater, 0.49 or 94%?

EXAMPLE 2 Real-Life Application

You, your sister, and a friend each take the same number of shots at a soccer goal. You make 72% of your shots, your sister makes $\frac{19}{25}$ of her shots, and your friend makes 0.67 of his shots. Who made the fewest shots?

Write 72% and $\frac{19}{25}$ as decimals.

You: 72% = 72.% = 0.72

Sister: $\frac{19}{25} = \frac{76}{100} = 0.76$ (numerator and denominator × 4)

Remember

To order numbers from least to greatest, write them as they appear on a number line from left to right.

Graph the decimals on a number line.

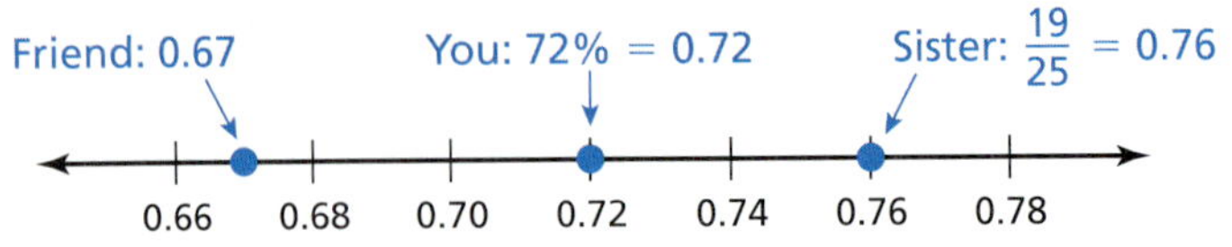

0.67 is the least number. So, your friend made the fewest shots.

On Your Own

Now You're Ready
Exercises 16–21

3. You make 75% of your shots, your sister makes $\frac{13}{20}$ of her shots, and your friend makes 0.7 of his shots. Who made the most shots?

EXAMPLE 3 Real-Life Application

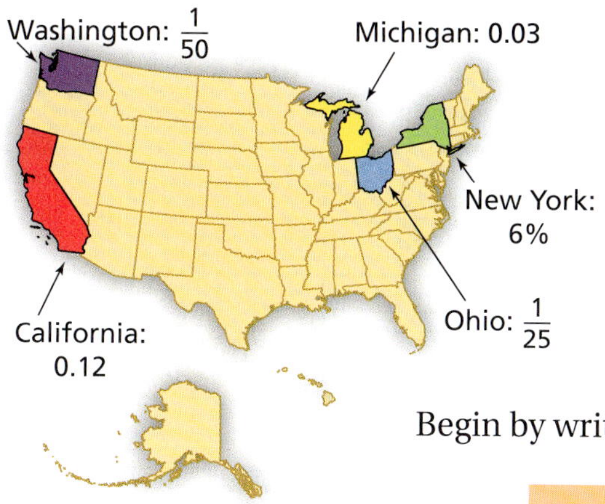

The map shows the portions of the U.S. population that live in five states.

List the five states in order by population from least to greatest.

Begin by writing each portion as a fraction, a decimal, and a percent.

State	Fraction	Decimal	Percent
Michigan	$\frac{3}{100}$	0.03	3%
New York	$\frac{6}{100}$	0.06	6%
Washington	$\frac{1}{50}$	0.02	2%
California	$\frac{12}{100}$	0.12	12%
Ohio	$\frac{1}{25}$	0.04	4%

Graph the percent for each state on a number line.

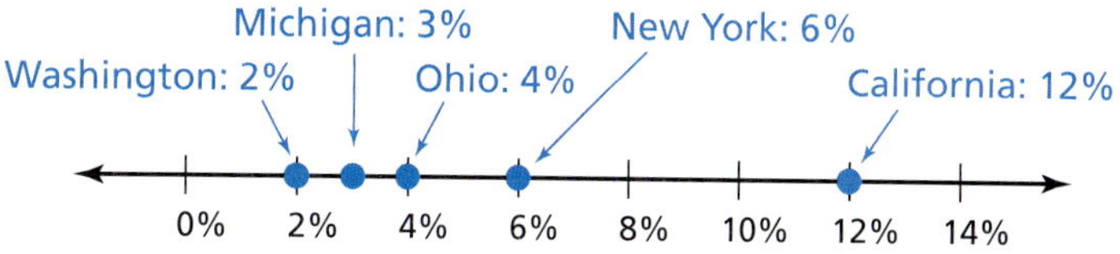

∴ The states in order by population from least to greatest are Washington, Michigan, Ohio, New York, and California.

On Your Own

4. The portion of the U.S. population that lives in Texas is $\frac{2}{25}$. The portion that lives in Illinois is 0.042. Reorder the states in Example 3 including Texas and Illinois.

4.7 Exercises

Check It Out
Help with Homework
BigIdeasMath.com

Vocabulary and Concept Check

1. **NUMBER SENSE** Copy and complete the table.

Fraction	Decimal	Percent
$\frac{18}{25}$	0.72	
$\frac{17}{20}$		85%
$\frac{13}{50}$		
	0.62	
		45%

2. **NUMBER SENSE** How would you decide whether $\frac{3}{5}$ or 59% is greater? Explain.

3. **WHICH ONE DOESN'T BELONG?** Which one does *not* belong with the other three? Explain your reasoning.

40%	$\frac{2}{5}$
0.4	0.04

Practice and Problem Solving

Tell which number is greater.

(1) 4. 0.9, 95%

5. 20%, 0.02

6. $\frac{37}{50}$, 37%

7. 50%, $\frac{13}{25}$

8. 0.086, 86%

9. 76%, 0.67

10. 60%, $\frac{5}{8}$

11. 0.12, 1.2%

12. 17%, $\frac{4}{25}$

13. 140%, 0.14

14. $\frac{1}{3}$, 30%

15. 80%, $\frac{7}{9}$

Use a number line to order the numbers from least to greatest.

(2) 16. 38%, $\frac{8}{25}$, 0.41

17. 68%, 0.63, $\frac{13}{20}$

18. $\frac{43}{50}$, 0.91, $\frac{7}{8}$, 84%

19. 0.15%, $\frac{3}{20}$, 0.015

20. 2.62, $2\frac{2}{5}$, 26.8%, 2.26, 271%

21. $\frac{87}{200}$, 0.44, 43.7%, $\frac{21}{50}$

22. **TEST** You answered 21 out of 25 questions correctly on a test. Did you reach your goal of getting at least 80%?

23. **POPULATION** The table shows the portions of the world population that live in four countries. Order the countries by population from least to greatest.

Country	Brazil	India	Russia	United States
Portion of World Population	2.8%	$\frac{7}{40}$	$\frac{1}{50}$	0.044

PRECISION **Order the numbers from least to greatest.**

24. 66.1%, 0.66, $\frac{2}{3}$, 0.667

25. $\frac{2}{9}$, 21%, $0.2\overline{1}$, $\frac{11}{50}$

Tell which letter shows the graph of the number.

26. $\frac{2}{5}$

27. 45.2%

28. 0.435

29. $\frac{4}{9}$

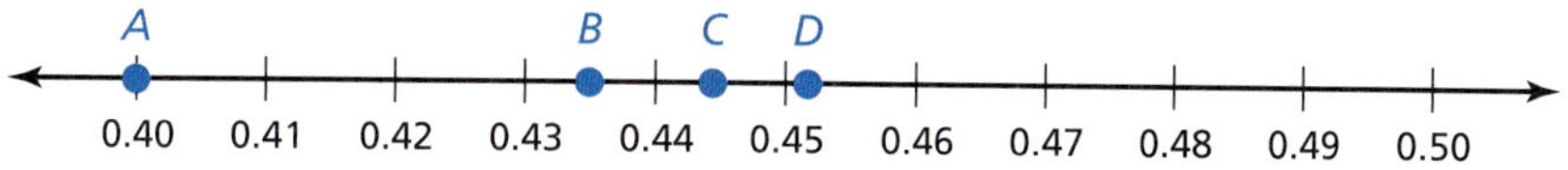

30. **TOUR DE FRANCE** The Tour de France is a bicycle road race. The whole race is made up of 21 small races called *stages*. The table shows how several stages compare to the whole Tour de France in a recent year. Order the stages from shortest to longest.

Stage	1	7	8	17	21
Portion of Total Distance	$\frac{11}{200}$	0.044	$\frac{6}{125}$	0.06	4%

31. **SLEEP** The table shows the portions of the day that several animals sleep.

a. Order the animals by sleep time from least to greatest.

b. Estimate the portion of the day that you sleep.

c. Where do you fit on the ordered list?

Animal	Portion of Day Sleeping
Dolphin	0.433
Lion	56.3%
Rabbit	$\frac{19}{40}$
Squirrel	$\frac{31}{50}$
Tiger	65.8%

32. Number Sense Tell what whole number you can substitute for a in each list so the numbers are ordered from least to greatest. If there is none, explain why.

a. $\frac{2}{a}$, $\frac{a}{22}$, 33%

b. $\frac{1}{a}$, $\frac{a}{8}$, 33%

Fair Game Review What you learned in previous grades & lessons

Multiply.

33. $-3(5)$

34. $0(-7)$

35. $-5(2)(-2)$

36. **MULTIPLE CHOICE** What is the value of $4 + 8 \div 2 - 1$?

Ⓐ 5 Ⓑ 5.5 Ⓒ 7 Ⓓ 12

4 Study Help

Check It Out
Graphic Organizer
BigIdeasMath.com

You can use a **summary triangle** to explain a concept. Here is an example of a summary triangle for writing a percent as a decimal.

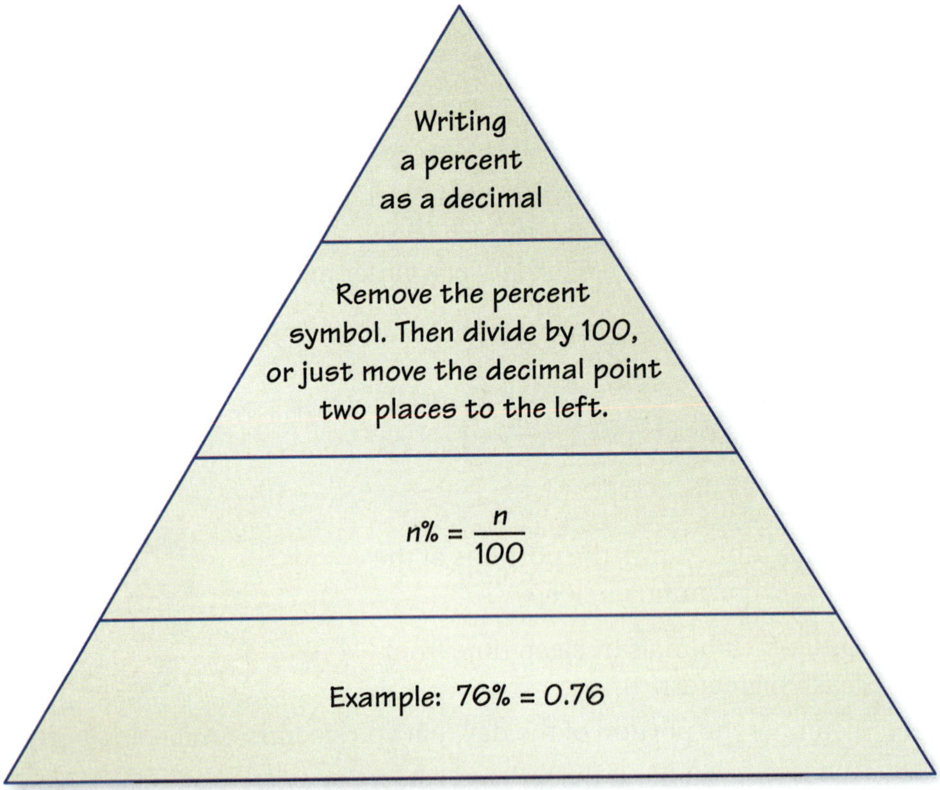

On Your Own

Make summary triangles to help you study these topics.

1. adding and subtracting decimals
2. multiplying decimals by whole numbers
3. multiplying decimals by decimals
4. dividing decimals by whole numbers
5. dividing decimals by decimals
6. writing rational numbers as decimals
7. percent
8. writing a decimal as a percent
9. comparing and ordering fractions, decimals, and percents

"I found this great summary triangle in my *Beautiful Beagle Magazine*."

4 Chapter Review

Check It Out
Vocabulary Help
BigIdeasMath.com

Review Key Vocabulary

rational number, *p. 134*
terminating decimal, *p. 134*
repeating decimal, *p. 134*
percent, *p. 140*

Review Examples and Exercises

4.1 Adding and Subtracting Decimals *(pp. 110–115)*

a. Add 7.36 + 2.22.

Line up the decimal points.

$$\begin{array}{r} 7.36 \\ +\ 2.22 \\ \hline 9.58 \end{array}$$

Add.

b. Subtract 5.467 − 2.736.

Line up the decimal points.

$$\begin{array}{r} \overset{4\,14}{\cancel{5}.\cancel{4}67} \\ -\ 2.736 \\ \hline 2.731 \end{array}$$

Subtract.

Exercises

Add or subtract.

1. $3.78 + 8.94$
2. $19.89 + 4.372$
3. $7.638 - 2.365$
4. $14.21 - 4.103$

4.2 Multiplying Decimals *(pp. 116–123)*

Find 7.5 × 5.3.

$$\begin{array}{r} 7.5 \\ \times\ 5.3 \\ \hline 2\,2\,5 \\ +\ 3\,7\,5 \\ \hline 3\,9.7\,5 \end{array}$$

7.5 ← 1 decimal place
× 5.3 ← + 1 decimal place
39.75 ← 2 decimal places

So, $7.5 \times 5.3 = 39.75$.

Exercises

Multiply. Use estimation to check your answer.

5. 5.3×8
6. 6.1×7
7. 4.68×3
8. 9.475×8.03
9. 0.27×4.42
10. 0.051×0.244

4.3 Dividing Decimals (pp. 124–131)

Find 22.8 ÷ 1.2.

Multiply 1.2 by 10.

Multiply 22.8 by 10.

Place the decimal point above the decimal point in the dividend 228.

$$1.2\overline{)22.8} \rightarrow 12\overline{)228.}$$

$$\begin{array}{r} 19. \\ 12\overline{)228.} \\ -\underline{12} \\ 108 \\ -\underline{108} \\ 0 \end{array}$$

So, 22.8 ÷ 1.2 = 19.

Exercises

Divide. Use estimation to check your answer.

11. 6.8 ÷ 4 **12.** $0.12\overline{)3.6}$ **13.** $3.9\overline{)22.23}$

4.4 Rational Numbers (pp. 132–137)

a. Write $4\frac{3}{5}$ as a decimal.

Notice that $4\frac{3}{5} = \frac{23}{5}$.

Divide 23 by 5.

$$\begin{array}{r} 4.6 \\ 5\overline{)23.0} \\ -\underline{20} \\ 3\,0 \\ -\underline{3\,0} \\ 0 \end{array}$$

The remainder is 0. So, it is a terminating decimal.

So, $4\frac{3}{5} = 4.6$.

b. Write 0.14 as a fraction in simplest form.

$$0.14 = \frac{14}{100} = \frac{7}{50}$$

Exercises

Write the rational number as a decimal.

14. $\frac{8}{15}$ **15.** $\frac{5}{8}$ **16.** $\frac{13}{6}$ **17.** $1\frac{7}{16}$

Write the decimal as a fraction or a mixed number in simplest form.

18. 0.6 **19.** 0.35 **20.** 5.8 **21.** 24.23

4.5 Percents *(pp. 138–143)*

Write $\frac{3}{20}$ as a percent.

$\frac{3}{20} = \frac{15}{100} = 15\%$

Because $20 \times 5 = 100$, multiply the numerator and denominator by 5. Write the numerator with a percent symbol.

Exercises

Write the percent as a fraction or mixed number in simplest form.

22. 12% **23.** 88% **24.** 0.8%

Write the fraction or mixed number as a percent.

25. $\frac{3}{5}$ **26.** $\frac{43}{25}$ **27.** $1\frac{21}{50}$

4.6 Percents and Decimals *(pp. 144–149)*

a. Write 64% as a decimal.

$64\% = 64.\% = 0.64$

b. Write 0.023 as a percent.

$0.023 = 0.023 = 2.3\%$

Exercises

Write the percent as a decimal. Use a model to check your answer.

28. 76% **29.** 6% **30.** 334%

Write the decimal as a percent. Use a model to check your answer.

31. 0.15 **32.** 1.24 **33.** 0.097

4.7 Comparing and Ordering Fractions, Decimals, and Percents
(pp. 150–155)

Which is greater, $\frac{9}{10}$ or 88%?

Write $\frac{9}{10}$ as a percent: $\frac{9}{10} = \frac{90}{100} = 90\%$

88% is less than 90%. So, $\frac{9}{10}$ is the greater number.

Exercises

Tell which number is greater.

34. $\frac{1}{2}$, 52% **35.** $\frac{12}{5}$, 245% **36.** 0.46, 43% **37.** 0.023, 22%

Use a number line to order the numbers from least to greatest.

38. $\frac{41}{50}$, 0.83, 80% **39.** $\frac{9}{4}$, 220%, 2.15 **40.** 0.67, 66%, $\frac{2}{3}$

5 Ratios, Rates, and Proportions

What You Learned Before

Identifying Patterns

Example 1 Using the numbers from the table, find and state the rule in words. Then find the missing value.

x	y
1	6
2	12
3	18
4	

Each y-value is 6 times the x-value.

The x-value times 6 equals the y-value.
The missing value is $6(4) = 24$.

"I wonder if our rate is proportional to the slope of the hill."

Try It Yourself

Using the numbers from the table, find and state the rule in words. Then find the missing value.

1.

x	y
1	2
3	6
5	10
7	

2.

x	y
2	8
4	16
6	24
8	

3.

x	y
1	5
2	10
3	15
4	

Multiplying and Dividing by Fractions

Example 2 Find $\frac{5}{6} \cdot \frac{3}{4}$.

$$\frac{5}{6} \cdot \frac{3}{4} = \frac{5 \cdot \overset{1}{\cancel{3}}}{\underset{2}{\cancel{6}} \cdot 4}$$

$$= \frac{5}{8}$$

Example 3 Find $2 \div \frac{9}{10}$.

$$2 \div \frac{9}{10} = 2 \cdot \frac{10}{9}$$

Multiply by the reciprocal of the divisor.

$$= \frac{2 \cdot 10}{9}$$

$$= \frac{20}{9}$$

Try It Yourself

Evaluate the expression. Write the answer in simplest form.

4. $\frac{1}{5} \cdot \frac{13}{20}$ **5.** $\frac{3}{4} \cdot \frac{13}{25}$ **6.** $7 \div \frac{9}{10}$ **7.** $4 \div \frac{16}{17}$

5.1 Ratios

Essential Question How can you represent a relationship between two quantities?

1 ACTIVITY: Comparing Quantities

Work with a partner. Use the collection of objects to complete each statement.

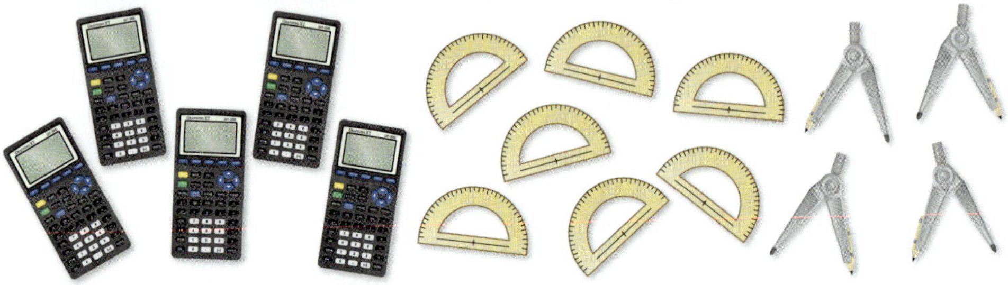

There are ▢ graphing calculators to ▢ protractors.

There are ▢ protractors to ▢ graphing calculators.

There are ▢ compasses to ▢ protractors.

There are ▢ graphing calculators to ▢ compasses.

There are ▢ protractors to ▢ total objects.

The number of graphing calculators is $\frac{\square}{\square}$ of the total number of objects.

2 ACTIVITY: Playing Garbage Basketball

Work with a partner.

- **Take turns shooting a ball or other object into a wastebasket from a reasonable distance.**
- **Organize the numbers of shots you made and shots you missed in a chart.**

a. Write a statement similar to those in Activity 1 that describes the relationship between the number of shots you made and the number of shots you missed.

b. Write a statement similar to those in Activity 1 that describes the relationship between the number of shots you made and the total number of shots.

c. What fraction of your shots did you make? What fraction did you miss?

Ratios

In this lesson, you will
- understand the concept of a ratio.
- use ratios to describe the relationship between two quantities.

3 ACTIVITY: Reading a Diagram

Work with a partner. You mix different amounts of paint to create new colors. Write a statement that describes the relationship between the amounts of paint shown in each diagram.

a. Blue 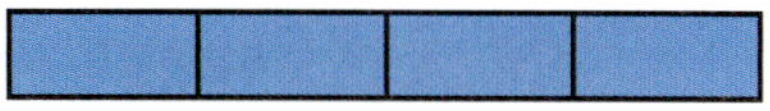

Green 

There are ____ parts blue for every ____ parts green.

b. Orange 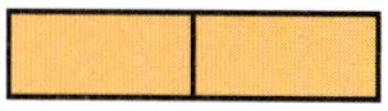

Yellow 

There are ____ for every ____.

c. Red 

Blue 

____.

d. White 

Purple

____.

4 ACTIVITY: Describing Relationships

Math Process

Use a Table or Diagram

What are the quantities in this problem? How does a table or diagram represent the relationship between the quantities?

Work with a partner. Use a table or a diagram to represent the relationship between the two quantities.

a. For every 3 boys standing in a line, there are 4 girls.

b. For each vote Brian received, Sasha received 6 votes.

c. A class counts the number of vehicles that pass by its school from 1:00 to 2:00 P.M. There are 3 times as many cars as trucks.

d. A hand sanitizer contains 5 parts aloe for every 2 parts distilled water.

What Is Your Answer?

5. **IN YOUR OWN WORDS** How can you represent a relationship between two quantities? Give examples to support your explanation.

6. **MODELING** You make 48 pints of pink paint by using 5 pints of red paint for every 3 pints of white paint. Use a diagram to find the number of pints of red paint and white paint in your mixture. Explain.

Practice Use what you learned about comparing two quantities to complete Exercises 4 and 5 on page 166.

5.1 Lesson

Check It Out
Lesson Tutorials
BigIdeasMath.com

Key Vocabulary
ratio, *p. 164*

Key Idea

Ratio

Words A **ratio** is a comparison of two quantities. Ratios can be part-to-part, part-to-whole, or whole-to-part comparisons.

Examples
2 red crayons *to* 6 blue crayons
1 red crayon *for every* 3 blue crayons
3 blue crayons *per* 1 red crayon
3 blue crayons *for each* red crayon
3 blue crayons *out of every* 4 crayons
2 red crayons *out of* 8 crayons

Algebra The ratio of a to b can be written as $a : b$. For a part-to-whole relationship, the ratio of a to b can also be written as $\frac{a}{b}$.

EXAMPLE 1 Writing Ratios

You have the coins shown.

a. Write the ratio of pennies to quarters.

6 pennies → 6 to 7 ← 7 quarters

So, the ratio of pennies to quarters is 6 to 7 or 6 : 7.

b. Write the ratio of dimes to the total number of coins.

3 dimes → 3 to 16 ← 16 coins

So, the ratio of dimes to the total number of coins is 3 to 16, 3 : 16, or $\frac{3}{16}$.

Remember

Part-to-whole relationships compare a part of a whole to the whole. Fractions represent part-to-whole relationships. Part-to-part relationships compare a part of a whole to another part of the whole.

On Your Own

Now You're Ready
Exercises 6–13

1. In Example 1, write the ratio of dimes to pennies.
2. The circle graph shows the favorite ice-cream toppings of several students. Use ratio language to compare the number of students who favor peanuts to the total number of students.

Favorite Toppings

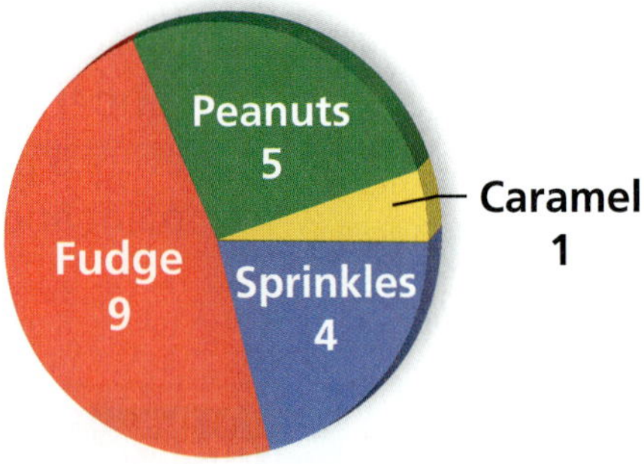

Multi-Language Glossary at BigIdeasMath.com

A *tape diagram* is a diagram that looks like a segment of tape. It shows the relationship between two quantities.

EXAMPLE 2 Using a Tape Diagram

The ratio of your monthly allowance to your friend's monthly allowance is 5 : 3. The monthly allowances total \$40. How much is each allowance?

To help visualize the problem, express the ratio 5 : 3 using a tape diagram.

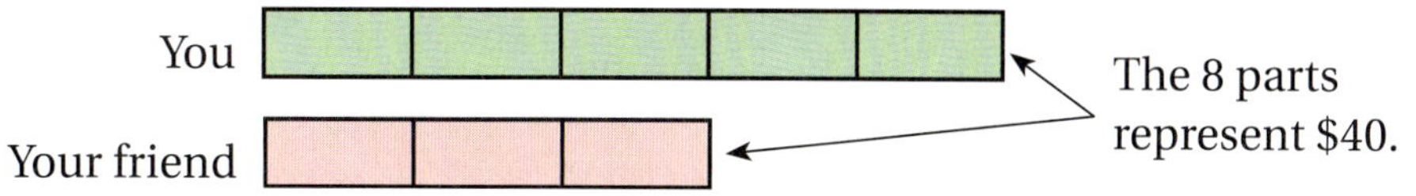

Because there are 8 parts, you know that 1 part represent \$40 ÷ 8 = \$5.

5 parts represent \$5 • 5 = \$25.

3 parts represent \$5 • 3 = \$15.

∴ So, your monthly allowance is \$25, and your friend's monthly allowance is \$15.

EXAMPLE 3 Using a Tape Diagram

You separate 42 bulbs of garlic into two groups: one for planting and one for cooking. You will plant 3 bulbs for every 4 bulbs that you will use for cooking. Each bulb has about 8 cloves. About how many cloves will you plant?

To help visualize the problem, express the ratio *3 for every 4* using a tape diagram.

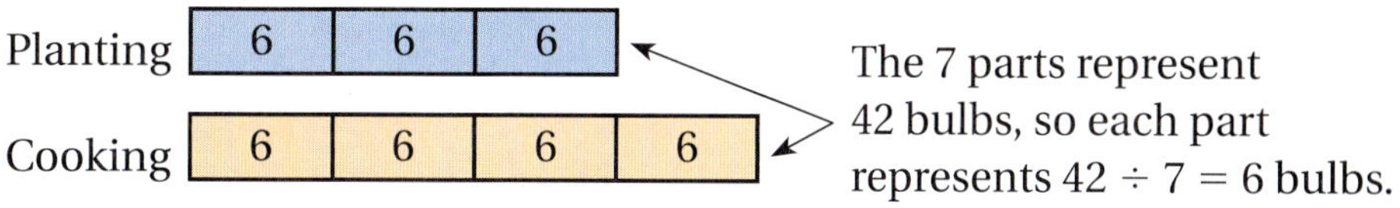

There are 3 • 6 = 18 bulbs for planting and 4 • 6 = 24 bulbs for cooking. The group of 18 bulbs has about 18 • 8 = 144 cloves.

∴ So, you will plant about 144 cloves.

On Your Own

Now You're Ready
Exercises 15 and 16

3. **WHAT IF?** In Example 2, the ratio is 2 to 3. How much is each allowance?

4. **WHAT IF?** In Example 3, you will plant 1 bulb for every 2 bulbs that you will use for cooking. Will you plant more or fewer cloves than originally planned? Explain your reasoning.

5.1 Exercises

Check It Out
Help with Homework
BigIdeasMath.com

Vocabulary and Concept Check

1. **VOCABULARY** The ratio of vowels to consonants in a word is 5 to 7. Are there more vowels or consonants in the word? Explain.

2. **NUMBER SENSE** You are comparing apples to oranges in a fruit bowl. Is the ratio 2 : 3 the same as the ratio 3 : 2? Explain.

3. **WHICH ONE DOESN'T BELONG?** Which ratio does *not* belong with the other three? Explain your reasoning.

2 parts to 5 parts	2 out of every 5	2 for each 5	2 for every 5

Practice and Problem Solving

Use a table or a diagram to represent the relationship between the two quantities.

4. For each lion, there are 7 giraffes.

5. For every 5 seats, there are 4 fans.

Write the ratio. Explain what the ratio means.

6. frogs to turtles

7. basketballs to soccer balls

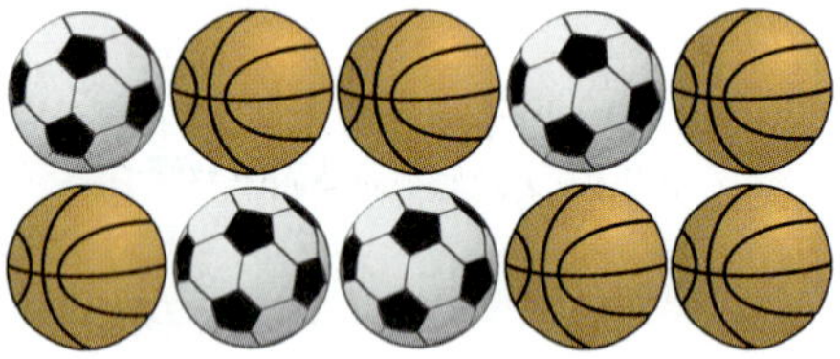

8. calculators : pencils

9. shirts : pants

Use the table to write the ratio. Explain what the ratio means.

10. dramas to movies

11. comedies to movies

12. movies : action

13. movies : dramas

Movie	Number
Drama	3
Comedy	8
Action	4

Topic	Stamps
Birds	7
Celebrity	14
Horses	5
Ships	9

14. **STAMP COLLECTING** The table shows the numbers of stamps in a new stamp collection. Use ratio language to compare the number of celebrity stamps to the total number of stamps.

You and a friend tutor for a total of 12 hours. Use the tape diagram to find how many hours you tutor.

15. 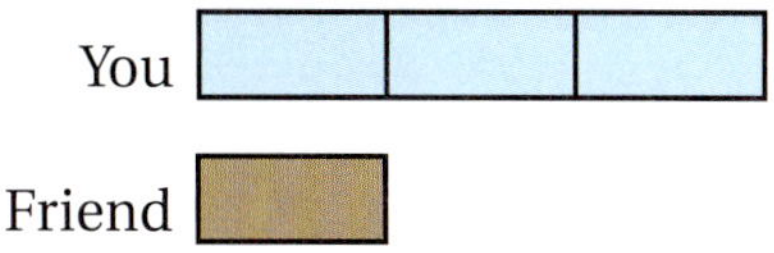

16. 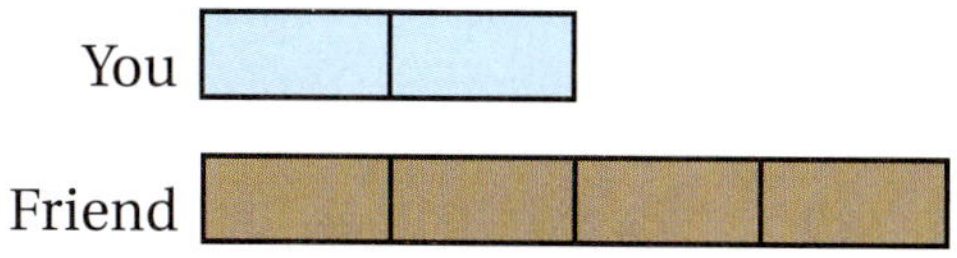

17. REASONING Twelve of the 28 students in a class have a dog. What is the ratio of students who have a dog to students who do not?

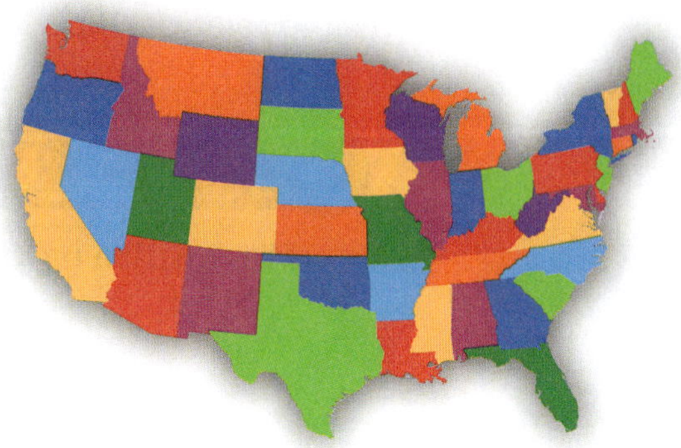

18. GEOGRAPHY In the continental United States, the ratio of states that border an ocean to states that do not border an ocean is 7 : 9. How many of the states border an ocean?

19. CHECKERS During a checkers game, there are 16 pieces left. The ratio of black to red is 3 : 5. How many black pieces are on the board? Explain how you found your answer.

20. SCHOOL PLAY There are 48 students in a school play. The ratio of boys to girls is 5 : 7. How many more girls than boys are in the play? Explain how you found your answer.

21. GEOMETRY Use the blue and green rectangles.

a. Find the ratio of the length of the blue rectangle to the length of the green rectangle. Repeat this for width, perimeter, and area.

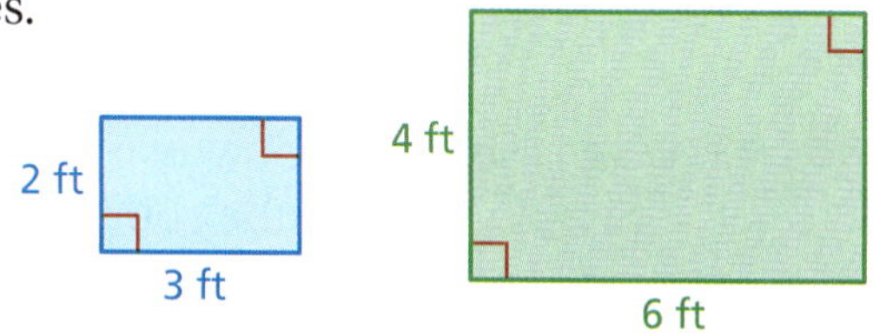

b. Compare and contrast your ratios in part (a).

22. PERIMETER The ratio of the side lengths of a triangle is 2 : 3 : 4. The shortest side is 15 inches. What is the perimeter? Explain.

23. PRECISION You mix soda water, fruit punch concentrate, and ginger ale in the ratio of 1 : 2 : 5 to make fruit punch. How many pints of each ingredient should you use to make 4 gallons of fruit punch? Is your answer reasonable? Explain.

24. Reasoning There are 12 boys and 10 girls in your gym class. If 6 boys joined the class, how many girls would need to join for the ratio of boys to girls to remain the same? Justify your answer.

Fair Game Review What you learned in previous grades & lessons

Divide.

25. 13.8 ÷ 3 **26.** 16.45 ÷ 5 **27.** 53.13 ÷ 21 **28.** 19.214 ÷ 13

29. MULTIPLE CHOICE What is the value of 30 ÷ 18?

Ⓐ $\frac{3}{5}$ Ⓑ $1\frac{2}{3}$ Ⓒ 12 Ⓓ 48

5.2 Ratio Tables

Essential Question How can you find two ratios that describe the same relationship?

1 ACTIVITY: Making a Mixture

Work with a partner. A mixture calls for 1 cup of lemonade and 3 cups of iced tea.

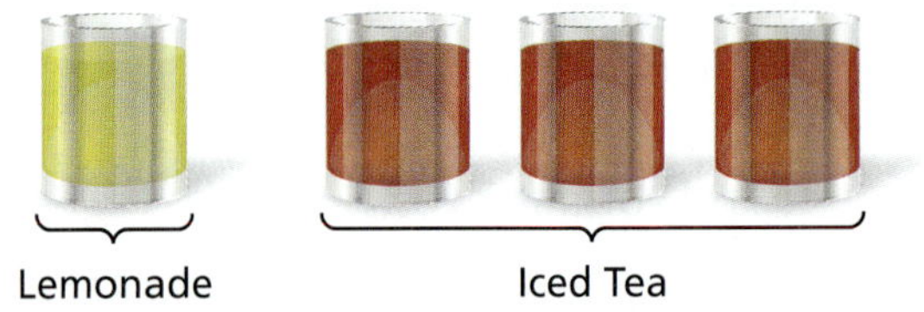

a. How many total cups does the mixture contain? ____ cups

For every ____ cup of lemonade, there are ____ cups of iced tea.

b. How do you make a larger batch of this mixture? Describe your procedure and use the table below to organize your results. Add more columns to the table if needed.

Cups of Lemonade						
Cups of Iced Tea						
Total Cups						

c. Which operations did you use to complete your table? Do you think there is more than one way to complete the table? Explain.

d. How many total cups are in your final mixture? How many of those cups are lemonade? How many are iced tea? Compare your results with those of other groups in your class.

e. Suppose you take a sip from every group's final mixture. Do you think all the mixtures should taste the same? Do you think the color of all the mixtures should be the same? Explain your reasoning.

f. Why do you think it is useful to use a table when organizing your results in this activity? Explain.

Ratios

In this lesson, you will

- use ratio tables to find equivalent ratios.
- solve real-life problems.

2 ACTIVITY: Using a Multiplication Table

Math Process
Use Operations
For each part of this problem, how do you know which operation to use?

Work with a partner. Use the information in Activity 1 and the multiplication table below.

	1	2	3	4	5	6	7	8	9	10	11	12
1	1	2	3	4	5	6	7	8	9	10	11	12
2	2	4	6	8	10	12	14	16	18	20	22	24
3	3	6	9	12	15	18	21	24	27	30	33	36
4	4	8	12	16	20	24	28	32	36	40	44	48

a. A mixture contains 8 cups of lemonade. How many cups of iced tea are in the mixture?

b. A mixture contains 21 cups of iced tea. How many cups of lemonade are in the mixture?

c. A mixture has a total of 40 cups. How many cups are lemonade? How many are iced tea?

d. **REPEATED REASONING** Explain how a multiplication table may have helped you in Activity 1.

3 ACTIVITY: Using More than One Ratio to Describe a Quantity

Work with a partner.

a. Find the ratio of pitchers of lemonade to pitchers of iced tea.

b. How can you divide the pitchers into equal groups? Is there more than one way? Use your results to describe the entire collection of pitchers.

c. Three more pitchers of lemonade are added. Is there more than one way to divide the pitchers into equal groups? Explain.

d. The number of pitchers of lemonade and iced tea are doubled. Can you use the ratio in part (b) to describe the entire collection of pitchers? Explain.

What Is Your Answer?

4. **IN YOUR OWN WORDS** How can you find two ratios that describe the same relationship? Give examples to support your explanation.

Practice Use what you learned about ratios to complete Exercises 4 and 5 on page 173.

5.2 Lesson

Check It Out
Lesson Tutorials
BigIdeasMath.com

Key Vocabulary

equivalent ratios, *p. 170*

ratio table, *p. 170*

Two ratios that describe the same relationship are **equivalent ratios**. You can find equivalent ratios by:

- adding or subtracting quantities in equivalent ratios.
- multiplying or dividing each quantity in a ratio by the same number.

You can find and organize equivalent ratios in a **ratio table**.

EXAMPLE 1 Completing Ratio Tables

Find the missing value(s) in each ratio table. Then write the equivalent ratios.

a.

Pens	1	2	
Pencils	3		9

b.

Dogs	4		24
Cats	6	12	

a. You can use repeated addition with the original ratio to find the missing values.

+1 +1

Pens	1	2	3
Pencils	3	6	9

+3 +3

The equivalent ratios are 1 : 3, 2 : 6, and 3 : 9.

b. You can use multiplication to find the missing values.

×2 ×3

Dogs	4	8	24
Cats	6	12	36

×2 ×3

The equivalent ratios are 4 : 6, 8 : 12, and 24 : 36.

On Your Own

Now You're Ready
Exercises 6–9

Find the missing value(s) in the ratio table. Then write the equivalent ratios.

1.

Plantains	4		12
Bananas	3	6	

2.

Euros	5	10	
Dollars	4		32

Multi-Language Glossary at BigIdeasMath.com

EXAMPLE 2 Making a Ratio Table

You are making sugar water for your hummingbird feeder. A website indicates to use 4 parts of water for every 1 part of sugar. You use 20 cups of water. How much sugar do you need?

You can solve this problem by using equivalent ratios. The ratio of water to sugar is 4 parts to 1 part. So, for every 4 cups of water, you need 1 cup of sugar. Find an equivalent ratio with 20 parts water.

Method 1: Use a ratio table and addition.

You can think of making a larger batch of sugar water as combining several batches of 4 to 1 mixtures. Use addition to obtain 20 in the water column.

+4 +4 +4 +4

Water (cups)	4	8	12	16	20
Sugar (cups)	1	2	3	4	5

+1 +1 +1 +1

STEM VIDEO

The ratio 20 to 5 is equivalent to 4 to 1.

So, you need 5 cups of sugar.

Method 2: Use a ratio table and multiplication.

You multiplied the amount of water in the recipe by 5 because $20 \div 4 = 5$. So, you need to multiply the amount of sugar by 5. Multiply each part of the ratio in the original recipe by 5.

×5

Water (cups)	4	20
Sugar (cups)	1	5

×5

The ratio 20 to 5 is equivalent to 4 to 1.

So, you need 5 cups of sugar.

Study Tip

In Example 2, Method 1, notice that you can eliminate a step by adding columns 2 and 3 to obtain $8 + 12 = 20$ cups of water for $2 + 3 = 5$ cups of sugar.

On Your Own

Now You're Ready Exercises 13 and 14

3. **WHAT IF?** You use 24 cups of water. How much sugar do you need?
4. You make a sweeter mixture of sugar water for your hummingbird feeder using 3 parts of water for every 1 part of sugar. You use 9 quarts of water. How much sugar do you need?

EXAMPLE 3 Using a Ratio Table

The nutrition facts label on a box of crackers shows that there are 240 milligrams of sodium in every 36 crackers.

a. You eat 15 crackers. How much sodium do you consume?

The ratio of sodium to crackers is 240 to 36. Use a ratio table to find an equivalent ratio with 15 crackers.

$\div 2$ $\quad \div 6$ $\quad \times 5$

Sodium (milligrams)	240	120	20	100
Crackers	36	18	3	15

$\div 2$ $\quad \div 6$ $\quad \times 5$

The ratio 100 to 15 is equivalent to 240 to 36.

∴ So, you consume 100 milligrams of sodium.

b. You eat 21 crackers. How much sodium do you consume?

Notice that you can add the two middle columns in the table above.

∴ So, you consume $120 + 20 = 140$ milligrams of sodium in $18 + 3 = 21$ crackers.

Study Tip

In Example 3, notice that you could use one step in the ratio table: multiply by

$\frac{1}{2} \cdot \frac{1}{6} \cdot 5 = \frac{5}{12}$.

EXAMPLE 4 Using a Ratio Table

You mix 3 pints of yellow paint for every 4 pints of blue paint to make green paint. You use 10 pints of blue paint. How much green paint do you make?

The ratio of yellow paint to blue paint is 3 to 4. Use a ratio table to find an equivalent ratio with 10 parts blue paint.

$\div 2$ $\quad \times 5$

Yellow (pints)	3	$\frac{3}{2}$	$7\frac{1}{2}$
Blue (pints)	4	2	10

$\div 2$ $\quad \times 5$

You use $7\frac{1}{2}$ pints of yellow paint and 10 pints of blue paint.

∴ So, you make $7\frac{1}{2} + 10 = 17\frac{1}{2}$ pints of green paint.

Study Tip

In Example 4, notice that you could use one step in the ratio table: multiply by

$\frac{1}{2} \cdot 5 = \frac{5}{2}$.

On Your Own

Now You're Ready
Exercises 15 and 16

5. **WHAT IF?** In Example 3, you eat 24 crackers. How much sodium do you consume?

6. **WHAT IF?** In Example 4, you mix 2 pints of yellow paint for every 3 pints of blue paint. You use 5 pints of yellow paint. How much green paint do you make?

5.2 Exercises

Check It Out
Help with Homework
BigIdeasMath.com

Vocabulary and Concept Check

1. **VOCABULARY** How can you tell whether two ratios are equivalent?

2. **NUMBER SENSE** Consider the ratio 3 : 5. Can you create an equivalent ratio by adding the same number to each quantity in the ratio? Explain.

3. **WHICH ONE DOESN'T BELONG?** Which ratio does *not* belong with the other three? Explain your reasoning.

   3 : 4   9 : 12   12 : 15   12 : 16

Practice and Problem Solving

Write several ratios that describe the collection.

4. baseballs to gloves

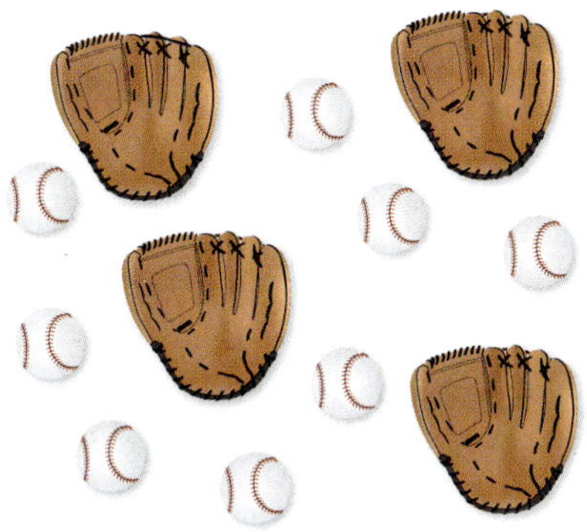

5. ladybugs to bees

Find the missing value(s) in the ratio table. Then write the equivalent ratios.

1 6.

Boys	1	
Girls	5	10

7.

Violins	8	24
Cellos	3	

8.

Taxis	6		36
Buses	5	15	

9.

Burgers	3		9
Hot Dogs	5	10	

Construct a ratio table for the ratio. Include at least three equivalent ratios.

10. 14 towels : 8 blankets

11. 16 forks : 10 spoons

12. **WORK** Your neighbor pays you $17 for every 2 hours you work. You work for 8 hours on Saturday. How much does your neighbor owe you?

Complete the ratio table to solve the problem.

2 **13.** For every 3 tickets you sell, your friend sells 4. You sell a total of 12 tickets. How many does your friend sell?

You	3			12
Friend	4			

14. A store sells 2 printers for every 5 computers. The store sells 40 computers. How many printers does the store sell?

Printers	2		8	
Computers	5	10		40

3 **15.** First and second place in a contest use a ratio to share a cash prize. When first place pays \$100, second place pays \$60. How much does first place pay when second place pays \$36?

First	100		
Second	60		36

16. A grade has 81 girls and 72 boys. The grade is split into groups that have the same ratio of girls to boys as the whole grade. How many girls are in a group that has 16 boys?

Girls	81		
Boys	72		16

ERROR ANALYSIS **Describe and correct the error in making the ratio table.**

17. ✗

A	3	8	13
B	7	12	17

18. ✗

A	5	25	125
B	3	9	27

19. **DONATION** A sports store donates basketballs and soccer balls to the boys and girls club. The ratio of basketballs to soccer balls is 7 : 6. The store donates 24 soccer balls. How many basketballs does the store donate?

20. **DOWNLOAD** You are downloading songs to your MP3 player. The ratio of pop songs to rock songs is 5 : 4. You download 40 pop songs. How many rock songs do you download?

SCRAMBLED EGGS **In Exercises 21–25, use the ratio table showing different batches of the same recipe for scrambled eggs.**

Recipe	A	B	C	D	E	F
Servings	4	2	6	3	5	9
Eggs	8	4	12	6	10	18
Milk (cups)	$\frac{1}{2}$	$\frac{1}{4}$	$\frac{3}{4}$	$\frac{3}{8}$	$\frac{5}{8}$	$1\frac{1}{8}$

21. How can you use Recipes B and D to create Recipe E?

22. How can you use Recipes C and D to create Recipe F?

23. How can you use Recipes B and C to create Recipe A?

24. How can you use Recipes C and F to create Recipe D?

25. Describe one way to use the recipes to create a batch with 11 servings.

Two whole numbers A and B satisfy the following conditions. Find A and B.

26. $A + B = 30$
$A : B$ is equivalent to $2 : 3$.

27. $A + B = 44$
$A : B$ is equivalent to $4 : 7$.

28. $A - B = 18$
$A : B$ is equivalent to $11 : 5$.

29. $A - B = 25$
$A : B$ is equivalent to $13 : 8$.

Nutrition Facts
Serving Size: 1 ounce (28g)

Amount Per Serving	
Calories 161	Calories from Fat 109
	% Daily Value*
Total Fat 13g	20%
Saturated Fat 3g	13%
Trans Fat	
Cholesterol 0mg	0%
Sodium 4mg	0%
Total Carbohydrate 9g	3%
Dietary Fiber 1g	3%
Sugars 1g	
Protein 4g	
Vitamin A 0% • Vitamin C	0%
Calcium 1% • Iron	9%

*Percent Daily Values are based on a 2,000 calorie diet. Your daily values may be higher or lower depending on your calorie needs.

30. CASHEWS The nutrition facts label on a container of dry roasted cashews indicates there are 161 calories in 28 grams. You eat 9 cashews totaling 12 grams.

a. How many calories do you consume?

b. How many cashews are in one serving?

31. REASONING The ratio of three numbers is $4 : 3 : 1$. The sum of the numbers is 64. What is the greatest number?

32. SURVEY Seven out of every 8 students surveyed owns a bike. The difference between the number of students who own a bike and those who do not is 72. How many students were surveyed?

33. BUG COLLECTION You and a classmate have a bug collection for science class. You find 5 out of every 9 bugs in the collection. You find 4 more bugs than your classmate. How many bugs are in the collection?

34. Problem Solving You and a friend each have a collection of tokens. Initially, for every 8 tokens you had, your friend had 3. After you give half of your tokens to your friend, your friend now has 18 more tokens than you. Initially, how many more tokens did you have than your friend?

Fair Game Review What you learned in previous grades & lessons

Find the GCF.

35. 54, 27

36. 60, 84

37. 42, 28

38. MULTIPLE CHOICE Which expression does *not* give the area of the shaded figure?

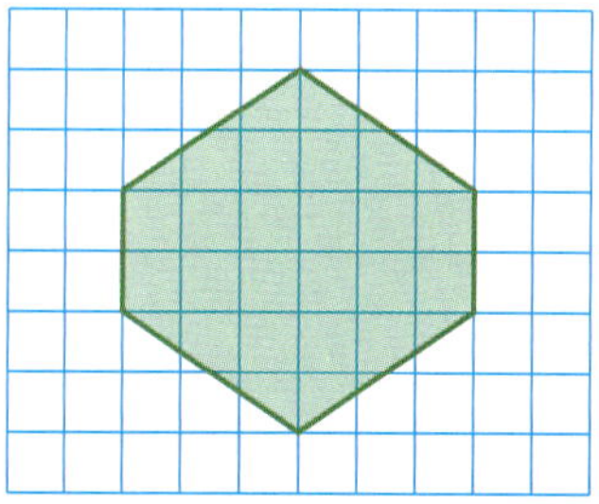

Ⓐ $2(6) + 2\left(\frac{1}{2}(6)(2)\right)$

Ⓑ $2\left(\frac{1}{2}(3)(2 + 6)\right)$

Ⓒ $6(6) - 4\left(\frac{1}{2}(3)(2)\right)$

Ⓓ $6(6) - \frac{1}{2}(6)(2)$

5.3 Rates

Essential Question How can you use rates to describe changes in real-life problems?

1 ACTIVITY: Stories Without Words

Work with a partner. Each diagram shows a story problem.

- **Describe the story problem in your own words.**
- **Write the rate indicated by the diagram. What are the units?**

a.

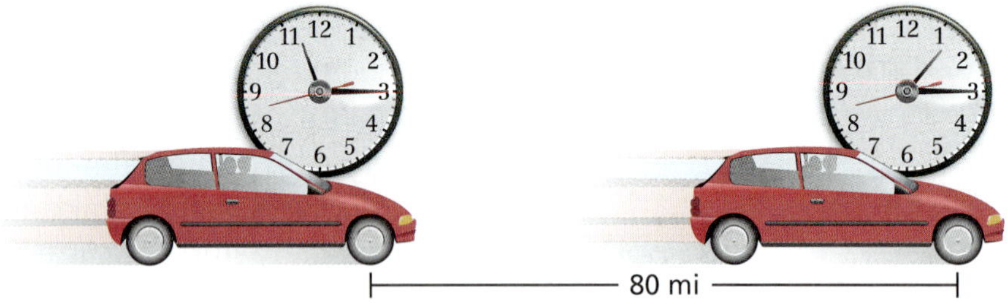

b.

c.

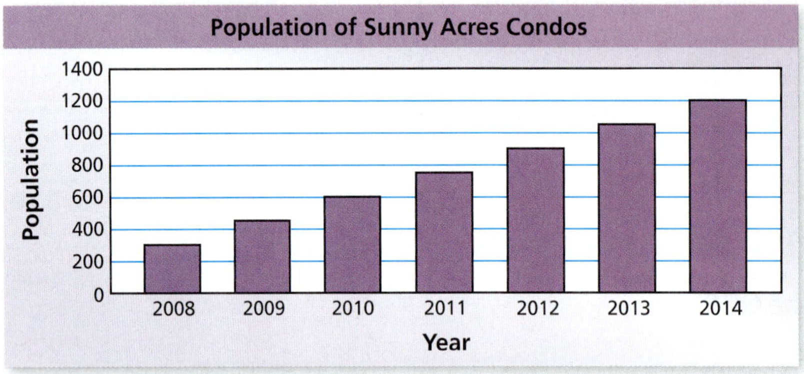

d.

Rates

In this lesson, you will
- understand the concepts of rates and unit rates.
- write unit rates.
- solve real-life problems.

2 ACTIVITY: Finding Equivalent Rates

Work with a partner. Use the diagrams in Activity 1. Explain how you found each answer.

a. How many miles does the car travel in 1 hour?

b. How much money does the person earn every hour?

c. How much does the population of Sunny Acres Condos increase each year?

d. How many feet does the alligator grow per year?

Math Process

Specify Units

How do the given units help you find the units for your answer?

3 ACTIVITY: Using a Double Number Line

Work with a partner. Count the number of times you can clap your hands in 12 seconds. Have your partner keep track of the time and record your results.

a. Use the results to complete the double number line.

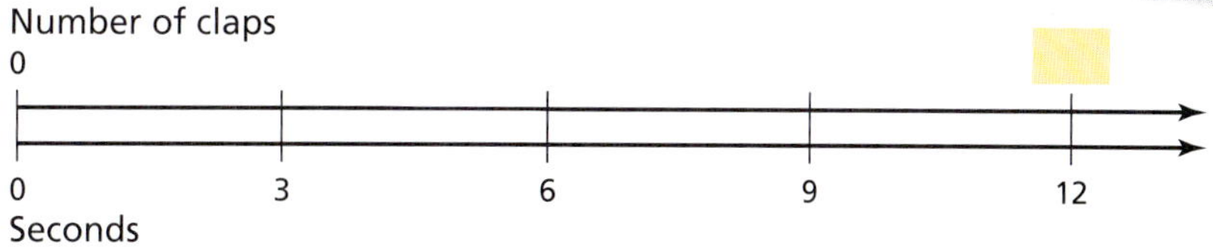

b. Explain how to use the double number line to find the number of times you clap your hands in 6 seconds and in 4 seconds.

c. Find the number of times you can clap your hands in 1 minute. Explain how you found your answer.

d. How can you find the number of times you can clap your hands in 2 minutes? 3 minutes? Explain.

What Is Your Answer?

4. **IN YOUR OWN WORDS** How can you use rates to describe changes in real-life problems? Give examples to support your explanation.

5. **MODELING** Use a double number line to model each story in Activity 1. Show how to use the double number line to answer each question in Activity 2. Why is a double number line a good problem-solving tool for these types of problems?

Practice Use what you learned about rates to complete Exercises 3 and 4 on page 180.

5.3 Lesson

Check It Out
Lesson Tutorials
BigIdeasMath.com

Key Vocabulary
rate, *p. 178*
unit rate, *p. 178*
equivalent rates, *p. 178*

Key Idea

Rate and Unit Rate

Words A **rate** is a ratio of two quantities using different units. A **unit rate** compares a quantity to one unit of another quantity. **Equivalent rates** have the same unit rate.

Numbers You pay $27 for 3 pizzas.

Rate: $27 : 3 pizzas

Unit rate: $9 : 1 pizza

Algebra Rate: a units : b units Unit rate: $\frac{a}{b}$ units : 1 unit

Study Tip

In a rate $a : b$, you can divide both a and b by b to find the unit rate.

EXAMPLE 1 Writing a Rate

The double number line shows the rate at which you earn points for successfully hitting notes in a music video game. Write a rate that represents this situation.

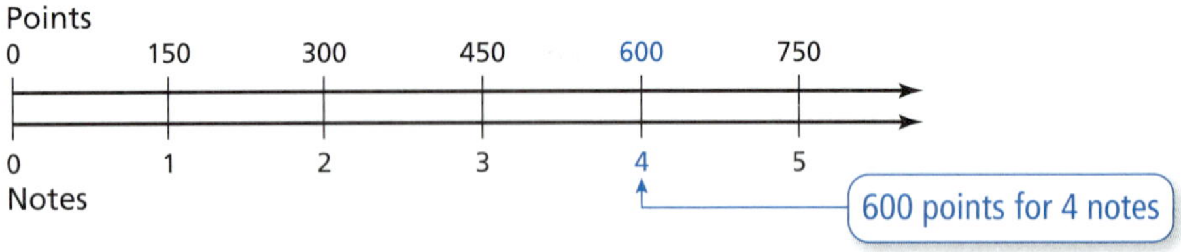

One possible rate is 600 points for every 4 notes.

EXAMPLE 2 Finding a Unit Rate

A piece of space junk travels 5 miles in 8 seconds. How far does it travel per second?

Use a ratio table and divide by 8 to write an equivalent rate in which the time is 1 second.

	÷ 8	
Distance (miles)	5	$\frac{5}{8}$
Time (seconds)	8	1
	÷ 8	

The rate 5 miles : 8 seconds is equivalent to $\frac{5}{8}$ mile : 1 second.

So, the space junk travels $\frac{5}{8}$ mile per second.

Multi-Language Glossary at BigIdeasMath.com

On Your Own

Now You're Ready
Exercises 3–10

1. Write another rate that represents the situation in Example 1.
2. A Japanese bullet train travels 558 miles in 3 hours. How far does it travel every hour?
3. You pay $8 for 16 ounces of sliced turkey. Write a rate that gives the price for each ounce of turkey.

EXAMPLE 3 Finding Equivalent Rates

a. A chef buys 6 pounds of salmon fillets for $51. How much will the chef pay for 9 more pounds of salmon fillets?

Using a ratio table, divide to find the unit rate and then multiply to find the cost for 9 pounds of salmon fillets.

$\div 6$ $\times 9$

Cost (dollars)	51	8.5	76.5
Salmon (pounds)	6	1	9

$\div 6$ $\times 9$

So, the chef will pay $76.50 for 9 more pounds of salmon fillets.

Study Tip

The unit rate of cost per unit is called *unit cost*. The unit cost of the salmon in Example 3(a) is $8.50 per pound.

b. You buy 2 pounds of tilapia fillets for $16. What is the cost for 7 pounds of tilapia fillets?

Because $16 is easily divided into halves, fourths, and eighths, it is appropriate to model the rate using a double number line.

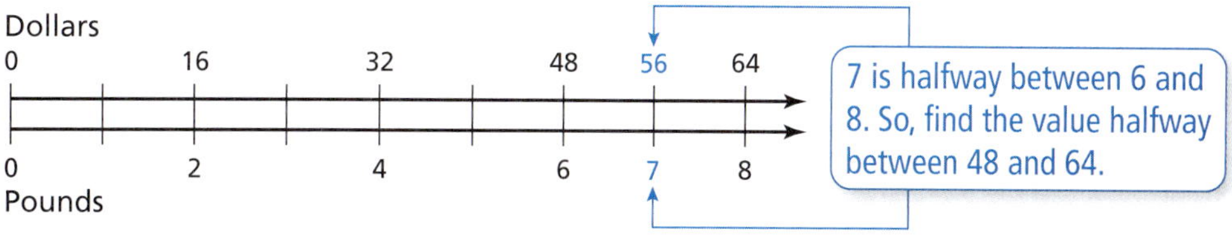

So, the cost for 7 pounds of tilapia fillets is $56.

On Your Own

Now You're Ready
Exercises 14 and 15

4. Your download speed is 3 megabytes every 4 seconds.
   a. How many megabytes can you download in 1 minute?
   b. Construct a double number line that represents the situation. How many megabytes can you download in 10 seconds?

5.3 Exercises

Check It Out
Help with Homework
BigIdeasMath.com

Vocabulary and Concept Check

1. **WRITING** Describe a unit rate that you use in real life.
2. **DIFFERENT WORDS, SAME QUESTION** Which is different? Find "both" answers.

What is the cost per bagel?	What is the cost per dozen bagels?
What is the unit cost of a bagel?	How much does each bagel cost?

Practice and Problem Solving

Write a rate that represents the situation.

1 3.
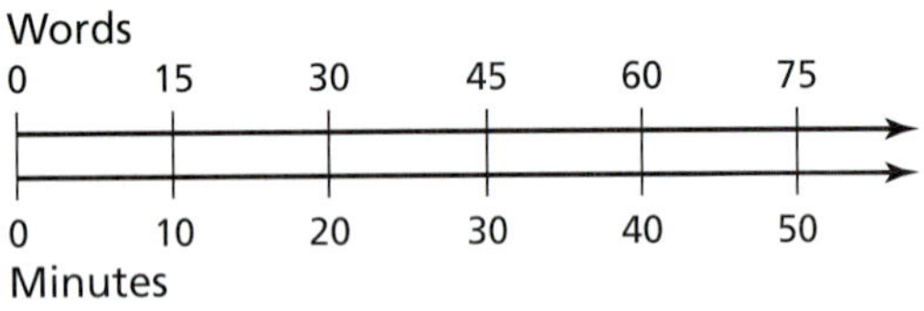

4.
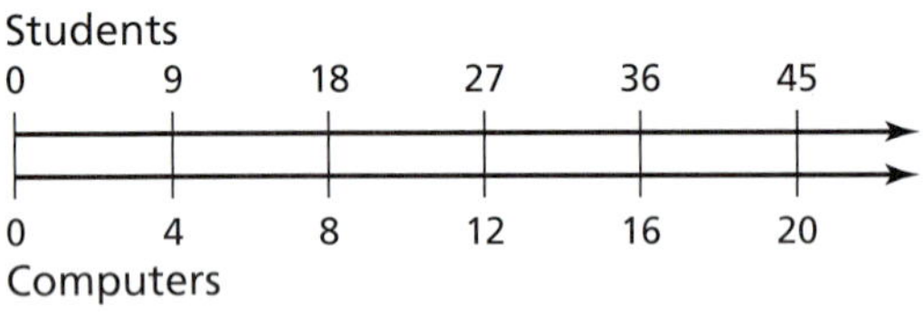

5.
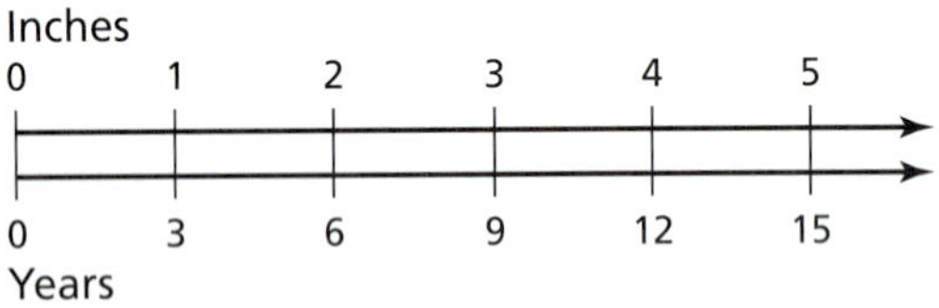

6.
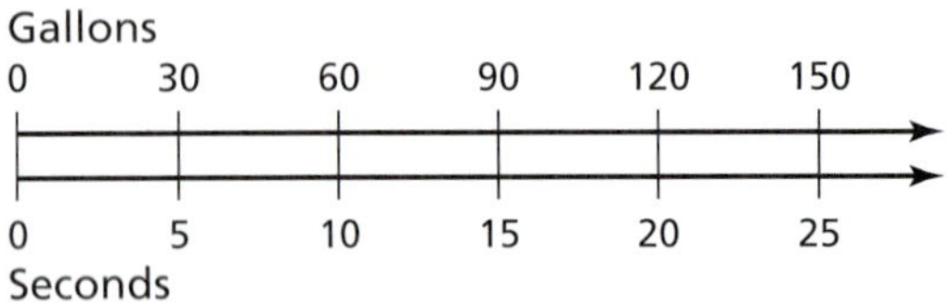

Write a unit rate for the situation.

2 7. $28 saved in 4 weeks

8. 18 necklaces made in 3 hours

9. 270 miles in 6 hours

10. 228 students in 12 classes

Write a unit rate for the table.

11.

Calories	880	440	220
Servings	8	4	2

12.

Data (kilobytes)	2520	5040	7560
Time (seconds)	18	36	54

13. **LIGHTNING** Lightning strikes Earth 1000 times in 10 seconds. How many times does lightning strike per second?

3 14. **CAR WASH** You earn $35 for washing 7 cars. How much do you earn for washing 4 cars?

15. **5K RACE** You jog 2 kilometers in 12 minutes. At this rate, how long will it take you to complete a 5-kilometer race?

Find the missing values in the ratio table. What is the unit rate?

16.

Points	126			252
Games	3	1	5	

17.

Weight (pounds)	4		10	
Cost (dollars)	16	1		22.5

18. **PRINTER** A printer prints 28 photos in 8 minutes.
   a. How many minutes does it take to print 21 more photos?
   b. Construct a double number line diagram that represents the situation. How many minutes does it take to print 35 more photos?

19. **SUN VISOR** An athletic director pays $90 for 12 sun visors for the softball team.
   a. How much will the athletic director pay to buy 15 more sun visors?
   b. Construct a double number line diagram that represents the situation. What is the cost of 16 sun visors?

20. **FOOD DRIVE** The table shows the amounts of food collected by two homerooms. Homeroom A collects 21 additional items of food. How many more items does Homeroom B need to collect to have more items per student?

	Homeroom A	Homeroom B
Students	24	16
Canned Food	30	22
Dry Food	42	24

21. **MARATHON** A runner completed a 26.2-mile marathon in 210 minutes.
   a. Estimate the unit rate, in miles per minute.
   b. Estimate the unit rate, in minutes per mile.
   c. Another runner says, "I averaged 10-minute miles in the marathon." Is this runner talking about the kind of rate described in part (a) or in part (b)? Explain your reasoning.

22. **Logic** You can do one-half of a job in an hour. Your friend can do one-third of the same job in an hour. How long will it take to do the job if you work together?

Fair Game Review What you learned in previous grades & lessons

Write two fractions that are equivalent to the given fraction.

23. $\frac{1}{3}$ 24. $\frac{5}{6}$ 25. $\frac{2}{5}$ 26. $\frac{4}{9}$

27. **MULTIPLE CHOICE** Which expression is equal to $6(3) - 6(2)$?

Ⓐ $2(3 - 6)$ Ⓑ $6(3 - 2)$ Ⓒ $12(3 - 1)$ Ⓓ $36(3 - 2)$

5.4 Comparing and Graphing Ratios

Essential Question How can you compare two ratios?

1 ACTIVITY: Comparing Ratio Tables

Work with a partner.

- **You make colored frosting by adding 3 drops of red food coloring for every 1 drop of blue food coloring.**
- **Your teacher makes colored frosting by adding 5 drops of red food coloring for every 3 drops of blue food coloring.**

a. Copy and complete the ratio table for each frosting mixture.

Your Frosting	
Drops of Blue	Drops of Red
1	
2	
3	
4	
5	

Your Teacher's Frosting	
Drops of Blue	Drops of Red
3	
6	
9	
12	
15	

b. Whose frosting is bluer? Whose frosting is redder? Justify your answers.

c. **STRUCTURE** Insert and complete a new column for each ratio table above that shows the total number of drops. How can you use this column to answer part (b)?

2 ACTIVITY: Graphing from a Ratio Table

Work with a partner.

a. Explain how you can use the values from the ratio table for your frosting to create a graph in the coordinate plane.

b. Use the values in the table to plot the points. Then connect the points and describe the graph. What do you notice?

c. What does the line represent?

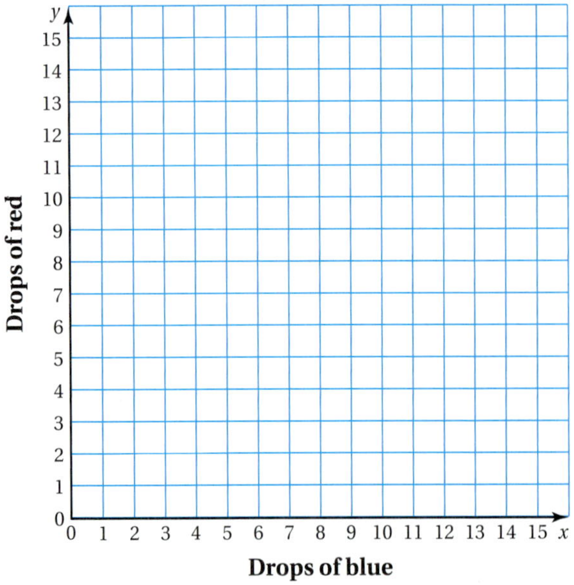

Ratios and Rates

In this lesson, you will

- compare ratios.
- compare unit rates.
- graph ordered pairs to compare ratios and rates.

3 ACTIVITY: Comparing Graphs from Ratio Tables

Math Process

Look for Patterns

What patterns do you notice in the graph? What does this tell you about the problem?

Work with a partner. The graph shows the values from the ratio table for your teacher's frosting.

a. Complete the table and the graph.

Your Teacher's Frosting	
Drops of Blue	Drops of Red
3	
6	
9	
12	
15	

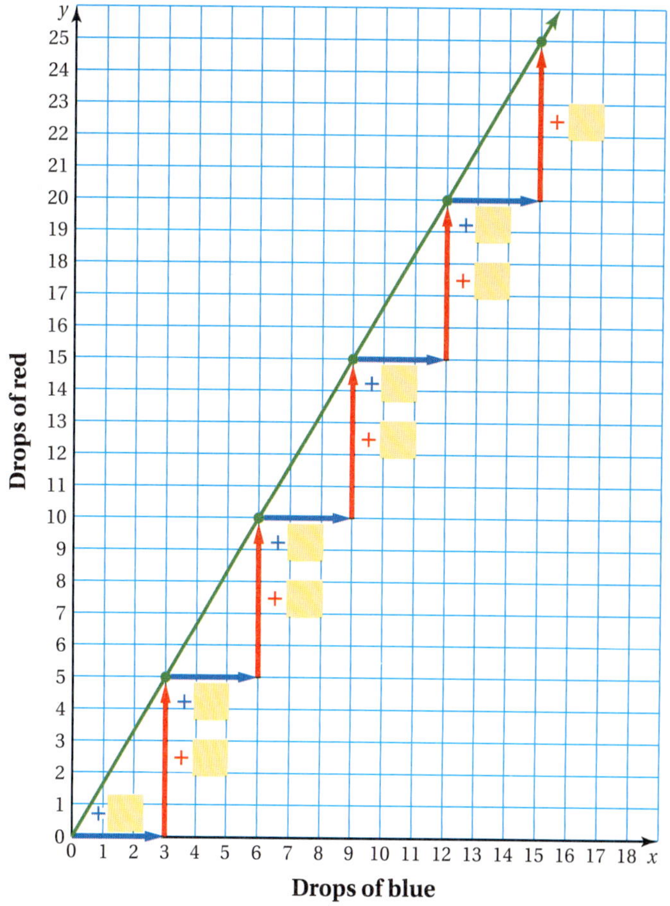

b. Explain the relationship between the entries in the ratio table and the points on the graph.

c. How is this graph similar to the graph in Activity 2? How is it different?

d. How can you use the graphs to determine whose frosting has more red or blue in it? Explain.

What Is Your Answer?

4. **IN YOUR OWN WORDS** How can you compare two ratios?

5. **PRECISION** Your teacher's frosting mixture has 7 drops of blue in it. How can you use the graph to find how many drops of red are needed to make the frosting? Is your answer exact? Explain.

Practice Use what you learned about comparing ratios to complete Exercises 3 and 4 on page 186.

5.4 Lesson

Check It Out
Lesson Tutorials
BigIdeasMath.com

One way to compare ratios is by using ratio tables.

EXAMPLE 1 Comparing Ratios

You mix 8 tablespoons of hot sauce and 3 cups of salsa in a green bowl. You mix 12 tablespoons of hot sauce and 4 cups of salsa in an orange bowl. Which mixture is hotter?

Use ratio tables to compare the mixtures. Find a larger batch of each mixture in which the amount of hot sauce or salsa is the same.

Green Bowl ($\times 4$)

Hot Sauce (tablespoons)	8	32
Salsa (cups)	3	12

Orange Bowl ($\times 3$)

Hot Sauce (tablespoons)	12	36
Salsa (cups)	4	12

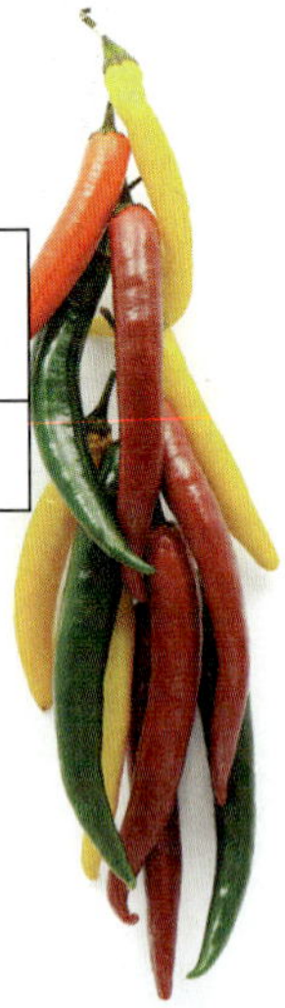

The tables show that for a larger batch of each mixture using 12 cups of salsa, the orange bowl would have $36 - 32 = 4$ more tablespoons of hot sauce.

So, the mixture in the orange bowl is hotter.

EXAMPLE 2 Comparing Unit Rates

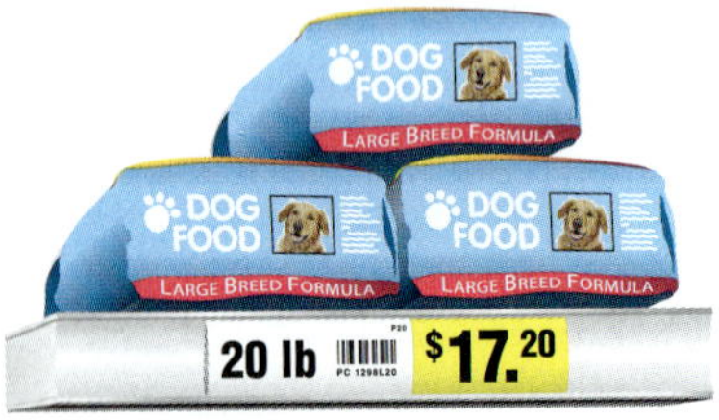

Which bag of dog food is the better buy?

Use ratio tables to find and compare the unit costs.

20-Pound Bag ($\div 20$)

Cost (dollars)	17.20	0.86
Food (pounds)	20	1

30-Pound Bag ($\div 30$)

Cost (dollars)	25.20	0.84
Food (pounds)	30	1

The 20-pound bag costs \$0.86 per pound, and the 30-pound bag costs \$0.84 per pound.

Because \$0.84 is less than \$0.86, the 30-pound bag is the better buy.

On Your Own

Now You're Ready
Exercises 3–10

1. In Example 1, you mix 10 tablespoons of hot sauce and 3 cups of salsa in a red bowl. Which mixture is the mildest? Explain.
2. A 30-pack of paper towels costs \$48.30. A 32-pack costs \$49.60. Which is the better buy? Explain.

EXAMPLE 3 Graphing Values from Ratio Tables

A hot-air balloon rises 9 meters every 3 seconds. A blimp rises 7 meters every 2 seconds.

Rises 9 meters every 3 seconds.

a. Complete the ratio table for each aircraft. Which rises faster?

Balloon	
Time (seconds)	Height (meters)
3	9
6	18
9	27
12	36

×2, ×3, ×4

Blimp	
Time (seconds)	Height (meters)
2	7
4	14
6	21
8	28

×2, ×3, ×4

Every 6 seconds, the balloon rises 18 meters and the blimp rises 21 meters.

∴ So, the blimp rises faster.

b. Graph the ordered pairs (time, height) from the tables in part (a). What can you conclude?

Write the ordered pairs.

Balloon: (3, 9), (6, 18), (9, 27), (12, 36)

Blimp: (2, 7), (4, 14), (6, 21), (8, 28)

Study Tip

When graphing speed, you often place time on the horizontal axis and distance on the vertical axis.

Plot and label each set of ordered pairs. Then draw a line through each set of points.

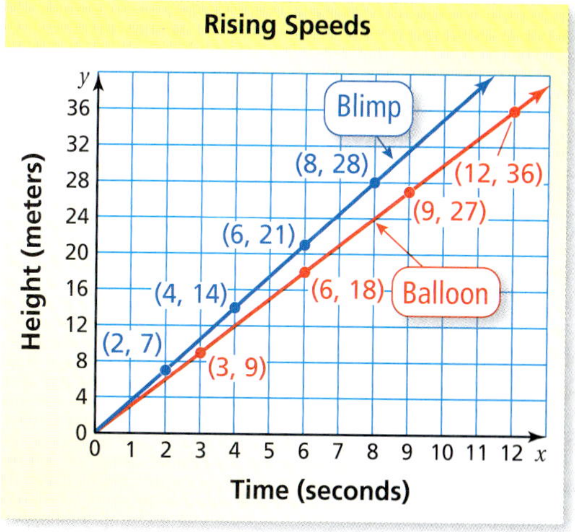

∴ Both graphs begin at (0, 0). The graph for the blimp is steeper, so the blimp rises faster than the hot-air balloon.

On Your Own

Now You're Ready
Exercises 12 and 13

3. **WHAT IF?** The blimp rises 6 meters every 2 seconds. How does this affect your conclusion?

5.4 Exercises

Check It Out
Help with Homework
BigIdeasMath.com

Vocabulary and Concept Check

1. **WRITING** Explain how to use tables to compare ratios.

2. **NUMBER SENSE** Just by looking at the graph, determine who earns a greater hourly wage. Explain.

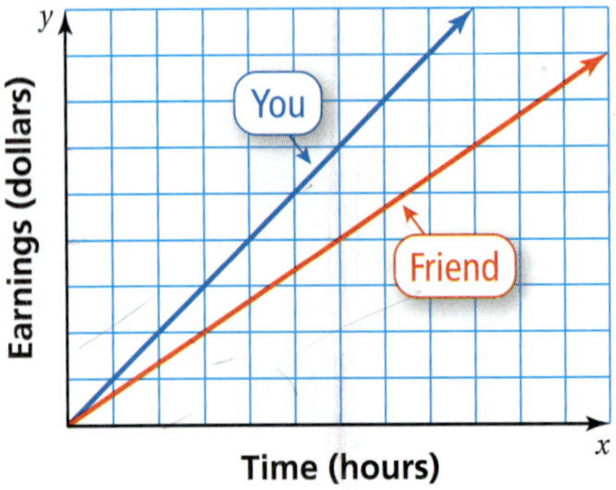

Practice and Problem Solving

Determine which car gets the better gas mileage.

1 3.

Car	A	B
Distance (miles)	125	120
Gallons Used	5	6

4.

Car	A	B
Distance (miles)	300	320
Gallons Used	8	10

5.

Car	A	B
Distance (miles)	450	405
Gallons Used	15	12

6.

Car	A	B
Distance (miles)	360	270
Gallons Used	20	18

Determine which is the better buy.

2 7.

Air Freshener	A	B
Cost (dollars)	6	12
Refills	2	3

8.

Kitten Food	A	B
Cost (dollars)	15	9
Cans	18	12

9.

Ham	A	B
Cost (dollars)	5.70	8.75
Pounds	3	5

10.

Cheese	A	B
Cost (dollars)	3.59	5.12
Slices	10	16

11. **SALT WATER GARGLE** Salt water gargle can temporarily relieve a sore throat. One recipe calls for $\frac{3}{4}$ teaspoon of salt in 1 cup of water. A second recipe calls for 1 teaspoon of salt in 2 cups of water. Which recipe will taste saltier?

Complete the ratio tables and graph the ordered pairs from the tables. What can you conclude?

3 **12.**

Water Tank	
Time (min)	Liters Leaked
2	4
4	
6	
8	

Swimming Pool	
Time (min)	Liters Leaked
3	2
6	
9	
12	

13.

Zoo	
People	Cost (dollars)
4	60
8	
12	
16	

Museum	
People	Cost (dollars)
5	95
10	
15	
20	

14. **MILK** In whole milk, 13 parts out of 400 are milk fat. In 2% milk, 1 part out of 50 is milk fat. Which type of milk has more milk fat per cup?

15. **HEART RATE** A horse's heart beats 440 times in 10 minutes. A cow's heart beats 390 times in 6 minutes. Which animal has a greater heart rate?

16. **CHOOSE TOOLS** A chemist prepares two acid solutions.

a. Use a ratio table to determine which solution is more acidic.

b. Use a graph to determine which solution is more acidic.

c. Which method do you prefer? Explain.

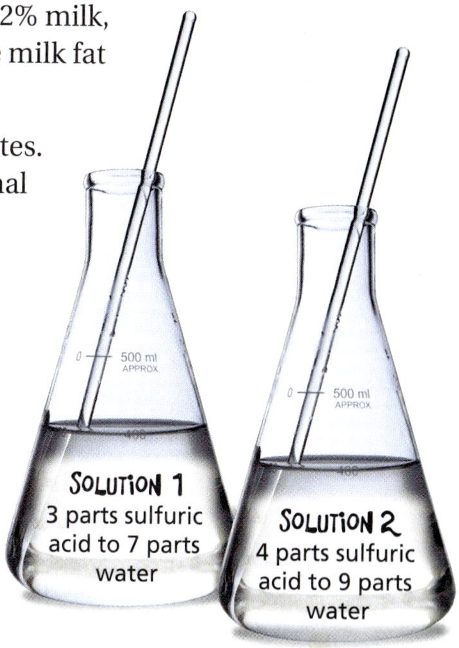

17. **NUT MIXTURE** A company offers a nut mixture with 7 peanuts for every 4 almonds. The company changes the mixture to have 8 peanuts for every 5 almonds, but the number of nuts per container does not change.

a. Create a ratio table for each mixture. How many nuts are in the smallest possible container?

b. Graph the ordered pairs from the tables. What can you conclude?

c. Almonds cost more than peanuts. Should the company charge more or less for the new mixture? Explain your reasoning.

18. **Structure** The point (p, q) is on the graph of values from a ratio table. What is another point on the graph?

Fair Game Review What you learned in previous grades & lessons

Divide.

19. $544 \div 34$ **20.** $1520 \div 83$ **21.** $8439 \div 245$

22. **MULTIPLE CHOICE** Which of the following numbers is equal to 9.32 when you increase it by 4.65?

Ⓐ 4.33 Ⓑ 4.67 Ⓒ 5.67 Ⓓ 13.97

5.5 Proportions

Essential Question How can you determine whether two quantities are in a proportional relationship?

The Meaning of a Word ● Proportional

When you work toward a goal, your success is usually **proportional** to the amount of work you put in.

An equation stating that two ratios are equal is a **proportion**.

1 ACTIVITY: Determining Proportions

Work with a partner. Tell whether the two ratios are equivalent. If they are not equivalent, change the next day to make the ratios equivalent. Explain your reasoning.

a. On the first day, you pay \$5 for 2 boxes of popcorn. The next day, you pay \$7.50 for 3 boxes.

First Day / Next Day

$$\frac{\$5.00}{2 \text{ boxes}} \stackrel{?}{=} \frac{\$7.50}{3 \text{ boxes}}$$

b. On the first day, it takes you $3\frac{1}{2}$ hours to drive 175 miles. The next day, it takes you 5 hours to drive 200 miles.

First Day / Next Day

$$\frac{3\frac{1}{2}\text{ h}}{175 \text{ mi}} \stackrel{?}{=} \frac{5 \text{ h}}{200 \text{ mi}}$$

c. On the first day, you walk 4 miles and burn 300 calories. The next day, you walk $3\frac{1}{3}$ miles and burn 250 calories.

First Day / Next Day

$$\frac{4 \text{ mi}}{300 \text{ cal}} \stackrel{?}{=} \frac{3\frac{1}{3}\text{ mi}}{250 \text{ cal}}$$

Proportions

In this lesson, you will

- use equivalent ratios to determine whether two ratios form a proportion.
- determine whether two quantities are in a proportional relationship.

d. On the first day, you paint 150 square feet in $2\frac{1}{2}$ hours. The next day, you paint 200 square feet in 4 hours.

First Day / Next Day

$$\frac{150 \text{ ft}^2}{2\frac{1}{2}\text{ h}} \stackrel{?}{=} \frac{200 \text{ ft}^2}{4 \text{ h}}$$

2 ACTIVITY: Checking a Proportion

Work with a partner.

a. It is said that "one year in a dog's life is equivalent to seven years in a human's life." Explain why Newton thinks he has a score of 105 points. Did he solve the proportion correctly?

$$\frac{1 \text{ year}}{7 \text{ years}} \stackrel{?}{=} \frac{15 \text{ points}}{105 \text{ points}}$$

"I got 15 on my online test. That's 105 in dog points! Isn't that an A+?"

b. If Newton thinks his score is 98 points, how many points does he actually have? Explain your reasoning.

3 ACTIVITY: Modeling Proportional Relationships

Math Process

Justify Conclusions

What information can you use to justify your conclusion?

Work with a partner. There is a proportional relationship between the number of T-shirts you buy at a clothing store and the total cost of the T-shirts. The store advertises a price of $40 for 5 T-shirts.

a. Copy and complete the table using equivalent ratios.

T-shirts	1	2	3	4	5
Total Cost (dollars)					40

b. What is the unit rate of the proportional relationship? Explain.

c. What is the relationship between the number of T-shirts and the total cost of the T-shirts? Write a rule for the total cost of a given number of T-shirts.

d. How is your rule for the total cost of a given number of T-shirts related to the unit rate of the proportional relationship?

What Is Your Answer?

4. Find a recipe for something you like to eat. Then show how two of the ingredient amounts are proportional when you double or triple the recipe.

5. **IN YOUR OWN WORDS** How can you determine whether two quantities are in a proportional relationship?

Practice Use what you discovered about proportions to complete Exercises 13 and 14 on page 192.

Check It Out
Lesson Tutorials
BigIdeasMath.com

Key Vocabulary
proportion, *p. 190*
proportional, *p. 190*

Key Idea

Proportions

Words A **proportion** is an equation stating that two ratios are equivalent. Two quantities that form a proportion are **proportional**.

Numbers $\frac{2}{3} = \frac{4}{6}$ The proportion is read "2 is to 3 as 4 is to 6."

EXAMPLE 1 Determining Whether Ratios Form a Proportion

Tell whether $\frac{6}{4}$ and $\frac{8}{12}$ form a proportion.

Compare the ratios in simplest form.

$$\frac{6}{4} = \frac{6 \div 2}{4 \div 2} = \frac{3}{2}$$

$$\frac{8}{12} = \frac{8 \div 4}{12 \div 4} = \frac{2}{3}$$

The ratios are *not* equivalent.

So, $\frac{6}{4}$ and $\frac{8}{12}$ do *not* form a proportion.

EXAMPLE 2 Determining Whether Two Quantities Are Proportional

Tell whether x and y are proportional.

x	y
$\frac{1}{2}$	3
1	6
$\frac{3}{2}$	9
2	12

Compare each ratio x to y in simplest form.

$$\frac{\frac{1}{2}}{3} = \frac{1}{6} \qquad \frac{1}{6} \qquad \frac{\frac{3}{2}}{9} = \frac{1}{6} \qquad \frac{2}{12} = \frac{1}{6}$$

The ratios are equivalent.

So, x and y are proportional.

Reading

Two quantities that are proportional are in a *proportional relationship.*

On Your Own

Now You're Ready
Exercises 3–12

Tell whether the ratios form a proportion.

1. $\frac{1}{2}, \frac{5}{10}$
2. $\frac{4}{6}, \frac{18}{24}$
3. $\frac{10}{3}, \frac{5}{6}$
4. $\frac{25}{20}, \frac{15}{12}$
5. Tell whether x and y are proportional.

Birdhouses Built, x	1	2	4	6
Nails Used, y	12	24	48	72

Multi-Language Glossary at BigIdeasMath.com

Key Ideas

Proportional Relationships

In a proportional relationship between two quantities, you can find a measure of the second quantity by multiplying the corresponding measure of the first quantity by a constant.

Proportional

x	y
2×6 →	12
3×6 →	18
4×6 →	24

Multiplicative relationship

Not Proportional

x	y
$2 + 4$ →	6
$3 + 4$ →	7
$4 + 4$ →	8

Additive relationship

EXAMPLE 3 Identifying Proportional Relationships

Study Tip

You can use a table of equivalent ratios to represent a proportional relationship.

For each online store, determine whether there is a proportional relationship between the number of comic books and the total cost. Justify your answer.

a. Store A charges \$3.50 for each comic book and offers free shipping.

Comic Books	$1 \times \$3.50$	$2 \times \$3.50$	$3 \times \$3.50$	$4 \times \$3.50$
Total Cost (dollars)	3.50	7.00	10.50	14.00

To find the total cost, multiply the number of comic books by \$3.50.

So, the total cost is proportional to the number of comic books.

b. Store B charges \$3.00 for each comic book and \$7.00 for shipping.

Comic Books	1	2	3	4
Total Cost (dollars)	10	13	16	19

There is no constant that can be multiplied by the number of comic books to find the total cost.

So, the total cost is not proportional to the number of comic books.

On Your Own

Now You're Ready
Exercises 15–18

6. You read 4 pages in 5 minutes, and you read 8 pages in 10 minutes. Determine whether there is a proportional relationship between the number of pages you read and the time. Justify your answer.

5.5 Exercises

Check It Out
Help with Homework
BigIdeasMath.com

Vocabulary and Concept Check

1. **VOCABULARY** What does it mean for two ratios to form a proportion?

2. **OPEN-ENDED** Write two ratios that are equivalent to $\frac{3}{5}$.

Practice and Problem Solving

Tell whether the ratios form a proportion.

(1) 3. $\frac{1}{3}, \frac{7}{21}$

4. $\frac{1}{5}, \frac{6}{30}$

5. $\frac{3}{4}, \frac{24}{18}$

6. $\frac{2}{5}, \frac{40}{16}$

7. $\frac{48}{9}, \frac{16}{3}$

8. $\frac{18}{27}, \frac{33}{44}$

9. $\frac{7}{2}, \frac{16}{6}$

10. $\frac{12}{10}, \frac{14}{12}$

Tell whether x and y are proportional.

(2) 11.

x	1	2	3	4
y	7	8	9	10

12.

x	2	4	6	8
y	5	10	15	20

Determine whether there is a proportional relationship between the two quantities. Justify your answer.

(3) 13. There are 150 calories in each serving of yogurt.

Servings	1	2	3	4
Calories	150	300	450	600

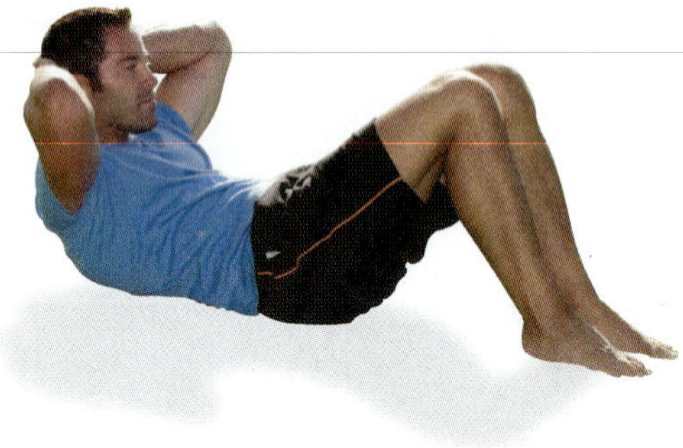

14. An oak tree is 12 years older than a pine tree.

Age of Pine (years)	1	2	3	4
Age of Oak (years)	13	14	15	16

Tell whether the two rates form a proportion.

15. 440 calories in 4 servings; 300 calories in 3 servings

16. 120 units made in 5 days; 88 units made in 4 days

17. 66 wins in 82 games; 99 wins in 123 games

18. 68 hits in 172 at bats; 43 hits in 123 at bats

19. **FITNESS** You can do 90 sit-ups in 2 minutes. Your friend can do 135 sit-ups in 3 minutes. Do these rates form a proportion? Explain.

20. **HEART RATES** Find the heart rates of you and your friend. Do these rates form a proportion? Explain.

	Heartbeats	Seconds
You	22	20
Friend	18	15

Tell whether the ratios form a proportion.

21. $\frac{2.5}{4}, \frac{7}{11.2}$

22. 2 to 4, 11 to $\frac{11}{2}$

23. $2 : \frac{4}{5}, \frac{3}{4} : \frac{3}{10}$

24. **PAY RATE** You earn \$56 walking your neighbor's dog for 8 hours. Your friend earns \$36 painting your neighbor's fence for 4 hours.

- **a.** What is your pay rate?
- **b.** What is your friend's pay rate?
- **c.** Are the pay rates equivalent? Explain.

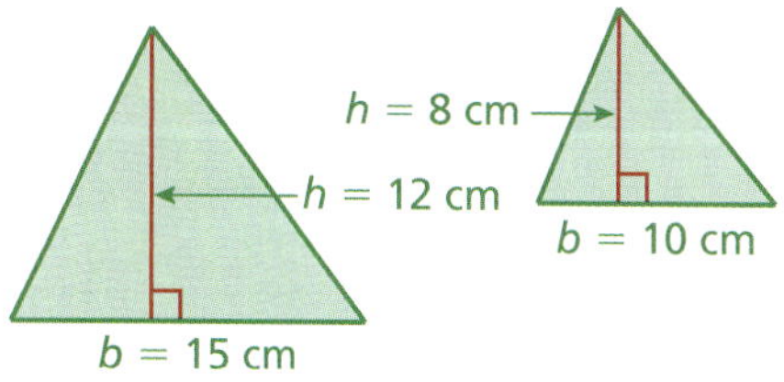

25. **GEOMETRY** Are the heights and bases of the two triangles proportional? Explain.

26. **BASEBALL** A pitcher coming back from an injury limits the number of pitches thrown in bull pen sessions as shown.

Session Number, x	Pitches, y	Curveballs, z
1	10	4
2	20	8
3	30	12
4	40	16

- **a.** Which quantities are proportional?
- **b.** How many pitches that are not curveballs do you think the pitcher will throw in Session 5?

27. **NAIL POLISH** A specific shade of red nail polish requires 7 parts red to 2 parts yellow. A mixture contains 35 quarts of red and 8 quarts of yellow. How can you fix the mixture to make the correct shade of red?

28. **COIN COLLECTION** The ratio of quarters to dimes in a coin collection is 5 : 3. You add the same number of new quarters as dimes to the collection.

- **a.** Is the ratio of quarters to dimes still 5 : 3?
- **b.** If so, illustrate your answer with an example. If not, show why with a "counterexample."

29. **AGE** You are 13 years old, and your cousin is 19 years old. As you grow older, is your age proportional to your cousin's age? Explain your reasoning.

30. **Critical Thinking** Ratio A is equivalent to Ratio B. Ratio B is equivalent to Ratio C. Is Ratio A equivalent to Ratio C? Explain.

Fair Game Review What you learned in previous grades & lessons

Add or subtract.

31. $-28 + 15$

32. $-6 + (-11)$

33. $-10 - 8$

34. $-17 - (-14)$

35. **MULTIPLE CHOICE** Which fraction is not equivalent to $\frac{2}{6}$?

Ⓐ $\frac{1}{3}$ Ⓑ $\frac{12}{36}$ Ⓒ $\frac{4}{12}$ Ⓓ $\frac{6}{9}$

Graphing Proportional Relationships

Check It Out
Lesson Tutorials
BigIdeasMath.com

Recall that you can graph the values from a ratio table.

Time, *x* (seconds)	Height, *y* (meters)
3	2
6	4
9	6
12	8

+ 3 (between each row of *x*), + 2 (between each row of *y*)

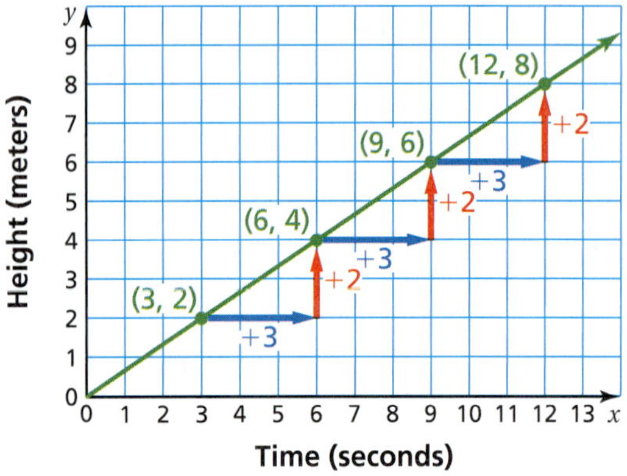

The structure in the ratio table shows why the graph has a constant *rate of change*. You can use the constant rate of change to show that the graph passes through the origin. The graph of every proportional relationship is a line through the origin.

EXAMPLE 1 Determining Whether Two Quantities Are Proportional

Use a graph to tell whether x and y are in a proportional relationship.

a.

x	2	4	6
y	6	8	10

Plot (2, 6), (4, 8), and (6, 10). Draw a line through the points.

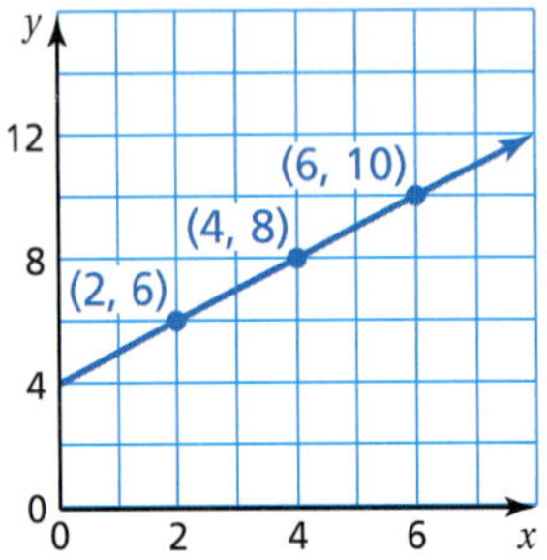

The graph is a line that does not pass through the origin.

So, x and y are not in a proportional relationship.

b.

x	1	2	3
y	2	4	6

Plot (1, 2), (2, 4), and (3, 6). Draw a line through the points.

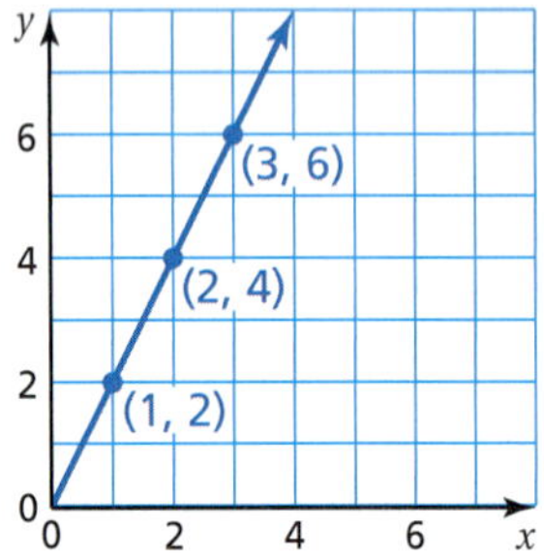

The graph is a line that passes through the origin.

So, x and y are in a proportional relationship.

Proportions

In this extension, you will

- use graphs to determine whether two ratios form a proportion.
- interpret graphs of proportional relationships.

Practice

Use a graph to tell whether x and y are in a proportional relationship.

1.

x	1	2	3	4
y	3	4	5	6

2.

x	1	3	5	7
y	0.5	1.5	2.5	3.5

EXAMPLE 2 Interpreting the Graph of a Proportional Relationship

The graph shows that the distance traveled by the Mars rover *Curiosity* is proportional to the time traveled. Interpret each plotted point in the graph.

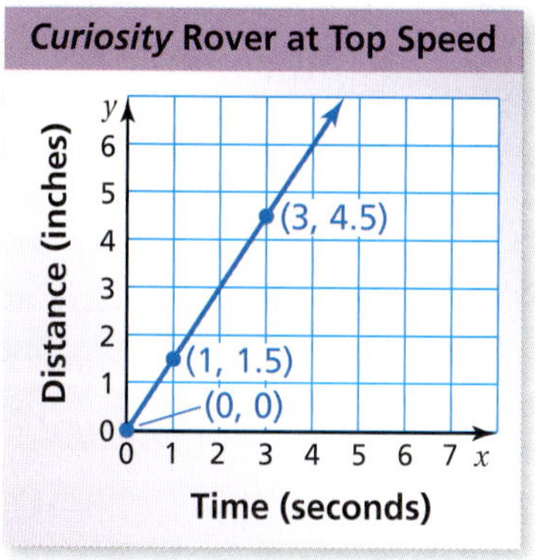

(0, 0): The rover travels 0 inches in 0 seconds.

(1, 1.5): The rover travels 1.5 inches in 1 second. So, the unit rate is 1.5 inches per second.

(3, 4.5): The rover travels 4.5 inches in 3 seconds. Because the relationship is proportional, you can also use this point to find the unit rate.

$$\frac{4.5 \text{ in.}}{3 \text{ sec}} = \frac{1.5 \text{ in.}}{1 \text{ sec}}, \text{ or } 1.5 \text{ inches per second}$$

Study Tip

In the graph of a proportional relationship, you can find the unit rate from the point $(1, y)$.

Practice

Interpret each plotted point in the graph of the proportional relationship.

3.

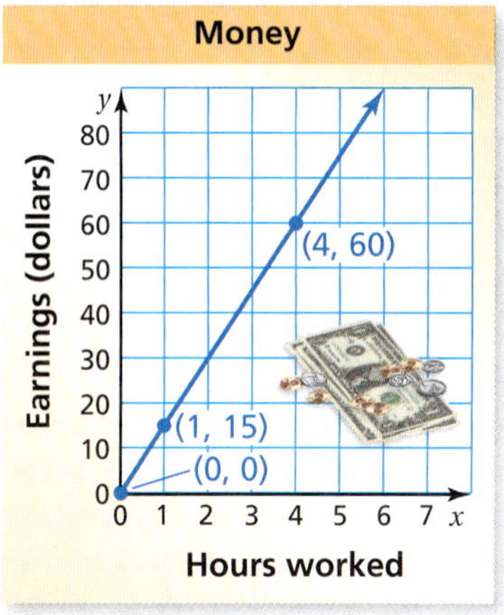

4.

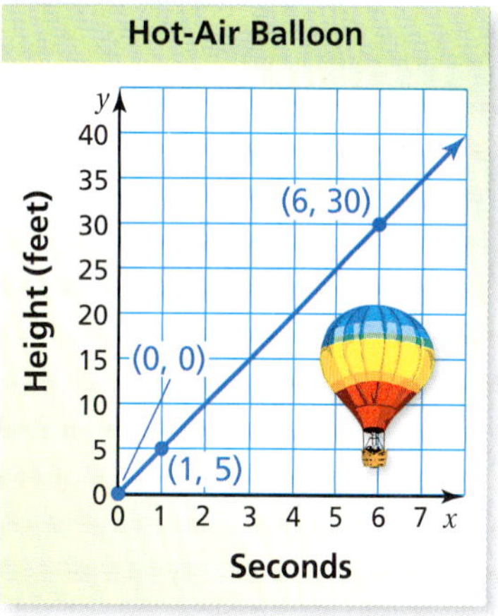

Tell whether x and y are in a proportional relationship. If so, find the unit rate.

5.

x (hours)	1	4	7	10
y (feet)	5	20	35	50

6. Let y be the temperature x hours after midnight. The temperature is 60°F at midnight and decreases 2°F every $\frac{1}{2}$ hour.

7. **REASONING** The graph of a proportional relationship passes through (12, 16) and $(1, y)$. Find y.

8. **MOVIE RENTAL** You pay \$1 to rent a movie plus an additional \$0.50 per day until you return the movie. Your friend pays \$1.25 per day to rent a movie.

a. Make tables showing the costs to rent a movie up to 5 days.

b. Which person pays an amount proportional to the number of days rented?

5 Study Help

Check It Out
Graphic Organizer
BigIdeasMath.com

You can use a **definition and example chart** to organize information about a concept. Here is an example of a definition and example chart for ratio.

Ratio: a comparison of two quantities. Ratios can be part-to-part, part-to-whole, or whole-to-part comparisons.

- Example: 4 to 5
- Example: 2 : 5
- Example: teachers : students

On Your Own

Make definition and example charts to help you study these topics.

1. equivalent ratios
2. ratio table
3. rate
4. unit rate
5. equivalent rates
6. proportion
7. proportional
8. graph of a proportional relationship

"My math teacher taught us how to make a definition and example chart."

5 Chapter Review

Check It Out
Vocabulary Help
BigIdeasMath.com

Review Key Vocabulary

ratio, *p. 164*
equivalent ratios, *p. 170*
ratio table, *p. 170*
rate, *p. 178*
unit rate, *p. 178*
equivalent rates, *p. 178*
proportion, *p. 190*
proportional, *p. 190*

Review Examples and Exercises

5.1 Ratios *(pp. 162–167)*

Write the ratio of apples to oranges. Explain what the ratio means.

3 apples → 3 to 5 ← 5 oranges

So, the ratio of apples to oranges is 3 to 5, or 3 : 5. That means that for every 3 apples, there are 5 oranges.

Exercises

Write the ratio. Explain what the ratio means.

1. butterflies : caterpillars

2. saxophones : total instruments

5.2 Ratio Tables *(pp. 168–175)*

Find the missing values in the ratio table. Then write the equivalent ratios.

Trees	2	6	
Birds	5		30

You can use multiplication to find the missing values.

×3 ×2

Trees	2	6	12
Birds	5	15	30

×3 ×2

The equivalent ratios are 2 : 5, 6 : 15, and 12 : 30.

Exercises

Find the missing values in the ratio table. Then write the equivalent ratios.

3.

Levers	6		18
Pulleys	3	6	

4.

Cars	3	6	
Trucks	4		24

5. Construct a ratio table for 12 cats : 10 dogs. Include at least three equivalent ratios.

5.3 Rates *(pp. 176–181)*

A horse can run 165 feet in 3 seconds. At this rate, how far can the horse run in 5 seconds?

Using a ratio table, divide to find the unit rate. Then multiply to find the distance that the horse can run in 5 seconds.

	÷3	×5	
Distance (feet)	165	55	275
Time (seconds)	3	1	5
	÷3	×5	

So, the horse can run 275 feet in 5 seconds.

Exercises

Write a unit rate for the situation.

6. 12 stunts in 4 movies

7. 3600 stitches in 3 minutes

8. Write a unit rate for the table.

Cars Washed	90	225	360
Time (hours)	2	5	8

9. **MUSIC** A song has 28 beats in 4 seconds. At this rate, how many beats are there in 30 seconds?

5.4 Comparing and Graphing Ratios *(pp. 182–187)*

There are 24 grams of sugar in 6 fluid ounces of Soft Drink A, and there are 15 grams of sugar in 4 fluid ounces of Soft Drink B. Which soft drink contains more sugar in a 12-ounce can?

Use ratio tables to compare the soft drinks.

Soft Drink A

		×2
Sugar (grams)	24	48
Volume (fluid ounces)	6	12
		×2

Soft Drink B

		×3
Sugar (grams)	15	45
Volume (fluid ounces)	4	12
		×3

The tables show that a 12-ounce can of Soft Drink A has $48 - 45 = 3$ more grams of sugar than Soft Drink B.

So, a 12-ounce can of Soft Drink A has more sugar.

Exercises

10. **TUNA** A 5-ounce can of tuna costs \$0.90. A 12-ounce can of tuna costs \$2.40. Which is the better buy?

5.5 Proportions *(pp. 188–195)*

Tell whether the ratios $\frac{9}{12}$ and $\frac{6}{8}$ form a proportion.

$$\frac{9}{12} = \frac{9 \div 3}{12 \div 3} = \frac{3}{4}$$

$$\frac{6}{8} = \frac{6 \div 2}{8 \div 2} = \frac{3}{4}$$

The ratios are equivalent.

So, $\frac{9}{12}$ and $\frac{6}{8}$ form a proportion.

Exercises

Tell whether the ratios form a proportion.

11. $\frac{4}{9}, \frac{2}{3}$

12. $\frac{12}{22}, \frac{18}{33}$

13. $\frac{8}{50}, \frac{4}{10}$

14. $\frac{32}{40}, \frac{12}{15}$

Determine whether there is a proportional relationship between the two quantities.

15.

Concert Tickets	1	2	3	4
Total Cost (dollars)	55	110	165	220

16.

Your Cousin's Age (years)	1	2	3	4
Your Age (years)	6	7	8	9

Tell whether the two rates form a proportion.

17. 420 calories in 7 servings; 840 calories in 14 servings

18. 12 players from 21 teams; 15 players from 24 teams

19. Use a graph to determine whether x and y are in a proportional relationship.

x	1	3	6	8
y	4	12	24	32

6 Algebraic Expressions and Properties

"Did you know that $5 \times 6 = 6 \times 5$, but $5 \div 6 \neq 6 \div 5$?"

"Only certain operations like addition and multiplication preserve equality when you switch the numbers around."

"Descartes, evaluate this expression when $x = 2$ to determine the number of cat treats you are going to eat today."

"Remember that you evaluate an algebraic expression by substituting the value of x into the expression."

What You Learned Before

"Great! You're up to $x = 2$. Let's keep going."

Interpreting Numerical Expressions

Example 1 Write a sentence interpreting the expression $3 \times (19{,}762 + 418)$.

$3 \times (19{,}762 + 418)$ is 3 times as large as $19{,}762 + 418$.

Example 2 Write a sentence interpreting the expression $(316 + 43{,}449) + 5$.

$(316 + 43{,}449) + 5$ is 5 more than $316 + 43{,}449$.

Example 3 Write a sentence interpreting the expression $(20{,}008 - 752) \div 2$.

$(20{,}008 - 752) \div 2$ is half as large as $20{,}008 - 752$.

Try It Yourself

Write a sentence interpreting the expression.

1. $3 \times (372 + 20{,}967)$
2. $2 \times (432 + 346{,}322)$
3. $4 \times (6722 + 4086)$
4. $(115 + 36{,}372) + 6$
5. $(392 + 75{,}325) + 78$
6. $(352 + 46{,}795) + 100$
7. $(30{,}929 + 425) \div 2$
8. $(58{,}742 - 721) \div 2$
9. $(96{,}792 + 564) \div 3$

Using Order of Operations

Example 4 Simplify $4^2 - 3(9 - 5)$.

First: Parentheses
Second: Exponents
Third: Multiplication and Division (from left to right)
Fourth: Addition and Subtraction (from left to right)

$$\begin{aligned} 4^2 - 3(9 - 5) &= 4^2 - 3 \cdot 4 \\ &= 16 - 3 \cdot 4 \\ &= 16 - 12 \\ &= 4 \end{aligned}$$

Try It Yourself

Simplify the expression.

10. $3^2 - 5(4 - 2)$
11. $3 + 4 \div 2$
12. $-10 \div 5 \cdot 3$
13. $(3^3 - 7) \div (-2)$
14. $3 \cdot 6 - 4 \div 2$
15. $12 + 7 \cdot 3 - 24$

6.1 Algebraic Expressions

Essential Question How can you write and evaluate an expression that represents a real-life problem?

1 ACTIVITY: Reading and Re-Reading

Work with a partner.

a. You babysit for 3 hours. You receive $12. What is your hourly wage?

- Write the problem. Underline the important numbers and units you need to solve the problem.
- Read the problem carefully a second time. Circle the key word for the question.

- Write each important number or word, with its units, on a piece of paper. Write +, −, ×, ÷, and = on five other pieces of paper.

- Arrange the pieces of paper to answer the key word question, "What is your hourly wage?"
- Evaluate the expression that represents the hourly wage.

hourly wage = ___ ÷ ___   Write.

= ___   Evaluate.

So, your hourly wage is $___ per hour.

b. How can you use your hourly wage to find how much you will receive for any number of hours worked?

Algebraic Expressions

In this lesson, you will

- use order of operations to evaluate algebraic expressions.
- solve real-life problems.

2 ACTIVITY: Reading and Re-Reading

Math Process

Make Sense of Quantities

What are the units in the problem? How does this help you write an expression?

Work with a partner. Use the strategy shown in Activity 1 to write an expression for each problem. After you have written the expression, evaluate it using mental math or some other method.

a. You wash cars for 2 hours. You receive $6. How much do you earn per hour?

b. You have $60. You buy a pair of jeans and a shirt. The pair of jeans costs $27. You come home with $15. How much did you spend on the shirt?

c. For lunch, you buy 5 sandwiches that cost $3 each. How much do you spend?

d. You are running a 4500-foot race. How much farther do you have to go after running 2000 feet?

e. A young rattlesnake grows at a rate of about 20 centimeters per year. How much does a young rattlesnake grow in 2 years?

What Is Your Answer?

3. IN YOUR OWN WORDS How can you write and evaluate an expression that represents a real-life problem? Give one example with addition, one with subtraction, one with multiplication, and one with division.

Practice Use what you learned about evaluating expressions to complete Exercises 4–7 on page 207.

6.1 Lesson

Check It Out
Lesson Tutorials
BigIdeasMath.com

Key Vocabulary
algebraic expression, *p. 204*
terms, *p. 204*
variable, *p. 204*
coefficient, *p. 204*
constant, *p. 204*

An **algebraic expression** is an expression that may contain numbers, operations, and one or more symbols. Parts of an algebraic expression are called **terms**.

A symbol that represents one or more numbers is called a **variable**.

$$5p + 4$$

The numerical factor of a term that contains a variable is a **coefficient**.

A term without a variable is called a **constant**.

EXAMPLE 1 Identifying Parts of an Algebraic Expression

Identify the terms, coefficients, and constants in each expression.

a. $5x + 13$

$5x + 13$

Terms: $5x$, 13

Coefficient: 5

Constant: 13

b. $2z^2 + y + 3$

$2z^2 + y + 3$

Terms: $2z^2$, $1y$, 3

Coefficients: 2, 1

Constant: 3

Study Tip
A variable by itself has a coefficient of 1. So, the term *y* in Example 1(b) has a coefficient of 1.

On Your Own

Now You're Ready
Exercises 8–13

Identify the terms, coefficients, and constants in the expression.

1. $12 + 10c$ **2.** $15 + 3w + \frac{1}{2}$ **3.** $z^2 + 9z$

EXAMPLE 2 Writing Algebraic Expressions Using Exponents

Write each expression using exponents.

a. $d \cdot d \cdot d \cdot d$

Because d is used as a factor 4 times, its exponent is 4.

So, $d \cdot d \cdot d \cdot d = d^4$.

b. $1.5 \cdot h \cdot h \cdot h$

Because h is used as a factor 3 times, its exponent is 3.

So, $1.5 \cdot h \cdot h \cdot h = 1.5h^3$.

Multi-Language Glossary at BigIdeasMath.com

On Your Own

Now You're Ready
Exercises 16–21

Write the expression using exponents.

4. $j \cdot j \cdot j \cdot j \cdot j \cdot j$

5. $9 \cdot k \cdot k \cdot k \cdot k \cdot k$

To evaluate an algebraic expression, substitute a number for each variable. Then use the order of operations to find the value of the numerical expression.

EXAMPLE 3 Evaluating Algebraic Expressions

a. Evaluate $k + 10$ when $k = 25$.

$k + 10 = 25 + 10$ — Substitute 25 for *k*.

$= 35$ — Add 25 and 10.

b. Evaluate $4 \cdot n$ when $n = -12$.

$4 \cdot n = 4 \cdot -12$ — Substitute -12 for *n*.

$= -48$ — Multiply 4 and -12.

Study Tip

You can write the product of 4 and *n* in several ways.

$4 \cdot n$

$4n$

$4(n)$

On Your Own

Now You're Ready
Exercises 25–32

6. Evaluate $24 + c$ when $c = 9$.

7. Evaluate $d - 17$ when $d = -30$.

EXAMPLE 4 Evaluating an Expression with Two Variables

Evaluate $a \div b$ when $a = 16$ and $b = \frac{2}{3}$.

$a \div b = 16 \div \frac{2}{3}$ — Substitute 16 for *a* and $\frac{2}{3}$ for *b*.

$= 16 \cdot \frac{3}{2}$ — Multiply by the reciprocal of $\frac{2}{3}$, which is $\frac{3}{2}$.

$= 24$ — Multiply.

On Your Own

Now You're Ready
Exercises 33–36

Evaluate the expression when $p = 24$ and $q = 8$.

8. $p \div q$

9. $q + p$

10. $p - q$

11. pq

EXAMPLE 5 Evaluating Expressions with Two Operations

a. Evaluate $3x - 14$ when $x = 5$.

$3x - 14 = 3(5) - 14$ — Substitute 5 for *x*.

$= 15 - 14$ — Using order of operations, multiply 3 and 5.

$= 1$ — Subtract 14 from 15.

b. Evaluate $z^2 + 8.5$ when $z = 2$.

$z^2 + 8.5 = 2^2 + 8.5$ — Substitute 2 for *z*.

$= 4 + 8.5$ — Using order of operations, evaluate 2^2.

$= 12.5$ — Add 4 and 8.5.

On Your Own

Now You're Ready
Exercises 43–51

Evaluate the expression when $y = 6$.

12. $5y + 1$ **13.** $30 - 24 \div y$ **14.** $y^2 - 7$ **15.** $1.5 + y^2$

EXAMPLE 6 Real-Life Application

You are saving money to buy a skateboard. You begin with $45 and you save $3 each week. The expression $45 + 3w$ gives the amount of money you save after w weeks.

a. How much will you have after 4 weeks, 10 weeks, and 20 weeks?

b. After 20 weeks, can you buy the skateboard? Explain.

a. Substitute the given number of weeks for *w*.

Number of Weeks, *w*	$45 + 3w$	Amount Saved
4	$45 + 3(4)$	$45 + 12 = \$57$
10	$45 + 3(10)$	$45 + 30 = \$75$
20	$45 + 3(20)$	$45 + 60 = \$105$

b. After 20 weeks, you have $105. So, you cannot buy the $125 skateboard.

On Your Own

16. WHAT IF? In Example 6, the expression for how much money you have after w weeks is $45 + 4w$. Can you buy the skateboard after 20 weeks? Explain.

6.1 Exercises

Check It Out
Help with Homework
BigIdeasMath.com

Vocabulary and Concept Check

1. **WHICH ONE DOESN'T BELONG?** Which expression does *not* belong with the other three? Explain your reasoning.

$2x + 1$	$5w \cdot c$	$3(4) + 5$	$y \div z$

2. **NUMBER SENSE** Which step in the order of operations is first? second? third? fourth?

Add or subtract from left to right.	Multiply or divide from left to right.
Evaluate terms with exponents.	Perform operations in parentheses.

3. **NUMBER SENSE** Will the value of the expression $20 - x$ *increase*, *decrease*, or *stay the same* as x increases? Explain.

Practice and Problem Solving

Write and evaluate an expression for the problem.

4. You receive \$8 for raking leaves for 2 hours. What is your hourly wage?
5. Music lessons cost \$20 per week. How much do 6 weeks of lessons cost?
6. The scores on your first two history tests were 82 and 95. By how many points did you improve on your second test?
7. You buy a hat for \$12 and give the cashier a \$20 bill. How much change do you receive?

Identify the terms, coefficients, and constants in the expression.

1 8. $7h + 3$

9. $g + 12 + 9g$

10. $5c^2 + 7d$

11. $2m^2 + 15 + 2p^2$

12. $6 + n^2 + \frac{1}{2}d$

13. $8x + \frac{x^2}{3}$

> ✗ Terms: 2, x^2, y
> Coefficient: 2
> Constant: none

14. **ERROR ANALYSIS** Describe and correct the error in identifying the terms, coefficients, and constants in the algebraic expression $2x^2y$.

15. **PERIMETER** You can use the expression $2\ell + 2w$ to find the perimeter of a rectangle where ℓ is the length and w is the width.

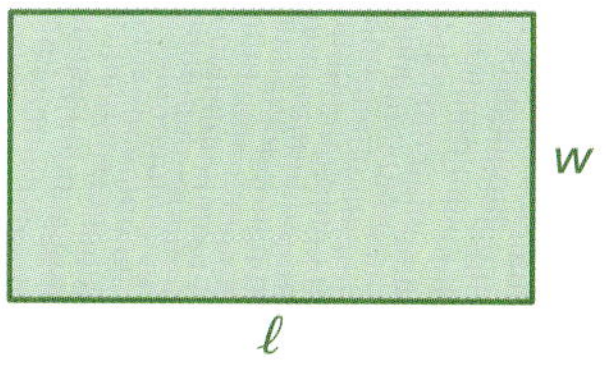

 a. Identify the terms, coefficients, and constants in the expression.

 b. Interpret the coefficients of the terms.

Write each expression using exponents.

16. $b \cdot b \cdot b$ **17.** $g \cdot g \cdot g \cdot g \cdot g$ **18.** $8 \cdot w \cdot w \cdot w \cdot w$

19. $5.2 \cdot y \cdot y \cdot y$ **20.** $a \cdot a \cdot c \cdot c$ **21.** $2.1 \cdot x \cdot z \cdot z \cdot z \cdot z$

22. ERROR ANALYSIS Describe and correct the error in writing the product using exponents.

✗ $3 \cdot n \cdot n \cdot n \cdot n = 4n^3$

23. AREA Write an expression using exponents that represents the area of the square.

As I was going to St. Ives
I met a man with seven wives
Each wife had seven sacks
Each sack had seven cats
Each cat had seven kits
Kits, cats, sacks, wives
How many were going to St. Ives?

24. ST. IVES Suppose the man in the St. Ives poem has x wives, each wife has x sacks, each sack has x cats, and each cat has x kits. Write an expression using exponents that represents the total number of kits, cats, sacks, and wives going to St. Ives.

ALGEBRA Evaluate the expression when $a = 3$, $b = 2$, and $c = 12$.

25. $6 + a$ **26.** $b \cdot 5$ **27.** $c - 1$ **28.** $27 \div a$

29. $12 - b$ **30.** $c + 5$ **31.** $2a$ **32.** $c \div 6$

33. $a + b$ **34.** $c - a$ **35.** $\frac{c}{a}$ **36.** $b \cdot c$

37. ERROR ANALYSIS Describe and correct the error in evaluating the expression when $m = 8$.

✗
$$\begin{aligned} 5m + 3 &= 5 \cdot 8 + 3 \\ &= 5 \cdot 11 \\ &= 55 \end{aligned}$$

38. LAWNS You earn $15n$ dollars for mowing n lawns. How much do you earn for mowing one lawn? seven lawns?

39. PLANT After m months, the height of a plant is $10 + 3m$ millimeters. How tall is the plant after eight months? three years?

Copy and complete the table.

40.

x	3	6	9
$x \cdot 8$			

41.

x	2	4	8
$64 \div x$			

42. FALLING OBJECT An object falls $16t^2$ feet in t seconds. You drop a rock from a bridge that is 75 feet above the water. Will the rock hit the water in 2 seconds? Explain.

ALGEBRA **Evaluate the expression when $a = 10$, $b = 9$, and $c = 4$.**

5 **43.** $2a + 3$ **44.** $4c - 7.8$ **45.** $\frac{a}{4} + \frac{1}{3}$

46. $\frac{24}{b} + 8$ **47.** $c^2 + 6$ **48.** $a^2 - 18$

49. $a + 9c$ **50.** $bc + 12.3$ **51.** $3a + 2b - 6c$

Standard Rentals
$3

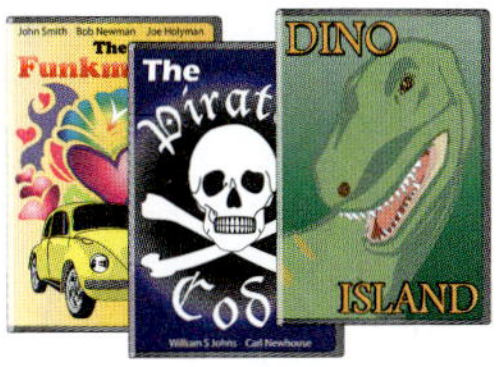

New Releases
$4

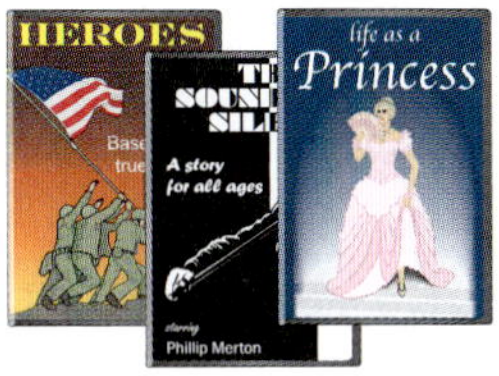

52. **MOVIES** You rent x new releases and y standard rentals. Which expression tells you how much money you will need?

$3x + 4y$ $4x + 3y$ $7(x + y)$

53. **WATER PARK** You float 2000 feet along a "Lazy River" water ride. The ride takes less than 10 minutes. Give two examples of possible times and speeds.

54. **SCIENCE CENTER** The expression $20a + 13c$ is the cost (in dollars) for a adults and c students to enter a science center.

a. How much does it cost for an adult? a student? Explain your reasoning.

b. Find the total cost for 4 adults and 24 students.

c. You find the cost for a group. Then the numbers of adults and students in the group both double. Does the cost double? Explain your answer using an example.

d. In part (b), the number of adults is cut in half, but the number of students doubles. Is the cost the same? Explain your answer.

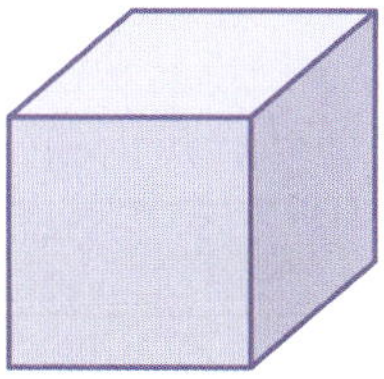

x in.

55. Reasoning The volume of the cube is equal to four times the area of one of its faces. What is the volume of the cube?

Fair Game Review What you learned in previous grades & lessons

Find the value of the power.

56. 3^5 **57.** 8^3 **58.** 7^4 **59.** 2^8

60. **MULTIPLE CHOICE** Which numbers have a least common multiple of 24?

Ⓐ 4, 6 Ⓑ 2, 22 Ⓒ 3, 8 Ⓓ 6, 12

6.2 Writing Expressions

Essential Question How can you write an expression that represents an unknown quantity?

1 ACTIVITY: Ordering Lunch

Work with a partner. You use a $20 bill to buy lunch at a café. You order a sandwich from the menu board shown.

a. Complete the table. In the last column, write a numerical expression for the amount of change received.

Sandwich	Price (dollars)	Change Received (dollars)
Reuben		
BLT		
Egg salad		
Roast beef		

b. **REPEATED REASONING** Write an expression for the amount of change you receive when you order any sandwich from the menu board.

c. Compare the expression you wrote in part (b) with the expressions in the last column of the table in part (a).

d. The café offers several side dishes, each at the same price. You order a chicken salad sandwich and two side dishes. Write an expression for the total amount of money you spend. Explain how you wrote your expression.

e. The expression $20 - 4.65s$ represents the amount of change one customer receives after ordering from the menu board. Explain what each part of the expression represents. Do you know what the customer ordered? Explain your reasoning.

Algebraic Expressions

In this lesson, you will

- use variables to represent numbers in algebraic expressions.
- write algebraic expressions.

2 ACTIVITY: Words That Imply Addition or Subtraction

Math Process

Use Expressions

How do the key words in the phrase help you write the given relationship as an expression?

Work with a partner.

a. Complete the table.

Variable	Phrase	Expression
n	4 **more than** a number	
m	the **difference** of a number and 3	
x	the **sum** of a number and -8	
p	10 **less than** a number	
n	7 units **farther** away	
t	8 minutes **sooner**	
w	12 minutes **later**	
y	a number **increased** by 9	

b. Here is a word problem that uses one of the expressions in the table.

You arrive at the café 8 minutes sooner than your friend. Your friend arrives at 6:42 P.M. When did you arrive?

Which expression from the table can you use to solve the problem?

c. Write a problem that uses a different expression from the table.

3 ACTIVITY: Words That Imply Multiplication or Division

Work with a partner. Match each phrase with an expression.

the product of a number and 3	$n \div 3$
the quotient of 3 and a number	$-4p$
-4 times a number	$n \cdot 3$
a number divided by 3	$2m$
twice a number	$3 \div n$

What Is Your Answer?

4. **IN YOUR OWN WORDS** How can you write an expression that represents an unknown quantity? Give examples to support your explanation.

Practice

Use what you learned about writing expressions to complete Exercises 9–12 on page 214.

6.2 Lesson

Check It Out
Lesson Tutorials
BigIdeasMath.com

Some words imply math operations.

Operation	Addition	Subtraction	Multiplication	Division
Key Words and Phrases	added to plus sum of more than increased by total of and	subtracted from minus difference of less than decreased by fewer than take away	multiplied by times product of twice of	divided by quotient of

EXAMPLE 1 Writing Numerical Expressions

Write the phrase as an expression.

a. 8 fewer than 21

$21 - 8$ — The phrase *fewer than* means *subtraction*.

b. the product of -30 and 9

-30×9, or $-30 \cdot 9$ — The phrase *product of* means *multiplication*.

EXAMPLE 2 Writing Algebraic Expressions

Common Error

When writing expressions involving subtraction or division, order is important. For example, the quotient of a number x and 2 means

$x \div 2$, not $2 \div x$.

Write the phrase as an expression.

a. 14 more than a number x

$x + 14$ — The phrase *more than* means *addition*.

b. a number y minus 75

$y - 75$ — The word *minus* means *subtraction*.

c. the quotient of -3 and a number z

$-3 \div z$, or $\frac{-3}{z}$ — The phrase *quotient of* means *division*.

On Your Own

Now You're Ready
Exercises 3–18

Write the phrase as an expression.

1. the sum of -18 and 35
2. 6 times 50
3. 25 less than a number b
4. a number x divided by -4
5. the total of a number t and 11
6. 100 decreased by a number k

EXAMPLE 3 Writing an Algebraic Expression

The length of Interstate 90 from the West Coast to the East Coast is 153.5 miles more than 2 times the length of Interstate 15 from southern California to northern Montana. Let m be the length of Interstate 15. Which expression can you use to represent the length of Interstate 90?

Ⓐ $2m + 153.5$ Ⓑ $2m - 153.5$ Ⓒ $153.5 - 2m$ Ⓓ $153.5m + 2$

The word *times* means *multiplication*. So, multiply 2 and m.

$2m + 153.5$

The phrase *more than* means *addition*. So, add $2m$ and 153.5.

The correct answer is Ⓐ.

EXAMPLE 4 Real-Life Application

You plant a cypress tree that is 10 inches tall. Each year, its height increases by 15 inches.

a. Make a table that shows the height of the tree for 4 years. Then write an expression for the height after t years.

b. What is the height after 9 years?

a. The height is *increasing*, so *add* 15 each year as shown in the table.

Year, t	Height (inches)
0	10
1	$10 + 15(1) = 25$
2	$10 + 15(2) = 40$
3	$10 + 15(3) = 55$
4	$10 + 15(4) = 70$

When t is 0, the height is 10 inches.

You can see that an expression is $10 + 15t$.

STEM VIDEO

So, the height after year t is $10 + 15t$.

b. Evaluate $10 + 15t$ when $t = 9$.

$$10 + 15t = 10 + 15(9) = 145$$

After 9 years, the height of the tree is 145 inches.

Study Tip

Sometimes, like in Example 3, a variable represents a single value. Other times, like in Example 4, a variable can represent more than one value.

On Your Own

Now You're Ready
Exercises 27–30

7. Your friend has 5 more than twice as many game tokens as your sister. Let t be the number of game tokens your sister has. Write an expression for the number of game tokens your friend has.

8. **WHAT IF?** In Example 4, what is the height of the cypress tree after 16 years?

...ercises

Check It Out
Help with Homework
BigIdeasMath.com

Vocabulary and Concept Check

1. **DIFFERENT WORDS, SAME QUESTION** Which is different? Write "both" expressions.

12 more than x	x increased by 12	x take away 12	the sum of x and 12

2. **REASONING** You pay $0.25p$ dollars to print p photos. What does the coefficient represent?

Practice and Problem Solving

Write the phrase as an expression.

(1) (2)

3. 5 less than 8
4. the product of 3 and -12
5. 28 divided by 7
6. the total of 6 and 10
7. 3 fewer than -18
8. -17 added to -15
9. 13 subtracted from a number x
10. -5 times a number d
11. the quotient of 18 and a number a
12. the difference of a number s and 6
13. -7 increased by a number w
14. a number b squared
15. the sum of a number y and -4
16. the difference of -12 and a number x
17. twice a number z
18. a number t cubed

ERROR ANALYSIS **Describe and correct the error in writing the phrase as an expression.**

19. the quotient of 8 and a number y

✗ $\frac{y}{8}$

20. 16 decreased by a number x

✗ $x - 16$

21. **DINNER** Five friends share the cost of a dinner equally.
    a. Write an expression for the cost per person.
    b. Make up a total cost and test your expression. Is the result reasonable?

22. **TV SHOW** A television show has 19 episodes per season.
    a. Copy and complete the table.
    b. Write an expression for the number of episodes in n seasons.

Seasons	1	2	3	4	5
Episodes					

Give two ways to write the expression as a phrase.

23. $n + 6$
24. $4w$
25. $-15 - b$
26. $14 - 3z$

③ ④ **Write the phrase as an expression. Then evaluate when $x = -5$ and $y = 20$.**

27. 3 less than the quotient of a number y and 4

28. the sum of a number x and -4, all divided by 3

29. 6 more than the product of -8 and a number x

30. the quotient of 40 and the difference of a number y and 16

31. MODELING It costs \$3 to bowl a game and \$2 for shoe rental.

a. Make a table for the cost of up to 5 games.

b. Write an expression for the cost of g games.

c. Use your expression to find the cost of 8 games.

32. PUZZLE Florida has 8 less than 5 times the number of counties in Arizona. Georgia has 25 more than twice the number of counties in Florida.

a. Write an expression for the number of counties in Florida.

b. Write an expression for the number of counties in Georgia.

c. Arizona has 15 counties. How many do Florida and Georgia have?

33. PATTERNS There are 140 people in a singing competition. The graph shows the results for the first five rounds.

a. Write an expression for the number of people after each round.

b. How many people compete in the ninth round? Explain your reasoning.

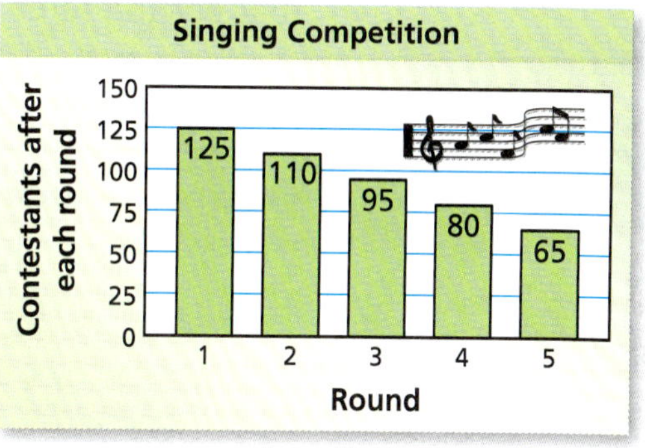

34. NUMBER SENSE The difference between two numbers is 8. The lesser number is a. Write an expression for the greater number.

35. Reasoning One positive number is four times another. The greater number is x. Write an expression for the lesser number.

Fair Game Review What you learned in previous grades & lessons

Evaluate the expression.

36. $8 + (22 + 15)$ **37.** $(13 + 9) + 37$ **38.** $(13 \times 6) \times 5$ **39.** $4 \times (7 \times 5)$

40. MULTIPLE CHOICE A grocery store is making fruit baskets using 144 apples, 108 oranges, and 90 pears. Each basket will be identical. What is the greatest number of fruit baskets the store can make using all the fruit?

Ⓐ 6 Ⓑ 9 Ⓒ 16 Ⓓ 18

Properties of Addition and Multiplication

Essential Question Does the order in which you perform an operation matter?

1 ACTIVITY: Does Order Matter?

Work with a partner. Place each statement in the correct oval.

a. Fasten 5 shirt buttons.
b. Put on a shirt and tie.
c. Fill and seal an envelope.
d. Floss your teeth.
e. Put on your shoes.
f. Chew and swallow.

Order Matters **Order Doesn't Matter**

Think of three math problems using the four operations where order matters and three where order doesn't matter.

The Meaning of a Word ● Commute

When you **commute** the positions of two stuffed animals on a shelf,

you switch their positions.

Equivalent Expressions
In this lesson, you will
- use properties of operations to generate equivalent expressions.

2 ACTIVITY: Commutative Properties

Work with a partner.

a. Which of the following are true?

$3 + 5 \stackrel{?}{=} 5 + 3$ $3 - 5 \stackrel{?}{=} 5 - 3$

$9 \times 3 \stackrel{?}{=} 3 \times 9$ $9 \div 3 \stackrel{?}{=} 3 \div 9$

b. The true equations show the Commutative Properties of Addition and Multiplication. Why do you think they are called *commutative*?

The Meaning of a Word ● Associate

You have two best friends. Sometimes you **associate** with one of them.

And sometimes you **associate** with the other.

3 ACTIVITY: Associative Properties

Math Process

Use Counterexamples

What do the false equations tell you about the Associative Properties?

Work with a partner.

a. Which of the following are true?

$8 + (3 + 1) \stackrel{?}{=} (8 + 3) + 1$ $\qquad$ $8 - (3 - 1) \stackrel{?}{=} (8 - 3) - 1$

$12 \times (6 \times 2) \stackrel{?}{=} (12 \times 6) \times 2$ $\qquad$ $12 \div (6 \div 2) \stackrel{?}{=} (12 \div 6) \div 2$

b. The true equations show the Associative Properties of Addition and Multiplication. Why do you think they are called *associative*?

What Is Your Answer?

4. **IN YOUR OWN WORDS** Does the order in which you perform an operation matter? Give examples to support your explanation.

5. **MENTAL MATH** Explain how you can add the sum in your head.

$$11 + 7 + 12 + 13 + 8 + 9$$

6. **SECRET CODE** The creatures on a distant planet use the symbols ■, ◆, ★, and ● for the four operations.

   a. Use the codes to decide which symbol represents addition and which symbol represents multiplication. Explain your reasoning.

   3 ● 4 = 4 ● 3

   3 ★ 4 = 4 ★ 3

   2 ● (5 ● 3) = (2 ● 5) ● 3

   2 ★ (5 ★ 3) = (2 ★ 5) ★ 3

   0 ● 4 = 0

   0 ★ 4 = 4

   b. Make up your own symbols for addition and multiplication. Write codes using your symbols. Trade codes with a classmate. Decide which symbol represents addition and which symbol represents multiplication.

Practice Use what you learned about the properties of addition and multiplication to complete Exercises 5–8 on page 220.

6.3 Lesson

Check It Out
Lesson Tutorials
BigIdeasMath.com

Key Vocabulary
equivalent expressions, *p. 218*

Expressions with the same value, like $12 + 7$ and $7 + 12$, are **equivalent expressions**. You can use the Commutative and Associative Properties to write equivalent expressions.

Key Ideas

Commutative Properties

Words Changing the order of addends or factors does not change the sum or product.

Numbers $5 + 8 = 8 + 5$
$5 \cdot 8 = 8 \cdot 5$

Algebra $a + b = b + a$
$a \cdot b = b \cdot a$

Associative Properties

Words Changing the grouping of addends or factors does not change the sum or product.

Numbers $(7 + 4) + 2 = 7 + (4 + 2)$
$(7 \cdot 4) \cdot 2 = 7 \cdot (4 \cdot 2)$

Algebra $(a + b) + c = a + (b + c)$
$(a \cdot b) \cdot c = a \cdot (b \cdot c)$

EXAMPLE 1 Using Properties to Write Equivalent Expressions

a. Simplify the expression $7 + (12 + x)$.

$7 + (12 + x) = (7 + 12) + x$ Associative Property of Addition

$= 19 + x$ Add 7 and 12.

b. Simplify the expression $(6.1 + x) + 8.4$.

$(6.1 + x) + 8.4 = (x + 6.1) + 8.4$ Commutative Property of Addition

$= x + (6.1 + 8.4)$ Associative Property of Addition

$= x + 14.5$ Add 6.1 and 8.4.

c. Simplify the expression $-5(11y)$.

$-5(11y) = (-5 \cdot 11)y$ Associative Property of Multiplication

$= -55y$ Multiply -5 and 11.

Study Tip

One way to check whether expressions are equivalent is to evaluate each expression for any value of the variable. In Example 1(a), use $x = 2$.

$7 + (12 + x) = 19 + x$

$7 + (12 + 2) \stackrel{?}{=} 19 + 2$

$21 = 21$ ✓

On Your Own

Now You're Ready
Exercises 5–8

Simplify the expression. Explain each step.

1. $-10 + (a + 9)$
2. $\left(c + \frac{2}{3}\right) + \frac{1}{2}$
3. $5(4n)$

Multi-Language Glossary at BigIdeasMath.com

Key Ideas

Addition Property of Zero

Words The sum of any number and 0 is that number.

Numbers $7 + 0 = 7$ **Algebra** $a + 0 = a$

Multiplication Properties of Zero and One

Words The product of any number and 0 is 0.

The product of any number and 1 is that number.

Numbers $9 \cdot 0 = 0$ **Algebra** $a \cdot 0 = 0$

$-4 \cdot 1 = -4$ $a \cdot 1 = a$

EXAMPLE 2 Using Properties to Write Equivalent Expressions

a. Simplify the expression $9 \cdot 0 \cdot p$.

$9 \cdot 0 \cdot p = (9 \cdot 0) \cdot p$ Associative Property of Multiplication

$= 0 \cdot p = 0$ Multiplication Property of Zero

b. Simplify the expression $4.5 \cdot r \cdot 1$.

$4.5 \cdot r \cdot 1 = 4.5 \cdot (r \cdot 1)$ Associative Property of Multiplication

$= 4.5 \cdot r$ Multiplication Property of One

$= 4.5r$

EXAMPLE 3 Real-Life Application

Common Error

You **and** six friends are on the team, so use the expression 7*x*, not 6*x*, to represent the cost of the T-shirts.

You and six friends play on a basketball team. A sponsor paid $100 for the league fee, *x* dollars for each player's T-shirt, and $68.25 for trophies. Write an expression for the total amount the sponsor paid.

Add the league fee, the cost of the T-shirts, and the cost of the trophies.

$100 + 7x + 68.25 = 7x + 100 + 68.25$ Commutative Property of Addition

$= 7x + 168.25$ Add 100 and 68.25.

An expression for the total amount is $7x + 168.25$.

On Your Own

Now You're Ready
Exercises 9–23

Simplify the expression. Explain each step.

4. $-12 \cdot b \cdot 0$ **5.** $1 \cdot m \cdot 24$ **6.** $(t + 15) + 0$

7. **WHAT IF?** In Example 3, your sponsor paid $54.75 for trophies. Write an expression for the total amount the sponsor paid.

6.3 Exercises

Check It Out
Help with Homework
BigIdeasMath.com

Vocabulary and Concept Check

1. **NUMBER SENSE** Write an example of a sum of fractions. Show that the Commutative Property of Addition is true for the sum.
2. **OPEN-ENDED** Write an algebraic expression that can be simplified using the Associative Property of Addition.
3. **OPEN-ENDED** Write an algebraic expression that can be simplified using the Associative Property of Multiplication and the Multiplication Property of One.
4. **WHICH ONE DOESN'T BELONG?** Which statement does *not* belong with the other three? Explain your reasoning.

$7 + (x + 4) = 7 + (4 + x)$	$(3 + b) + 2 = (b + 3) + 2$
$9 + (7 + w) = (9 + 7) + w$	$(4 + n) + 6 = (n + 4) + 6$

Practice and Problem Solving

Tell which property the statement illustrates.

1 5. $5 \cdot p = p \cdot 5$

6. $2 + (12 + r) = (2 + 12) + r$

7. $-4 \cdot (x \cdot 10) = (-4 \cdot x) \cdot 10$

8. $x + 7.5 = 7.5 + x$

2 9. $(c + 2) + 0 = c + 2$

10. $a \cdot 1 = a$

11. **ERROR ANALYSIS** Describe and correct the error in stating the property that the statement illustrates.

✗ $(7 + x) + 3 = (x + 7) + 3$
Associative Property of Addition

Simplify the expression. Explain each step.

12. $6 + (5 + x)$

13. $(14 + y) + 3$

14. $6(2b)$

15. $-7(9w)$

16. $3.2 + (x + 5.1)$

17. $-8 + (a + 0)$

18. $9 \cdot c \cdot 4$

19. $(18.6 \cdot d) \cdot 1$

20. $\left(3k + 4\frac{1}{5}\right) + 8\frac{3}{5}$

21. $(2.4 + 4n) + 9$

22. $(3s) \cdot 8$

23. $z \cdot 0 \cdot (-12)$

24. **BICYCLING** The expression $12 + x + 4$ represents the distance you rode your bicycle in three days. Simplify the expression.

25. **SCOUT COOKIES** A case of Scout cookies has 10 cartons. A carton has 12 boxes. The amount you earn on a whole case is $10(12x)$ dollars.

 a. What does x represent?

 b. Simplify the expression.

26. **STRUCTURE** The volume of the rectangular prism is $12.5 \cdot x \cdot 1$.

a. Simplify the expression.

b. Match $x = 0.25$, 12.5, and 144 with the object. Explain.

A. siding for a house   B. ruler   C. square floor tile

Write the phrase as an expression. Then simplify the expression.

27. 7 plus the sum of a number x and 5

28. the product of 8 and a number y multiplied by 9

Copy and complete the statement using the specified property.

	Property	Statement
29.	Associative Property of Multiplication	$7(2y) =$
30.	Commutative Property of Multiplication	$13.2 \cdot (x \cdot 1) =$
31.	Associative Property of Addition	$-17 + (6 + 2x) =$
32.	Addition Property of Zero	$2 + (c + 0) =$
33.	Multiplication Property of One	$1 \cdot w \cdot 16 =$

34. **HATS** You and a friend sell hats at a fair booth. You sell 16 hats on the first shift and 21 hats on the third shift. Your friend sells x hats on the second shift.

a. Write an expression for the number of hats sold.

b. The expression $37(14) + 10x$ represents the amount that you both earned. How can you tell that your friend was selling the hats for a discounted price?

c. **Reasoning** You earned more money than your friend. What can you say about the value of x?

Fair Game Review What you learned in previous grades & lessons

Evaluate the expression.

35. $7(10 + 4)$ 36. $12(10 - 1)$ 37. $6(5 + 10)$ 38. $8(30 - 5)$

Find the prime factorization of the number.

39. 37   40. 144   41. 147   42. 205

43. **MULTIPLE CHOICE** A bag has 16 blue, 20 red, and 24 green marbles. What fraction of the marbles in the bag are blue?

Ⓐ $\frac{1}{5}$ Ⓑ $\frac{4}{15}$ Ⓒ $\frac{4}{11}$ Ⓓ $\frac{11}{15}$

6.4 The Distributive Property

Essential Question How do you use mental math to multiply two numbers?

The Meaning of a Word ● Distribute

When you **distribute** something to each person in a group, you give that thing to each person in the group.

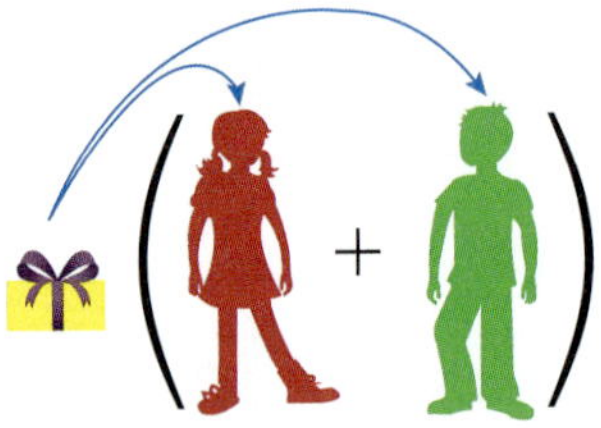

1 ACTIVITY: Modeling a Property

Work with a partner.

a. **MODELING** Draw two rectangles of the same width but with different lengths on a piece of grid paper. Label the dimensions.

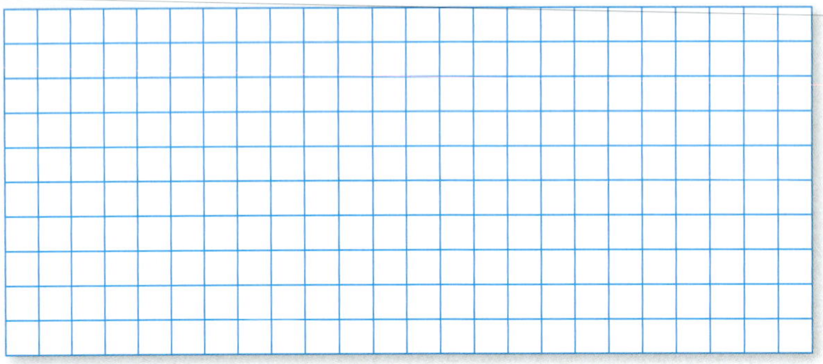

b. Write an expression for the total area of the rectangles.

$$(\square \times \square) + (\square \times \square)$$

c. Rearrange the rectangles by aligning the shortest sides to form one rectangle. Label the dimensions. Write an expression for the area.

$$\square \times (\square + \square)$$

d. Can the expressions from parts (b) and (c) be set equal to each other? Explain.

e. **REPEATED REASONING** Repeat this activity using different rectangles. Explain how this illustrates the Distributive Property. Write a rule for the Distributive Property.

Equivalent Expressions

In this lesson, you will
- use the Distributive Property to find products.
- use the Distributive Property to simplify algebraic expressions.

2 ACTIVITY: Using Mental Math

Math Process

Find Entry Points

How can you rewrite the larger number as the sum of two numbers so that you can use mental math?

Work with a partner. Use the method shown to find the product.

a. Sample: 23×6

$$\begin{array}{r} 23 \\ \times\ \ 6 \\ \hline 120 \\ +\ 18 \\ \hline 138 \end{array}$$

23 ← 23 is 20 + 3.

120: Multiply 20 and 6.

+ 18: Multiply 3 and 6.

138: Add.

So, $23 \times 6 = 138$.

b. 33×7

c. 47×9

d. $28 \times (-5)$

e. $17 \times (-4)$

3 ACTIVITY: Using Mental Math

Work with a partner. Use the Distributive Property and mental math to find the product.

a. Sample: 6×23

$6 \times 23 = 6 \times (20 + 3)$	Write 23 as the sum of 20 and 3.
$= (6 \times 20) + (6 \times 3)$	Distribute the 6 over the sum.
$= 120 + 18$	Find the products.
$= 138$	Add.

So, $6 \times 23 = 138$.

b. 5×17

c. -8×26

d. 20×19

e. 40×29

f. -25×39

g. -15×47

What Is Your Answer?

4. Compare the methods in Activities 2 and 3.

5. **IN YOUR OWN WORDS** How do you use mental math to multiply two numbers? Give examples to support your explanation.

Practice Use what you learned about the Distributive Property to complete Exercises 5–8 on page 227.

6.4 Lesson

Check It Out
Lesson Tutorials
BigIdeasMath.com

Key Vocabulary
like terms, *p. 226*

Key Idea

Distributive Property

Words To multiply a sum or difference by a number, multiply each number in the sum or difference by the number outside the parentheses. Then evaluate.

Numbers $3(7 + 2) = 3 \times 7 + 3 \times 2$

$3(7 - 2) = 3 \times 7 - 3 \times 2$

Algebra $a(b + c) = ab + ac$

$a(b - c) = ab - ac$

EXAMPLE 1 Using Mental Math

Use the Distributive Property and mental math to find 8 × 53.

$8 \times 53 = 8(50 + 3)$ Write 53 as 50 + 3.

$= 8(50) + 8(3)$ Distributive Property

$= 400 + 24$ Multiply.

$= 424$ Add.

EXAMPLE 2 Using the Distributive Property

Use the Distributive Property to find $\frac{1}{2} \times 2\frac{3}{4}$.

$\frac{1}{2} \times 2\frac{3}{4} = \frac{1}{2} \times \left(2 + \frac{3}{4}\right)$ Rewrite $2\frac{3}{4}$ as the sum $2 + \frac{3}{4}$.

$= \left(\frac{1}{2} \times 2\right) + \left(\frac{1}{2} \times \frac{3}{4}\right)$ Distributive Property

$= 1 + \frac{3}{8}$ Multiply.

$= 1\frac{3}{8}$ Add.

On Your Own

Now You're Ready
Exercises 5–16

Use the Distributive Property to find the product.

1. 5×41
2. -9×19
3. $-6(37)$
4. $\frac{2}{3} \times 1\frac{1}{2}$
5. $\frac{1}{4} \times 4\frac{1}{5}$
6. $\frac{2}{7} \times 3\frac{3}{4}$

Multi-Language Glossary at BigIdeasMath.com

EXAMPLE 3 Simplifying Algebraic Expressions

Use the Distributive Property to simplify the expression.

a. $4(n + 5)$

$4(n + 5) = 4(n) + 4(5)$	Distributive Property
$= 4n + 20$	Multiply.

b. $-12(2y - 3)$

$-12(2y - 3) = -12(2y) + 12(3)$	Distributive Property
$= -24y + 36$	Multiply.

c. $9(6 + x + 2)$

$9(6 + x + 2) = 9(6) + 9(x) + 9(2)$	Distributive Property
$= 54 + 9x + 18$	Multiply.
$= 9x + 54 + 18$	Commutative Property of Addition
$= 9x + 72$	Add 54 and 18.

Study Tip

You can use the Distributive Property when there are more than two terms in the sum or difference.

On Your Own

Now You're Ready
Exercises 17–32

Use the Distributive Property to simplify the expression.

7. $-7(a + 2)$ **8.** $3(d - 11)$ **9.** $-7(2 + 6 - 4d)$

EXAMPLE 4 Real-Life Application

José is x years old. His brother, Felipe, is 2 years older than José. Their aunt, Maria, is three times as old as Felipe. Write and simplify an expression that represents Maria's age in years.

Name	Description	Expression
José	He is x years old.	x
Felipe	He is 2 years *older* than José. So, *add* 2 to x.	$x + 2$
Maria	She is three *times* as old as Felipe. So, *multiply* 3 and $(x + 2)$.	$3(x + 2)$

$3(x + 2) = 3(x) + 3(2)$	Distributive Property
$= 3x + 6$	Multiply.

Maria's age in years is represented by the expression $3x + 6$.

On Your Own

10. Alexis is x years old. Her sister, Gloria, is 7 years older than Alexis. Their grandfather is five times as old as Gloria. Write and simplify an expression that represents their grandfather's age in years.

In an algebraic expression, **like terms** are terms that have the same variables raised to the same exponents. Constant terms are also like terms.

Like terms ($5x$ and $2x$)

$$5x + 19 + 2x + 2$$

Like terms (19 and 2)

Use the Distributive Property to *combine* like terms.

EXAMPLE 5 Combining Like Terms

Simplify each expression.

a. $3x + 9 + 2x - 5$

$3x + 9 + 2x - 5$	$= 3x + 2x + 9 - 5$	Commutative Property of Addition
	$= (3 + 2)x + 9 - 5$	Distributive Property
	$= 5x + 4$	Simplify.

b. $y + y + y$

$y + y + y$	$= 1y + 1y + 1y$	Multiplication Property of One
	$= (1 + 1 + 1)y$	Distributive Property
	$= 3y$	Add coefficients.

c. $7z + 2(z - 5y)$

$7z + 2(z - 5y)$	$= 7z + 2(z) - 2(5y)$	Distributive Property
	$= 7z + 2z - 10y$	Multiply.
	$= (7 + 2)z - 10y$	Distributive Property
	$= 9z - 10y$	Add coefficients.

On Your Own

Now You're Ready
Exercises 39–53

Simplify the expression.

11. $8 + 3z - z$

12. $-3(b + 5) + b + 2$

6.4 Exercises

Check It Out
Help with Homework
BigIdeasMath.com

Vocabulary and Concept Check

1. **WRITING** One meaning of the word *distribute* is "to give something to each member of a group." How can this help you remember the Distributive Property?

2. **OPEN-ENDED** Write an algebraic expression in which you use the Distributive Property and then the Associative Property of Addition to simplify.

3. **WHICH ONE DOESN'T BELONG?** Which expression does *not* belong with the other three? Explain your reasoning.

   $2(x + 2)$ $5(x - 8)$ $4 + (x \cdot 4)$ $8(9 - x)$

4. Identify the like terms in the expression $8x + 1 + 7x + 4$.

Practice and Problem Solving

Use the Distributive Property and mental math to find the product.

① **5.** 3×21 **6.** 9×76 **7.** $-12(43)$ **8.** $-5(88)$

9. 18×52 **10.** -8×27 **11.** $-8(63)$ **12.** $7(28)$

Use the Distributive Property to find the product.

② **13.** $\frac{1}{4} \times 2\frac{2}{7}$ **14.** $-\frac{5}{6} \times 2\frac{2}{5}$ **15.** $\frac{5}{9} \times 4\frac{1}{2}$ **16.** $\frac{2}{15} \times 5\frac{5}{8}$

Use the Distributive Property to simplify the expression.

③ **17.** $3(x + 4)$ **18.** $10(b - 6)$ **19.** $6(s - 9)$ **20.** $-7(8 + y)$

21. $-8(12 + a)$ **22.** $9(2n + 1)$ **23.** $12(6 - k)$ **24.** $-18(5 - 3w)$

25. $9(3 + c + 4)$ **26.** $7(8 + x + 2)$ **27.** $-8(5g + 5 - 2)$ **28.** $6(10 + z + 3)$

29. $-4(x + y)$ **30.** $-25(x - y)$ **31.** $7(p + q + 9)$ **32.** $13(n + 4 + 7m)$

33. **ERROR ANALYSIS** Describe and correct the error in rewriting the expression.

✗ $6(y + 8) = 6y + 8$

34. **ART MUSEUM** A class of 30 students visits an art museum and a special exhibit while there.

a. Use the Distributive Property to write and simplify an expression for the cost.

b. Estimate a reasonable value for x. Explain.

c. Use your estimate for x to evaluate the original expression and the simplified expression in part (a). Are the values the same?

PRICES

	Museum	Exhibit
Child (under 5)	Free	Free
Student	$8	$x
Regular	$12	$4
Senior	$10	$3

35. **FITNESS** Each day, you run on a treadmill for r minutes and lift weights for 15 minutes. Which expressions can you use to find how many minutes of exercise you do in 5 days? Explain your reasoning.

$5(r + 15)$ $5r + 5 \cdot 15$ $5r + 15$ $r(5 + 15)$

36. **SPEED** A cheetah can run 103 feet per second. A zebra can run x feet per second. Use the Distributive Property to write and simplify an expression for how much farther the cheetah can run in 10 seconds.

UNIFORMS Your baseball team has 16 players. Use the Distributive Property to write and simplify an expression for the total cost of buying the items shown for all the players.

37.

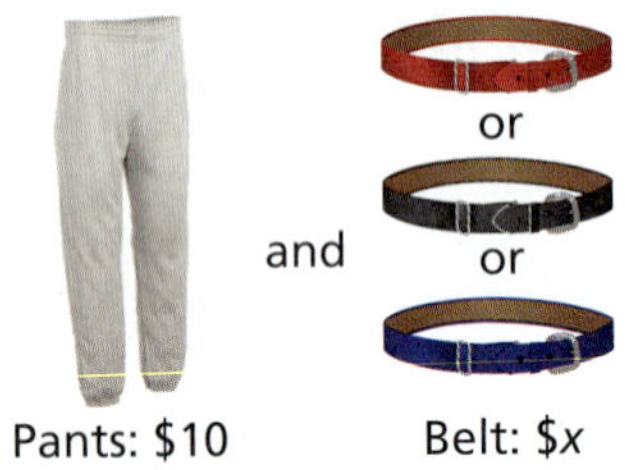

38.

5 **Simplify the expression.**

39. $6(x + 4) + 1$
40. $5 + 8(3 + x)$
41. $-7(8 + 4k) + 12$
42. $x + 3 + 5x$
43. $7y + 6 - 1 + 12y$
44. $w + w + 5w$
45. $4d + 9 - d - 8$
46. $n - 3(n - 1)$
47. $2v + 8v - 5v$
48. $-5(z + 4) + 5(2 + z)$
49. $2.7(w - 5.2)$
50. $\frac{2}{3}y + \frac{1}{6}y + y$
51. $\frac{3}{4}\left(z + \frac{2}{5}\right) + 2z$
52. $7(x + y) - 7x$
53. $4x + 9y - 3(x + y)$

54. **ERROR ANALYSIS** Describe and correct the error in simplifying the expression.

$$\begin{aligned} 8x - 2x + 5x &= 8x - 7x \\ &= (8 - 7)x \\ &= x \end{aligned}$$

ALGEBRA Find the value of x that makes the expressions equivalent.

55. $4(x - 5);\ 32 - 20$
56. $2(x + 9);\ -30 + 18$
57. $7(8 - x);\ 56 - 21$

58. **REASONING** Simplify the expressions and compare. What do you notice? Explain.

$4(x + 6)$ $(x + 6) + (x + 6) + (x + 6) + (x + 6)$

GEOMETRY **Write and simplify expressions for the area and perimeter of the rectangle.**

59.

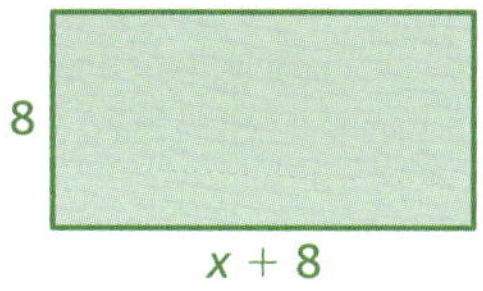

60.

61.

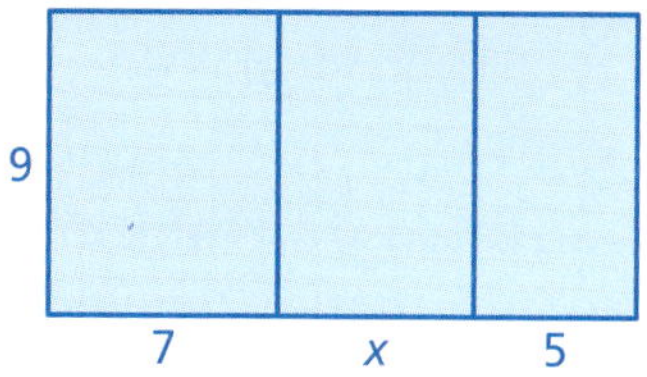

62. **FUNDRAISER** An art club sells 42 large candles and 56 small candles.

a. Use the Distributive Property to write and simplify an expression for the profit.

b. A large candle costs $5, and a small candle costs $3. What is the club's profit?

Profit = Price − Cost

63. **REASONING** Evaluate each expression by (1) using the Distributive Property and (2) evaluating inside the parentheses first. Which method do you prefer? Is your preference the same for both expressions? Explain your reasoning.

a. $2(3.22 - 0.12)$ **b.** $12\left(\frac{1}{2} + \frac{2}{3}\right)$

64. **REASONING** Write and simplify an expression for the difference between the perimeters of the rectangle and the hexagon. Interpret your answer.

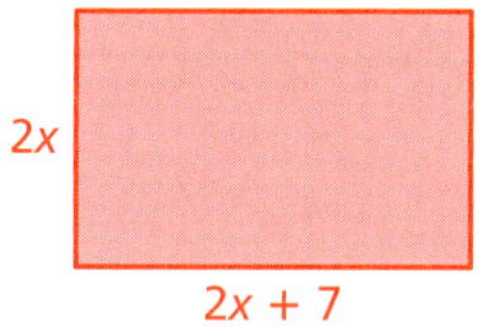

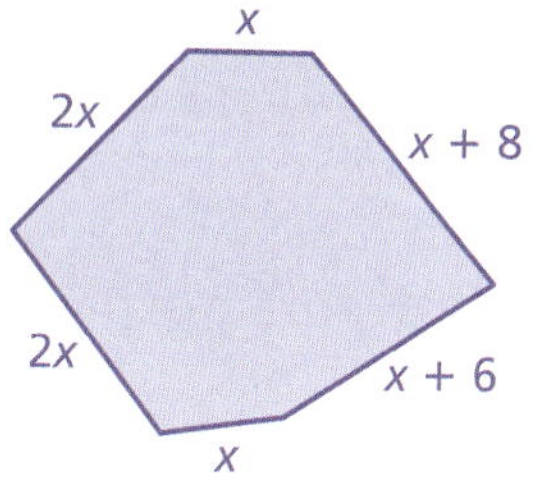

65. **Puzzle** Add one set of parentheses to the expression $7 \cdot x + 3 + 8 \cdot x + 3 \cdot x + 8 - 9$ so that it is equivalent to $2(9x + 10)$.

Fair Game Review What you learned in previous grades & lessons

Evaluate the expression.

66. $4.871 + 7.4 - 1.63$

67. $25.06 - 0.049 + 8.995$

68. $15.3 \cdot 9.1 - 4.017$

69. $29.24 \div 3.4 \cdot 0.045$

70. **MULTIPLE CHOICE** Which statement is true?

Ⓐ $-6 > |-3|$

Ⓑ $-|2| = -2$

Ⓒ $|-3| = -3$

Ⓓ $|-7| < |5|$

6 Study Help

Check It Out
Graphic Organizer
BigIdeasMath.com

You can use an **information wheel** to organize information about a topic. Here is an example of an information wheel for identifying parts of an algebraic expression.

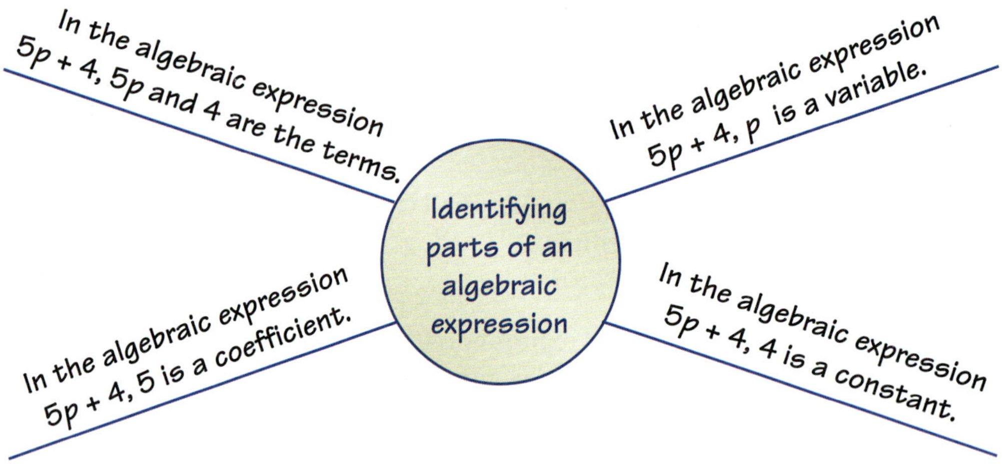

On Your Own

Make information wheels to help you study these topics.

1. evaluating algebraic expressions
2. writing algebraic expressions
3. Commutative Properties of Addition and Multiplication
4. Associative Properties of Addition and Multiplication
5. Addition Property of Zero
6. Multiplication Properties of Zero and One
7. Distributive Property

"My information wheel for Fluffy has matching adjectives and nouns."

6 Chapter Review

Check It Out
Vocabulary Help
BigIdeasMath.com

Review Key Vocabulary

algebraic expression, *p. 204*
terms, *p. 204*
variable, *p. 204*
coefficient, *p. 204*
constant, *p. 204*
equivalent expressions, *p. 218*
like terms, *p. 226*

Review Examples and Exercises

6.1 Algebraic Expressions (pp. 202–209)

a. Evaluate $a \div b$ when $a = -48$ and $b = 8$.

$a \div b = -48 \div 8$ Substitute −48 for *a* and 8 for *b*.

$= -6$ Divide −48 by 8.

b. Evaluate $y^2 - 14$ when $y = 5$.

$y^2 - 14 = 5^2 - 14$ Substitute 5 for *y*.

$= 25 - 14$ Using order of operations, evaluate 5^2.

$= 11$ Subtract 14 from 25.

Exercises

Evaluate the expression when $x = 20$ and $y = -4$.

1. $x \div 5$
2. $y + x$
3. $8y - x$

4. **GAMING** In a video game, you score p game points and b triple bonus points. An expression for your score is $p + 3b$. What is your score when you earn 245 game points and 20 triple bonus points?

6.2 Writing Expressions (pp. 210–215)

Write the phrase as an expression.

a. a number z decreased by 18

$z - 18$ The phrase *decreased by* means *subtraction.*

b. the sum of −7 and the product of a number x and 12

$-7 + 12x$ The phrase *sum of* means *addition.*
The phrase *product of* means *multiplication.*

Exercises

Write the phrase as an expression.

5. 11 fewer than a number b

6. the product of a number d and -32

7. 18 added to a number n

8. a number t decreased by 17

9. **BASKETBALL** Your basketball team scored 4 fewer than twice as many points as the other team.

a. Write an expression for the number of points your team scored.

b. The other team scored 24 points. How many points did your team score?

6.3 Properties of Addition and Multiplication *(pp. 216–221)*

a. Simplify the expression $(x + 18) + 4$.

$(x + 18) + 4 = x + (18 + 4)$ — Associative Property of Addition

$= x + 22$ — Add 18 and 4.

b. Simplify the expression $(5.2 + a) + 0$.

$(5.2 + a) + 0 = 5.2 + (a + 0)$ — Associative Property of Addition

$= 5.2 + a$ — Addition Property of Zero

c. Simplify the expression $-36 \cdot r \cdot 1$.

$-36 \cdot r \cdot 1 = -36 \cdot (r \cdot 1)$ — Associative Property of Multiplication

$= -36 \cdot r$ — Multiplication Property of One

$= -36r$

Exercises

Simplify the expression. Explain each step.

10. $10 + (2 + y)$

11. $(21 + b) + 1$

12. $-3(7x)$

13. $1(3.2w)$

14. $5.3 + (w + 1.2)$

15. $(0 + t) + (-9)$

16. **GEOMETRY** The expression $7 + 3x + 4$ represents the perimeter of the triangle. Simplify the expression.

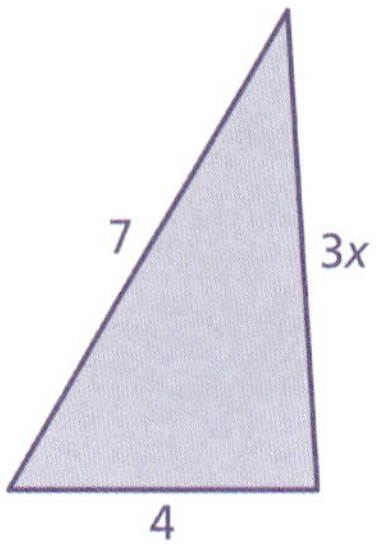

6.4 The Distributive Property (pp. 222–229)

a. Use the Distributive Property to find $\frac{1}{3} \times 6\frac{2}{5}$.

$$\frac{1}{3} \times 6\frac{2}{5} = \frac{1}{3} \times \left(6 + \frac{2}{5}\right)$$ Rewrite $6\frac{2}{5}$ as the sum $6 + \frac{2}{5}$.

$$= \left(\frac{1}{3} \times 6\right) + \left(\frac{1}{3} \times \frac{2}{5}\right)$$ Distributive Property

$$= 2 + \frac{2}{15}$$ Multiply.

$$= 2\frac{2}{15}$$ Add.

b. Use the Distributive Property to simplify $3(n + 9)$.

$$3(n + 9) = 3(n) + 3(9)$$ Distributive Property

$$= 3n + 27$$ Multiply.

c. Simplify $-5x + 7 + 3x - 2$.

$$-5x + 7 + 3x - 2 = -5x + 3x + 7 - 2$$ Commutative Property of Addition

$$= (-5 + 3)x + 7 - 2$$ Distributive Property

$$= -2x + 5$$ Simplify.

Exercises

Use the Distributive Property to find the product.

17. $\frac{3}{4} \times 2\frac{1}{3}$ **18.** $\frac{4}{7} \times 4\frac{5}{8}$ **19.** $\frac{1}{5} \times 5\frac{10}{11}$

Use the Distributive Property to simplify the expression.

20. $2(x + 12)$ **21.** $11(b - 3)$

22. $-8(s - 1)$ **23.** $-6(6 + y)$

24. $25(z - 4)$ **25.** $35(w - 2)$

26. HAIRCUT A family of four goes to a salon for haircuts. The cost of each haircut is $13. Use the Distributive Property and mental math to find the product 4×13 for the total cost.

Simplify the expression.

27. $5(n + 3) + 4n$ **28.** $t + 2 - 6t$ **29.** $-3z + 4 + 5z - 9$

7 Equations and Inequalities

What You Learned Before

"Dear Sir: I have the answer to the contest question, 'How many seconds are in a year?' There are 12: January 2nd, February 2nd, ..."

Evaluating Expressions

Example 1 **Evaluate $7x + 3y$ when $x = 2$ and $y = 4$.**

$7x + 3y = 7 \cdot 2 + 3 \cdot 4$ — Substitute 2 for x and 4 for y.

$= 14 + 12$ — Using order of operations, multiply from left to right.

$= 26$ — Add 14 and 12.

Example 2 **Evaluate $5x^2 - 2(y + 1) + 9$ when $x = 2$ and $y = 1$.**

$5x^2 - 2(y + 1) + 9 = 5(2)^2 - 2(1 + 1) + 9$ — Substitute 2 for x and 1 for y.

$= 5(2)^2 - 2 \cdot 2 + 9$ — Using order of operations, evaluate within the parentheses.

$= 5 \cdot 4 - 2 \cdot 2 + 9$ — Using order of operations, evaluate the exponent.

$= 20 - 4 + 9$ — Using order of operations, multiply from left to right.

$= 25$ — Subtract 4 from 20. Add the result to 9.

Try It Yourself

Evaluate the expression when $a = \frac{1}{2}$ and $b = 7$.

1. $6ab$ **2.** $16a - b$ **3.** $3b - 2a - 9$ **4.** $b^2 - 16a + 5$

Writing Expressions

Example 3 **Write the phrase as an expression.**

a. the sum of twice a number n and five

$2n + 5$

b. twelve less than four times a number y

$4y - 12$

Try It Yourself

Write the phrase as an expression.

5. six more than three times a number w

6. the quotient of seven and a number p

7. negative two minus a number t

8. the product of a number x and five

9. five more than six divided by a number r

10. four less than three times a number b

7.1 Writing Equations in One Variable

Essential Question How does rewriting a word problem help you solve the word problem?

1 ACTIVITY: Rewriting a Word Problem

Work with a partner. Read the problem several times. Think about how you could rewrite the problem. Leave out information that you do not need to solve the problem.

Given Problem (63 words)

Your minivan has a flat, rectangular area in the back. When you fold down the rear seats of the van and move them forward, the width of the rectangular area in the van is increased by 2 feet, as shown in the diagram.

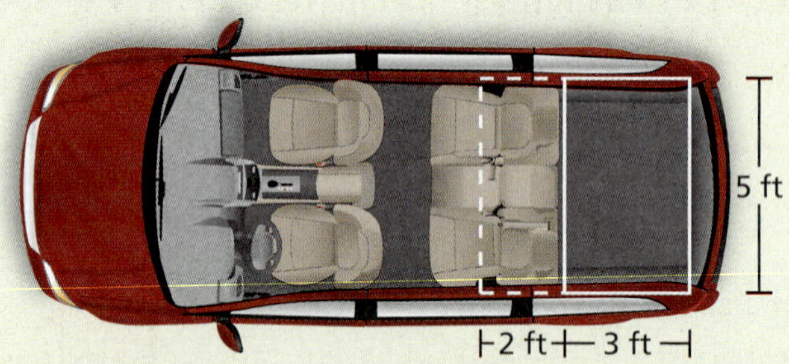

By how many square feet does the rectangular area increase when the rear seats are folded down and moved forward?

Rewritten Problem (28 words)

When you fold down the back seats of a minivan, the added area is a 5-foot by 2-foot rectangle. What is the area of this rectangle?

Can you make the problem even simpler?

Rewritten Problem (words)

Explain why your rewritten problem is easier to read.

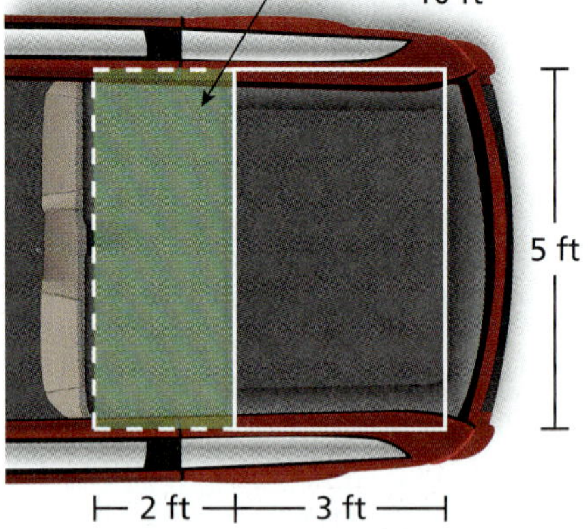

Writing Equations
In this lesson, you will
- write word sentences as equations.

Math Process

Analyze Givens
What information do you need to solve the problem?

2 ACTIVITY: Rewriting a Word Problem

Work with a partner. Rewrite each problem using fewer words. Leave out information that you do not need to solve the problem. Then solve the problem.

a. (63 words)

A supermarket is having its grand opening on Saturday morning. Every fifth customer will receive a $10 coupon for a free turkey. Every seventh customer will receive a $3 coupon for 2 gallons of ice cream. You are the manager of the store and you expect to have 400 customers. How many of each type of coupon should you plan to give away?

b. (71 words)

You and your friend are at a football game. The stadium is 4 miles from your home. You each brought $5 to spend on refreshments. During the third quarter of the game, you say, "I read that the greatest distance that a baseball has been thrown is 445 feet 10 inches." Your friend says, "That's about one and a half times the length of the football field." Is your friend correct?

c. (90 words)

You are visiting your cousin who lives in the city. To get back home, you take a taxi. The taxi charges $2.10 for the first mile and $0.90 for each additional mile. After riding 13 miles, you decide that the fare is going to be more than the $20 you have with you. So, you tell the driver to stop and let you out. Then you call a friend and ask your friend to come and pick you up. After paying the driver, how much of your $20 is left?

What Is Your Answer?

3. **IN YOUR OWN WORDS** How does rewriting a word problem help you solve the word problem? Make up a word problem that has more than 50 words. Then show how you can rewrite the problem using at most 25 words.

"Solving a math word problem is like making maple syrup."

"You need to boil down 40 gallons of sap from a sugar maple tree to get 1 gallon of syrup."

Practice Use what you learned about writing equations to complete Exercises 4 and 5 on page 240.

7.1 Lesson

Check It Out
Lesson Tutorials
BigIdeasMath.com

Key Vocabulary
equation, *p. 238*

An **equation** is a mathematical sentence that uses an equal sign, =, to show that two expressions are equal.

Expressions	*Equations*
$4 + 8$	$4 + 8 = 12$
$x + 8$	$x + 8 = 12$

To write a word sentence as an equation, look for key words or phrases such as *is*, *the same as*, or *equals* to determine where to place the equal sign.

EXAMPLE 1 Writing Equations

Write the word sentence as an equation.

a. The sum of a number n and 7 is 15.

The sum of a number n and 7 is 15.

$n + 7 \quad = 15$ *Sum of* means *addition.*

An equation is $n + 7 = 15$.

b. A number y decreased by 4 is -3.

A number y decreased by 4 is -3.

$y - 4 \quad = -3$ *Decreased by* means *subtraction.*

An equation is $y - 4 = -3$.

c. 12 times a number p equals 48.

12 times a number p equals 48.

$12p \quad = \quad 48$ *Times* means *multiplication.*

An equation is $12p = 48$.

On Your Own

Now You're Ready
Exercises 6–13

Write the word sentence as an equation.

1. 9 less than a number b equals 2.
2. The product of a number g and -5 is 30.
3. A number k increased by 10 is the same as 24.
4. The quotient of a number q and 4 is -12.

EXAMPLE 2 Writing an Equation

Ten servers decorate 25 tables for a wedding. Each table is decorated as shown. Let *c* be the total number of white and purple candles. Which equation can you use to find *c*?

Ⓐ $c = 25 + (4 \times 6)$ Ⓑ $c = 25(4 + 6)$

Ⓒ $c = 10(25 + 4 + 6)$ Ⓓ $c = 10(4 + 6)$

Words The total number of candles | is | the number of tables | times | the number of candles on each table.

Variable Let c be the total number of candles.

Equation $c = 25 \times (4 + 6)$

∴ The correct answer is Ⓑ.

EXAMPLE 3 Real-Life Application

After two rounds, 24 students are eliminated from a spelling bee. There are 96 students remaining. Write an equation you can use to find the number of students that started the spelling bee.

Reading

The word *eliminated* means *subtraction*.

Words The number of students that started | minus | the number of students eliminated | is | the number of students remaining.

Variable Let s be the number of students that started.

Equation $s - 24 = 96$

∴ An equation is $s - 24 = 96$.

On Your Own

5. You enter an elevator and go down 7 floors. You exit on the 10th floor. Write an equation you can use to find the floor where you entered the elevator.
6. Together you and a friend have $52. Your friend has $28. Write an equation you can use to find how much money you have.
7. A typical person takes about 24,000 breaths each day. Write an equation you can use to find the number of breaths a typical person takes each minute.

7.1 Exercises

Check It Out
Help with Homework
BigIdeasMath.com

Vocabulary and Concept Check

1. **VOCABULARY** How are expressions and equations different?
2. **DIFFERENT WORDS, SAME QUESTION** Which is different? Write "both" equations.

4 less than a number n is 8.	A number n is 4 less than 8.
A number n minus 4 equals 8.	4 subtracted from a number n is 8.

3. **OPEN-ENDED** Write a word sentence for the equation $28 - n = 5$.

Practice and Problem Solving

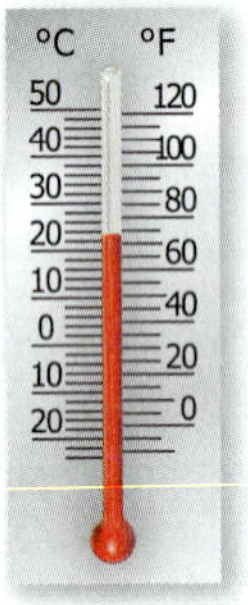

Rewrite the problem using fewer words. Leave out information that you do not need to solve the problem. Then solve the problem.

4. In a cross-country race you run at a steady rate of 7 minutes per mile. After 21 minutes, you finish in fourth place. How long is the race?
5. For a science project, you record the high temperature each day. The high temperature on Day 1 was 6° less than on Day 4 and 4° less than on Day 10. The high temperature on Day 10 was 62°F. What was the high temperature on Day 1?

Write the word sentence as an equation.

1 6. The sum of a number x and 4 equals -12.
7. A number y decreased by 9 is 8.
8. 9 times a number b is 36.
9. A number w divided by 5 equals 6.
10. 54 equals 9 more than a number t.
11. -5 is one-fourth of a number c.
12. 11 is the quotient of a number y and 6.
13. 9 less than a number n equals 27.

14. **ERROR ANALYSIS** Describe the error in writing the sentence as an equation.

> ✗ A number n is 5 more than 12.
> $n + 5 = 12$

15. **FUNDRAISING** Students and faculty raised \$6042 for band uniforms. The faculty raised \$1780. Write an equation you can use to find the amount a raised by the students.

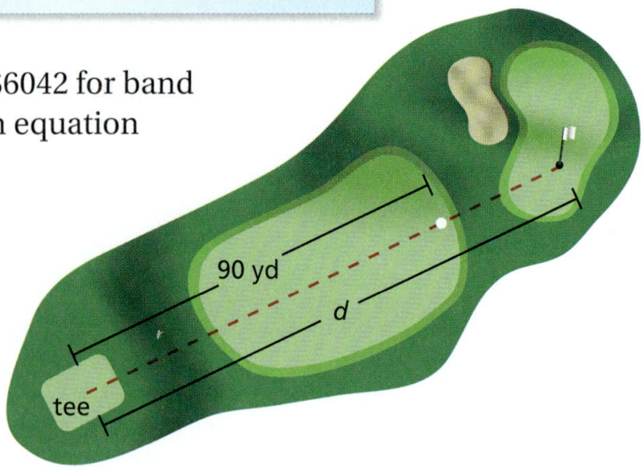

16. **GOLF** You hit a golf ball 90 yards. It travels three-fourths of the distance to the hole. Write an equation you can use to find the distance d from the tee to the hole.

GEOMETRY **Write an equation that you can use to find the value of x.**

17. Perimeter of triangle: 16 in.

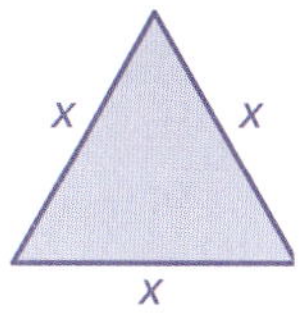

18. Perimeter of square: 30 mm

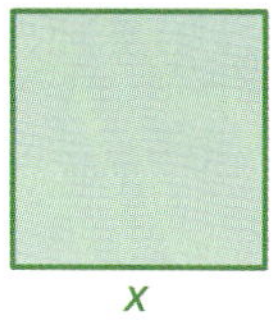

19. **MUSIC** You sell instruments at a Caribbean music festival. You earn \$326 by selling 12 sets of maracas, 6 sets of claves, and x *djembe* drums. Write an equation you can use to find the number of *djembe* drums you sold.

20. **SALES TAX** Find a sales receipt from a store that shows the total price and the total amount paid including sales tax.

a. Write an equation you can use to find the sales tax rate r.

b. Can you use r to find the *percent* for the sales tax? Explain.

21. **STRAWBERRIES** You buy a basket of 24 strawberries. You eat them as you walk to the beach. It takes the same amount of time to walk each block. When you are halfway there, half of the berries are gone. After walking 3 more blocks, you still have 5 blocks to go. You reach the beach 28 minutes after you began. One-sixth of your strawberries are left.

a. Is there enough information to find the time it takes to walk each block? Explain.

b. Is there enough information to find how many strawberries you ate while walking the last block? Explain.

22. **Geometry** A triangle is cut from a rectangle. The height of the triangle is half of the unknown side length s. The area of the shaded region is 84 square inches. Write an equation you can use to find the side length s.

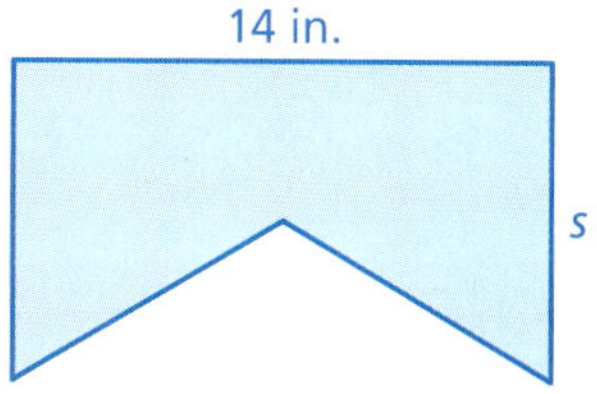

Fair Game Review What you learned in previous grades & lessons

Evaluate the expression when $a = 7$.

23. $6 + a$ **24.** $a - 4$ **25.** $4a$ **26.** $\frac{35}{a}$

27. **MULTIPLE CHOICE** Which expression is equivalent to $8(x + 3)$?

Ⓐ $8x + 3$ Ⓑ $8x + 24$ Ⓒ $8x + 11$ Ⓓ $x + 24$

7.2 Solving Equations Using Addition or Subtraction

Essential Question How can you use addition or subtraction to solve an equation?

When two sides of a scale weigh the same, the scale will balance.

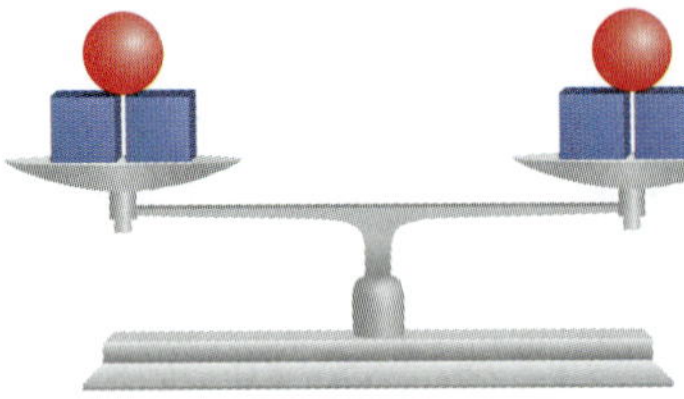

When you add or subtract the same amount on each side of the scale, it will still balance.

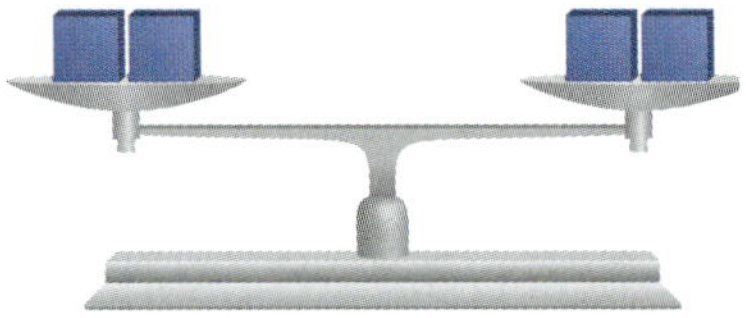

1 ACTIVITY: Solving an Equation

Work with a partner.

a. Use a model to solve $n + 3 = 7$.

- Explain how the model represents the equation $n + 3 = 7$.

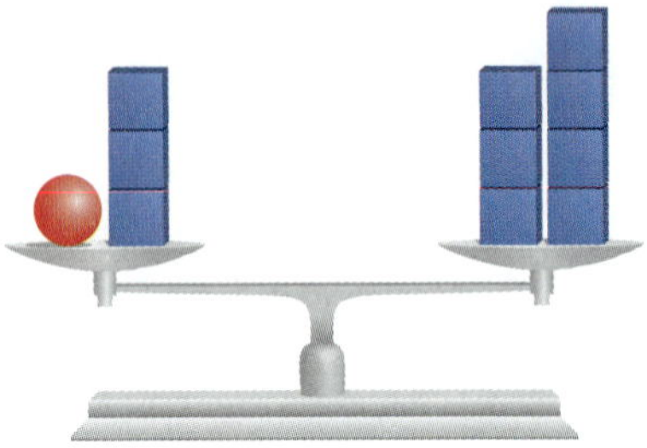

- How much does one  weigh? How do you know?

The solution is $n = $ ▭.

b. Describe how you could check your answer in part (a).

c. Which model below represents the solution of $n + 1 = 9$? How do you know?

Solving Equations

In this lesson, you will

- use addition or subtraction to solve equations.
- use substitution to check answers.
- solve real-life problems.

2 ACTIVITY: Solving Equations

Work with a partner. Solve the equation using the method in Activity 1.

Math Process

Understand Quantities

What does the variable represent in the equation?

a.

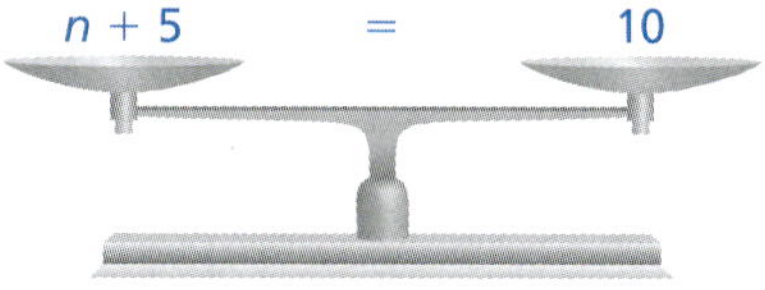

b.

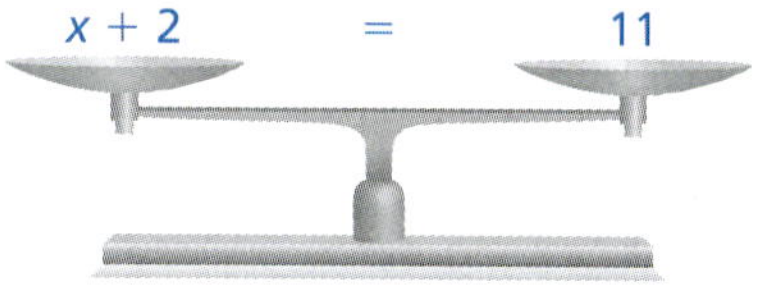

c.

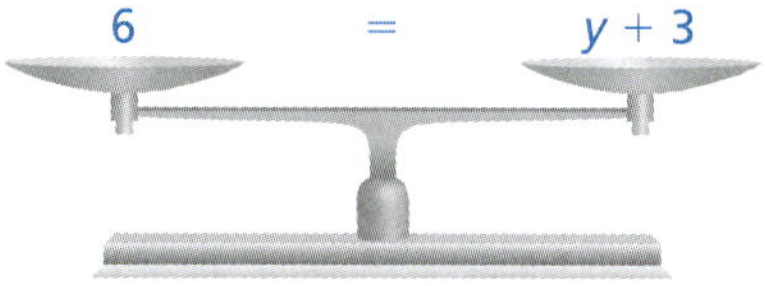

d.

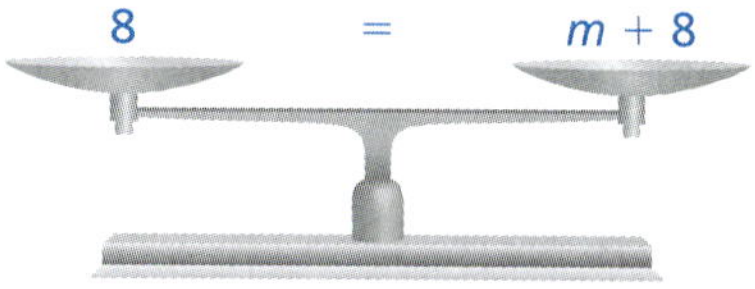

3 ACTIVITY: Solving Equations Using Mental Math

Work with a partner. Write a question that represents the equation. Use mental math to answer the question. Then check your solution.

Equation	Question	Solution	Check
a. $x + 1 = 5$			
b. $4 + m = 11$			
c. $8 = a + 3$			
d. $x - 9 = 21$			
e. $13 = p - 4$			

What Is Your Answer?

4. **REPEATED REASONING** In Activity 3, how are parts (d) and (e) different from parts (a)–(c)? Did your process to find the solution change? Explain.
5. Decide whether the statement is *true* or *false*. If false, explain your reasoning.
   a. In an equation, you can use any letter as a variable.
   b. The goal in solving an equation is to get the variable by itself.
   c. In the solution, the variable must always be on the left side of the equal sign.
   d. If you add a number to one side, you should subtract it from the other side.
6. **IN YOUR OWN WORDS** How can you use addition or subtraction to solve an equation? Give two examples to show how your procedure works.
7. Are the following equations equivalent? Explain your reasoning.

$$x - 5 = 12 \qquad \text{and} \qquad 12 = x - 5$$

Practice Use what you learned about solving equations to complete Exercises 12–17 on page 247.

7.2 Lesson

Check It Out
Lesson Tutorials
BigIdeasMath.com

Key Vocabulary
solution, *p. 244*
inverse operations, *p. 245*

Reading
The symbol ≠ means *is not equal to.*

Equations may be true for some values and false for others. A **solution** of an equation is a value that makes the equation true.

Value of x	$x + 3 = 7$	Are both sides equal?
3	$3 + 3 \stackrel{?}{=} 7$ $6 \neq 7$ ✗	no
4	$4 + 3 \stackrel{?}{=} 7$ $7 = 7$ ✓	yes
5	$5 + 3 \stackrel{?}{=} 7$ $8 \neq 7$ ✗	no

So, the value $x = 4$ is a solution of the equation $x + 3 = 7$.

EXAMPLE 1 Checking Solutions

Tell whether the given value is a solution of the equation.

a. $p + 10 = 38;\ p = 18$

$18 + 10 \stackrel{?}{=} 38$ — Substitute 18 for *p*.

$28 \neq 38$ ✗ — Sides are *not* equal.

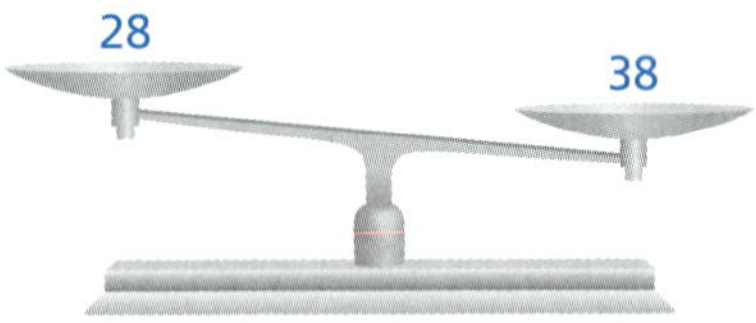

So, $p = 18$ is *not* a solution.

b. $4y = 56;\ y = 14$

$4(14) \stackrel{?}{=} 56$ — Substitute 14 for *y*.

$56 = 56$ ✓ — Sides are equal.

So, $y = 14$ is a solution.

On Your Own

Now You're Ready
Exercises 6–11

Tell whether the given value is a solution of the equation.

1. $a + 6 = 17;\ a = 9$

2. $9 - g = 5;\ g = 3$

3. $-35 = 7n;\ n = -5$

4. $\frac{q}{2} = 28;\ q = 14$

You can use *inverse operations* to solve equations. **Inverse operations** "undo" each other. Addition and subtraction are inverse operations.

Key Ideas

Addition Property of Equality

Words When you add the same number to each side of an equation, the two sides remain equal.

Numbers

$$\begin{aligned} 8 &= 8 \\ +5 \quad & \quad +5 \\ 13 &= 13 \end{aligned}$$

Algebra

$$\begin{aligned} x - 4 &= 5 \\ +4 \quad & \quad +4 \\ x &= 9 \end{aligned}$$

Subtraction Property of Equality

Words When you subtract the same number from each side of an equation, the two sides remain equal.

Numbers

$$\begin{aligned} 8 &= 8 \\ -5 \quad & \quad -5 \\ 3 &= 3 \end{aligned}$$

Algebra

$$\begin{aligned} x + 4 &= 5 \\ -4 \quad & \quad -4 \\ x &= 1 \end{aligned}$$

EXAMPLE 2 Solving Equations Using Addition

a. Solve $x - 2 = 6$.

$x - 2 = 6$	Write the equation.
$+2 \quad +2$	Addition Property of Equality
$x = 8$	Simplify.

Undo the subtraction.

The solution is $x = 8$.

Check

$x - 2 = 6$

$8 - 2 \stackrel{?}{=} 6$

$6 = 6$ ✓

b. Solve $18 = x - 7$.

$18 = x - 7$	Write the equation.
$+7 \quad +7$	Addition Property of Equality
$25 = x$	Simplify.

The solution is $x = 25$.

Check

$18 = x - 7$

$18 \stackrel{?}{=} 25 - 7$

$18 = 18$ ✓

Study Tip

You can check your solution by substituting it for the variable in the original equation.

On Your Own

Now You're Ready
Exercises 18–20

Solve the equation. Check your solution.

5. $k - 3 = 1$ **6.** $n - 10 = 4$ **7.** $-15 = r - 6$

EXAMPLE 3 Solving Equations Using Subtraction

a. Solve $x + 2 = -9$.

$$x + 2 = -9 \quad \text{Write the equation.}$$

Undo the addition. →

$$\underline{-2} \quad \underline{-2} \quad \text{Subtraction Property of Equality}$$

$$x = -11 \quad \text{Simplify.}$$

The solution is $x = -11$.

Check

$x + 2 = -9$

$-11 + 2 \stackrel{?}{=} -9$

$-9 = -9$ ✓

b. Solve $26 = 11 + x$.

A solution can be represented as a point on the number line.

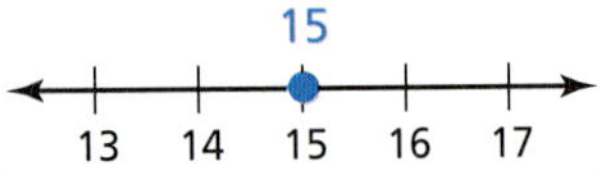

$$26 = 11 + x \quad \text{Write the equation.}$$

$$\underline{-11} \quad \underline{-11} \quad \text{Subtraction Property of Equality}$$

$$15 = x \quad \text{Simplify.}$$

The solution is $x = 15$.

Check

$26 = 11 + x$

$26 \stackrel{?}{=} 11 + 15$

$26 = 26$ ✓

EXAMPLE 4 Real-Life Application

Your parents give you \$20 to help buy the new pair of shoes shown. After you buy the shoes, you have \$5.50 left. Write and solve an equation to find how much money you had before your parents gave you \$20.

Words	The starting amount	plus	the amount your parents gave you	minus	the cost of the shoes	is	the amount left.
Variable	Let s be the starting amount.						
Equation	s	$+$	20	$-$	59.95	$=$	5.50

$s + 20 - 59.95 = 5.50$ — Write the equation.

$s + 20 - 59.95 + 59.95 = 5.50 + 59.95$ — Addition Property of Equality

$s + 20 = 65.45$ — Simplify.

$s + 20 - 20 = 65.45 - 20$ — Subtraction Property of Equality

$s = 45.45$ — Simplify.

You had \$45.45 before your parents gave you money.

Study Tip

In Example 4, you can solve the problem arithmetically by working backwards from \$5.50.

$5.50 + 59.95 - 20 = 45.45$

So, your answer is reasonable.

On Your Own

Now You're Ready Exercises 21–23

Solve the equation. Check your solution.

8. $s + 8 = 17$ **9.** $9 = y + 6$ **10.** $13 + m = -20$

11. You eat 8 blueberries and your friend eats 11 blueberries from a package. There are 23 blueberries left. Write and solve an equation to find the number of blueberries in a full package.

7.2 Exercises

Check It Out
Help with Homework
BigIdeasMath.com

Vocabulary and Concept Check

1. **WRITING** How can you check the solution of an equation?

Name the inverse operation you can use to solve the equation.

2. $x - 8 = 12$
3. $n + 3 = -13$
4. $b + 14 = 33$

5. **WRITING** When solving $x + 5 = 16$, why do you subtract 5 from the left side of the equation? Why do you subtract 5 from the right side of the equation?

Practice and Problem Solving

Tell whether the given value is a solution of the equation.

(1) 6. $x + 42 = 85;\ x = 43$

7. $-8b = 48;\ b = -6$

8. $19 - g = 7;\ g = 15$

9. $\frac{m}{4} = 16;\ m = 4$

10. $w + (-28) = 16;\ w = 12$

11. $s - 68 = 11;\ s = 79$

Use a scale to model and solve the equation.

12. $n + 7 = 9$
13. $t + 4 = 5$
14. $c + 2 = 8$

Write a question that represents the equation. Use mental math to answer the question. Then check your solution.

15. $a + 5 = 12$
16. $v + 9 = 18$
17. $20 = d - 6$

Solve the equation. Check your solution.

(2) 18. $y - 7 = 3$

19. $z - 3 = -13$

20. $8 = r - 14$

(3) 21. $p + 5 = 8$

22. $k + (-6) = 18$

23. $64 = h + 30$

24. $f - 27 = 19$

25. $25 = q + 14$

26. $-3 = j - 1$

27. $x + 3 = -10$

28. $1 = m - 2$

29. $a + 5 = 17$

ERROR ANALYSIS **Describe and correct the error in solving the equation.**

30. ✗

$$\begin{array}{rcl} x + 7 & = & 13 \\ +7 & & +7 \\ \hline x & = & 20 \end{array}$$

31. ✗

$$\begin{array}{rcl} 34 & = & y - 12 \\ -12 & & +12 \\ \hline 22 & = & y \end{array}$$

32. **PENGUINS** An emperor penguin is 45 inches tall. It is 24 inches taller than a rockhopper penguin. Write and solve an equation to find the height of a rockhopper penguin. Is your answer reasonable? Explain.

33. **ELEVATOR** You get in an elevator and go down 8 floors. You exit on the 16th floor. Write and solve an equation to find what floor you got on the elevator.

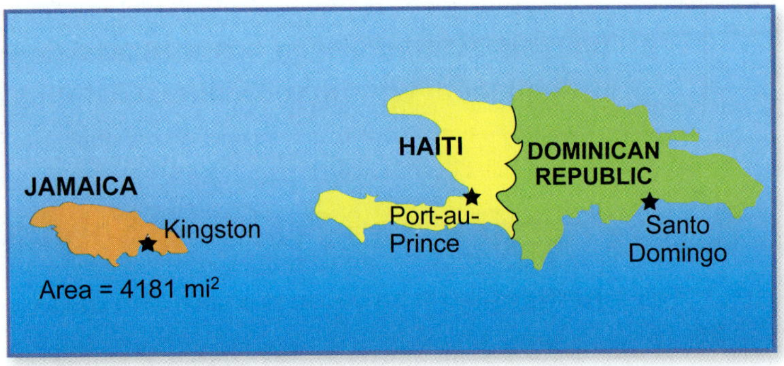

34. **AREA** The area of Jamaica is 6460 square miles less than the area of Haiti. Write and solve an equation to find the area of Haiti.

35. **REASONING** The solution of the equation $x + 3 = 12$ is shown. Explain each step. Use a property, if possible.

$x + 3 = 12$	Write the equation.
$x + 3 - 3 = 12 - 3$	
$x + 0 = 9$	
$x = 9$	

Write the word sentence as an equation. Then solve the equation.

36. 13 subtracted from a number w is 15.

37. A number k increased by 7 is -34.

38. 9 is the difference of a number n and -7.

39. 93 is the sum of a number g and 58.

Solve the equation. Check your solution.

40. $b + 7 + 12 = 30$

41. $y + 4 - 1 = -18$

42. $m + 18 + 23 = 71$

43. $v - 7 = 9 + 12$

44. $5 + 44 = -2 + r$

45. $22 + 15 = d - 17$

GEOMETRY Write and solve an addition equation to find *x*.

46. Perimeter = 48 ft

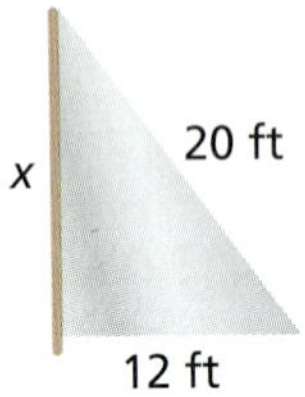

47. Perimeter = 132 in.

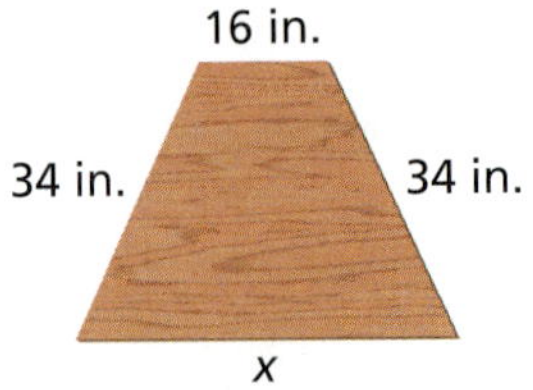

48. Perimeter = 93 ft

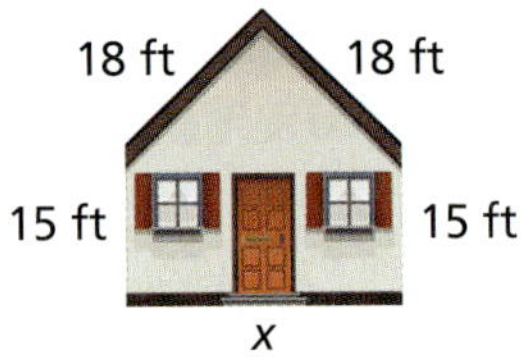

49. **REASONING** Explain why the equations $x + 4 = 13$ and $4 + x = 13$ have the same solution.

50. **REASONING** Explain why the equations $x - 13 = 4$ and $13 - x = 4$ do *not* have the same solution.

51. **SIMPLIFYING AND SOLVING** Compare and contrast the two problems.

Simplify the expression $2(x + 3) - 4$.

$$\begin{aligned} 2(x + 3) - 4 &= 2x + 6 - 4 \\ &= 2x + 2 \end{aligned}$$

Solve the equation $x + 3 = 4$.

$$\begin{aligned} x + 3 &= 4 \\ \underline{-3} &\quad \underline{-3} \\ x &= 1 \end{aligned}$$

52. **PUZZLE** In a *magic square*, the sum of the numbers in each row, column, and diagonal is the same. Write and solve equations to find the values of a, b, and c.

a	37	16
19	25	b
34	c	28

53. **FUNDRAISER** You participate in a dance-a-thon fundraiser. After your parents pledge \$15 and your neighbor pledges \$8, you have \$55. Write and solve an equation to find how much money you had before your parents and neighbor pledged.

54. **MONEY** On Saturday, you spend \$33, give \$15 to a friend, and receive \$20 for mowing your neighbor's lawn. You have \$21 left. Use two methods to find how much money you started with that day.

55. **AMUSEMENT PARK** You have \$25.

a. How much money do you have left if you ride each ride once?

b. Do you have enough money to ride each ride twice? Explain.

56. **Critical Thinking** Consider the equation $x + y = 15$. The value of x increases by 3. What has to happen to the value of y so that $x + y = 15$ remains true?

Fair Game Review What you learned in previous grades & lessons

Find the value of the expression. Use estimation to check your answer.

57. 12×8 58. 13×16 59. $75 \div 15$ 60. $72 \div 3$

61. **MULTIPLE CHOICE** You buy a burrito for \$5.69 and a bottle of orange juice for \$1.99. You pay with a \$10 bill. How much change will you receive?

(A) \$2.32 (B) \$4.31 (C) \$7.68 (D) \$8.01

7.3 Solving Equations Using Multiplication or Division

Essential Question How can you use multiplication or division to solve an equation?

1 ACTIVITY: Finding Missing Dimensions

Work with a partner. Describe how you would find the value of *x*. Then find the value and check your result.

a. rectangle

b. rectangle

c. right triangle

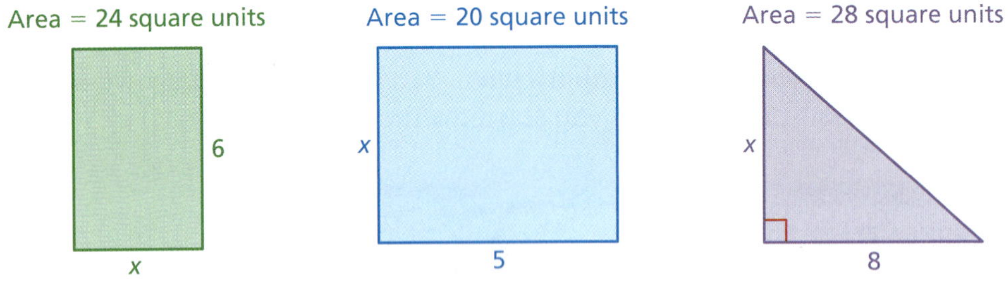

2 ACTIVITY: Using an Equation to Model a Story

Work with a partner.

a. Use a model to solve the problem.

> Three people go out to lunch. They decide to share the $12 bill evenly. How much does each person pay?

- What equation does the model represent? Explain how this represents the problem.

- How much does one  weigh? How do you know?

∴ Each person pays ___.

b. Describe how you can check your answer in part (a).

Solving Equations
In this lesson, you will
- use multiplication or division to solve equations.
- use substitution to check answers.
- solve real-life problems.

3 ACTIVITY: Using Equations to Model a Story

Work with a partner.

- **What is the unknown?**
- **Write an equation that represents each problem.**
- **What does the variable in your equation represent?**
- **Explain how you can solve the equation.**
- **Answer the question.**

> **Math Process**
>
> **Interpret Results**
>
> What does the solution represent? Does the answer make sense?

	Problem	Equation
a.	Three robots go out to lunch. They decide to share the $15 bill evenly. How much does each robot pay?	
b.	On Earth, objects weigh 6 times what they weigh on the Moon. A robot weighs 96 pounds on Earth. What does it weigh on the Moon?	
c.	At maximum speed, a robot runs 6 feet in 1 second. How many feet does the robot run in 1 minute?	
d.	Four identical robots lie on the ground head-to-toe and measure 14 feet. How tall is each robot?	

What Is Your Answer?

4. Complete each sentence by matching.

- The inverse operation of addition
- The inverse operation of subtraction
- The inverse operation of multiplication
- The inverse operation of division

- is multiplication.
- is subtraction.
- is addition.
- is division.

5. **IN YOUR OWN WORDS** How can you use multiplication or division to solve an equation? Give two examples to show how your procedure works.

Practice Use what you learned about solving equations to complete Exercises 15–18 on page 254.

7.3 Lesson

Check It Out Lesson Tutorials BigIdeasMath.com

Key Ideas

Remember

Inverse operations "undo" each other. Multiplication and division are inverse operations.

Multiplication Property of Equality

Words When you multiply each side of an equation by the same nonzero number, the two sides remain equal.

Numbers $\frac{8}{4} = 2$

$\frac{8}{4} \cdot 4 = 2 \cdot 4$

$8 = 8$

Algebra $\frac{x}{4} = 2$

$\frac{x}{4} \cdot 4 = 2 \cdot 4$

$x = 8$

Multiplicative Inverse Property

Words The product of a nonzero number n and its reciprocal, $\frac{1}{n}$, is 1.

Numbers $5 \cdot \frac{1}{5} = 1$

Algebra $n \cdot \frac{1}{n} = \frac{1}{n} \cdot n = 1, n \neq 0$

EXAMPLE 1 Solving Equations Using Multiplication

a. Solve $\frac{w}{4} = 12$.

$\frac{w}{4} = 12$ Write the equation.

Undo the division. → $\frac{w}{4} \cdot 4 = 12 \cdot 4$ Multiplication Property of Equality

$w = 48$ Simplify.

The solution is $w = 48$.

Check

$\frac{w}{4} = 12$

$\frac{48}{4} \stackrel{?}{=} 12$

$12 = 12$ ✓

b. Solve $\frac{1}{7}x = -6$.

$\frac{1}{7}x = -6$ Write the equation.

Use the Multiplicative Inverse Property. → $\frac{7}{1} \cdot \left(\frac{1}{7}x\right) = \frac{7}{1} \cdot (-6)$ Multiplication Property of Equality

$x = -42$ Simplify.

The solution is $x = -42$.

On Your Own

Now You're Ready Exercises 7–10

Solve the equation. Check your solution.

1. $\frac{a}{8} = -6$
2. $4 = \frac{1}{5}y$
3. $z \div 2 = 9$

Key Idea

Division Property of Equality

Words When you divide each side of an equation by the same nonzero number, the two sides remain equal.

Numbers

$$8 \cdot 4 = 32$$
$$8 \cdot 4 \div 4 = 32 \div 4$$
$$8 = 8$$

Algebra

$$4x = 32$$
$$\frac{4x}{4} = \frac{32}{4}$$
$$x = 8$$

EXAMPLE 2 Solving an Equation Using Division

Solve $5b = 65$.

$5b = 65$	Write the equation.
$\frac{5b}{5} = \frac{65}{5}$	Division Property of Equality
$b = 13$	Simplify.

Undo the multiplication.

Check

$5b = 65$

$5(13) \stackrel{?}{=} 65$

$65 = 65$ ✓

The solution is $b = 13$.

EXAMPLE 3 Real-Life Application

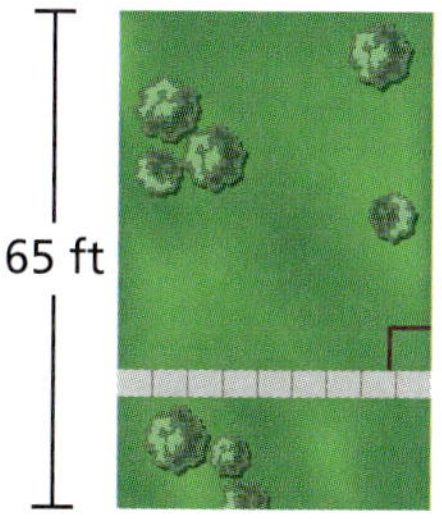

The area of the rectangular courtyard is 2730 square feet. What is the length of the sidewalk?

The width of the rectangle represents the length of the sidewalk.

$A = \ell w$	Use the formula for the area of a rectangle.
$2730 = 65w$	Substitute 2730 for A and 65 for ℓ.
$\frac{2730}{65} = \frac{65w}{65}$	Division Property of Equality
$42 = w$	Simplify.

So, the sidewalk is 42 feet long.

On Your Own

Now You're Ready
Exercises 11–14

Solve the equation. Check your solution.

4. $p \cdot 3 = 18$
5. $-12q = 60$
6. $81 = 9r$
7. You and four friends buy tickets to a baseball game. The total cost is \$70. Write and solve an equation to find the cost of each ticket.

7.3 Exercises

Check It Out
Help with Homework
BigIdeasMath.com

Vocabulary and Concept Check

1. **NUMBER SENSE** What number divided by 12 equals 1?

2. **WRITING** What property of equality would you use to solve $\frac{x}{6} = 7$? Explain how you would use the property.

Copy and complete the first step in the solution.

3. $4x = 24$

   $\frac{4x}{\square} = \frac{24}{\square}$

4. $\frac{x}{3} = 11$

   $\frac{x}{3} \cdot \square = 11 \cdot \square$

5. $8 = n \div 3$

   $8 \cdot \square = (n \div 3) \cdot \square$

6. **OPEN-ENDED** Write an equation that can be solved using the Division Property of Equality.

Practice and Problem Solving

Solve the equation. Check your solution.

1 7. $\frac{s}{10} = 7$ 8. $6 = \frac{t}{5}$ 9. $x \div (-6) = 20$ 10. $24 = \frac{1}{4}r$

2 11. $3a = 12$ 12. $5 \cdot z = -35$ 13. $40 = 4y$ 14. $42 = 7k$

15. $-7x = -105$ 16. $75 = 6 \cdot w$ 17. $13 = d \div 6$ 18. $9 = v \div 5$

19. $\frac{1}{15}c = 3$ 20. $b \div 12 = -4$ 21. $64 \cdot n = 32$ 22. $-3m = 120$

23. **ERROR ANALYSIS** Describe and correct the error in solving the equation.

✗
$x \div 4 = 28$
$\frac{x \div 4}{4} = \frac{28}{4}$
$x = 7$

24. **ANOTHER WAY** Show how you can solve the equation $3x = 9$ by multiplying each side by the reciprocal of 3.

25. **BASKETBALL** Forty-five basketball players participate in a tournament. Write and solve an equation to find the number of 3-person teams that they can form.

26. **THEATER** A theater has 1200 seats. Each row has 20 seats. Write and solve an equation to find the number of rows in the theater.

Solve for *x*. Check your answer.

27. rectangle

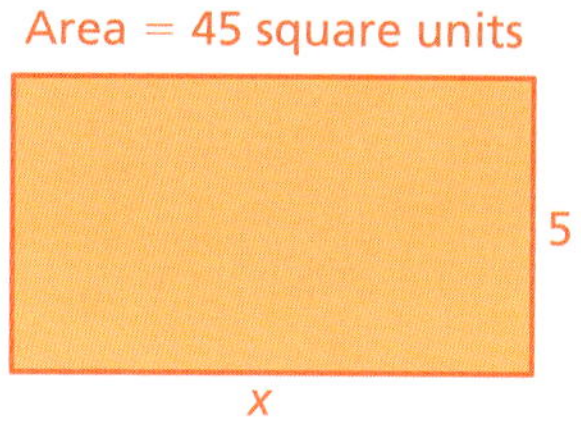

28. rectangle

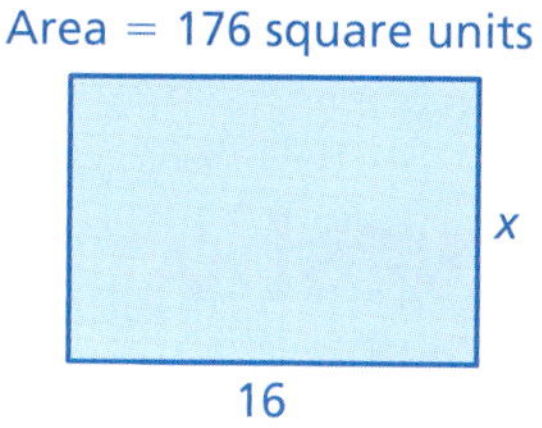

29. right triangle

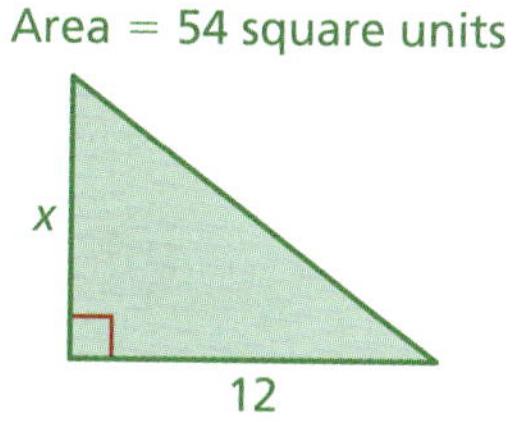

30. GAME SHOW On a game show, you correctly answer six 5-point questions and five 2-point questions. You earn $\frac{1}{3}$ of the possible points in the game. What is the greatest number of points p a player can earn in the game?

31. CARD GAME You use index cards to play a homemade game. The object is to be the first to get rid of all your cards. How many cards are in your friend's stack?

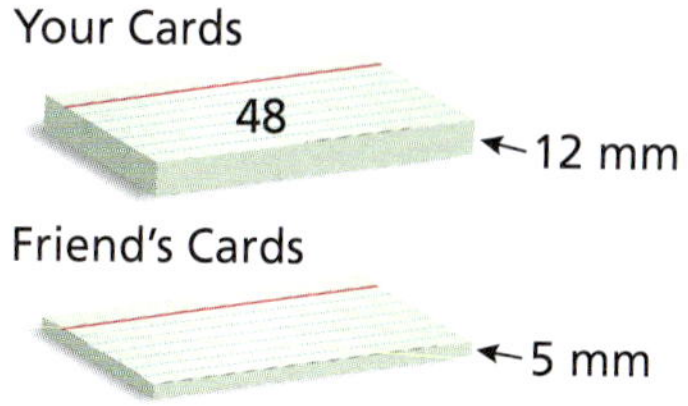

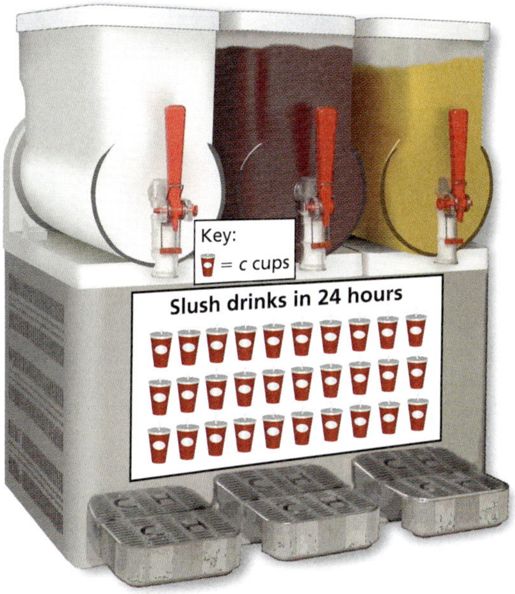

32. SLUSH DRINKS A slush drink machine fills 1440 cups in 24 hours.

a. Write and solve an equation to find the number c of cups each symbol represents.

b. To lower costs, you replace the cups with paper cones that hold $\frac{1}{2}$ as much. Write and solve an equation to find the number n of paper cones that the machine can fill in 24 hours.

STRUCTURE Solve the equation. Explain how you found your answer.

33. $5x + 3x = 5x + 18$

34. $8y + 2y = 2y + 40$

35. Number Sense The area of the picture is 100 square inches. The length is 4 times the width. Find the length and width of the picture.

Fair Game Review What you learned in previous grades & lessons

Write the word sentence as an equation.

36. The sum of a number b and 8 is 17.

37. A number t divided by 3 is 7.

38. MULTIPLE CHOICE What is the value of a^3 when $a = 4$?

Ⓐ 12 Ⓑ 43 Ⓒ 64 Ⓓ 81

7.4 Writing and Graphing Inequalities

Essential Question How can you use a number line to represent solutions of an inequality?

1 ACTIVITY: Understanding Inequality Statements

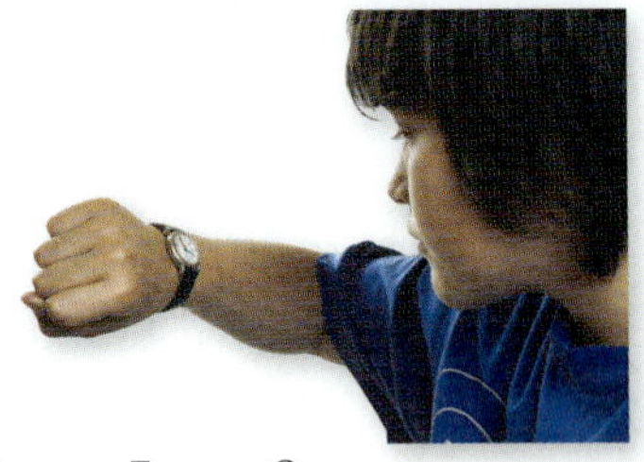

Work with a partner. Read the statement. Circle each number that makes the statement true, and then answer the questions.

a. "Your friend is more than 3 minutes late."

−3 −2 −1 0 1 2 3 4 5 6

- What do you notice about the numbers that you circled?
- Is the number 3 included? Why or why not?
- Write four other numbers that make the statement true.

b. "The temperature is at most 2 degrees."

−5 −4 −3 −2 −1 0 1 2 3 4

- What do you notice about the numbers that you circled?
- Can the temperature be exactly 2 degrees? Explain.
- Write four other numbers that make the statement true.

c. "You need at least 4 pieces of paper for your math homework."

−3 −2 −1 0 1 2 3 4 5 6

- What do you notice about the numbers that you circled?
- Can you have exactly 4 pieces of paper? Explain.
- Write four other numbers that make the statement true.

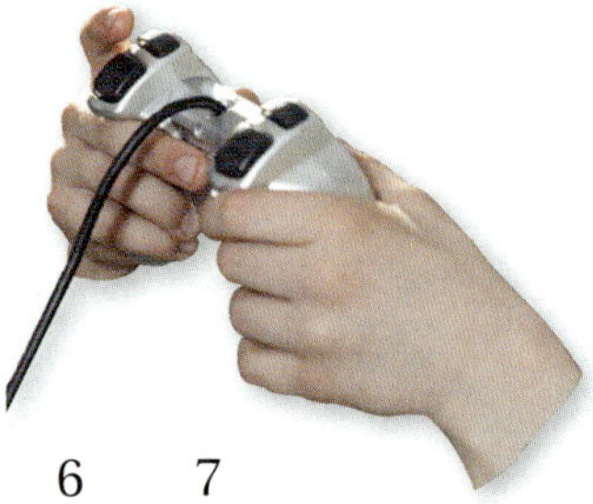

d. "After playing a video game for 20 minutes, you have fewer than 6 points."

−2 −1 0 1 2 3 4 5 6 7

- What do you notice about the numbers that you circled?
- Is the number 6 included? Why or why not?
- Write four other numbers that make the statement true.

Writing Inequalities

In this lesson, you will
- write word sentences as inequalities.
- use a number line to graph the solution set of inequalities.
- use inequalities to represent real-life situations.

2 ACTIVITY: Understanding Inequality Symbols

Work with a partner.

a. Consider the statement "x is a number such that $x < 2$."

- Can the number be exactly 2? Explain.
- Circle each number that makes the statement true.

  −5 −4 −3 −2 −1 0 1 2 3 4

- Write four other numbers that make the statement true.

Math Process

State the Meaning of Symbols

What do the symbols < and ≥ mean?

b. Consider the statement "x is a number such that $x \geq 1$."

- Can the number be exactly 1? Explain.
- Circle each number that makes the statement true.

  −5 −4 −3 −2 −1 0 1 2 3 4

- Write four other numbers that make the statement true.

3 ACTIVITY: How Close Can You Come to 0?

Work with a partner.

a. Which number line shows $x > 0$? Which number line shows $x \geq 0$? Explain your reasoning.

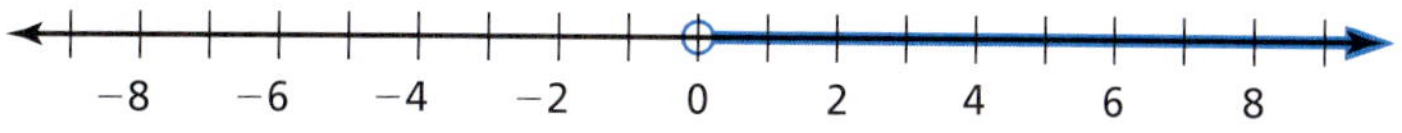

b. Write the least positive number you can think of that is still a solution of the inequality $x > 0$. Explain your reasoning.

What Is Your Answer?

4. **IN YOUR OWN WORDS** How can you use a number line to represent solutions of an inequality?
5. Write an inequality. Graph all solutions of your inequality on a number line.
6. Graph the inequalities $x > 9$ and $9 < x$ on different number lines. What do you notice?

Practice Use what you learned about graphing inequalities to complete Exercises 17–20 on page 261.

7.4 Lesson

Check It Out
Lesson Tutorials
BigIdeasMath.com

Key Vocabulary
inequality, *p. 258*
solution of an inequality, *p. 259*
solution set, *p. 259*
graph of an inequality, *p. 260*

An **inequality** is a mathematical sentence that compares expressions. It contains the symbols $<$, $>$, $\leq$, or $\geq$. To write an inequality, look for the following phrases to determine where to place the inequality symbol.

Inequality Symbols				
Symbol	$<$	$>$	$\leq$	$\geq$
Key Phrases	• is less than • is fewer than	• is greater than • is more than	• is less than or equal to • is at most • is no more than	• is greater than or equal to • is at least • is no less than

EXAMPLE 1 Writing Inequalities

Write the word sentence as an inequality.

a. A number c is less than -4.

A number c | is less than | -4.

c $\quad <\quad$ -4

An inequality is $c < -4$.

b. A number k plus 5 is greater than or equal to 8.

A number k plus 5 | is greater than or equal to | 8.

$k + 5$ $\quad\geq\quad$ 8

An inequality is $k + 5 \geq 8$.

c. Four times a number q is at most 16.

Four times a number q | is at most | 16.

$4q$ $\quad\leq\quad$ 16

An inequality is $4q \leq 16$.

On Your Own

Now You're Ready
Exercises 5–10

Write the word sentence as an inequality.

1. A number n is greater than 1.
2. Twice a number p is fewer than 7.
3. A number w minus 3 is less than or equal to 10.
4. A number z divided by 2 is at least -6.

A **solution of an inequality** is a value that makes the inequality true. An inequality can have more than one solution. The set of all solutions of an inequality is called the **solution set**.

Value of x	$x + 3 \leq 7$	Is the inequality true?
3	$3 + 3 \overset{?}{\leq} 7$ $6 \leq 7$ ✓	yes
4	$4 + 3 \overset{?}{\leq} 7$ $7 \leq 7$ ✓	yes
5	$5 + 3 \overset{?}{\leq} 7$ $8 \nleq 7$ ✗	no

Reading

The symbol $\nleq$ means *is not less than or equal to.*

EXAMPLE 2 Checking Solutions

Tell whether the given value is a solution of the inequality.

a. $x + 1 > 7;\ x = 8$

$x + 1 > 7$ — Write the inequality.

$8 + 1 \overset{?}{>} 7$ — Substitute 8 for x.

$9 > 7$ ✓ — Add. 9 is greater than 7.

So, 8 is a solution of the inequality.

b. $7y < 27;\ y = 4$

$7y < 27$ — Write the inequality.

$7(4) \overset{?}{<} 27$ — Substitute 4 for y.

$28 \nless 27$ ✗ — Multiply. 28 is *not* less than 27.

So, 4 is *not* a solution of the inequality.

c. $\frac{z}{3} \geq 5;\ z = 15$

$\frac{z}{3} \geq 5$ — Write the inequality.

$\frac{15}{3} \overset{?}{\geq} 5$ — Substitute 15 for z.

$5 \geq 5$ ✓ — Divide. 5 is greater than or equal to 5.

So, 15 is a solution of the inequality.

On Your Own

Now You're Ready
Exercises 11–16

Tell whether 3 is a solution of the inequality.

5. $b + 4 < 6$ **6.** $9 - n \geq 6$ **7.** $18 \div x \leq 10$

The **graph of an inequality** shows all the solutions of the inequality on a number line. An open circle ○ is used when a number is *not* a solution. A closed circle ● is used when a number is a solution. An arrow to the left or right shows that the graph continues in that direction.

EXAMPLE 3 Graphing an Inequality

Reading

The inequality $g > 2$ is the same as $2 < g$.

Graph $g > 2$.

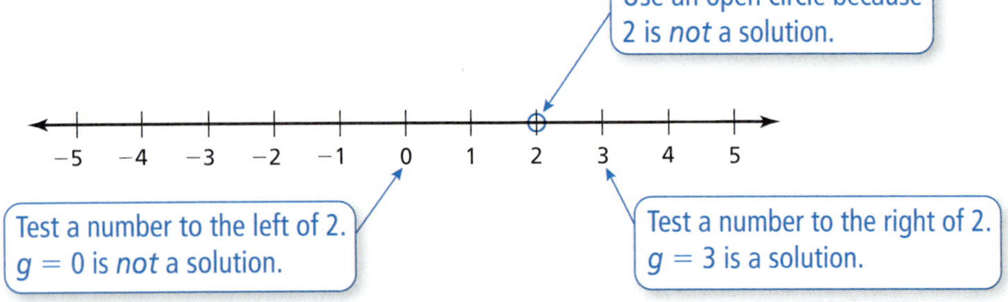

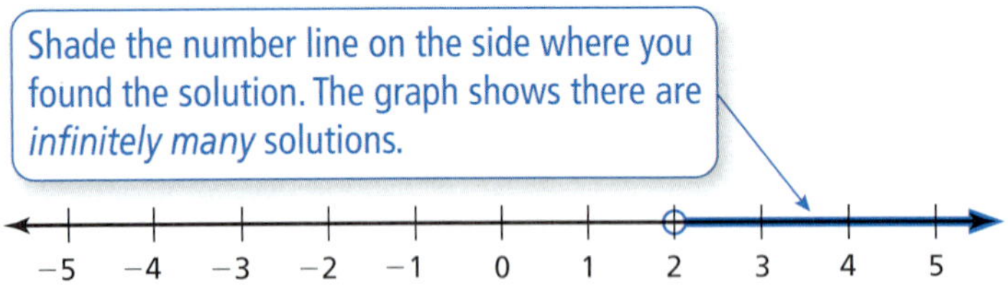

EXAMPLE 4 Real-Life Application

The NASA Solar Probe Plus can withstand temperatures up to and including 2600°F. Write and graph an inequality that represents the temperatures the probe can withstand.

Words	temperatures	up to and including	2600°F
Variable	Let t be the temperatures the probe can withstand.		
Inequality	t	$\leq$	2600

STEM VIDEO

∴ An inequality is $t \leq 2600$.

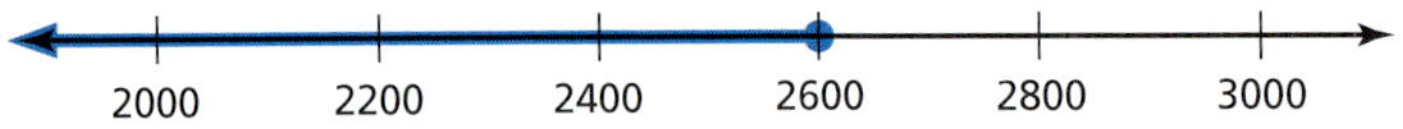

On Your Own

Now You're Ready
Exercises 25–36

Graph the inequality on a number line.

8. $a < 4$ **9.** $f \leq 7$ **10.** $n > 0$ **11.** $p \geq -3$

Write and graph an inequality for the situation.

12. A cruise ship can carry at most 3500 passengers.

13. A board game is designed for ages 12 and up.

7.4 Exercises

Check It Out
Help with Homework
BigIdeasMath.com

Vocabulary and Concept Check

1. **VOCABULARY** How are *greater than* and *greater than or equal to* similar? How are they different?

2. **DIFFERENT WORDS, SAME QUESTION** Which is different? Write "both" inequalities.

A number n is at most 3.	A number n is at least 3.
A number n is less than or equal to 3.	A number n is no more than 3.

3. **WRITING** Explain how the graph of $x \le 6$ is different from the graph of $x < 6$.

4. **WRITING** Are the graphs of $x \le 5$ and $5 \ge x$ the same or different? Explain.

Practice and Problem Solving

Write the word sentence as an inequality.

1 5. A number k is less than 10.

6. A number a is more than 6.

7. A number z is fewer than $\frac{3}{4}$.

8. A number b is at least -3.

9. One plus a number y is no more than -13.

10. A number x divided by 3 is at most 5.

Tell whether the given value is a solution of the inequality.

2 11. $x - 1 \le 7$; $x = 6$

12. $y + 5 < 13$; $y = 17$

13. $3z > 6$; $z = 3$

14. $\frac{b}{2} \ge 6$; $b = 10$

15. $c + 2.5 < 4.3$; $c = 1.8$

16. $a \le 0$; $a = -5$

Match the inequality with its graph.

17. $x \ge 2$

18. $x < 2$

19. $x > -2$

20. $x \le -2$

A.
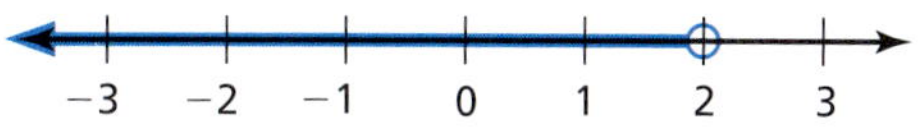

B.
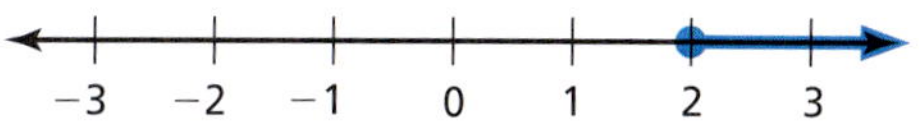

C.
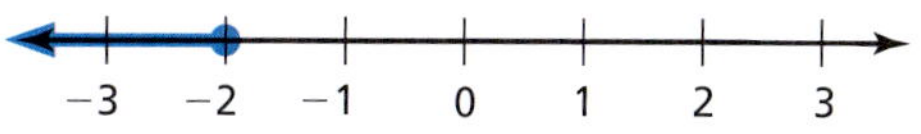

D.
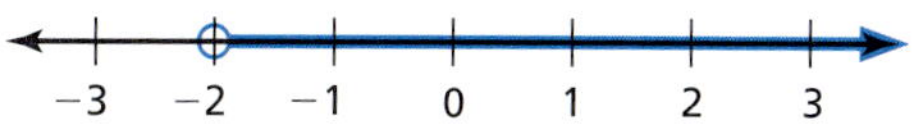

Write an inequality and a word sentence that represent the graph.

21. 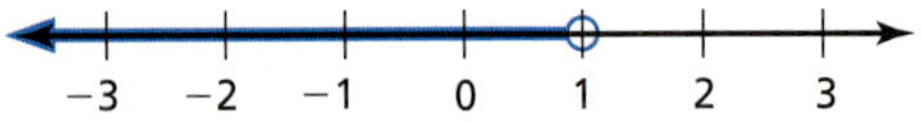

22. 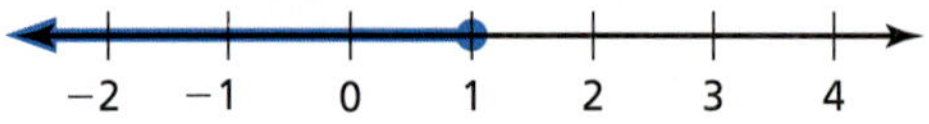

23. 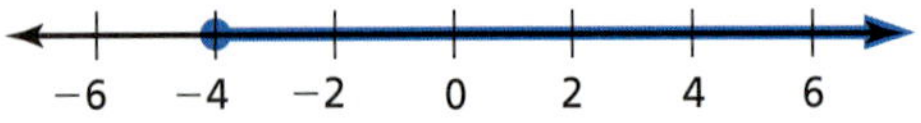

24. 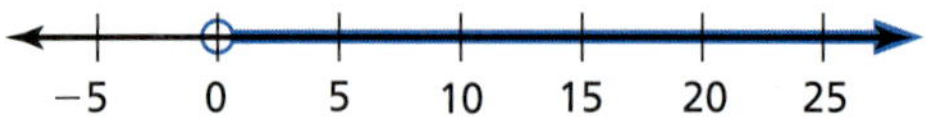

Graph the inequality on a number line.

3 **25.** $a > 4$ **26.** $n \geq 8$ **27.** $3 \geq x$ **28.** $y < \frac{1}{2}$

29. $x < \frac{2}{9}$ **30.** $-3 \geq c$ **31.** $m > -5$ **32.** $0 \leq b$

33. $1.5 > f$ **34.** $t \geq -\frac{1}{2}$ **35.** $p > -1.6$ **36.** $\frac{7}{3} \geq z$

ERROR ANALYSIS **Describe and correct the error in graphing the inequality.**

37. 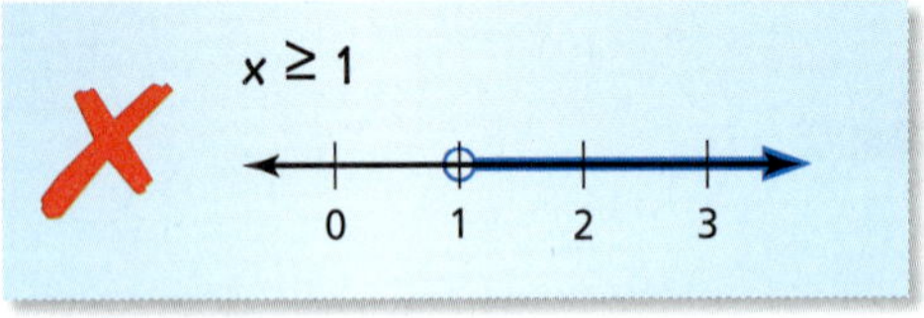

38. 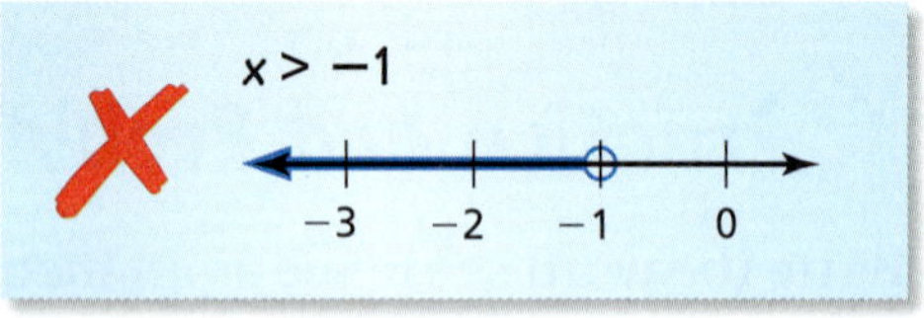

39. **FISHING** You are fishing and are allowed to catch at most 3 striped bass. Each striped bass must be no less than 18 inches long.

a. Write and graph an inequality to represent the number of striped bass you are allowed to catch.

b. Write and graph an inequality to represent the length of each striped bass you are allowed to catch.

40. **MODELING** For a food to be labeled *low sodium,* there must be no more than 140 milligrams of sodium per serving.

a. Write and graph an inequality to represent the amount of sodium in a low-sodium serving.

b. Write and graph an inequality to represent the amount of sodium in a serving that does *not* qualify as low sodium.

c. Does the food represented by the nutrition facts label qualify as a low-sodium food? Explain.

Nutrition Facts

Serving Size ½cup (114g)
Servings Per Container 4

Amount Per Serving	
Calories 90	Calories from fat 30
	% Daily Value*
Total Fat 3g	**5%**
Saturated Fat 0g	**0%**
Cholesterol 0mg	**0%**
Sodium 300mg	**13%**
Total Carbohydrate 13g	**4%**
Dietary Fiber 3g	**12%**
Sugars 3g	
Protein 3g	
Vitamin A 80% •	Vitamin C 60%
Calcium 4% •	Iron 4%

41. **SHOPPING** You have \$33. You want to buy a necklace and one other item from the list.

a. Write an inequality to represent the situation.

b. Can the other item be a T-shirt? Explain.

c. Can the other item be a book? Explain.

Item	Price (with tax)
T-shirt	\$ 15
Book	\$ 20
DVD	\$ 13
Necklace	\$ 16

Determine whether the statement is *sometimes, always,* or *never* true. Explain your reasoning.

42. A number that is a solution of the inequality $x > 5$ is also a solution of the inequality $x \geq 5$.

43. A number that is a solution of the inequality $5 \leq x$ is also a solution of the inequality $x > 5$.

44. **BUS RIDE** A bus ride costs \$1.50. A 30-day bus pass costs \$36. Write an inequality to represent the number of bus rides you would need to take for the bus pass to be a better deal.

45. **MOVIE THEATER** Fifty people are seated in a movie theater. The maximum capacity of the theater is 425 people. Write an inequality to represent the number of additional people who can still be seated.

46. Critical Thinking The map shows the elevations above sea level for an area of land.

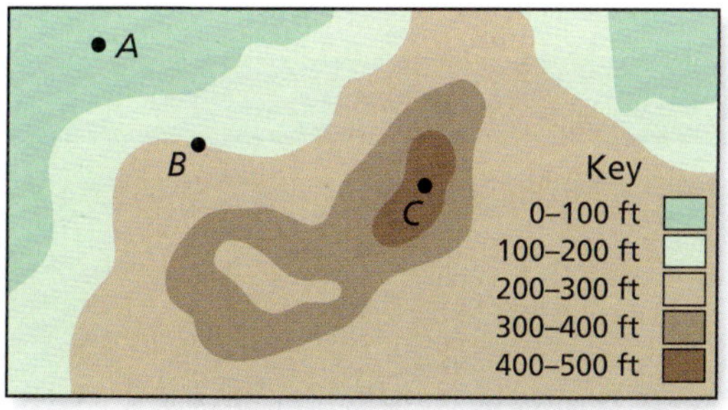

a. Graph the possible elevations of A. Write the set of elevations as two inequalities.

b. Graph the possible elevations of C. How can you write this set of elevations as a single inequality? Explain.

c. What is the elevation of B? Explain.

Fair Game Review What you learned in previous grades & lessons

Solve the equation. Check your solution.

47. $x + 3 = 12$

48. $x - 6 = 8$

49. $16 + x = 44$

50. $7.6 = x - 6.5$

51. **MULTIPLE CHOICE** A stack of boards is 24 inches high. Each board is $\frac{3}{8}$ of an inch thick. How many boards are in the stack?

Ⓐ $\frac{1}{9}$ Ⓑ $\frac{1}{6}$ Ⓒ 9 Ⓓ 64

7.5 Solving Inequalities Using Addition or Subtraction

Essential Question How can you use addition or subtraction to solve an inequality?

1 ACTIVITY: Writing an Inequality

Work with a partner. In 3 years, your friend will still not be old enough to vote.

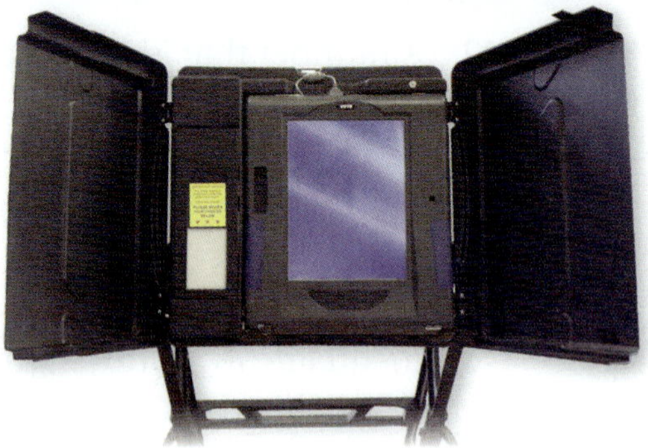

a. Which of the following represents your friend's situation? What does x represent? Explain your reasoning.

$x + 3 < 18$ $\qquad$ $x + 3 \leq 18$

$x + 3 > 18$ $\qquad$ $x + 3 \geq 18$

b. Graph the possible ages of your friend on a number line. Explain how you decided what to graph.

2 ACTIVITY: Writing an Inequality

Work with a partner. Baby manatees are about 4 feet long at birth. They grow to a maximum length of 13 feet.

a. Which of the following can represent a baby manatee's growth? What does x represent? Explain your reasoning.

$x + 4 < 13$ $\qquad$ $x + 4 \leq 13$

$x - 4 > 13$ $\qquad$ $x - 4 \geq 13$

b. Graph the solution on a number line. Explain how you decided what to graph.

Solving Inequalities
In this lesson, you will
- use addition or subtraction to solve inequalities.
- use a number line to graph the solution set of inequalities.
- solve real-life problems.

3 ACTIVITY: Solving Inequalities

Work with a partner. Complete the following steps for Activity 1. Then repeat the steps for Activity 2.

> **Math Process**
> **Interpret Results**
> What does the solution of the inequality represent?

- Use your inequality from part (a). Replace the inequality symbol with an equal sign.
- Solve the equation.
- Replace the equal sign with the original inequality symbol.
- Graph this new inequality.
- Compare the graph with your graph in part (b). What do you notice?

4 ACTIVITY: The Triangle Inequality

Work with a partner. Draw different triangles whose sides have lengths 10 cm, 6 cm, and *x* cm.

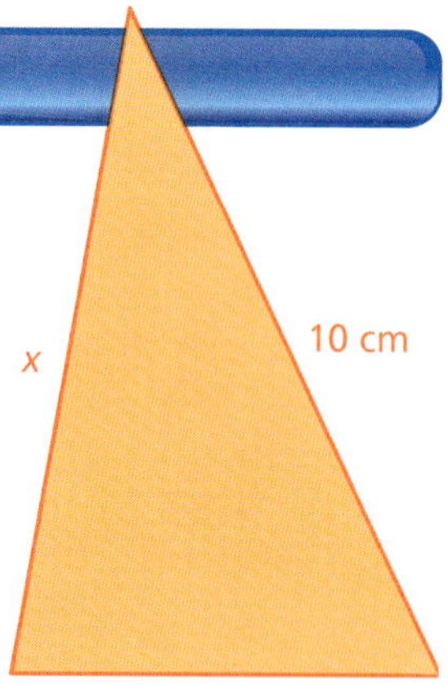

a. Which of the following describes how *small* x can be? Explain your reasoning.

$6 + x < 10$ $6 + x \le 10$

$6 + x > 10$ $6 + x \ge 10$

b. Which of the following describes how *large* x can be? Explain your reasoning.

$x - 6 < 10$ $x - 6 \le 10$ $x - 6 > 10$ $x - 6 \ge 10$

c. Graph the possible values of x on a number line.

What Is Your Answer?

5. **IN YOUR OWN WORDS** How can you use addition or subtraction to solve an inequality?
6. Describe a real-life situation that you can represent with an inequality. Write the inequality. Graph the solution on a number line.

Practice Use what you learned about solving inequalities to complete Exercises 5–7 on page 268.

7.5 Lesson

Check It Out
Lesson Tutorials
BigIdeasMath.com

Study Tip

You can solve inequalities the same way you solve equations. Use inverse operations to get the variable by itself.

Key Ideas

Addition Property of Inequality

Words When you add the same number to each side of an inequality, the inequality remains true.

Numbers

$$\begin{array}{rcr} 3 & < & 5 \\ +2 & & +2 \\ \hline 5 & < & 7 \end{array}$$

Algebra

$$\begin{array}{rcr} x-4 & > & 5 \\ +4 & & +4 \\ \hline x & > & 9 \end{array}$$

Graph

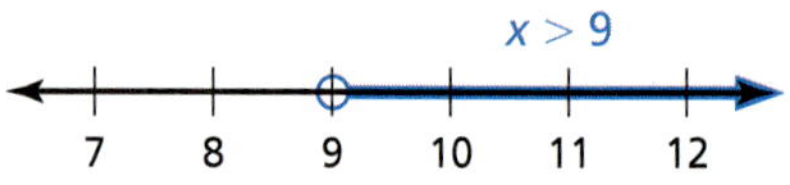

Subtraction Property of Inequality

Words When you subtract the same number from each side of an inequality, the inequality remains true.

Numbers

$$\begin{array}{rcr} 3 & < & 5 \\ -2 & & -2 \\ \hline 1 & < & 3 \end{array}$$

Algebra

$$\begin{array}{rcr} x+4 & > & 5 \\ -4 & & -4 \\ \hline x & > & 1 \end{array}$$

Graph

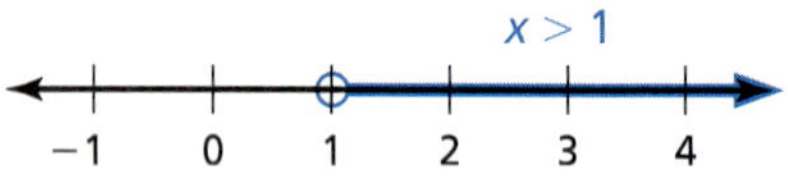

These properties are also true for $\le$ and $\ge$.

EXAMPLE 1 Solving an Inequality Using Addition

Solve $x - 3 > -1$. Graph the solution.

$$\begin{array}{rcrl} x-3 & > & -1 & \text{Write the inequality.} \\ +3 & & +3 & \text{Addition Property of Inequality} \\ \hline x & > & 2 & \text{Simplify.} \end{array}$$

Undo the subtraction. (points to $+3$ $+3$)

The solution is $x > 2$.

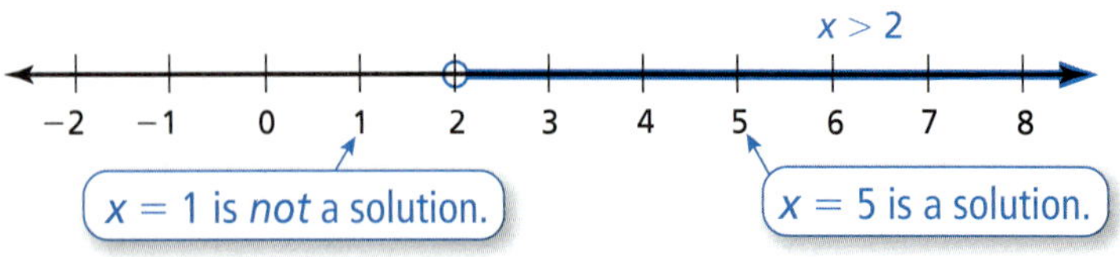

Check:

$x = 1$: $1 - 3 \overset{?}{>} -1$

$-2 \not> -1$ ✗

$x = 5$: $5 - 3 \overset{?}{>} -1$

$2 > -1$ ✓

On Your Own

Solve the inequality. Graph the solution.

1. $x - 2 < -1$
2. $x - 6 \ge -4$
3. $10 \ge x - 1$

EXAMPLE 2 Solving an Inequality Using Subtraction

Solve $15 \geq 6 + x$. Graph the solution.

Undo the addition.

$15 \geq 6 + x$	Write the inequality.
$-6 \quad -6$	Subtraction Property of Inequality
$9 \geq x$	Simplify.

The solution is $x \leq 9$.

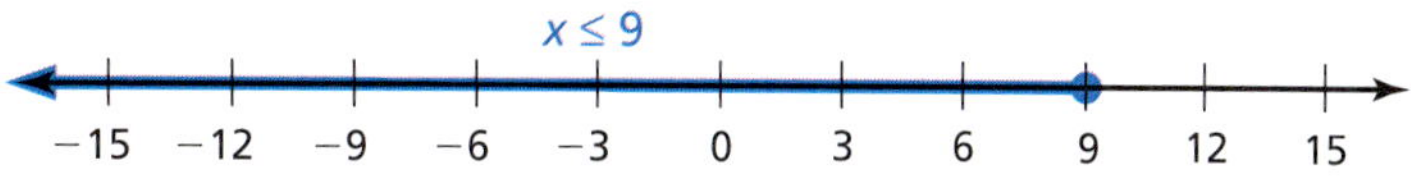

Reading

The inequality $x \leq 9$ is the same as $9 \geq x$.

On Your Own

Now You're Ready
Exercises 5–16

Solve the inequality. Graph the solution.

4. $x + 3 > 7$ **5.** $y + 2 < 17$ **6.** $-2 \leq m + 9$

EXAMPLE 3 Real-Life Application

A flea market advertises that it has more than 250 vending booths. Of these, 184 are currently filled. Write and solve an inequality to represent the number of vending booths still available.

Words	The number of booths filled	plus	the number of remaining booths	is greater than	the total number of booths.
Variable	Let b be the number of remaining booths.				
Inequality	184	+	b	>	250

$184 + b > 250$	Write the inequality.
$-184 \quad -184$	Subtraction Property of Inequality
$b > 66$	Simplify.

More than 66 vending booths are still available.

On Your Own

7. You have already spent \$24 shopping online for clothes. Write and solve an inequality to represent the additional amount you must spend to get free shipping.

7.5 Exercises

Check It Out
Help with Homework
BigIdeasMath.com

Vocabulary and Concept Check

1. **OPEN-ENDED** Write an inequality that can be solved by subtracting 7 from each side.
2. **WRITING** Explain how to solve the inequality $x - 6 > 3$.
3. **WRITING** Describe the graph of the solution of $x + 3 \le 4$.
4. **OPEN-ENDED** Write an inequality that the graph represents. Then use the Subtraction Property of Inequality to write another inequality that the graph represents.

Practice and Problem Solving

Solve the inequality. Graph the solution.

(1) (2)

5. $x - 4 < -3$
6. $5 + h > 7$
7. $3 \ge y - 2$
8. $-9 \le c - (-1)$
9. $18 > 12 + x$
10. $37 + z \le 54$
11. $y - 21 < 85$
12. $g - 17 \ge 17$
13. $-4 < x + 3$
14. $12 \ge s - 5$
15. $1 \le -2 + n$
16. $3 + b > 3$

17. **ERROR ANALYSIS** Describe and correct the error in solving the inequality.

$$\begin{array}{rcl} 28 & \ge & t - 9 \\ -9 & & -9 \\ \hline 19 & \ge & t \end{array}$$

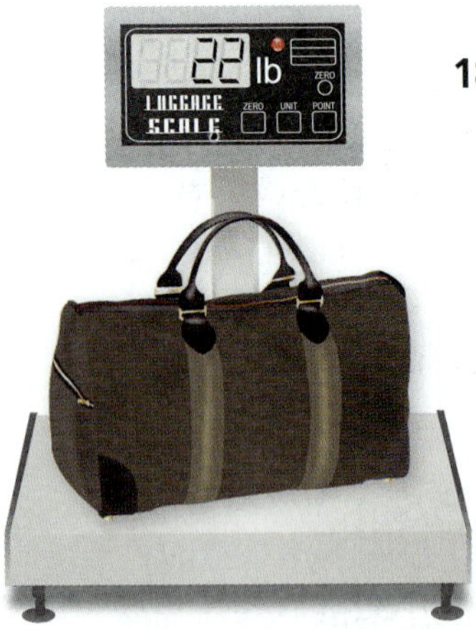

18. **AIR TRAVEL** Your carry-on bag can weigh at most 40 pounds. Write and solve an inequality to represent how much more weight you can add to the bag and still meet the requirement.

19. **SHOPPING** It costs $\$x$ for a round-trip bus ticket to the mall. You have \$24. Write and solve an inequality to represent how much money you can spend for the bus fare and still have enough to buy the baseball cap.

Write the word sentence as an inequality. Then solve the inequality.

20. Five more than a number is less than 17.
21. Three less than a number is more than 15.

Solve the inequality. Graph the solution.

22. $x + 9 - 3 \leq 14$ **23.** $44 > 7 + s + 26$ **24.** $6.1 - 0.3 \geq c + 1$

25. VIDEO GAME The high score for a video game is 36,480. Your current score is 34,280. Each dragonfly you catch is worth 1 point. You also get a 1000-point bonus for reaching 35,000 points. Write and solve an inequality to represent the number of dragonflies you must catch to earn a new high score.

26. PICKUP TRUCKS You can register a pickup truck as a passenger vehicle if the truck is not used for commercial purposes and the weight of the truck with its contents does not exceed 8500 pounds.

a. Your pickup truck weighs 4200 pounds. Write an inequality to represent the number of pounds your truck can carry and still qualify as a passenger vehicle. Then solve the inequality.

b. A cubic yard of sand weighs about 1600 pounds. How many cubic yards of sand can you haul in your truck and still qualify as a passenger vehicle? Explain your reasoning.

27. TRIATHLON You complete two events of a triathlon. Your goal is to finish with an overall time of less than 100 minutes.

a. Write and solve an inequality to represent how many minutes you can take to finish the running event and still meet your goal.

b. The running event is 3.1 miles long. Estimate how many minutes it would take you to run 3.1 miles. Would this time allow you to reach your goal? Explain your reasoning.

Triathlon

Event	Your Time (minutes)
Swimming	18.2
Biking	45.4
Running	?

28. Number Sense The possible values of x are given by $x - 3 \geq 2$. What is the least possible value of $5x$?

Fair Game Review What you learned in previous grades & lessons

Solve the equation. Check your solution.

29. $\frac{t}{12} = 4$ **30.** $6 = \frac{s}{9}$ **31.** $8x = 72$ **32.** $9 = 3z$

33. MULTIPLE CHOICE Which brand of turkey is the best buy?

Ⓐ Brand A Ⓑ Brand B
Ⓒ Brand C Ⓓ Brand D

Brand	A	B	C	D
Cost (dollars)	10.38	13.47	21.45	34.93
Pounds	2	3	5	7

7 Study Help

Check It Out
Graphic Organizer
BigIdeasMath.com

You can use an **example and non-example chart** to list examples and non-examples of a vocabulary word or term. Here is an example and non-example chart for equations.

Equations

Examples	Non-Examples
$x = 5$	5
$2a = 16$	$2a$
$x + 4 = 19$	$x + 4$
$5 = x + 3$	$x + 3$
$12 - 7 = 5$	$12 - 7$
$\frac{1}{4}y = 6$	$\frac{1}{4}$

On Your Own

Make example and non-example charts to help you study these topics.

1. inverse operations
2. equations solved using addition or subtraction
3. equations solved using multiplication or division
4. inequalities
5. graphs of inequalities
6. inequalities solved using addition or subtraction

"I need a good non-example of a cool animal for my example and non-example chart."

7 Chapter Review

Check It Out
Vocabulary Help
BigIdeasMath.com

Review Key Vocabulary

equation, *p. 238*
solution, *p. 244*
inverse operations, *p. 245*
inequality, *p. 258*
solution of an inequality, *p. 259*
solution set, *p. 259*
graph of an inequality, *p. 260*

Review Examples and Exercises

7.1 Writing Equations in One Variable *(pp. 236–241)*

Write the word sentence "The quotient of a number b and 6 is 9" as an equation.

The quotient of a number b and 6 is 9.

$b \div 6 = 9$ *Quotient of means division.*

An equation is $b \div 6 = 9$.

Exercises

Write the word sentence as an equation.

1. The product of a number m and -2 is 8.
2. 6 less than a number t is 7.
3. A number m increased by 5 is 7.
4. 8 is the quotient of a number g and 3.

7.2 Solving Equations Using Addition or Subtraction *(pp. 242–249)*

Solve $z + 5 = 13$.

$z + 5 = 13$	Write the equation.
$\underline{-5} \quad \underline{-5}$	Subtraction Property of Equality
$z = 8$	Simplify.

Undo the addition.

The solution is $z = 8$.

Check

$z + 5 = 13$

$8 + 5 \stackrel{?}{=} 13$

$13 = 13$ ✓

Exercises

Solve the equation. Check your solution.

5. $x - 1 = 8$
6. $m + 7 = -11$
7. $21 = p - 12$

7.3 Solving Equations Using Multiplication or Division (pp. 250–255)

Solve $4c = 32$.

$4c = 32$	Write the equation.
$\frac{4c}{4} = \frac{32}{4}$	Division Property of Equality
$c = 8$	Simplify.

Undo the multiplication.

Check

$4c = 32$

$4(8) \stackrel{?}{=} 32$

$32 = 32$ ✓

Exercises

Solve the equation. Check your solution.

8. $7 \cdot q = 42$ **9.** $7k = 21$ **10.** $\frac{a}{7} = -25$

7.4 Writing and Graphing Inequalities (pp. 256–263)

Write the word sentence as an inequality.

a. A number x is more than -9.

A number x | is more than | -9.

x $>$ -9

An inequality is $x > -9$.

b. A number r divided by 2 is at most 4.

A number r divided by 2 | is at most | 4.

$\frac{r}{2}$ $\leq$ 4

An inequality is $\frac{r}{2} \leq 4$.

Exercises

Write the word sentence as an inequality.

11. A number m is less than 5.

12. A number h is at least -12.

Tell whether the given value is a solution of the inequality.

13. $n + 7 < 9; n = 3$ **14.** $p - 4 > 6; p = 10$ **15.** $g + 3 \leq 8; g = 5$

Graph the inequality on a number line.

16. $x < 0$ **17.** $a \geq 3$ **18.** $n \leq -1$

7.5 Solving Inequalities Using Addition or Subtraction *(pp. 264–269)*

Solve the inequality. Graph the solution.

a. $1 \le x - 4$

	$1 \le x - 4$	Write the inequality.
Undo the subtraction. →	$\underline{+4} \quad \underline{+4}$	Addition Property of Inequality
	$5 \le x$	Simplify.

The inequality $5 \le x$ is the same as $x \ge 5$.

∴ The solution is $x \ge 5$.

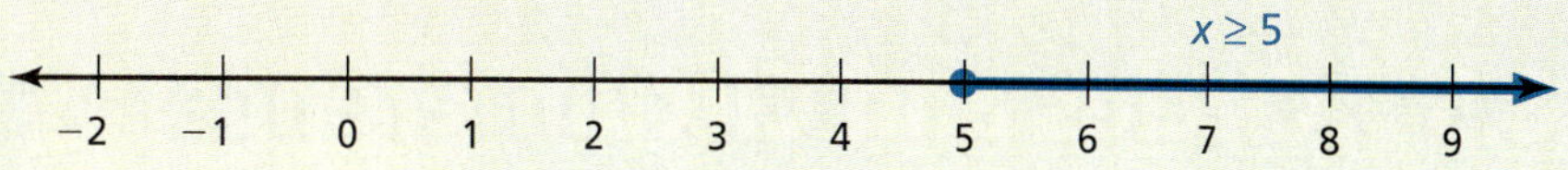

b. $t + 3 > -4$

	$t + 3 > -4$	Write the inequality.
Undo the addition. →	$\underline{-3} \quad \underline{-3}$	Subtraction Property of Inequality
	$t > -7$	Simplify.

∴ The solution is $t > -7$.

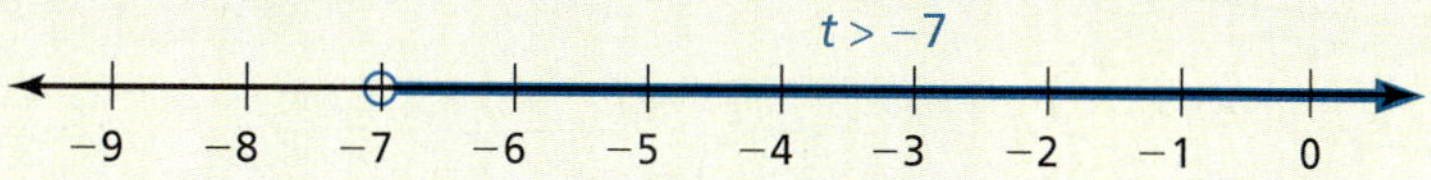

Exercises

Solve the inequality. Graph the solution.

19. $x + 1 > 3$

20. $k - 7 \le 0$

21. $y + 8 \ge 9$

22. $24 < 11 + x$

23. $4 \le n - 4$

24. $x - 20 > 24$

25. $b + 12 \le 26$

26. $s - 1 < -2$

27. $3 + m \le 10$

28. $-5 \ge a - 5$

29. **FORECAST** A weather forecast calls for less than 4 inches of snow. It has already snowed 1 inch. How much more snow is expected?

30. **OPEN-ENDED** Write a real-life problem that can be solved using the Subtraction Property of Inequality, and has a solution that can be represented by the number line. Justify your answer.

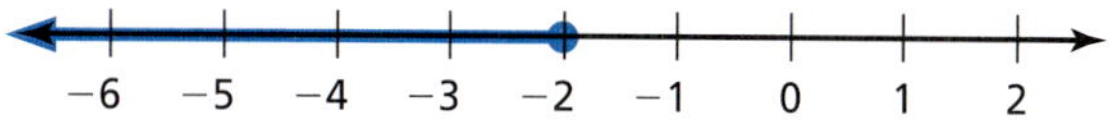

8 Geometry

π≈3.141592...
"Think of any number between 1 and 9."
"Okay, now add 4 to the number, multiply by 3, subtract 12, and divide by your original number."
Can I start over?
"You end up with 3, don't you?"

"What do you get when you divide the circumference of a jack-o-lantern by its diameter?"
I love math!
"Pumpkin pi, HE HE HE."

What You Learned Before

Classifying Figures

Identify the basic shapes in the figure.

Example 1

Rectangle, right triangle

Example 2

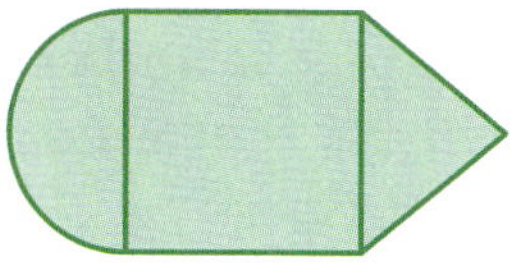

Semicircle, square, and triangle

Try It Yourself

Identify the basic shapes in the figure.

1.

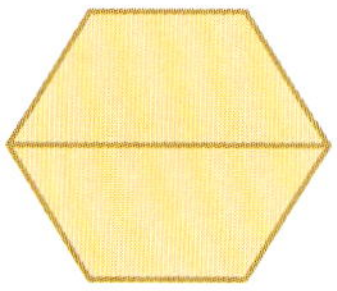

2.

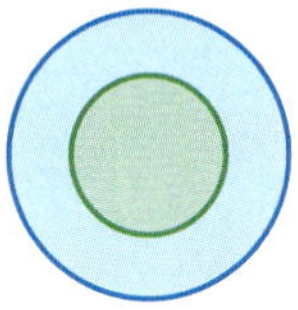

3.

4.

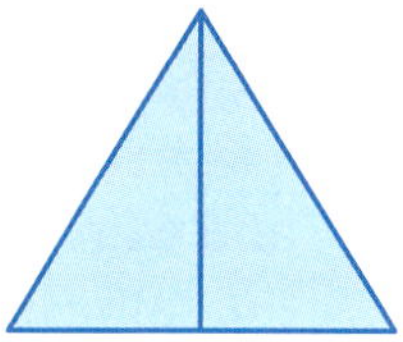

5.

6.

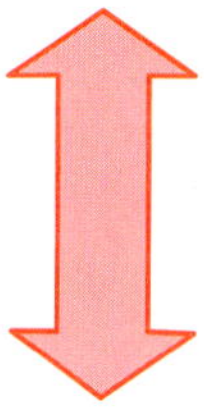

Squaring Numbers and Using Order of Operations

Example 3 Evaluate 4^2.

$$4^2 = 4 \cdot 4 = 16$$

4^2 means to multiply 4 by itself.

Example 4 Evaluate $3 \cdot 6^2$.

$$3 \cdot 6^2 = 3 \cdot (6 \cdot 6) = 3 \cdot 36 = 108$$

Use order of operations. Evaluate the exponent, and then multiply.

Try It Yourself

Evaluate the expression.

7. 5^2

8. 12^2

9. $3 \cdot 2^2$

10. $4 \cdot 7^2$

11. $3(1 + 8)^2$

12. $2(3 + 7)^2 - 3 \cdot 4$

8.1 Regular Polygons and Symmetry

Essential Question How can you tell whether a figure is a regular polygon?

1 ACTIVITY: Classifying Polygons

Work with a partner. Name each polygon. Then, in your own words, describe each type of polygon.

		Polygon	*Number of Sides*	*Name*	*Description*
Sample:	**a.**	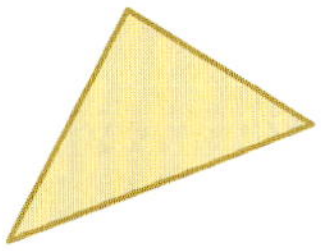	3	Triangle	A polygon with 3 sides
	b.	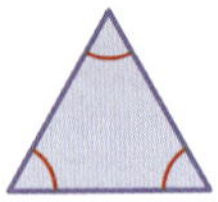			
	c.	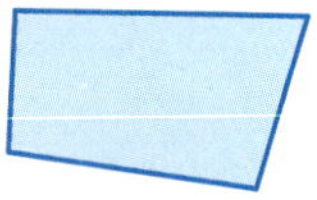			
Sample:	**d.**		4	Square	A quadrilateral with 4 right interior angles and whose sides have the same length
	e.	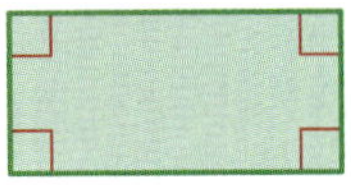			
	f.				
	g.				
	h.	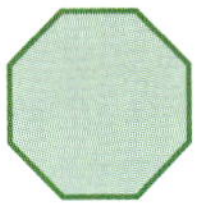			

Geometry
In this lesson, you will
- identify regular polygons.
- draw lines of symmetry of regular polygons.

2 ACTIVITY: Determining Side Lengths and Angle Measures

In Activity 1, measure the side lengths and interior angle measures of each polygon. Which have equal side lengths? Which have equal interior angle measures? Which have both equal side lengths and equal interior angle measures?

3 ACTIVITY: Dividing Figures

Work with a partner. Determine whether each line divides the figure into two parts, each of which is the mirror image of the other. Write *yes* or *no*.

a.
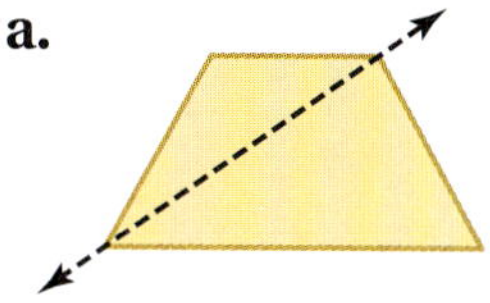

b.
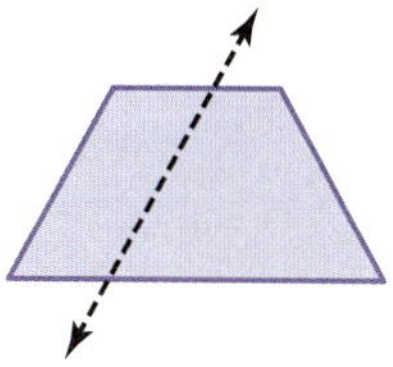

c.
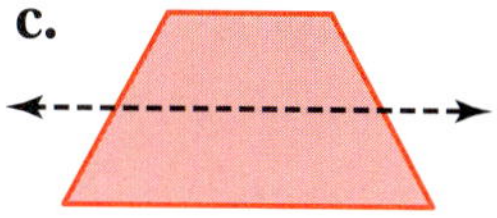

d.
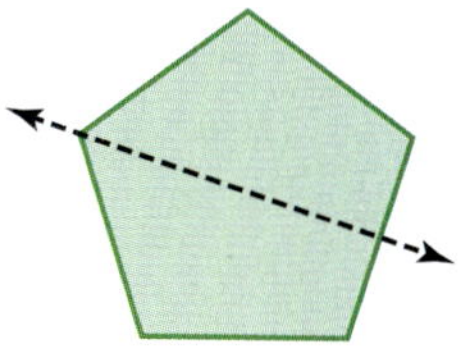

e.
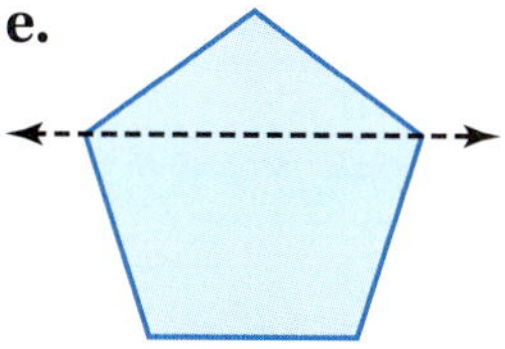

f.
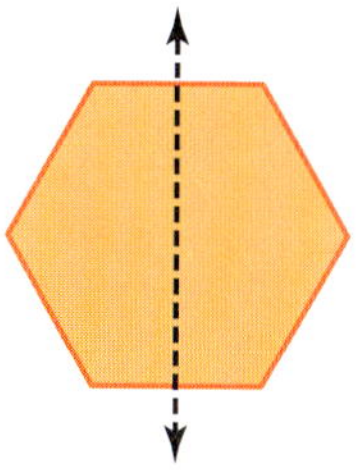

g.
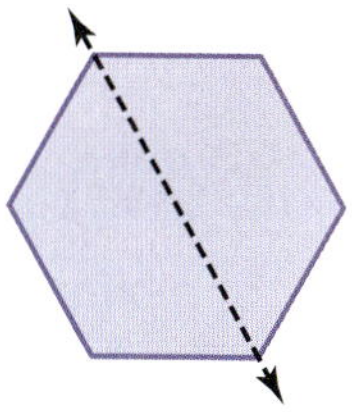

h.
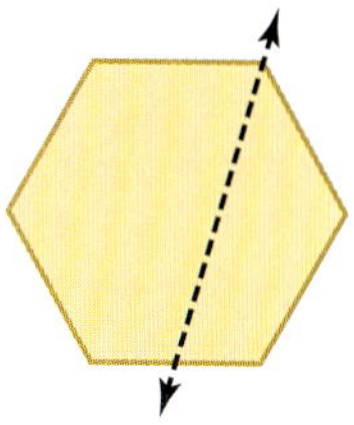

What Is Your Answer?

4. **IN YOUR OWN WORDS** In Activity 1, the figures in parts (b), (d), (f), (g), and (h) are regular polygons. Identify what makes a figure a regular polygon.

5. Determine whether each description is of a regular polygon. Explain.
   a. an equilateral triangle
   b. a rhombus with one pair of interior angles measuring 80° and one pair of interior angles measuring 100°
   c. a trapezoid

6. When two figures or two parts of one figure have symmetry, they are mirror images of each other. Describe what you think a line of symmetry might be. In Activity 3, which lines are lines of symmetry?

7. Are lines of symmetry always horizontal or vertical? Explain.

8. How many lines of symmetry does a 3-sided regular polygon have? 4-sided? n-sided?

Math Process

Make Conjectures

How can you use the results of the first two parts of Question 8 to answer the third part?

Practice Use what you learned about regular polygons to complete Exercises 7–9 on page 280.

Check It Out
Lesson Tutorials
BigIdeasMath.com

Key Vocabulary
regular polygon, *p. 278*
congruent, *p. 278*
line of symmetry, *p. 279*

A **regular polygon** has **congruent** sides and congruent interior angles.

Recall that congruent sides are equal in length. They are indicated by tick marks, or hash marks. An equal number of tick marks indicates the sides are congruent.

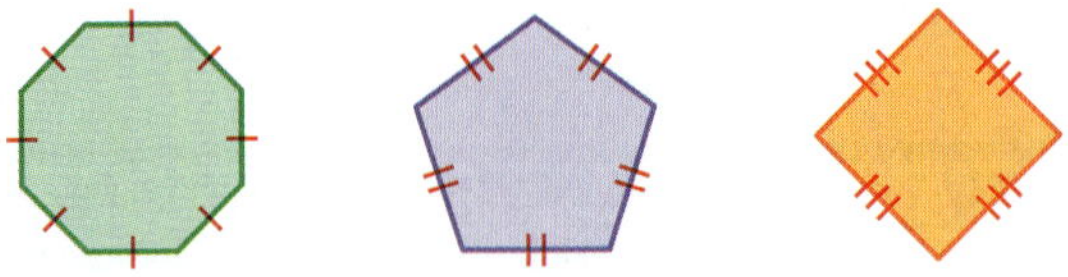

congruent sides of regular polygons

Congruent angles are equal in measure. They are indicated by arcs, or angle curves. An equal number of arcs indicates the angles are congruent.

congruent interior angles of regular polygons

EXAMPLE 1 Identifying Regular Polygons

Determine whether each triangle is a regular polygon.

a.

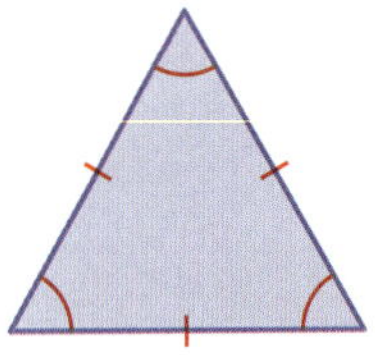

All 3 sides are congruent and all 3 angles are congruent. So, the triangle is a regular polygon. (It is an equilateral triangle.)

b.

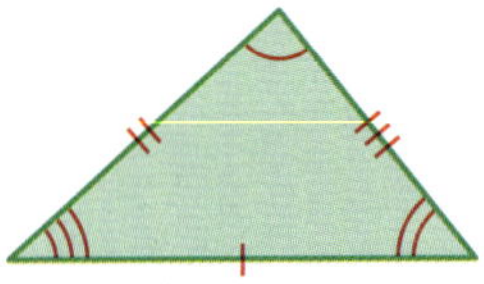

No sides are congruent and no angles are congruent. So, the triangle is not a regular polygon.

c.

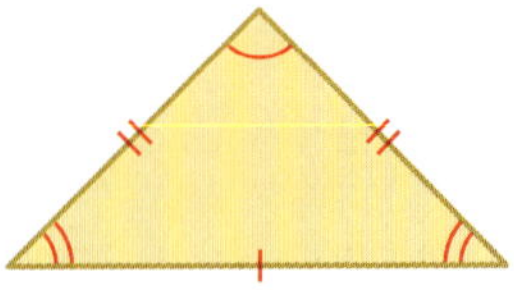

Only 2 sides are congruent and only 2 angles are congruent. So, the triangle is not a regular polygon.

On Your Own

Now You're Ready
Exercises 10–12

Determine whether the pentagon is a regular polygon. Explain.

1.

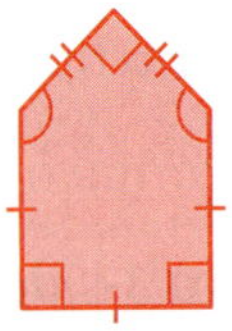

2.

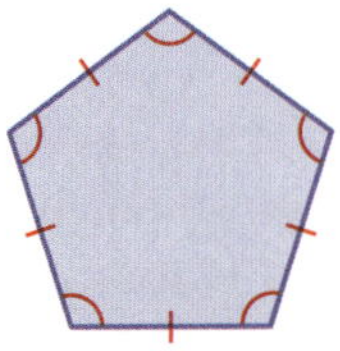

3. **THINK ABOUT IT** The Pentagon building in Arlington County, Virginia, is in the shape of a regular pentagon. The sum of the interior angle measures of any pentagon is 540°. What is the measure of each interior angle of the Pentagon building?

Multi-Language Glossary at BigIdeasMath.com.

A **line of symmetry** divides a figure into two parts, each of which is the mirror image of the other. The number of lines of symmetry of a regular polygon is equal to the number of sides of the polygon. Note that a polygon may not be regular but still could have at least one line of symmetry.

EXAMPLE 2 Drawing Lines of Symmetry of Regular Polygons

Draw all the lines of symmetry of each polygon.

a. **square** **b.** **regular pentagon** **c.** **isosceles triangle**

a. A square is a 4-sided regular polygon. So, it has 4 lines of symmetry. One is horizontal, one is vertical, and two are diagonal.

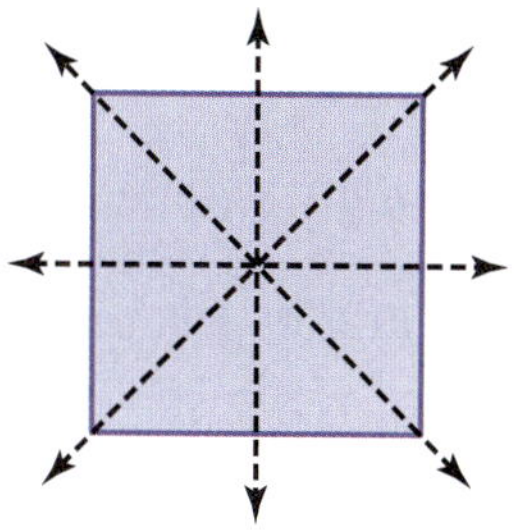

b. A regular pentagon is a 5-sided regular polygon. So, it has 5 lines of symmetry. Each line of symmetry divides the pentagon in half through a vertex and the side opposite the vertex.

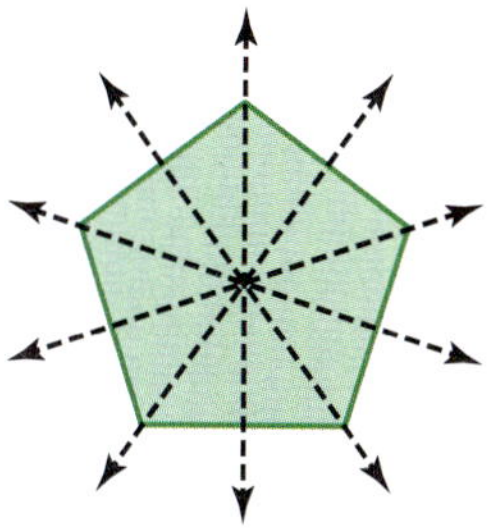

c. An isosceles triangle is not a regular polygon. It has two congruent sides and two congruent angles, but only one line of symmetry.

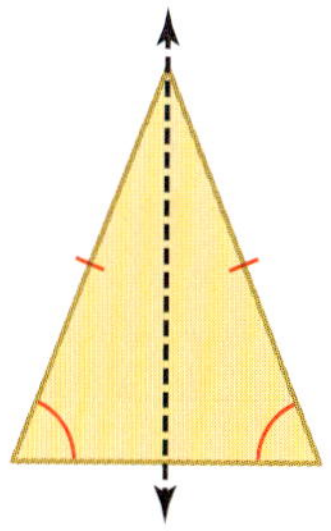

On Your Own

Now You're Ready
Exercises 21–23

Draw all the lines of symmetry on each polygon.

4.

5.

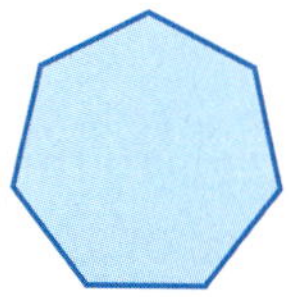

6.

8.1 Exercises

Check It Out
Help with Homework
BigIdeasMath.com

Vocabulary and Concept Check

1. **VOCABULARY** Identify the regular polygon.

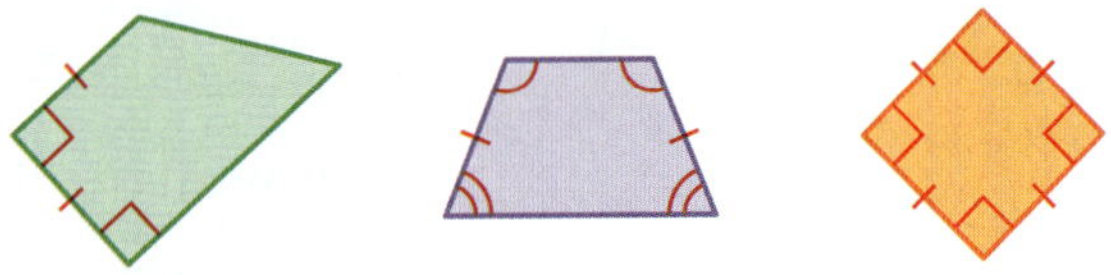

2. **VOCABULARY** What is a line of symmetry of a polygon?

VOCABULARY Tell whether the statement is *true* or *false*. Explain your reasoning.

3. A rhombus is a regular polygon.
4. A right triangle can be a regular polygon.
5. All regular polygons have at least three lines of symmetry.
6. Any polygon with congruent interior angles is a regular polygon.

Practice and Problem Solving

Determine whether the figure is a regular polygon.

7. 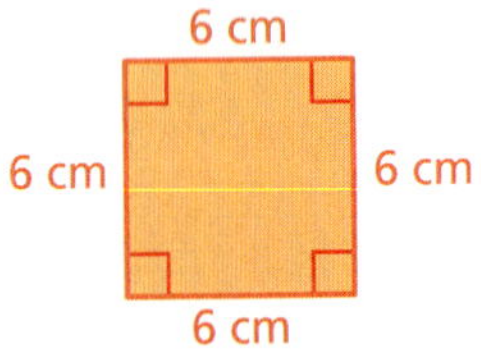

8. 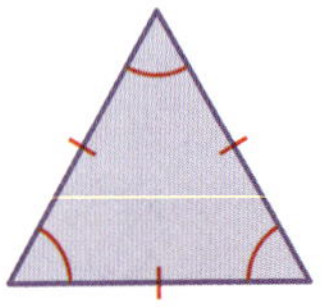

9. 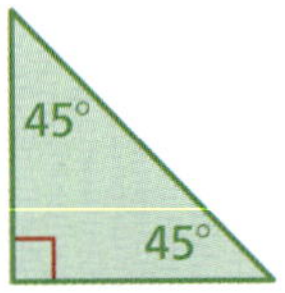

10. 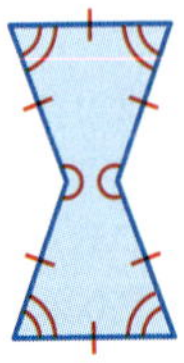

11. 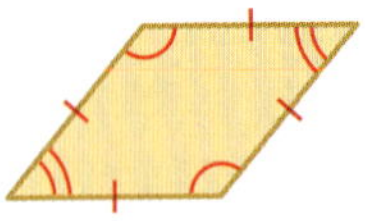

12. 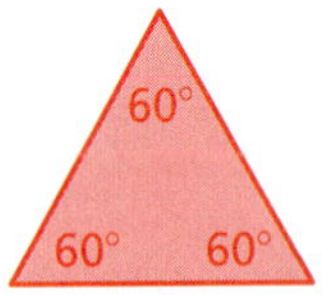

13. 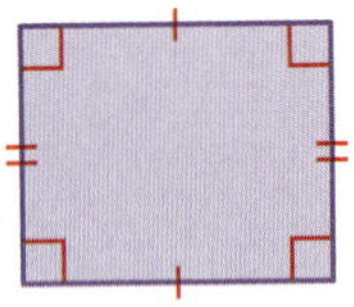

14. 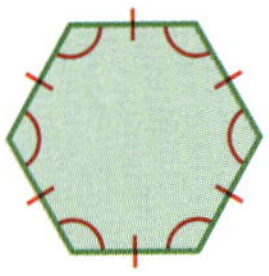

15. 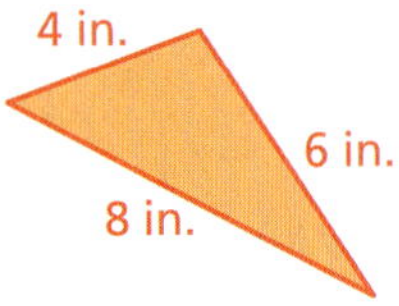

16. 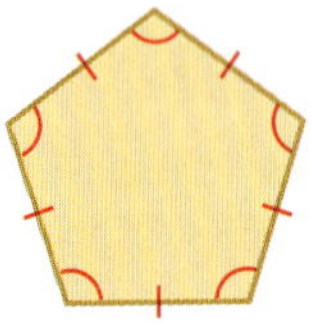

17. 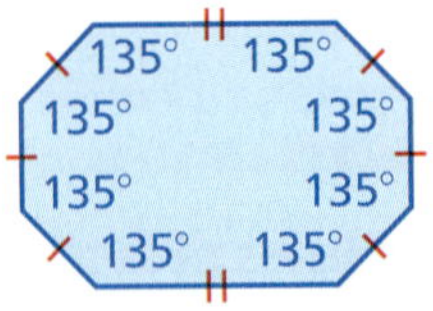

18. 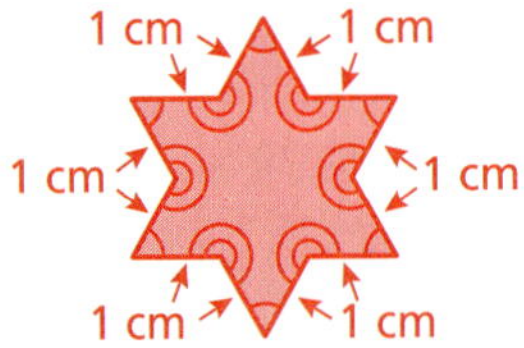

19. **STOP SIGN** A stop sign is in the shape of a regular octagon. The sum of the interior angle measures of any octagon is 1080°. What is the measure of each angle of a stop sign?

20. **SUSAN B. ANTHONY DOLLAR** A Susan B. Anthony dollar coin is in the shape of a regular hendecagon (an 11-sided polygon). The sum of the interior angle measures of any hendecagon is 1620°. What is the measure of each interior angle of a Susan B. Anthony dollar coin?

Draw all lines of symmetry on each polygon (if possible).

2 **21.**

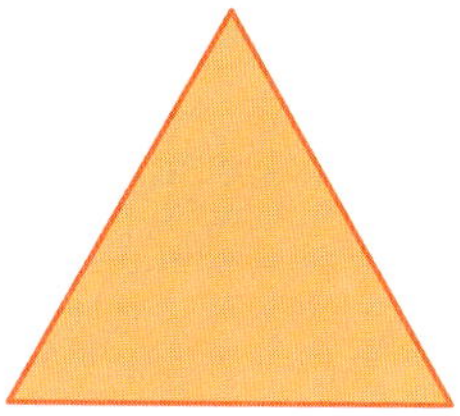

22.

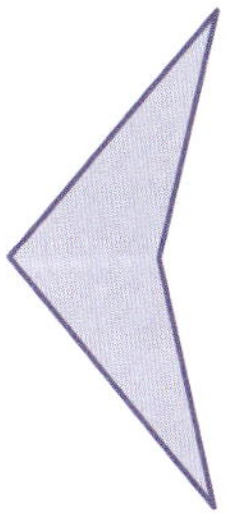

23.

24.

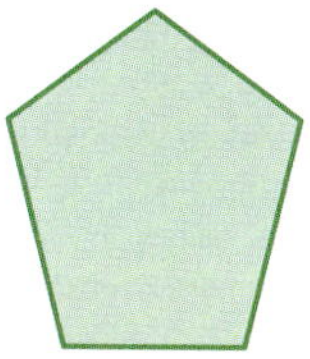

25.

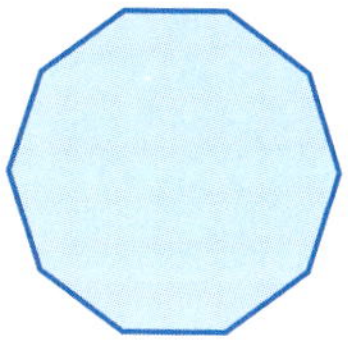

26.

27. **REASONING** If all of the sides of a rectangle are congruent, is it a regular polygon? Explain.

28. **Critical Thinking** Describe the relationship between the number of sides that a regular polygon has and the number of lines of symmetry it has.

29. **Critical Thinking** A hexagon is shown. Draw any lines of symmetry. Is this hexagon a regular polygon? Explain.

30. **REASONING** A regular dodecagon is shown. How many more lines of symmetry does this dodecagon have than a regular hexagon? Explain your answer.

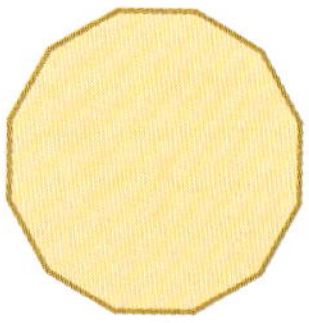

Fair Game Review What you learned in previous grades & lessons

Multiply.

31. $\frac{1}{2} \times \frac{4}{7}$ **32.** $\frac{63}{10} \times \frac{8}{9}$ **33.** 3.5×4.9 **34.** 0.068×12.7

35. **MULTIPLE CHOICE** Major League Baseball teams play 162 games during the regular season. Suppose your favorite team wins $\frac{2}{3}$ of its games. How many games would the team win?

Ⓐ 54 Ⓑ 81 Ⓒ 108 Ⓓ 243

8.2 Congruent Figures

Essential Question How can you identify congruent triangles?

Two figures are congruent when they have the same size and the same shape.

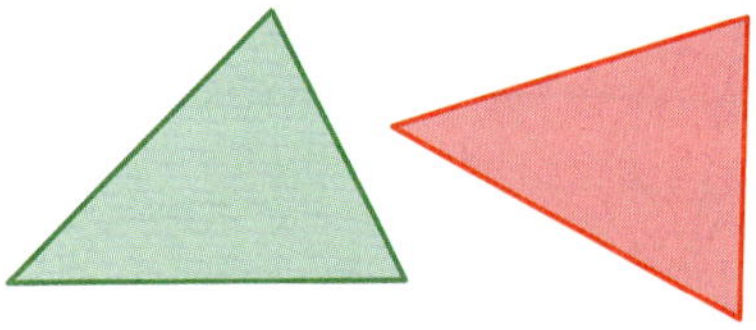

Congruent
Same size *and* shape

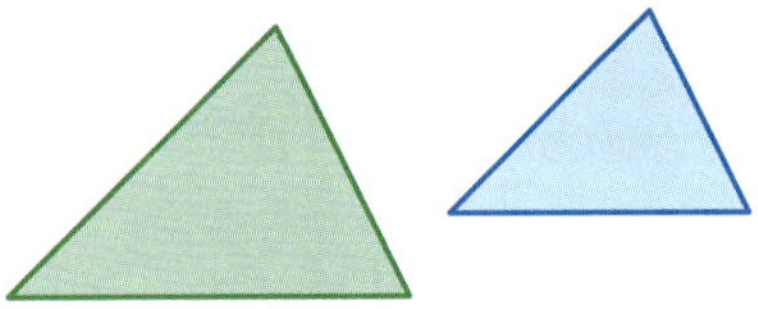

Not Congruent
Same shape, but not same size

1 ACTIVITY: Identifying Congruent Triangles

Work with a partner.

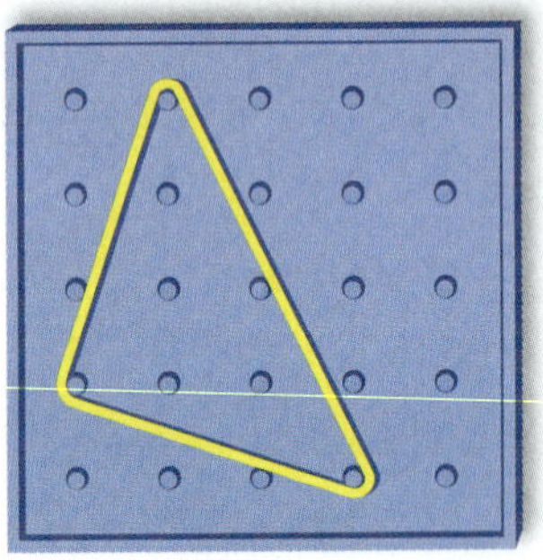

- **Which of the geoboard triangles below are congruent to the geoboard triangle at the right?**
- **Form each triangle on a geoboard.**
- **Measure each side with a ruler. Record your results in a table.**
- **Write a conclusion about the side lengths of triangles that are congruent.**

a.

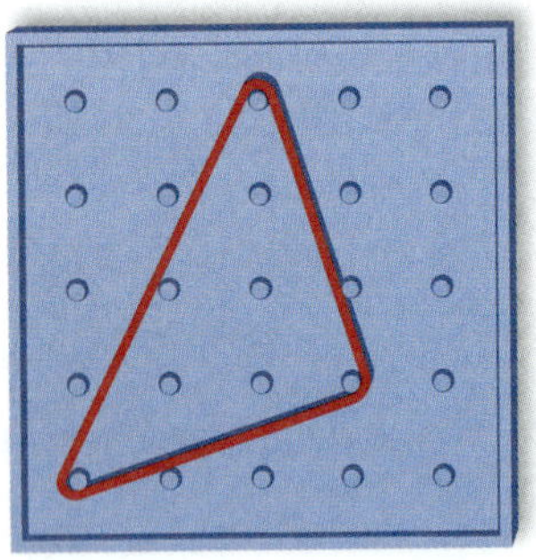

b.

c.

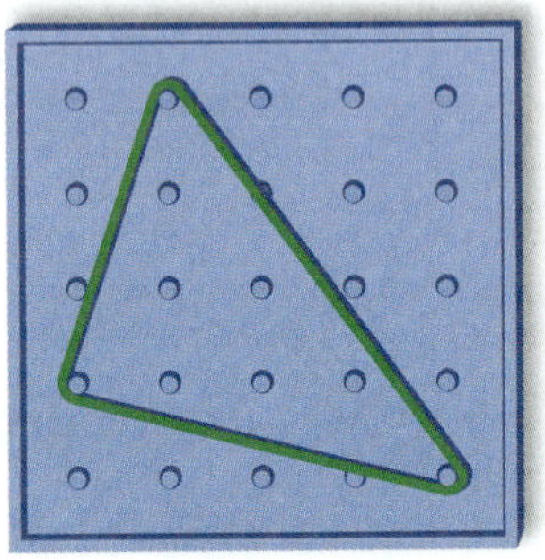

d.

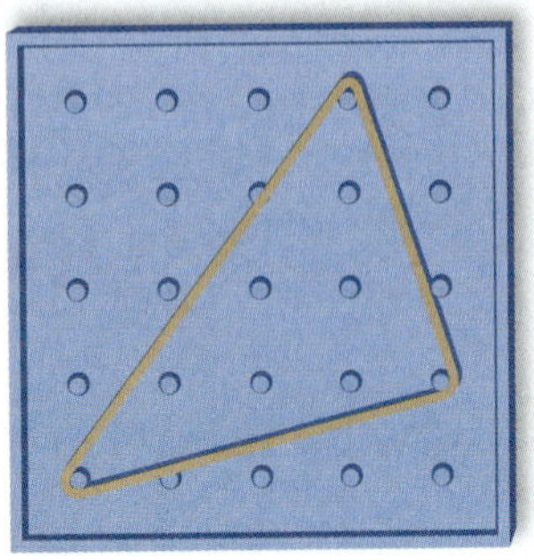

e.

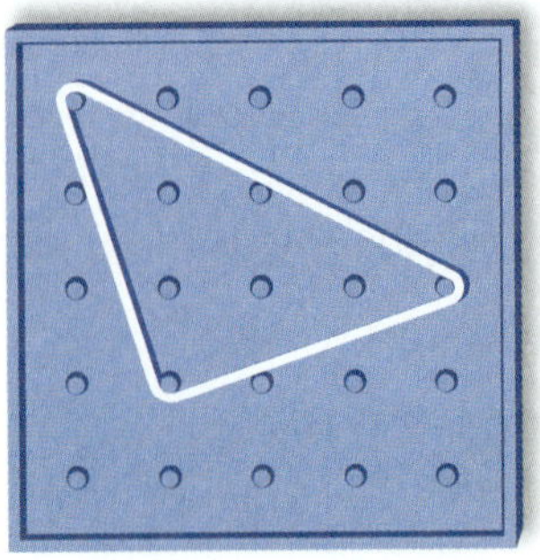

f.

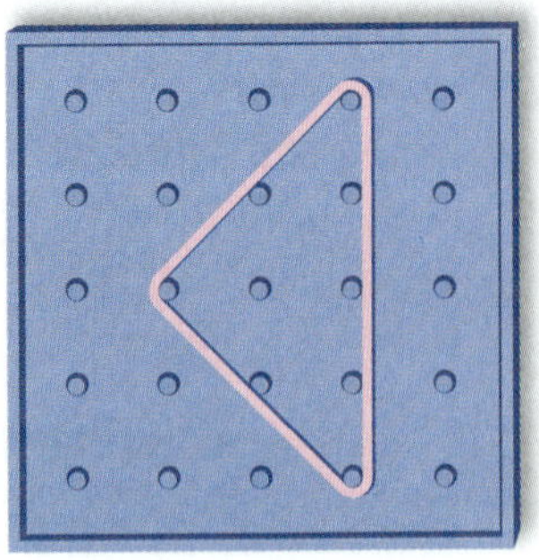

Geometry
In this lesson, you will
- name corresponding angles and corresponding sides of congruent figures.
- identify congruent figures.

Math Process

Recognize Usefulness of Tools

What are some advantages and disadvantages of using a geoboard to construct congruent triangles?

The geoboard at the right shows three congruent triangles.

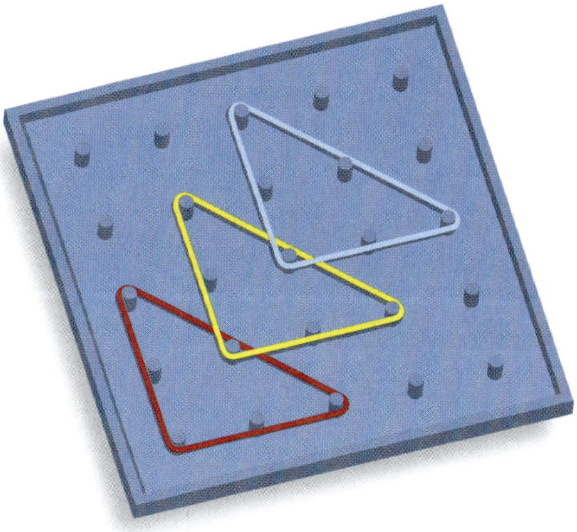

2 ACTIVITY: Forming Congruent Triangles

Work with a partner.

a. Form the yellow triangle in Activity 1 on your geoboard. Record the triangle on geoboard dot paper.

b. Move each vertex of the triangle one peg to the right. Is the new triangle congruent to the original triangle? How can you tell?

c. On a 5-by-5 geoboard, make as many different triangles as possible, each of which is congruent to the yellow triangle in Activity 1. Record each triangle on geoboard dot paper.

What Is Your Answer?

3. **IN YOUR OWN WORDS** How can you identify congruent triangles? Use the conclusion you wrote in Activity 1 as part of your answer.

4. Can you form a triangle on your geoboard whose side lengths are 3, 4, and 5 units? If so, draw such a triangle on geoboard dot paper.

Practice Use what you learned about congruent triangles to complete Exercises 4 and 5 on page 286.

Check It Out
Lesson Tutorials
BigIdeasMath.com

Key Vocabulary
congruent figures, *p. 284*
corresponding angles, *p. 284*
corresponding sides, *p. 284*

Key Idea

Congruent Figures

Figures that have the same size and the same shape are called **congruent figures**. The triangles below are congruent.

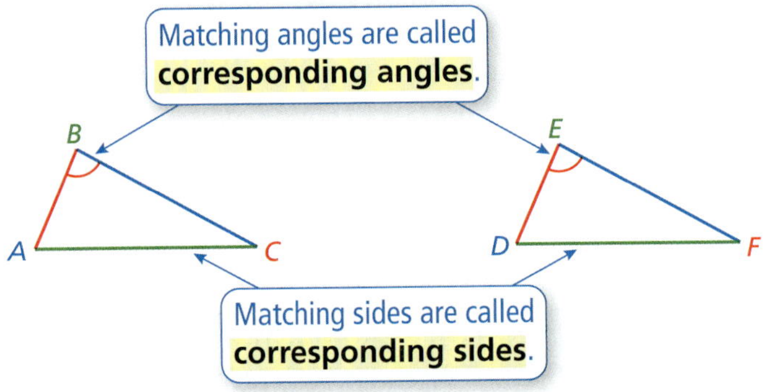

EXAMPLE 1 Naming Corresponding Parts

The figures are congruent. Name the corresponding angles and the corresponding sides.

Corresponding Angles	*Corresponding Sides*
$\angle A$ and $\angle W$	Side AB and Side WX
$\angle B$ and $\angle X$	Side BC and Side XY
$\angle C$ and $\angle Y$	Side CD and Side YZ
$\angle D$ and $\angle Z$	Side AD and Side WZ

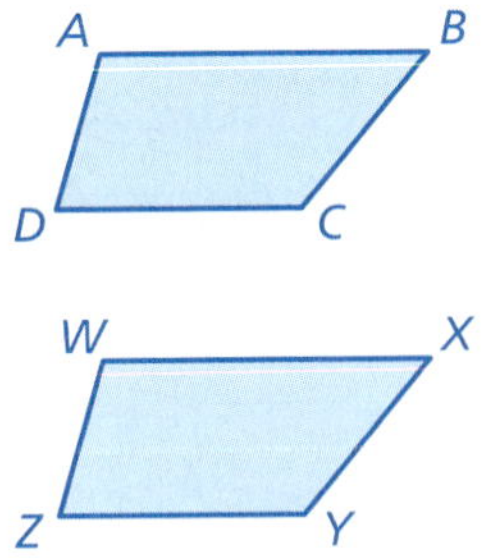

On Your Own

Now You're Ready
Exercises 6 and 7

1. The figures are congruent. Name the corresponding angles and the corresponding sides.

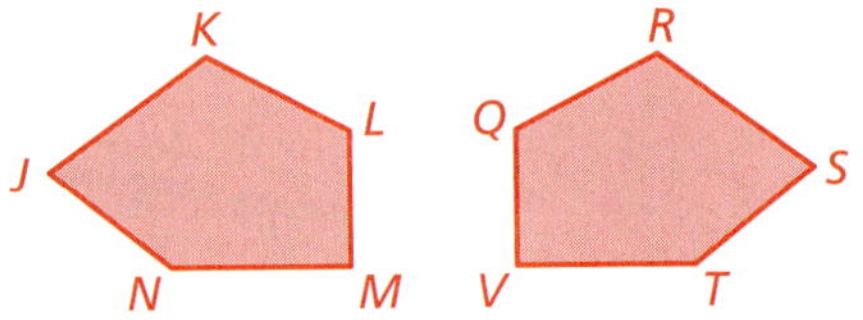

Key Idea

Identifying Congruent Figures

Two figures are congruent when corresponding angles and corresponding sides are congruent.

Triangle ABC is congruent to Triangle DEF.

$\triangle ABC \cong \triangle DEF$

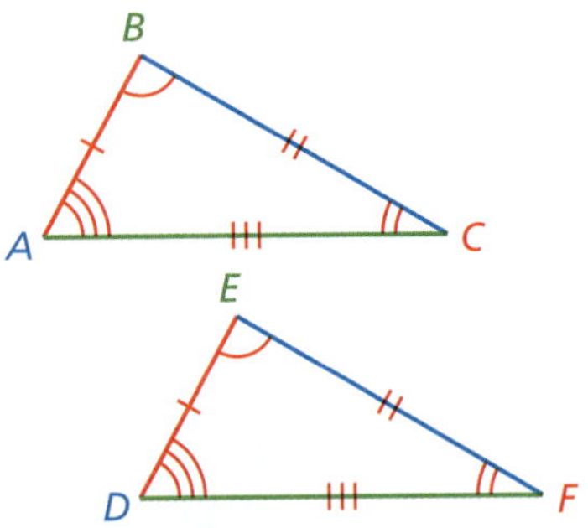

Reading

The symbol $\cong$ means *is congruent to.*

Multi-Language Glossary at BigIdeasMath.com

EXAMPLE 2 Identifying Congruent Figures

Which square is congruent to Square A?

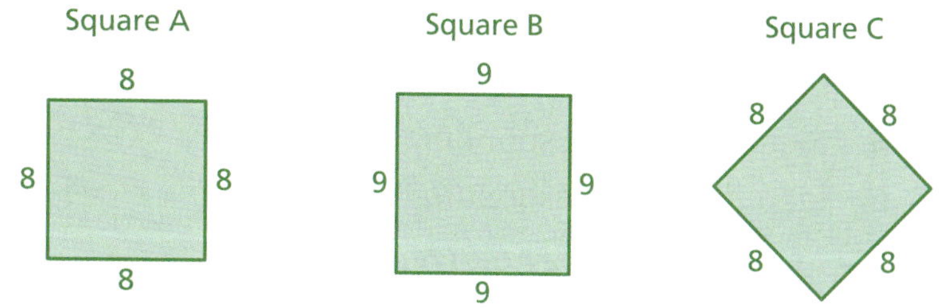

Each square has four right angles. So, corresponding angles are congruent. Check to see if corresponding sides are congruent.

Square A and Square B

Each side length of Square A is 8, and each side length of Square B is 9. So, corresponding sides are not congruent.

Square A and Square C

Each side length of Square A and Square C is 8. So, corresponding sides are congruent.

So, Square C is congruent to Square A.

EXAMPLE 3 Using Congruent Figures

Trapezoids *ABCD* and *JKLM* are congruent.

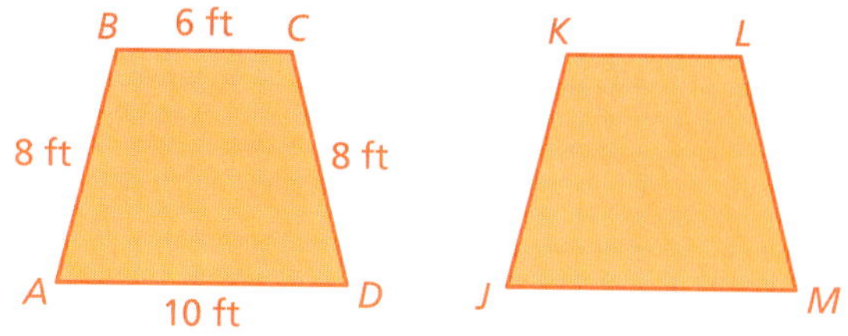

a. What is the length of side *JM*?

Side *JM* corresponds to side *AD*.

So, the length of side *JM* is 10 feet.

b. What is the perimeter of *JKLM*?

The perimeter of *ABCD* is $10 + 8 + 6 + 8 = 32$ feet. Because the trapezoids are congruent, their corresponding sides are congruent.

So, the perimeter of *JKLM* is also 32 feet.

On Your Own

Now You're Ready
Exercises 8, 9, and 12

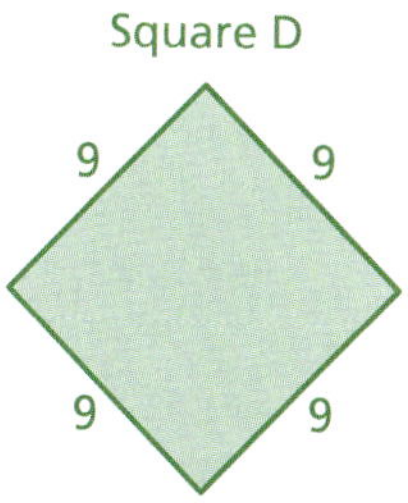

2. Which square in Example 2 is congruent to Square D?

3. In Example 3, which angle of *JKLM* corresponds to $\angle C$? What is the length of side *KJ*?

8.2 Exercises

Check It Out
Help with Homework
BigIdeasMath.com

Vocabulary and Concept Check

1. **VOCABULARY** $\triangle ABC$ is congruent to $\triangle DEF$.

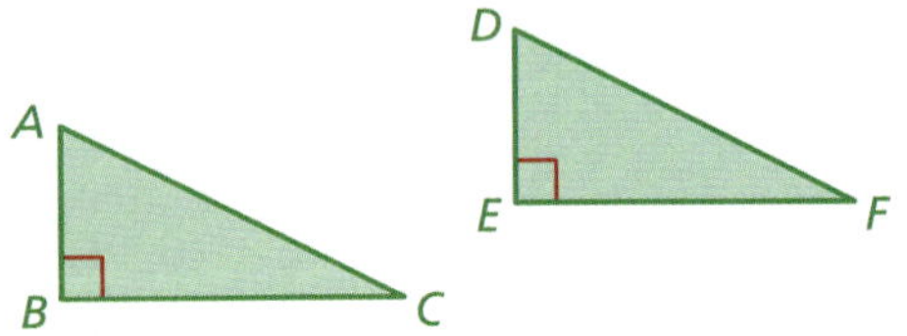

   a. Identify the corresponding angles.

   b. Identify the corresponding sides.

2. **VOCABULARY** Explain how you can tell that two figures are congruent.

3. **WHICH ONE DOESN'T BELONG?** Which one does *not* belong with the other three? Explain your reasoning.

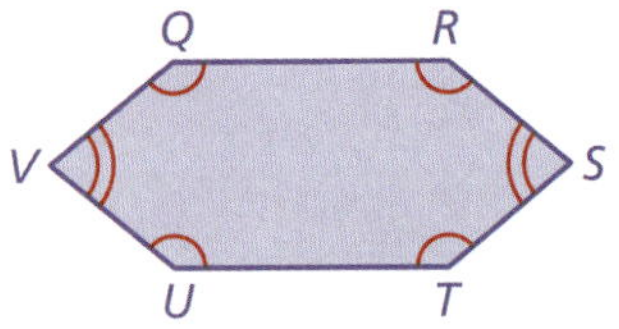

$\angle R$	$\angle U$	$\angle V$	$\angle Q$

Practice and Problem Solving

Tell whether the triangles are *congruent* or *not congruent*.

4.

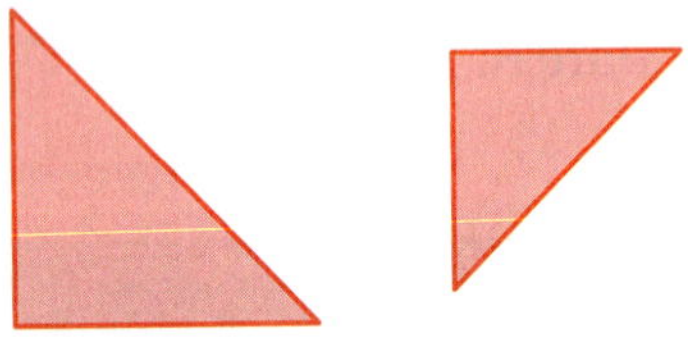

5.

The figures are congruent. Name the corresponding angles and the corresponding sides.

1 6.

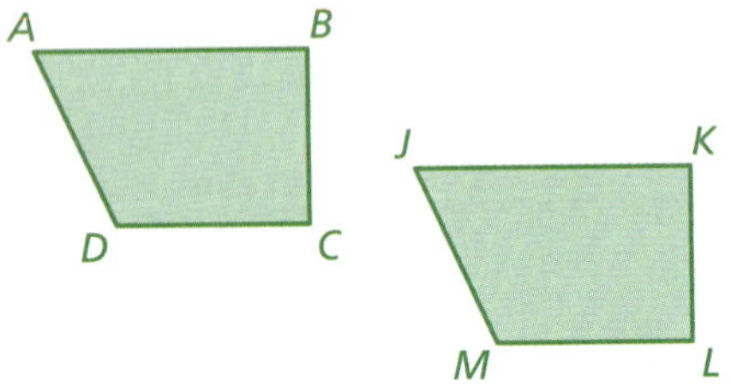

7.

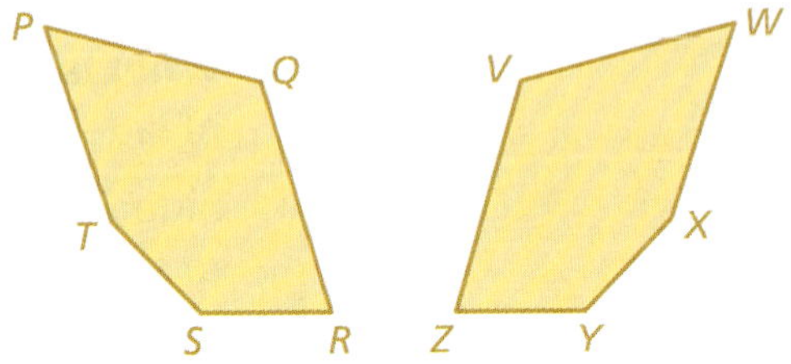

Tell whether the two figures are congruent. Explain your reasoning.

2 8.

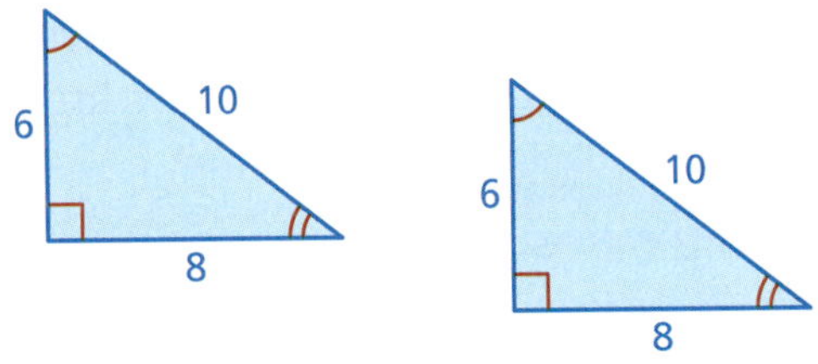

9.

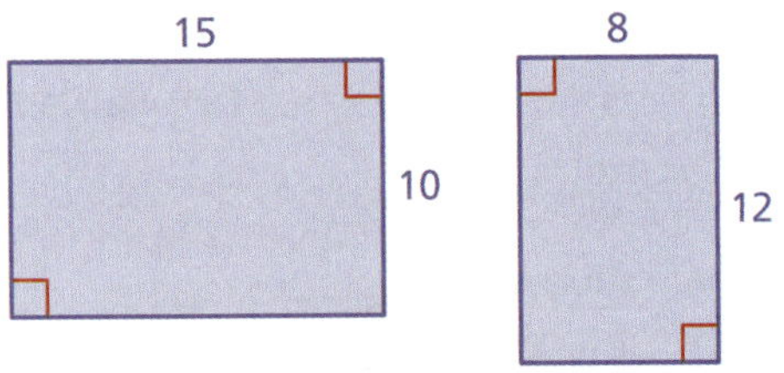

10. **PUZZLE** Describe the relationship between the unfinished puzzle and the missing piece.

11. ERROR ANALYSIS Describe and correct the error in telling whether the two figures are congruent.

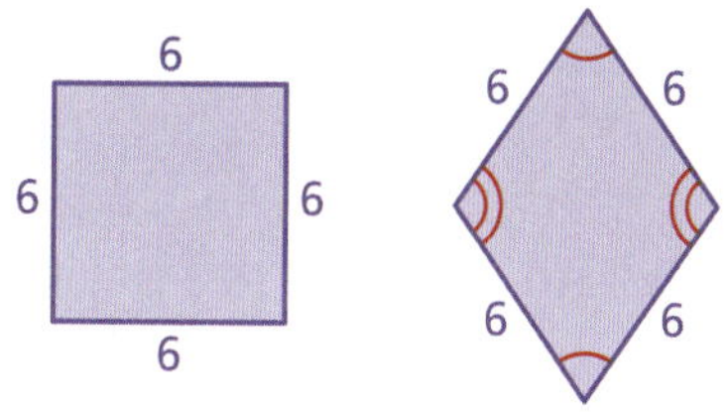

✗ Both figures have four sides, and the corresponding side lengths are equal. So, they are congruent.

3 **12. HOUSES** The fronts of the houses are identical.

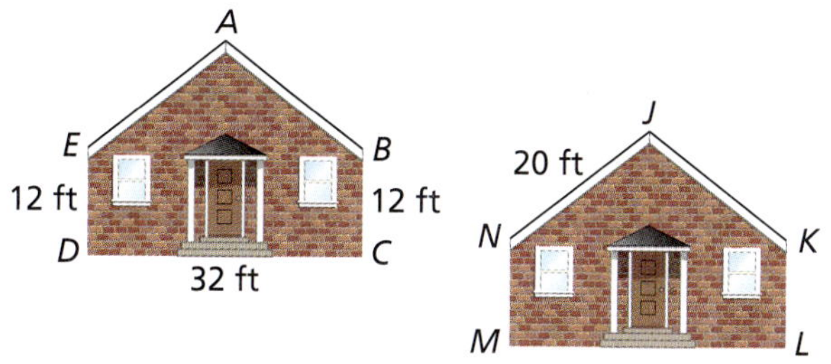

a. What is the length of side *LM*?

b. Which angle of *JKLMN* corresponds to $\angle D$?

c. Side *AB* is congruent to side *AE*. What is the length of side *AB*?

d. What is the perimeter of *ABCDE*?

13. REASONING Here are two ways to draw *one* line to divide a rectangle into two congruent figures. Draw three other ways.

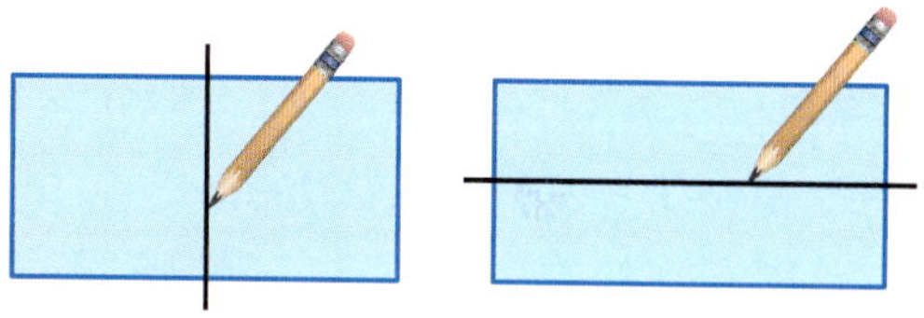

14. CRITICAL THINKING Are the areas of two congruent figures equal? Explain. Draw a diagram to support your answer.

15. True or False? The trapezoids are congruent. Determine whether the statement is *true* or *false*. Explain your reasoning.

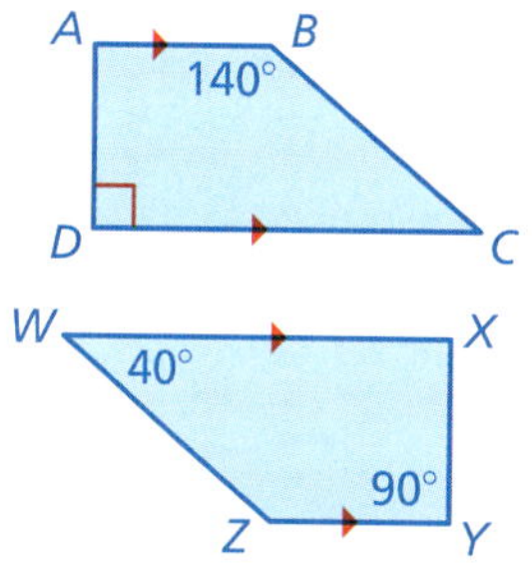

a. Side *AB* is congruent to side *YZ*.

b. $\angle A$ is congruent to $\angle X$.

c. $\angle A$ corresponds to $\angle X$.

d. The sum of the angle measures of *ABCD* is 360°.

Fair Game Review What you learned in previous grades & lessons

Plot and label the ordered pair in a coordinate plane.

16. $A(5, 3)$ **17.** $B(4, -1)$ **18.** $C(-2, 6)$ **19.** $D(-4, -2)$

20. MULTIPLE CHOICE You have 2 quarters and 5 dimes in your pocket. Write the ratio of quarters to the total number of coins.

Ⓐ $\frac{2}{5}$ Ⓑ 2 : 7 Ⓒ 5 to 7 Ⓓ $\frac{7}{2}$

8.3 Perimeters of Rectangles and Triangles

Essential Question How can you find the perimeter of a triangle or a rectangle?

1 ACTIVITY: Finding Perimeter

Work with a partner. Classify each figure as a scalene triangle, isosceles triangle, equilateral triangle, rectangle, or square. Then find the perimeter of each figure.

	Figure	*Classification*	*Perimeter*
a.	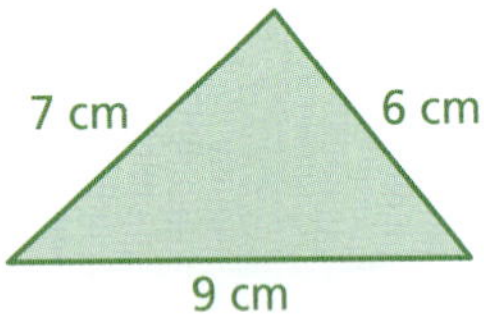		
b.	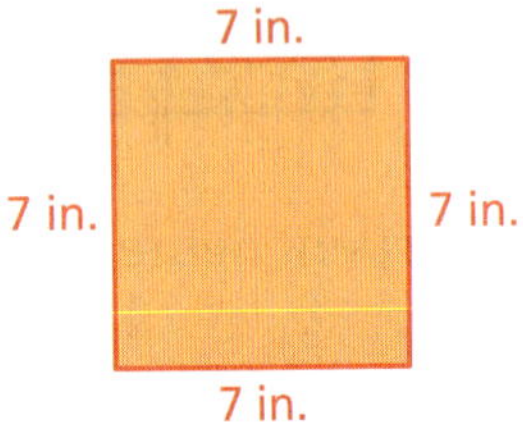		
c.	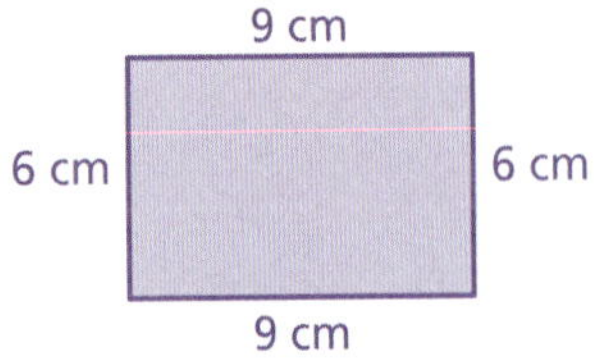		

2 ACTIVITY: Constructing Rectangles

Work with a partner. Arrange the line segments to make three different rectangles that each have a perimeter of 12 mm. Then record the length and width of each rectangle in the table.

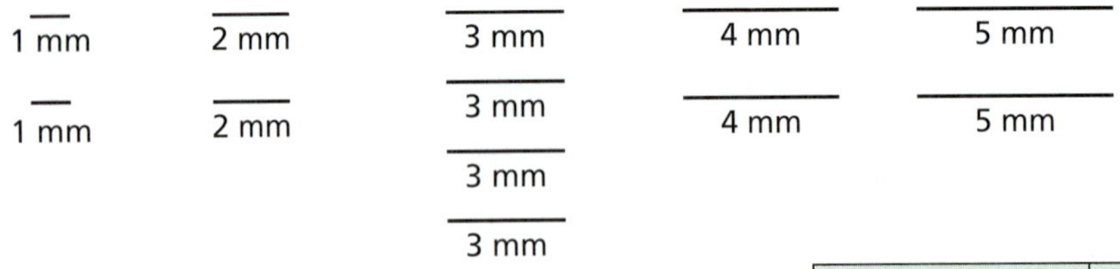

	Length (mm)	Width (mm)
First Rectangle		
Second Rectangle		
Third Rectangle		

Geometry

In this lesson, you will

- find perimeters of triangles.
- find perimeters of rectangles.
- solve real-life problems.

3 ACTIVITY: Creating Perimeters

Work with a partner. Solve each problem.

a. A landscaper fences a rectangular field that has a length of 28 yards and a width of 24 yards. How many yards of fencing does the landscaper need?

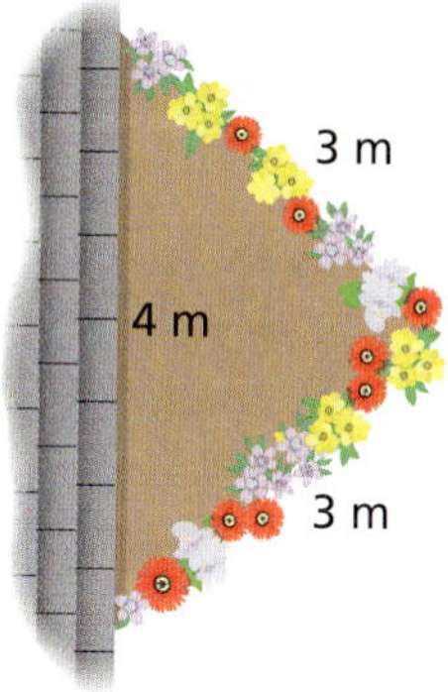

b. A gardner creates a decorative border around two sides of a triangular garden. The garden has side lengths of 3 meters, 3 meters, and 4 meters. The longest side of the garden rests against a house and does not need a border. How many feet of decorative border does the gardener need?

c. A pet expert uses fencing to surround a square playpen. The playpen has a side length of 8 feet. How many feet of fencing does the pet expert need?

d. The pet expert from part (c) extends the playpen. The new playpen is rectangular with a length of 12 feet and a width of 10 feet. The expert reuses the old fencing. How many feet of new fencing does the pet expert need?

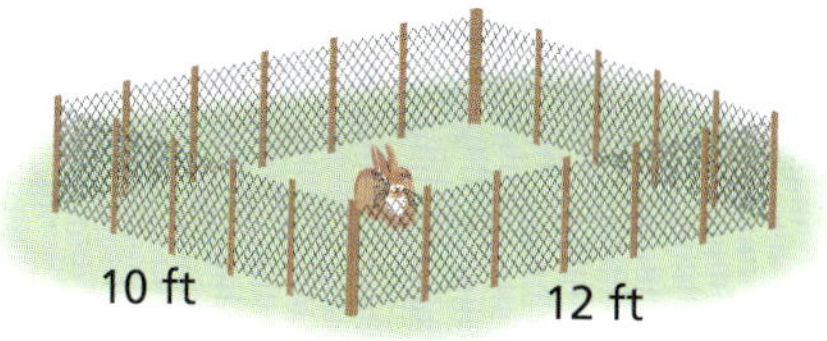

What Is Your Answer?

4. **IN YOUR OWN WORDS** How can you find the perimeter of a figure?
5. Draw two different rectangles that have the same perimeter.
6. Draw two different triangles that have the same perimeter.
7. Give an example of how "finding a perimeter" is helpful in each of the following careers.

a.

Carpenter

b.

Architect

c.

Pilot

Practice Use what you learned about the perimeters of triangles to complete Exercises 3–5 on page 292.

8.3 Lesson

Check It Out
Lesson Tutorials
BigIdeasMath.com

The distance around a figure is called its perimeter. To find the perimeter of a figure, find the sum of its side lengths.

EXAMPLE 1 Finding the Perimeter of a Triangle

Remember

Perimeter is measured in *linear* units such as inches, feet, or centimeters.

Find the perimeter of the triangle.

P = sum of side lengths

$= 5 + 12 + 13$

$= 30$

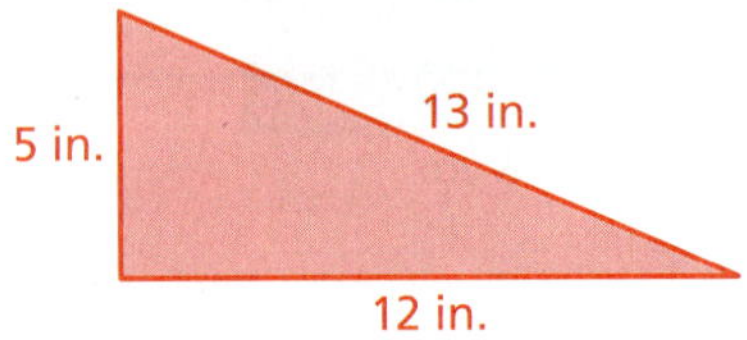

∴ The perimeter of the triangle is 30 inches.

Key Ideas

Perimeter of a Square

Words The perimeter P of a square is 4 times its side length s.

Algebra $P = 4s$

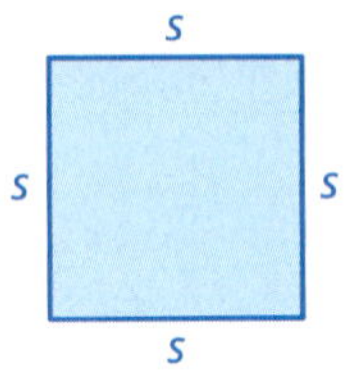

Perimeter of a Rectangle

Words The perimeter P of a rectangle is twice its length ℓ plus twice its width w.

Algebra $P = 2\ell + 2w$

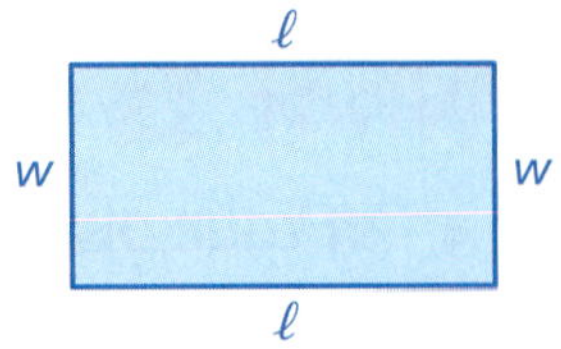

Study Tip

Using the Distributive Property, you can write the perimeter of a rectangle as $P = 2(\ell + w)$.

EXAMPLE 2 Finding the Perimeter of a Square and a Rectangle

Find the perimeter of the square or rectangle.

a.

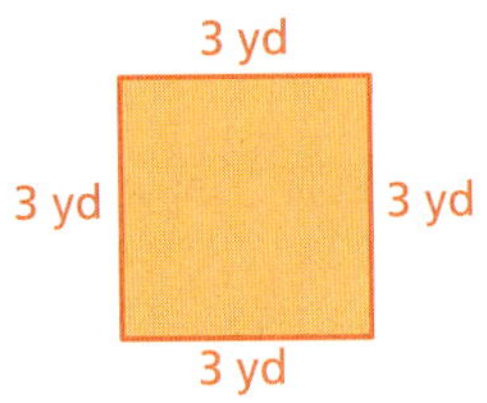

$P = 4s$ — Write formula.

$= 4(3)$ — Substitute.

$= 12$ — Simplify.

∴ The perimeter of the square is 12 yards.

b.

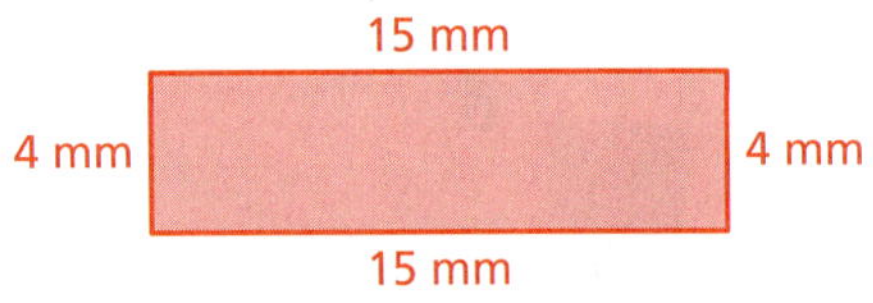

$P = 2\ell + 2w$

$= 2(15) + 2(4)$

$= 38$

∴ The perimeter of the rectangle is 38 millimeters.

On Your Own

Now You're Ready Exercises 3–8

Find the perimeter of the figure.

1.

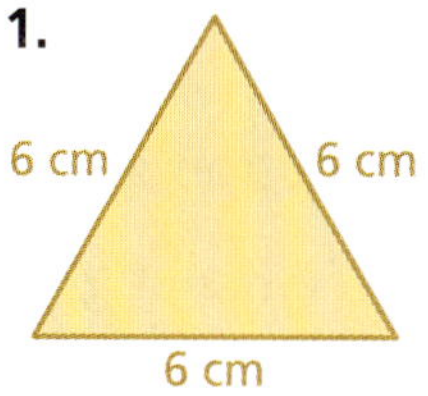

2.

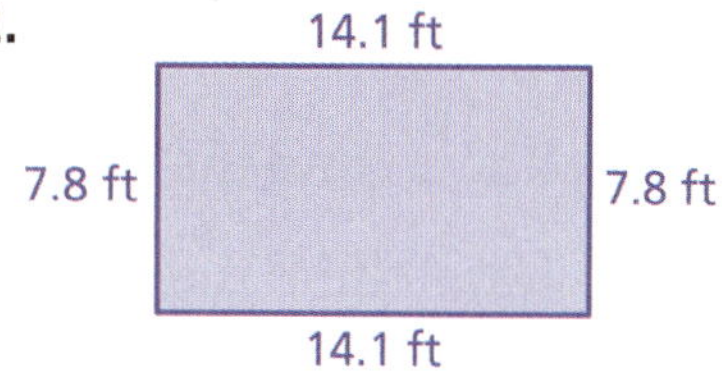

3.

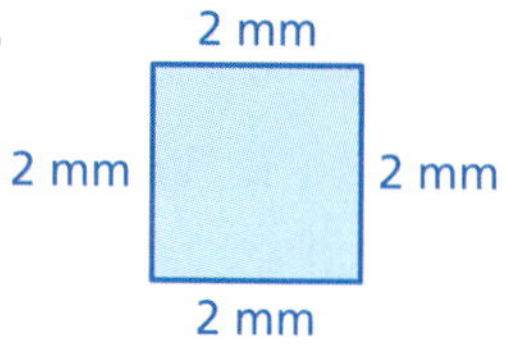

EXAMPLE 3 Real-Life Application

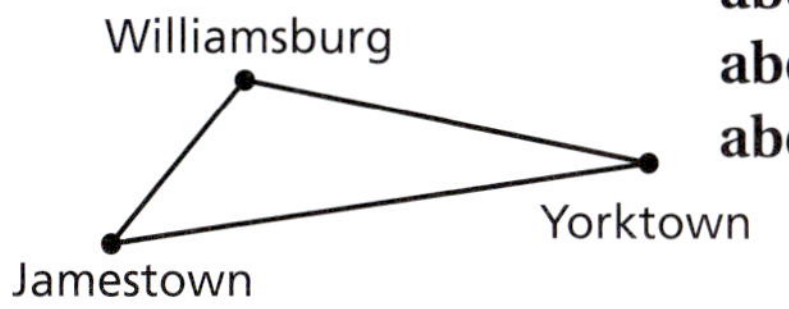

The Historic Triangle in Virginia connects Jamestown, Williamsburg, and Yorktown. The distance between Jamestown and Williamsburg is about 5.67 miles. The distance between Williamsburg and Yorktown is about 11.11 miles. The distance between Jamestown and Yorktown is about 14.71 miles. Estimate the perimeter of the Historic Triangle.

$P = \text{sum of side lengths} = 5.67 + 11.11 + 14.71 = 31.49$

∴ The perimeter of the Historic Triangle is about 31.49 miles.

EXAMPLE 4 Real-Life Application

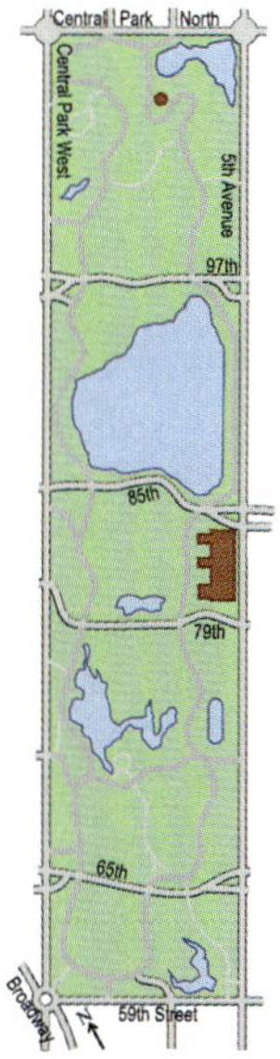

Central Park

Central Park in New York City is rectangular. Its width is about 800 meters. Its length is 5 times its width. Estimate the perimeter of the park.

The length is 5 times the width.

$\ell = 5(800) = 4000$

So, the length is 4000 meters. Use the formula for the perimeter of a rectangle to estimate the perimeter of the park.

$P = 2\ell + 2w$	Write formula.
$= 2(4000) + 2(800)$	Substitute 4000 for ℓ and 800 for w.
$= 8000 + 1600$	Multiply.
$= 9600$	Add.

∴ The perimeter is about 9600 meters, or 9.6 kilometers.

On Your Own

Now You're Ready Exercises 11–13

4. A triangular display case has side lengths of 18 inches, 18 inches, and 26 inches. What is the perimeter of the case?

5. The width of a rectangular field is 16 feet. The length is 3 times the width. What is the perimeter of the rectangular field?

8.3 Exercises

Check It Out
Help with Homework
BigIdeasMath.com

Vocabulary and Concept Check

1. **WRITING** Explain how to find the perimeter of a triangle.
2. **WRITING** Explain how to find the perimeter of a rectangle.

Practice and Problem Solving

1 **Find the perimeter of each triangle.**

3.
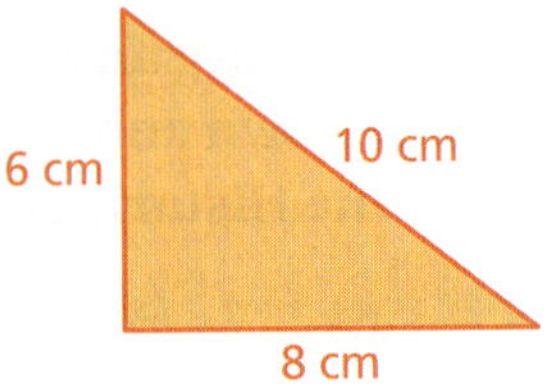

4.
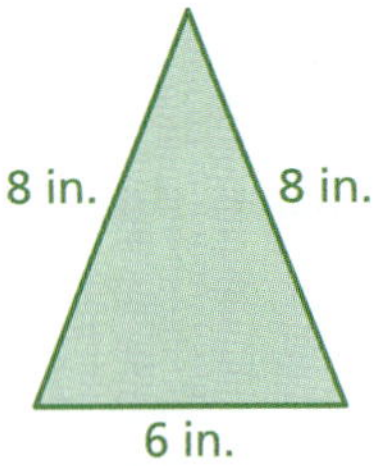

5.

6. **ERROR ANALYSIS** Describe and correct the error in finding the perimeter of the polygon.

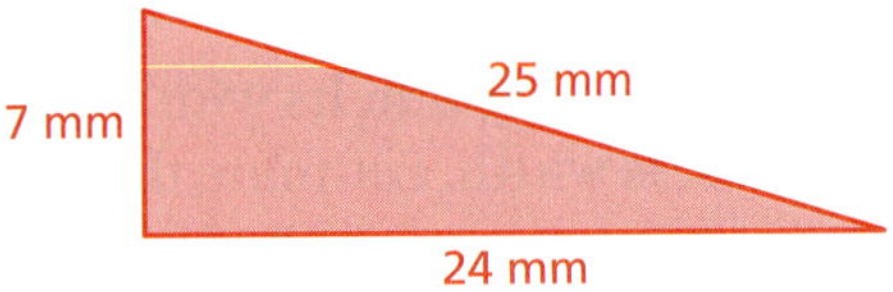

✗ Perimeter $= 7 \times 24 \times 25$
$= 4200$ mm

2 **Find the perimeter of each square or rectangle.**

7.
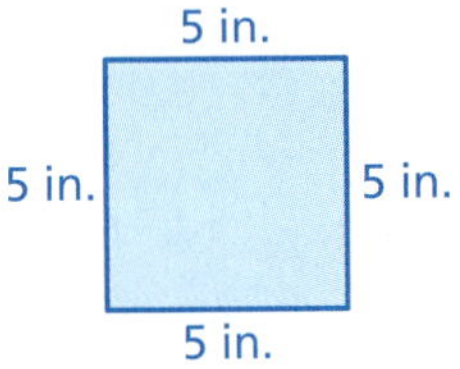

8.
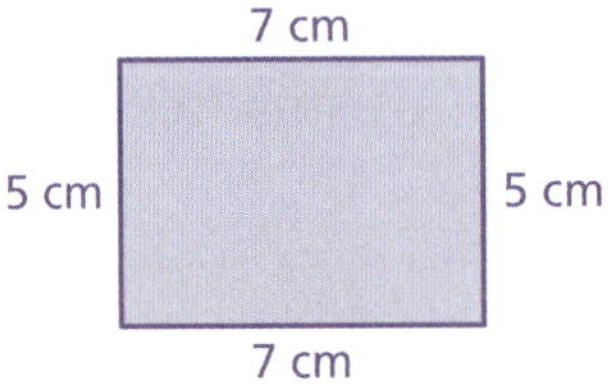

9.
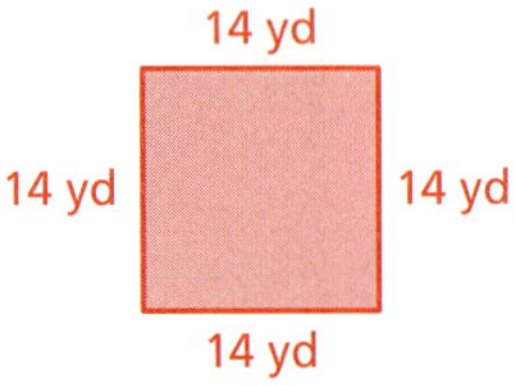

10.
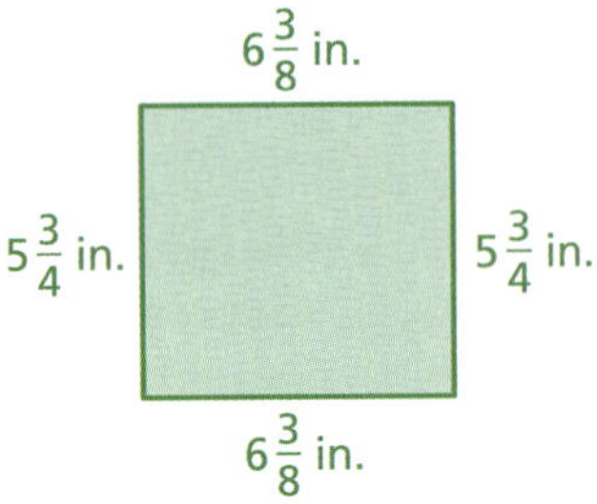

11.
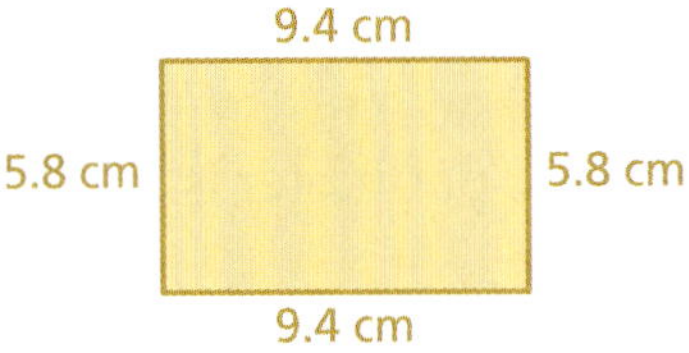

12.
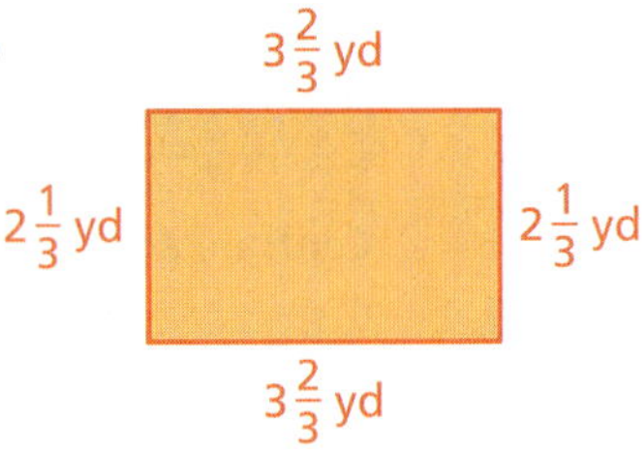

13. **CRITICAL THINKING** An equilateral triangle has a perimeter of 36 feet. What is the length of each side of the triangle? Explain your reasoning.

14. **GARDEN** Your aunt designs a triangular flower garden. Find the perimeter of the garden.

15. **REASONING** The length of a rectangle is 24 meters. The length is 4 times the width. What is the perimeter of the rectangle?

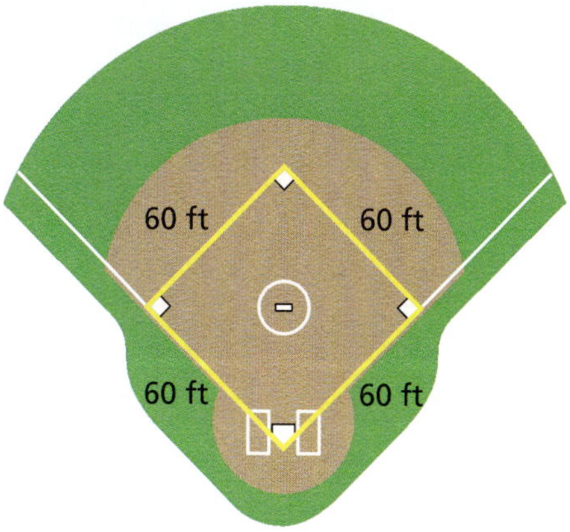

16. **SOFTBALL DIAMOND** Find the perimeter of the softball diamond.

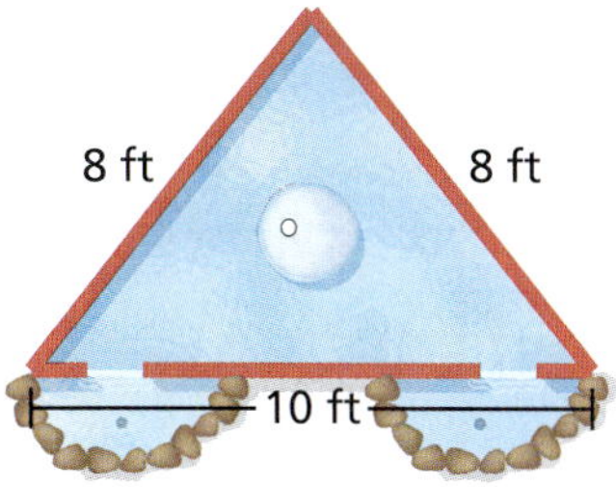

17. **FOUNTAIN** A homeowner designs a fountain with a brick border in the shape of an isosceles triangle. Each leg is 8 feet long and the base is 10 feet long. The base will have two sections of 1 foot each that will not be covered by brick, so that the water can flow. How many feet of brick are needed for the border?

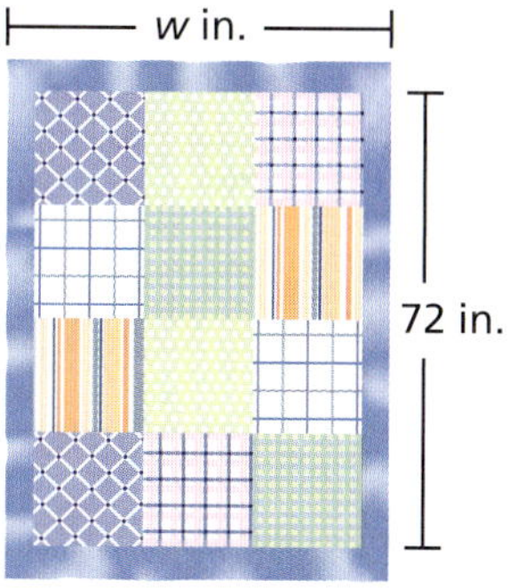

18. **QUILT** You are bordering a quilt with a blue ribbon. Which expression tells you how much ribbon you will need? Draw a diagram to help explain your reasoning.

$2(w + 72)$ $2w + 72$

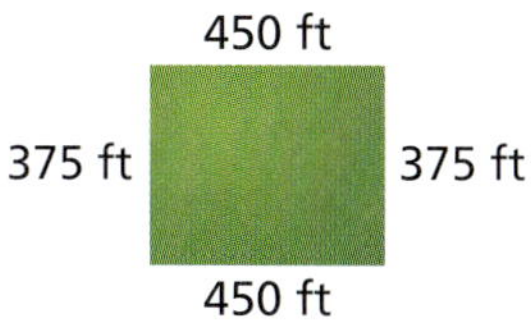

19. **PASTURE** A farmer wants to build a fence around a pasture. From which store should the farmer buy the fencing? Explain your reasoning. How much will the farmer save by buying all of the fencing at this store?

- Store A: \$11 per foot
- Store B: \$30 per yard

20. **Critical Thinking** How does the perimeter of a square change when its side lengths double? triple?

Fair Game Review What you learned in previous grades & lessons

Use the Distributive Property to simplify the expression.

21. $2(x + 3)$ 22. $4(8 + r)$ 23. $7(w - 1)$ 24. $8(s - 4)$

25. **MULTIPLE CHOICE** Which expression represents "5 less than the product of 2 and a number y?"

Ⓐ $(5 - 2)y$ Ⓑ $5 - 2y$ Ⓒ $\frac{5}{2y}$ Ⓓ $2y - 5$

8.4 Areas of Rectangles and Triangles

Essential Question How can you derive a formula for the area of a triangle?

1 ACTIVITY: Finding the Area of a Rectangle

Work with a partner. Each grid square represents 1 square inch.

a. Copy and complete the table.

Rectangle	Length	Width	Area
A			
B			
C			
D			

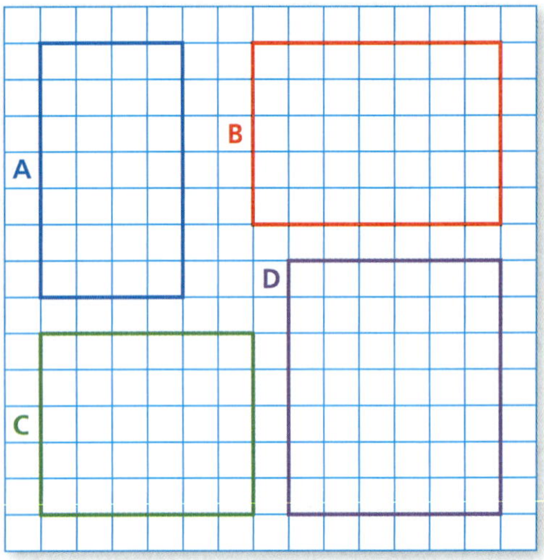

b. Describe two ways to find the areas of the rectangles in part (a).

2 ACTIVITY: Deriving the Area Formula of a Triangle

Work with a partner.

a. Fold a piece of grid paper in half. Draw a triangle so that its base lies on one of the horizontal lines of the paper. Do not use a right triangle. Label the height and the base *inside* the triangle.

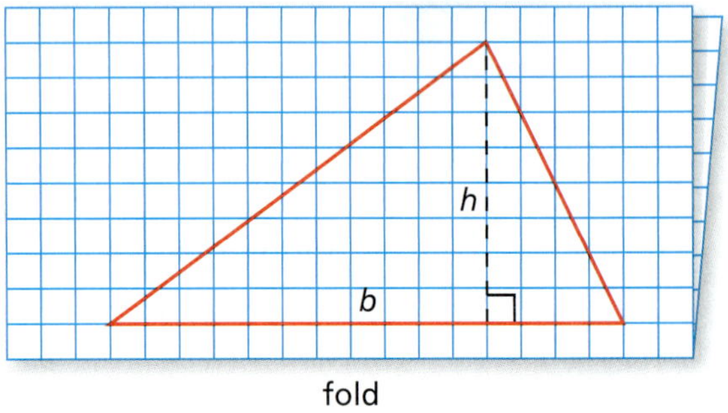

b. Estimate the area of your triangle by counting unit squares.

Area ≈ ______ Estimate

c. Cut out the triangle so that you end up with two identical triangles. Form a quadrilateral whose area you know. What type of quadrilateral is it? Explain how you *know* it is this type.

d. Use your results to write a formula for the area of a triangle. Then use your formula to find the exact area of your triangle. Compare this area with your estimate in part (b).

Geometry

In this lesson, you will
- find areas of rectangles.
- find areas of triangles.
- solve real-life problems.

Math Process

Calculate Accurately

How can you estimate the area of each triangle so that the answer is close to the exact area?

3 ACTIVITY: Estimating and Finding the Area of a Triangle

Work with a partner. Each grid square represents 1 square centimeter.

- **Use estimation to match each triangle with its area.**
- **Then check your work by finding the exact area of each triangle.**

	Area	*Estimate Match*	*Exact Match*
a.	15 cm^2		
b.	20 cm^2		
c.	9 cm^2		
d.	12 cm^2		
e.	60 cm^2		
f.	$12\frac{1}{2}$ cm^2		
g.	$24\frac{1}{2}$ cm^2		
h.	8 cm^2		

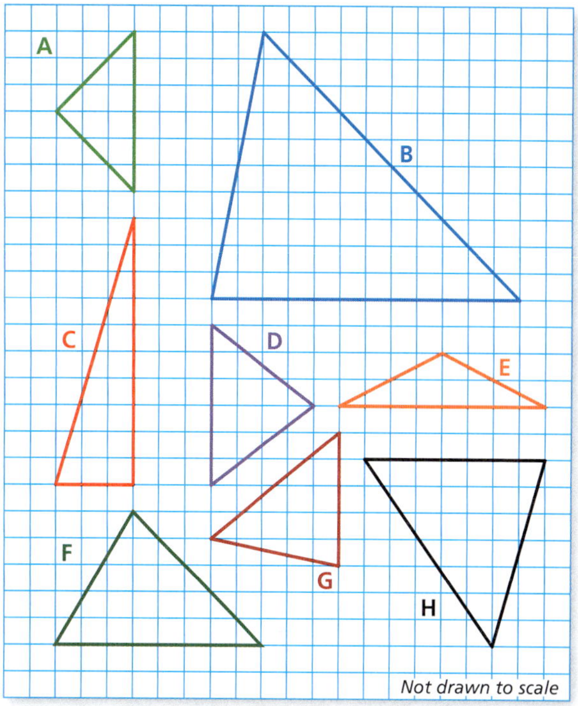

What Is Your Answer?

4. **PARTNER ACTIVITY** Use a piece of centimeter grid paper to create your own "area matching activity." Include rectangles and triangles. Trade with your partner and solve each other's matching activity.

5. **IN YOUR OWN WORDS** How can you derive a formula for the area of a triangle?

Practice Use what you learned about the areas of triangles to complete Exercises 6–8 on page 298.

8.4 Lesson

Check It Out
Lesson Tutorials
BigIdeasMath.com

Key Idea

Area of a Rectangle

Words The area A of a rectangle is the product of its length ℓ and its width w.

Algebra $A = \ell w$

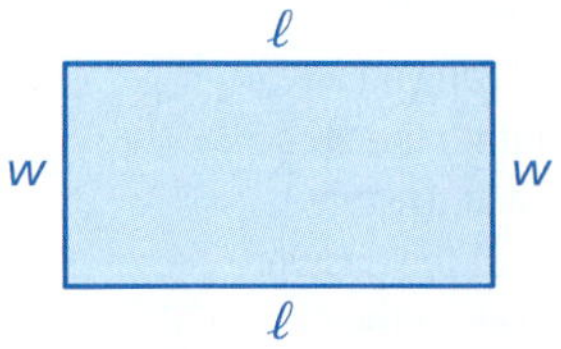

EXAMPLE 1 Finding the Area of a Rectangle

Find the area of the rectangle.

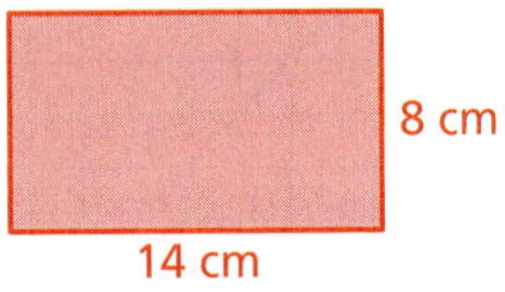

$A = \ell w$ Write formula.

$= (14)(8)$ Substitute 14 for ℓ and 8 for w.

$= 112$ Multiply.

The area of the rectangle is 112 square centimeters.

Key Idea

Area of a Triangle

Words The area A of a triangle is one-half the product of its base b and its height h.

Algebra $A = \frac{1}{2}bh$

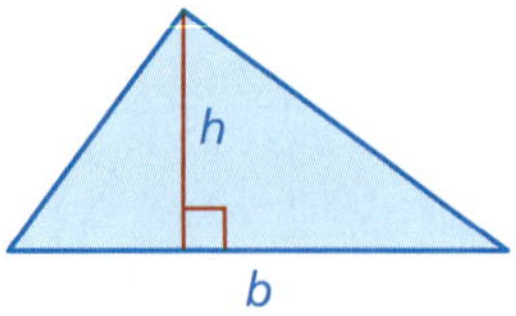

EXAMPLE 2 Finding the Area of a Triangle

Find the area of the triangle.

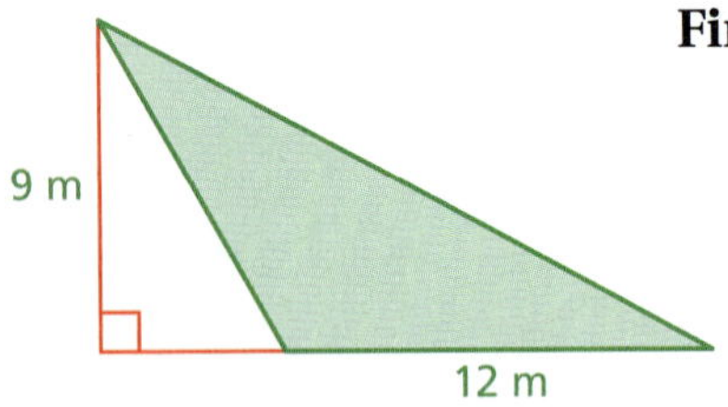

$A = \frac{1}{2}bh$ Write formula.

$= \frac{1}{2}(12)(9)$ Substitute 12 for b and 9 for h.

$= 54$ Multiply.

The area of the triangle is 54 square meters.

On Your Own

Now You're Ready
Exercises 3–11

Find the area of the rectangle or triangle.

1. 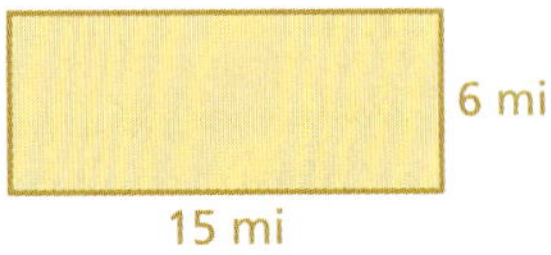

2. 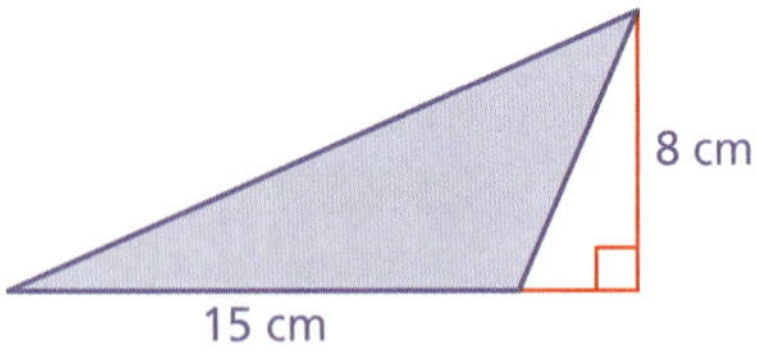

EXAMPLE 3 Real-Life Application

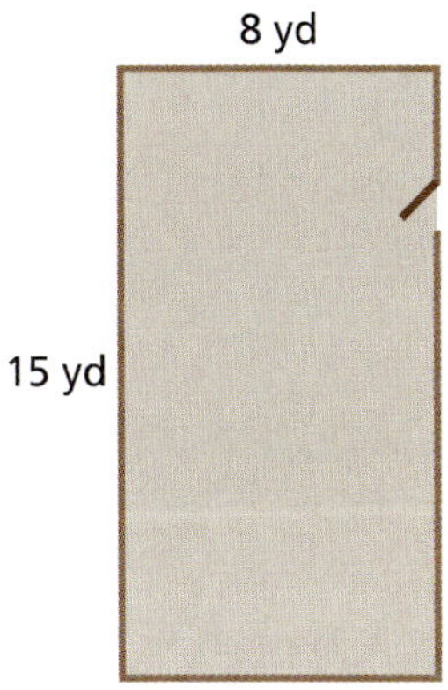

Your uncle buys carpet for the rectangular room. The carpet costs $36 per square yard. What is the total cost of the carpet?

Find the area of the room.

$A = \ell w$	Write formula.
$= (15)(8)$	Substitute 15 for ℓ and 8 for w.
$= 120$	Multiply.

The area of the room is 120 square yards. Multiply by the cost per square yard.

$120(\$36) = \$4320$

∴ The total cost of the carpet is $4320.

EXAMPLE 4 Real-Life Application

The base and height of the red butterfly wing are two times greater than the base and height of the blue butterfly wing. How many times greater is the area of the red wing than the area of the blue wing?

Find the area of the blue wing.

$A = \frac{1}{2}bh$	Write formula.
$= \frac{1}{2}(2)(1)$	Substitute 2 for b and 1 for h.
$= 1 \text{ cm}^2$	Multiply.

The red wing dimensions are 2 times greater, so the base is $2 \times 2 = 4$ cm and the height is $2 \times 1 = 2$ cm. Find the area of the red wing.

$A = \frac{1}{2}bh$	Write formula.
$= \frac{1}{2}(4)(2)$	Substitute 4 for b and 2 for h.
$= 4 \text{ cm}^2$	Multiply.

∴ Because $\frac{4 \cancel{\text{cm}^2}}{1 \cancel{\text{cm}^2}} = 4$, the area of the red wing is 4 times greater.

On Your Own

3. In Example 3, a rectangular closet is 2 yards long and 1.5 yards wide. What is the cost of the carpet for the closet?

4. How many times greater is the area of a triangle with a height of 3 feet and a base of 6 feet than the area of a triangle with a height of 1 foot and a base of 2 feet?

8.4 Exercises

Check It Out
Help with Homework
BigIdeasMath.com

Vocabulary and Concept Check

1. **OPEN-ENDED** List the dimensions of two rectangles with areas of 36 square feet.

2. **DIFFERENT WORDS, SAME QUESTION** Which is different? Find "both" answers.

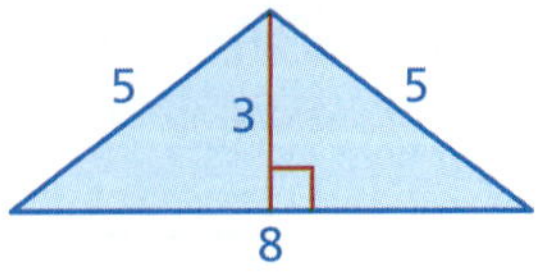

What is the area of the triangle?

What is the distance around the triangle?

How many unit squares fit in the triangle?

What is one-half the product of the base and the height?

Practice and Problem Solving

Find the area of the rectangle.

1 3.

4.

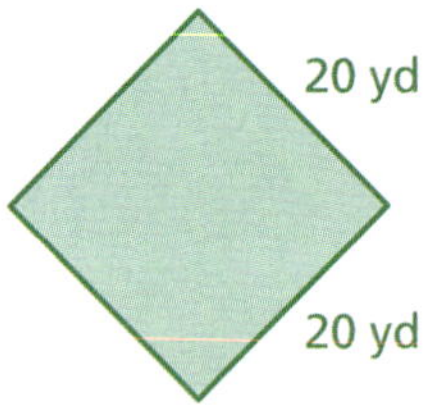

5.

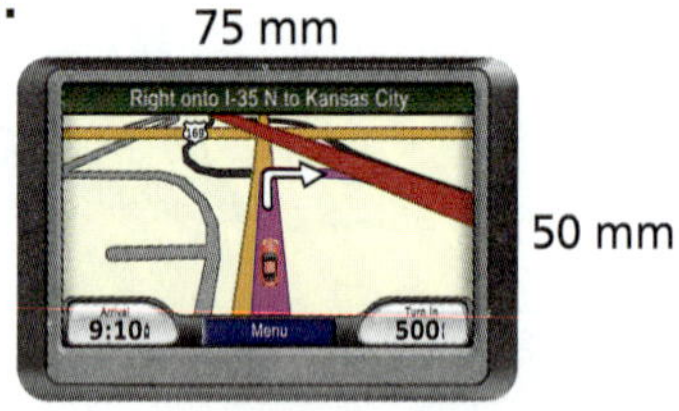

Find the area of the triangle.

2 6.

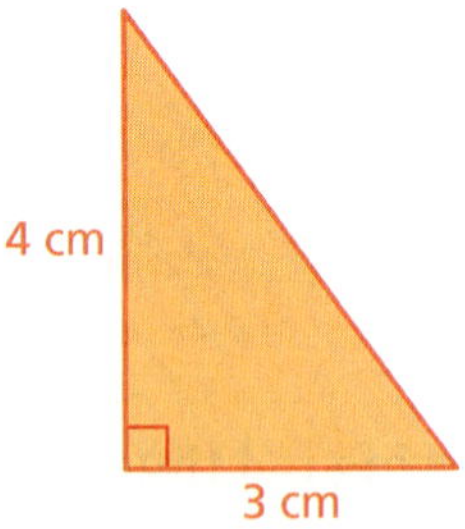

7.

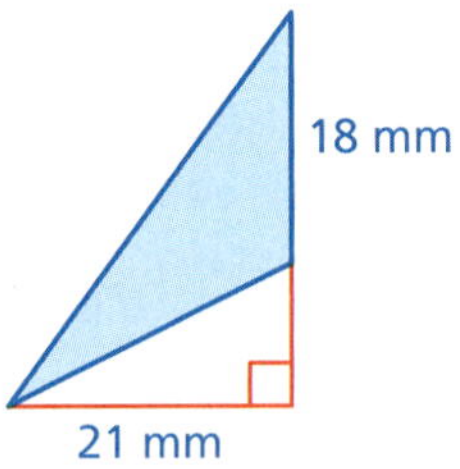

8.

9.

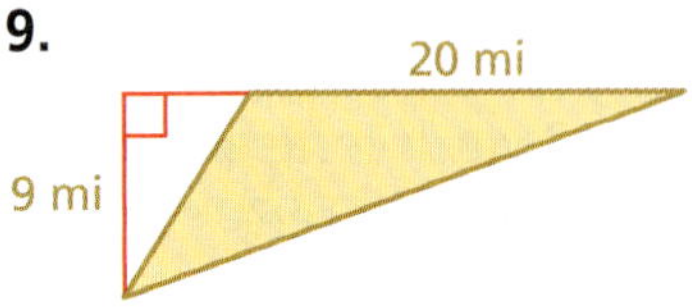

10.

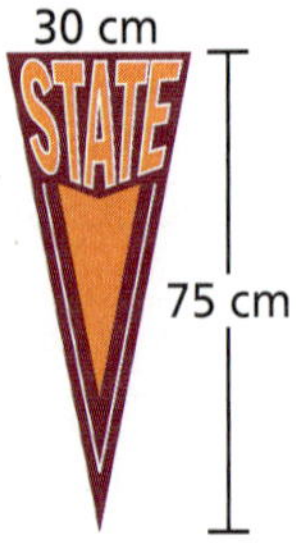

11.

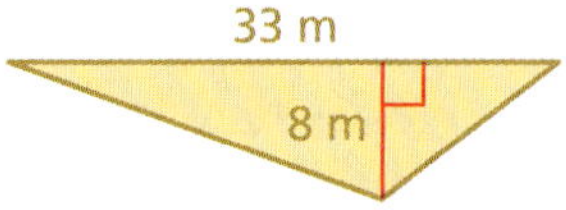

12. **ERROR ANALYSIS** Describe and correct the error in finding the area of the triangle.

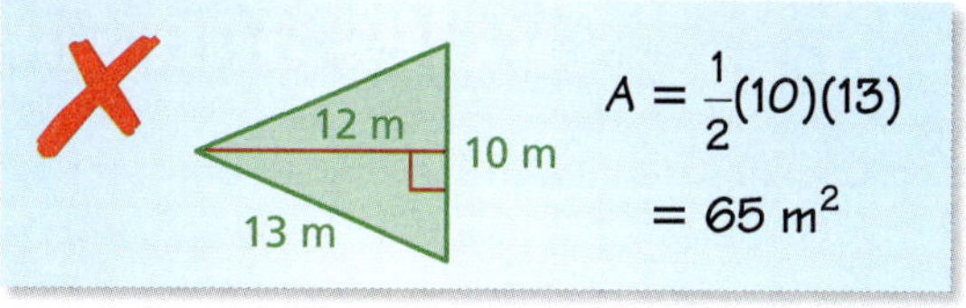

13. **WALLPAPER** You are hanging wallpaper on a wall that is 16 feet long and 8 feet high. There are two windows on the wall that each measure 3 feet by 6 feet. How much wallpaper do you need?

14. **WRITING** The perimeter of a square room is 64 feet. Explain how to find the total cost to carpet the room at \$3 per square foot. Then find the total cost of the carpet.

15. **OPEN-ENDED** Draw and label two rectangles and two triangles that each have an area of 24 square feet.

16. **HANG GLIDING** The wingspan of the triangular hang glider is 30 feet.

    a. How much fabric is needed to make the sail?

    b. **RESEARCH** Use the Internet or some other source to find how the area of the sail is related to the weight limit of the pilot.

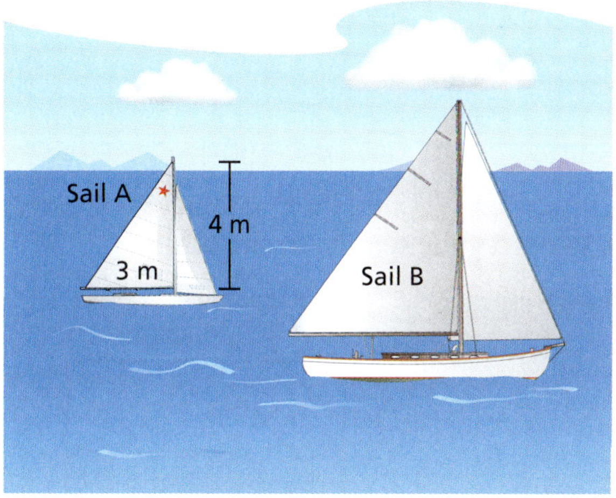

17. **SAILBOATS** The base and the height of Sail B are x times greater than the base and the height of Sail A. How many times greater is the area of Sail B? Write your answer as a power.

18. **WRITING** You know the height and the perimeter of an equilateral triangle. Explain how to find the area of the triangle. Draw a diagram to support your reasoning.

19. **REASONING** The base and the height of Triangle A are half the base and the height of Triangle B. How many times greater is the area of Triangle B?

20. **Critical Thinking** The total area of the polygon is 176 square feet. Find the value of x.

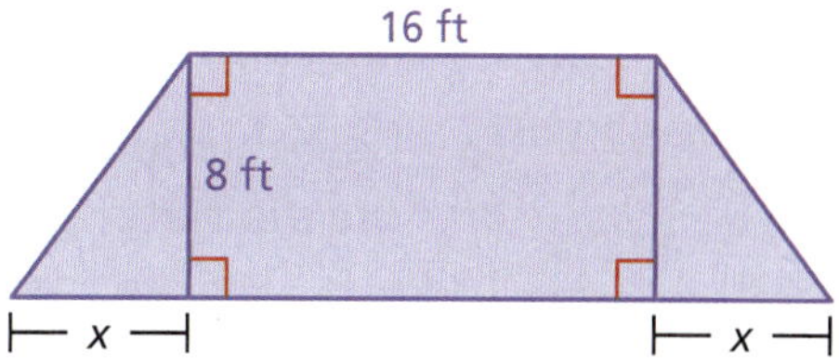

Fair Game Review What you learned in previous grades & lessons

Tell which property is illustrated by the statement.

21. $n \cdot 1 = n$

22. $4 \cdot m = m \cdot 4$

23. $(x + 2) + 5 = x + (2 + 5)$

24. **MULTIPLE CHOICE** What is the first step when using order of operations?

    (A) Multiply or divide from left to right.

    (B) Add or subtract from left to right.

    (C) Perform operations in parentheses.

    (D) Evaluate numbers with exponents.

8.5 Circles and Circumference

Essential Question How can you find the circumference of a circle?

Archimedes was a Greek mathematician, physicist, engineer, and astronomer.

Archimedes discovered that in any circle the ratio of circumference to diameter is always the same. Archimedes called this ratio pi, or π (a letter from the Greek alphabet).

$$\pi = \frac{\text{circumference}}{\text{diameter}}$$

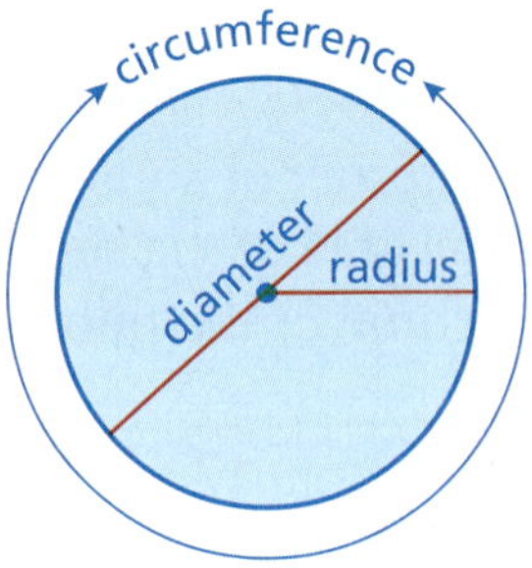

In Activities 1 and 2, you will use the same strategy Archimedes used to approximate π.

1 ACTIVITY: Approximating Pi

Work with a partner. Copy the table. Record your results in the table.

- **Measure the perimeter of the large square in millimeters.**
- **Measure the diameter of the circle in millimeters.**
- **Measure the perimeter of the small square in millimeters.**
- **Calculate the ratios of the two perimeters to the diameter.**
- **The average of these two ratios is an approximation of π.**

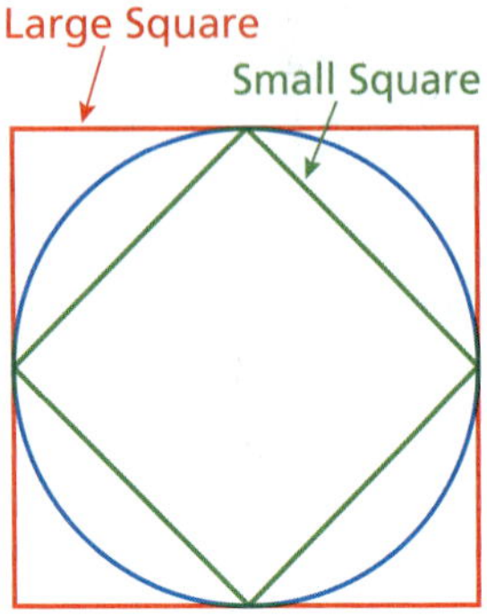

Sides	Large Perimeter	Diameter of Circle	Small Perimeter	$\frac{\text{Large Perimeter}}{\text{Diameter}}$	$\frac{\text{Small Perimeter}}{\text{Diameter}}$	Average of Ratios
4						
6						
8						
10						

Geometry

In this lesson, you will
- describe a circle in terms of radius and diameter.
- understand the concept of pi.
- find circumferences of circles and perimeters of semicircles.

2 ACTIVITY: Approximating Pi

Math Process

Make Conjectures

How can you use the results of the activity to find an approximation of pi?

Continue your approximation of pi. Complete the table from Activity 1 using a hexagon (6 sides), an octagon (8 sides), and a decagon (10 sides).

a.

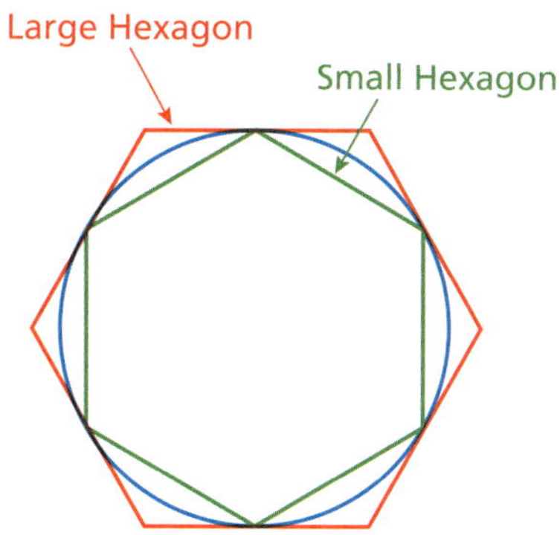

b.

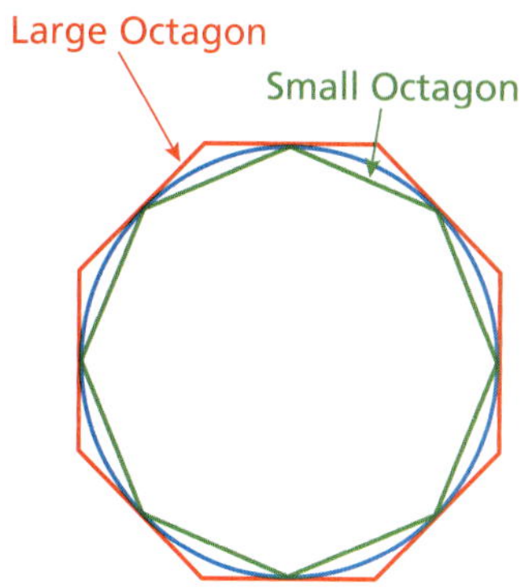

c.

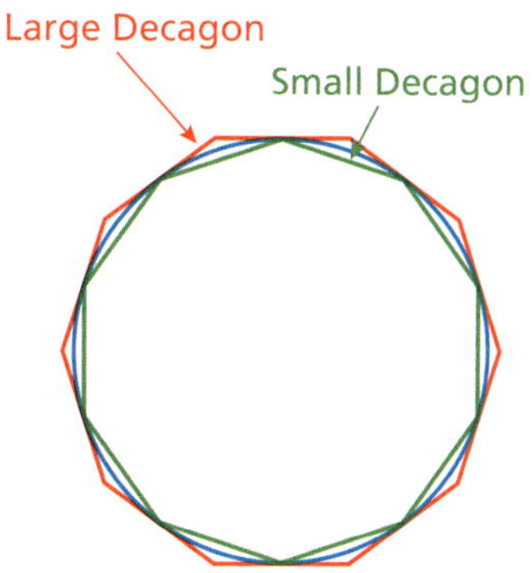

d. From the table, what can you conclude about the value of π? Explain your reasoning.

e. Archimedes calculated the value of π using polygons with 96 sides. Do you think his calculations were more or less accurate than yours?

What Is Your Answer?

3. **IN YOUR OWN WORDS** Now that you know an approximation for pi, explain how you can use it to find the circumference of a circle. Write a formula for the circumference C of a circle whose diameter is d.

4. **CONSTRUCTION** Use a compass to draw three circles. Use your formula from Question 3 to find the circumference of each circle.

Practice Use what you learned about circles and circumference to complete Exercises 9–11 on page 305.

8.5 Lesson

Check It Out
Lesson Tutorials
BigIdeasMath.com

Key Vocabulary
circle, *p. 302*
center, *p. 302*
radius, *p. 302*
diameter, *p. 302*
circumference, *p. 303*
pi, *p. 303*
semicircle, *p. 304*

A **circle** is the set of all points in a plane that are the same distance from a point called the **center**.

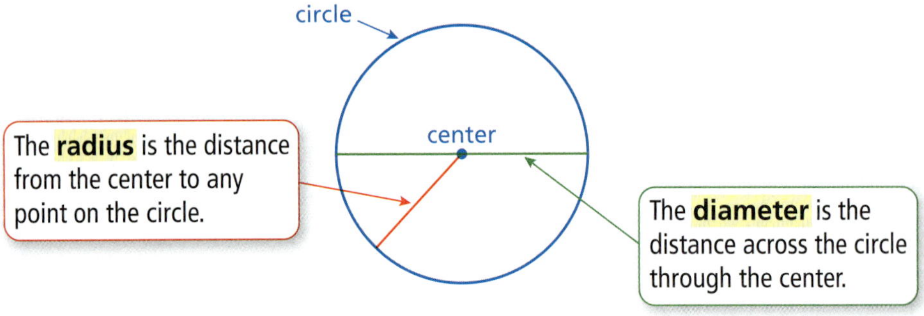

Key Idea

Radius and Diameter

Words The diameter d of a circle is twice the radius r. The radius r of a circle is one-half the diameter d.

Algebra **Diameter:** $d = 2r$ **Radius:** $r = \frac{d}{2}$

EXAMPLE 1 Finding a Radius and a Diameter

a. The diameter of a circle is 20 feet. Find the radius.

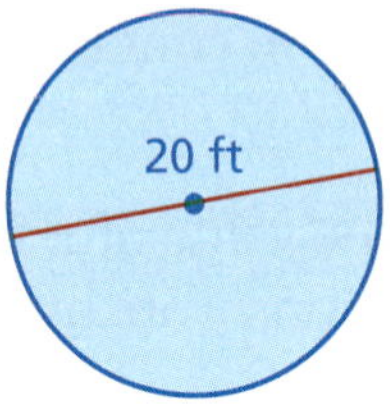

$r = \frac{d}{2}$ Radius of a circle

$= \frac{20}{2}$ Substitute 20 for d.

$= 10$ Divide.

∴ The radius is 10 feet.

b. The radius of a circle is 7 meters. Find the diameter.

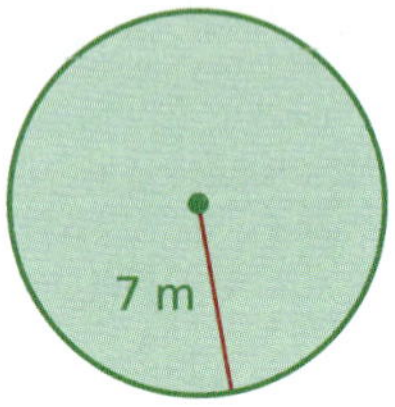

$d = 2r$ Diameter of a circle

$= 2(7)$ Substitute 7 for r.

$= 14$ Multiply.

∴ The diameter is 14 meters.

On Your Own

Now You're Ready
Exercises 3–8

1. The diameter of a circle is 16 centimeters. Find the radius.
2. The radius of a circle is 9 yards. Find the diameter.

Multi-Language Glossary at BigIdeasMath.com

The distance around a circle is called the **circumference**. The ratio $\frac{\text{circumference}}{\text{diameter}}$ is the same for *every* circle and is represented by the Greek letter π, called **pi**. The value of π can be approximated as 3.14 or $\frac{22}{7}$.

Study Tip

When the radius or diameter is a multiple of 7, it is easier to use $\frac{22}{7}$ as the estimate of π.

Key Idea

Circumference of a Circle

Words The circumference C of a circle is equal to π times the diameter d or π times twice the radius r.

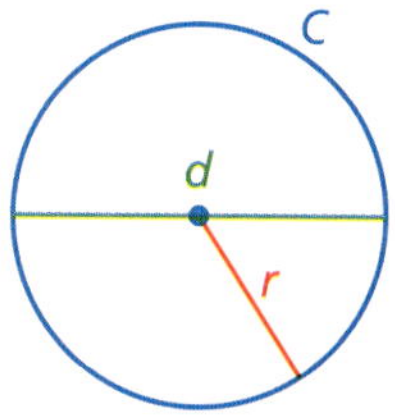

Algebra $C = \pi d$ or $C = 2\pi r$

EXAMPLE 2 Finding Circumferences of Circles

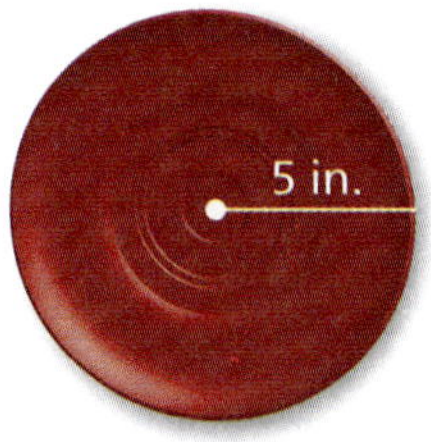

a. Find the circumference of the flying disc. Use 3.14 for π.

$C = 2\pi r$	Write formula for circumference.
$\approx 2 \cdot 3.14 \cdot 5$	Substitute 3.14 for π and 5 for r.
$= 31.4$	Multiply.

The circumference is about 31.4 inches.

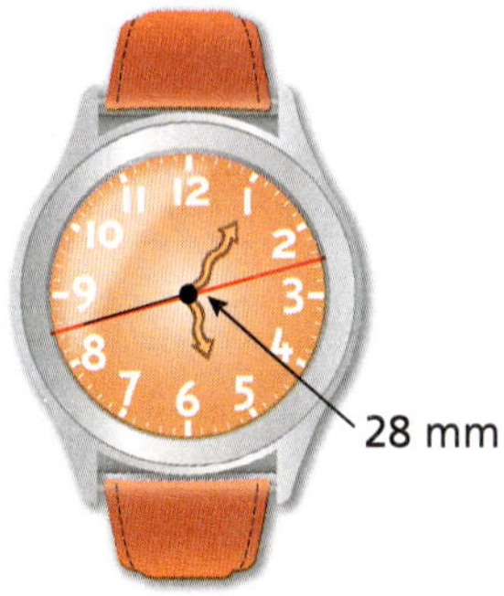

b. Find the circumference of the watch face. Use $\frac{22}{7}$ for π.

$C = \pi d$	Write formula for circumference.
$\approx \frac{22}{7} \cdot 28$	Substitute $\frac{22}{7}$ for π and 28 for d.
$= 88$	Multiply.

The circumference is about 88 millimeters.

On Your Own

Now You're Ready
Exercises 9–11

Find the circumference of the object. Use 3.14 or $\frac{22}{7}$ for π.

3.

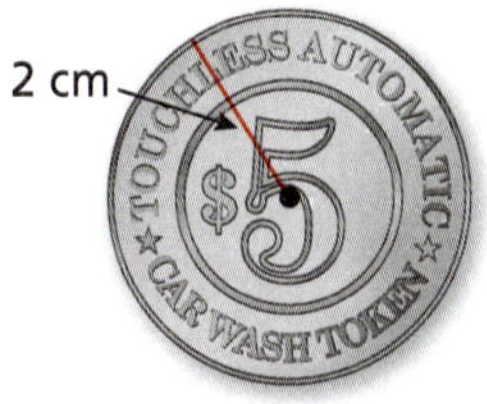

4.

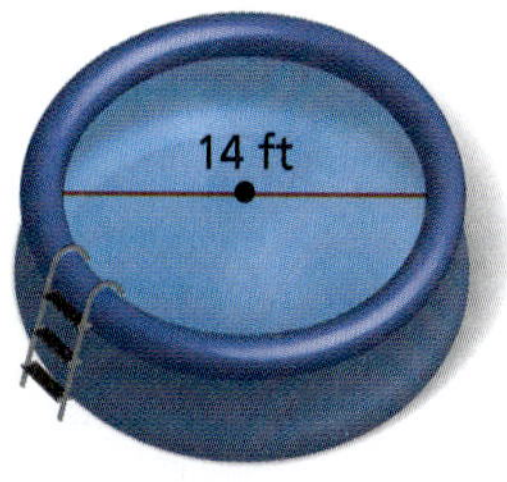

5.

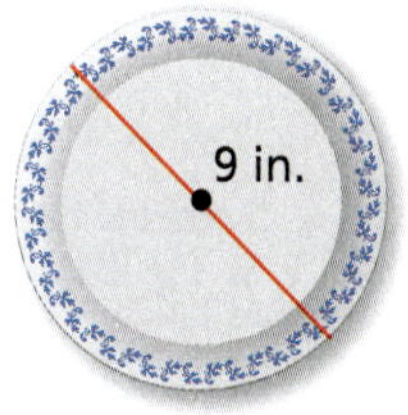

EXAMPLE 3 Estimating a Diameter

$C = 31.4$ in.

The circumference of the roll of caution tape decreases 10.5 inches after a construction worker uses some of the tape. Which is the best estimate of the diameter of the roll after the decrease?

Ⓐ 5 inches   Ⓑ 7 inches   Ⓒ 10 inches   Ⓓ 12 inches

After the decrease, the circumference of the roll is $31.4 - 10.5 = 20.9$ inches.

$C = \pi d$	Write formula for circumference.
$20.9 \approx 3.14 \cdot d$	Substitute 20.9 for C and 3.14 for π.
$21 \approx 3d$	Round 20.9 up to 21. Round 3.14 down to 3.
$7 = d$	Divide each side by 3.

∴ The correct answer is Ⓑ.

On Your Own

6. **WHAT IF?** The circumference of the roll of tape decreases 5.25 inches. Estimate the diameter of the roll after the decrease.

EXAMPLE 4 Finding the Perimeter of a Semicircular Region

A semicircle is one-half of a circle. Find the perimeter of the semicircular region.

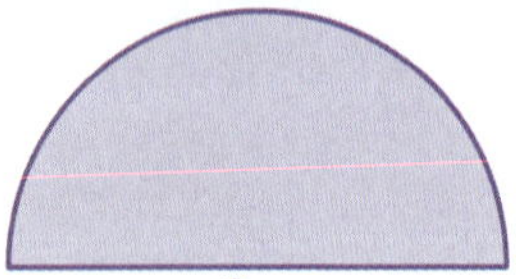

The straight side is 6 meters long. The distance around the curved part is one-half the circumference of a circle with a diameter of 6 meters.

$\frac{C}{2} = \frac{\pi d}{2}$	Divide the circumference by 2.
$\approx \frac{3.14 \cdot 6}{2}$	Substitute 3.14 for π and 6 for d.
$= 9.42$	Simplify.

∴ So, the perimeter is about $6 + 9.42 = 15.42$ meters.

On Your Own

Now You're Ready
Exercises 15 and 16

Find the perimeter of the semicircular region.

7.
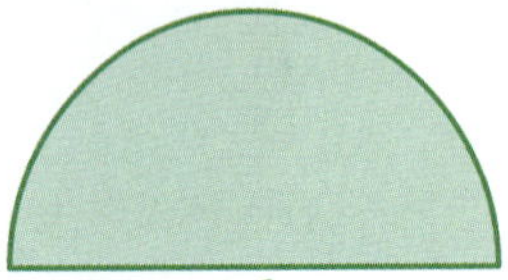

8.
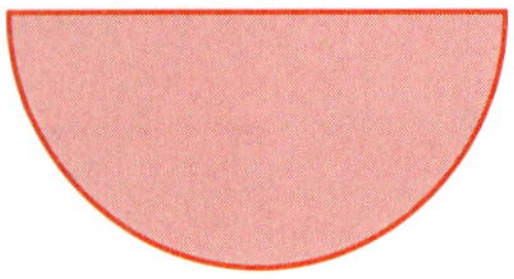

9.
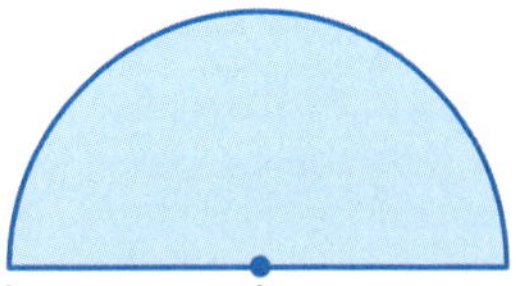

8.5 Exercises

Check It Out
Help with Homework
BigIdeasMath.com

Vocabulary and Concept Check

1. **VOCABULARY** What is the relationship between the radius and the diameter of a circle?

2. **WHICH ONE DOESN'T BELONG?** Which phrase does *not* belong with the other three? Explain your reasoning.

the distance around a circle	π times twice the radius
π times the diameter	the distance from the center to any point on the circle

Practice and Problem Solving

Find the radius of the button.

3. 

4. 

5. 

Find the diameter of the object.

6. 

7. 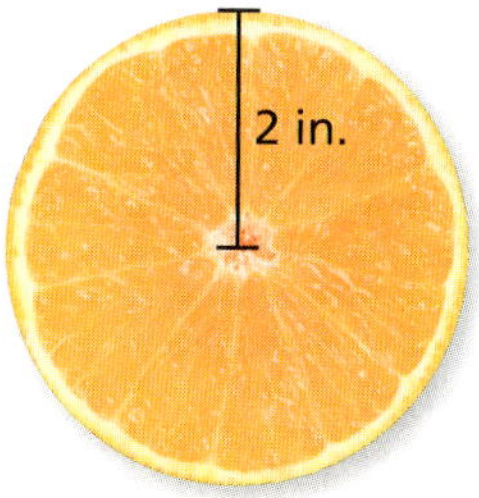

8. 

Find the circumference of the pizza. Use 3.14 or $\frac{22}{7}$ for π.

9. 

10. 

11. 

12. **CHOOSE TOOLS** Choose a real-life circular object. Explain why you might need to know its circumference. Then find the circumference.

13. **SINKHOLE** A circular sinkhole has a circumference of 75.36 meters. A week later, it has a circumference of 150.42 meters.

a. Estimate the diameter of the sinkhole each week.

b. How many times greater is the diameter of the sinkhole now compared to the previous week?

STEM VIDEO

14. **REASONING** Consider the circles A, B, C, and D.

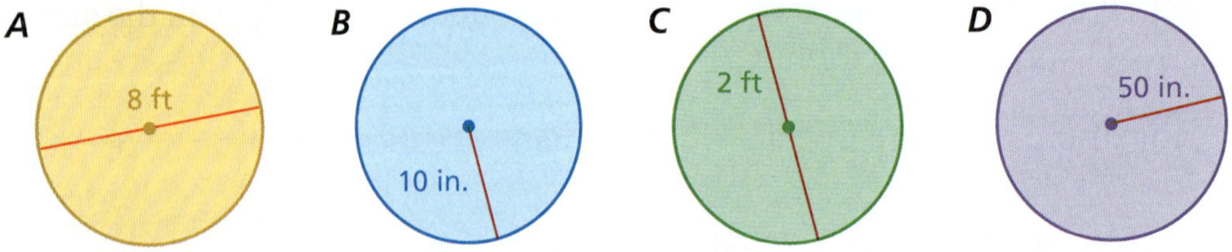

a. Without calculating, which circle has the greatest circumference?

b. Without calculating, which circle has the least circumference?

Find the perimeter of the window.

4 15.

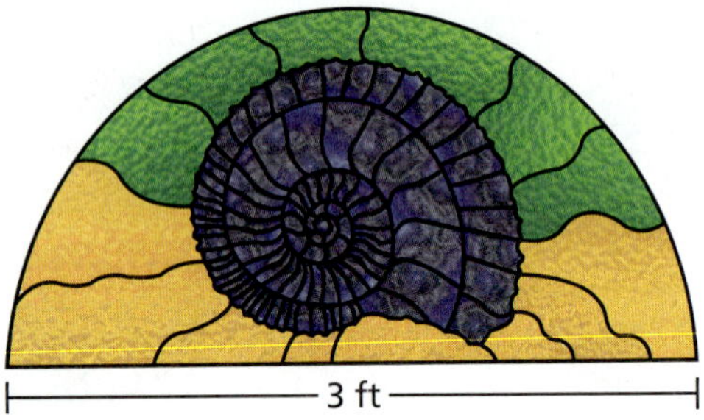

16.

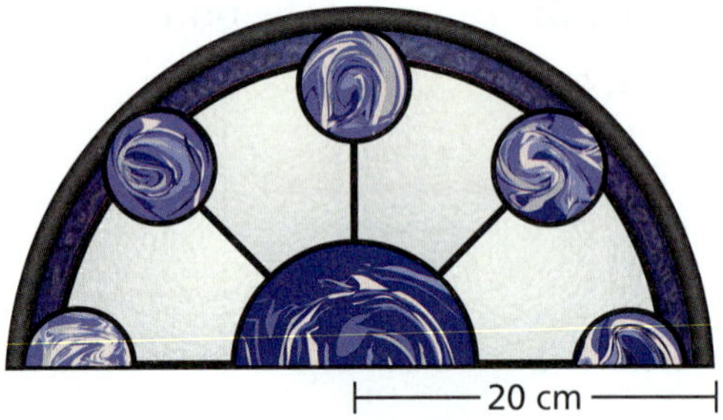

Find the circumferences of both circles.

17.

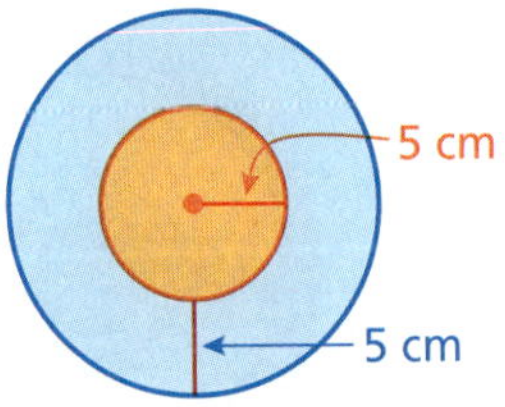

18.

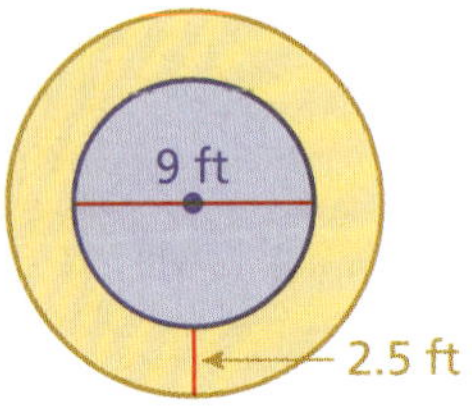

19.

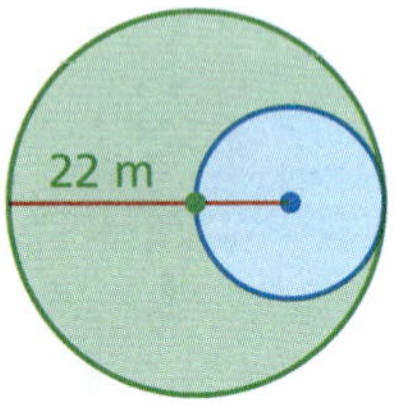

20. **STRUCTURE** Because the ratio $\frac{\text{circumference}}{\text{diameter}}$ is the same for every circle, is the ratio $\frac{\text{circumference}}{\text{radius}}$ the same for every circle? Explain.

21. **WIRE** A wire is bent to form four semicircles. How long is the wire?

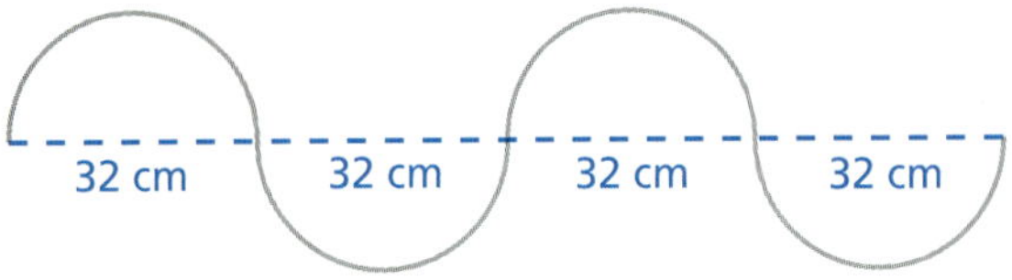

22. **CRITICAL THINKING** Explain how to draw a circle with a circumference of π^2 inches. Then draw the circle.

23. AROUND THE WORLD "Lines" of latitude on Earth are actually circles. The Tropic of Cancer is the northernmost line of latitude at which the Sun appears directly overhead at noon. The Tropic of Cancer has a radius of 5854 kilometers.

To qualify for an around-the-world speed record, a pilot must cover a distance no less than the circumference of the Tropic of Cancer, cross all meridians, and land on the same airfield where he started.

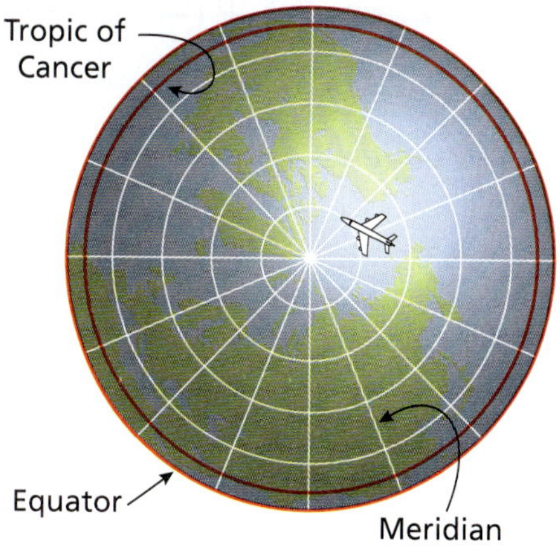

a. What is the minimum distance that a pilot must fly to qualify for an around-the-world speed record?

b. RESEARCH Estimate the time it would take for a pilot to qualify for the speed record.

24. PROBLEM SOLVING Bicycles in the late 1800s looked very different than they do today.

a. How many rotations does each tire make after traveling 600 feet? Round your answers to the nearest whole number.

b. Would you rather ride a bicycle made with two large wheels or two small wheels? Explain.

25. **Logic** The length of the minute hand is 150% of the length of the hour hand.

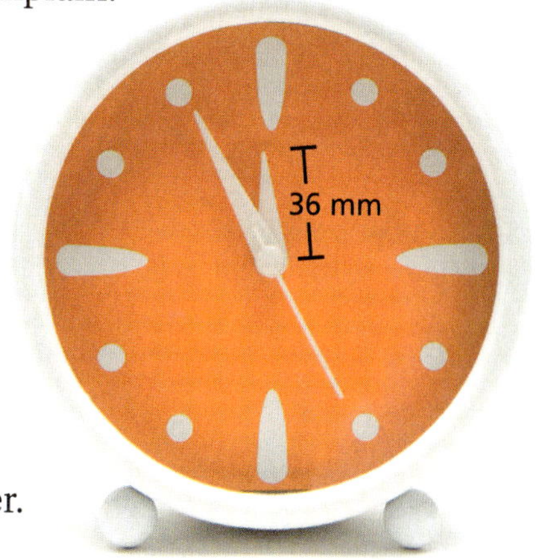

a. What distance will the tip of the minute hand move in 45 minutes? Explain how you found your answer.

b. In 1 hour, how much farther does the tip of the minute hand move than the tip of the hour hand? Explain how you found your answer.

Fair Game Review What you learned in previous grades & lessons

Find the perimeter of the polygon.

26.

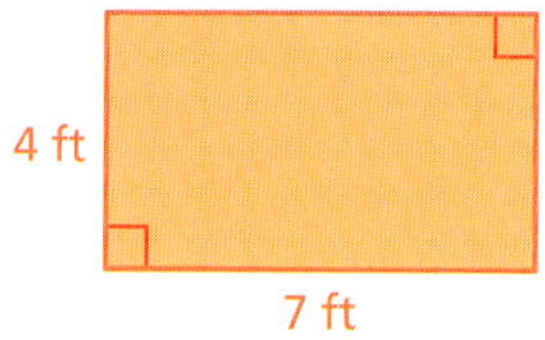

27.

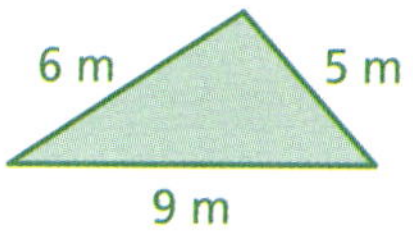

28.

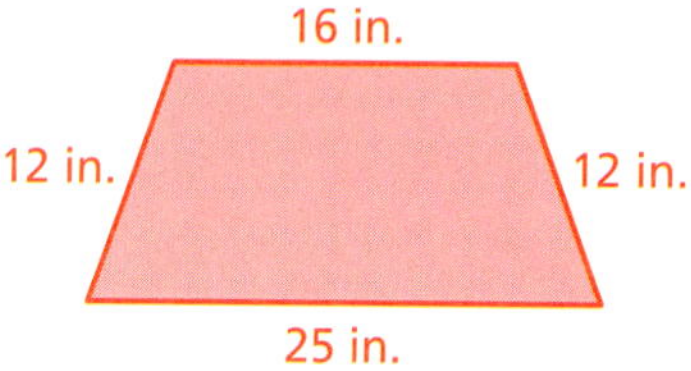

29. MULTIPLE CHOICE What is the median of the data set?

12, 25, 16, 9, 5, 22, 27, 20

Ⓐ 7 Ⓑ 16 Ⓒ 17 Ⓓ 18

8.6 Areas of Circles

Essential Question How can you find the area of a circle?

1 ACTIVITY: Estimating the Area of a Circle

Work with a partner. Each square in the grid is 1 unit by 1 unit.

a. Find the area of the large 10-by-10 square.

b. Copy and complete the table.

Region			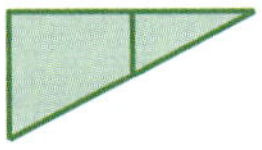
Area (square units)			

c. Use your results to estimate the area of the circle. Explain your reasoning.

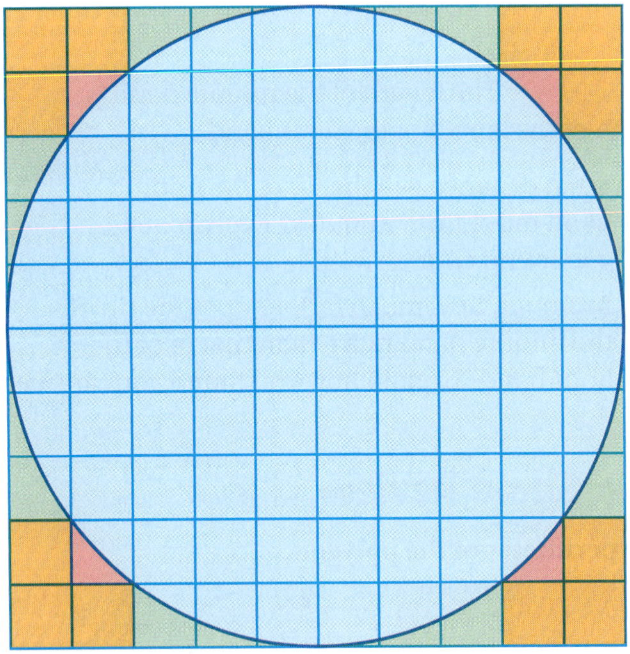

Geometry
In this lesson, you will
- find areas of circles and semicircles.

d. Fill in the blanks. Explain your reasoning.

Area of large square = ____ • 5^2 square units

Area of circle ≈ ____ • 5^2 square units

e. What dimension of the circle does 5 represent? What can you conclude?

2 ACTIVITY: Approximating the Area of a Circle

Work with a partner.

a. Draw a circle. Label the radius as r.

b. Divide the circle into 24 equal sections.

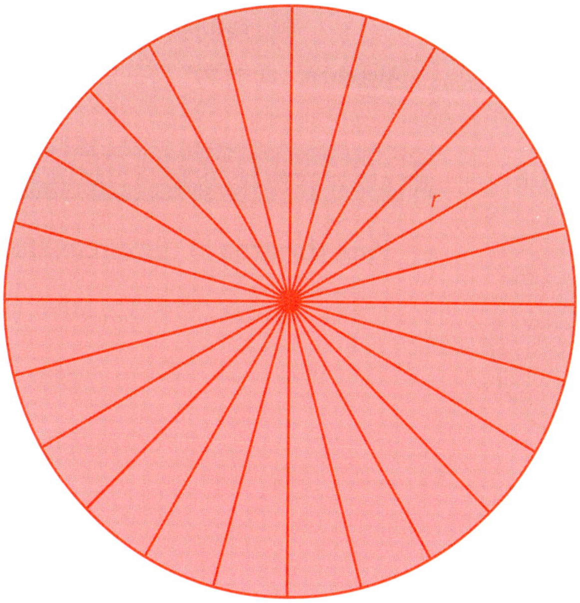

c. Cut the sections apart. Then arrange them to approximate a parallelogram.

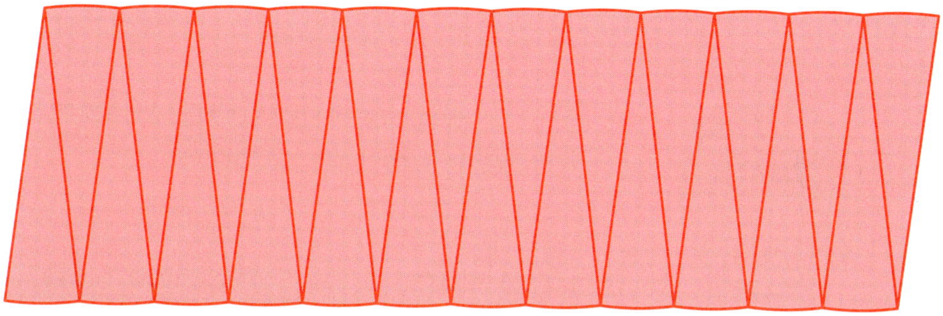

Math Process

Interpret a Solution

What does the area of the parallelogram represent? Explain.

d. What is the approximate height and base of the parallelogram?

e. Find the area of the parallelogram. What can you conclude?

What Is Your Answer?

3. **IN YOUR OWN WORDS** How can you find the area of a circle?

4. Write a formula for the area of a circle with radius r. Find an object that is circular. Use your formula to find the area.

Practice Use what you learned about areas of circles to complete Exercises 3–5 on page 312.

Check It Out
Lesson Tutorials
BigIdeasMath.com

Key Idea

Area of a Circle

Words The area A of a circle is the product of π and the square of the radius.

Algebra $A = \pi r^2$

EXAMPLE 1 Finding Areas of Circles

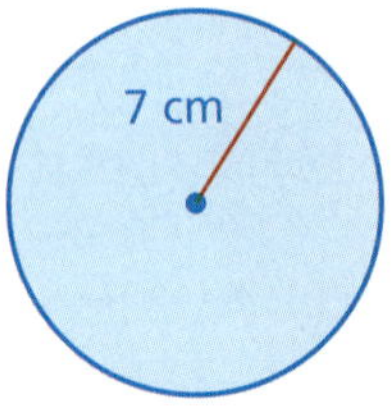

a. Find the area of the circle. Use $\frac{22}{7}$ for π.

Estimate $3 \times 7^2 \approx 3 \times 50 = 150$

$A = \pi r^2$	Write formula for area.
$\approx \frac{22}{7} \cdot 7^2$	Substitute $\frac{22}{7}$ for π and 7 for r.
$= \frac{22}{\cancel{7}_1} \cdot \cancel{49}^{7}$	Evaluate 7^2. Divide out the common factor.
$= 154$	Multiply.

The area is about 154 square centimeters.

Reasonable? $154 \approx 150$ ✓

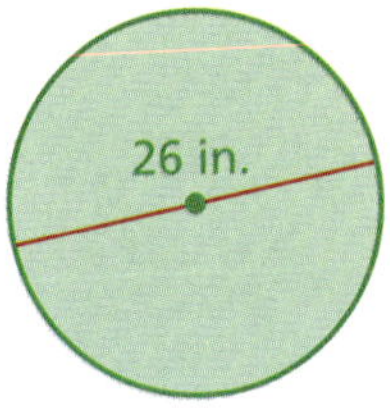

b. Find the area of the circle. Use 3.14 for π.

The radius is $26 \div 2 = 13$ inches.

Estimate $3 \times 13^2 \approx 3 \times 170 = 510$

$A = \pi r^2$	Write formula for area.
$\approx 3.14 \cdot 13^2$	Substitute 3.14 for π and 13 for r.
$= 3.14 \cdot 169$	Evaluate 13^2.
$= 530.66$	Multiply.

The area is about 530.66 square inches.

Reasonable? $530.66 \approx 510$ ✓

On Your Own

Now You're Ready
Exercises 3–10

1. Find the area of a circle with a radius of 6 feet. Use 3.14 for π.
2. Find the area of a circle with a diameter of 28 meters. Use $\frac{22}{7}$ for π.

EXAMPLE 2 Describing a Distance

You want to find the distance the monster truck travels when the tires make one 360-degree rotation. Which best describes this distance?

Ⓐ the radius of the tire Ⓑ the diameter of the tire
Ⓒ the circumference of the tire Ⓓ the area of the tire

The distance the truck travels after one rotation is the same as the distance *around* the tire. So, the circumference of the tire best describes the distance in one rotation.

∴ The correct answer is Ⓒ.

On Your Own

3. You want to find the height of one of the tires. Which measurement would best describe the height?

EXAMPLE 3 Finding the Area of a Semicircle

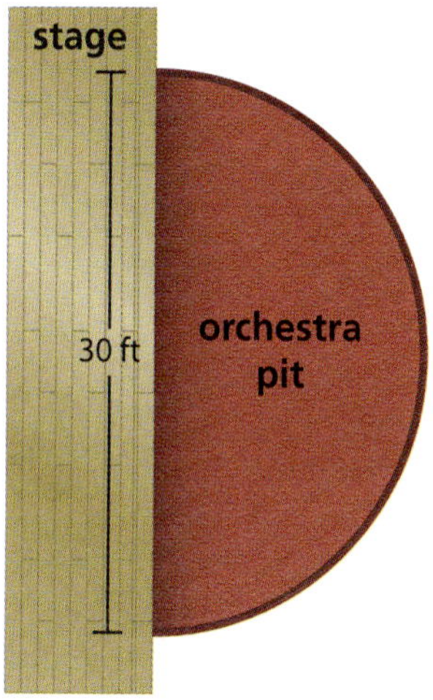

Find the area of the semicircular orchestra pit.

The area of the orchestra pit is one-half the area of a circle with a diameter of 30 feet.

The radius of the circle is 30 ÷ 2 = 15 feet.

$$\frac{A}{2} = \frac{\pi r^2}{2}$$ Divide the area by 2.

$$\approx \frac{3.14 \cdot 15^2}{2}$$ Substitute 3.14 for π and 15 for r.

$$= \frac{3.14 \cdot 225}{2}$$ Evaluate 15^2.

$$= 353.25$$ Simplify.

∴ So, the area of the orchestra pit is about 353.25 square feet.

On Your Own

Now You're Ready
Exercises 13–15

Find the area of the semicircle.

4.

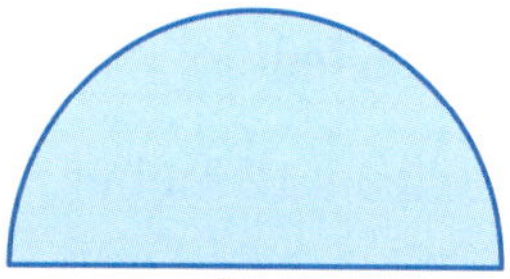

5.

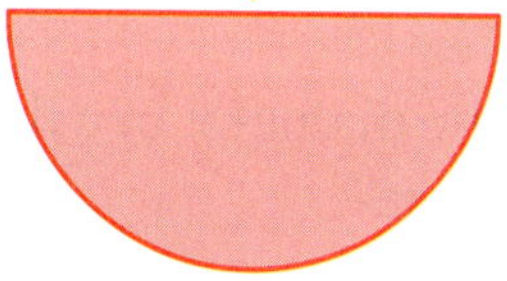

6.

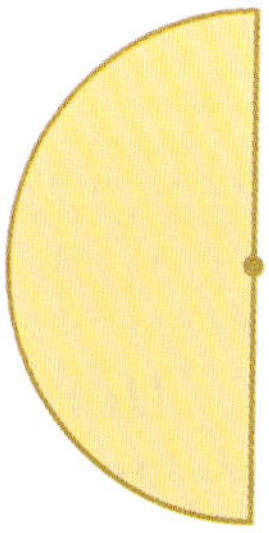

8.6 Exercises

Check It Out
Help with Homework
BigIdeasMath.com

Vocabulary and Concept Check

1. **VOCABULARY** Explain how to find the area of a circle given its diameter.

2. **DIFFERENT WORDS, SAME QUESTION** Which is different? Find "both" answers.

What is the area of a circle with a diameter of 1 m?	What is the area of a circle with a diameter of 100 cm?
What is the area of a circle with a radius of 100 cm?	What is the area of a circle with a radius of 500 mm?

Practice and Problem Solving

Find the area of the circle. Use 3.14 or $\frac{22}{7}$ for π.

1 3.
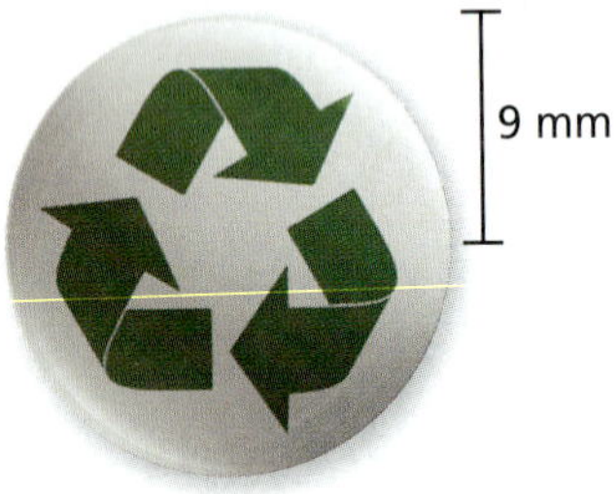

4.

5.

6.
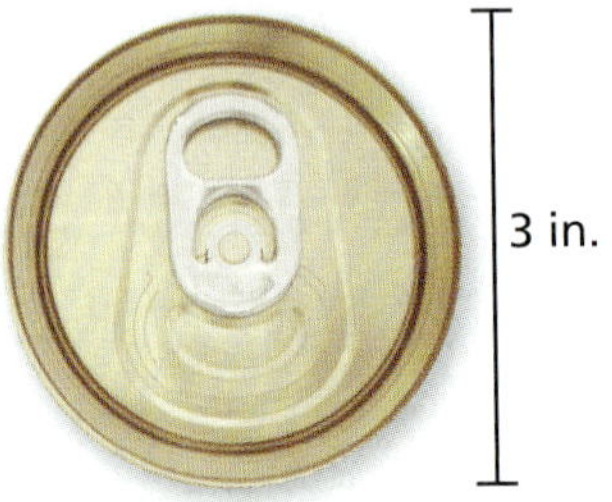

7.
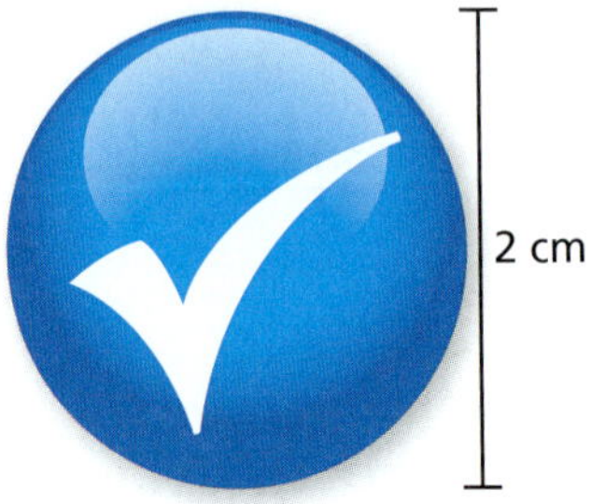

8.

9. Find the area of a circle with a diameter of 56 millimeters.

10. Find the area of a circle with a radius of 5 feet.

11. **TORTILLA** The diameter of a flour tortilla is 12 inches. What is the area?

12. **LIGHTHOUSE** The Hillsboro Inlet Lighthouse lights up how much more area than the Jupiter Inlet Lighthouse?

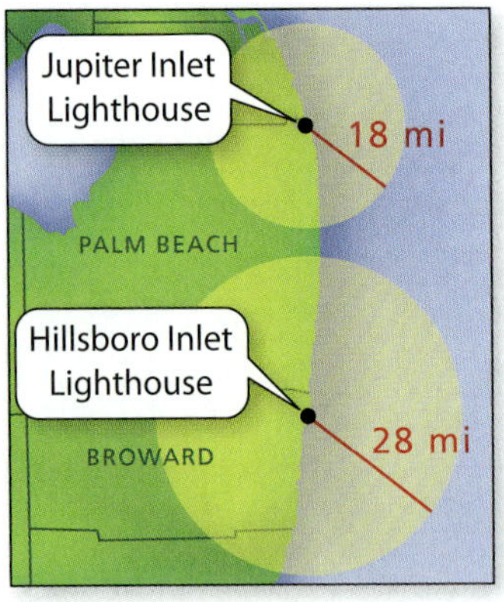

Find the area of the semicircle.

3 **13.**

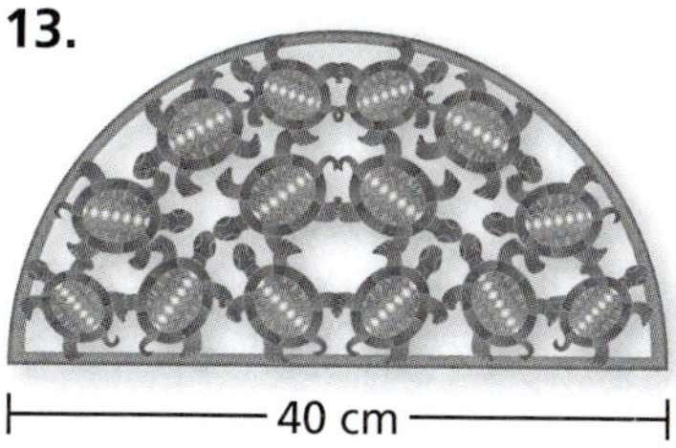

14.

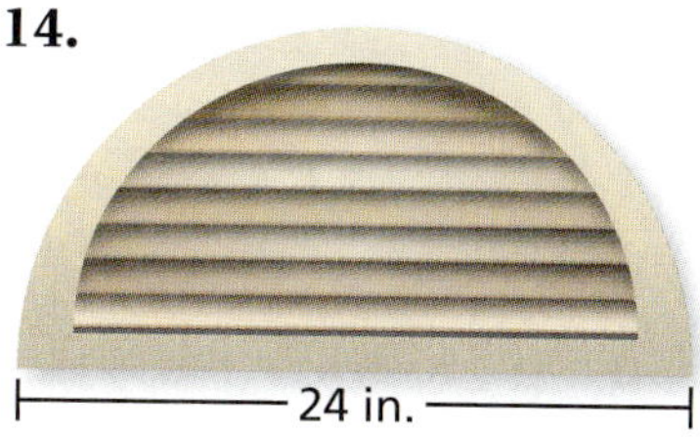

15.

16. **REPEATED REASONING** Consider five circles with radii of 1, 2, 4, 8, and 16 inches.

a. Copy and complete the table. Write your answers in terms of π.

b. Compare the areas and circumferences. What happens to the circumference of a circle when you double the radius? What happens to the area?

c. What happens when you triple the radius?

Radius	Circumference	Area
1	2π in.	π in.^{2}
2		
4		
8		
16		

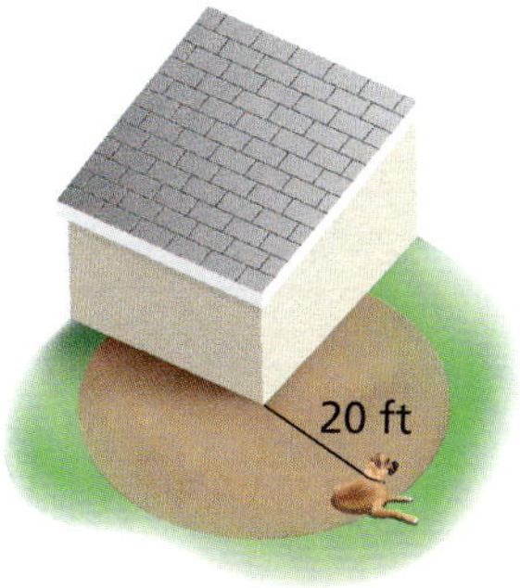

17. **DOG** A dog is leashed to the corner of a house. How much running area does the dog have? Explain how you found your answer.

18. **CRITICAL THINKING** Is the area of a semicircle with a diameter of x *greater than*, *less than*, or *equal to* the area of a circle with a diameter of $\frac{1}{2}x$? Explain.

Reasoning **Find the area of the shaded region. Explain how you found your answer.**

19.

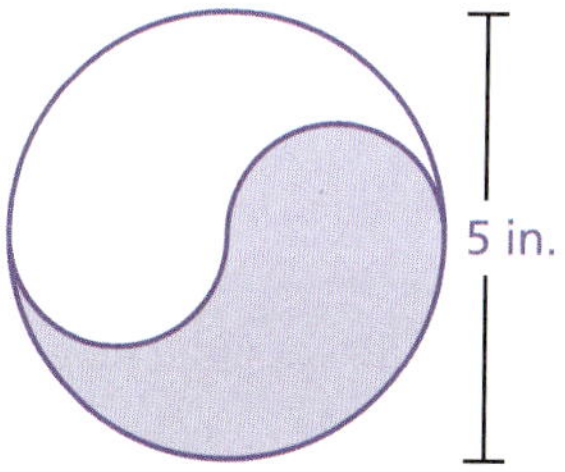

20.

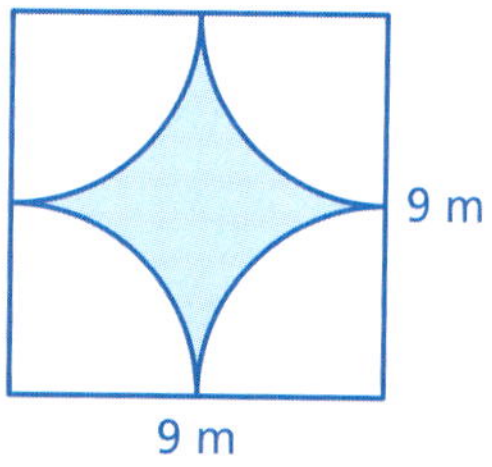

21.

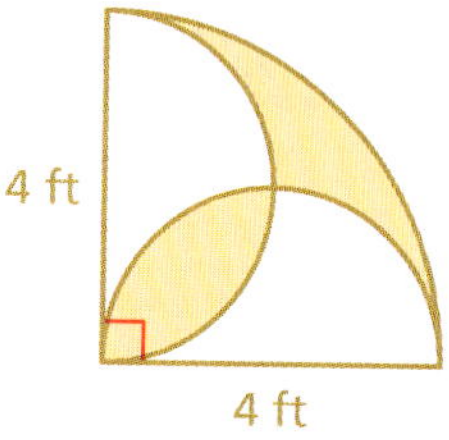

Fair Game Review What you learned in previous grades & lessons

Evaluate the expression.

22. $\frac{1}{2}(7)(4) + 6(5)$

23. $\frac{1}{2} \cdot 8^2 + 3(7)$

24. $12(6) + \frac{1}{4} \cdot 2^2$

25. **MULTIPLE CHOICE** What is the product of $8\frac{1}{3}$ and $3\frac{2}{5}$?

Ⓐ $4\frac{14}{15}$ Ⓑ $11\frac{11}{15}$ Ⓒ $24\frac{2}{15}$ Ⓓ $28\frac{1}{3}$

8 Study Help

Check It Out
Graphic Organizer
BigIdeasMath.com

You can use a **word magnet** to organize formulas or phrases that are associated with a vocabulary word or term. Here is an example of a word magnet for circle.

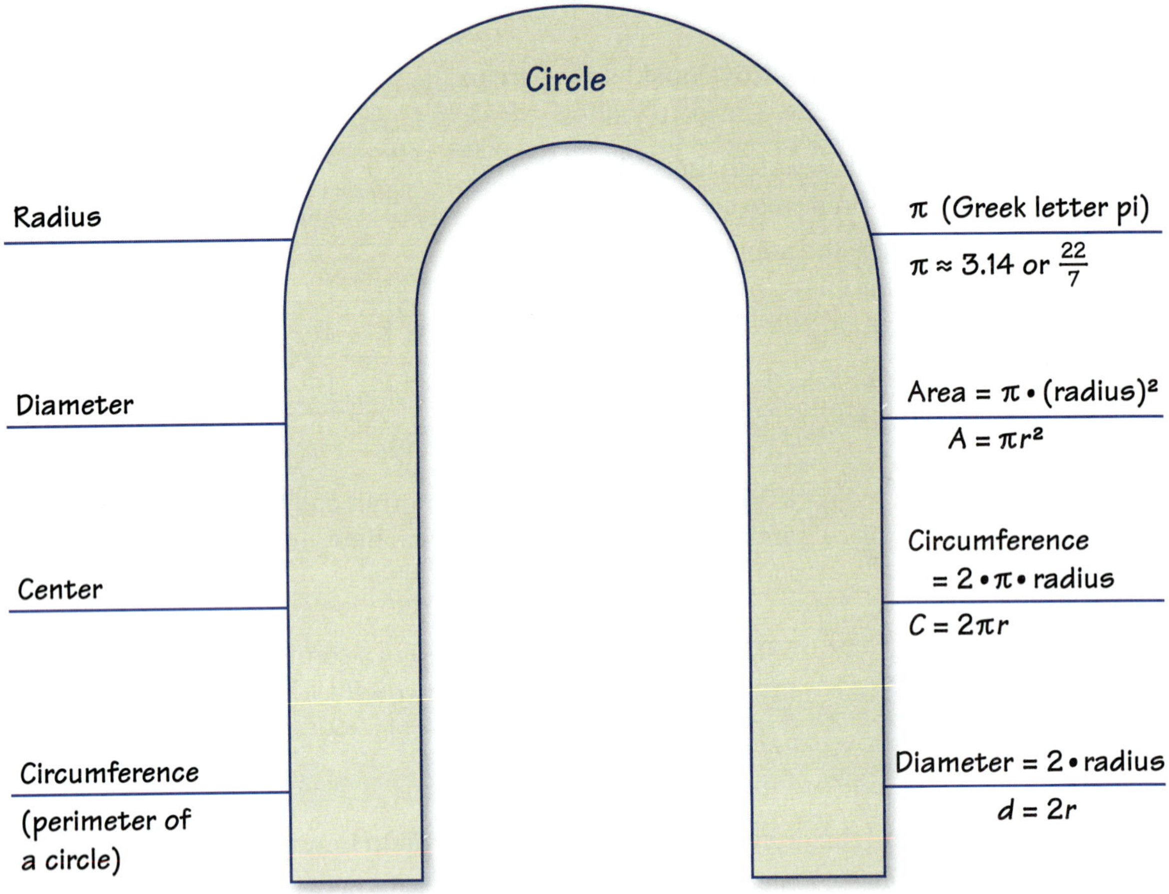

On Your Own

Make word magnets to help you study these topics.

1. regular polygon
2. symmetry
3. perimeter
4. area of a triangle
5. area of a circle

"I'm trying to make a word magnet for happiness, but I can only think of two words."

8 Chapter Review

Check It Out
Vocabulary Help
BigIdeasMath.com

Review Key Vocabulary

regular polygon, *p. 278*
congruent, *p. 278*
line of symmetry, *p. 279*
congruent figures, *p. 284*
corresponding angles, *p. 284*
corresponding sides, *p. 284*
circle, *p. 302*
center, *p. 302*
radius, *p. 302*
diameter, *p. 302*
circumference, *p. 303*
pi, *p. 303*
semicircle, *p. 304*

Review Examples and Exercises

8.1 Regular Polygons and Symmetry *(pp. 276–281)*

Determine whether the hexagon is a regular polygon. Then draw all the lines of symmetry on the hexagon.

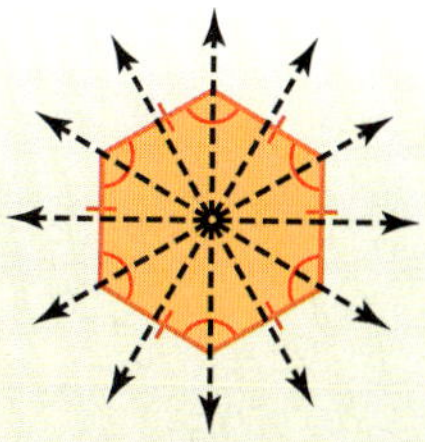

All 6 sides are congruent and all 6 angles are congruent. So, the hexagon is a regular polygon.

A regular hexagon has 6 sides, so it has 6 lines of symmetry.

∴ The polygon is a regular hexagon with 6 lines of symmetry.

Exercises

1. Draw all the lines of symmetry on the polygon.

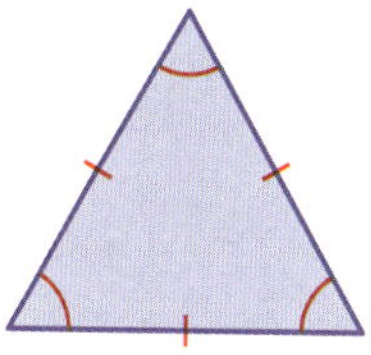

8.2 Congruent Figures *(pp. 282–287)*

Trapezoids *EFGH* and *QRST* are congruent.

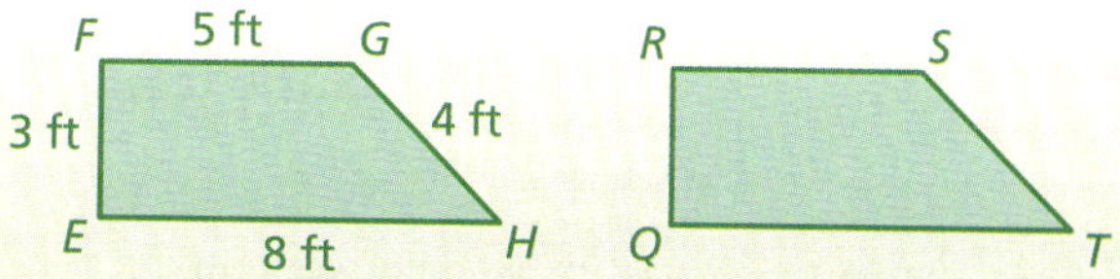

a. What is the length of side *QT*?

Side *QT* corresponds to side *EH*.

∴ So, the length of side *QT* is 8 feet.

b. Which angle of *QRST* corresponds to $\angle H$?

∴ $\angle T$ corresponds to $\angle H$.

Exercises

The figures are congruent. Name the corresponding angles and the corresponding sides.

2.

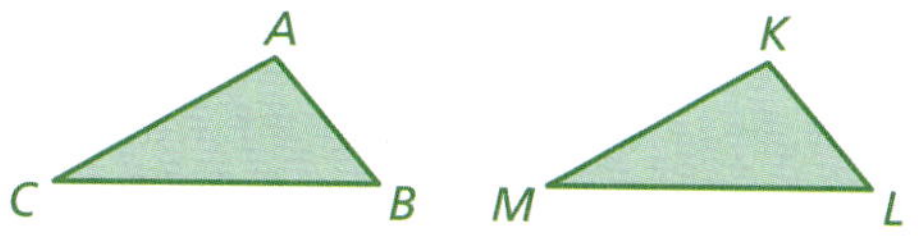

3.

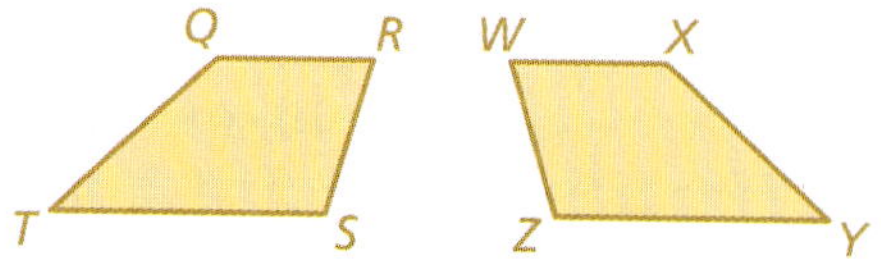

8.3 Perimeters of Rectangles and Triangles *(pp. 288–293)*

Find the perimeter of the triangle or rectangle.

a.

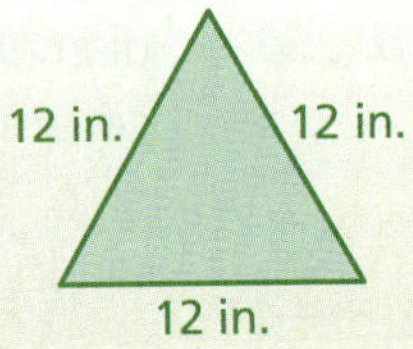

P = sum of side lengths

$= 12 + 12 + 12$

$= 36$

The perimeter of the triangle is 36 inches.

b.

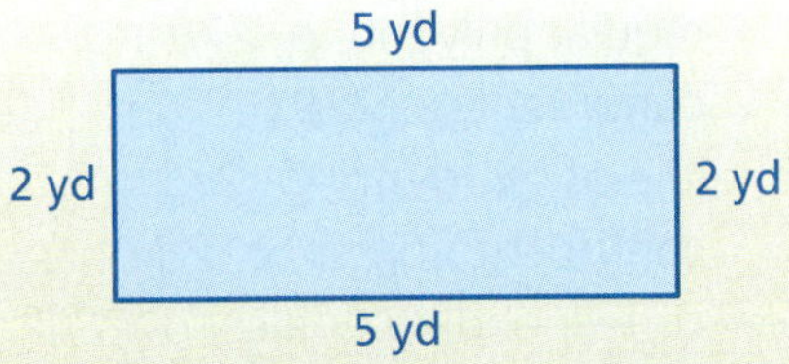

P = sum of side lengths

$= 2 + 5 + 2 + 5$

$= 14$

The perimeter of the rectangle is 14 yards.

Exercises

Find the perimeter of the triangle or rectangle.

4.

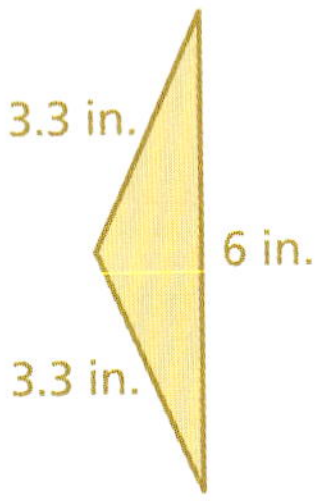

5.

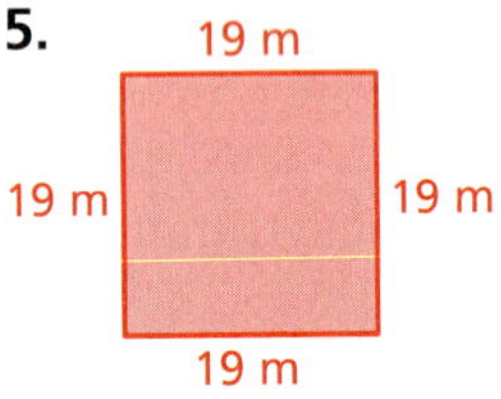

6.

8.4 Areas of Rectangles and Triangles *(pp. 294–299)*

Find the area of the triangle or rectangle.

a.

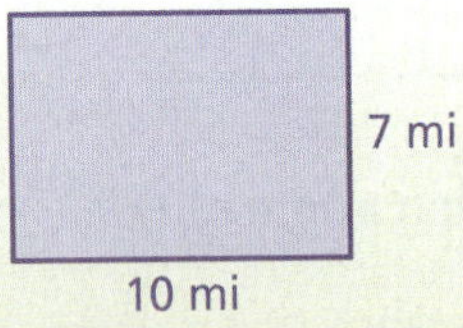

$A = \ell w$ Write formula.

$= (10)(7)$ Substitute.

$= 70$ Multiply.

The area of the rectangle is 70 square miles.

b.

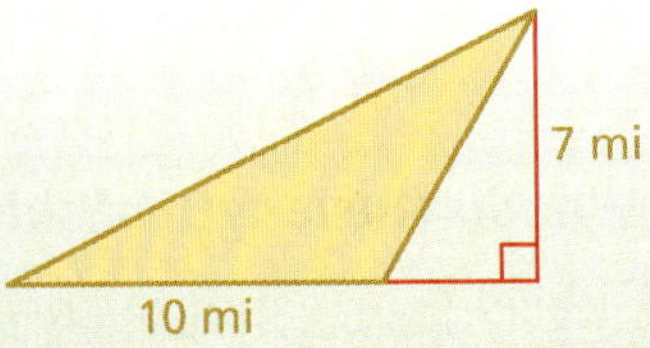

$A = \frac{1}{2}bh$

$= \frac{1}{2}(10)(7)$

$= 35$

The area of the triangle is 35 square miles.

Exercises

Find the area of the triangle or rectangle.

7.

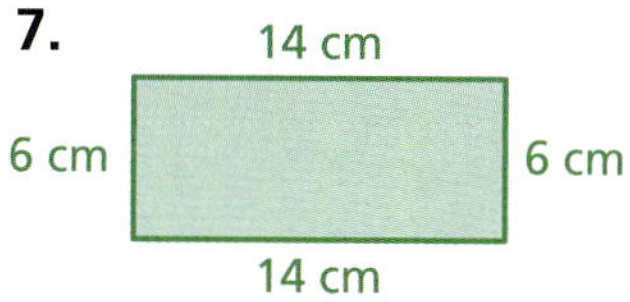

8.

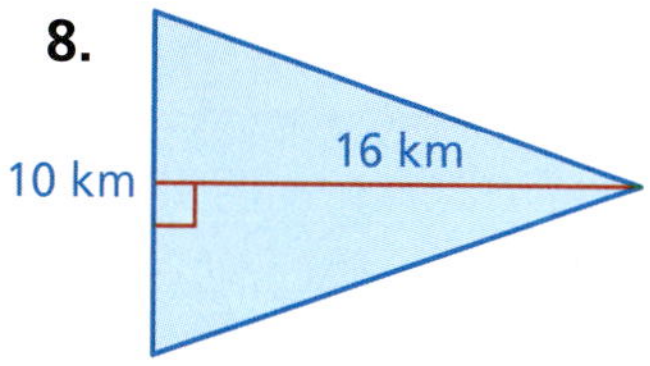

9.

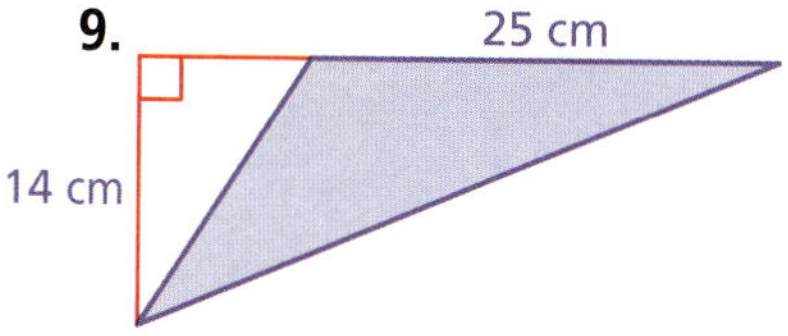

8.5 Circles and Circumference *(pp. 300–307)*

Find the circumference of the circle. Use 3.14 for π.

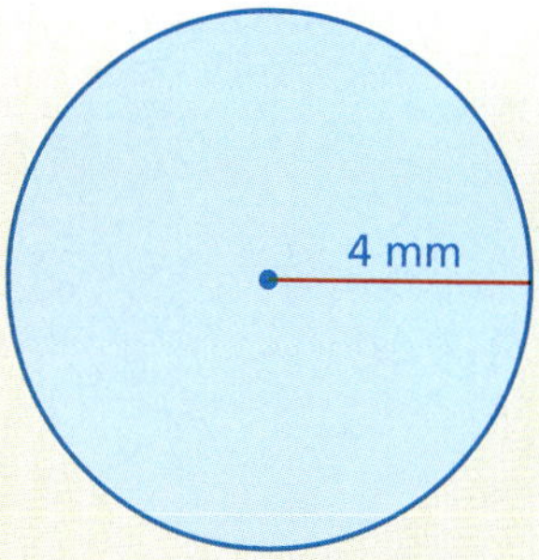

The radius is 4 millimeters.

$C = 2\pi r$	Write formula for circumference.
$\approx 2 \cdot 3.14 \cdot 4$	Substitute 3.14 for π and 4 for r.
$= 25.12$	Multiply.

The circumference is about 25.12 millimeters.

Exercises

Find the circumference of the circle. Use 3.14 or $\frac{22}{7}$ for π.

10.

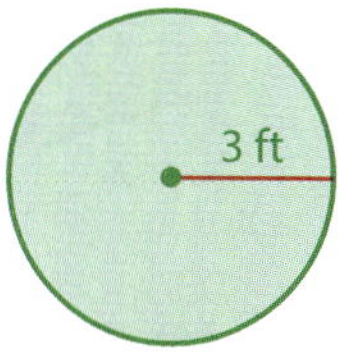

11.

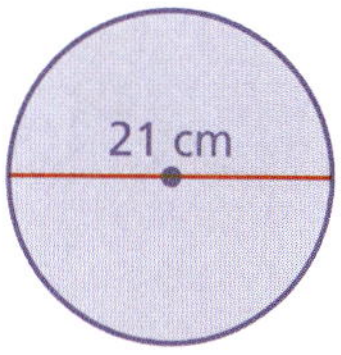

12.

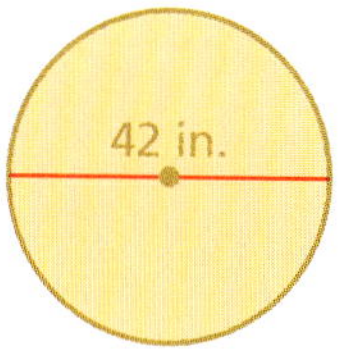

8.6 Areas of Circles *(pp. 308–313)*

Find the area of the circle. Use 3.14 for π.

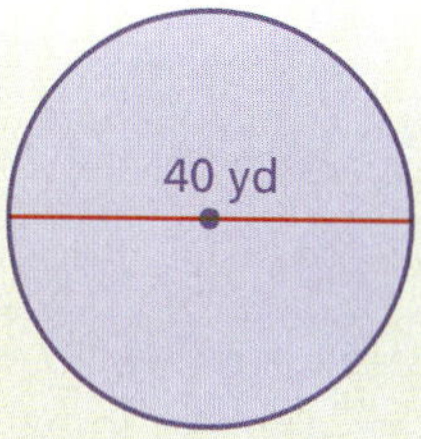

$A = \pi r^2$	Write formula for area.
$\approx 3.14 \cdot 20^2$	Substitute 3.14 for π and 20 for r.
$= 1256$	Multiply.

The area is about 1256 square yards.

Exercises

Find the area of the circle. Use 3.14 or $\frac{22}{7}$ for π.

13.

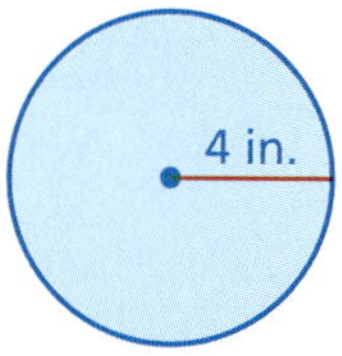

14.

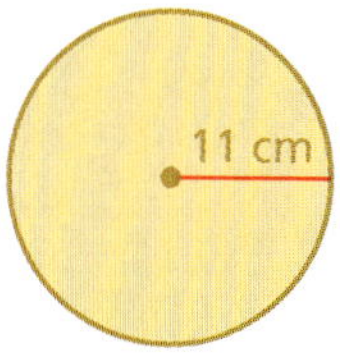

15.

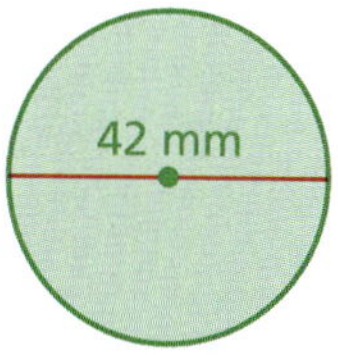

9 Statistical Measures and Data Analysis

9.1 Mean

9.2 Measures of Center

9.3 Circle Graphs

"Please hold still. I am trying to find the mean of 6, 8, and 10 by dividing their sum into three equal piles."

What You Learned Before

"Our mean weight is 18 pounds."

Ordering Decimals

Example 1 **Use a number line to order 8, 6.5, 7.25, 5.5, 4.25, and 7 from least to greatest.**

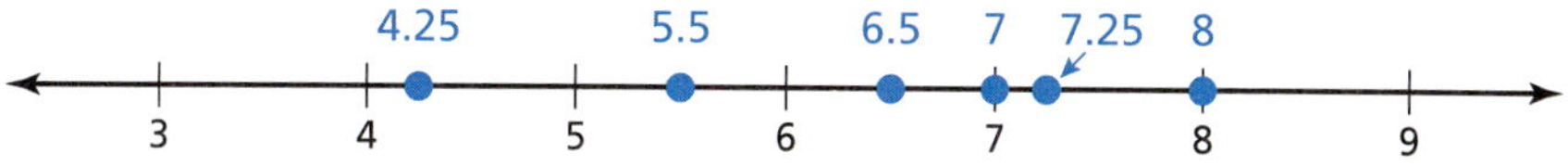

Try It Yourself

Use a number line to order the numbers from least to greatest.

1. 7.25, 4.5, 6.5, 6, 5.5, 8.75

2. 4, 2.5, 3.25, 5.5, 4.5, 6.75

3. 6.25, 3, 2.5, 3.5, 5.75, 5

4. 1.25, 5.5, 4.75, 4.5, 3.5, 2.25

Analyzing Double Bar Graphs

Example 2 **How many more male athletes than female athletes participated in the 1992 Summer Olympics?**

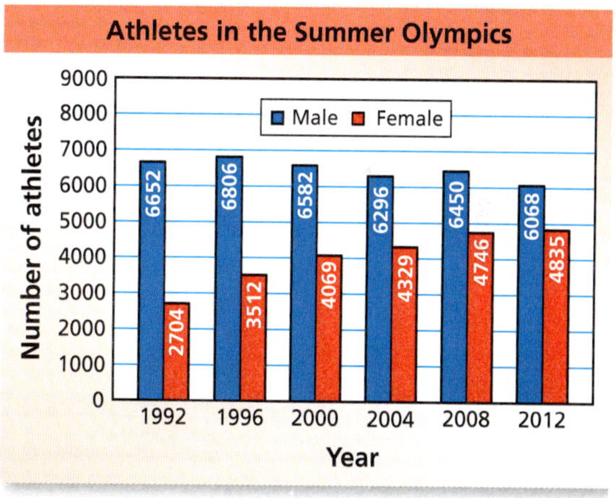

$6652 - 2704 = 3948$

Number of male athletes in 1992

Number of female athletes in 1992

3948 more male athletes participated.

Example 3 **How many athletes participated in the 2000 Summer Olympics?**

$6582 + 4069 = 10{,}651$ athletes participated in the 2000 Summer Olympics.

Try It Yourself

5. How many more female athletes participated in the 2012 Summer Olympics than in the 1992 Summer Olympics?

6. Describe the relationship between the number of athletes in the 2000 Summer Olympics and the number of athletes in the 2004 Summer Olympics.

9.1 Mean

Essential Question How can you find an average value of a data set?

1 ACTIVITY: Finding a Balance Point

Work with a partner. Discuss the distribution of the data. Where on the number line do you think the data set is *balanced*? Is this a good representation of the average? Explain.

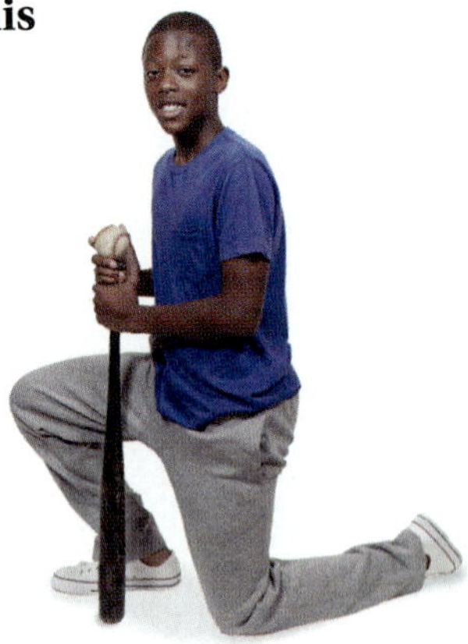

a. number of quarters brought to a batting cage

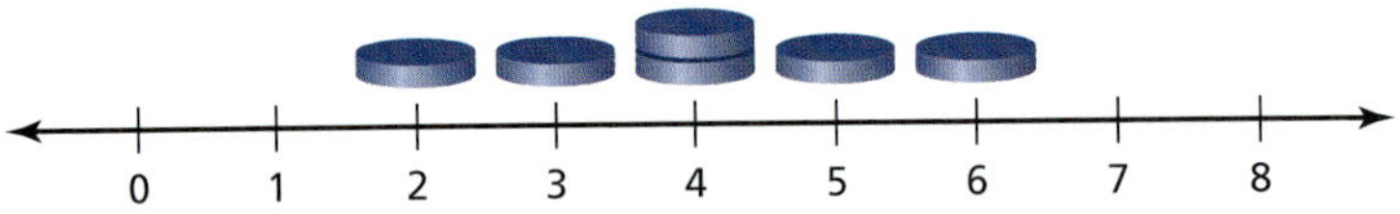

b. annual income of recent graduates (in thousands of dollars)

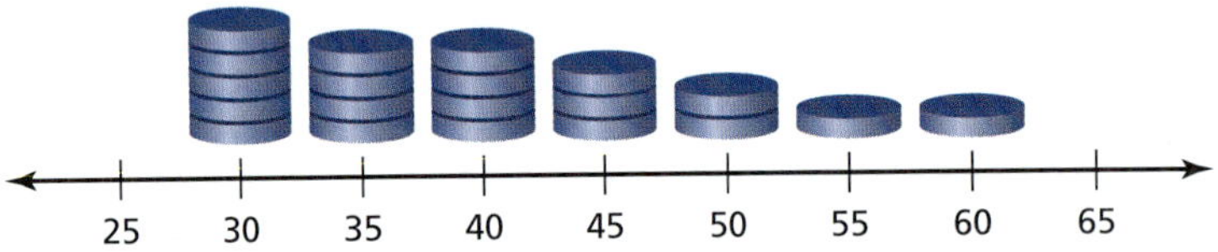

c. hybrid fuel economy (miles per gallon)

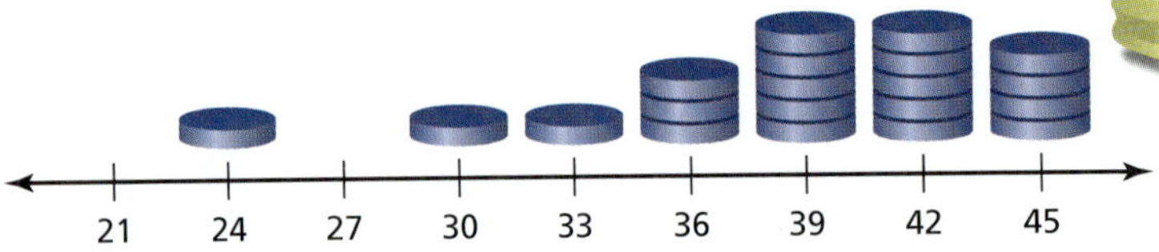

2 ACTIVITY: Finding a Fair Share

Statistics

In this lesson, you will

- understand the concept of the mean of data sets.
- find the mean of data sets.
- compare and interpret the means of data sets.

Work with a partner. It costs $0.25 to hit 12 baseballs in a batting cage. The table shows the numbers of quarters six friends bring to the batting cage. They want to group the quarters so that everyone has the same amount.

Quarters					
John	Lisa	Miguel	Matt	Cheryl	Jean
6	3	4	5	2	4

Use counters to represent each number in the table. How can you use the counters to determine how many times each friend can use the batting cage? Explain how this procedure results in a "fair share."

3 ACTIVITY: Finding an Average

Work with a partner. Use the information in Activity 2.

a. What is the total number of quarters the group of friends brought to the batting cage?

b. **REASONING** How can you use math to find the average number of quarters that each friend brought to the batting cage? Find the average number of quarters. Why do you think this average represents a fair share?

4 ACTIVITY: Answering a Statistical Question

Work with a partner. The table shows the numbers of quarters several people bring to a batting cage. You want to answer the question:

"How many quarters do people bring to a batting cage?"

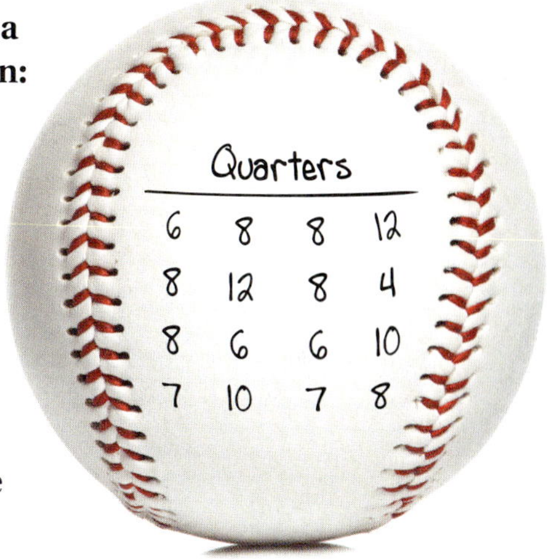

a. Explain why this question is a statistical question.

b. **MODELING** Make a dot plot of the data. Use the distribution of the data to answer the question. Explain your reasoning.

c. **REASONING** Use an average to answer the question. Explain your reasoning.

Math Process

Use Clear Definitions

What does it mean for data to have an average? How does this help you answer the question?

What Is Your Answer?

5. **IN YOUR OWN WORDS** How can you find an average value of a data set?

6. Give two real-life examples of averages.

7. Explain what it means to say the average of a data set is the point on a number line where the data set is balanced.

8. There are 5 students in the cartoon. Four of the students are 66 inches tall. One is 96 inches tall.

   a. How do you think the students decided that their average height is 6 feet?

   b. Does a height of 6 feet seem like a good representation of the average height of the 5 students? Explain why or why not.

"Yup, the average height in our class is 6 feet."

Practice Use what you learned about averages to complete Exercises 4 and 5 on page 324.

9.1 Lesson

Check It Out
Lesson Tutorials
BigIdeasMath.com

Key Vocabulary
mean, *p. 322*
outlier, *p. 323*

A mean is a type of average.

Key Idea

Mean

Words The **mean** of a data set is the sum of the data divided by the number of data values.

Numbers **Data:** 8, 5, 6, 9 **Mean:** $\frac{8+5+6+9}{4} = \frac{28}{4} = 7$

4 data values

EXAMPLE 1 Finding the Mean

Text Messages Sent
Mark: 120
Laura: 95
Stacy: 101
Josh: 125
Kevin: 82
Maria: 108
Manny: 90

The table shows the number of text messages sent by a group of friends over 1 week. What is the mean number of messages sent?

Ⓐ 100 Ⓑ 102 Ⓒ 103 Ⓓ 104

$$\text{mean} = \frac{120+95+101+125+82+108+90}{7}$$

Sum of the data

Number of values

$$= \frac{721}{7}, \text{ or } 103$$ Simplify.

The mean number of text messages sent is 103. The correct answer is Ⓒ.

EXAMPLE 2 Comparing Means

The double bar graph shows the monthly rainfall amounts for two cities over a six-month period. Compare the mean monthly rainfalls.

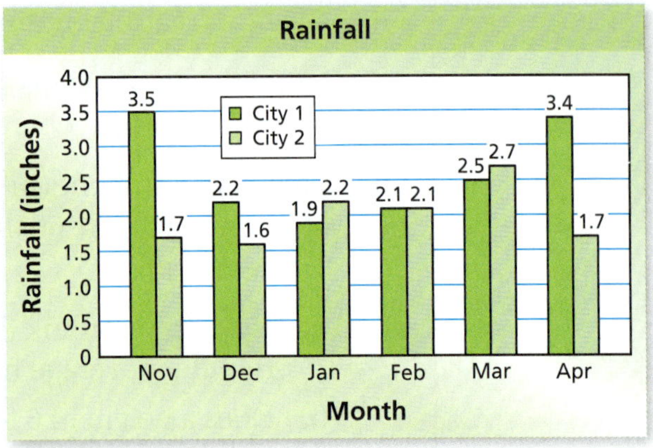

City 1 mean: $\frac{3.5+2.2+1.9+2.1+2.5+3.4}{6} = \frac{15.6}{6}$, or 2.6

City 2 mean: $\frac{1.7+1.6+2.2+2.1+2.7+1.7}{6} = \frac{12}{6}$, or 2

Because 2.6 is greater than 2, City 1 averaged more rainfall.

Multi-Language Glossary at BigIdeasMath.com

On Your Own

Now You're Ready
Exercises 6–9

Find the mean of the data.

1. 49, 62, 52, 54, 61, 70, 55, 53
2. 7.2, 8.5, 7.0, 8.1, 6.7

An **outlier** is a data value that is much greater or much less than the other values. When included in a data set, it can affect the mean.

EXAMPLE 3 Finding the Mean With and Without an Outlier

Shetland Pony Heights (inches)				
40	37	39	40	42
38	38	37	28	40

The table shows the heights of several Shetland ponies.

a. Identify the outlier.

b. Find the mean with and without the outlier.

c. Describe how the outlier affects the mean.

STEM VIDEO

a. Display the data in a dot plot.

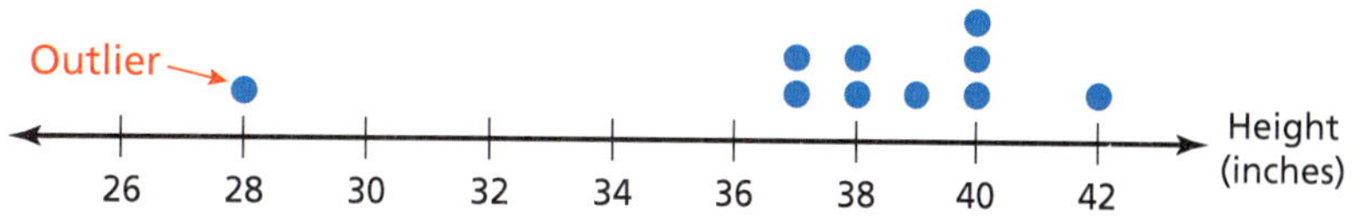

The height of 28 inches is much less than the other heights. So, it is an outlier.

b. Mean with outlier:

$$\frac{40 + 37 + 39 + 40 + 42 + 38 + 38 + 37 + 28 + 40}{10} = \frac{379}{10}, \text{ or } 37.9$$

Mean without outlier:

$$\frac{40 + 37 + 39 + 40 + 42 + 38 + 38 + 37 + 40}{9} = \frac{351}{9}, \text{ or } 39$$

c. With the outlier, the mean is less than all but three of the heights. Without the outlier, the mean better represents the heights.

On Your Own

Now You're Ready
Exercise 14

For each data set, identify the outlier. Then describe how it affects the mean.

3. Weights (in pounds) of dogs at a kennel:

   48, 50, 55, 60, 8, 37, 50

4. Prices for flights from Miami, Florida, to San Juan, Puerto Rico:

   $456, $512, $516, $900, $436, $516

9.1 Exercises

Check It Out
Help with Homework
BigIdeasMath.com

Vocabulary and Concept Check

1. **VOCABULARY** Arrange the words to explain how to find a mean.

the data values	divide by	the number of data values	add	then

2. **NUMBER SENSE** Is the mean always equal to a value in the data set? Explain.

3. **REASONING** Can you use the mean to answer a statistical question? Explain.

Practice and Problem Solving

Describe an average value of the data.

4. Ages in a class: 11, 12, 12, 12, 12, 12, 13

5. Movies seen this week: 0, 0, 0, 1, 1, 2, 3

Find the mean of the data.

1 6.

Pets Owned	
Brandon	I
Jill	III
Mark	II
Nicole	IIII
Steve	0

7.

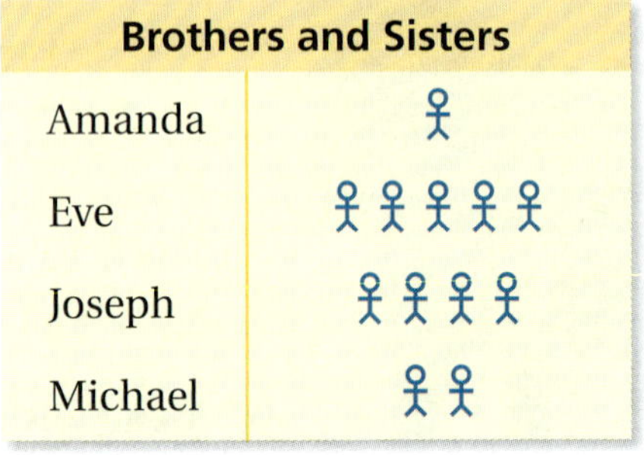

8.

Sit-ups		
108	85	94
103	112	115
98	119	126
105	82	89

9.

10. **GOLF** The table shows tournament finishes for a golfer.

    a. What was the golfer's mean finish?

    b. Identify two outliers for the data.

Tournament Finishes							
1	1	2	1	1	12	6	2
15	37	1	2	1	26	9	1

11. **COMMERCIALS** You and your friends are watching a television show. One of your friends asks, "How long are the commercial breaks during this show?"

    a. Is this a statistical question? Explain.

    b. Use the mean of the values in the table to answer the question.

Time (minutes)				
4.2	3.5	4.55	2.75	2.25

Month	Rainfall (inches)	Month	Rainfall (inches)
Jan	2.22	Jul	3.27
Feb	1.51	Aug	5.40
Mar	1.86	Sep	5.45
Apr	2.06	Oct	4.34
May	3.48	Nov	2.64
Jun	4.57	Dec	2.14

12. RAINFALL The table shows the monthly rainfall at a measuring station. What is the mean monthly rainfall?

13. OPEN-ENDED Create two different sets of data that have six values and a mean of 21.

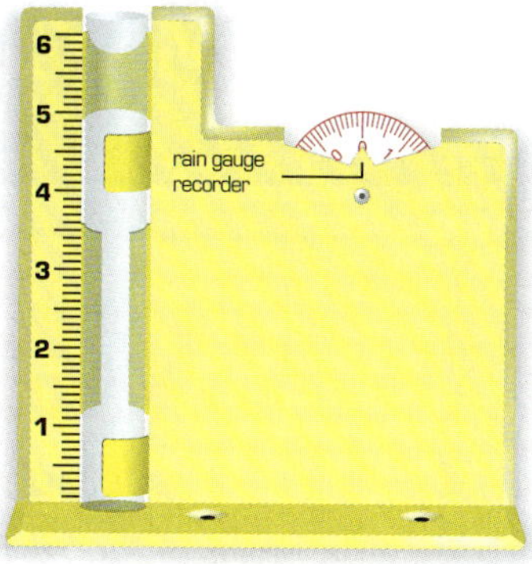

③ **14. CELL PHONE** The bar graph shows your cell phone usage for five months.

a. Which data value is an outlier? Explain.

b. Find the mean with and without the outlier. Then describe how the outlier affects the mean.

c. Describe a situation that could have caused the outlier in this problem.

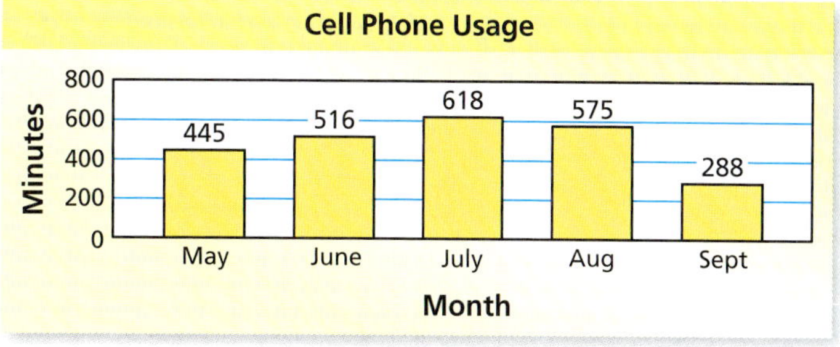

15. HEIGHT The table shows the heights of the volleyball players from two schools. What is the difference between the mean heights of the two teams? Do outliers affect either mean? Explain.

	Player Height (inches)														
Dolphins	59	65	53	56	58	61	64	68	51	56	54	57			
Tigers	63	68	66	58	54	55	61	62	53	70	64	64	62	67	69

16. REASONING Make a dot plot of the data set 11, 13, 17, 15, 12, 18, and 12. Use the dot plot to explain how the mean is the point where the data set is balanced.

17. ALLOWANCE In your class, 7 students do not receive a weekly allowance, 5 students receive \$3, 7 students receive \$5, 3 students receive \$6, and 2 students receive \$8. What is the mean weekly allowance? Explain how you found your answer.

18. **Precision** A collection of 8 backpacks has a mean weight of 14 pounds. A different collection of 12 backpacks has a mean weight of 9 pounds. What is the mean weight of the 20 backpacks? Explain how you found your answer.

Fair Game Review *What you learned in previous grades & lessons*

Evaluate the expression.

19. $\frac{8 + 10}{2}$ **20.** $\frac{26 + 34}{2}$ **21.** $\frac{18 + 19}{2}$ **22.** $\frac{14 + 17}{2}$

23. MULTIPLE CHOICE 60% of what number is 105?

Ⓐ 63 Ⓑ 175 Ⓒ 630 Ⓓ 1750

9.2 Measures of Center

Essential Question In what other ways can you describe an average of a data set?

1 ACTIVITY: Finding a Median

Work with a partner.

a. Write the total number of letters in the first and last names of 19 celebrities, historical figures, or people you know. Organize your data in a table. One person is already listed for you.

Person	Number of letters in first and last name
Abraham Lincoln	14

b. Order the values in your data set from least to greatest. Then write the data on a strip of grid paper with 19 boxes.

c. Place a finger on the square at each end of the strip. Move your fingers toward the center of the ordered data set until your fingers touch. On what value do your fingers touch?

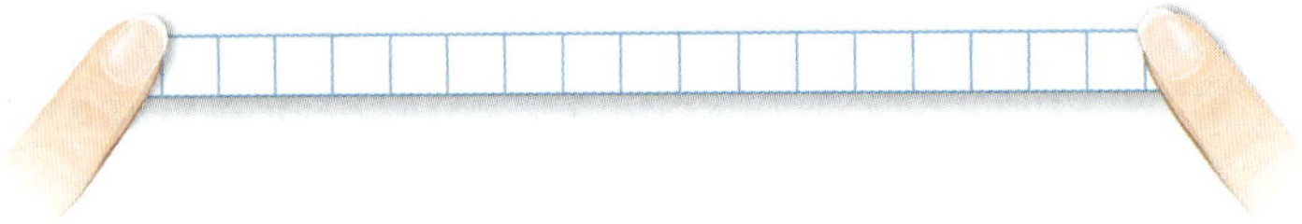

Statistics
In this lesson, you will
- understand the concept of measures of center.
- find the median and mode of data sets.

d. Now take your strip of grid paper and fold it in half. On what number is the crease? What do you notice? This value is called the *median*. How would you describe to another student what the median of a data set represents?

e. How many values are greater than the median? How many are less than the median?

f. Why do you think the median is considered an average of a data set?

2 ACTIVITY: Adding a Value to a Data Set

Work with a partner.

a. How many total letters are in your first name and last name? Add this value to the ordered data set in Activity 1. How many values are now in your data set?

b. Write the ordered data, including your new value from part (a), on a strip of grid paper.

c. Repeat parts (c) and (d) from Activity 1. Explain your findings. How do you think you can find the median of this data set?

d. Compare the medians in Activities 1 and 2. Then answer the following questions. Explain your reasoning.

- Do you think the median always has to be a value in the data set?
- Do you think the median always has to be a whole number?

3 ACTIVITY: Finding a Mode

Work with a partner.

a. Make a dot plot for the data set in Activity 2. Describe the distribution of the data.

b. Which value occurs most often in the data set? This value is called the *mode.*

c. Do you think a data set can have no mode or more than one mode? Explain.

d. Do you think the mode always has to be a value in the data set? Explain.

e. Why do you think the mode is considered an average of a data set?

Math Process

Use a Graph

How can you use the dot plot to find the mode?

What Is Your Answer?

4. **IN YOUR OWN WORDS** In what other ways can you describe an average of a data set?

5. Find the mean of your data set in Activity 2. Then compare the mean, median, and mode. Is there one measure that you think best represents your data set? Explain your reasoning.

Practice Use what you learned about the median of a data set to complete Exercises 5 and 6 on page 331.

9.2 Lesson

Check It Out
Lesson Tutorials
BigIdeasMath.com

Key Vocabulary
measure of center, *p. 328*
median, *p. 328*
mode, *p. 328*

A **measure of center** is a measure that describes the typical value of a data set. The mean is one type of measure of center. Here are two others.

Key Ideas

Median

Words Order the data. For a set with an odd number of values, the **median** is the middle value. For a set with an even number of values, the **median** is the mean of the two middle values.

Numbers **Data:** 5, 8, 9, 12, 14 The median is 9.

Data: 2, 3, 5, 7, 10, 11 The median is $\frac{5+7}{2}$, or 6.

Mode

Words The **mode** of a data set is the value or values that occur most often. Data can have one mode, more than one mode, or no mode. When all values occur only once, there is no mode.

Numbers **Data:** 11, 13, 15, 15, 18, 21, 24, 24

The modes are 15 and 24.

Study Tip
The mode is the only measure of center that you can use to describe a set of data that is *not* made up of numbers.

EXAMPLE 1 Finding the Median and Mode

Bowling Scores				
120	135	160	125	90
205	160	175	105	145

Find the median and mode of the bowling scores.

90, 105, 120, 125, 135, 145, 160, 160, 175, 205 Order the data.

Median: $\frac{135 + 145}{2} = \frac{280}{2}$, or 140 Add the two middle values and divide by 2.

Mode: 90, 105, 120, 125, 135, 145, 160, 160, 175, 205

The value 160 occurs most often.

∴ The median is 140. The mode is 160.

On Your Own

Now You're Ready
Exercises 7–12

Find the median and mode of the data.

1. 20, 4, 17, 8, 12, 9, 5, 20, 13
2. 100, 75, 90, 80, 110, 102

EXAMPLE 2 Finding the Mode

Favorite Types of Movies

Comedy	Drama	Horror
Horror	Drama	Horror
Comedy	Comedy	Action
Action	Comedy	Action
Horror	Drama	Comedy
Comedy	Comedy	Horror
Horror	Comedy	Action
Horror	Action	Drama

The list shows the favorite types of movies for students in a class. Organize the data in a frequency table. Then find the mode.

Type	Tally	Frequency
Action	𝍸	5
Comedy	𝍸 III	8
Drama	IIII	4
Horror	𝍸 II	7

The number of tally marks is the frequency.

Make a tally for each vote.

Comedy received the most votes.

∴ So, the mode is comedy.

On Your Own

Now You're Ready
Exercises 14–15

3. One member of the class was absent and ends up voting for horror. Does this change the mode? Explain.

EXAMPLE 3 Choosing the Best Measure of Center

Find the mean, median, and mode of the sneaker prices. Which measure best represents the data?

Mean: $\dfrac{20 + 31 + 122 + 48 + 37 + 20 + 45 + 65}{8} = \dfrac{388}{8}$, or 48.5

Median: 20, 20, 31, 37, 45, 48, 65, 122 — Order from least to greatest.

$\dfrac{37 + 45}{2} = \dfrac{82}{2}$, or 41

Mode: 20, 20, 31, 37, 45, 48, 65, 122 — The value 20 occurs most often.

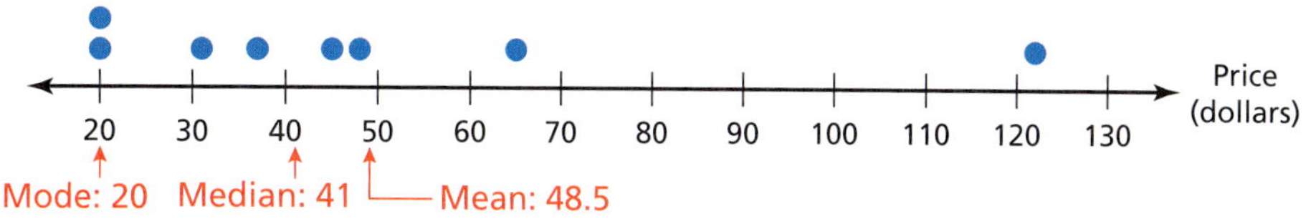

∴ The median best represents the data. The mode is less than most of the data, and the mean is greater than most of the data.

On Your Own

Now You're Ready
Exercises 17–20

Find the mean, median, and mode of the data. Choose the measure that best represents the data. Explain your reasoning.

4. 1, 93, 46, 48, 34, 194, 67, 55

5. 96, 150, 102, 87, 150, 75

EXAMPLE 4 Removing an Outlier

Identify the outlier in Example 3. Find the mean, median, and mode without the outlier. Which measure does the outlier affect the most?

The price of $122 is much greater than any other price. So, it is the outlier.

	Mean	Median	Mode
With Outlier (Example 3)	48.5	41	20
Without Outlier	38	37	20

∴ The mean is affected the most by the outlier.

On Your Own

Now You're Ready
Exercises 21–22

6. The times (in minutes) it takes six students to travel to school are 8, 10, 10, 15, 20, and 45. Identify the outlier. Find the mean, median, and mode with and without the outlier. Which measure does the outlier affect the most?

EXAMPLE 5 Changing the Values of a Data Set

The prices of six video games at an online store are shown in the table. The price of each game increases by $4.98 when a shipping charge is included. How does this increase affect the mean, median, and mode?

Video Game Prices	
$53.42	$35.69
$18.99	$25.13
$27.97	$53.42

Make a new table by adding $4.98 to each price. Then find the mean, median, and mode of both data sets.

Video Game Prices with Shipping Charge	
$58.40	$40.67
$23.97	$30.11
$32.95	$58.40

	Mean	Median	Mode
Original Price	35.77	31.83	53.42
Price with Shipping Charge	40.75	36.81	58.4

Compare:

Mean: $40.75 - 35.77 = 4.98$

Median: $36.81 - 31.83 = 4.98$

Mode: $58.4 - 53.42 = 4.98$

∴ By increasing each video game price by $4.98 for shipping, the mean, median, and mode all increase by $4.98.

On Your Own

7. **WHAT IF?** The store decreases the price of each video game by $3. How does this decrease affect the mean, median, and mode?

9.2 Exercises

Check It Out
Help with Homework
BigIdeasMath.com

Vocabulary and Concept Check

1. **NUMBER SENSE** Give an example of a data set that has no mode.
2. **WRITING** Which is affected most by an outlier: the mean, median, or mode? Explain.
3. **WHICH ONE DOESN'T BELONG** Which word does *not* belong with the other three? Explain.

   median   outlier   mode   mean

4. **NUMBER SENSE** A data set has a mean of 7, a median of 5, and a mode of 8. Which of the numbers 7, 5, and 8 *must* be in the data set? Explain.

Practice and Problem Solving

Use grid paper to find the median of the data.

5. 9, 7, 2, 4, 3, 5, 9, 6, 8, 0, 3, 8
6. 16, 24, 13, 36, 22, 26, 22, 28, 25

Find the median and mode(s) of the data.

(1) 7. 3, 5, 7, 9, 11, 3, 8
8. 14, 19, 16, 13, 16, 14
9. 93, 81, 94, 71, 89, 92, 94, 99
10. 44, 13, 36, 52, 19, 27, 33
11. 12, 33, 18, 28, 29, 12, 17, 4, 2
12. 55, 44, 40, 55, 48, 44, 58, 67

13. **ERROR ANALYSIS** Describe and correct the error in finding the median of the data.

    ✗ The median is 58.

    63, 55, 49, 58, 50, 59, 51

Find the mode(s) of the data.

(2) 14.

Shirt Color		
Black	Blue	Red
Pink	Black	Black
Gray	Green	Blue
Blue	Blue	Red
Yellow	Blue	Blue
Black	Orange	Black
Black		

15.

Talent Show Acts		
Singing	Dancing	Comedy
Singing	Singing	Dancing
Juggling	Dancing	Singing
Singing	Poetry	Dancing
Comedy	Magic	Dancing
Poetry	Singing	Singing

16. **REASONING** In Exercises 14 and 15, can you find the mean and median of the data? Explain.

Find the mean, median, and mode(s) of the data. Choose the measure that best represents the data. Explain your reasoning.

③ **17.** 48, 12, 11, 45, 48, 48, 43, 32

18. 12, 13, 40, 95, 88, 7, 95

19. 2, 8, 10, 12, 56, 9, 5, 2, 4

20. 126, 62, 144, 81, 144, 103

Find the mean, median, and mode(s) of the data with and without the outlier. Describe the effect of the outlier on the measures of center.

④ **21.** 45, 52, 17, 63, 57, 42, 54, 58

22. 85, 77, 211, 88, 91, 84, 85

Find the mean, median, and mode(s) of the data.

23. 4.7, 8.51, 6.5, 7.42, 9.64, 7.2, 9.3

24. $8\frac{1}{2}, 6\frac{5}{8}, 3\frac{1}{8}, 5\frac{3}{4}, 6\frac{5}{8}, 5\frac{1}{4}, 10\frac{5}{8}, 4\frac{1}{2}$

25. WEATHER The weather forecast for a week is shown.

	Sun	Mon	Tue	Wed	Thu	Fri	Sat

High	90° F	91° F	89° F	97° F	101° F	99° F	91° F
Low	74° F	78° F	77° F	77° F	83° F	78° F	72° F

a. Find the mean, median, and mode(s) of the high temperatures. Which measure best represents the data? Explain your reasoning.

b. Repeat part (a) for the low temperatures.

26. RESEARCH Find the unit costs of 10 different kinds of cereal. Choose one cereal whose unit cost will be an outlier.

a. Find the mean, median, and mode(s) of the data. Which measure best represents the data? Explain your reasoning.

b. Identify the outlier in the data set. Find the mean, median, and mode(s) of the data set without the outlier. Which measure does the outlier affect the most?

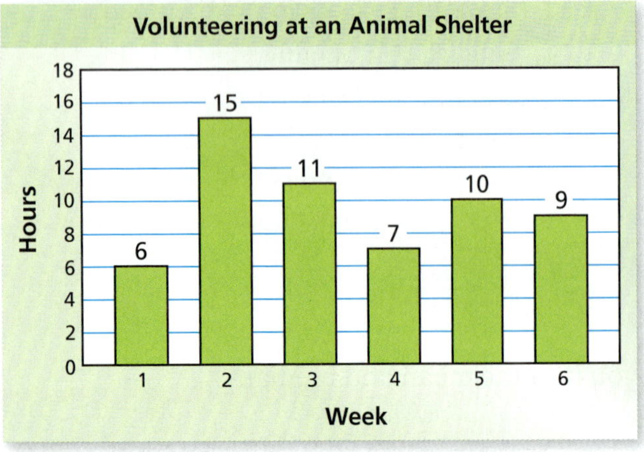

27. PROBLEM SOLVING The bar graph shows the numbers of hours you volunteered at an animal shelter. What is the minimum number of hours you need to work in the seventh week to justify that you worked an average of 10 hours for the 7 weeks? Explain your answer using measures of center.

28. REASONING Why do you think the mode is the least frequently used measure to describe a data set? Explain.

29. MOTOCROSS The ages of the racers in a bicycle motocross race are 14, 22, 20, 25, 26, 17, 21, 30, 27, 25, 14, and 29. The 30-year-old drops out of the race and is replaced with a 15-year-old. How are the mean, median, and mode of the ages affected?

30. CAMERAS The data are the prices of several digital cameras at a store.

$130 $170 $230 $130
$250 $275 $130 $185

a. Does the price shown in the advertisement represent the prices well? Explain.

b. Why might the store use this advertisement?

c. In this situation, why might a person want to know the mean? the median? the mode? Explain.

31. SALARIES The table shows the monthly salaries for employees at a company.

Monthly Salaries (dollars)				
1940	1660	1860	2100	1720
1540	1760	1940	1820	1600

a. Find the mean, median, and mode of the data.

b. Each employee receives a 5% raise. Find the mean, median, and mode of the data with the raise. How does this increase affect the mean, median, and mode of the data?

c. Use the original monthly salaries to calculate the annual salaries. Find the mean, median, and mode of the annual salaries. How are these values related to the mean, median, and mode of the monthly salaries?

32. Critical Thinking Consider the algebraic expressions $3x$, $9x$, $4x$, $23x$, $6x$, and $3x$. Assume $x > 0$.

a. Find the mean, median, and mode.

b. Is there an outlier? If so, what is it?

Fair Game Review What you learned in previous grades & lessons

Find the value of the expression.

33. $48 - 35$ **34.** $188 - 123$ **35.** $416 - 297$ **36.** $6249 - 3374$

37. MULTIPLE CHOICE A shelf in your room can hold at most 30 pounds. There are 12 pounds of books already on it. Which inequality represents the number of pounds you can add to the shelf?

Ⓐ $x < 18$ Ⓑ $x \geq 18$ Ⓒ $x \leq 42$ Ⓓ $x \leq 18$

9.3 Circle Graphs

Essential Question How can you use a circle graph to show the results of a survey?

1 ACTIVITY: Reading a Circle Graph

Work with a partner. Six hundred middle school students were asked "What is your favorite sport?" The circle graph shows the results of the survey.

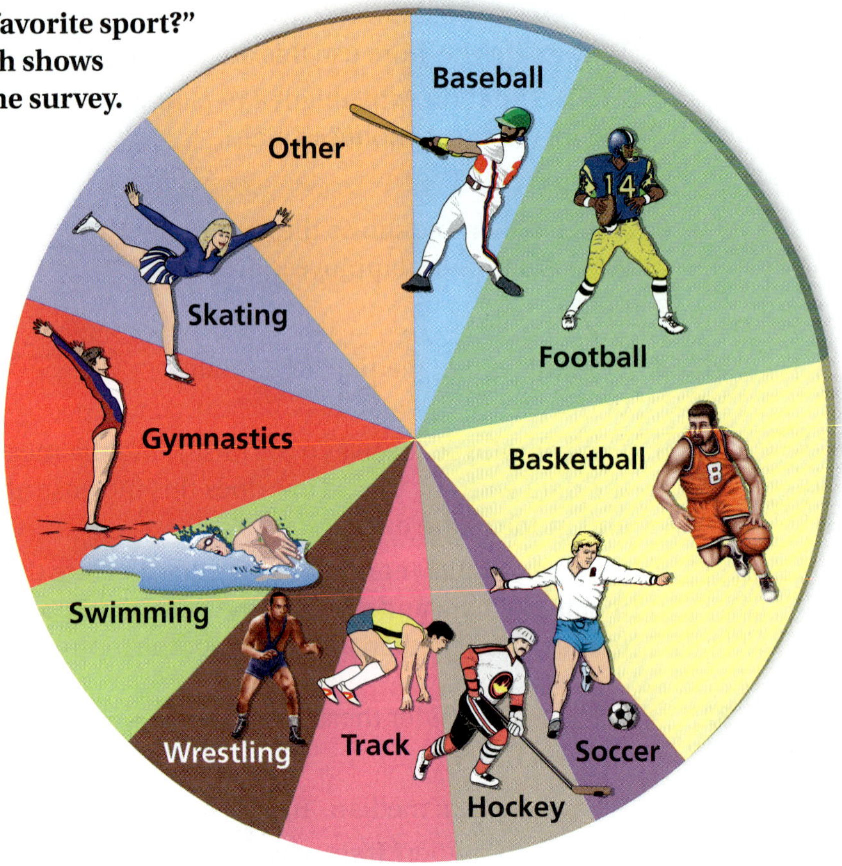

Statistics

In this lesson, you will

- represent data in a circle graph.
- make inferences about data represented in a circle graph.

a. Use a protractor to find the angle measure (in degrees) of the section (pie piece) for football.

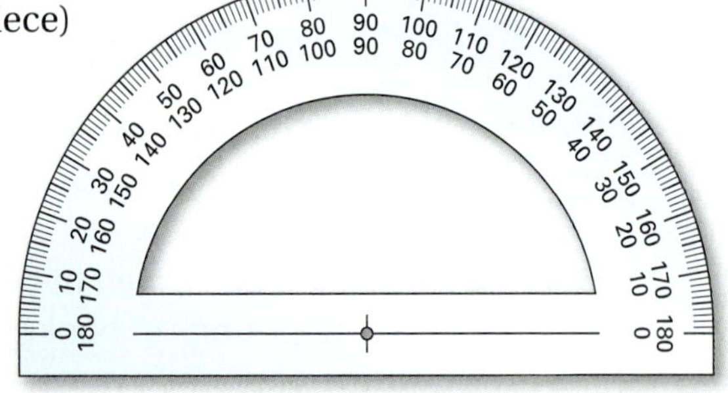

b. How many degrees are in a full circle?

c. Use your answers from parts (a) and (b) to find the number of students who said that football is their favorite sport.

d. Repeat the process for the other sections of the circle graph.

2 ACTIVITY: Making a Circle Graph

Work with a partner.

a. Conduct a survey in your class. Each student should check his or her favorite sport on a piece of paper similar to the one shown below.

What is your favorite sport?

Baseball	❑	Skating	❑
Basketball	❑	Soccer	❑
Football	❑	Swimming	❑
Gymnastics	❑	Track	❑
Hockey	❑	Wrestling	❑
		Other	❑

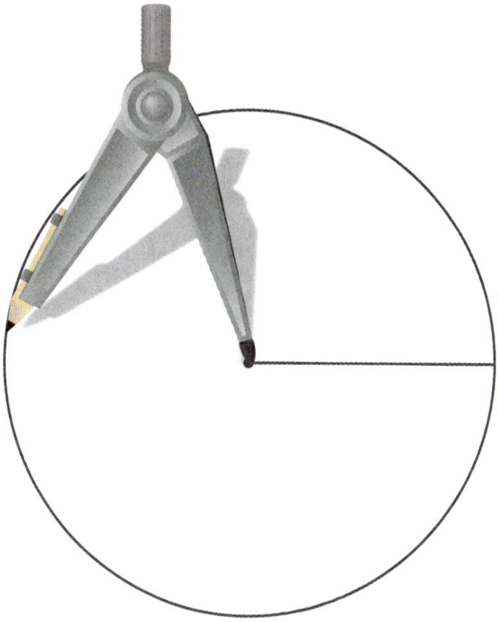

b. Organize the results on the board.

c. Display the results in a circle graph.

d. Compare and contrast your class survey with the survey in Activity 1.

What Is Your Answer?

3. **IN YOUR OWN WORDS** How can you use a circle graph to show the results of a survey?

4. Find a circle graph in a newspaper, in a magazine, or on the Internet. Copy it and describe the results that it shows.

"I conducted a survey and asked 30 people if they would like a million dollars."

"I organized the results in a circle graph."

Practice Use what you learned about circle graphs to complete Exercises 5–7 on page 339.

9.3 Lesson

Check It Out
Lesson Tutorials
BigIdeasMath.com

Key Vocabulary
circle graph, *p. 336*

Key Idea

Circle Graphs

A **circle graph** displays data as sections of a circle. The sum of the angle measures in a circle graph is 360°.

Favorite Fruit

When the data are given in percents, multiply the fraction form of each percent by 360° to find the angle measure for each section.

EXAMPLE 1 Making a Circle Graph

Favorite Amusement Park	People
Disney World	25
Busch Gardens	15
Universal Studios	12
Marineland	8

The table shows the results of a survey. Display the data in a circle graph.

Step 1: Find the total number of people.

$$25 + 15 + 12 + 8 = 60$$

Step 2: Find the angle measure for each section of the graph. Multiply the fraction of people that chose each park by 360°.

Disney World

$$\frac{25}{60} \cdot 360° = 150°$$

Busch Gardens

$$\frac{15}{60} \cdot 360° = 90°$$

Universal Studios

$$\frac{12}{60} \cdot 360° = 72°$$

Marineland

$$\frac{8}{60} \cdot 360° = 48°$$

Check

$$\frac{25}{60} + \frac{15}{60} + \frac{12}{60} + \frac{8}{60} = 1$$

$$150° + 90° + 72° + 48° = 360° \checkmark$$

Step 3: Use a protractor to draw the angle measures found in Step 2 on a circle. Then label the sections.

Favorite Amusement Park

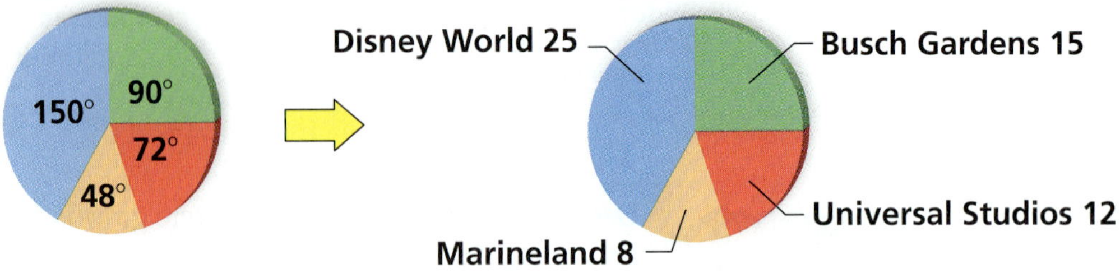

Multi-Language Glossary at BigIdeasMath.com.

On Your Own

Now You're Ready
Exercises 8–13

1. The table shows the dog and cat ownership among teachers in a school. Display the data in a circle graph.

Kind of pet	Dogs only	Cats only	Both	Neither
Percent	30%	30%	15%	25%

EXAMPLE 2 Using a Circle Graph

Students chose one of four topics for their science projects. (a) What fraction of the students chose *Earth's Atmosphere*? (b) How many students are in the class? (c) How many students chose *Atoms*?

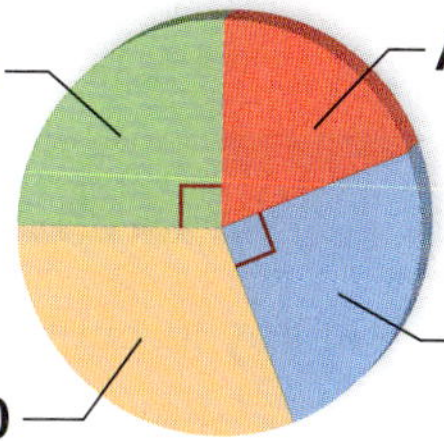

a. Because the *Earth's Atmosphere* section has a right angle, this section represents $\frac{90^\circ}{360^\circ} = \frac{1}{4}$ of the data.

One-fourth of the students chose *Earth's Atmosphere*.

b. From the circle graph and part (a), you know that one-fourth, or 8, of the students chose *Earth's Atmosphere*.

Think: 8 is one-fourth of what number? $\frac{1}{4} \times 32 = 8$

So, there are 32 students in the class.

c. Because the *Solar System* and *Earth's Atmosphere* sections have the same angle measure, the same number of students chose each project. So, 8 students chose *Solar System*. Subtract to find the number of students who chose *Atoms*.

$$32 - 8 - 8 - 10 = 6$$

Six students chose *Atoms*.

On Your Own

2. What percent of the students chose *Natural Resources*? What percent of the students chose either *Earth's Atmosphere* or *Solar System*?

EXAMPLE 3 Making a Prediction from a Circle Graph

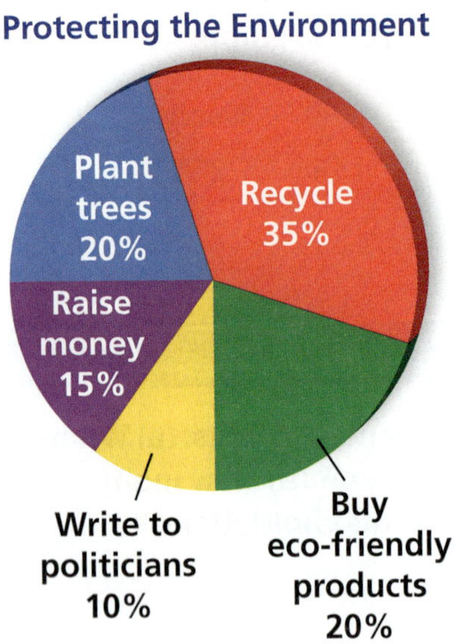

A survey asked students to name the most important thing people can do to protect the environment. The results are shown in the circle graph. You survey 50 more students. How many can you expect to say *Plant trees*?

The circle graph shows that 20% of students surveyed said *Plant trees*. To predict how many of the 50 additional students will say *Plant trees*, find 20% of 50.

$$20\% \text{ of } 50 = \frac{1}{5} \times 50$$ Write 20% as a fraction.

$$= 10$$ Multiply.

So, you can expect 10 more students to say *Plant trees*.

EXAMPLE 4 Comparing Data Displays

A survey asked students to choose their favorite school uniform color. The results are shown in the two data displays. You want to compare the portion of students who chose *Red* to all of the student responses. Which data display should you use? Explain.

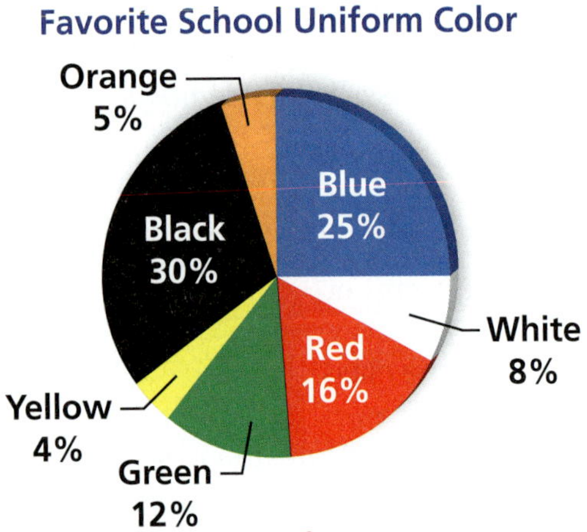

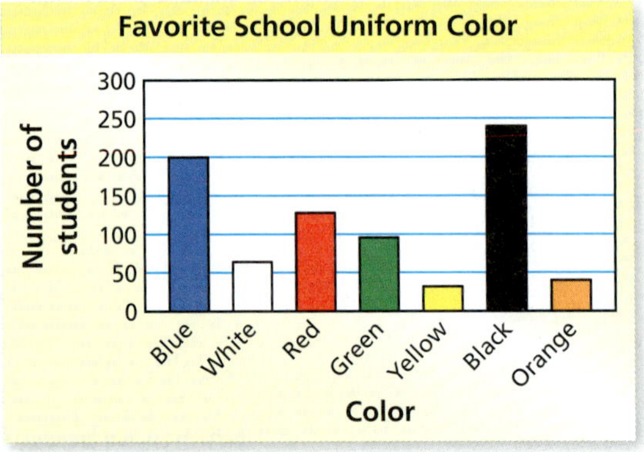

To use the bar graph, you have to estimate the number of students surveyed and the number of students that chose *Red*. The circle graph shows exact percents, so it is the better choice.

On Your Own

Now You're Ready
Exercises 14–19

3. **WHAT IF?** In Example 3, you survey 60 more students. How many can you expect to say *Recycle*?
4. **WHAT IF?** In Example 4, you want to estimate the number of students that chose *Black* as their favorite school uniform color. Which data display should you use? Explain.

9.3 Exercises

Check It Out
Help with Homework
BigIdeasMath.com

Vocabulary and Concept Check

1. **VOCABULARY** How do you make a circle graph when the data are given in percents?

2. **REASONING** Can one section of a circle graph be 110%? Explain.

3. **WHICH ONE DOESN'T BELONG?** Which one does *not* belong with the other three? Explain your reasoning.

| 360° | 100% | 1 | $\frac{1}{2}$ |

4. **DIFFERENT WORDS, SAME QUESTION** Which is different? Find "both" answers.

| How many people chose drama? | What is 25% of 120? |
| What is 90% of 120? | What is $\frac{1}{4}$ of 120? |

Favorite Movie

Total: 120

Practice and Problem Solving

The circle graph shows the results of a survey on favorite fruit.

5. Which fruit is the most popular?

6. Compare the number of students who chose oranges with the number of students who chose apples.

7. The survey included 80 students. How many students chose bananas?

Favorite Fruit

Find the angle measure that corresponds to the percent of a circle.

1 8. 20%   9. 15%   10. 70%   11. 3%

Display the data in a circle graph.

12.

Season	Rainfall (inches)
Spring	9
Summer	18
Fall	6
Winter	3

13.

Expense	Cost (dollars)
Play rights	400
Costume rental	650
Programs/tickets	300
Advertising	250
Other	400

Types of Pets Treated

PET HOSPITAL The circle graph shows the types of pets treated at a pet hospital.

(3) **14.** How many of the next 20 pets treated do you expect to be cats?

15. How many of the next 25 pets treated do you expect to be dogs?

16. How many of the next 40 pets treated do you expect to be cats or lizards?

17. **TIME** Your uncle says "It is a quarter to three." What does he mean? Explain.

(4) **18.** **COMPARING DISPLAYS** The pictograph shows the results of a survey asking students to name their favorite season.

a. Make a circle graph to represent the data in the pictograph.

b. You want to find the number of students who named *summer* as their favorite season. Which data display should you use? Explain.

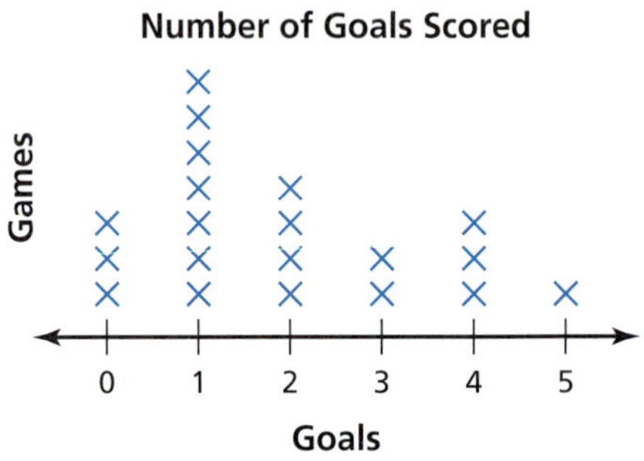

19. **COMPARING DISPLAYS** The line plot shows the numbers of goals the Tigers scored in 20 soccer games.

a. Make a circle graph to represent the data in the line plot.

b. Describe a situation where you would rather use a line plot than a circle graph and a situation where you would rather use a circle graph than a line plot.

20. **REASONING** A survey asks a group of students what they like to do during summer vacation. The results show that 68% like to go to the beach, 45% like to go camping, 72% like to go to amusement parks, and 29% like to go to the mall. Can a circle graph be used to display these data? Explain your reasoning.

21. **COMPARING DISPLAYS** Make a circle graph and a bar graph of the data in the table. Compare and contrast the two data displays. Which of the two better represents the data? Explain your reasoning.

Favorite Subject	Students
Art	12
English	56
Math	82
Music	28
Science	22

22. **REASONING** The table shows the height of a candle as it burns. Should you use a *circle graph, line graph,* or *stem-and-leaf plot* to represent the situation? Explain. Then make the display.

Time (hours)	0	1	2	3	4	5	6	7
Height (centimeters)	30	22	15	10	6	3	1	0

23. **LAND AREA** The table shows the land areas, in millions of square miles, of all the countries in North America.

Country	United States	Mexico	Canada	Other
Land Area	3.72	0.76	3.85	1.12
Percent				
Angle in Circle Graph				

a. Copy and complete the table. Round each angle to the nearest 5 degrees.

b. Display the data in a circle graph.

c. Find a map of North America. Do Canada and the United States appear to have the same area? Explain why or why not.

24. **RETAIL** A department store had \$7200 in sales.

a. Find the amount collected for each category.

b. Long sleeve shirts were $\frac{1}{4}$ of the shirt sales. Find the angle measure of the section that would represent long sleeve shirts on the circle graph.

c. How much of the next \$900 in sales do you expect to be from pants?

Department Store Sales

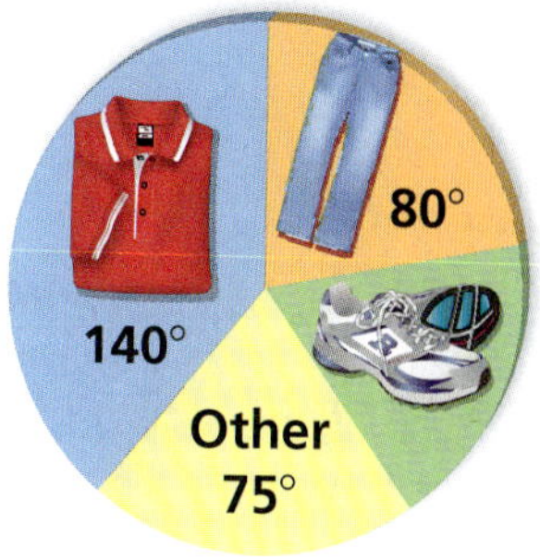

College Student Ages

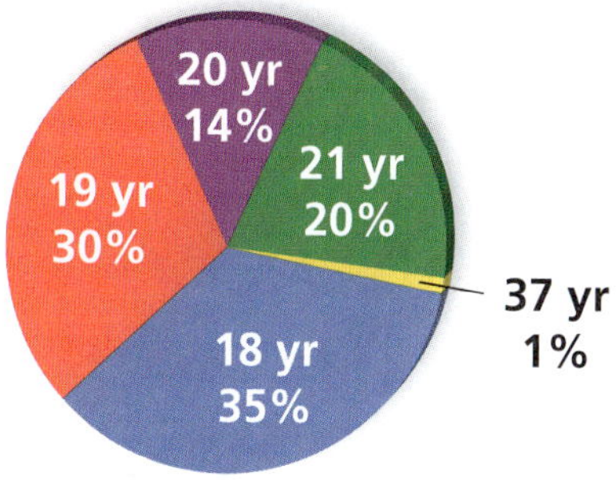

25. **WRITING** What math skills are needed to interpret data in a circle graph?

26. **Critical Thinking** The circle graph shows the ages of 200 students in a college psychology class.

a. Find the mean, median, and mode of the students' ages.

b. Identify the outliers. How do the outliers affect the mean, median, and mode?

Fair Game Review What you learned in previous grades & lessons

Write the phrase as an expression.

27. 7 less than a number x

28. a number y divided by 2

29. a number b increased by 50

30. the product of 14 and a number w

31. **MULTIPLE CHOICE** Which hamburger weighs the most?

(A) quarter pound

(B) third pound

(C) half pound

(D) eighth pound

9 Study Help

Check It Out
Graphic Organizer
BigIdeasMath.com

You can use a **process diagram** to show the steps involved in a procedure. Here is an example of a process diagram for finding the mean.

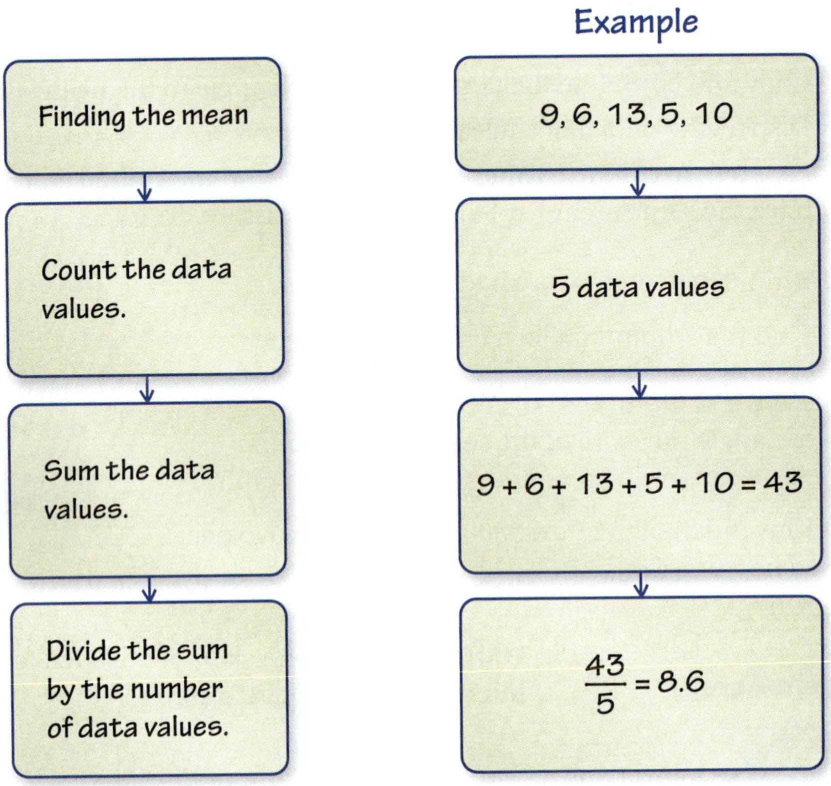

On Your Own

Make process diagrams with examples to help you study these topics.

1. finding the median
2. finding the mode
3. choosing the best measure of center
4. making a circle graph

"Descartes, you should use my process diagram when you eat your treats."

9 Chapter Review

Check It Out
Vocabulary Help
BigIdeasMath.com

Review Key Vocabulary

mean, *p. 322*
outlier, *p. 323*
measure of center, *p. 328*
median, *p. 328*
mode, *p. 328*
circle graph, *p. 336*

Review Examples and Exercises

9.1 Mean *(pp. 320–325)*

The table shows the weights of several dogs.

a. Identify the outlier.

b. Find the mean with and without the outlier.

c. Describe how the outlier affects the mean.

Dog Weights (pounds)				
43	14	50	64	57
54	51	38	62	49

a. Display the data in a dot plot.

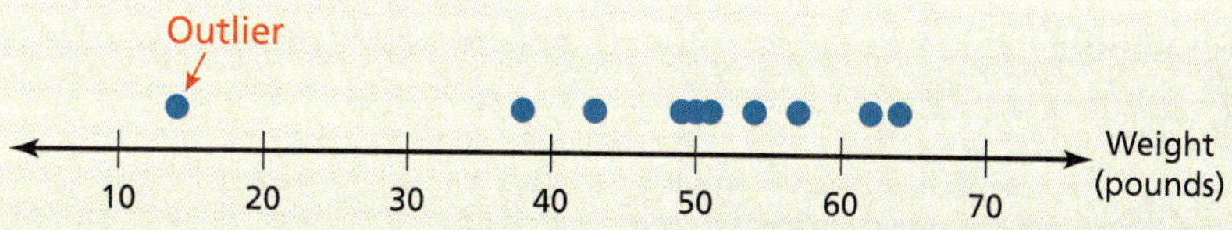

The weight of 14 pounds is much less than the other weights. So, it is an outlier.

b. Mean with outlier:

$$\frac{43 + 14 + 50 + 64 + 57 + 54 + 51 + 38 + 62 + 49}{10} = \frac{482}{10} = 48.2$$

Mean without outlier:

$$\frac{43 + 50 + 64 + 57 + 54 + 51 + 38 + 62 + 49}{9} = \frac{468}{9} = 52$$

c. With the outlier, the mean is less than all but three of the weights. Without the outlier, the mean better represents the weights.

Exercises

Find the mean of the data.

1. 4, 5, 7, 14, 17, 12, 18

2. 15, 5, 8, 12, 5, 9, 4, 10, 2, 11

3. The prices of several tablet computers are shown below. (a) Identify the outlier, (b) find the mean price with and without the outlier, and (c) describe how the outlier affects the mean.

$410, $260, $390, $400, $920, $500, $370, $440

9.2 Measures of Center *(pp. 326–333)*

The paper shows the number of states visited by each student in a sixth grade class.

a. Find the mean, median, and mode of the numbers of states visited.

b. Which measure best represents the data?

c. Identify the outlier. Find the mean, median, and mode without the outlier. Which measure does the outlier affect the most?

Number of States Visited

1	7	5	21
11	6	3	2
4	7	1	6
2	2	1	8
10	3	12	5

a. Mean: $\dfrac{1+7+5+21+\cdots+5}{20} = \dfrac{117}{20} = 5.85$

Order the data from least to greatest.

Median: 1, 1, 1, 2, 2, 2, 3, 3, 4, 5, 5, 6, 6, 7, 7, 8, 10, 11, 12, 21

$\dfrac{5+5}{2} = 5$ Add the two middle values and divide by 2.

Mode: 1, 1, 1, 2, 2, 2, 3, 3, 4, 5, 5, 6, 6, 7, 7, 8, 10, 11, 12, 21

The values 1 and 2 occur most often.

b. The mean and median both represent the data well. The modes are less than most of the data.

c. The number 21 is much greater than any other number. So, it is the outlier.

	Mean	Median	Mode(s)
With Outlier (part a)	5.85	5	1 and 2
Without Outlier	About 5.05	5	1 and 2

∴ The mean is affected the most by the outlier.

Exercises

Find the median and the mode(s) of the data.

4. 8, 8, 6, 8, 4, 5, 6

5. 24, 74, 61, 29, 38, 27, 68, 54

6. The lengths (in minutes) of several movies are shown below. (a) Find the mean, median, and mode of the lengths. (b) Which measure best represents the data? (c) Identify the outlier. Which measure does the outlier affect the most?

124, 92, 87, 144, 122, 228, 118, 101, 142, 91, 112, 144

9.3 Circle Graphs (pp. 334–341)

Favorite P.E. Activity	Students
Badminton	15
Volleyball	10
Kickball	25

a. Display the data in a circle graph.

Step 1: Find the angle measure for each section of the graph.

Badminton	***Volleyball***	***Kickball***
$\frac{15}{50} \cdot 360° = 108°$	$\frac{10}{50} \cdot 360° = 72°$	$\frac{25}{50} \cdot 360° = 180°$

Step 2: Use a protractor to draw the angle measures on a circle. Label the sections.

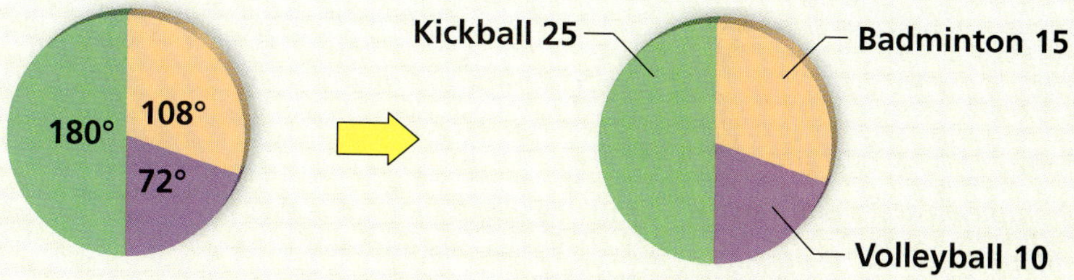

b. A survey asked students to name their favorite type of art. The results are shown in the circle graph. You survey 50 more students. How many can you expect to say *Virtual/Computer*?

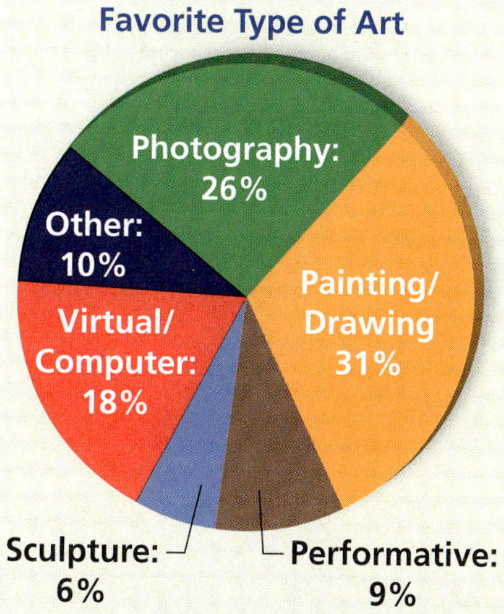

The circle graph shows that 18% of students surveyed said *Virtual/Computer*. To predict how many of the 50 additional students will say *Virtual/Computer*, find 18% of 50.

$18\% \text{ of } 50 = \frac{9}{50} \times 50$ — Write 18% as a fraction.

$= 9$ — Multiply.

So, you can expect 9 more students to say *Virtual/Computer.*

Exercises

Display the data in a circle graph.

7.

Singing Part	Students
Soprano	12
Alto	20
Tenor	18
Bass	10

8.

Candidate	Votes
Jon	60
Isabelle	35
Carmen	50
Ernesto	55

9. In part (b), you survey 200 more students. How many can you expect to say *Photography*?

Selected Answers

Section 1.1 Integers
(pages 6 and 7)

1. 8, −9, 22

3. *Sample answer:* below, under, lose

5.
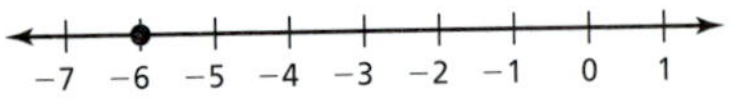

7.
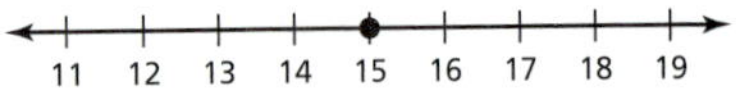

9. 37,500

11. −56

13. 5

15. −318

17.
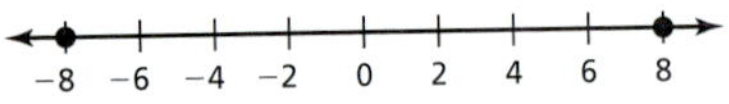

19.
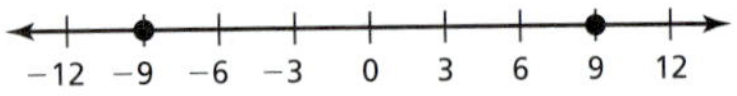

21.
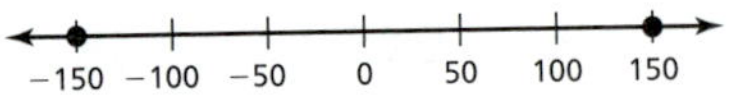

23.
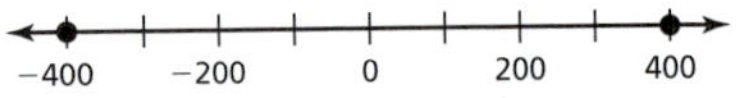

25.
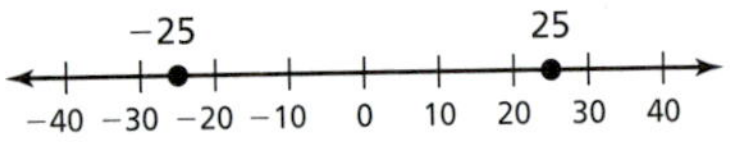

27. −8

29. 18

31. **a.** *Sample answer:* Choosing 8, the opposite is −8.

b. *Sample answer:* 8

c. The opposite of the opposite of an integer is the integer; Yes;
Sample answer:

Case 1:
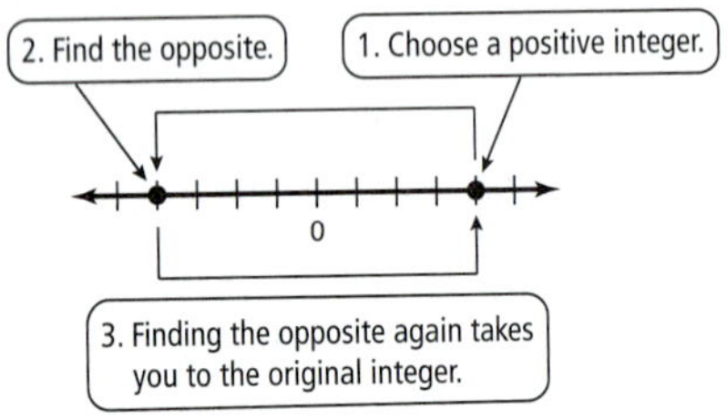

Case 2:
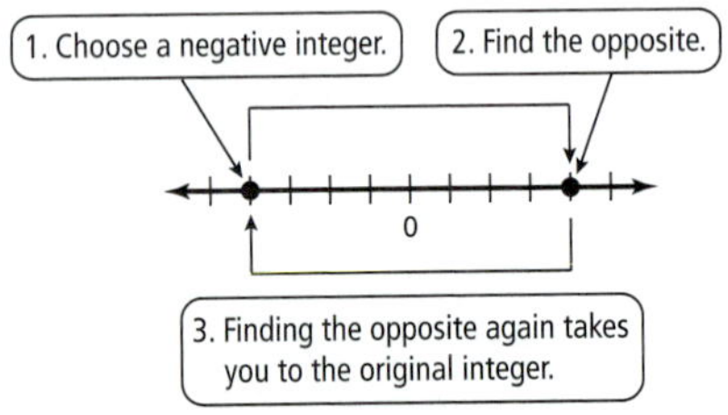

Case 3: Choose 0. The opposite of 0 is 0, so the opposite of the opposite of 0 is 0.

d. $-(-(-6))$ is the opposite of the opposite of −6; $-(-(-6)) = -6$

33. $\frac{3}{8}, \frac{1}{2}, \frac{3}{4}, \frac{7}{8}$

35. B

Section 1.2 Comparing and Ordering Integers
(pages 12 and 13)

1. On a number line, numbers to the left are less than numbers to the right. Numbers to the right are greater than numbers to the left.

3. The value of a is less than the value of b because a is to the left of b.

5. $<$

7. $>$

9. $>$

11. $>$

13. The explanation about where the integers are located on a number line is incorrect; $-7 < -3$; So, −7 is to the left of −3 on a number line.

15. −4, −3, −2, 1, 2

17. −7, −4, 2, 3, 6

19. −20, −10, −5, 15, 25

21. oxygen

23. always; The opposite of a positive integer is a negative integer. Positive integers are greater than negative integers.

25. **a.** Florida, Louisiana, Arkansas, Tennessee, California

b. California, Louisiana, Florida, Arkansas, Tennessee

c. An elevation of 0 feet represents sea level.

27. no; In order for the median to be below 0°F, at least 6 of the temperatures must be below 0°F.

29. 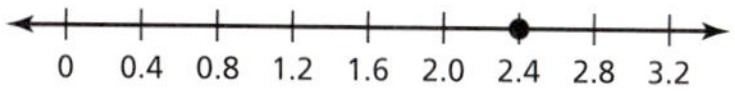

31. 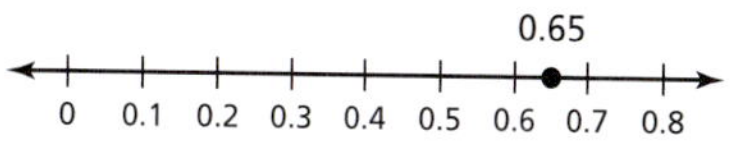

33. B

Section 1.3 Integers and Absolute Value

(pages 18 and 19)

1. 9, −1, 15

3. −6; All of the other expressions are equal to 6.

5. 6 7. 10 9. 13 11. 12 13. 8 15. 18

17. 45 19. 125 21. $|-4| < 7$ 23. $|-4| > -6$ 25. $|5| = |-5|$

27. Because $|-5| = 5$, the statement is incorrect; $|-5| > 4$

29. −8, 5

31. $-7, -6, |5|, |-6|, 8$

33. $-17, |-11|, |20|, 21, |-34|$

35. −4

37. **a.** 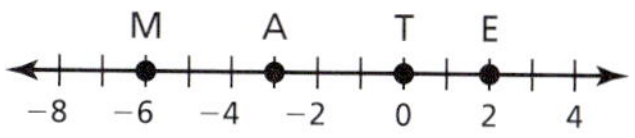

; MATE

b. 

; TEAM

39. $n \geq 0$

41. The number closer to 0 is the greater integer.

43. **a.** Player 3 **b.** Player 2 **c.** Player 1

45. false; The absolute value of zero is zero, which is neither positive nor negative.

47. 144

49. 3170

Section 1.4 The Coordinate Plane

(pages 25–27)

1. 4

3. (2, −3); (2, −3) is in Quadrant IV. The other three points are in Quadrant II.

5. (3, 1) 7. (−2, 4) 9. (2, −2) 11. (−4, 2) 13. (4, 0)

15–21. See graph below.

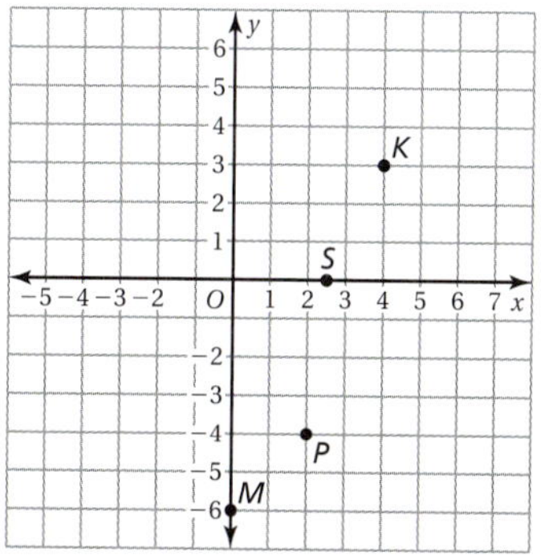

15. Quadrant I

17. y-axis

19. Quadrant IV

21. x-axis

Section 1.4 The Coordinate Plane *(continued)* *(pages 25–27)*

23. The numbers are reversed. To plot (4, 5), start at (0, 0) and move 4 units right and 5 units up.

25. 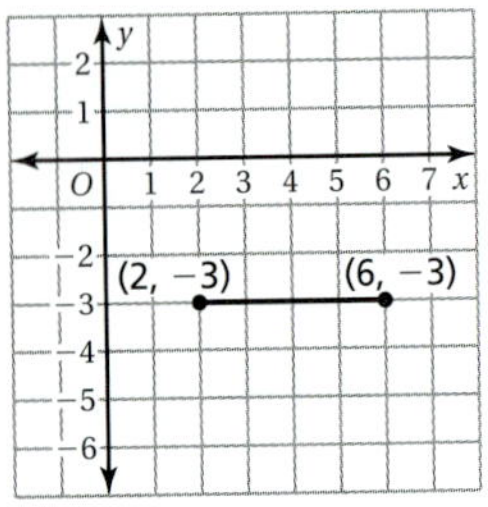

4

27. 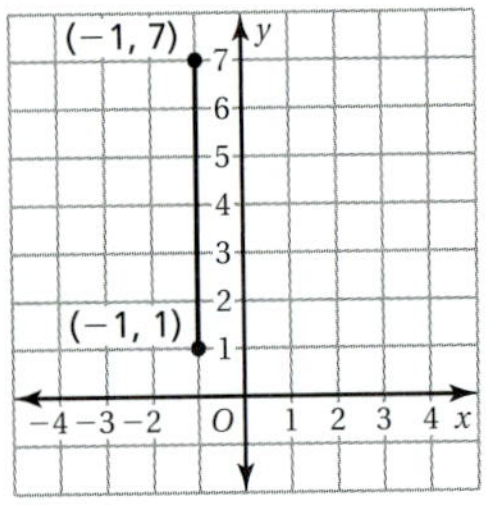

6

29. 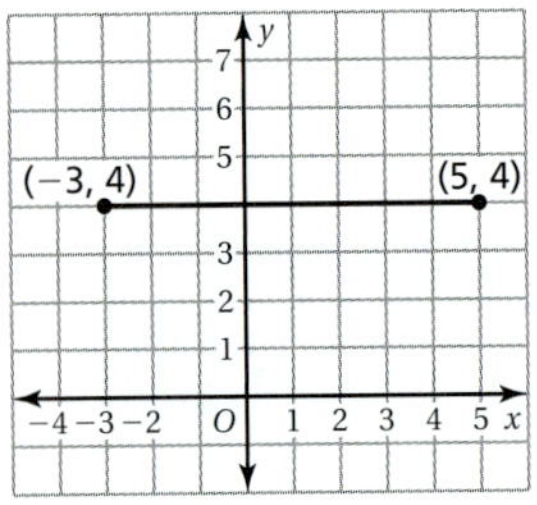

8

31. (−2, 1)

33. 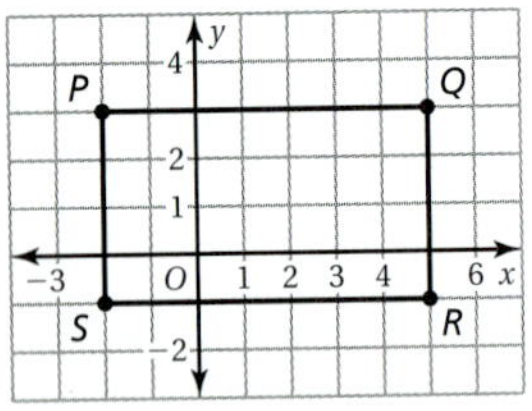

22 units; 28 units^2

35. a. about 142,000

b. 2011 and 2012

c. increase of about 10,000 people

37. a. 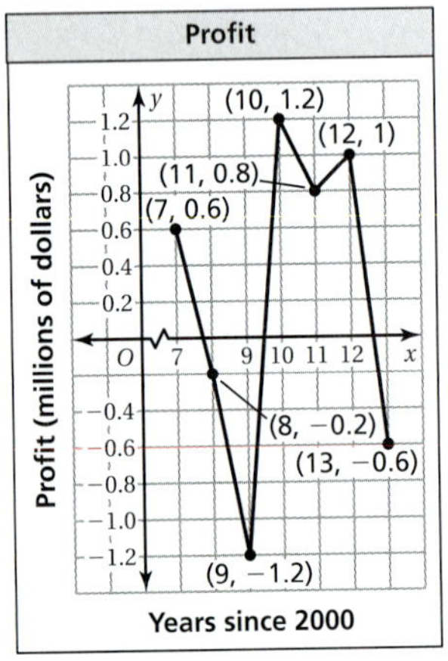

b. *Sample answer:* There are four years where the profit is positive and three years where the profit is negative. The profit decreased from 2007 to 2009. The profit increased the most from 2009 to 2010.

c. Because the x-axis represents the number of years since 2000, then 0 represents 2000. So, you could graph the profits for 1990 to 2006 by using x-values from −10 to 6.

39. Quadrant III

41. Quadrant I, Quadrant IV, or the positive x-axis

43. origin

45. never; All points in Quadrant III have negative y-coordinates.

47. Reptiles

49. no; Quadrants III or IV

51. Because (−8, −3) is in Quadrant III, consider exhibits in Quadrant III.

53. *Sample answer:* (−6, 3), (−2, 3), (−2, −9), (2, −9)

55. 34

57. 5

59. C

Section 2.1 Adding Integers

(pages 38 and 39)

1. Change the sign of the integer.

3. positive; 20 has the greater absolute value and is positive.

5. negative; The common sign is a negative sign.

7. false; A positive integer and its absolute value are equal, not opposites.

9. -10 **11.** 7 **13.** 0 **15.** 10

17. -4 **19.** -11 **21.** -4 **23.** -34

25. -10 and -10 are not opposites; $-10 + (-10) = -20$

27. $48

29. Use the Associative Property to add 13 and -13 first; -8

31. *Sample answer:* Use the Commutative Property to switch the last two terms; -12

33. *Sample answer:* Use the Commutative Property to switch the last two terms; 11

35. -27 **37.** 21 **39.** -85

41. *Sample answer:* $-26 + 1$; $-12 + (-13)$

43. -3 **45.** $d = -10$ **47.** $m = -7$

49. Find the number in each row or column that already has two numbers in it before guessing.

51. 8 **53.** 183

Section 2.2 Subtracting Integers

(pages 44 and 45)

1. You add the integer's opposite. **3.** What is 3 less than -2?; -5; 5

5. C **7.** B **9.** 13 **11.** -5

13. -10 **15.** 3 **17.** 17 **19.** 1

21. -22 **23.** -20 **25.** $-3 - 9$ **27.** 6

29. 9 **31.** 8 **33.** $m = 14$ **35.** $c = 15$

37. 2 **39.** 3

41. *Sample answer:* $x = -2, y = -1$; $x = -3, y = -2$

43. sometimes; It's positive only if the first integer is greater.

45. always; It's always positive because the first integer is always greater.

47. all values of a and b

49. when a and b have the same sign and $|a| \geq |b|$ or $b = 0$

51. -45 **53.** 468 **55.** 2378

Selected Answers

Section 2.3 Multiplying and Dividing Integers
(pages 50 and 51)

1. **a.** They are the same.

   b. They are different.

3. negative; different signs

5. negative; different signs

7. false; The product of the first two negative integers is positive. The product of the positive result and the third negative integer is negative.

9. -54

11. -88

13. -81

15. 0

17. -3

19. 6

21. 7

23. -10

25. 54

27. -700

29. 0

31. $-240{,}000$

33. -12 alligators/year

35. The quotient should be zero; $0 \div (-5) = 0$

37. $-8, 4$

39. **a.** 153; 141; 129

    b. The price drops \$12 every month.

    c. no; yes; In August, you have \$135 but the cost is \$141. In September, you have \$153 and the cost is only \$129.

41. 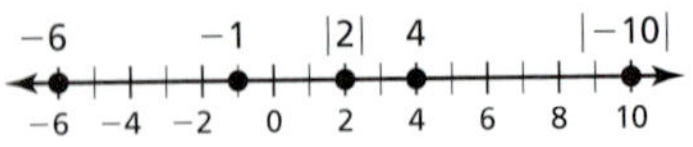

    $-6, -1, |2|, 4, |-10|$

43. 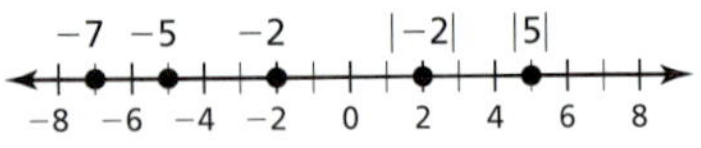

    $-7, -5, -2, |-2|, |5|$

Section 2.4 Powers and Exponents
(pages 56 and 57)

1. An exponent indicates the number of times the base is used as a factor. A power is the entire expression (base and exponent). A power is a product of repeated factors.

3. $3 + 3 + 3 + 3 = 3(4)$ does not belong because it shows a product as a sum of repeated addends, whereas the other three show powers as products of repeated factors.

5. 13^2

7. 2^5

9. 8^4

11. 7^6

13. The base is written as the exponent and the exponent is written as the base.
    $4 \cdot 4 \cdot 4 = 4^3$

15. 64

17. 1

19. 65,536

21. 1,419,857

23. 8,000,000 people

25. not a perfect square

27. perfect square

29. perfect square

31. not a perfect square

33. 40,000 cm^2

35. 8 squares

37.

Power	4^6	4^5	4^4	4^3	4^2	4^1
Value	4096	1024	256	64	16	4

As the exponent decreases, the value of the power is divided by 4; $4^0 = 1$

39. 13 blocks; add $7^2 - 6^2$ blocks; 19 blocks; add $10^2 - 9^2$ blocks; 39 blocks; add $20^2 - 19^2$ blocks

41. 165

43. 7

Section 2.5 Order of Operations
(pages 62 and 63)

1. Using the order of operations for $12 - 8 \div 2$, you divide 8 by 2 and then subtract the result from 12. Using the order of operations for $(12 - 8) \div 2$, you subtract 8 from 12 and then divide by 2.

3. 57
5. 2
7. -3
9. 24
11. -52
13. 2
15. Addition was performed before multiplication; $9 + (-2) \times 3 = 9 + (-6) = 3$
17. 8 pages
19. 17
21. -15
23. 47
25. 22 people
27. -2
29. $34
31. $23; Add the prices of the items you buy. Then subtract the amount of the gift card from the total.
33. **a.** $27 \div 3 + 5 \times 2 = 19$

    b. *Sample answer:* $9^2 + 11 - 8 \times 4 \div 1 = 60$

    c. $5 \times 6 - 15 + 9 = 24$

    d. $14 \times 2 \div 7 - 3 + 9 = 10$
35. 6.1
37. 0.9

Section 3.1 Adding Fractions and Mixed Numbers
(pages 74 and 75)

1. Use the LCD of 8 to rewrite the addition expression as $2\frac{7}{8} + \frac{6}{8}$. Then, add the whole numbers and add the fractions.
3. What is the distance between $4\frac{6}{7}$ and $\frac{3}{7}$?; $4\frac{3}{7}$; $5\frac{2}{7}$
5. $1\frac{4}{5}$
7. $\frac{13}{14}$
9. $8\frac{1}{12}$
11. $6\frac{17}{24}$
13. The whole numbers are not added; $2\frac{4}{9} + 2\frac{1}{3} = 2\frac{4}{9} + 2\frac{3}{9} = 4\frac{7}{9}$
15. $4\frac{1}{6}$ hours
17. 7
19. 1
21. Rewrite the fractions using the LCD. Then add the numerators and keep the denominators. Simplify if needed.
23. 2 feet
25. $5\frac{1}{2}$
27. Associative Property of Multiplication; -72
29. Commutative Property of Multiplication; $\frac{12}{35}$

Selected Answers

Section 3.2 Subtracting Fractions and Mixed Numbers
(pages 80 and 81)

1. Write the mixed number as an improper fraction. Rewrite the fractions using a common denominator. Then subtract the numerators to get $\frac{38}{15}$, or $2\frac{8}{15}$.

3. $\frac{1}{4}$
5. $1\frac{3}{5}$
7. $1\frac{19}{24}$
9. $3\frac{1}{3}$
11. $6\frac{7}{20}$
13. $3\frac{1}{4}$
15. $2\frac{11}{40}$
17. **a.** $\frac{5}{12}$ kilometer
    b. $\frac{5}{24}$ kilometer
19. $7\frac{5}{8}$
21. The difference is an integer when the two fraction parts are equivalent.
23. $1\frac{7}{8}$ miles
25. $8\frac{7}{30}$ inches
27. The difference is greater than 1 because the fraction part of the first mixed number is greater than the fraction part of the second mixed number.
29. 3, 10
31. 26
33. -16

Section 3.3 Multiplying Fractions and Mixed Numbers
(pages 87–89)

1. Multiply numerators and multiply denominators, then simplify the fraction.
3. *Sample answer:* $3\frac{1}{2} \times 3\frac{1}{7} = 11$
5. $\frac{5}{16}$
7. $\frac{3}{28}$
9. $\frac{5}{8}$
11. $\frac{1}{3}$
13. $5\frac{1}{4}$
15. $\frac{16}{45}$
17. $\frac{5}{27}$
19. $1\frac{19}{30}$
21. $\frac{3}{10}$
23. $\frac{4}{7} > \left(\frac{9}{10} \times \frac{4}{7}\right)$; Because $\frac{9}{10} < 1$, the product will be less than $\frac{4}{7}$.
25. $\frac{5}{6} = \left(\frac{5}{6} \times \frac{7}{7}\right)$; Because $\frac{7}{7} = 1$, by the Multiplication Property of One, the two expressions are equal.
27. 2
29. 2
31. 2
33. $1\frac{1}{2}$
35. $1\frac{3}{14}$
37. $36\frac{2}{3}$
39. $6\frac{4}{9}$
41. $11\frac{3}{8}$
43. You must first rewrite the mixed number as improper fractions and then multiply.

$$2\frac{1}{2} \times 7\frac{4}{5} = \frac{5}{2} \times \frac{39}{5} = \frac{\cancel{5}^{1} \times 39}{2 \times \cancel{5}_{1}} = \frac{39}{2}, \text{ or } 19\frac{1}{2}$$

45. **a.** 7 ft^2 **b.** $10\frac{1}{3}$ ft^2

47. $\frac{2}{15}$

49. $26\frac{2}{5}$

51. $\frac{9}{25}$

53. 462 in.^{2}

55. 4 mi

57. Which units of measure would make the calculations easier?

59. a. $\frac{3}{50}$ b. 45 people

61. $3^2 \cdot 5$

63. $2^2 \cdot 3 \cdot 5$

Section 3.4 Dividing Fractions
(pages 95–97)

1. *Sample answer:* $\frac{2}{5}, \frac{5}{2}$

3. B

5. A

7. $\frac{1}{8}$

9. $\frac{5}{2}$

11. $\frac{1}{2}$

13. 16

15. $\frac{1}{14}$

17. $\frac{1}{3}$

19. 3

21. $\frac{2}{27}$

23. $\frac{27}{28}$

25. $20\frac{1}{4}$

27. You need to invert the second fraction before you multiply.

$$\frac{4}{7} \div \frac{13}{28} = \frac{4}{7} \times \frac{28}{13} = \frac{4 \times \cancel{28}^{4}}{{}_{1}\cancel{7} \times 13} = \frac{16}{13}, \text{ or } 1\frac{3}{13}$$

29. Round $\frac{2}{5}$ to $\frac{1}{2}$ and $\frac{8}{9}$ to 1. $\frac{1}{2} \div 1 = \frac{1}{2}$, which is not close to the incorrect answer of $\frac{20}{9}$.

31. $5\frac{5}{8}$ times

33. yes

35. yes

37. $\frac{1}{3}$

39. >; When you divide a number by a fraction less than 1, the quotient is greater than the number.

41. >; When you divide a number by a fraction less than 1, the quotient is greater than the number.

43. $\frac{1}{216}$

45. $1\frac{1}{6}$

47. 2

49. $\frac{3}{26}$

51. $\frac{2}{3}$

53. $2\frac{2}{5}$ hours, or 2 hours 24 minutes

55. a. $3\frac{3}{4}$ times b. $3\frac{1}{3}$ times c. $\frac{1}{4}$

57. a. $67\frac{1}{5}$ gal b. $8\frac{2}{5}$ gal c. $33\frac{3}{5}$ gal

59. 6

61. 5

Section 3.5 Dividing Mixed Numbers
(pages 102 and 103)

1. $\frac{3}{22}$

3. sometimes; The reciprocal of $\frac{2}{2}$ is $\frac{2}{2}$, which is improper.

5. 3

7. $9\frac{3}{4}$

9. $3\frac{18}{19}$

11. $\frac{9}{10}$

13. $12\frac{1}{2}$

15. $1\frac{1}{5}$

17. $\frac{2}{7}$

19. $1\frac{5}{18}$

Section 3.5 Dividing Mixed Numbers *(continued)* *(pages 102 and 103)*

21. The mixed number $1\frac{2}{3}$ was not written as an improper fraction before inverting.

$3\frac{1}{2} \div 1\frac{2}{3} = \frac{7}{2} \div \frac{5}{3} = \frac{7}{2} \times \frac{3}{5} = \frac{7 \times 3}{2 \times 5} = \frac{21}{10}$, or $2\frac{1}{10}$

23. 14 hamburgers

25. no; The model shows $2\frac{1}{2} \div 1\frac{1}{6} = 2\frac{1}{7}$. There are 2 full groups of $1\frac{1}{6}$ plus one piece remaining, which represents $\frac{1}{7}$ of $1\frac{1}{6}$.

27. 4 **29.** $1\frac{1}{3}$ **31.** $5\frac{1}{6}$

33. $\frac{7}{54}$ **35.** $12\frac{1}{2}$ **37.** $\frac{22}{35}$

39. **a.** 6 ramps; *Sample answer:* The estimate is reasonable because $12\frac{1}{2}$ was rounded down.

b. 6 ramps; $1\frac{1}{4}$ feet left over

41. 0.43 **43.** 3.8 **45.** C

Section 4.1 Adding and Subtracting Decimals *(pages 114 and 115)*

1. Estimating allows you to check that your answer is reasonable.

3. $1.15 + 0.43 = 1.58$ **5.** 11.029 **7.** 22.899

9. 29.937 **11.** 1.46 **13.** 4.366 **15.** 2.644

17. Line up the decimal points before adding. Insert a 0 at the end of the second number so that both numbers have the same number of decimal places; $6.058 + 3.95 = 10.008$

19. \$8.30 **21.** 19.58 **23.** 10 **25.** 15.606

27. the decimal parts in the sum total 1; the decimal parts in the difference are exactly the same

29. 34.995 m **31.** 4.816 AU **33.** 20.189 AU **35.** 6.85 units

37. $\frac{1}{4}$ **39.** $\frac{1}{20}$

Section 4.2 Multiplying Decimals *(pages 121–123)*

1. Place the decimal point so that there are two decimal places; $1.2 \times 2.4 = 2.88$

3. 8.722 **5.** 19.5750 **7.** 4 **9.** 3.15

11. 0.21 **13.** 33.6 **15.** 115.04 **17.** 21.45

19. 13.888 **21.** 2.4 **23.** 0.0342

25. The decimal is in the wrong place; $0.0045 \times 9 = 0.0405$

27. 30.06 lb
29. 3 mm; 9 mm
31. 0.024
33. 0.000072
35. 0.03
37. 0.000012
39. 109.74
41. 3.886
43. 13.7104
45. 51.3156
47. \$3.24
49. \$1284.78

51. $7.12 \times 8.22 \times 100 = 7.12 \times 822 = 5852.64$

53. 137
55. 23.112
57. 71.984
59. 36.225

61. 2; 3; 4; There is one decimal place in each factor.

63. Each number is 0.1 times the previous number; 0.0015, 0.00015, 0.000015

65. Each number is 1.5 times the previous number; 25.3125, 37.96875, 56.953125

67. **a.** 190.06 mi

    b. 91.29 mi

69. Which framing is thicker?

71. 5
73. 7

Section 4.3 Dividing Decimals

(pages 129–131)

1. $4\overline{)2.44}$ with quotient 0.61
3. $6.38 \div 11 = 0.58$
5. $47\overline{)136}$
7. $216\overline{)1850}$
9. 13
11. 9
13. 6.7
15. 1.3
17. 9.4
19. 3.2
21. 0.098
23. 3.57

25. A zero should be placed before the 8 in the quotient.

$$\begin{array}{r} 0.086 \\ 6\overline{)0.516} \\ \underline{48} \\ 36 \\ \underline{36} \\ 0 \end{array}$$

27. the 5-ounce bottle; The price per ounce is \$2.06 for the 5-ounce bottle and \$2.12 for the 4-ounce bottle.

29. 1.62
31. 10.12
33. 8.046
35. \$26.96
37. 9
39. 0.08
41. 400
43. 460
45. about 1.33
47. about 12.21
49. 113 tickets
51. 850 songs
53. =
55. <

57. about 5357 bees

59. When dividing, make sure your units cancel.

61. $1\frac{1}{6}$
63. $\frac{1}{20}$

65. B

Section 4.4 Rational Numbers

(pages 136 and 137)

1. no; The denominator cannot be 0.

3. rational numbers, integers

5. rational numbers, integers, whole numbers

7. repeating

9. terminating

11. 0.875

13. $0.\overline{7}$

15. $1.8\overline{3}$

17. $5.58\overline{3}$

19. The bar should be over both digits to the right of the decimal point.

$\frac{7}{11} = 0.\overline{63}$

21. $\frac{9}{20}$

23. $\frac{39}{125}$

25. $1\frac{16}{25}$

27. $12\frac{81}{200}$

29. $0.8, 1.1, \frac{9}{5}, 2.5$

31. $\frac{6}{10}, \frac{5}{3}, 2.1, \frac{9}{4}$

33. $\frac{15}{10}, 1.6, 2.25, 2.4$

35. the robin's nest

37. $1.82 > 1.81$

39. $4\frac{6}{10} < 4.65$

41. $2\frac{13}{16} > 2\frac{11}{14}$

43. Michelle

45. no; The base of the skating pool is 10 feet deep, which is deeper than $9\frac{5}{6}$ feet.

47. **a.** when a is negative

b. when a and b have the same sign, $a \neq 0 \neq b$

49. $\frac{7}{30}$

51. 21.15

Section 4.5 Percents

(pages 142 and 143)

1. You can shade 42 out of 100 squares to model 42%.

3. *Sample answer:* $\frac{3}{20}, \frac{23}{100}, \frac{1}{8}$

5.

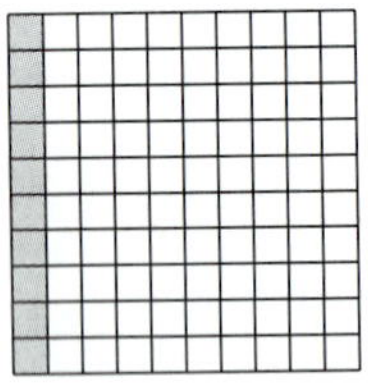

7.

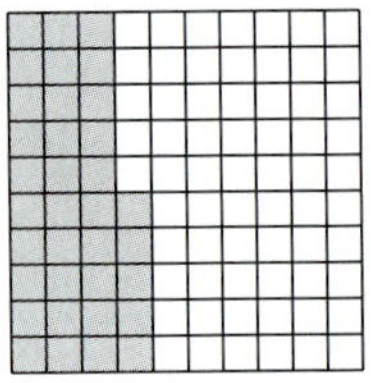

9. $\frac{9}{10}$

11. $\frac{7}{100}$

13. $\frac{79}{100}$

15. $1\frac{22}{25}$

17. $2\frac{6}{25}$

19. $\frac{1}{250}$

21. 10%

23. 55%

25. 54%

27. 185%

29. The decimal point should not have been added to the percent expression.

$\frac{14}{25} = \frac{14 \times 4}{25 \times 4} = \frac{56}{100} = 56\%$

31. $\frac{5}{4}$; No, you have more than you need.

33. 81.25%

35. 82.5%

37. Organize the percents and fractions in a table. What operation should you use to compare Illinois to Hawaii?

39. You can shade half of one of the squares.

41. $\frac{1}{2}$ **43.** 16 **45.** D

Section 4.6 Percents and Decimals *(pages 148 and 149)*

1. B **3.** C

5. *Sample answer:* 0.11, 0.13, 0.19

7. 0.78 **9.** 0.185 **11.** 0.33 **13.** 0.4763 **15.** 1.66 **17.** 0.0006

19. 74% **21.** 89% **23.** 99% **25.** 48.7% **27.** 368% **29.** 3.71%

31. The decimal point was moved in the wrong direction; 0.86 = 0.86 = 86%

33. 34% **35.** $\frac{9}{25} = 0.36$ **37.** $\frac{203}{1250} = 0.1624$ **39.** 40%

41. **a.** $16.\overline{6}\%$, or $16\frac{2}{3}\%$ **b.** $\frac{5}{6}$

43. $\frac{31}{100}$ **45.** $4\frac{8}{25}$ **47.** $|-6| = |6|$ **49.** $|-3| > |-1|$

Section 4.7 Comparing and Ordering Fractions, Decimals, and Percents *(pages 154 and 155)*

1.

$\frac{18}{25}$	0.72	72%
$\frac{17}{20}$	0.85	85%
$\frac{13}{50}$	0.26	26%
$\frac{31}{50}$	0.62	62%
$\frac{9}{20}$	0.45	45%

3. 0.04; 0.04 = 4%, but 40%, $\frac{2}{5}$, and 0.4 are all equal to 40%.

5. 20% **7.** $\frac{13}{25}$ **9.** 76% **11.** 0.12 **13.** 140% **15.** 80%

17.

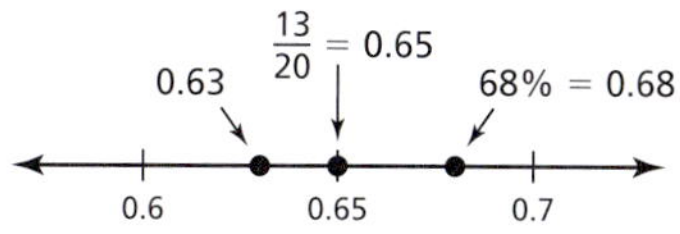

19.

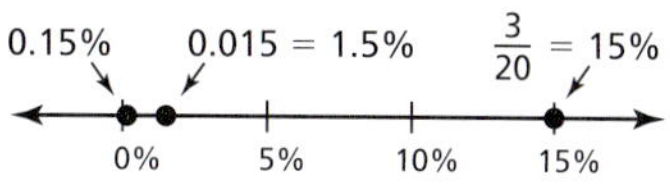

21.

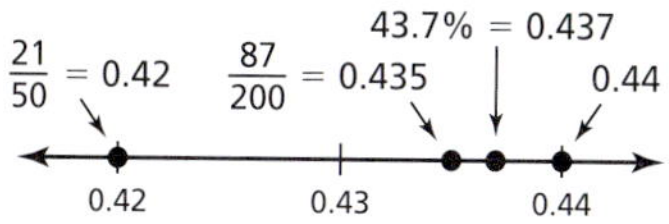

23. Russia, Brazil, United States, India **25.** 21%, $0.2\overline{1}$, $\frac{11}{50}$, $\frac{2}{9}$

27. *D* **29.** *C*

31. **a.** dolphin, rabbit, lion, squirrel, tiger **b.** About $\frac{1}{3}$ of the day $\left(\frac{8}{24}\text{ hours}\right)$ **c.** first

33. −15 **35.** 20

Section 5.1 Ratios
(pages 166 and 167)

1. consonants; For every 5 vowels there are 7 consonants, so consonants outnumber the vowels.

3. 2 out of every 5; This ratio is 2 : 3, all other ratios are 2 : 5.

5. 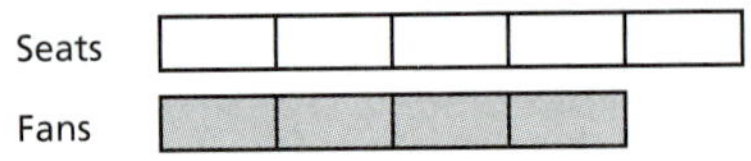

7. 6 to 4 or 6 : 4; For every 6 basketballs, there are 4 soccer balls.

9. 3 to 7 or 3 : 7; For every 3 shirts, there are 7 pants.

11. 8 to 15, 8 : 15, or $\frac{8}{15}$; 8 out of 15 movies are comedies.

13. 15 to 3 or 15 : 3; Out of 15 movies, 3 are dramas.

15. 9 h

17. 12 : 16

19. 6 black pieces; The ratio of black to red is 3 : 5, so each part is $16 \div 8 = 2$. So, there are $3 \cdot 2 = 6$ black pieces and $5 \cdot 2 = 10$ red pieces.

21. It may be helpful to organize your results in a table.

23. 4 pints of soda water, 8 pints of fruit punch concentrate, 20 pints of ginger ale; Yes; *Sample answer:* There is twice as much fruit punch as soda water (as in the original ratio). There is 5 times as much ginger ale as soda water (as in the original ratio).

25. 4.6

27. 2.53

29. B

Section 5.2 Ratio Tables
(pages 173–175)

1. Two ratios are equivalent if they can be written as the same ratio.

3. 12 : 15 does not belong because all other ratios are equivalent.

5. The ratio of ladybugs to bees can be described by 12 : 4, 6 : 2, or 3 : 1.

7.

Violins	8	24
Cellos	3	9

8 : 3 and 24 : 9

9.

Burgers	3	6	9
Hot Dogs	5	10	15

3 : 5, 6 : 10, and 9 : 15

11.

Forks	16	8	48
Spoons	10	5	30

16 : 10, 8 : 5, and 48 : 30

13.

You	3	6	9	12
Friend	4	8	12	16

16 tickets

15.

First	100	10	60
Second	60	6	36

$60

17. Adding the same number, 5 in this case, to each part of the ratio does not create equivalent ratios. You can add corresponding parts of equivalent ratios to create new equivalent ratios.

Sample answer:

A	3	6	9
B	7	14	21

19. 28 basketballs

21. Add the corresponding quantities of Recipes B and D to create Recipe E.

23. Subtract the corresponding quantities of Recipe B from Recipe C to create Recipe A.

25. *Sample answer:* Add the corresponding quantities of Recipes B and F to create a batch with 11 servings.

27. $A = 16, B = 28$

29. $A = 65, B = 40$

31. 32

33. 36 bugs

35. 27

37. 14

Section 5.3 Rates
(pages 180 and 181)

1. *Sample answer:* You walk at a rate of 2 blocks per minute, so you walk 12 blocks in 6 minutes.

3. *Sample answer:* 45 words for every 30 minutes

5. *Sample answer:* 4 inches for every 12 years

7. \$7 per week

9. 45 miles per hour

11. 110 calories per second

13. 100 times per second

15. 30 minutes

17.

Weight (pounds)	4	0.25	10	5.625
Cost (dollars)	16	1	40	22.5

0.25 pound per dollar

19. **a.** \$112.50

b.

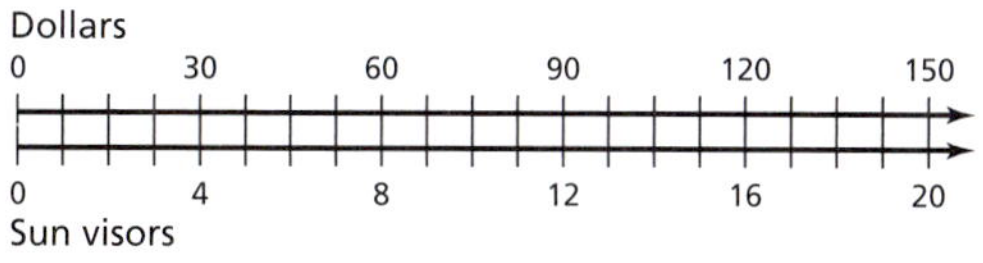

\$120

21. **a.** about 0.12 mile per minute

b. about 8.0 minutes per mile

c. The runner is talking about the rate in part (b) because "10-minute miles" is a way of talking about the rate in minutes per mile.

23. *Sample answer:* $\frac{2}{6}, \frac{3}{9}$

25. *Sample answer:* $\frac{4}{10}, \frac{8}{20}$

27. B

Section 5.4 Comparing and Graphing Ratios
(pages 186 and 187)

1. Use ratio tables to write equivalent ratios where one part from each ratio has the same numerical value. Compare the other part.

3. A

5. B

7. A

9. B

11. the first recipe

13.

Zoo	
People	**Cost (dollars)**
4	60
8	120
12	180
16	240

Museum	
People	**Cost (dollars)**
5	95
10	190
15	285
20	380

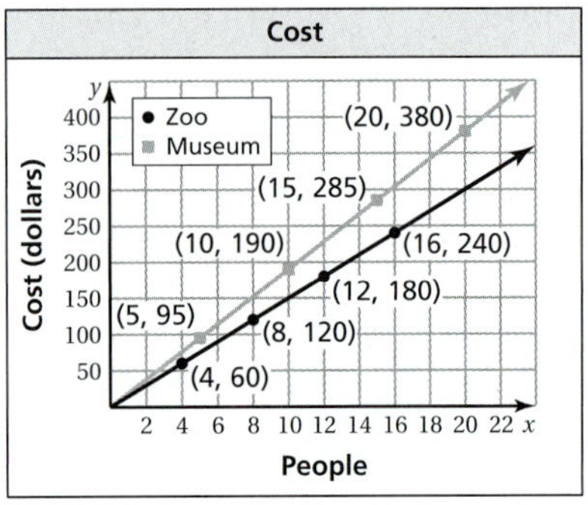

Both graphs begin at (0, 0). The graph for the museum is steeper, so the cost to attend the museum is greater than the cost to attend the zoo.

15. Begin by using double number lines to represent the situations.

17. **a.** *Sample answer:*

Old Mixture														
	Peanuts	7	14	21	28	35	42	49	56	63	70	77	84	91
	Almonds	4	8	12	16	20	24	28	32	36	40	44	48	52
	Total	11	22	33	44	55	66	77	88	99	110	121	132	**143**

New Mixture												
	Peanuts	8	16	24	32	40	48	56	64	72	80	88
	Almonds	5	10	15	20	25	30	35	40	45	50	55
	Total	13	26	39	52	65	78	91	104	117	130	**143**

143 nuts

b.

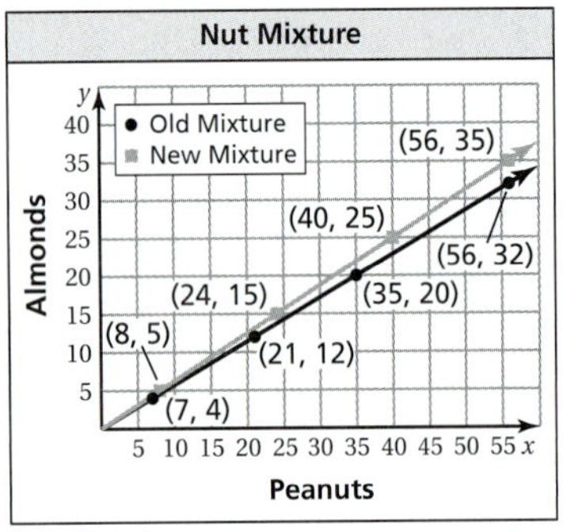

Both graphs begin at (0, 0). The graph for the new mixture is slightly steeper, so it has a greater concentration of almonds.

c. more; Almonds cost more and there are more of them in the new mixture than in the old mixture.

19. 16

21. 34 R109

Section 5.5 Proportions
(pages 192 and 193)

1. Both ratios are equal.

3. yes **5.** no **7.** yes **9.** no **11.** no

13. The number of calories is proportional to the number of servings. To find the number of calories, multiply the number of servings by 150.

15. no **17.** yes

19. yes; Both can do 45 sit-ups per minute.

21. yes **23.** yes

25. yes; The ratio of height to base for both triangles is $\frac{4}{5}$.

27. Add 2 quarts of yellow.

29. no; The ratios are not equivalent; $\frac{13}{19} \neq \frac{14}{20} \neq \frac{15}{21}$ etc.

31. -13 **33.** -18 **35.** D

Extension 5.5 Graphing Proportional Relationships
(pages 194 and 195)

1.

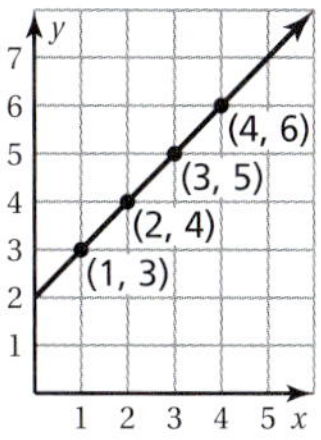

no

3. (0, 0): You earn \$0 for working 0 hours.

(1, 15): You earn \$15 for working 1 hour; unit rate: $\frac{\$15}{1\text{ h}}$

(4, 60): You earn \$60 for working 4 hours; unit rate: $\frac{\$60}{4\text{ h}} = \frac{\$15}{1\text{ h}}$

5. yes; 5 ft/h

7. $y = \frac{4}{3}$

Section 6.1 Algebraic Expressions
(pages 207–209)

1. $3(4) + 5$ does not belong because it is a numerical expression and the other three are algebraic expressions.

3. decrease; When you subtract greater and greater values from 20, you will have less and less left.

5. \$120 **7.** \$8

9. Terms: g, 12, $9g$
Coefficients: 1, 9
Constant: 12

11. Terms: $2m^2$, 15, $2p^2$
Coefficients: 2, 2
Constant: 15

13. Terms: $8x$, $\frac{x^2}{3}$
Coefficients: 8, $\frac{1}{3}$
Constant: none

15. **a.** Terms: 2ℓ, $2w$; Coefficients: 2, 2: Constant: none

b. The coefficient 2 of ℓ represents that there are 2 lengths on the rectangle. The coefficient 2 of w represents that there are 2 widths on the rectangle.

Section 6.1 Algebraic Expressions *(continued)* *(pages 207–209)*

17. g^5 **19.** $5.2y^3$ **21.** $2.1xz^4$ **23.** $25d^2$ **25.** 9

27. 11 **29.** 10 **31.** 6 **33.** 5 **35.** 4

37. Multiplication should be done first, then addition.

$5m + 3 = 5 \cdot 8 + 3 = 40 + 3 = 43$

39. 34 mm; 118 mm

41.

x	2	4	8
$64 \div x$	32	16	8

43. 23 **45.** $2\frac{5}{6}$ **47.** 22 **49.** 46 **51.** 24

53. Start by drawing a visual image of moving 2000 feet in exactly 10 minutes.

55. 64 in.^3 **57.** 512 **59.** 256

Section 6.2 Writing Expressions *(pages 214 and 215)*

1. x take away 12; $x - 12$; $x + 12$

3. $8 - 5$ **5.** $28 \div 7$

7. $-18 - 3$ **9.** $x - 13$ **11.** $18 \div a$

13. $-7 + w$ or $w + (-7)$ **15.** $y + (-4)$ or $-4 + y$ **17.** $2 \cdot z$ or $z \cdot 2$

19. The expression is not written in the correct order; $\frac{8}{y}$

21. **a.** $x \div 5$

b. *Sample answer:* If the total cost is \$30, then the cost per person is $x \div 5 = 30 \div 5 = \$6$. The result is reasonable.

23. *Sample answer:* The sum of n and 6; 6 more than a number n

25. *Sample answer:* A number b less than -15; -15 take away a number b

27. $\frac{y}{4} - 3$; 2 **29.** $-8x + 6$; 46

31. **a.**

Game	1	2	3	4	5
Cost	\$5	\$8	\$11	\$14	\$17

b. $2 + 3g$

c. \$26

33. It might help to see the pattern if you make a table of the data in the bar graph.

35. $\frac{x}{4}$ **37.** 59 **39.** 140

Section 6.3 Properties of Addition and Multiplication

(pages 220 and 221)

1. *Sample answer:* $\frac{1}{5} + \frac{3}{5} = \frac{3}{5} + \frac{1}{5}$

$\frac{4}{5} = \frac{4}{5}$

3. *Sample answer:* $(5 \cdot x) \cdot 1 = 5 \cdot (x \cdot 1)$

$= 5x$

5. Comm. Prop. of Mult.

7. Assoc. Prop. of Mult.

9. Add. Prop. of Zero

11. The grouping of the numbers did not change. The statement illustrates the Commutative Property of Addition because the order of the addends changed.

13.

$(14 + y) + 3 = (y + 14) + 3$	Comm. Prop. of Add.
$= y + (14 + 3)$	Assoc. Prop. of Add.
$= y + 17$	Add 14 and 3.

15.

$-7(9w) = (-7 \cdot 9)w$	Assoc. Prop. of Mult.
$= -63w$	Multiply −7 and 9.

17. $-8 + (a + 0) = -8 + a$ Add. Prop. of Zero

19.

$(18.6 \cdot d) \cdot 1 = 18.6 \cdot (d \cdot 1)$	Assoc. Prop. of Mult.
$= 18.6d$	Mult. Prop. of One

21.

$(2.4 + 4n) + 9 = (4n + 2.4) + 9$	Comm. Prop. of Add.
$= 4n + (2.4 + 9)$	Assoc. Prop. of Add.
$= 4n + 11.4$	Add 2.4 and 9.

23.

$z \cdot 0 \cdot (-12) = (z \cdot 0) \cdot (-12)$	Assoc. Prop. of Mult.
$= 0 \cdot (-12)$	Mult. Prop. of Zero
$= 0$	Mult. Prop. of Zero

25. **a.** x represents the cost of a box of cookies. **b.** $120x$

27. $7 + (x + 5) = x + 12$

29. $(7 \cdot 2) \cdot y$

31. $(-17 + 6) + 2x$

33. $w \cdot 16$

35. 98

37. 90

39. 37 is already prime.

41. 3×7^2

43. B

Section 6.4 The Distributive Property

(pages 227–229)

1. *Sample answer:* You must distribute or give the number outside the parentheses to the numbers inside the parentheses.

3. $4 + (x \cdot 4)$ does not belong because it does not represent the Distributive Property.

5. 63

7. −516

9. 936

11. −504

13. $\frac{4}{7}$

15. $2\frac{1}{2}$

17. $3x + 12$

19. $6s - 54$

21. $-96 - 8a$

23. $72 - 12k$

25. $63 + 9c$

27. $-40g - 24$

29. $-4x - 4y$

31. $7p + 7q + 63$

33. The 6 was not distributed to the 8 inside the parentheses; $6(y + 8) = 6y + 48$

35. $5(r + 15)$ and $5r + 5 \cdot 15$, because they are equivalent expressions.

Section 6.4 The Distributive Property *(continued)* *(pages 227–229)*

37. $16(10 + x) = 160 + 16x$

39. $6x + 25$

41. $-44 - 28k$

43. $19y + 5$

45. $3d + 1$

47. $5v$

49. $2.7w - 14.04$

51. $\frac{11}{4}z + \frac{3}{10}$

53. $x + 6y$

55. $x = 8$

57. $x = 3$

59. Area: $8x + 64$
Perimeter: $2x + 32$

61. Area: $9x + 108$
Perimeter: $2x + 42$

63. **a.** 6.2 **b.** 14

Sample answer: The preferred method is not the same for both expressions.
For part (a), evaluating inside the parentheses first requires easier and less calculations.
For part (b), using the Distributive Property will eliminate the fractions.

65. $7(x + 3) + 8 \cdot x + 3 \cdot x + 8 - 9 = 2(9x + 10)$

67. 34.006

69. 0.387

Section 7.1 Writing Equations in One Variable *(pages 240 and 241)*

1. An equation has an equal sign and an expression does not.

3. *Sample answer:* A number n subtracted from 28 is 5.

5. What was the high temperature if it was 4° less than 62°F? 58°F

7. $y - 9 = 8$

9. $w \div 5 = 6$

11. $-5 = \frac{1}{4}c$

13. $n - 9 = 27$

15. $6042 = 1780 + a$

17. $16 = 3x$

19. $326 = 12(14) + 6(5) + 16x$

21. It might be helpful to organize the given information visually.

23. 13

25. 28

27. B

Section 7.2 Solving Equations Using Addition or Subtraction *(pages 247–249)*

1. Substitute your solution back into the original equation and see if you obtain a true statement.

3. subtraction

5. so that x is by itself; so that the two sides remain equal

7. yes

9. no

11. yes

13. $t = 1$

15. What number plus 5 equals 12?; $a = 7$

17. 20 is what number minus 6?; $d = 26$

19. $z = -10$

21. $p = 3$

23. $h = 34$

25. $q = 11$

27. $x = -13$

29. $a = 12$

31. They must apply the same operations to both sides.

$$\begin{aligned} 34 &= y - 12 \\ +12 &\quad\ +12 \\ 46 &= y \end{aligned}$$

33. $x - 8 = 16$; 24th floor

35. Subtract 3 from each side. (Subtraction Property of Equality); Subtract 3 from 3. (Subtract.); Add x and 0. (Addition Property of Zero)

37. $k + 7 = -34$; $k = -41$

39. $93 = g + 58$; $g = 35$

41. $y = -21$

43. $v = 28$

45. $d = 54$

47. $x + 34 + 34 + 16 = 132$; 48 in.

49. Addition is commutative.

51. Begin by writing the characteristics of each problem.

53. $x + 15 + 8 = 55$; \$32

55. **a.** \$12

b. no; You have \$12 left and it costs \$13 to ride each ride once.

57. 96

59. 5

61. A

Section 7.3 Solving Equations Using Multiplication or Division *(pages 254 and 255)*

1. 12

3. $\frac{4x}{4} = \frac{24}{4}$

5. $8 \cdot 3 = (n \div 3) \cdot 3$

7. $s = 70$

9. $x = -120$

11. $a = 4$

13. $y = 10$

15. $x = 15$

17. $d = 78$

19. $c = 45$

21. $n = \frac{1}{2}$

23. They should have multiplied by 4.

$$\begin{aligned} x \div 4 &= 28 \\ (x \div 4) \cdot 4 &= 28 \cdot 4 \\ x &= 112 \end{aligned}$$

25. $3x = 45$; 15 items

27. 9 units

29. 9 units

31. 20 cards

33. $x = 6$; Because $5x$ is on both sides of the equation, $3x$ must be equal to 18 so that the equation is true.

35. length: 20 in.; width: 5 in.

37. $\frac{t}{3} = 7$

Section 7.4 Writing and Graphing Inequalities *(pages 261–263)*

1. Both phrases refer to numbers that are greater than a given number. The difference is that "greater than or equal to" includes the number itself, whereas "greater than" does not.

3. The graph of $x \leq 6$ has a closed circle at 6. The graph of $x < 6$ has an open circle at 6.

5. $k < 10$

7. $z < \frac{3}{4}$

9. $1 + y \leq -13$

Section 7.4 Writing and Graphing Inequalities *(continued)* *(pages 261–263)*

11. yes **13.** yes **15.** no **17.** B **19.** D

21. $x < 1$; A number x is less than 1. **23.** $x \geq -4$; A number x is at least -4.

25. 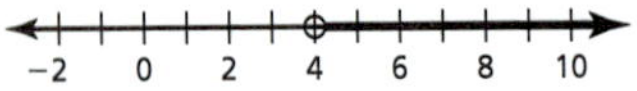

27. 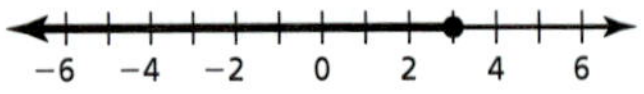

29. 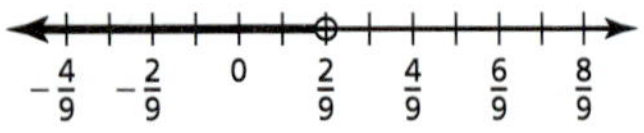

31. 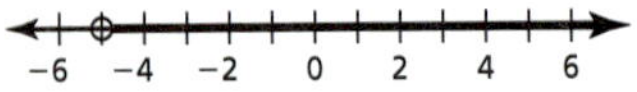

33. 

35. 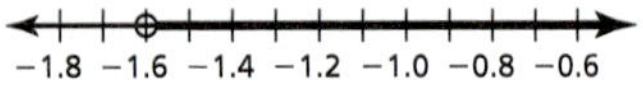

37. $x \geq 1$ means that 1 is also a solution, so a closed circle should be used.

39. **a.** $b \leq 3$; 

b. $\ell \geq 18$; 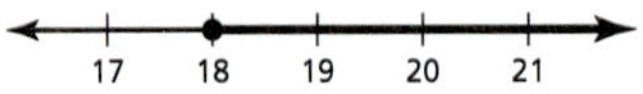

41. The cost of the necklace and another item should be less than or equal to \$33.

43. sometimes; The only time this is not true is if $x = 5$.

45. $p \leq 375$ **47.** $x = 9$

49. $x = 28$ **51.** D

Section 7.5 Solving Inequalities Using Addition or Subtraction *(pages 268 and 269)*

1. *Sample answer:* $x + 7 \geq 143$

3. By solving the inequality to obtain $x \leq 1$, the graph has a closed circle at 1 and an arrow pointing in the negative direction.

5. $x < 1$;

7. $5 \geq y$;

9. $6 > x$;

11. $y < 106$;

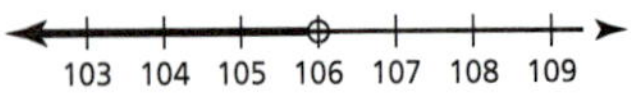

13. $-7 < x$;

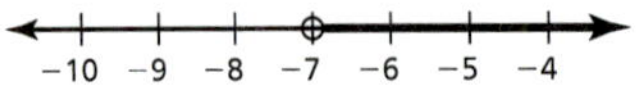

15. $3 \leq n$;

17. To solve the inequality, 9 should be added to both sides, not subtracted.

$$\begin{array}{rcl} 28 & \geq & t - 9 \\ +9 & & +9 \\ \hline 37 & \geq & t \end{array}$$

19. $x + 19 \leq 24$; $x \leq \$5$

21. $x - 3 > 15$; $x > 18$

23. $11 > s$; 

25. $34{,}280 + d + 1000 > 36{,}480$; $d > 1200$ dragonflies

27. The estimate for running a mile should be greater than 4 minutes, because the world record is under 4 minutes.

29. $t = 48$ **31.** $x = 9$ **33.** C

Section 8.1 Regular Polygons and Symmetry
(pages 280 and 281)

1. 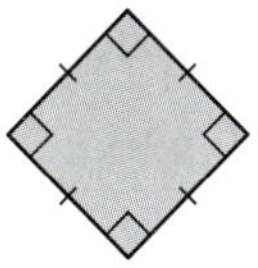

3. false; A rhombus does not always have all congruent interior angles.

5. true; n-sided regular polygons have n lines of symmetry.

7. yes

9. no

11. no

13. no

15. no

17. no

19. 135°

21. 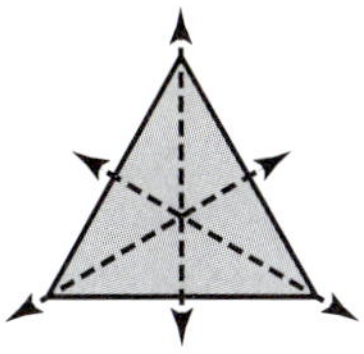

23. 

25. 

27. yes; The interior angles of a rectangle are congruent, all 90°, so both the sides and the angles are congruent.

29. no; The sides are not all congruent.

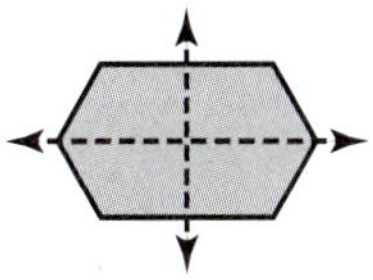

31. $\frac{2}{7}$

33. 17.15

35. C

Section 8.2 Congruent Figures
(pages 286 and 287)

1. **a.** $\angle A$ and $\angle D$, $\angle B$ and $\angle E$, $\angle C$ and $\angle F$

   b. Side AB and Side DE, Side BC and Side EF, Side AC and Side DF

3. $\angle V$ does not belong. The other three angles are congruent to each other, but not to $\angle V$.

5. congruent

7. $\angle P$ and $\angle W$, $\angle Q$ and $\angle V$, $\angle R$ and $\angle Z$, $\angle S$ and $\angle Y$, $\angle T$ and $\angle X$; Side PQ and Side WV, Side QR and Side VZ, Side RS and Side ZY, Side ST and Side YX, Side TP and Side XW

9. not congruent; Corresponding sides are not congruent.

11. The corresponding angles are not congruent, so the two figures are not congruent.

Section 8.2 Congruent Figures *(continued)*

(pages 286 and 287)

13. *Sample answers:*

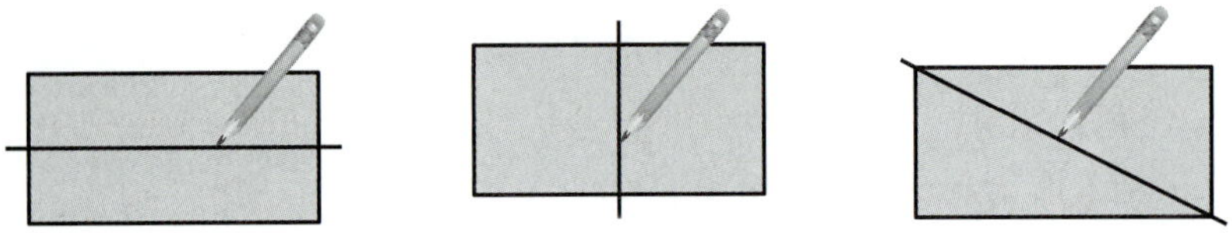

15. **a.** true; Side AB corresponds to Side YZ.

b. true; $\angle A$ and $\angle X$ have the same measure.

c. false; $\angle A$ corresponds to $\angle Y$.

d. true; The measure of $\angle A$ is 90°, the measure of $\angle B$ is 140°, the measure of $\angle C$ is 40°, and the measure of $\angle D$ is 90°. So, the sum of the angle measures of $ABCD$ is $90° + 140° + 40° + 90° = 360°$.

17 and 19.

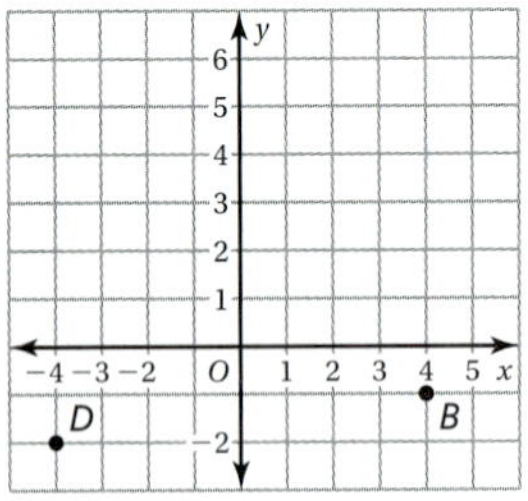

Section 8.3 Perimeters of Rectangles and Triangles

(pages 292 and 293)

1. Find the sum of the side lengths.

3. 24 cm

5. $46\frac{1}{2}$ in.

7. 20 in.

9. 56 yd

11. 30.4 cm

13. 12 ft; Each side of an equilateral triangle has the same length, and 36 divided by 3 is 12.

15. 60 m

17. 24 ft

19. Store B; Fencing is less expensive ($10 per foot); $1650

21. $2x + 6$

23. $7w - 7$

25. D

Section 8.4 Areas of Rectangles and Triangles

(pages 298 and 299)

1. *Sample answer:* length: 9 ft, width: 4 ft; length: 12 ft, width: 3 ft

3. 40 ft^2

5. 3750 mm^2

7. 189 mm^2

9. 90 mi^2

11. 132 m^2

13. 92 ft^2

15. *Sample answer:*

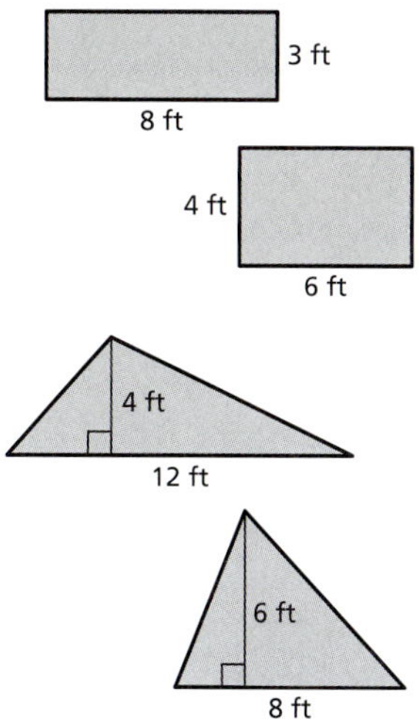

17. x^2 times greater

19. 4 times greater

21. Mult. Prop. of One

23. Assoc. Prop. of Add.

Section 8.5 Circles and Circumference
(pages 305–307)

1. The radius is one-half the diameter.

3. 2.5 cm

5. $1\frac{3}{4}$ in.

7. 4 in.

9. about 31.4 in.

11. about 56.52 in.

13. **a.** about 25 m; about 50 m **b.** about 2 times greater

15. about 7.71 ft

17. about 31.4 cm; about 62.8 cm

19. about 69.08 m; about 138.16 m

21. about 200.96 cm

23. Draw a diagram of the given information.

25. **a.** about 254.34 mm; First find the length of the minute hand. Then find $\frac{3}{4}$ of the circumference of a circle whose radius is the length of the minute hand.

    b. about 320.28 mm; Subtract $\frac{1}{12}$ the circumference of a circle whose radius is the length of the hour hand from the circumference of a circle whose radius is the length of the minute hand.

27. 20 m

29. D

Section 8.6 Areas of Circles
(pages 312 and 313)

1. Divide the diameter by 2 to get the radius. Then use the formula $A = \pi r^2$ to find the area.

3. about 254.34 mm^2

5. about 314 in.^{2}

7. about 3.14 cm^2

9. about 2461.76 mm^2

11. about 113.04 in.^{2}

13. about 628 cm^2

15. about 1.57 ft^2

17. What fraction of the circle is the dog's running area?

Section 8.6 Areas of Circles *(continued)*

(pages 312 and 313)

19. about 9.8125 in.^{2}; The two regions are identical, so find one-half the area of the circle.

21. about 4.56 ft^2; Find the area of the shaded regions by subtracting the areas of both unshaded regions from the area of the quarter-circle containing them. The area of each unshaded region can be found by subtracting the area of the smaller shaded region from the semicircle. The area of the smaller shaded region can be found by drawing a square about the region.

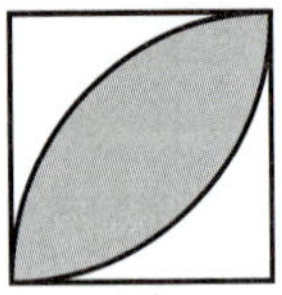

Subtract the area of a quarter-circle from the area of the square to find an unshaded area. Then subtract both unshaded areas from the square's area to find the shaded region's area.

23. 53

25. D

Section 9.1 Mean

(pages 324 and 325)

1. Add the data values then divide by the number of data values.

3. yes; Because of the variability of the answers to a statistical question, the mean gives an average of the answers. That way, you can use only one value, the mean, to answer the statistical question.

5. 1 movie seen this week; Find the total number of movies and divide by the number of people.

7. 3 brothers and sisters

9. 16 visits

11. **a.** yes; There will be variability in the lengths of the commercial breaks.

b. 3.45 minutes

13. *Sample answer:* 20, 21, 21, 21, 21, 22; 20, 20.5, 20.5, 21.5, 21.5, 22

15. 3.9 inches; No, neither team has a height that is much shorter or taller than the other heights. So, you can say that the Tigers are taller than the Dolphins on average.

17. There are 5 different allowance amounts and 24 students. Each amount is used more than once.

19. 9

21. 18.5

23. B

Section 9.2 Measures of Center

(pages 331–333)

1. *Sample answer:* 1, 2, 3, 4, 5, 6

3. outlier; The other three are measures of center.

5. 5.5

7. median: 7; mode: 3

9. median: 92.5; mode: 94

11. median: 17; mode: 12

13. The data were not ordered from least to greatest; The median is 55. 49, 50, 51, 55, 58, 59, 63

15. singing

17. mean: 35.875; median: 44; mode: 48
Sample answer: The median is probably best, because it is close to most of the data. The mean is less than most of the data and the mode is the greatest value.

19. mean: 12; median: 8; mode: 2
Sample answer: The median is the best measure, because the mean is greater than most of the data and the mode is the least value.

21.

With Outlier	*Without Outlier*
mean: 48.5	mean: 53
median: 53	median: 54
mode: none	mode: none

The outlier reduces the median slightly, but reduces the mean more. There is no mode with or without the outlier.

23. mean: 7.61; median: 7.42; no mode

25. **a.** mean: 94°F; median: 91°F; mode: 91°F
Sample answer: Both the median and mode are the best measures for the data, because both are very close to most of the values.

b. mean: 77°F; median: 77°F; modes: 77°F and 78°F
Sample answer: Both the mean and median are the best measures for the data, because there are two modes.

27. 10 hours; Using the mean as the average, you would need to work 12 hours. Using the median as the average, you would need to work 10 or more hours. Using the mode as the average, you would need to work 10 hours. So, the minimum number of hours is 10 and you can use the median or mode to justify your answer.

29. Ordering the data makes it easier to find the median and the mode.

31. **a.** mean: $1794; median: $1790; mode: $1940

b. mean: $1883.70; median: $1879.50; mode: $2037
The mean, median, and mode all increased by 5%.

c. annual salaries: $23,280, $19,920, $22,320, $25,200, $20,640, $18,480, $21,120, $23,280, $21,840, $19,200; mean: $21,528; median: $21,480; mode: $23,280; They are 12 times the mean, median, and mode of the monthly salary.

33. 13

35. 119

37. D

Section 9.3 Circle Graphs

(pages 339–341)

1. Multiply the decimal form of each percent by 360° to find the angle measure for each section.

3. $\frac{1}{2}$ does not belong because it does not represent an entire circle.

5. orange

7. 20 students

9. 54°

11. 10.8°

Circle Graphs *(continued)*

(pages 339–341)

13.

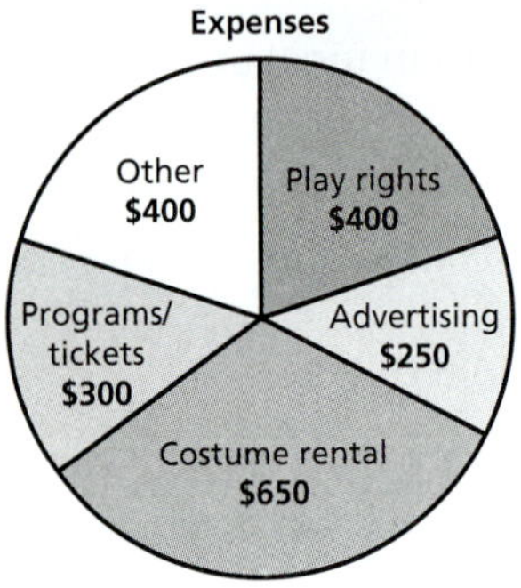

15. 10 pets

17. The time is 15 minutes before 3:00 or 2:45. "A quarter to" is short for "a quarter of an hour before," and a quarter $\left(\frac{1}{4}\right)$ of an hour is 15 minutes.

19. **a.**

b. Answers will vary. *Sample answer:* Use a line plot when you want to show the number of times each value occurs in a data set. Use a circle graph when you want to show a percent of the total.

21.

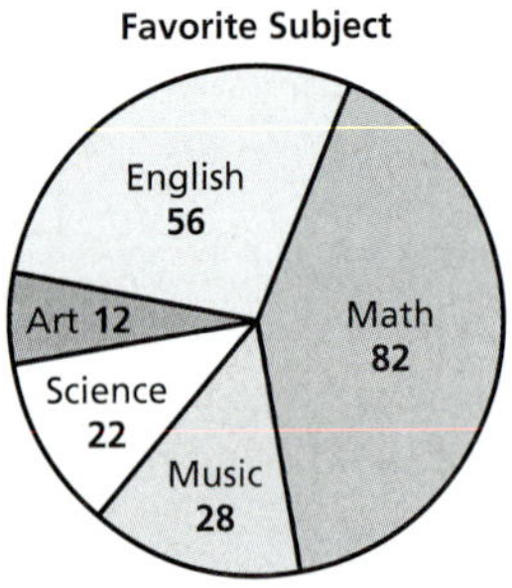

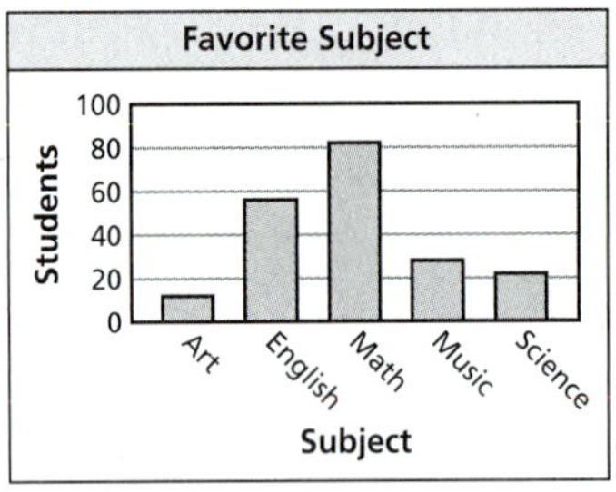

Sample answer: The circle graph better represents the data because it allows you to easily compare categories of data as well as compare a category of data to all of the data. With the bar graph, you can compare categories of data but it is difficult to compare a category of data to all of the data.

23. **a.**

	U.S.	Mexico	Canada	Other
Area	3.72	0.76	3.85	1.12
Percent	39.4%	8.0%	40.7%	11.9%
Angle	140°	30°	145°	45°

b.

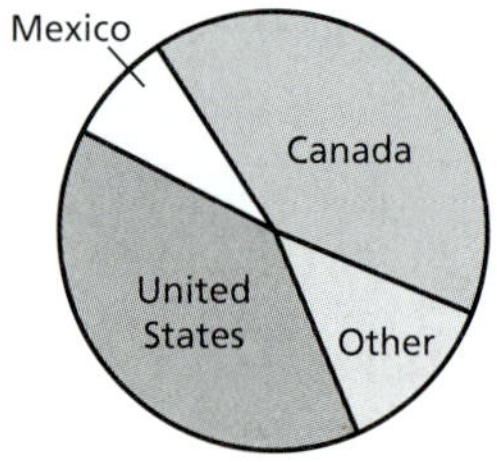

c. On a flat map, Canada appears much larger because the land area is exaggerated from the change in shape. On a globe, the land area appears to be the same.

25. *Sample answer:* Writing percents as fractions and decimals, finding a percent of a number, and finding the number of degrees in a section of a circle

27. $x - 7$

29. $b + 50$

31. C

English-Spanish Glossary

English / Spanish

A

absolute value *(p. 16)* The distance between a number and 0 on a number line; The absolute value of a number a is written as $|a|$

valor absoluto *(p. 16)* La distancia entre un número y 0 en una recta numérica; El valor absoluto de un número a es escrito como $|a|$

additive inverse *(p. 36)* The opposite of a number

inverso aditivo *(p. 36)* El opuesto de un número

algebraic expression *(p. 204)* An expression that contains numbers, operations, and one or more symbols

expresión algebraica *(p. 204)* Una expresión que contiene números, operaciones, y uno o más símbolos

B

base (of a power) *(p. 54)* The base of a power is the repeated factor

base (de una potencia) *(p. 54)* La base de una potencia es el factor repetido

C

center (of a circle) *(p. 302)* The point inside a circle that is the same distance from all points on the circle

centro (de un círculo) *(p. 302)* El punto dentro de un círculo que es la misma distancia de todos los puntos en el círculo

circle *(p. 302)* The set of all points in a plane that are the same distance from a point called the center

círculo *(p. 302)* El conjunto de todos los puntos en un plano que están a la misma distancia de un punto llamado el centro

circle graph *(p. 336)* A graph that displays data as sections of a circle

gráfico circular *(p. 336)* Gráfica que muestra datos como secciones de un círculo

circumference *(p. 303)* The distance around a circle

circunferencia *(p. 303)* La distancia alrededor de un círculo

coefficient *(p. 204)* The numerical factor of a term that contains a variable

coeficiente *(p. 204)* El factor numérico de un término que contiene una variable

congruent *(p. 278)* Equal in measure or length

congruente *(p. 278)* De misma medida o longitud

congruent figures *(p. 284)* Figures that have the same size and the same shape

figuras congruentes *(p. 284)* Figuras que tienen exactamente el mismo tamaño y la misma forma

constant *(p. 204)* A term without a variable

constante *(p. 204)* Un término que no tiene una variable

coordinate plane *(p. 22)* A coordinate plane is formed by the intersection of a horizontal number line and a vertical number line

plano de coordenadas *(p. 22)* Un plano de coordenadas es formado por la intersección de una recta numérica horizontal y una recta numérica vertical

corresponding angles *(p. 284)* Matching angles of two congruent figures

ángulos correspondientes *(p. 284)* Ángulos coincidentes de dos figuras congruentes

corresponding sides *(p. 284)* Matching sides of two congruent figures

lados correspondientes *(p. 284)* Lados coincidentes de dos figuras congruentes

D

diameter (of a circle) *(p. 302)* The distance across a circle through the center

diámetro (de un círculo) *(p. 302)* La distancia a través de un círculo por el centro

E

equation *(p. 238)* A mathematical sentence that uses an equal sign, =, to show that two expressions are equal

ecuación *(p. 238)* Una expresión matemática que usa un signo de igualdad, =, para mostrar que dos expresiones son iguales

equivalent expressions *(p. 218)* Expressions with the same value

expresiones equivalentes *(p. 218)* Expresiones con el mismo valor

equivalent rates *(p. 178)* Rates that have the same unit rate

tasas equivalentes *(p. 178)* Razones que tienen la misma tasa por unidad

equivalent ratios *(p. 170)* Two ratios that describe the same relationship

razones equivalentes *(p. 170)* Dos razones que describen la misma relación

evaluate (a numerical expression) *(p. 60)* Use the order of operations to find the value of a numerical expression

evaluar (una expresión numérica) *(p. 60)* Usar el orden de operaciones para hallar el valor de una expresión numérica

exponent *(p. 54)* The exponent of a power indicates the number of times the base is used as a factor

exponente *(p. 54)* El exponente de una potencia indica el número de veces que una base es usada como un factor

G

graph of an inequality *(p. 260)* A graph that shows all the solutions of an inequality on a number line

gráfica de una desigualdad *(p. 260)* Una gráfica que muestra todas las soluciones de una desigualdad en una recta numérica

I

inequality *(p. 258)* A mathematical sentence that compares expressions; It contains the symbols $<$, $>$, $\leq$, or $\geq$

desigualdad *(p. 258)* Una expresión matemática que compara las expresiones; Contiene los símbolos $<$, $>$, $\leq$, o $\geq$

integers *(p. 4)* The set of whole numbers and their opposites

números enteros *(p. 4)* El conjunto de números naturales y sus opuestos

inverse operations *(p. 245)* Operations that "undo" each other, such as addition and subtraction or multiplication and division

operaciones inversas *(p. 245)* Operaciones que deshacer unos de otros, tales como suma y resta o multiplicación y división

L

like terms *(p. 226)* Terms of an algebraic expression that have the same variables raised to the same exponents

términos semejantes *(p. 226)* Términos de una expresión algebraica que tienen las mismas variables elevadas a los mismos exponentes

line of symmetry *(p. 279)* A line that divides a figure into two parts that are mirror images of each other

línea de simetría *(p. 279)* Una recta que divide una figura en dos partes que son imágenes especulares de la otra

M

mean *(p. 322)* The sum of the data divided by the number of data values

media *(p. 322)* La suma de los datos dividido por el número de valores de datos

measure of center *(p. 328)* A measure that describes the typical value of a data set

medida de centro *(p. 328)* Una medida que describe el valor típico de un conjunto de datos

median *(p. 328)* For a data set with an odd number of ordered values, the median is the middle value. For a data set with an even number of ordered values, the median is the mean of the two middle values.

mediana *(p. 328)* Para un conjunto de datos con un número impar de valores ordenados, la mediana es el valor del medio. Para un conjunto de datos con un número par de valores ordenados, la mediana es la media de los dos valores del medio

mode *(p. 328)* The data value or values that occur most often; Data can have one mode, more than one mode, or no mode

moda *(p. 328)* El valor o valores de datos que ocurre(n) con más frecuencia; Los datos pueden tener una moda, más que una moda, o ninguna moda

N

negative numbers *(p. 4)* Numbers that are less than 0

números negativos *(p. 4)* Números que son menos de 0

numerical expression *(p. 60)* An expression that contains only numbers and operations

expresión numérica *(p. 60)* Una expresión que contiene solamente números y operaciones

O

opposites *(p. 4)* Two numbers that are the same distance from 0 on a number line, but on opposite sides of 0

opuestos *(p. 4)* Dos números que están a la misma distancia de 0 en una recta numérica, pero en lados opuestos de 0

order of operations *(p. 60)* The order in which to perform operations when evaluating expressions with more than one operation

orden de operaciones *(p. 60)* El orden en el que para realizar operaciones al evaluar expresiones con más de una operación

origin *(p. 22)* The point, represented by the ordered pair (0, 0), where the horizontal and vertical number lines intersect in a coordinate plane

origen *(p. 22)* El punto, representado por el par ordenado (0, 0), donde las rectas numéricas horizontales y verticales se intersecan en un plano de coordenadas

outlier *(p. 323)* A data value that is much greater or much less than the other values

outlier *(p. 323)* Un valor de datos que es mucho mayor o mucho menor que los otros valores

P

percent *(p. 140)* A part-to-whole ratio where the whole is 100

porcentaje *(p. 140)* La razón de número de partes por un entero en donde el entero es 100

perfect square *(p. 55)* The square of a whole number

cuadrado perfecto *(p. 55)* El cuadrado de un número naturales

pi (π) *(p. 303)* The ratio of the circumference of a circle to its diameter

pi(π) *(p. 303)* La razón de la circunferencia de un círculo a su diámetro

positive numbers *(p. 4)* Numbers that are greater than 0

números positivos *(p. 4)* Números que son mayores que 0

power *(p. 54)* A product of repeated factors

potencia *(p. 54)* Un producto de factores repetidos

proportion *(p. 190)* An equation stating that two ratios are equivalent

proporción *(p. 190)* Una ecuación que se indica que dos razones son equivalentes

proportional *(p. 190)* Two quantities that form a proportion are proportional

proporcional *(p. 190)* Dos cantidades que forman una proporción son proporcionales

Q

quadrants *(p. 22)* The four regions created by the intersection of the horizontal and vertical number lines in a coordinate plane

cuadrantes *(p. 22)* Las cuatro regiones creadas por la intersección de las rectas numéricas horizontales y verticales en un plano de coordenadas

R

radius (of a circle) *(p. 302)* The distance from the center of a circle to any point on the circle

radio (de un círculo) *(p. 302)* La distancia del centro de un círculo a cualquier punto en el círculo

rate *(p. 178)* A ratio of two quantities using different units

tasa *(p. 178)* Una razón de dos cantidades usando unidades diferentes

ratio *(p. 164)* A comparison of two quantities; The ratio of a to b can be written as $a : b$

razón *(p. 164)* Una comparación de dos cantidades; la razón de a a b puede escribirse como $a : b$

ratio table *(p. 170)* A table used to find and organize equivalent ratios

tabla de razones *(p. 170)* Una tabla usada para encontrar y organizar las razones equivalentes

rational number *(p. 134)* A number that can be written as $\frac{a}{b}$ where a and b are integers and $b \neq 0$

número racional *(p. 134)* Un número que puede ser escrito como $\frac{a}{b}$ donde a y b son enteros y $b \neq 0$

reciprocals *(p. 92)* Two numbers whose product is 1

recíprocos *(p. 92)* Dos números cuyo producto es 1

regular polygon *(p. 278)* A polygon with congruent sides and congruent angles

polígono regular *(p. 278)* Un polígono con lados congruentes y ángulos congruentes

repeating decimal *(p. 134)* A decimal that has a pattern that repeats

decimal periódico *(p. 134)* Un decimal que tiene una pauta que se repite

S

semicircle *(p. 304)* One-half of a circle

semicírculo *(p. 304)* La mitad de un círculo

solution (of an equation) *(p. 244)* A value that makes an equation true

solución (de una ecuación) *(p. 244)* Un valor que hace una ecuación verdadera

solution of an inequality *(p. 259)* A value that makes an inequality true

solución de una desigualdad *(p. 259)* Un valor que hace una desigualdad verdadera

solution set *(p. 259)* The set of all solutions of an inequality

conjunto de solución *(p. 259)* El conjunto de todas las soluciones de una desigualdad

T

term (of an algebraic expression) *(p. 204)* The parts of an algebraic expression

términos (de una expresión algebraica) *(p. 204)* Las partes de una expression algebraica

terminating decimal *(p. 134)* A decimal that ends

decimal finito *(p. 134)* Un deicmal que termina

U

unit rate *(p. 178)* A rate that compares a quantity to one unit of another quantity

tasa unitaria *(p. 178)* Una tasa que compara una cantidad a una unidad de otra cantidad

V

variable *(p. 204)* A symbol that represents one or more numbers

variable *(p. 204)* Un símbolo que representa a uno o más números

Student Index

This student-friendly index will help you find vocabulary, key ideas, and concepts. It is easily accessible and designed to be a reference for you whether you are looking for a definition, real-life application, or help with avoiding common errors.

Student Index

G

I

L

M

N

Q

R

Student Index

T

U

V

W

Photo Credits

Front matter

iv Big Ideas Learning, LLC; **viii** *top* ©iStockphoto.com/Jonathan Larsen; *bottom* ©iStockphoto.com/Jane norton; **ix** *top* ©iStockphoto.com/ALEAIMAGE, ©iStockphoto.com/Ann Marie Kurtz; *bottom* wavebreakermedia ltd/Shutterstock.com; **x** *top* ©iStockphoto.com/ALEAIMAGE, ©iStockphoto.com/Ann Marie Kurtz; *bottom* Odua Images/Shutterstock.com; **xi** *top* Kasiap/Shutterstock.com, ©iStockphoto.com/Ann Marie Kurtz; *bottom* ©iStockphoto.com/kate_sept2004; **xii** *top* ©iStockphoto.com/Lisa Thornberg, ©iStockphoto.com/Ann Marie Kurtz; *bottom* william casey/Shutterstock.com; **xiii** *top* stephan kerkhofs/Shutterstock.com, Cigdem Sean Cooper/Shutterstock.com, ©iStockphoto.com/Andreas Gradin; *bottom* Edyta Pawlowska/Shutterstock.com; **xiv** *top* Varina and Jay Patel/Shutterstock.com, ©iStockphoto.com/Ann Marie Kurtz; *bottom* PETER CLOSE/Shutterstock.com; **xv** *top* ©iStockphoto/Michael Flippo, ©iStockphoto.com/Ann Marie Kurtz; *bottom* ©iStockphoto.com/ranplett; **xvi** *top* Chiyacat/Shutterstock.com, Zoom Team/Shutterstock.com; *bottom* ©iStockphoto.com/Noraznen Azit; **xvii** ©iStockphoto.com/Thomas Perkins; **xviii** Ljupco Smokovski/Shuterstock.com

Chapter 1

0 ©iStockphoto.com/Jonathan Larsen;**1** ©iStockphoto.com/Egor Mopanko; **7** haveseen/Shutterstock.com; **8** NASA/Kim Shiflett; **8** NASA; **9** NASA; **13** ©iStockphoto.com/Andrew Penner; **24** Christophe Testi/Shutterstock.com

Chapter 2

32 ©iStockphoto.com/ALEAIMAGE, ©iStockphoto.com/Ann Marie Kurtz; **51** Dmitry Melnikov/Shutterstock.com; **52** Danomyte/Shutterstock.com; **53** Nicole Gordine/Shutterstock.com; **55** vonDUCK/Shutterstock.com; **57** ©iStockphoto.com/WestLight; **62** ©iStockphoto.com/clu; **63** ©iStockphoto.com/mladn61; **67** Liem Bahneman/Shutterstock.com

Chapter 3

68 ©iStockphoto.com/ALEAIMAGE, ©iStockphoto.com/Ann Marie Kurtz; **74** margouillat photo/Shutterstock.com; **75** Heide Hellebrand/Shutterstock.com; **87** *center left* fivespots/Shutterstock.com; *center right* bluehand/Shutterstock.com; **96** tele52/Shutterstock.com, lithian/Shutterstock.com, Galina Barskaya/Shutterstock.com; **97** *center left* ©iStockphoto.com/Michael Plumb; *center right* g215/Shutterstock.com; **101** ©iStockphoto.com/bonchan

Chapter 4

108 Kasiap/Shutterstock.com, ©iStockphoto.com/Ann Marie Kurtz; **113** Vacclav/Shutterstock.com; **114** Peredniankina/Shutterstock.com; **115** SSSCCC/Shutterstock.com; **121** Luba V Nel/Shutterstock.com; **122** KENCKOphotography/Shutterstock.com; **129** ©iStockphoto.com/bananahuman; **131** ©iStockphoto.com/Janis Litavnieks; **155** ©iStockphoto.com/Eric Isselée

Chapter 5

160 ©iStockphoto.com/Lisa Thornberg, ©iStockphoto.com/Ann Marie Kurtz; **162** Elnur/Shutterstock.com; **164** Vladimir Wrangel/Shutterstock.com; **165** Lepas/Shutterstock.com; **168** *top* foxie/Shutterstock.com; *center right* Constantinos/Shutterstock.com; **169** Danny Smythe/Shutterstock.com; **171** South 12th Photography/Shutterstock.com; **172** Petr Malyshev/Shutterstock.com; **174** ©iStockphoto.com/otakumania; **175** Anneka/Shutterstock.com; **177** vita khorzhevska/Shutterstock.com; **179** Alex Staroseltsev/Shutterstock.com; **180** *top right* ©iStockphoto.com/Gord Horne; *bottom right* leonid_tit/Shutterstock.com; **181** *top left* ©iStockphoto.com/ljpat; *bottom right* ©iStockphoto.com/Birgitte Magnus; **182** Mike Flippo/Shutterstock.com; **184** *top right* ultimathule/Shutterstock.com; *top left* Christopher Kolaczan/Shutterstock.com; **185** ©iStockphoto.com/Bart Wolczyk; **186** Catalin Petolea/Shutterstock.com, Kaspri/Shutterstock.com; **187** R. Gino Santa Maria/Shutterstock.com; **192** ©iStockphoto.com/Kemter; **193** ©iStockphoto.com/VikaValter

Chapter 6

200 stephan kerkhofs/Shutterstock.com, Cigdem Sean Cooper/Shutterstock.com, ©iStockphoto.com/Andreas Gradin; **213** Kateryna Larina/Shutterstock.com; **228** Pal Teravagimov/Shutterstock.com; **231** Helder Almeida/Shutterstock.com

Chapter 7

234 Varina and Jay Patel/Shutterstock.com, ©iStockphoto.com/Ann Marie Kurtz; **241** *top right* ©iStockphoto.com/Joop Snijder, ©iStockphoto.com/Michael MacFadden, ©iStockphoto.com/Steve Goodwin; *center left* ©iStockphoto.com/Kenneth C. Zirkel; **246** jocic/Shutterstock.com, Marko Poplasen/Shutterstock.com; **248** *top left* ©iStockphoto.com/Jeremy Wee; *top right* ©iStockphoto.com/Jan Will; **249** ©iStockphoto.com/Keith Reicher; **251** ©iStockphoto.com/Vladyslav Otsiatsia; **254** ©iStockphoto.com/Christopher Futcher; **255** ©iStockphoto.com/Eric Isselée; **256** *top right* ©iStockphoto.com/Studio-Annika; *center right* ©iStockphoto.com/nicholas belton; *bottom right* ©iStockphoto.com/Robert Dant; **260** NASA/Johns Hopkins University Applied Physics Laboratory; **262** ©iStockphoto.com/George Peters; **263** ©iStockphoto.com/Anthony Ladd; **264** *top right* CLS Design/Shutterstock.com; *bottom right* Liquid Productions, LLC / Shutterstock.com; **269** *top left* ©iStockphoto.com/o-che; *center left* ©iStockphoto.com/sunygraphics

Chapter 8

274 ©iStockphoto.com/Michael Flippo, ©iStockphoto.com/Ann Marie Kurtz; **291** MapMaster / CC-BY-SA-3.0; **299** ©iStockphoto.com/bamse009; **300** ©iStockphoto.com/HultonArchive; **305** *Exercises 3 and 4* ©iStockphoto.com/zentillia; *Exercise 5* ©iStockphoto.com/Dave Hopkins; *Exercise 6* ©iStockphoto.com/Boris Yankov; *Exercise 8* ©iStockphoto.com/ALEAIMAGE; *Exercise 8* ©iStockphoto.com/iLexx; *Exercises 9–11* ©iStockphoto.com/alexander mychko; **307** *center left* ©iStockphoto.com/HultonArchive; *center right* ©iStockphoto.com/winterling; **311** Mechanik/Shutterstock.com; **312** *Exercise 3* ©iStockphoto.com/zentillia; *Exercises 4 and 5* ©iStockphoto.com/PhotoHamster; *Exercise 6* ©iStockphoto.com/subjug; *Exercise 7* ©iStockphoto.com/Dave Hopkins; *Exercise 8* ©iStockphoto.com/7nuit

Chapter 9

318 Chiyacat/Shutterstock.com, Zoom Team/Shutterstock.com; **320** Rob Byron/Shutterstock.com; **321** Denis Vrublevski/Shutterstock.com; **323** ©iStockphoto.com/Eric Isselée; **326** *top right* Hein Nouwens/Shutterstock.com; *bottom* ivelly/Shutterstock.com; **327** ©iStockphoto.com/Andrew Rich; **333** *top right* ©iStockphoto.com/suemack; *top left* ©iStockphoto.com/muratkoc

Cartoon illustrations Tyler Stout

Mathematics Reference Sheet

Conversion

U.S. Customary
1 foot = 12 inches
1 yard = 3 feet
1 mile = 5280 feet
1 acre ≈ 43,560 square feet
1 cup = 8 fluid ounces
1 pint = 2 cups
1 quart = 2 pints
1 gallon = 4 quarts
1 gallon = 231 cubic inches
1 pound = 16 ounces
1 ton = 2000 pounds
1 cubic foot ≈ 7.5 gallons

U.S. Customary to Metric
1 inch = 2.54 centimeters
1 foot ≈ 0.3 meter
1 mile ≈ 1.61 kilometers
1 quart ≈ 0.95 liter
1 gallon ≈ 3.79 liters
1 cup ≈ 237 milliliters
1 pound ≈ 0.45 kilogram
1 ounce ≈ 28.3 grams
1 gallon ≈ 3785 cubic centimeters

Time
1 minute = 60 seconds
1 hour = 60 minutes
1 hour = 3600 seconds
1 year = 52 weeks

Temperature
$$C = \frac{5}{9}(F - 32)$$
$$F = \frac{9}{5}C + 32$$

Metric
1 centimeter = 10 millimeters
1 meter = 100 centimeters
1 kilometer = 1000 meters
1 liter = 1000 milliliters
1 kiloliter = 1000 liters
1 milliliter = 1 cubic centimeter
1 liter = 1000 cubic centimeters
1 cubic millimeter = 0.001 milliliter
1 gram = 1000 milligrams
1 kilogram = 1000 grams

Metric to U.S. Customary
1 centimeter ≈ 0.39 inch
1 meter ≈ 3.28 feet
1 kilometer ≈ 0.62 mile
1 liter ≈ 1.06 quarts
1 liter ≈ 0.26 gallon
1 kilogram ≈ 2.2 pounds
1 gram ≈ 0.035 ounce
1 cubic meter ≈ 264 gallons

Number Properties

Commutative Properties of Addition and Multiplication

$$a + b = b + a$$
$$a \cdot b = b \cdot a$$

Associative Properties of Addition and Multiplication

$$(a + b) + c = a + (b + c)$$
$$(a \cdot b) \cdot c = a \cdot (b \cdot c)$$

Distributive Property:

$$a(b + c) = ab + ac$$
$$a(b - c) = ab - ac$$

Addition Property of Zero

$$a + 0 = a$$

Multiplication Properties of Zero and One

$$a \cdot 0 = 0$$
$$a \cdot 1 = a$$

Additive Inverse Property

$$a + (-a) = (-a) + a = 0$$

Multiplicative Inverse Property

$$n \cdot \frac{1}{n} = \frac{1}{n} \cdot n = 1, n \neq 0$$

Properties of Equality

Addition Property of Equality

If $a = b$, then $a + c = b + c$.

Subtraction Property of Equality

If $a = b$, then $a - c = b - c$.

Substitution Property of Equality

If $a = b$, then a can be substituted for b (or b for a) in any equation or expression.

Multiplication Property of Equality

If $a = b$, then $a \cdot c = b \cdot c$.

Division Property of Equality

If $a = b$, then $a \div c = b \div c$, $c \neq 0$.

Properties of Inequality

Addition Property of Inequality

If $a > b$, then $a + c > b + c$.

Subtraction Property of Inequality

If $a > b$, then $a - c > b - c$.

Perimeter and Area

Square	Rectangle	Parallelogram	Triangle	Trapezoid
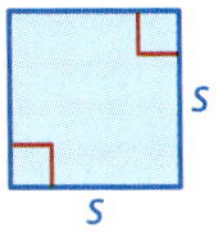	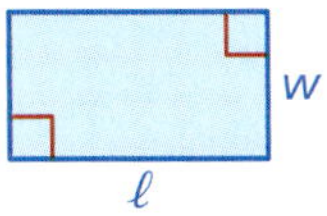	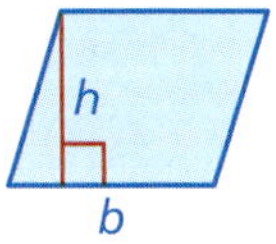	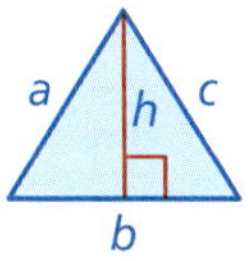	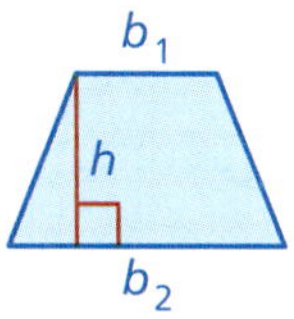
$P = 4s$ $A = s^2$	$P = 2\ell + 2w$ $A = \ell w$	$A = bh$	$P = a + b + c$ $A = \frac{1}{2}bh$	$A = \frac{1}{2}h(b_1 + b_2)$

Circumference and Area of a Circle

$C = \pi d$ or $C = 2\pi r$

$A = \pi r^2$

$\pi \approx \frac{22}{7}$, or 3.14

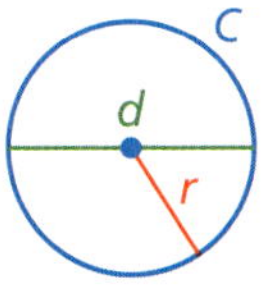

The Coordinate Plane

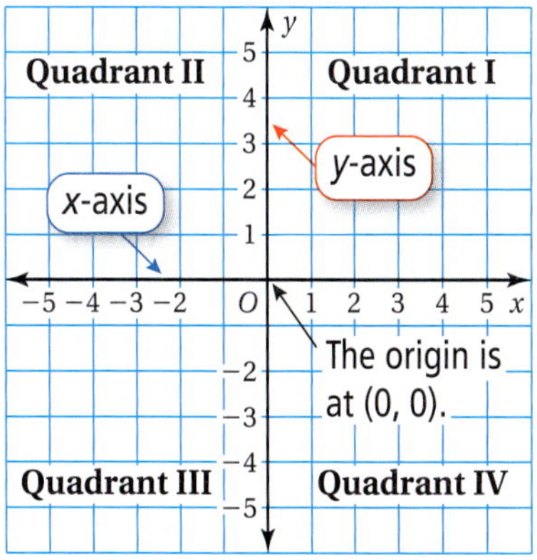